New Perspectives on

Microsoft® Office Excel 2003

CourseCard Edition

Introductory

THOMSON
COURSE TECHNOLOGY

Australia • Canada • Mexico • Singapore • Spain • United Kingdom

What does this logo mean?

It means this courseware has been approved by the Microsoft® Office Specialist Program to be among the finest available for learning Microsoft Office Word 2003, Microsoft Office Excel 2003, Microsoft Office Access 2003, and Microsoft Office PowerPoint® 2003. It also means that upon completion of this courseware, you may be prepared to take an exam for Microsoft Office Specialist qualification.

What is a Microsoft Office Specialist?

A Microsoft Office Specialist is an individual who has passed exams for certifying his or her skills in one or more of the Microsoft Office desktop applications such as Microsoft Word, Microsoft Excel, Microsoft PowerPoint, Microsoft Outlook®, Microsoft Access, or Microsoft Project. The Microsoft Office Specialist Program is the only program in the world approved by Microsoft for testing proficiency in Microsoft Office desktop applications and Microsoft Project.* This testing program can be a valuable asset in any job search or career advancement.

More Information:

To learn more about becoming a Microsoft Office Specialist, visit www.microsoft.com/officespecialist

To learn about other Microsoft Office Specialist approved courseware from Course Technology, visit **www.course.com/newperspectives/teacherslounge**

New Perspectives on

Microsoft® Office Excel 2003

CourseCard Edition

Introductory

June Jamrich Parsons

Dan Oja

Patrick Carey

Roy Ageloff
University of Rhode Island

THOMSON
™
COURSE TECHNOLOGY

Australia • Canada • Mexico • Singapore • Spain • United Kingdom • United States

THOMSON

COURSE TECHNOLOGY

New Perspectives on Microsoft® Office Excel 2003—Introductory, CourseCard Edition

is published by Course Technology.

Senior Managing Editor:
Rachel Goldberg

Senior Product Managers:
Kathy Finnegan, Karen Stevens

Senior Technology Product Manager:
Amanda Young Shelton

Product Manager:
Brianna Germain

Associate Product Manager:
Emilie Perreault

Editorial Assistant:
Shana Rosenthal

Marketing Manager:
Joy Stark

Developmental Editor:
Jane Pedicini

Cover Artist:
Ed Carpenter
www.edcarpenter.net

Production Editor:
Philippa Lehar

Composition:
GEX Publishing Services

Text Designer:
Steve Deschene

Cover Designer:
Nancy Goulet

Preface

Real, Thought-Provoking, Engaging, Dynamic, Interactive—these are just a few of the words that are used to describe the New Perspectives Series' approach to learning and building computer skills.

Without our critical-thinking and problem-solving methodology, computer skills could be learned but not retained. By teaching with a case-based approach, the New Perspectives Series challenges students to apply what they've learned to real-life situations.

Our ever-growing community of users understands why they're learning what they're learning. Now you can too!

See what instructors and students are saying about the best-selling New Perspectives Series:

"I have used books from the New Perspectives series for about ten years now. I haven't been able to find anything else that approaches their quality when it comes to covering intermediate and advanced software application topics."
— Kathleen Nordquist, College of St. Benedict & St. John's University

...and about New Perspectives on Microsoft Office Excel 2003:

"The layout in this textbook is thoughtfully designed and organized. It is very easy to locate concepts and step-by-step instructions. The Case Problems provide different scenarios that cover material in the tutorial with plenty of exercises."
— Shui-lien Huang, Mt. San Antonio College

"I have used the New Perspectives Excel textbooks for several years since they are the best on the market. The New Perspectives Excel 2003 textbook—which can best be described as clear, concise, practical, and interesting—puts the competitors even further behind."
— Joe Pidutti, Durham College

Why *New Perspectives* will work for you

Context
Each tutorial begins with a problem presented in a "real-world" case that is meaningful to students. The case sets the scene to help students understand what they will do in the tutorial.

Hands-on Approach
Each tutorial is divided into manageable sessions that combine reading and hands-on, step-by-step work. Screenshots—now 20% larger for enhanced readability—help guide students through the steps. **Trouble?** tips anticipate common mistakes or problems to help students stay on track and continue with the tutorial.

Review
In New Perspectives, retention is a key component to learning. At the end of each session, a series of Quick Check questions helps students test their understanding of the concepts before moving on. And now each tutorial contains an end-of-tutorial summary and a list of key terms for further reinforcement.

Assessment
Engaging and challenging Review Assignments and Case Problems have always been a hallmark feature of the New Perspectives Series. Now we've added new features to make them more accessible! Colorful icons and brief descriptions accompany the exercises, making it easy to understand, at a glance, both the goal and level of challenge a particular exercise holds.

Reference
While contextual learning is excellent for retention, there are times when students will want a high-level understanding of how to accomplish a task. Within each tutorial, Reference Windows appear before a set of steps to provide a succinct summary and preview of how to perform a task. In addition, a complete Task Reference at the back of the book provides quick access to information on how to carry out common tasks. Finally, each book includes a combination Glossary/Index to promote easy reference of material.

Lab Assignments
Certain tutorials in this book contain Lab Assignments, which provide additional reinforcement of important skills in a simulated environment. These labs have been hailed by students and teachers alike for years as the most comprehensive and accurate on the market. Great for pre-work or remediation, the labs help students learn concepts and skills in a structured environment.

Student Online Companion
This book has an accompanying online companion Web site designed to enhance learning. This Web site includes:
- Internet Assignments and Lab Assignments for selected tutorials
- Student Data Files and PowerPoint presentations
- Microsoft Office Specialist Certification Grids

Certification
The logo on the front of this book means that this book has been independently reviewed and approved by ProCert Labs. If you are interested in acquiring Microsoft Office Specialist certification, you may use this book as courseware in your preparation. For more information on this certification, go to www.microsoft.com/officespecialist.

www.course.com/NewPerspectives

New Perspectives offers an entire system of instruction

The New Perspectives Series is more than just a handful of books. It's a complete system of offerings:

New Perspectives catalog
Our online catalog is never out of date! Go to the catalog link on our Web site to check out our available titles, request a desk copy, download a book preview, or locate online files.

Coverage to meet your needs!
Whether you're looking for just a small amount of coverage or enough to fill a semester-long class, we can provide you with a textbook that meets your needs.
- Brief books typically cover the essential skills in just 2 to 4 tutorials.
- Introductory books build and expand on those skills and contain an average of 5 to 8 tutorials.
- Comprehensive books are great for a full-semester class, and contain 9 to 12+ tutorials.
- Power Users or Advanced books are perfect for a highly accelerated introductory class or a second course in a given topic.

So if the book you're holding does not provide the right amount of coverage for you, there's probably another offering available. Go to our Web site or contact your Course Technology sales representative to find out what else we offer.

Instructor Resources
We offer more than just a book. We have all the tools you need to enhance your lectures, check students' work, and generate exams in a new, easier-to-use and completely revised package. This book's Instuctor's Manual, ExamView testbank, PowerPoint presentations, data files, solution files, figure files, and sample syllabus are all available on a single CD-ROM or for downloading at www.course.com.

How will your students master Microsoft Office?
SAM (Skills Assessment Manager) 2003 helps you energize your class exams and training assignments by allowing students to learn and test important computer skills in an active, hands-on environment. With SAM 2003, you create powerful interactive exams on critical Microsoft Office 2003 applications, including Word, Excel, Access, and PowerPoint. The exams simulate the application environment, allowing your students to demonstrate their knowledge and to think through the skills by performing real-world tasks. Designed to be used with the New Perspectives Series, SAM 2003 includes built-in page references so students can create study guides that match the New Perspectives textbooks you use in class. Powerful administrative options allow you to schedule exams and assignments, secure your tests, and run reports with almost limitless flexibility. Find out more about SAM 2003 by going to www.course.com or speaking with your Course Technology sales representative.

Distance Learning
Enhance your course with any of our online learning platforms. Go to www.course.com or speak with your Course Technology sales representative to find the platform or the content that's right for you.

www.course.com/NewPerspectives

About This Book

This book is ideal for an introductory course on the latest version of Microsoft Excel, covering topics ranging from working with formulas and functions, to using templates and recording macros.

- New! Now includes a free, tear-off Excel 2003 CourseCard that provides students with a great way to have Excel skills at their fingertips.
- Updated for the new software! This book includes coverage of new Excel 2003 features, including the new Research task pane, creating a list range, and saving a workbook as an XML file.
- Tutorials 1 and 2 have been restructured and simplified, with new case scenarios that present topics within a more accessible context. Greater focus is placed on essential tasks, such as calculating totals with AutoSum, and on working with more basic functions, such as SUM, AVERAGE, and MAX. Streamlined coverage of Financial and Logical functions is provided in an *optional* session.
- Students also learn how to format worksheets, create and modify charts, work with Excel lists, manage multiple worksheets and workbooks, work with Excel's editing and Web tools, and develop an Excel application.
- Two appendices cover working with Logical functions, Database functions, and advanced filtering; and integrating Excel with other Windows programs.
- This book meets Microsoft Office Specialist certification requirements for the Microsoft Office Excel 2003 exam!

Features of the New Perspectives series include:

- Large screenshots offer improved readability.
- Sequential page numbering makes it easier to refer to specific pages in the book.
- The Tutorial Summary and Key Terms sections at the end of each tutorial provide additional conceptual review for students.
- Meaningful labels and descriptions for the end-of-tutorial exercises make it easy for you to select the right exercises for your students.

Acknowledgments

We would like to thank the many people whose invaluable contributions made this book possible. First, thanks go to our reviewers: Rory De Simone, University of Florida; Shui-lien Huang, Mt. San Antonio College; Glen Johansson, Spokane Community College; Mary Logan, Delgado Community College; Karleen Nordquist, College of St. Benedict & St. John's University; Joe Pidutti, Durham College; Kate Pulling, Community College of Southern Nevada; Donna Ulmer, St. Louis Community College at Meramec; and Kathy Winters, The University of Tennessee at Chattanooga. At Course Technology we would like to thank Rachel Goldberg, Senior Managing Editor; Kathy Finnegan and Karen Stevens, Senior Product Managers; Brianna Germain, Product Manager; Emilie Perreault, Associate Product Manager; Shana Rosenthal, Editorial Assistant; Philippa Lehar, Production Editor; John Bosco and John Freitas, Quality Assurance Managers; Shawn Day, Sean Franey, Danielle Shaw, Marc Sporto, and Ashlee Welz, Quality Assurance Testers; and Steven Freund, Dave Nuscher and Rebekah Tidwell for their work on the Instructor Resources. A special thanks to Jane Pedicini, Developmental Editor, for another great effort, keeping us focused and level-headed as we worked to complete this text.

June Jamrich Parsons
Dan Oja
Patrick Carey
Roy Ageloff

www.course.com/NewPerspectives

Brief Contents

Table of Contents

Tutorial 2   EX 51

Working with Formulas and Functions .... EX 51

Developing a Family Budget ....EX 51

Tutorial 3   EX 95

Developing a Professional-Looking Worksheet... EX 95

Formatting a Sales Report ....EX 95

Tutorial 6   EX 253

Working with Multiple Worksheets and Workbooks . . . . **EX 253**

Tracking Cash Flow . . . . .EX 253

Tutorial 7   EX 301

Working with Excel's Editing and Web Tools . . . EX 301

Collaborating on a Workbook and Web Page . . . . . .EX 301

New Perspectives on

Using Common Features of Microsoft® Office 2003

Preparing Promotional Materials   OFF 3

Read This Before You Begin

To the Student

Data Files

To complete the Using Common Features of Microsoft Office 2003 tutorial, you need the starting student Data Files. Your instructor will either provide you with these Data Files or ask you to obtain them yourself.

The Using Common Features of Microsoft Office 2003 tutorial requires the folder named "OFF" to complete the Tutorial, Review Assignments, and Case Problems. You will need to copy this folder from a file server, a stand-alone computer, or the Web to the drive and folder where you will be storing your Data Files. Your instructor will tell you which computer, drive letter, and folder(s) contain the files you need. You can also download the files by going to www.course.com; see the inside back or front cover for

more information on downloading the files, or ask your instructor or technical support person for assistance.

If you are storing your Data Files on floppy disks, you will need one blank, formatted, high-density disk for this tutorial. Label your disk as shown, and place on it the folder indicated.

▼**Common Features of Office: Data Disk**
    OFF folder

When you begin this tutorial, refer to the Student Data Files section at the bottom of the tutorial opener page, which indicates which folders and files you need for the tutorial. Each end-of-tutorial exercise also indicates the files you need to complete that exercise.

To the Instructor

The Data Files are available on the Instructor Resources CD for this title. Follow the instructions in the Help file on the CD to install the programs to your network or standalone computer. See the "To the Student" section above for information on how to set up the Data Files that accompany this text.

You are granted a license to copy the Data Files to any computer or computer network used by students who have purchased this book.

System Requirements

If you are going to work through this book using your own computer, you need:

• **Computer System** Microsoft Windows 2000 or Windows XP Professional or higher must be installed on your computer. This tutorial assumes a typical installation of Microsoft Office 2003. Additionally, to

complete the steps for accessing Microsoft's Online Help for Office, an Internet connection and a Web browser are required.

• **Data Files** You will not be able to complete the tutorials or exercises in this book using your own computer until you have the necessary starting Data Files.

www.course.com/NewPerspectives

Objectives

- Explore the programs that comprise Microsoft Office
- Start programs and switch between them
- Explore common window elements
- Minimize, maximize, and restore windows
- Use personalized menus and toolbars
- Work with task panes
- Create, save, close, and open a file
- Use the Help system
- Print a file
- Exit programs

Using Common Features of Microsoft Office 2003

Preparing Promotional Materials

Case

Delmar Office Supplies

Delmar Office Supplies, a company in Wisconsin founded by Jake Alexander in 1996, sells recycled office supplies to businesses and home-based offices around the world. The demand for quality recycled papers, reconditioned toner cartridges, and renovated office furniture has been growing each year. Jake and all his employees use Microsoft Office 2003, which provides everyone in the company the power and flexibility to store a variety of information, create consistent files, and share data. In this tutorial, you'll review how the company's employees use Microsoft Office 2003.

Student Data Files

▼ **OFF folder**

▽ **Tutorial folder**

    (no starting Data Files)

▽ **Review folder**

    Finances.xls

    Letter.doc

Exploring Microsoft Office 2003

Microsoft Office 2003, or simply **Office**, is a collection of the most popular Microsoft programs: Word, Excel, PowerPoint, Access, and Outlook. Each Office program contains valuable tools to help you accomplish many tasks, such as composing reports, analyzing data, preparing presentations, compiling information, sending e-mail, and planning schedules.

Microsoft Word 2003, or simply **Word**, is a word-processing program you use to create text documents. The files you create in Word are called **documents**. Word offers many special features that help you compose and update all types of documents, ranging from letters and newsletters to reports, brochures, faxes, and even books—all in attractive and readable formats. You can also use Word to create, insert, and position figures, tables, and other graphics to enhance the look of your documents. The Delmar Office Supplies sales representatives create their business letters using Word.

Microsoft Excel 2003, or simply **Excel**, is a spreadsheet program you use to display, organize, and analyze numerical data. You can do some of this in Word with tables, but Excel provides many more tools for recording and formatting numbers as well as performing calculations. The graphics capabilities in Excel also enable you to display data visually. You might, for example, generate a pie chart or a bar chart to help readers quickly see the significance of and the connections between information. The files you create in Excel are called **workbooks**. The Delmar Office Supplies operations department uses a line chart in an Excel workbook to visually track the company's financial performance.

Microsoft Access 2003, or simply **Access**, is a database program you use to enter, organize, display, and retrieve related information. The files you create in Access are called **databases**. With Access you can create data entry forms to make data entry easier, and you can create professional reports to improve the readability of your data. The Delmar Office Supplies operations department tracks the company's inventory in a table in an Access database.

Microsoft PowerPoint 2003, or simply **PowerPoint**, is a presentation graphics program you use to create a collection of slides that can contain text, charts, pictures, and so on. The files you create in PowerPoint are called **presentations**. You can show these presentations on your computer monitor, project them onto a screen as a slide show, print them, share them over the Internet, or display them on the World Wide Web. You can also use PowerPoint to generate presentation-related documents such as audience handouts, outlines, and speakers' notes. The Delmar Office Supplies sales department has created an effective slide presentation with PowerPoint to promote the company's latest product line.

Microsoft Outlook 2003, or simply **Outlook**, is an information management program you use to send, receive, and organize e-mail; plan your schedule; arrange meetings; organize contacts; create a to-do list; and jot down notes. You can also use Outlook to print schedules, task lists, phone directories, and other documents. Jake Alexander uses Outlook to send and receive e-mail, plan his schedule, and create a to-do list.

Although each Office program individually is a strong tool, their potential is even greater when used together.

Integrating Office Programs

One of the main advantages of Office is **integration**, the ability to share information between programs. Integration ensures consistency and accuracy, and it saves time because you don't have to re-enter the same information in several Office programs. The staff at Delmar Office Supplies uses the integration features of Office daily, including the following examples:

- The accounting department created an Excel bar chart on the previous two years' fourth-quarter results, which they inserted into the quarterly financial report created in Word. They included a hyperlink in the Word report that employees can click to open the Excel workbook and view the original data.
- The operations department included an Excel pie chart of sales percentages by divisions of Delmar Office Supplies on a PowerPoint slide, which is part of a presentation to stockholders.
- The marketing department produced a mailing to promote the company's newest products by combining a form letter created in Word with an Access database that stores the names and addresses of customers.
- A sales representative wrote a letter in Word about a sales incentive program and merged the letter with an Outlook contact list containing the names and addresses of his customers.

These are just a few examples of how you can take information from one Office program and integrate it into another.

Starting Office Programs

You can start any Office program by clicking the Start button on the Windows taskbar, and then selecting the program you want from the All Programs menu. Once the program starts, you can immediately begin to create new files or work with existing ones. If you or another user has recently used one of the Office programs, then that program might appear on the most frequently used programs list on the left side of the Start menu. You can click the program name to start the program.

Starting Office Programs	Reference Window

- Click the Start button on the taskbar.
- Point to All Programs.
- Point to Microsoft Office.
- Click the name of the program you want to start.

or

- Click the name of the program you want to start on the most frequently used programs list on the left side of the Start menu.

You'll start Excel using the Start button.

To start Excel and open a new, blank workbook:

1. Make sure your computer is on and the Windows desktop appears on your screen.

   Trouble? If your screen varies slightly from those shown in the figures, then your computer might be set up differently. The figures in this book were created while running Windows XP in its default settings, but how your screen looks depends on a variety of things, including the version of Windows, background settings, and so forth.

2. Click the **Start** button on the taskbar, and then point to **All Programs** to display the All Programs menu.

3. Point to **Microsoft Office** on the All Programs menu, and then point to **Microsoft Office Excel 2003**. See Figure 1. Depending on how your computer is set up, your desktop and menu might contain different icons and commands.

Figure 1 Start menu with All Programs submenu displayed

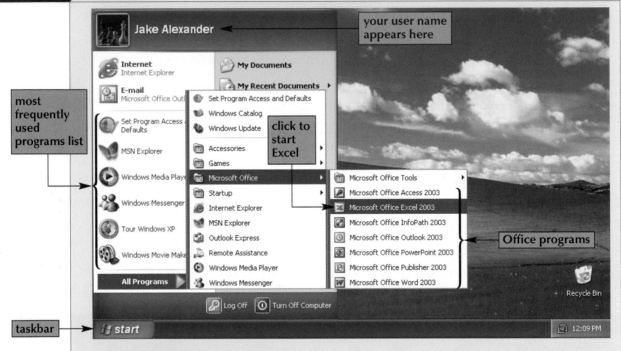

Trouble? If you don't see Microsoft Office on the All Programs menu, point to Microsoft Office Excel 2003. If you still don't see Microsoft Office Excel 2003, ask your instructor or technical support person for help.

4. Click **Microsoft Office Excel 2003** to start Excel and open a new, blank workbook. See Figure 2.

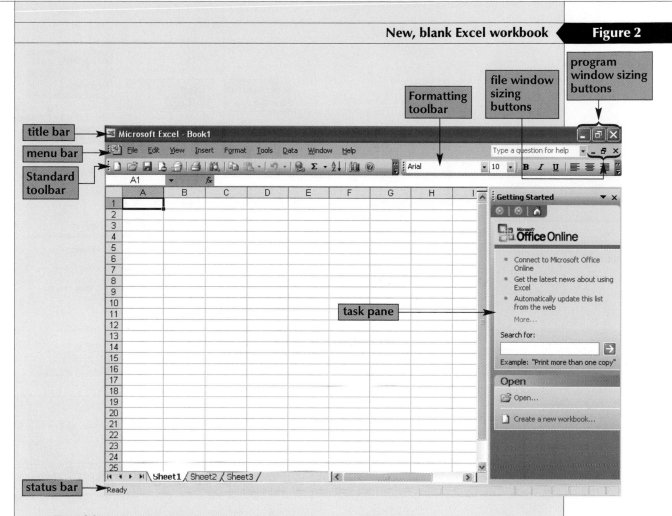

Trouble? If the Excel window doesn't fill your entire screen, the window is not maximized, or expanded to its full size. You'll maximize the window shortly.

You can have more than one Office program open at once. You'll use this same method to start Word and open a new, blank document.

To start Word and open a new, blank document:

▶ **1.** Click the **Start** button on the taskbar.

▶ **2.** Point to **All Programs** to display the All Programs menu.

▶ **3.** Point to **Microsoft Office** on the All Programs menu.

Trouble? If you don't see Microsoft Office on the All Programs menu, point to Microsoft Office Word 2003. If you still don't see Microsoft Office Word 2003, ask your instructor or technical support person for help.

▶ **4.** Click **Microsoft Office Word 2003**. Word opens with a new, blank document. See Figure 3.

Figure 3   New, blank document in Word

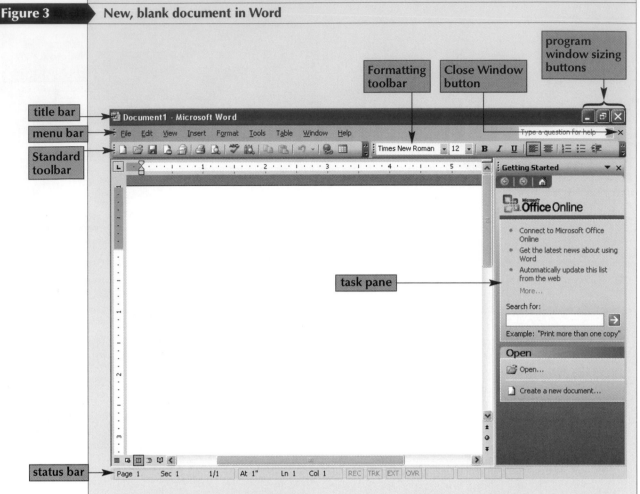

Trouble? If the Word window doesn't fill your entire screen, the window is not maximized. You'll maximize the window shortly.

When you have more than one program or file open at a time, you can switch between them.

Switching Between Open Programs and Files

Two programs are running at the same time—Excel and Word. The taskbar contains buttons for both programs. When you have two or more programs running, or two files within the same program open, you can use the taskbar buttons to switch from one program or file to another. The employees at Delmar Office Supplies often work in several programs at once.

To switch between Word and Excel:

▶ **1.** Click the **Microsoft Excel – Book1** button on the taskbar to switch from Word to Excel. See Figure 4.

Excel and Word programs opened simultaneously ◀ **Figure 4**

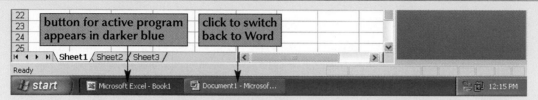

▶ **2.** Click the **Document1 – Microsoft Word** button on the taskbar to return to Word.

As you can see, you can start multiple programs and switch between them in seconds.

Exploring Common Window Elements

The Office programs consist of windows that have many similar features. As you can see in Figures 2 and 3, many of the elements you see in both the Excel program window and the Word program window are the same. In fact, all the Office programs have these same elements. Figure 5 describes some of the most common window elements.

Common window elements ◀ **Figure 5**

Element	Description
Title bar	A bar at the top of the window that contains the filename of the open file, the program name, and the program window sizing buttons
Menu bar	A collection of menus for commonly used commands
Toolbars	Collections of buttons that are shortcuts to commonly used menu commands
Sizing buttons	Buttons that resize and close the program window or the file window
Task pane	A window that provides access to commands for common tasks you'll perform in Office programs
Status bar	An area at the bottom of the program window that contains information about the open file or the current task on which you are working

Because these elements are the same in each program, once you've learned one program, it's easy to learn the others. The next sections explore the primary common features—the window sizing buttons, the menus and toolbars, and the task panes.

Using the Window Sizing Buttons

There are two sets of sizing buttons. The top set controls the program window and the bottom set controls the file window. There are three different sizing buttons. The Minimize button ⬜, which is the left button, hides a window so that only its program button is visible on the taskbar. The middle button changes name and function depending on the status of the window—the Maximize button 🔲 expands the window to the full screen size or to the program window size, and the Restore button 🗗 returns the window to a predefined size. The right button, the Close button ❌, exits the program or closes the file.

Most often you'll want to maximize the program and file windows as you work to take advantage of the full screen size you have available. If you have several files open, you might want to restore the files so that you can see more than one window at a time or you might want to minimize the programs with which you are not working at the moment. You'll try minimizing, maximizing, and restoring windows now.

To resize windows:

▶ 1. Click the **Minimize** button ▬ on the Word title bar to reduce the Word program window to a taskbar button. The Excel window is visible again.

▶ 2. If necessary, click the **Maximize** button ▢ on the Excel title bar. The Excel program window expands to fill the screen.

▶ 3. Click the **Restore Window** button 🗗 on the Excel menu bar. The file window, referred to as the workbook window in Excel, resizes smaller than the full program window. See Figure 6.

| Figure 6 | Resized Excel windows |

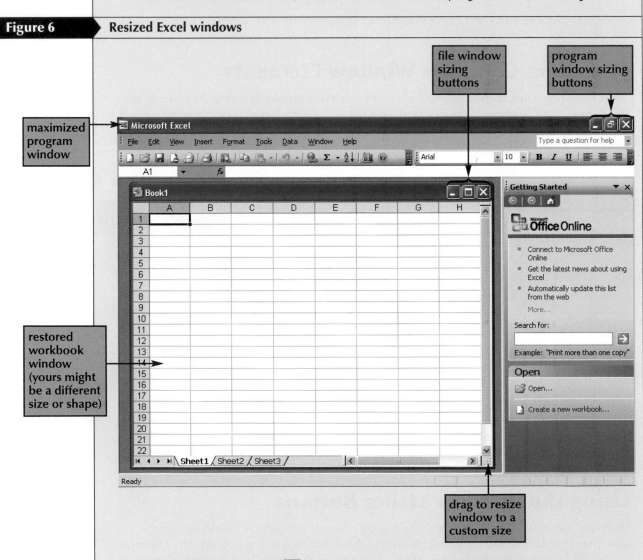

file window sizing buttons

program window sizing buttons

maximized program window

restored workbook window (yours might be a different size or shape)

drag to resize window to a custom size

▶ 4. Click the **Maximize** button ▢ on the Excel workbook window title bar. The Excel workbook window expands to fill the program window.

5. Click the **Document1 - Microsoft Word** button on the taskbar. The Word program window returns to its previous size.

6. If necessary, click the **Maximize** button ▣ on the Word title bar. The Word program window expands to fill the screen.

The sizing buttons give you the flexibility to arrange the program and file windows on your screen to best fit your needs.

Using Menus and Toolbars

In each Office program, you can perform tasks using a menu command, a toolbar button, or a keyboard shortcut. A **menu command** is a word on a menu that you click to execute a task; a **menu** is a group of related commands. For example, the File menu contains commands for managing files, such as the Open command and the Save command. The File, Edit, View, Insert, Format, Tools, Window, and Help menus appear on the menu bar in all the Office programs, although some of the commands they include differ from program to program. Other menus are program specific, such as the Table menu in Word and the Data menu in Excel.

A **toolbar** is a collection of buttons that correspond to commonly used menu commands. For example, the Standard toolbar contains an Open button and a Save button. The Standard and Formatting toolbars (as well as other toolbars) appear in all the Office programs, although some of the buttons they include differ from program to program. The Standard toolbar has buttons related to working with files. The Formatting toolbar has buttons related to changing the appearance of content. Each program also has program-specific toolbars, such as the Tables and Borders toolbar in Word for working with tables and the Chart toolbar in Excel for working with graphs and charts.

A **keyboard shortcut** is a combination of keys you press to perform a command. For example, Ctrl+S is the keyboard shortcut for the Save command (you hold down the Ctrl key while you press the S key). Keyboard shortcuts appear to the right of many menu commands.

Viewing Personalized Menus and Toolbars

When you first use a newly installed Office program, the menus and toolbars display only the basic and most commonly used commands and buttons, streamlining the program window. The other commands and buttons are available, but you have to click an extra button to see them (the Expand button on a menu and the Toolbar Options button on a toolbar). As you select commands and click buttons, the ones you use often are put on the short, personalized menu and on the visible part of the toolbars. The ones you don't use remain available on the full menus and toolbars. This means that the Office menus and toolbars might display different commands and buttons on each person's computer.

To view a personalized and full menu:

1. Click **Insert** on the Word menu bar to display the short, personalized menu. See Figure 7. The Bookmark command, for example, does not appear on the short menu.

Figure 7   Short, personalized menu

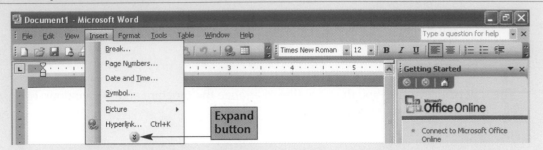

Trouble? If the Insert menu displays different commands than those shown in Figure 7, you need to reset the menus. Click Tools on the menu bar, click Customize (you might need to pause until the full menu appears to see the command), and then click the Options tab in the Customize dialog box. Click the Always show full menus check box to remove the check mark, if necessary, and then click the Show full menus after a short delay check box to insert a check mark, if necessary. Click the Reset menu and toolbar usage data button, and then click the Yes button to confirm that you want to reset the commands. Click the Close button. Repeat Step 1.

You can display the full menu in one of three ways: (1) pause until the full menu appears, which might happen as you read this; (2) click the Expand button at the bottom of the menu; or (3) double-click the menu name on the menu bar.

2. Pause until the full Insert menu appears, as shown in Figure 8. The Bookmark command and other commands are now visible.

Figure 8   Full, expanded menu

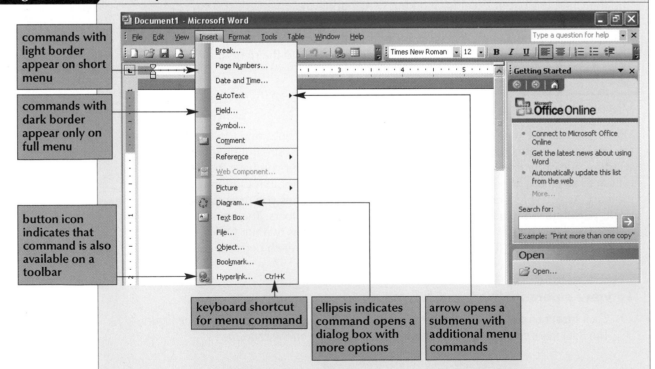

3. Click the **Bookmark** command. A dialog box opens when you click a command whose name is followed by an ellipsis (...). In this case, the Bookmark dialog box opens.

4. Click the **Cancel** button to close the Bookmark dialog box.

5. Click **Insert** on the menu bar again to display the short, personalized menu. The Bookmark command appears on the short, personalized menu because you have recently used it.

6. Press the **Esc** key on the keyboard twice to close the menu.

As you can see, the menu changed based on your actions. Over time, only the commands you use frequently will appear on the personalized menu. The toolbars work similarly.

To use the personalized toolbars:

1. Observe that the Standard and Formatting toolbars appear side by side below the menu bar.

   Trouble? If the toolbars appear on two rows, you need to reset them to their default state. Click Tools on the menu bar, click Customize, and then click the Options tab in the Customize dialog box. Click the Show Standard and Formatting toolbars on two rows check box to remove the check mark. Click the Reset menu and toolbar usage data button, and then click the Yes button to confirm you want to reset the commands. Click the Close button. Repeat Step 1.

2. Click the **Toolbar Options** button ⬚ on the Standard toolbar. See Figure 9.

Toolbar Options palette ◄ **Figure 9**

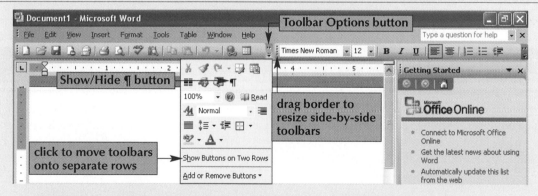

Trouble? If you see different buttons on the Toolbar Options palette, your side-by-side toolbars might be sized differently than the ones shown in Figure 9. Continue with Step 3.

3. Click the **Show/Hide ¶** button ▣ on the Toolbar Options palette to display the nonprinting screen characters. The Show/Hide ¶ button moves to the visible part of the Standard toolbar, and another button may be moved onto the Toolbar Options palette to make room for the new button.

   Trouble? If the Show/Hide ¶ button already appears on the Standard toolbar, click another button on the Toolbar Options palette. Then click that same button again in Step 4 to turn off that formatting, if necessary.

   Some buttons, like the Show/Hide ¶ button, act as a toggle switch—one click turns on the feature and a second click turns it off.

4. Click the **Show/Hide ¶** button ▣ on the Standard toolbar again to hide the nonprinting screen characters.

Some people like that the menus and toolbars change to meet their work habits. Others prefer to see all the menu commands or to display the default toolbars on two rows so that all the buttons are always visible. You'll change the toolbar setting now.

To turn off the personalized toolbars:

▶ 1. Click the **Toolbar Options** button ░ on the right side of the Standard toolbar.

▶ 2. Click the **Show Buttons on Two Rows** command. The toolbars move to separate rows (the Standard toolbar on top) and you can see all the buttons on each toolbar.

You can easily access any button on the Standard and Formatting toolbars with one mouse click. The drawback is that when the toolbars are displayed on two rows, they take up more space in the program window, limiting the space you have to work.

Using Task Panes

A **task pane** is a window that provides access to commands for common tasks you'll perform in Office programs. For example, the Getting Started task pane, which opens when you first start any Office program, enables you to create new files and open existing ones. Task panes also help you navigate through more complex, multi-step procedures. All the Office programs include the task panes described in Figure 10. The other available task panes vary by program.

| Figure 10 | Common task panes |

Task pane	Description
Getting Started	The home task pane; allows you to create new files, open existing files, search the online and offline Help system by keyword, and access Office online
Help	Allows you to search the online and offline Help system by keyword or table of contents, and access Microsoft Office Online
Search Results	Displays available Help topics related to entered keyword and enables you to initiate a new search
New	Allows you to create new files; name changes to New Document in Word, New Workbook in Excel, New File in Access, and New Presentation in PowerPoint
Clip Art	Allows you to search for all types of media clips (pictures, sound, video) and insert clips from the results
Clipboard	Allows you to paste some or all of the items that have been cut or copied from any Office program during the current work session
Research	Allows you to search a variety of reference material and other resources from within a file

No matter what their purpose, you use the same processes to open, close, and navigate between the task panes.

Opening and Closing Task Panes

When you first start any Office program, the Getting Started task pane opens by default along the right edge of the program window. You can resize or move the task pane to suit your work habits. You can also close the task pane to display the open file in the full available program window. For example, you might want to close the task pane when you are typing the body of a letter in Word or entering a lot of data in Excel.

You will open and close the task pane.

To open and close the task pane:

1. If necessary, click **View** on the menu bar, and then click **Task Pane**. The most recently viewed task pane opens on the right side of the screen. See Figure 11.

Getting Started task pane | **Figure 11**

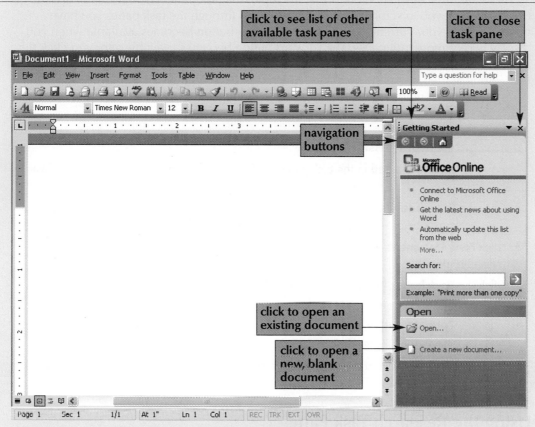

Trouble? If you do not see the task pane, you probably closed the open task pane in Step 1. Repeat Step 1 to reopen the task pane.

Trouble? If a different task pane than the Getting Started task pane opens, then another task pane was the most recently viewed task pane. You'll learn how to open different task panes in the next section; continue with Step 2.

2. Click the **Close** button ☒ on the task pane title bar. The task pane closes, leaving more room on the screen for the open file.

3. Click **View** on the menu bar, and then click **Task Pane**. The task pane reopens.

There are several ways to display different task panes.

Navigating Among Task Panes

Once the task pane is open, you can display different task panes to suit the task you are trying to complete. For example, you can display the New task pane when you want to create a new file from a template. The name of the New task pane varies, depending on the program you are using: Word has the New Document task pane, Excel has the New Workbook task pane, PowerPoint has the New Presentation task pane, and Access has the New File task pane.

One of the quickest ways to display a task pane is to use the Other Task Panes button. When you point to the name of the open task pane in the task pane title bar, it becomes the Other Task Panes button. When you click the Other Task Panes button, all the available task panes for that Office program are listed. Just click the name of the task pane you want to display to switch to that task pane.

There are three navigation buttons at the top of the task pane. The Back and Forward buttons enable you to scroll backward and forward through the task panes you have opened during your current work session. The Back button becomes available when you display two or more task panes. The Forward button becomes available after you click the Back button to return to a previously viewed task pane. The Home button returns you to the Getting Started task pane no matter which task pane is currently displayed.

You'll use each of these methods to navigate among the task panes.

To navigate among task panes:

1. Point to **Getting Started** in the task pane title bar. The title bar becomes the Other Task Panes button.

2. Click the **Other Task Panes** button. A list of the available task panes for Word is displayed. The check mark before Getting Started indicates that this is the currently displayed task pane.

3. Click **New Document**. The New Document task pane appears and the Back button is available.

4. Click the **Back** button ⊕ in the task pane. The Getting Started task pane reappears and the Forward button is available.

5. Click the **Forward** button ⊕ in the task pane. The New Document task pane reappears and the Back button is available.

6. Click the **Home** button ⌂ in the task pane. The Getting Started task pane reappears.

Using the Research Task Pane

The Research task pane allows you to search a variety of reference materials and other resources to find specific information while you are working on a file. You can insert the information you find directly into your open file. The thesaurus and language translation tools are installed with Office and therefore are stored locally on your computer. If you are connected to the Internet, you can also use the Research task pane to access a dictionary, an encyclopedia, research sites, as well as business and financial sources. Some of the sites that appear in the search results are fee-based, meaning that you'll need to pay to access information on that site.

To use the Research task pane, you type a keyword or phrase into the Search for text box and then select whether you want to search all the books, sites, and sources; one category; or a specific source. The search results appear in the Research task pane. Some of the results appear as links, which you can click to open your browser window and display that information. If you are using Internet Explorer 5.01 or later as your Web browser, the Research task pane is tiled (appears side by side) with your document. If you are using another Web browser, you'll need to return to the task pane in your open file to click another link.

The Research task pane functions independently in each file. So you can open multiple files and perform a different search in each. In addition, each Research task pane stores the results of up to 10 searches, so you can quickly return to the results from any of your most recent searches. To move among the saved searches, click the Back and Forward buttons in the task pane.

Reference Window

Using the Research Task Pane

- Type a keyword or phrase into the Search for text box.
- Select a search category, individual source, or all references.
- If necessary, click a link in the search results to display more information.
- Copy and paste selected content from the task pane into your file.

Jake plans to send a copy of the next quarter's sales report to the office in France. You'll use the bilingual dictionaries in the Research task pane to begin entering labels in French into an Excel workbook for the sales report.

To use the bilingual dictionaries in the Research task pane:

1. Click the **Microsoft Excel – Book1** button on the taskbar to switch to the Excel window.
2. Click the **Other Task Panes** button on the Getting Started task pane, and then click **Research**. The Research task pane opens.
3. Click in the **Search for** text box, and then type **paper**.
4. Click the **Search for** list arrow and then click **Translation**. The bilingual dictionary opens in the Research task pane. You can choose from among 12 languages to translate to and from, including Japanese, Russian, Spanish, Dutch, German, and French.

   Trouble? If a dialog box opens stating the translation feature is not installed, click the Yes button to install it.
5. If necessary, click the **To** list arrow, and then click **French (France)**. See Figure 12.

Research task pane | **Figure 12**

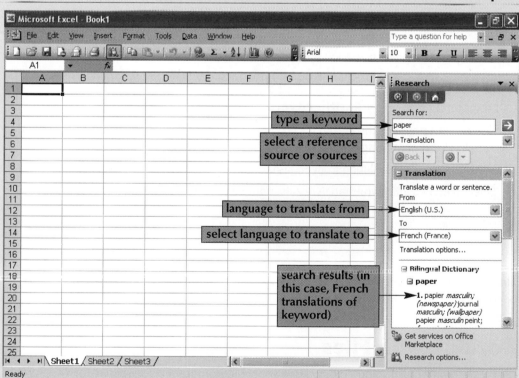

6. Scroll to read the different translations of "paper" in French.

After you locate specific information, you can quickly insert it into your open file. The information can be inserted by copying the selected content you want to insert, and then pasting it in the appropriate location in your file. In some instances, such as MSN Money Stock Quotes, a button appears enabling you to quickly insert the indicated information in your file at the location of the insertion point. Otherwise, you can use the standard Copy and Paste commands.

You'll copy the translation for "paper" into the Excel workbook.

To copy information from the Research task pane into a file:

1. Select **papier** in the Research task pane. This is the word you want to copy to the workbook.

2. Right-click the selected text, and then click **Copy** on the shortcut menu. The text is duplicated on the Office Clipboard.

3. Right-click cell **A1**, and then click **Paste**. The word "papier" is entered into the cell. See Figure 13.

Figure 13 | **Translation copied into Excel**

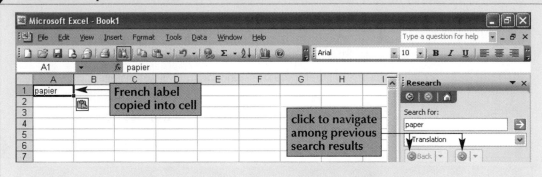

You'll repeat this process to look up the translation for "furniture" and copy it into cell A2.

To translate and copy another word into Excel:

1. Double-click **paper** in the Search for text box to select the text, type **furniture**, and then click the **Start searching** button ➡ in the Research task pane.

2. Verify that you're translating from English (U.S) to French (France).

3. Select **meubles** in the translation results, right-click the selected text, and then click **Copy**.

4. Right-click cell **A2**, and then click **Paste**. The second label appears in the cell.

The Research task pane works similarly in all the Office programs. You'll use other task panes later in this tutorial to perform specific tasks, including opening a file and getting assistance.

Working with Files

The most common tasks you'll perform in any Office program are to create, open, save, and close files. The processes for each of these tasks are the same in all the Office programs. In addition, there are several methods for performing most tasks in Office. This flexibility enables you to use Office in a way that fits how you like to work.

Creating a File

To begin working in a program, you need to create a new file or open an existing file. When you start Word, Excel, or PowerPoint, the program opens along with a blank file—ready for you to begin working on a new document, workbook, or presentation. When you start Access, the Getting Started task pane opens, displaying options for opening a new database or an existing one.

Jake has asked you to start working on the agenda for the stockholder meeting, which he suggests you create using Word. You enter text in a Word document by typing.

To enter text in a document:

1. Click the **Document1 – Microsoft Word** button on the taskbar to activate the Word program window.

2. Type **Delmar Office Supplies**, and then press the **Enter** key. The text you typed appears on one line in the Word document.

   Trouble? If you make a typing error, press the Backspace key to delete the incorrect letters, and then retype the text.

3. Type **Stockholder Meeting Agenda**, and then press the **Enter** key. The text you typed appears on the second line.

Next, you'll save the file.

Saving a File

As you create and modify Office files, your work is stored only in the computer's temporary memory, not on a hard disk. If you were to exit the programs, turn off your computer, or experience a power failure, your work would be lost. To prevent losing work, save your file to a disk frequently—at least every 10 minutes. You can save files to the hard disk located inside your computer or to portable storage disks, such as floppy disks, Zip disks, or read-write CD-ROMs.

The first time you save a file, you need to name it. This name is called a **filename**. When you choose a filename, select a descriptive one that accurately reflects the content of the document, workbook, presentation, or database, such as "Shipping Options Letter" or "Fourth Quarter Financial Analysis." Filenames can include a maximum of 255 letters, numbers, hyphens, and spaces in any combination. Office appends a **file extension** to the filename, which identifies the program in which that file was created. The file extensions are .doc for Word, .xls for Excel, .ppt for PowerPoint, and .mdb for Access. Whether you see file extensions depends on how Windows is set up on your computer.

You also need to decide where to save the file—on which disk and in what folder. A **folder** is a container for your files. Just as you organize paper documents within folders stored in a filing cabinet, you can organize your files within folders stored on your computer's hard disk or a removable disk. Store each file in a logical location that you will remember whenever you want to use the file again.

Reference Window | **Saving a File**

- Click the Save button on the Standard toolbar (*or* click File on the menu bar, and then click Save or Save As).
- In the Save As dialog box, click the Save in list arrow, and then navigate to the location where you want to save the file.
- Type a filename in the File name text box.
- Click the Save button.
- To resave the named file to the same location, click the Save button on the Standard toolbar (*or* click File on the menu bar, and then click Save).

The two lines of text you typed are not yet saved on disk. You'll do that now.

To save a file for the first time:

1. Click the **Save** button 🔲 on the Standard toolbar. The Save As dialog box opens. The first few words of the first line appear in the File name text box, as a suggested filename. You'll replace this with a more descriptive filename.

2. Click the **Save in** list arrow, and then click the location that contains your Data Files.

    Trouble? If you don't have the Common Office Features Data Files, you need to get them before you can proceed. Your instructor will either give you the Data Files or ask you to obtain them from a specified location (such as a network drive). In either case, be sure that you make a backup copy of your Data Files before you start using them, so that the original files will be available on your copied disk in case you need to start over because of an error or problem. If you have any questions about the Data Files, see your instructor or technical support person for assistance.

3. Double-click the **OFF** folder in the list box, and then double-click the **Tutorial** folder. This is the location where you want to save the document. See Figure 14.

4. Type **Stockholder Meeting Agenda** in the File name text box.

Figure 14 | **Completed Save As dialog box**

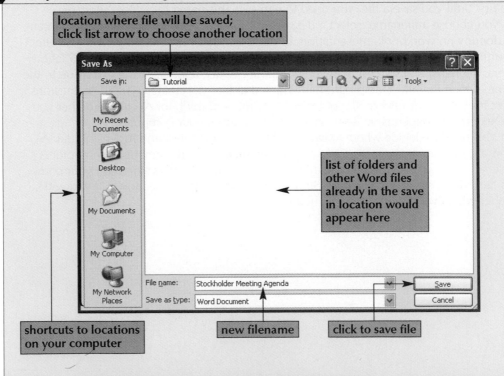

location where file will be saved; click list arrow to choose another location

list of folders and other Word files already in the save in location would appear here

shortcuts to locations on your computer

new filename

click to save file

Trouble? If the .doc file extension appears after the filename, then your computer is configured to show file extensions. Continue with Step 5.

5. Click the **Save** button. The Save As dialog box closes, and the name of your file appears in the program window title bar.

The saved file includes everything in the document at the time you last saved it. Any edits or additions you then make to the document exist only in the computer's memory and are not saved in the file on the disk. As you work, remember to save frequently so that the file is updated to reflect the latest content of the document.

Because you already named the document and selected a storage location, the second and subsequent times you save, the Save As dialog box doesn't open. If you wanted to save a copy of the file with a different filename or to a different location, you would reopen the Save As dialog box by clicking File on the menu bar, and then clicking Save As. The previous version of the file remains on your disk as well.

You need to add your name to the agenda. Then you'll save your changes.

To modify and save a file:

1. Type your name, and then press the **Enter** key. The text you typed appears on the next line.
2. Click the **Save** button 🖫 on the Standard toolbar to save your changes.

When you're done with a file, you can close it.

Closing a File

Although you can keep multiple files open at one time, you should close any file you are no longer working on to conserve system resources as well as to ensure that you don't inadvertently make changes to the file. You can close a file by clicking the Close command on the File menu or by clicking the Close Window button in the upper-right corner of the menu bar.

As a standard practice, you should save your file before closing it. If you're unsure whether the file is saved, it cannot hurt to save it again. However, Office has an added safeguard: If you attempt to close a file or exit a program without saving your changes, a dialog box opens asking whether you want to save the file. Click the Yes button to save the changes to the file before closing the file and program. Click the No button to close the file and program without saving changes. Click the Cancel button to return to the program window without saving changes or closing the file and program. This feature helps to ensure that you always save the most current version of any file.

You'll add the date to the agenda. Then, you'll attempt to close the document without saving.

To modify and close a file:

1. Type the date, and then press the **Enter** key. The text you typed appears under your name in the document.
2. Click the **Close Window** button ❌ on the Word menu bar to close the document. A dialog box opens, asking whether you want to save the changes you made to the document.

3. Click the **Yes** button. The current version of the document is saved to the file, and then the document closes, and Word is still running.

Trouble? If Word is not running, then you closed the program in Step 2. Start Word, click the Close Window button on the menu bar to close the blank document.

Once you have a program open, you can create additional new files for the open program or you can open previously created and saved files.

Opening a File

When you want to open a blank document, workbook, presentation, or database, you create a new file. When you want to work on a previously created file, you must first open it. Opening a file transfers a copy of the file from the storage disk (either a hard disk or a portable disk) to the computer's memory and displays it on your screen. The file is then in your computer's memory and on the disk.

Reference Window	**Opening an Existing or a New File**

- Click the Open button on the Standard toolbar (*or* click File on the menu bar, and then click Open *or* click the More link in the Open section of the Getting Started task pane).
- In the Open dialog box, click the Look in list arrow, and then navigate to the storage location of the file you want to open.
- Click the filename of the file you want to open.
- Click the Open button.

or

- Click the New button on the Standard toolbar (*or* click File on the menu bar, click New, and then (depending on the program) click the Blank document, Blank workbook, Blank presentation, or Blank database link in the New task pane).

Jake asks you to print the agenda. To do that, you'll reopen the file. You'll use the Open button on the Standard toolbar.

To open an existing file:

1. Click the **Open** button 📂 on the Standard toolbar. The Open dialog box, which works similarly to the Save As dialog box, opens.

2. Click the **Look in** list arrow, and then navigate to the **OFF\Tutorial** folder included with your Data Files. This is the location where you saved the agenda document.

3. Click **Stockholder Meeting Agenda** in the file list. See Figure 15.

Open dialog box | **Figure 15**

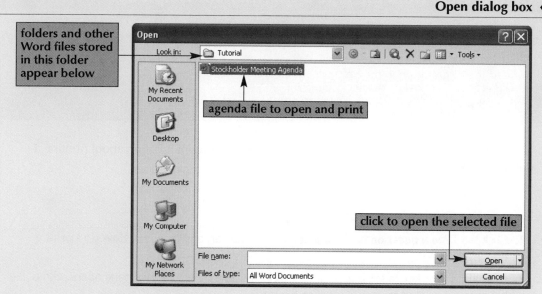

folders and other Word files stored in this folder appear below

agenda file to open and print

click to open the selected file

4. Click the **Open** button. The file containing the agenda opens in the Word program window.

Next, you'll get information about printing files in Word.

Getting Help

If you don't know how to perform a task or want more information about a feature, you can turn to Office itself for information on how to use it. This information, referred to simply as **Help**, is like a huge encyclopedia available from your desktop. You can access Help in a variety of ways, including ScreenTips, the Type a question for help box, the Help task pane, and Microsoft Office Online.

Using ScreenTips

ScreenTips are a fast and simple method you can use to get help about objects you see on the screen. A **ScreenTip** is a yellow box with the button's name. Just position the mouse pointer over a toolbar button to view its ScreenTip.

Using the Type a Question for Help Box

For answers to specific questions, you can use the **Type a question for help box**, located on the menu bar of every Office program, to find information in the Help system. You simply type a question using everyday language about a task you want to perform or a topic you need help with, and then press the Enter key to search the Help system. The Search Results task pane opens with a list of Help topics related to your query. You click a topic to open a Help window with step-by-step instructions that guide you through a specific procedure and explanations of difficult concepts in clear, easy-to-understand language. For example, you might ask how to format a cell in an Excel worksheet; a list of Help topics related to the words you typed will appear.

Reference Window	**Getting Help from the Type a Question for Help Box**

- Click the Type a question for help box on the menu bar.
- Type your question, and then press the Enter key.
- Click a Help topic in the Search Results task pane.
- Read the information in the Help window. For more information, click other topics or links.
- Click the Close button on the Help window title bar.

You'll use the Type a question for help box to obtain more information about printing a document in Word.

To use the Type a question for help box:

1. Click the **Type a question for help box** on the menu bar, and then type **How do I print a document?**

2. Press the **Enter** key to retrieve a list of topics. The Search Results task pane opens with a list of topics related to your query. See Figure 16.

Figure 16	**Search Results task pane displaying Help topics**

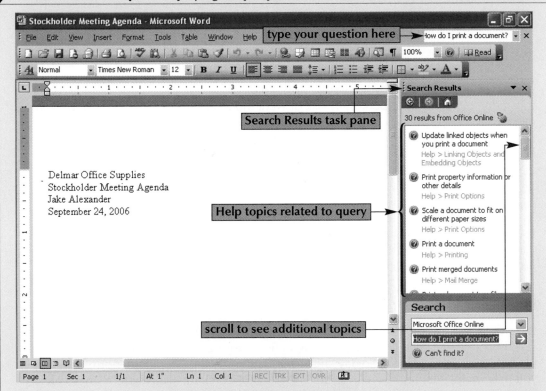

Trouble? If your search results list differs from the one shown in Figure 16, your computer is not connected to the Internet or Microsoft has updated the list of available Help topics since this book was published. Continue with Step 3.

3. Scroll through the list to review the Help topics.

4. Click **Print a document** to open the Help window and learn more about the various ways to print a document. See Figure 17.

Print a document Help window ◄ **Figure 17**

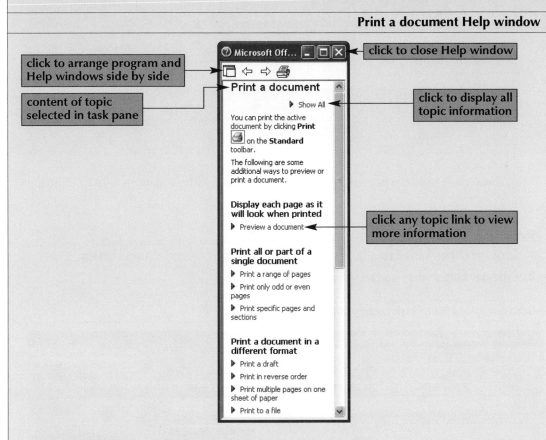

click to arrange program and Help windows side by side

content of topic selected in task pane

click to close Help window

click to display all topic information

click any topic link to view more information

Trouble? If the Word program window and the Help window do not appear side by side, then you need to tile the windows. Click the Auto Tile button on the toolbar in the Help window.

5. Read the information, and then when you're done, click the **Close** button ☒ on the Help window title bar to close the Help window.

The Help task pane works similarly.

Using the Help Task Pane

For more in-depth help, you can use the **Help task pane**, a task pane that enables you to search the Help system using keywords or phrases. You type a specific word or phrase in the Search for text box, and then click the Start searching button. The Search Results task pane opens with a list of topics related to the keyword or phrase you entered. If your computer is connected to the Internet, you might see more search results because some Help topics are stored only online and not locally on your computer. The task pane also has a Table of Contents link that organizes the Help system by subjects and topics, like in a book. You click main subject links to display related topic links.

Getting Help from the Help Task Pane

- Click the Other Task Panes button on the task pane title bar, and then click Help (*or* click Help on the menu bar, and then click Microsoft Word/Excel/PowerPoint/Access/ Outlook Help).
- Type a keyword or phrase in the Search for text box, and then click the Start searching button.
- Click a Help topic in the Search Results task pane.
- Read the information in the Help window. For more information, click other topics or links.
- Click the Close button on the Help window title bar.

You'll use the Help task pane to obtain more information about getting help in Office.

To use the Help task pane:

▶ 1. Click the **Other Task Panes** button on the task pane title bar, and then click **Help**.

▶ 2. Type **get help** in the Search for text box. See Figure 18.

Figure 18 Microsoft Word Help task pane with keyword

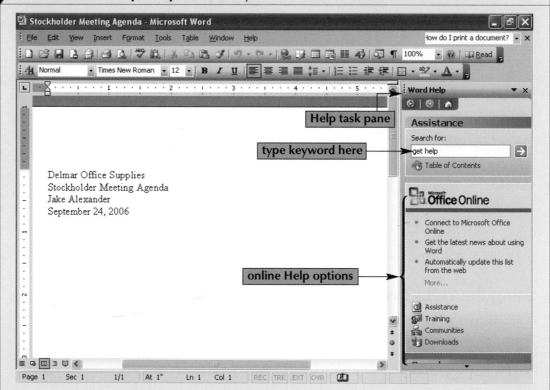

▶ 3. Click the **Start searching** button ➡. The Search Results task pane opens with a list of topics related to your keywords.

▶ 4. Scroll through the list to review the Help topics.

▶ 5. Click **About getting help while you work** to open the Microsoft Word Help window and learn more about the various ways to obtain help in Word. See Figure 19.

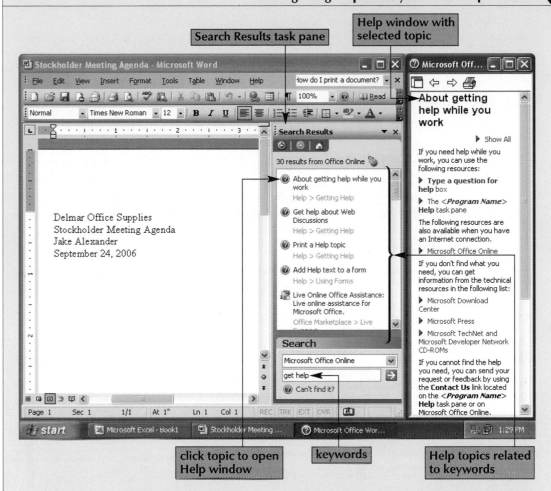

About getting help while you work Help window ◄ **Figure 19**

Trouble? If your search results list differs from the one shown in Figure 19, your computer is not connected to the Internet or Microsoft has updated the list of available Help topics since this book was published. Continue with Step 6.

Trouble? If the Word program window and the Help window do not appear side by side, then you need to tile the windows. Click the Auto Tile button on the toolbar in the Help window.

▶ 6. Click **Microsoft Office Online** in the right pane to display information about that topic. Read the information.

▶ 7. Click the other links about this feature and read the information.

▶ 8. When you're done, click the **Close** button ☒ on the Help window title bar to close the Help window. The task pane remains open.

If your computer has a connection to the Internet, you can get more help information from Microsoft Office Online.

Using Microsoft Office Online

Microsoft Office Online is a Web site maintained by Microsoft that provides access to additional Help resources. For example, you can access current Help topics, read how-to articles, and find tips for using Office. You can search all or part of a site to find information about tasks you want to perform, features you want to use, or anything else you want more help with. You can connect to Microsoft Office Online from the Getting Started task pane, the Help task pane, or the Help menu.

To connect to Microsoft Office Online, you'll need Internet access and a Web browser such as Internet Explorer.

To connect to Microsoft Office Online:

1. Click the **Back** button ⬅ in the Search Results task pane. The Word Help task pane reappears.

2. Click the **Connect to Microsoft Office Online** link in the task pane. Internet Explorer starts and the Microsoft Office Online home page opens. See Figure 20. This Web page offers links to Web pages focusing on getting help and for accessing additional Office resources, such as additional galleries of clip art, software downloads, and training opportunities.

| Figure 20 | Microsoft Office Online home page |

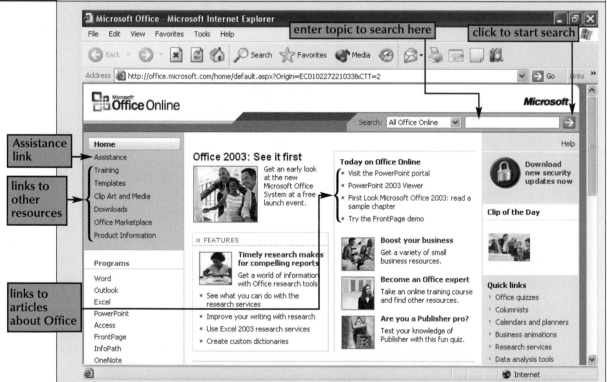

Trouble? If the content you see on the Microsoft Office Online home page differs from the figure, the site has been updated since this book was published. Continue with Step 3.

3. Click the **Assistance** link. The Assistance page opens. From this page, you browse for help in each of the different Office programs. You can also enter a keyword or phrase pertaining to a particular topic you wish to search for information on using the Search box in the upper-right corner of the window.

4. Click the **Close** button ☒ on the Internet Explorer title bar to close the browser.

The Help features enable the staff at Delmar Office Supplies to get answers to questions they have about any task or procedure when they need it. The more you practice getting information from the Help system, the more effective you will be at using Office to its full potential.

Printing a File

At times, you'll want a paper copy of your Office file. The first time you print during each session at the computer, you should use the Print menu command to open the Print dialog box so you can verify or adjust the printing settings. You can select a printer, the number of copies to print, the portion of the file to print, and so forth; the printing settings vary slightly from program to program. For subsequent print jobs, you can use the Print button to print without opening the dialog box, if you want to use the same default settings.

Reference Window

Printing a File

- Click File on the menu bar, and then click Print.
- Verify the print settings in the Print dialog box.
- Click the OK button.

or

- Click the Print button on the Standard toolbar.

Now that you know how to print, you'll print the agenda for Jake.

To print a file:

1. Make sure your printer is turned on and contains paper.
2. Click **File** on the menu bar, and then click **Print**. The Print dialog box opens. See Figure 21.

Print dialog box   Figure 21

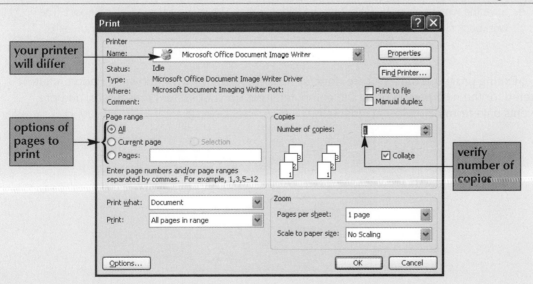

3. Verify that the correct printer appears in the Name list box in the Printer area. If the wrong printer appears, click the **Name** list arrow, and then click the correct printer from the list of available printers.

4. Verify that **1** appears in the Number of copies text box.

5. Click the **OK** button to print the document.

   Trouble? If the document does not print, see your instructor or technical support person for help.

Now that you have printed the agenda, you can close Word and Excel.

Exiting Programs

Whenever you finish working with a program, you should exit it. As with many other aspects of Office, you can exit programs with a button or from a menu. You'll use both methods to close Word and Excel. You can use the Exit command to exit a program and close an open file in one step. If you haven't saved the final version of the open file, a dialog box opens, asking whether you want to save your changes. Clicking the Yes button saves the open file, closes the file, and then exits the program.

To exit a program:

1. Click the **Close** button ⊠ on the Word title bar to exit Word. The Word document closes and the Word program exits. The Excel window is visible again on your screen.

   Trouble? If a dialog box opens, asking whether you want to save the document, you may have inadvertently made a change to the document. Click the No button.

2. Click **File** on the Excel menu bar, and then click **Exit**. A dialog box opens asking whether you want to save the changes you made to the workbook.

3. Click the **Yes** button. The Save As dialog box opens.

4. Save the workbook in the **OFF\Tutorial** folder with the filename **French Sales Report**. The workbook closes, saving a copy to the location you specified, and the Excel program exits.

Exiting programs after you are done using them keeps your Windows desktop uncluttered for the next person using the computer, frees up your system's resources, and prevents data from being lost accidentally.

Review

Quick Check

1. List the five programs included in Office.
2. How do you start an Office program?
3. Explain the difference between Save As and Save.
4. What is one method for opening an existing Office file?
5. What happens if you attempt to close a file or exit a program without saving the current version of the open file?
6. What are four ways to get help?

Review

Tutorial Summary

You have learned how to use features common to all the programs included in Microsoft Office 2003, including starting and exiting programs; resizing windows; using menus and toolbars; working with task panes; saving, opening, closing, and printing files; and getting help.

Key Terms

Access	menu	Outlook
database	menu bar	PowerPoint
document	menu command	presentation
Excel	Microsoft Access 2003	ScreenTip
file extension	Microsoft Excel 2003	task pane
filename	Microsoft Office 2003	toolbar
folder	Microsoft Office Online	Type a question for help box
Help	Microsoft Outlook 2003	Word
Help task pane	Microsoft PowerPoint 2003	workbook
integration	Microsoft Word 2003	
keyboard shortcut	Office	

Practice

Practice the skills you learned in the tutorial using the same case scenario.

Review Assignments

Data Files needed for the Review Assignments: Finances.xls, Letter.doc

Before the stockholders meeting at Delmar Office Supplies, you'll open and print documents for the upcoming presentation. Complete the following steps:

1. Start PowerPoint.
2. Use the Help task pane to learn how to change the toolbar buttons from small to large, and then do it. Use the same procedure to change the buttons back to regular size. Close the Help window when you're done.
3. Start Excel.
4. Switch to the PowerPoint window using the taskbar, and then close the presentation but leave open the PowerPoint program. (*Hint:* Click the Close Window button on the menu bar.)
5. Open a new, blank PowerPoint presentation from the Getting Started task pane. (*Hint:* Click Create a new presentation in the Open section of the Getting Started task pane.)
6. Close the PowerPoint presentation and program using the Close button on the PowerPoint title bar; do not save changes if asked.

7. Open the **Finances** workbook located in the **OFF\Review** folder included with your Data Files using the Open button on the Standard toolbar in Excel.

8. Use the Save As command to save the workbook as **Delmar Finances** in the **OFF\Review** folder.

9. Type your name, press the Enter key to insert your name at the top of the worksheet, and then save the workbook.

10. Print one copy of the worksheet using the Print command on the File menu.

11. Exit Excel using the File menu.

12. Start Word, and then use the Getting Started task pane to open the **Letter** document located in the **OFF\Review** folder included with your Data Files. (*Hint:* Click the More link in the Getting Started task pane to open the Open dialog box.)

13. Use the Save As command to save the document with the filename **Delmar Letter** in the **OFF\Review** folder.

14. Press and hold the Ctrl key, press the End key, and then release both keys to move the insertion point to the end of the letter, and then type your name.

15. Use the Save button on the Standard toolbar to save the change to the Delmar Letter document.

16. Print one copy of the document, and then close the document.

17. Exit the Word program using the Close button on the title bar.

Assess

SAM Assessment and Training

If you have a SAM user profile, you may have access to hands-on instruction, practice, and assessment of the skills covered in this tutorial. Log in to your SAM account and go to your assignments page to see what your instructor has assigned.

Review

Quick Check Answers

1. Word, Excel, PowerPoint, Access, Outlook

2. Click the Start button on the taskbar, point to All Programs, point to Microsoft Office, and then click the name of the program you want to open.

3. Save As enables you to change the filename and storage location of a file. Save updates a file to reflect its latest contents using its current filename and location.

4. Either click the Open button on the Standard toolbar or click the More link in the Getting Started task pane to open the Open dialog box.

5. A dialog box opens asking whether you want to save the changes to the file.

6. ScreenTips, Type a question for help box, Help task pane, Microsoft Office Online

New Perspectives on

Microsoft® Office Excel 2003

Read This Before You Begin: Tutorials 1–4

To the Student

Data Files

To complete the Level I Excel Tutorials (Tutorials 1 through 4), you need the starting student Data Files. Your instructor will either provide you with these Data Files or ask you to obtain them yourself.

The Level I Excel tutorials require the folders shown in the next column to complete the Tutorials, Review Assignments, and Case Problems. You will need to copy these folders from a file server, a standalone computer, or the Web to the drive and folder where you will be storing your Data Files. Your instructor will tell you which computer, drive letter, and folder(s) contain the files you need. You can also download the files by going to www.course.com; see the inside back or front cover for more information on downloading the files, or ask your instructor or technical support person for assistance.

If you are storing your Data Files on floppy disks, you will need **two** blank, formatted, high-density disks for these tutorials. Label your disks as shown, and place on them the folders indicated.

▼ **Excel 2003: Data Disk 1**
 Tutorial.01 folder
 Tutorial.02 folder

▼ **Excel 2003: Data Disk 2**
 Tutorial.03 folder
 Tutorial.04 folder

When you begin a tutorial, refer to the Student Data Files section at the bottom of the tutorial opener page, which indicates which folders and files you need for the tutorial. Each end-of-tutorial exercise also indicates the files you need to complete that exercise.

Course Labs

The Level I Excel tutorials feature an interactive Course Lab to help you understand spreadsheet concepts. There are Lab Assignments at the end of Tutorial 1 that relate to this lab. Contact your instructor or technical support person for assistance in accessing the lab.

To the Instructor

The Data Files and Course Labs are available on the Instructor Resources CD for this title. Follow the instructions in the Help file on the CD to install the programs to your network or standalone computer. See the "To the Student" section above for information on how to set up the Data Files that accompany this text.

You are granted a license to copy the Data Files and Course Labs to any computer or computer network used by students who have purchased this book.

System Requirements

If you are going to work through this book using your own computer, you need:

• **Computer System** Microsoft Windows 2000, Windows XP or higher must be installed on your computer. These tutorials assume a typical installation of Microsoft Excel 2003.

• **Data Files** You will not be able to complete the tutorials or exercises in this book using your own computer until you have the necessary starting Data Files.

• **Course Labs** See your instructor or technical support person to obtain the Course Lab software for use on your own computer.

Objectives

Session 1.1
- Learn about spreadsheets and how they work
- Identify major components of the Excel window
- Navigate within and between worksheets
- Enter text, dates, data, and formulas into a worksheet
- Change the size of a column or row

Session 1.2
- Select and move cell ranges
- Calculate totals with AutoSum
- Insert and delete a column or row
- Work in edit mode
- Undo an action
- Insert, move, and rename a worksheet
- Check the spelling in a workbook
- Preview and print a workbook
- Display the formulas within a worksheet

Lab

Student Data Files

Using Excel to Manage Data

Creating a Sales Order Report

Case

Dalton Food Co-op

Sandra Dalton and her husband, Kevin, own a farm in northern Florida. Recently, Sandra has been selling produce to local families to earn extra income. When she started, Sandra kept a paper record of customer orders, and all of the data was entered into a paper ledger with the calculations done on a tabletop calculator. Several months ago, Sandra and Kevin purchased a computer for the co-op. Bundled with the other software installed on the computer was a copy of **Microsoft Office Excel 2003** (or simply **Excel**), a computer program used to enter, analyze, and present quantitative data.

Sandra, who handles most of the financial aspects of the business, has been using Excel for several months, but as the business continues to grow and its busy season approaches, she has asked you to help. She wants you to use an Excel workbook to keep track of orders recently made at the Dalton Food Co-op.

▼**Tutorial.01**

▽ **Tutorial folder**

    (no starting Data Files)

▽ **Review folder**

    (no starting Data Files)

▽ **Cases folder**

    Balance1.xls
    CFlow1.xls
    Site1.xls

Session 1.1

Spreadsheets

Introducing Excel

Before you begin working with the recent orders at the co-op, you need to understand some of the key terms and concepts associated with a program such as Excel.

Understanding Spreadsheets

Excel is a computerized spreadsheet. A **spreadsheet** is an important tool used for analyzing and reporting information. Spreadsheets are often used in business for budgeting, inventory management, and decision making. For example, an accountant might use a paper-based spreadsheet like the one shown in Figure 1-1 to record a company's estimated and actual monthly cash flow.

| Figure 1-1 | A sample spreadsheet |

Cash Flow Comparison
Actual versus Budget

	Jan-06	
	Estimated	**Actual**
Cash balance(start of month)	$ 1,500.00	$ 1,500.00
Receipts		
Cash sales	1700.00	1852.00
Cash expenditures		
Advertising	200.00	211.00
Wages	900.00	900.00
Supplies	100.00	81.00
Total cash expenditures	1200.00	1192.00
Net cash flow	500.00	660.00
Cash balance(end of month)	$ 2,000.00	$ 2,160.00

In this spreadsheet, the accountant has recorded the estimated and actual cash flow for the month of January. Each line, or row, in this spreadsheet displays a different cash flow value. Each column contains the predicted or actual values, or text that describes those values. The accountant has also entered the total cash expenditures, net cash flow, and closing cash balance for the month, perhaps having used a calculator to do the calculations.

Figure 1-2 shows the same spreadsheet in Excel. The spreadsheet is now laid out in a grid in which the rows and columns are easily apparent. As you will see later, calculations are also part of this electronic spreadsheet, so that total cash expenditures, net cash flow, and cash balances are calculated automatically rather than entered manually. When you change an entry in the electronic spreadsheet, the spreadsheet automatically updates any calculated values based on the entry. You can also use an electronic spreadsheet to perform a **what-if analysis** in which you change one or more of the values in the worksheet and then examine the recalculated values to determine the effect of the change. (You will have a chance to explore this feature at the end of the tutorial.) So, an electronic spreadsheet provides more flexibility in entering and analyzing your data than the paper version.

The same spreadsheet in Excel ◀ **Figure 1-2**

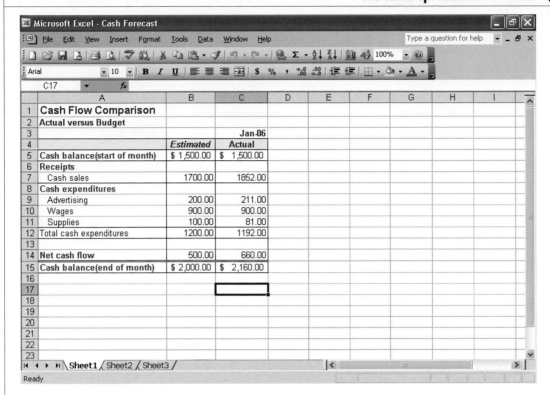

Excel stores electronic spreadsheets in files called **workbooks**. Each workbook is made up of individual **worksheets**, or **sheets**, just as a spiral-bound ledger, which an accountant would use, is made up of sheets of paper. You will learn more about multiple worksheets later in the tutorial. For now, keep in mind that the terms *worksheet* and *sheet* are often used interchangeably.

Parts of the Excel Window

Excel displays workbooks within a window that contains many tools for entering, editing, and viewing data. You will learn about some of these tools after starting Excel. By default, Excel opens with a blank workbook.

To start Excel:

▶ 1. Click the **Start** button on the taskbar, point to **All Programs**, point to **Microsoft Office**, and then click **Microsoft Office Excel 2003**. The Excel window opens. See Figure 1-3.

Figure 1-3 | **Parts of the Excel window**

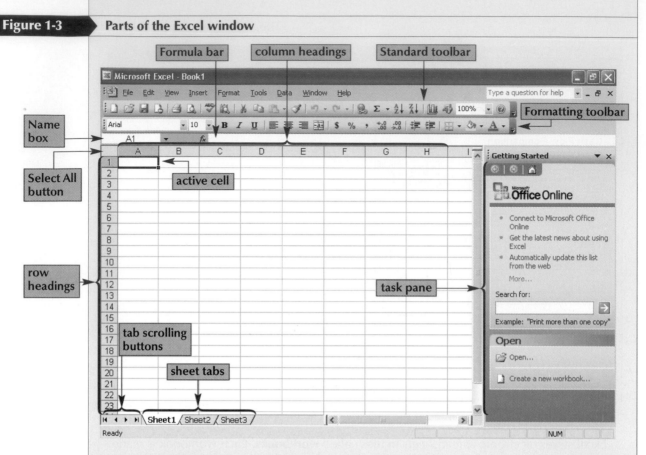

Trouble? If you don't see the Microsoft Office Excel 2003 option on the Microsoft Office submenu, look for it in a different submenu or as an option on the All Programs menu. If you still cannot find the Microsoft Office Excel 2003 option, ask your instructor or technical support person for help.

The Excel window contains many of the components that you find in other Windows programs, including a title bar, a menu bar, scroll bars, and a status bar. The Excel window also contains features that are unique to Excel. Within the Excel program window is another window, referred to as the **workbook window** or **worksheet window**. The worksheet window provides a grid of **columns** and **rows**, and the intersection of a column and row is called a **cell**. Each cell is identified by a **cell reference**, which is its column and row location. For example, the cell reference B6 indicates that the cell is located where column B and row 6 intersect. The column letter is always first in the cell reference: B6 is a correct reference; 6B is not. The cell in which you are working is called the **active cell**. Excel identifies the active cell by outlining it with a dark border. In Figure 1-3, cell A1 is the active cell. Notice that the cell reference for the active cell appears in the **Name box** next to the **Formula bar**. You can change the active cell by selecting another cell in the worksheet. As you review the layout of the Excel window shown in Figure 1-3, refer to Figure 1-4 for a description of each component.

Excel window components ◄ **Figure 1-4**

Feature	Description
Active cell	The cell in which you are currently working. A dark border outlining the cell identifies the active cell.
Column headings	The letters that appear along the top of the worksheet window. Columns are listed alphabetically from A to IV (a total of 256 possible columns).
Formula bar	The bar located immediately below the toolbars that displays the contents of the active cell. As you type or edit data, the changes appear in the Formula bar.
Name box	The box that displays the cell reference, or column and row location, of the active cell in the workbook window.
Row headings	The numbers that appear along the left side of the worksheet window. Rows are numbered consecutively from 1 to 65,536.
Select All button	Square button located at the intersection of the column and row headings that you click to select the entire contents of the worksheet.
Sheet tabs	Tabs located at the bottom of each worksheet in the workbook that display the names of the sheets. To move between worksheets, click the appropriate sheet tab.
Task pane	The pane that provides access to frequently used tasks. When you start Excel, the Getting Started task pane appears. The task pane disappears once you open a workbook. There are several task-specific panes available in Excel.
Tab scrolling buttons	Series of buttons located to the left of the sheet tabs that you can click to move between worksheets in the workbook.
Toolbars	Toolbars that provide quick access to commonly used commands. The Standard toolbar contains buttons for the most frequently used program commands, such as Save and Print. The Formatting toolbar contains buttons used to format the appearance of the workbook, such as Bold and Italics. Additional toolbars are available.

Now that you are familiar with the basic layout of an Excel window, you can try moving around within the workbook.

Navigating a Worksheet

Excel provides several ways of moving around within a worksheet. You can use your mouse to click a cell to make it the active cell, or you can use the vertical and horizontal scroll bars to display the area of the worksheet containing the cell you want to make active. You can also navigate a worksheet by using your keyboard. Figure 1-5 describes some of these keyboard shortcuts that Excel provides so you can move from cell to cell within the worksheet quickly and easily.

Shortcut keys for navigating a worksheet ◄ **Figure 1-5**

Keystroke	Action
↑ , ↓ ,←, →	Moves the active cell up, down, left, or right one cell
Ctrl + Home	Moves the active cell to cell A1
Ctrl + End	Moves to the last cell in the worksheet that contains data
Enter	Moves the active cell down one cell, or moves to the start of the next row in the selected range of cells
F5	Opens the Go To dialog box, in which you specify the cell you want to move to
Home	Moves the active cell to column A of the current row
Page Up, Page Down	Moves the active cell up or down one full screen
Tab, Shift + Tab	Moves the active cell to the right or left one cell

Try navigating the worksheet now.

To move around in the worksheet:

▶ 1. Click the **Close** button ✖ in the task pane to close it because you will not be using it in this session. The active cell is A1. The cell A1 is surrounded by a black border, indicating it is the active cell, and the Name box displays the cell reference A1.

▶ 2. With cell A1 the active cell, press the ↓ key on your keyboard four times to move to cell A5, and then press the → key twice to make cell C5 the active cell, as shown in Figure 1-6. Note that the column and row headings are highlighted and the cell reference appears in the Name box.

Figure 1-6	▶	Making cell C5 the active cell

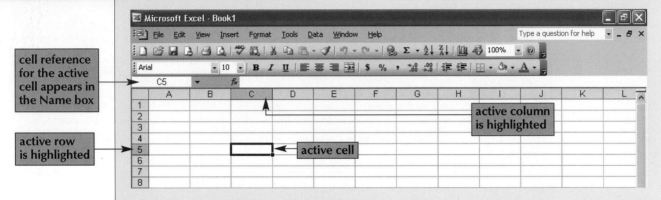

cell reference for the active cell appears in the Name box

active column is highlighted

active row is highlighted

active cell

▶ 3. Press the **Enter** key to move down one cell, and the press the **Tab** key to move to the right one cell. The active cell is now D6.

▶ 4. Press the **Page Down** key to move the display down one screen. The active cell should now be cell D29. If the actual number of columns and rows displayed on your screen differs from that shown in Figure 1-2, the active cell on your screen might not be cell D29. You will learn more about working with the number of columns and rows on your screen later in this tutorial; for now the active cell on your screen should be a screen full of rows down the worksheet.

▶ 5. Press the **Page Up** key to move the display back up one screen, making cell D6 the active cell again.

▶ 6. Press the **Home** key to move to the first cell in the current row, and then press the **Ctrl + Home** keys to make cell A1 active.

You will probably use the keyboard keys to navigate a worksheet the most frequently, but there will also be situations in which you will want to go directly to a cell on your worksheet. Although you can use the Page Up and Page Down keys or use the scroll bars, you have two other options: the Name box and the Go To dialog box. You can just click in the Name box and type the cell reference you want to go to, or you can open the Go To dialog box from any location in the worksheet by pressing the F5 function key. Try using these methods to navigate the worksheet.

To use the Go To dialog box and Name box:

▶ 1. Press the **F5** key to open the Go To dialog box, type **K55** in the Reference text box, and then click the **OK** button to make cell K55 the active cell.

▶ 2. Click in the **Name** box, type **E6**, and then press the **Enter** key to make cell E6 the active cell.

Navigating Between Worksheets

By default, a new Excel workbook contains three worksheets, labeled Sheet1, Sheet2, and Sheet3. Each sheet can be used to display different information. To move from one sheet to another, click the sheet tabs at the bottom of each sheet.

To move between worksheets:

▶ 1. Click the **Sheet2** tab. Sheet2, which is blank, appears in the workbook window. Notice that the Sheet2 tab is now white with the name "Sheet2" in a bold font. This is a visual indicator that Sheet2 is the active worksheet.

▶ 2. Click the **Sheet3** tab to move to the next worksheet in the workbook.

▶ 3. Click the **Sheet1** tab to make it the active worksheet.

Now that you have some basic skills navigating through a worksheet and a workbook, you can begin work on Sandra's worksheet.

Developing a Worksheet

Before you begin to enter data in a worksheet, you should think about the purpose of the worksheet and what will be needed to meet the challenge of that purpose. Effective worksheets are well planned and carefully designed. A well-designed worksheet should clearly identify its overall goal. It should present information in a clear, well-organized format and include all the data necessary to produce results that address the goal of the application. The process of developing a good worksheet includes the following planning and execution steps:

- Determine the worksheet's purpose, what it will include, and how it will be organized.
- Enter the data and formulas into the worksheet.
- Test the worksheet, and then edit the worksheet to correct any errors or to make modifications.
- Document the worksheet and format the worksheet's appearance.
- Save and print the complete worksheet.

To develop a worksheet that records orders made at the co-op, Sandra wants to develop a planning analysis sheet that will help her answer the following questions:

1. What is the goal of the worksheet? This helps to define its purpose or, in other words, the problem to solve.
2. What are the desired results? This information describes the output—the information required to help solve the problem.
3. What data is needed to calculate the results you want to see? This information is the input—data that must be entered.
4. What calculations are needed to produce the desired output? These calculations specify the formulas used in the worksheet.

After careful consideration of these questions, Sandra has developed the planning analysis sheet shown in Figure 1-7.

Figure 1-7 Planning analysis sheet

Planning Analysis Sheet
Author: Sandra Dalton, Dalton Food Co-op
Date: 4/26/2006

My goal
To develop a worksheet in which I can enter food co-op orders, calculating the total quantity of the items ordered and the revenue generated.

What results do I need to see?
▪ A listing of each order made by customers
▪ The total amount of each order
▪ The total quantity of items ordered by all of the customers
▪ The total revenue generated by all of the orders

What data do I need?
▪ The customer's name and address
▪ The date of the order
▪ The item purchased by the customer
▪ The price of each item
▪ The quantity of items ordered by the customer

What calculations must be performed by the worksheet?
▪ The total amount of each order (= price of the item x the quantity ordered)
▪ The total quantity of items ordered (= sum of the order quantities)
▪ The total revenue generated by all of the orders (= sum of the total amount of each order)

Sandra also knows the information that needs to go into the worksheet, including titles, column headings, row labels, and data values. Figure 1-8 shows how Sandra wants the sales data laid out, based on a sampling of customer orders.

Figure 1-8 Sales data for co-op worksheet

Name	Address	Date	Item	Price	Qty	Total
Alison Wilkes	45 Lincoln Street Midtown, FL 80481	4/16/2006	Red Grapefruit	$14	2	
David Wu	315 Oak Lane Midtown, FL 80422	4/16/2006	Navel Oranges	$17	1	
Carl Ramirez	900 South Street Crawford, FL 81891	4/17/2006	Navel Oranges	$17	2	
Jerry Dawson	781 Tree Lane Midtown, FL 80313	4/18/2006	Deluxe Combo	$21	4	
TOTAL						

The first two columns contain the name and address of the person ordering items from the co-op. The Date and Item columns indicate the date that the order was placed and the item ordered. The Price column displays the price of the item. The Qty column indicates the quantity of each item ordered by the customer. The Total column will display the total amount of each order. The TOTAL row will display the total quantity of items ordered and the total revenue generated by all of the sales. With this information in hand, you are now ready to create Sandra's worksheet in Excel.

Entering Data into a Worksheet

A worksheet can contain the following types of data: text, numeric values, dates, and calculated values. A text entry is simply any combination of words, letters, and numbers, typically used to label key features of the worksheet. Numeric values are numbers on which calculations can be made. Numeric values do not contain alphabetic characters, but may contain characters such as commas, dollar signs, and percent signs. Dates are special numeric values recognized by Excel and can be used to determine date-related calculations. The power of Excel lies in the formulas that you can enter into the worksheet cells, whose calculated values are based on the text, dates, and numeric values entered into other cells in the workbook (or in more complicated cases, other workbooks). If those values are changed, the calculated values will also be changed.

Worksheet cells in Excel can also be formatted to improve or enhance the appearance of the cell contents or an entire worksheet. You'll learn about formatting later in Tutorial 3.

Entering Text

To insert text into a worksheet cell, you first make the cell active by using one of the navigation techniques discussed earlier, and then you type the text you want the cell to contain. Excel automatically aligns the text with the left edge of the cell.

First, you'll enter the column headings that Sandra wants across the top row of her worksheet.

To enter the column headings in row 1:

1. Press the **Ctrl + Home** keys to make cell A1 the active cell on the Sheet1 worksheet.

2. Type **Name** and then press the **Tab** key. Pressing the Tab key enters the text in the cell and moves the insertion point to the right to cell B1, making it the active cell.

3. Type **Address** in cell B1, and then press the **Tab** key again. Cell C1 becomes the active cell.

4. Enter the remaining column headings **Date**, **Item**, **Price**, **Qty**, and **Total** in cells C1 through G1. Press the **Enter** key after you type the text for cell G1. Figure 1-9 shows the column headings for the worksheet.

Entering text into the worksheet ◄ **Figure 1-9**

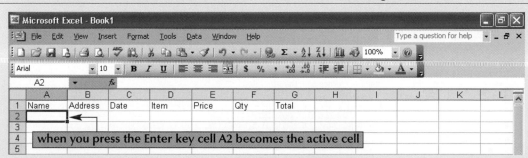

Trouble? If you make a mistake as you type, you can correct the error by clicking the cell and retyping the entry.

Note that when you press the Enter key, the active cell becomes cell A2, not cell G2. Excel recognizes that when you enter a row of data and then press the Enter key, you have completed the task of entering data in the current row, so the insertion point moves to the start of the next row. If you had started entering data in cell C1 rather than A1, pressing the Enter key would have made cell C2 the active cell.

Entering Several Lines of Text Within a Cell

In the next row, you'll enter actual sales information. One cell in this row contains the customer's address. In Sandra's records, this information is presented on two separate lines, with the street address on one line and the city, state, and ZIP code on the other. To place text on separate lines within the same cell, you press and hold the Alt key on the keyboard while pressing the Enter key.

Reference Window	**Entering Multiple Lines of Text Within a Cell**

- Click the cell in which you want to enter the text.
- Enter a line of text.
- Press and hold the Alt key, and then press the Enter key to move the insertion point to a new line within the cell.
- Enter the next line of text.
- Press the Alt + Enter keys for each new line of text you need to enter within the cell.

Try this technique now by entering the first customer's name and address.

To enter the address on two lines within a cell:

1. Verify that cell **A2** is the active cell, type **Alison Wilkes**, and then press the **Tab** key to move to column B, where you will enter the two-line address.

2. Type **45 Lincoln Street** in cell B2, but do *not* press the Tab or Enter key.

3. Press and hold the **Alt** key, and then press the **Enter** key to insert a line break, moving the insertion point to a new line within the cell.

4. Type **Midtown**, **FL 80481** on the second line of the cell, and then press the **Tab** key. Figure 1-10 shows the worksheet with the text you have entered so far.

Figure 1-10	**Entering the customer name and address**

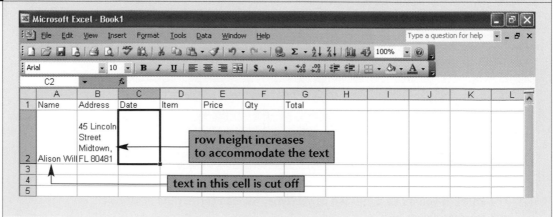

Excel has done a couple of things that you need to understand before entering more data. First, the name of the customer in cell A2 has been cut off, or truncated. When you enter more text than can be displayed within a cell, Excel will display the additional text in the cell or cells to the right as long as they are empty. If the cells to the right are not empty, Excel will truncate the display of the text when it encounters the first non-empty cell. The text itself is not affected. The complete name of the first customer is still entered in cell A2; it's just not displayed.

Second, the customer address in cell B2 does not extend into cell C2, even though that cell is empty. Instead, the height of row 2 has been increased to accommodate this text. If a cell contains multiple lines of text, Excel increases the height of the row to display all of the text entry. Note that the text in cell B2 "appears" to be on four lines, even though you entered the address on two lines. Excel wrapped the text in this way so that it would fit within the existing column width. Later in this session, you will learn how to adjust column widths and row heights to improve the worksheet's appearance.

Entering Dates

In Excel, dates are treated as numeric values, not text. This allows you to perform calculations with dates, such as determining the number of days between two dates. You'll learn how to work with date values in the next tutorial. For now, you need to know how to enter a date. You can enter a date using any of the following date formats, which are recognized by Excel:

- 4/16/2006
- 4/16/06
- 4-16-2006
- April 16, 2006
- 16-Apr-06

The appearance of a date, regardless of how you enter it in a cell, depends on the date format that has been set as the default in your version of Excel. For example, if you enter the date as the text string "April 26, 2006," Excel will automatically convert the entry to "26-Apr-2006" if the DD-MMM-YYYY format has been set as the default. You will learn about cell formats and date formats in Tutorial 3.

Sandra wants the date "4/16/2006" to appear in cell C2, so you will enter that next.

To insert the date in cell C2:

1. Verify that cell **C2** is the active cell.

2. Type **4/16/2006** and then press the **Tab** key.

   Trouble? If your computer is set up to display dates using a different date format, do not worry about their appearance at this time.

3. Type **Red Grapefruit** in cell D2, and then press the **Tab** key. Note that the text in cell D2 is completely displayed because, at this point, the cells to the right of D2 are still empty.

Entering Values

Values are numbers that represent a quantity of some type: the number of units in an inventory, stock prices, an exam score, and so on. Values can be numbers such as 378 and 25.275 or negative numbers such as –55.208. Values can also be expressed as currency such as $14.95 or as percentages such as 95%. Not all numbers are treated as values. For example, Excel treats a telephone number (1-800-555-8010) or a Social Security number (372-70-9654) as a text entry. As you type information into a cell, Excel determines whether the entry can be treated as a value, and if so, automatically right-aligns the value within the cell.

Next, you'll enter the price and quantity of the first order into cells E2 and F2.

To enter the price and quantity values:

1. Type **$14** in cell E2, and then press the **Tab** key.

2. Type **2** in cell F2, and then press the **Tab** key. Figure 1-11 shows the data for the first order. The last cell in the row is empty, but next you will enter a calculation that will give Sandra the total amount of the order.

| Figure 1-11 | Entering the price and quantity values |

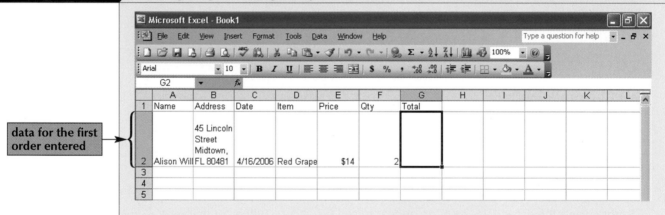

data for the first order entered

The remaining cell in this row will contain the total price of the order, which is equal to the price of the red grapefruit item multiplied by the quantity ordered. The total price of the first order is $14 multiplied by 2, or $28. Rather than entering this value into the cell, you'll let Excel calculate it for you by entering a formula.

Entering Formulas

The single most important reason for using a spreadsheet is to perform calculations on data. To accomplish that goal, you need to enter formulas. A **formula** is a mathematical expression that calculates a value. Excel formulas always begin with an equal sign (=) followed by an expression that describes the calculation to be done. A formula can contain one or more **arithmetic operators**, such as +, –, *, or /. For example, the formula =A1+A2 calculates the sum by adding the values of cells A1 and A2. Figure 1-12 gives examples of some other Excel formulas. Note that, by convention, cell references appear in uppercase letters, but this is not a requirement for Excel formulas. You can type the formula using either upper- or lowercase letters, and Excel will automatically convert the cell references to uppercase.

Sample Excel formulas using arithmetic operators   **Figure 1-12**

Operation	Operator	Example	Description
Addition	+	=10+A5	Adds 10 to the value in cell A5
		=B1+B2+B3	Adds the values of cells B1, B2, and B3
Subtraction	–	=C9–B2	Subtracts the value in cell B2 from the value in cell C9
		=1–D2	Subtracts the value in cell D2 from 1
Multiplication	*	=C9*B9	Multiplies the value in cell C9 by the value in cell B9
		=E5*0.06	Multiplies the value in cell E5 by 0.06
Division	/	=C9/B9	Divides the value in cell C9 by the value in cell B9
		=D15/12	Divides the value in cell D15 by 12
Exponentiation	^	=B5^3	Raises the value in cell B5 to the third power
		=3^B5	Raises 3 to the power specified in cell B5

Entering a Formula

Reference Window

- Click the cell where you want the formula result to appear.
- Type = and then type the expression that calculates the value you want.
- For a formula that includes cell references, such as B2 or D78, type the cell reference, or use the mouse or arrow keys to select each cell.
- When the formula is complete, press the Enter key (or press the Tab key or click the Enter button on the Formula bar).

If an expression contains more than one arithmetic operator, Excel performs the calculation in the order of precedence. The **order of precedence** is a set of predefined rules that Excel follows to calculate a formula by determining which operator is applied first, which operator is applied second, and so forth. First, Excel performs exponentiation (^). Second, Excel performs multiplication (*) or division (/). Third, Excel performs addition (+) or subtraction (–).

For example, because multiplication has precedence over addition, the formula =3+4*5 results in the value 23. If the expression contains two or more operators with the same level of precedence, Excel applies them from left to right in the expression. In the formula =4*10/8, Excel first multiplies 4 by 10 and then divides the result by 8 to produce the value 5.

When building a formula, you must add parentheses to change the order of operations. Excel will calculate any expression contained within the parentheses before any other part of the formula. The formula =(3+4)*5 first calculates the value of 3+4 and then multiplies the total by 5, resulting in the value 35. (Note that without the parentheses, Excel would produce a value of 23, as noted in the previous paragraph.) Figure 1-13 shows other examples of Excel formulas using the order of precedence rules.

Figure 1-13 Examples illustrating order of precedence rules

Formula (A1=50, B1=10, C1=5)	Order of precedence rule	Result
=A1+B1*C1	Multiplication before addition	100
=(A1+B1)*C1	Expression inside parentheses executed before expression outside	300
=A1/B1−C1	Division before subtraction	0
=A1/(B1−C1)	Expression inside parentheses executed before expression outside	10
=A1/B1*C1	Two operators at same precedence level, leftmost operator evaluated first	25
=A1/(B1*C1)	Expression inside parentheses executed before expression outside	1

Using what you know about formulas, you'll enter a formula in cell G2 to calculate the total amount of Alison Wilke's order.

To enter a formula to calculate the total amount of the first order:

1. Verify that cell **G2** is the active cell.

2. Type **=E2*F2** (the price of the item multiplied by the quantity ordered). Note that as you type the cell reference, Excel surrounds each cell with a different colored border that matches the color of the cell reference in the formula. As shown in Figure 1-14, Excel surrounds cell E2 with a blue border, matching the blue used for the cell reference. Green is used for the F2 cell border and cell reference.

Figure 1-14 Typing a formula into the active cell

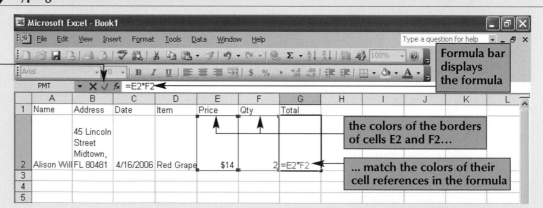

3. Press the **Enter** key. The total amount of the first order displayed in cell G2 is $28. Note that the value is displayed as currency because one of the components of the formula (cell E2) is a currency value. As you can see, the result of the formula is displayed in the worksheet. To see the formula itself, you need to select the cell and examine the formula in the Formula bar.

You can also enter formulas interactively by clicking each cell. In this technique, you type = (an equal sign) to begin the formula, and then click each cell that needs to be entered in the formula. Using this point-and-click method reduces the possibility of error caused by typing an incorrect cell reference.

Next, you'll enter the data for the second order, and then enter the formula =E3*F3 (the price of the item multiplied by the quantity ordered) using the point-and-click method.

To enter the same formula using the point-and-click method:

1. Enter **David Wu** in cell A3, **315 Oak Lane** on one line in cell B3 and **Midtown, FL 80422** on a second line in the cell, **4/16/2006** in cell C3, **Navel Oranges** in cell D3, **$17** in cell E3, and **1** in cell F3. Be sure to press the Alt + Enter keys to enter the address information on two separate lines as you did for the address in cell B2.

2. Make sure cell **G3** is the active cell, and then type **=** (but do *not* press the Enter or Tab key). When you type the equal sign, Excel knows that you are entering a formula. Any cell that you click from now on will cause Excel to insert the reference of the selected cell into the formula until you complete the formula by pressing the Enter or Tab key or by clicking the Enter button on the Formula bar (refer to Figure 1-14).

3. Click cell **E3**. Note that the cell is highlighted in the same color as the cell reference that now appears in the formula in cell G3.

4. Type ***** to enter the multiplication operator.

5. Click cell **F3** to enter this cell reference, and then press the **Enter** key. Cell G3 now contains the formula =E3*F3 and displays the value $17, which is the total amount of the second order.

Using AutoComplete

As you continue to work with Excel, you may find yourself entering the same text in different rows in the worksheet. To help make entering repetitive text easier, Excel provides the **AutoComplete** feature. Once you enter text in a worksheet, Excel tries to anticipate the text you are about to enter by displaying text that begins with the same letter as a previous entry. For example, two people—David Wu and Carl Ramirez—have ordered a box of navel oranges. You have already entered the data for David Wu's order. When you enter the data for Carl Ramirez's order, you will see how AutoComplete works.

To enter text using AutoComplete:

1. Enter **Carl Ramirez** in cell A4, **900 South Street Crawford, FL 81891** in cell B4 on two separate lines within the cell, and **4/17/2006** in cell C4. Do *not* enter the item for Carl's order yet.

2. Make sure cell **D4** is the active cell, and then type **N**. Note that Excel anticipates the entry by displaying "Navel Oranges," which is text you have already entered beginning with the letter N. See Figure 1-15. At this point, you can accept Excel's suggestion by pressing the Enter or Tab key to complete the text entry and to exit the cell. To override Excel's suggestion, you simply keep typing the text you want to enter into the cell.

Figure 1-15 **Entering text with the AutoComplete feature**

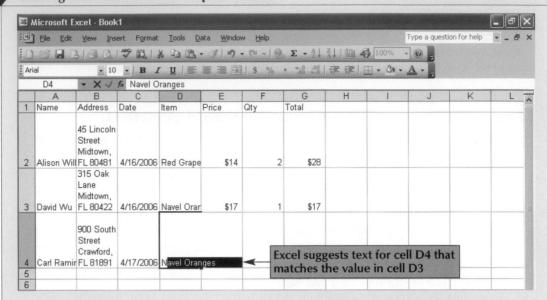

Trouble? If your version of Excel is not set up to use AutoComplete, you will not see the suggested text; therefore you must type "Navel Oranges".

3. Press the **Tab** key to accept Excel's AutoComplete suggestion and to move to cell E4.

4. Type **$17** in cell E4, press the **Tab** key, type **2** in cell F4, and then press the **Tab** key to move to cell G4.

5. Enter **=E4*F4** in cell G4 by typing the formula or by using the point-and-click method. Note that from now on in this text, when you are instructed to "enter" something versus "type" it, use the method that you most prefer; that is, press the Enter key, press the Tab key, or click the Enter button on the Formula bar. Clicking the Enter button not only enters the value in the cell, but also keeps that cell as the active cell.

Excel does not apply AutoComplete to dates or values. However, you can use another feature, AutoFill, to automatically fill in formulas. You'll learn more about AutoFill in the next tutorial.

Now you'll enter the last co-op order into the worksheet.

To enter the last order into the worksheet:

1. Enter **Jerry Dawson** in cell A5, **781 Tree Lane Midtown, FL 80313** in cell B5, **4/18/2006** in cell C5, **Deluxe Combo** in cell D5, **$21** in cell E5, and **4** in cell F5. (Remember to enter the address on two lines.)

2. In cell G5, enter the formula **=E5*F5**. Figure 1-16 shows the completed worksheet.

Four co-op orders entered | **Figure 1-16**

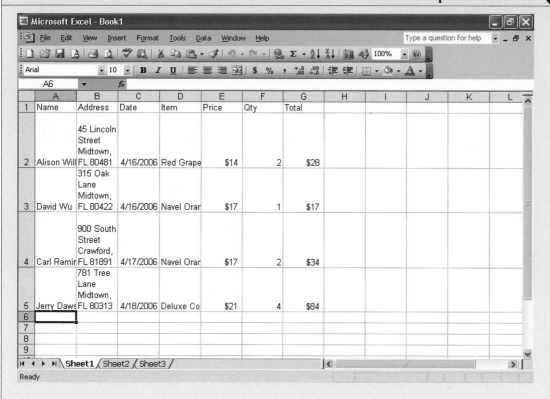

Changing the Size of a Column or Row

The default sizes of the columns and rows in an Excel worksheet may not always accommodate the information you need to enter. You can change the width of one column or multiple columns or the height of one row or multiple rows. Excel provides several methods for changing the width of a column or the height of a row. You can click the dividing line of the column or row, or you can drag the dividing line to change the width of the column or the height of the row. Heights and widths are expressed in terms of the number of characters that can be displayed in the cell, as well as the number of screen pixels, which are small units of measurement that appear as tiny dots on the screen.

Changing the Column Width or Row Height

Reference Window

- Click the column or row heading whose width or height you want to change.
- Click Format on the menu bar, point to Column or Row, and then click Width or Height (or click AutoFit or AutoFit Selection to make the column or row as large as the longest entry of the cells).
- In the Column Width or Row Height dialog box, enter the new column width or row height, and then click the OK button.

or

- Drag the column or row heading dividing line to the right or up to increase the column width or row height, or drag the dividing line to the left or down to decrease the column width or row height.

or

- Double-click the column or row heading dividing line to make the column or row as large as the longest entry of the cells in the column or row.

You'll use the drag technique to increase the width of the columns in which the data display has been truncated. As you drag the dividing line, a ScreenTip appears and displays the column width in characters and pixels.

To change the width of columns in the worksheet:

1. Move the mouse pointer to the dividing line between the column A and column B headings until the pointer changes to ✛.

2. Click and drag the pointer to the right to a length of about **20** characters (or **145 pixels**). See Figure 1-17.

Figure 1-17 ▸ **Increasing the width of column A**

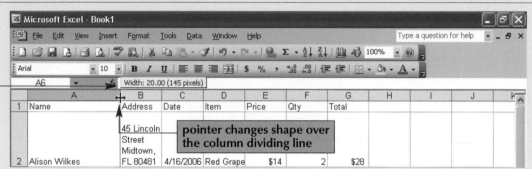

ScreenTip showing the width in characters and pixels

pointer changes shape over the column dividing line

3. Release the mouse button. All the names in column A should now be visible.

   Trouble? If the text in column A is still truncated, drag the dividing line further to the right.

4. Move the mouse pointer to the dividing line between column B and column C until the pointer changes to ✛, and then increase the width of column B to **25** characters (or **180** pixels).

5. Use your mouse to increase the width of column D to **15** characters (or **110** pixels).

Changing the width of the columns does not affect the height of the rows. However, now that column A is wider and the rows are taller, there is a great deal of empty space. To remove the empty space, you'll resize the rows. Rather than choosing a size for the rows, you'll let Excel make the adjustment automatically. If you double-click the dividing line of a column or row heading, the column width or row height adjusts to match the length of the longest entry in that column or row. You'll use this technique now to modify the height of the second row in the worksheet.

To change the height of the second row:

1. Move the mouse pointer to the dividing line between the second and third rows until the pointer changes to ✛.

2. Double-click the dividing line between the second and third rows. See Figure 1-18.

Changing the height of the second row | **Figure 1-18**

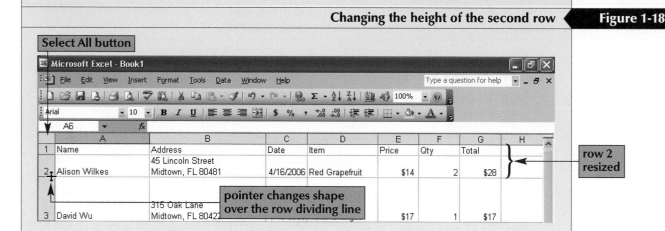

You can continue modifying the height of the remaining rows using this technique, but, for a worksheet containing a large amount of data, that would be extremely time-consuming. Another approach is to select the entire worksheet and then double-click the dividing line between any two row headings. When you do that, Excel changes the height of the rows to accommodate the data in them and reduces the amount of empty space. You can use this approach to resize columns, too.

You can select the entire worksheet by clicking the Select All button. You'll use this approach now to change the height of the remaining rows in the co-op order worksheet.

To change the height of the remaining rows:

1. Click the **Select All** button located at the junction of the row and column headings (see Figure 1-18). The row and column headings are displayed in black or dark blue, and all of the worksheet cells are displayed in light blue, indicating that the entire worksheet has been selected.

2. Move the mouse pointer to a dividing line between any two rows until the pointer changes to +.

3. Double-click the dividing line. Excel resizes the height of all the rows.

4. Click cell **A1** to make it the active cell and to remove the blue highlighting from the worksheet. Figure 1-19 shows the revised layout of the sheet.

Adjusting the height of the worksheet rows | **Figure 1-19**

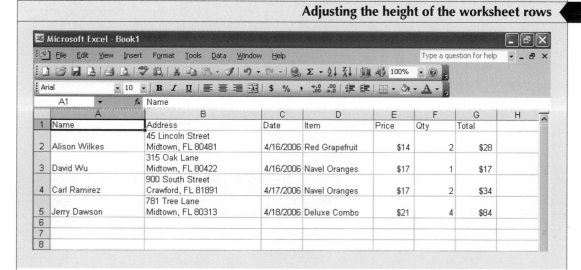

You've entered the data that Sandra wanted in the worksheet. Before proceeding further, she suggests that you save the file with the name "Dalton".

To save the workbook:

▶ 1. Click **File** on the menu bar, and then click **Save**. The Save As dialog box opens with the current workbook name, which is "Book1," in the File name text box.

▶ 2. Navigate to the Tutorial.01\Tutorial folder included with your Data Files.

    Trouble? If you don't have the Excel 2003 Data Files, you need to get them before you can proceed. Your instructor will either give you the Data Files or ask you to obtain them from a specified location (such as a network drive). In either case, be sure that you make a backup copy of your Data Files before you start using them, so that the original files will be available on your copied disk in case you need to start over because of an error or problem. If you have any questions about the Data Files, see your instructor or technical support person for assistance.

▶ 3. Replace the default filename with **Dalton**, make sure that **Microsoft Office Excel Workbook** is displayed in the Save as type list box, and then click the **Save** button. Excel saves the workbook with the name "Dalton" and closes the Save As dialog box. The new workbook name appears in the title bar of the Excel window.

    Trouble? If your computer has been set up to display file extensions, the filename "Dalton.xls" will appear in the title bar.

By default, Excel saves the workbook in Microsoft Excel Workbook format, and for most of the work you will do in this text, you will use this file format. If you are creating a workbook that will be read by applications other than Excel (or earlier versions of Excel), you can save your workbook in a different file format by following these steps:

1. Open the Save or Save As dialog box.
2. Display the location in which you want to save the file, and enter a filename, if necessary.
3. Click the Save as type list arrow, and then select the file format you want to apply.
4. Click the Save button.

Figure 1-20 describes some of the file formats in which you can save your workbooks.

Figure 1-20   **Some of the formats supported by Excel**

Format	Description
Microsoft Excel 4.0, 5.0, 97, 2000, 2002 Workbook	Saves the workbook in an earlier version of Excel
Single File Web Page	Saves the workbook as a single Web page file (MHTML file) that can be read by Internet Explorer 4.0 or later
Template	Saves the workbook as a template to be used for creating other Excel workbooks
Web Page	Saves the workbook in separate files that are used as the basis for a Web site, in a format that is readable by most browsers
XML Spreadsheet	Saves the workbook as an XML document

Sandra has some other changes to the workbook that she wants you to make. You'll continue working with the worksheet in the next session.

Session 1.1 Quick Check

1. A(n) _____ is the place on the worksheet where a column and row intersect.
2. Cell _____ refers to the intersection of the fourth column and second row.
3. What combination of keys can you press to make A1 the active cell in the worksheet?
4. To make Sheet2 the active worksheet, you _____.
5. Indicate whether Excel treats the following cell entries as text, a value, or a formula.
   a. 11/09/2006
   b. Net Income
   c. 321
   d. C11*225
   e. 201-19-1121
   f. =D1-D9
   g. 44 Evans Avenue
6. How do you enter multiple lines of text within a cell?
7. What formula would you enter to divide the value in cell E5 by the value in cell E6?

Session 1.2

Working with Ranges

Sandra has had a chance to study your work from the previous session. She likes the layout of her data, but she wants to have a title at the top of the worksheet that displays information about the sheet's contents. To make room for the title, you have to move the contents of the worksheet down a few rows. Before you attempt that, you have to first understand how Excel works with groups of cells.

A group of worksheet cells is called a **cell range**, or just **range**. Ranges can be either adjacent or nonadjacent. An **adjacent range** is a single rectangular block, such as all of the data entered in cells A1 through G5 of the Dalton workbook. A **nonadjacent range** consists of two or more separate adjacent ranges. For example, a nonadjacent range might be composed of the names of the customers in the cell range A1 through A5 and the total price of their orders in the cell range G1 through G5.

Just as a cell reference indicates the location of a cell on the worksheet, a **range reference** indicates the location and size of a cell range. For adjacent ranges, the range reference identifies the cells in the upper-left and lower-right corners of the rectangle, with the individual cell references separated by a colon. For example, the range reference for the order data you entered in the last session was A1:G5 because it included the range of cells from A1 through G5. If the range is nonadjacent, a semicolon separates the rectangular blocks A1:A5 and G1:G5, as in A1:A5;G1:G5. This nonadjacent range references the customer names in the range A1:A5 and the total amounts of their orders in the range G1:G5.

Selecting Ranges

Once you know how to select ranges of cells, you can move and copy the data anywhere in the worksheet or workbook.

Selecting Adjacent or Nonadjacent Ranges of Cells

To select an adjacent range of cells:
- Click a cell in the upper-left corner of the rectangle that comprises the adjacent range.
- Press and hold the left mouse button, and then drag the pointer through the cells you want selected.
- Release the mouse button.

To select a nonadjacent range of cells:
- Select an adjacent range of cells.
- Press and hold the Ctrl key, and then select another adjacent cell range.
- With the Ctrl key still pressed, continue to select other cell ranges until all of the ranges are selected.
- Release the mouse button and the Ctrl key.

To see how to select ranges, you'll start by selecting all of the cells containing order information.

To select the order data:

1. If you took a break at the end of the previous session, make sure that Excel is running and that the Dalton workbook is open.

2. Click cell **A1** on the Sheet1 worksheet, press and hold the left mouse button, and then drag the pointer to cell **G5**.

3. Release the mouse button. All the cells in the range A1:G5 are now highlighted, indicating that they are selected. See Figure 1-21.

Figure 1-21 — Selecting the range A1:G5

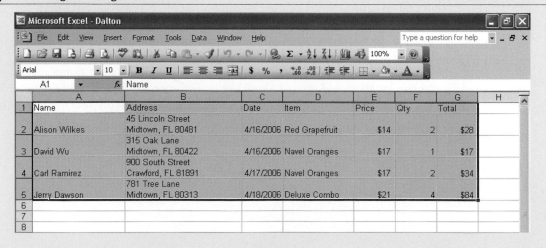

4. Click any cell in the worksheet to deselect the range.

Now try selecting the nonadjacent range A1:A5;G1:G5.

To select the nonadjacent range A1:A5;G1:G5:

▶ **1.** Select the range **A1:A5**, press and hold the **Ctrl** key, select the range **G1:G5**, and then release the mouse button and the Ctrl key. See Figure 1-22 for the selected nonadjacent range.

Selecting the nonadjacent range A1:A5;G1:G5 | **Figure 1-22**

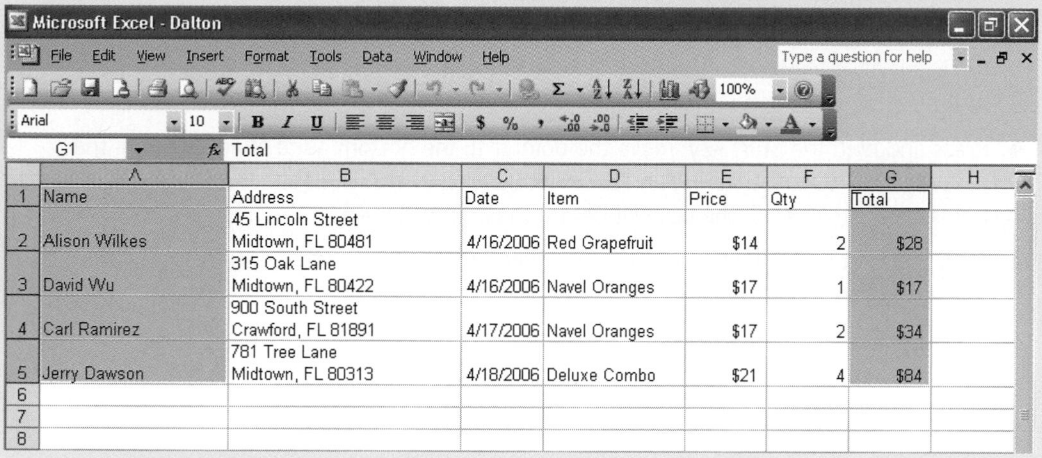

▶ **2.** Click any cell in the worksheet to deselect the range.

Other Selection Techniques

You can also select large cell ranges that extend beyond the borders of the workbook window. When this situation occurs, Excel automatically scrolls the workbook window horizontally or vertically to display additional cells in the worksheet. Selecting a large cell range using the mouse drag technique can be slow and frustrating. For this reason, Excel provides keyboard shortcuts that enable you to quickly select large blocks of data without having to drag through the worksheet to select the necessary cells. Figure 1-23 describes some of these selection techniques.

Other range selection techniques | **Figure 1-23**

To Select...	Action
A large range of cells	Click the first cell in the range, press and hold down the Shift key, and then click the last cell in the range. All of the cells between the first and last cell are selected.
All cells on the worksheet	Click the Select All button, the gray rectangle in the upper-left corner of the worksheet where the row and column headings meet.
All cells in an entire row or column	Click the row or column heading.
A range of cells containing data	Click the cell where you want to begin the selection of the range, press and hold down the Shift key, and then double-click the side of the cell in the direction that you want to extend the selection. Excel selects all adjacent cells that contain data, extending the selection of the range to the first empty cell.

Try some of the techniques described to select ranges of cells in the Dalton workbook.

To select a range of cells using keyboard shortcuts:

1. Click cell **A1** to make it the active cell.

2. Press and hold the **Shift** key, click cell **A5**, and then release the Shift key. Note that all of the cells between A1 and A5 are selected.

   Trouble? If the range A1:A5 is not selected, try again, but make sure you hold the Shift key while you click cell A5.

3. Click cell **A1** to make it the active cell again. Note that you don't have to deselect one range before clicking another cell.

4. Press and hold the **Shift** key, move the pointer to the bottom edge of cell A1 until the mouse pointer changes to ⁺⥍, and then double-click the bottom edge of cell **A1**. The selection extends to cell A5, the last cell before the empty cell A6.

5. With the Shift key still pressed, move the pointer to the right edge of the selection until, once again, the pointer changes to ⁺⥍, double-click the right edge of the selection, and then release the Shift key. The selection extends to the last nonblank column in the worksheet, selecting the range A1:G5.

6. Click the **A** column heading. All of the cells in column A are selected. Note that you didn't have to deselect the range A1:G5.

7. Click the **1** row heading. All of the cells in the first row are selected.

Moving a Selection of Cells

Now that you know various ways to select a range of cells, you can move the co-op data down a few rows in the worksheet. To move a cell range, you first select it; then you position the pointer over the selection border, and drag the selection to a new location. Try this technique to move the order data from the cell range A1:G5 to the cell range A5:G9.

To move the order data:

1. Select the range **A1:G5**, and then move the pointer over the bottom border of the selection until the pointer changes to ⁺⥍.

2. Press and hold the left mouse button, changing the pointer to ⟍, and then drag the selection down four rows. A ScreenTip appears indicating the new range reference of the selection. See Figure 1-24.

Moving the selection to the range A5:G9

Figure 1-24

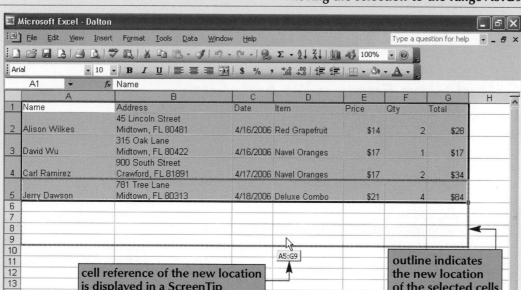

3. When the ScreenTip displays "A5:G9," release the left mouse button. The order data is now moved to range A5:G9.

Trouble? If you selected the wrong range or moved the selection to the wrong location, click the Undo button 🔄 on the Standard toolbar, and then repeat Steps 1 through 3.

4. Click cell **A1** to remove the selection and to make cell A1 the active cell so you can enter the new titles in the worksheet.

5. Type **Dalton Food Co-op** in cell A1, **List of Orders** in cell A2, **April, 2006** in cell A3, and then press the **Enter** key. Note that moving the cell range had no impact on the values in the worksheet; the values shown by the formulas in column G are also unchanged. This is because Excel automatically updated the cell references in the formulas to reflect the new location of the data. To confirm this, you'll examine the formula in cell G6.

6. Click cell **G6** and observe what is displayed in the Formula bar. The formula in cell G6 is now =E6*F6. Recall that when you originally entered Alison Wilke's order, the formula for this cell was =E2*G2 because the order was originally placed in the second row of the worksheet. When you moved the data, Excel automatically updated the formula to reflect the new location of Alison Wilke's order.

The technique you used to move the cell range is called "drag and drop." You can also use the drag-and-drop technique to copy a cell range. Copying a range of cells is similar to moving a range, except that you must press the Ctrl key while you drag the selection to its new location. A copy of the original data will then appear at the location of the pointer when you release the mouse button. You'll learn more about copying and pasting in the next two tutorials.

A cell range can also be moved from one worksheet in the workbook to another. To do this, press and hold the Alt key and then drag the selection over the sheet tab of the new worksheet. Excel will automatically make that worksheet the active sheet, so you can drag the selection into its new location on the worksheet.

Calculating Sums with AutoSum

Sandra reminds you that she wants the worksheet to also display summary information about the co-op orders, including the total number of items ordered and the amount of revenue generated from those orders. You could calculate the total quantity and total revenue using the formulas =F6+F7+F8+F9 and =G6+G7+G8+G9.

One problem with this approach is that as Sandra adds new orders to the worksheet, you will have to constantly update these formulas, adding cell references for the new orders. As you add more orders, the length of these two expressions will increase dramatically, increasing the possibility of making errors in the formulas.

One way to solve this problem is to use a **function**, which is a predefined formula that performs calculations using specific values. You will learn about and work with functions in more detail in the next tutorial. In this case, you'll insert one of Excel's most commonly used Financial functions, the SUM function, using the AutoSum button on the Standard toolbar. The **AutoSum** feature is a quick and convenient way to enter the SUM function. You use the **SUM function** to calculate the sum of values in a cell range. In this case, you want to calculate the sum of the values in the range F6:F9 and in the range G6:G9.

Now, you'll use AutoSum to calculate the total quantity and total revenue of the ordered items, putting these values in cells F10 and G10.

To calculate the total order quantity and revenue:

1. Click cell **A10**, type **TOTAL**, and then press the **Tab** key five times to move to cell F10.

2. With cell F10 as the active cell, click the **AutoSum** button ⟦Σ⟧ on the Standard toolbar. Excel automatically inserts the SUM function in the active cell and selects a cell range that it anticipates is the range of cells to be summed. See Figure 1-25. A ScreenTip also appears, showing the form of the SUM function. The mode indicator in the status bar changes to Point, indicating that you can point to the cell references. In this case, the range that Excel has selected for you is the correct range of cells, so all you need to do is indicate that you accept the range. You can complete the function and move to the next cell by pressing the Tab key.

Using the AutoSum button  **Figure 1-25**

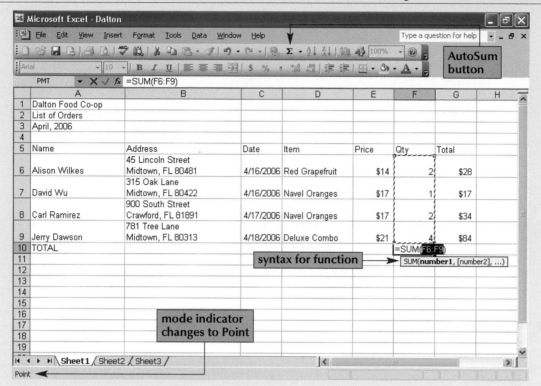

3. Press the **Tab** key to move to cell G10. The result of the formula *=SUM(F6:F9)* appears in cell F10, and you are in position to calculate the next set of values.

4. Click the **AutoSum** button Σ on the Standard toolbar to enter the SUM function in cell G10, and then press the **Enter** key to complete the formula *=SUM(G6:G9)*, accepting the range that Excel highlighted. See Figure 1-26. Nine items were sold, for a total of $163.

Calculating the total quantity and total income for the co-op **Figure 1-26**

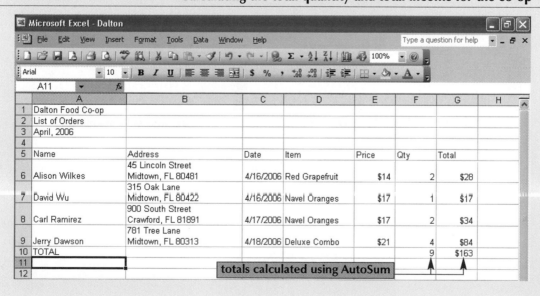

You can use AutoSum to calculate other summary values, such as the average, minimum, maximum, and total number of items in a cell range. You will learn more about using AutoSum to summarize values in Tutorial 2.

Working with Rows and Columns

Sandra has received a new order that she wants you to add to her worksheet. She wants to insert the new order right after Jerry Dawson's order, but wants to make sure the row containing the total values is still the last row. To do this, you need to insert a new row into the worksheet between row 9 and row 10.

Inserting a Row or Column

You can insert rows and columns in a worksheet, or you can insert individual cells within a row or column. When you insert rows, Excel shifts the existing rows down. When you insert columns, Excel shifts the existing columns to the right. If you insert cells within a row, Excel shifts the existing cells down; if you insert cells within a column, Excel shifts the existing cells to the right. Figure 1-27 illustrates what happens when you insert a row, a column, and cells within a row and within a column.

Figure 1-27 ▶ **Inserting new rows and columns**

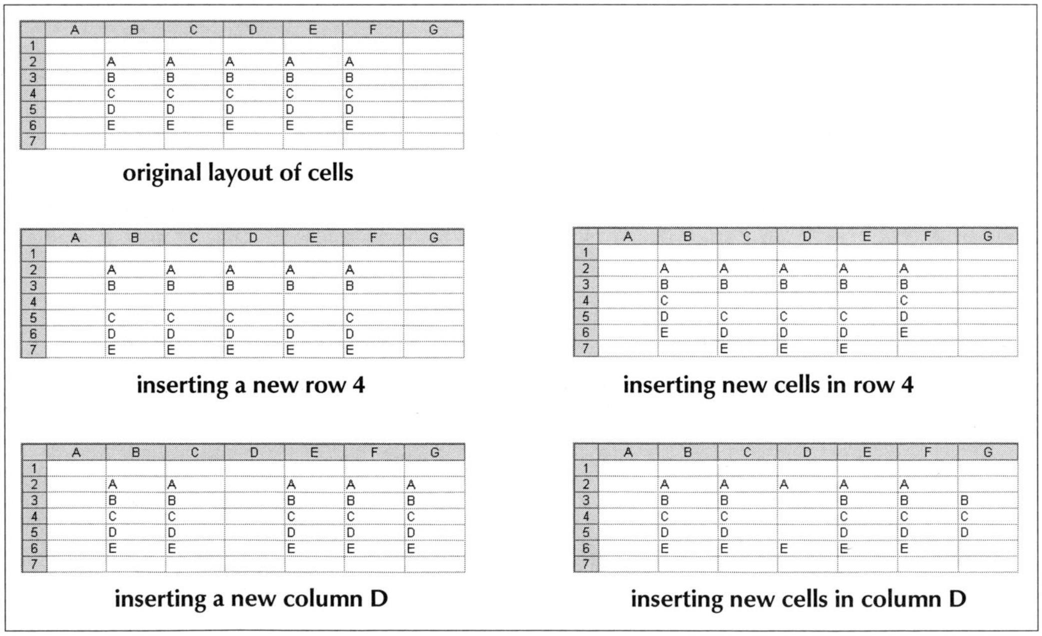

original layout of cells

inserting a new row 4

inserting new cells in row 4

inserting a new column D

inserting new cells in column D

You can use the Insert menu to insert cells, rows, and columns. You can also use the right-click method to display a shortcut menu that provides the Insert command, which opens the Insert dialog box.

Inserting a Row or Column into a Worksheet

Reference Window

- Select a cell where you want to insert the new row or column.
- Click Insert on the menu bar, and then click Rows or Columns.

or

- Right-click a cell where you want to insert a new row or column, and then click Insert on the shortcut menu.
- In the Insert dialog box, click the Entire row or Entire column option button, and then click the OK button.

To insert multiple rows or columns, you select a cell range that contains multiple rows or columns before applying the Insert command. For example, to insert two new blank rows, select two rows or any portion of two rows. To insert three blank columns, select three columns or any portion of three columns.

Sometimes you might need to insert individual cells, rather than an entire row or column, into a worksheet. To insert cells into a row or column, you must select the number of cells you want to insert, and then open the Insert dialog box. In this dialog box you indicate how Excel should shift the existing cells to accommodate the cells you want to insert.

Inserting Cells into a Worksheet

Reference Window

- Select a cell range equal to the number of cells you want to insert.
- Click Insert on the menu bar, and then click Cells; or right-click the selected range, and then click Insert on the shortcut menu.
- Click the Shift cells right option button to insert the new cells into the row, or click the Shift cells down button to insert the new cells into the column.

Sandra wants the data for the new order to be entered above the TOTAL row, row 10. You'll use the right-click method to insert a new row 10, and then you'll enter the data.

To insert a new row 10:

1. Right-click cell **A10**, which is where you want to insert the new row.
2. Click **Insert** on the shortcut menu. The Insert dialog box opens. See Figure 1-28.

Insert dialog box ◄ **Figure 1-28**

3. Click the **Entire row** option button, and then click the **OK** button. Excel inserts a new row 10 and shifts the calculations of the total values down one row.

4. Enter the data for Karen Paulson's order into row 10, as shown in Figure 1-29. Make sure that you press the Tab key to move from cell to cell and press the Alt + Enter keys to enter the address on two lines within cell B10.

Figure 1-29   **Data entered in the new row 10**

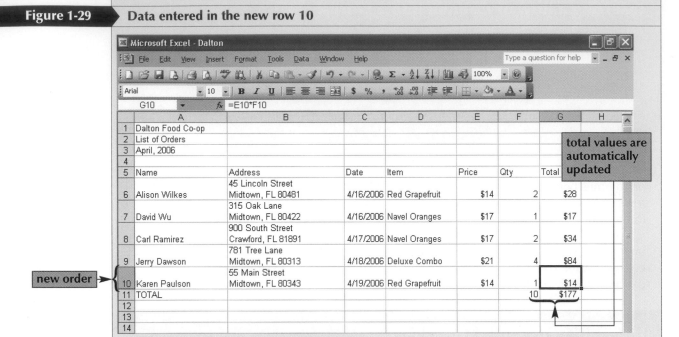

Note that Excel automatically inserts the formula *=E10*F10* into cell G10 for you. Excel recognizes that you are inserting a new set of values into a list of values and assumes that you intend to use the same formulas for the new order that you used for the previous ones. Also note that the calculations of the total quantity of items ordered and the total revenue from those orders have been updated. The functions now calculate the sums in the cell ranges F6:F10 and G6:G10. You'll learn more about how such formulas are automatically adjusted by Excel in the next tutorial.

Deleting a Row or Column

Sandra has also learned that David Wu has canceled his co-op order. You have two options for removing data from a worksheet. If you simply want to erase the contents of a cell, you can **clear** the cell, without actually removing the cell from the worksheet. If you want to remove not only the contents of the cells from the worksheet, but also the cells themselves, you can **delete** a cell range, and Excel then shifts the contents of the adjacent cells into the location of the deleted cells.

To clear the contents of a cell or range of cells, you select the range and then select the Clear command on the Edit menu or on the shortcut menu that you display by right-clicking the selection. Pressing the Delete key on the keyboard also clears the contents of the selected cells, without removing the cells themselves. To delete cells and their contents, you select the range and then choose the Delete command on the Edit menu, or right-click the selected cells, and click Delete on the shortcut menu. To adjust the adjacent cells, Excel opens the Delete Cells dialog box, which you can select to shift the remaining cells left or up, or choose to delete the entire row.

Because David Wu has canceled his order, you'll delete it from the worksheet.

To delete the row that contains David Wu's order:

▶ **1.** Click the row heading for row **7**, which contains the data you want to delete.

▶ **2.** Click **Edit** on the menu bar, and then click **Delete**. Excel deletes the row and shifts the next row up. See Figure 1-30. The total calculations in cells F10 and G10 are automatically updated to reflect the fact that David Wu's order has been deleted.

Deleting a row from the worksheet ◀ **Figure 1-30**

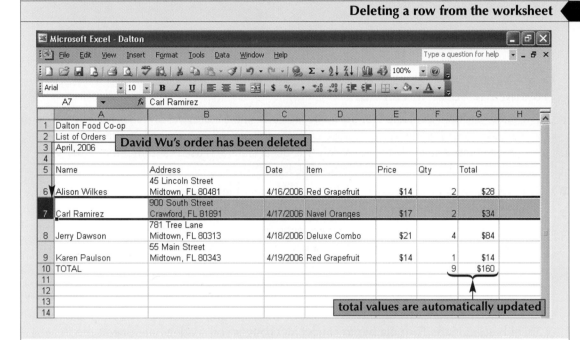

Editing Your Worksheet

When you work in Excel, you might make mistakes that you want to correct or undo. Sandra has noticed such a mistake in the Dalton workbook. The price for the Deluxe Combo box should be $23, not $21. You could simply clear the value in cell E8 and then type the correct value. However, there may be times when you will not want to change the entire contents of a cell, but merely edit a portion of the entry, especially if the cell contains a large block of text or a complicated formula. To edit the cell contents, you need to work in **edit mode**.

When you are working in edit mode, some of the keyboard shortcuts you've been using perform differently. For example, the Home, Delete, Backspace, and End keys do not move the insertion point to different cells in the worksheet; rather they move the insertion point to different locations within the cell. The Home key, for example, moves the insertion point to the beginning of whatever content has been entered into the cell. The End key moves the insertion point to the end of the cell's content. The left and right arrow keys move the insertion point backward and forward through the cell's content. The Backspace key deletes the character immediately to the left of the insertion point, and the Delete key deletes the character to the right of the insertion point.

| **Editing a Cell**

- Switch to edit mode by double-clicking the cell, clicking the cell and pressing the F2 key, or clicking the cell and then clicking in the Formula bar.
- Use the Home, End, ←, or → keys to move the insertion point within the cell's content, or use the Delete and Backspace keys to erase characters.
- Press the Enter key when finished, or if you are working in the Formula bar, click the Enter button.

You'll switch to edit mode and then change the value in cell E8.

To edit the value in cell E8:

▶ 1. Double-click cell **E8**. Note that the mode indicator in the status bar switches from Ready to Edit. Also note that the value 21 appears in the cell, not $21. This is because the cell contains a numeric value, not a text string. The dollar sign ($) is used to format the value. You'll learn more about formats in Tutorial 3.

▶ 2. Press the **End** key to move the blinking insertion point to the end of the cell.

▶ 3. Press the **Backspace** key once to delete the 1 character, type **3** to update the value, and then press the **Enter** key to accept the change. The value $23 appears in cell E8, and the total amount of this order in cell G8 changes to $92. Note that the mode indicator on the status bar switches back to Ready.

If you make a mistake as you type in edit mode, you can press the Esc key or click the Cancel button on the Formula bar to cancel all changes you made while in edit mode.

Undoing an Action

As you revise your worksheet, you may find that you need to undo one of your changes. To undo an action, click the Undo button on the Standard toolbar. As you work, Excel maintains a list of your actions, so you can undo most of the actions you perform in your workbook during the current session. To reverse more than one action, click the list arrow next to the Undo button and click the action you want to undo from the list. To see how this works, you'll use the Undo button to remove the edit you just made to cell E8.

To undo your last action:

▶ 1. Click the **Undo** button 🔄 on the Standard toolbar. The value $21 appears again in cell E8, indicating that your last action, editing the value in this cell, has been undone.

If you find that you have gone too far in undoing your previous actions, you can go forward in the action list and redo those actions. To redo an action, you click the Redo button on the Standard toolbar. Now you'll use the Redo button to return the value in cell E8 to $23.

To redo your last action:

▶ 1. Click the **Redo** button 🔁 on the Standard toolbar. The value in cell E8 changes back to $23.

Through the use of edit mode and the Undo and Redo buttons, you should be able to correct almost any mistake you make in your Excel workbook. The Undo and Redo commands are also available on the Edit menu or by using the shortcut keys Ctrl + Z, to undo an action, and Ctrl + Y, to redo an action.

Working with Worksheets

By default, Excel workbooks contain three worksheets, labeled Sheet1, Sheet2, and Sheet3. You can add new worksheets or remove old ones. You can also give your worksheets more descriptive names. In the Dalton workbook, there is no data entered in the Sheet2 or Sheet3 worksheets. Sandra suggests that you remove these sheets from the workbook.

Adding and Removing Worksheets

To delete a worksheet, you first select its sheet tab to make the worksheet the active sheet; then right-click the sheet tab and choose Delete from the shortcut menu. Try this now by deleting the Sheet2 and Sheet3 worksheets.

To delete the Sheet2 and Sheet3 worksheets:

▶ **1.** Click the **Sheet2** tab to make Sheet2 the active sheet.

▶ **2.** Right-click the sheet tab, and then click **Delete** on the shortcut menu. Sheet2 is deleted and Sheet3 becomes the active sheet.

▶ **3.** Right-click the **Sheet3** tab, and then click **Delete**. There is now only one worksheet in the workbook.

After you delete the two unused sheets, Sandra informs you that she wants to include a description of the workbook's content and purpose. In other words, Sandra wants to include a **documentation sheet**, a worksheet that provides information about the content and purpose of the workbook. A documentation sheet can be any information that you feel is important, for example, the name of the person who created the workbook or instructions on how to use the workbook. A documentation sheet is a valuable element if you intend to share the workbook with others. The documentation sheet is often the first worksheet in the workbook, though in this case, Sandra wants to place it at the end of the workbook.

To insert a new worksheet, you can either use the Worksheet command on the Insert menu or the right-click method. Both methods insert a new worksheet *before* the active sheet.

To insert a new worksheet in the workbook:

▶ **1.** Click **Insert** on the menu bar, and then click **Worksheet**. A new worksheet with the name "Sheet4" is placed at the beginning of your workbook. Your worksheet might be named Sheet2 or another name.

Sandra wants the documentation sheet to include the following information:

• The name of the co-op
• The date that this workbook was originally created
• The person who created the workbook
• The purpose of the workbook

You'll add this information to the new sheet in the Dalton workbook.

To insert the documentation information in the new worksheet:

1. Click cell **A1**, if necessary, type **Dalton Food Co-op**, and then press the **Enter** key twice.

2. Type **Date:** in cell A3, and then press the **Tab** key.

3. Enter the *current date* in cell B3, and then press the **Enter** key.

4. Type **Created By:** in cell A4, and then press the **Tab** key.

5. Enter *your name* in cell B4, and then press the **Enter** key.

6. Type **Purpose:** in cell A5, and then press the **Tab** key.

7. Type **To enter orders for the Dalton Food Co-op** in cell B5, and then press the **Enter** key.

8. Increase the width of column A to **15** characters (**110** pixels). Figure 1-31 shows the completed documentation sheet.

Figure 1-31 **Completed documentation sheet**

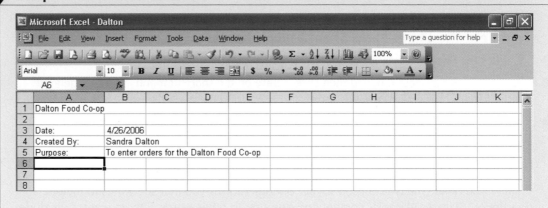

Renaming a Worksheet

The current sheet names, "Sheet4" and "Sheet1," are not very descriptive. Sandra suggests that you rename Sheet4 "Documentation" and Sheet1 "Orders." To rename a worksheet, you double-click the sheet tab to select the sheet name, and then you type a new name for the sheet. Sheet names cannot exceed 31 characters in length, including blank spaces.

To rename the worksheets:

1. Double-click the **Sheet4** tab. Note that the name of the sheet is selected.

2. Type **Documentation** and then press the **Enter** key. The width of the sheet tab adjusts to the length of the name you type.

3. Double-click the **Sheet1** tab.

4. Type **Orders** and then press the **Enter** key. Both worksheets are renamed.

Moving a Worksheet

You can change the placement of the worksheets in the workbook. To move the position of a worksheet in the workbook, click the sheet tab and then drag and drop it to a new location relative to the other worksheets. You can also make a copy of a worksheet using a similar drag-and-drop technique. To create a copy of a worksheet, press the Ctrl key as you drag and drop the sheet tab of the worksheet you want duplicated.

Moving or Copying a Worksheet
• Click the sheet tab of the worksheet you want to move (or copy). • Drag the sheet tab along the row of sheet tabs until the small arrow appears in the new location. To create a copy of the worksheet, press and hold the Ctrl key as you drag the sheet tab to the new location. • Release the mouse button. Release the Ctrl key if necessary.

Reference Window

Try this now by switching the location of the Documentation and Orders worksheets.

To reposition the worksheets:

1. Click the **Orders** tab, and then press and hold the left mouse button so the pointer changes to ⬚ and a small arrow appears in the upper-left corner of the tab.

2. Drag the pointer to the left of the sheet tab for the Documentation sheet, and then release the mouse button. The Documentation sheet is now the second sheet in the workbook, but Sandra would prefer that the documentation sheet be the first sheet.

3. Click the **Orders** tab, and then drag the sheet tab to the right of the Documentation sheet tab to place it back in its original location.

When you create a copy of a worksheet, you move the copy of the original worksheet to a new location, while the original sheet remains at its initial position.

Using the Spell Checker

One of Excel's editing tools is the **Spell Checker**. This feature checks the words in the workbook against the program's internal dictionary. If the Spell Checker comes across a word not in its dictionary, it displays the word in a dialog box along with a list of suggested replacements. You can replace the word with one from the list, or you can choose to ignore the word and go to the next word that might be misspelled. You can also add the word to the dictionary to prevent it from being flagged in the future. There are words that are not included in the online dictionary (for example, some uncommon personal names or last names). The Spell Checker will stop at these words. You can then choose to ignore all occurrences of the word, change the word, or add the word to the dictionary. Excel checks the spelling on the current worksheet only.

To see how the Spell Checker works, you'll make an intentional spelling error in the Orders worksheet.

To check the spelling in the Orders sheet:

1. Make sure the Orders sheet is the active sheet, and then click cell **G5**. You will enter the error in this cell.

2. Type **Totale** and then click cell **A1**. The Spell Checker always starts at the active cell in the worksheet. You can start from other cells, and the Spell Checker will cycle back to the first cell in the worksheet to continue checking each cell for spelling errors. However, you will find it helpful and more efficient to begin spell checking with the first cell in the sheet, cell A1.

3. Click the **Spelling** button 🔤 on the Standard toolbar. The Spelling dialog box opens, with the first word that the spell checker does not recognize, "Totale." See Figure 1-32.

| Figure 1-32 | Spelling dialog box |

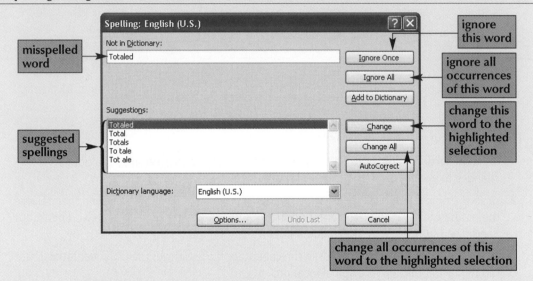

4. Click **Total** in the list of suggestions, and then click the **Change** button. The word "Totale" changes to "Total," and then Spell Checker continues to look for other potential spelling errors. There shouldn't be any other errors in this workbook.

   Trouble? If there are any other errors (you may have misspelled a name, address, or item), fix them before continuing to the next step.

5. Click the **OK** button to close the Spell Checker.

Previewing and Printing a Worksheet

Sandra would like a printed hard copy of the Dalton workbook for her records. You can print the contents of your workbook either by using the Print command on the File menu or by clicking the Print button on the Standard toolbar. If you use the Print command, Excel opens the Print dialog box in which you can specify which worksheets you want to print, the number of copies, and the print quality. If you click the Print button, your worksheet will print using the options already set in the Print dialog box. If you want to change a setting, you must open the Print dialog box using the File menu.

Before sending a worksheet to the printer, you should preview how the worksheet will appear as a printed page. You can display the worksheet in the Print Preview window either by selecting the Print Preview command on the File menu or by clicking the Print Preview button on the Standard toolbar. You can also click the Preview button in the Print dialog box. Previewing the printout is a helpful way to avoid printing errors.

If you are printing to a shared printer on a network, other people might be sending print jobs at the same time you do. To avoid confusion, you will print the contents of both the Documentation sheet and the Orders sheet. You will use the Print command on the File menu because you need to print the entire workbook and not just the active worksheet (which is the default print setting).

To open the Print dialog box:

▶ **1.** Click **File** on the menu bar, and then click **Print** to open the Print dialog box.

▶ **2.** Click the **Name** list box, and then select the printer to which you want to print, if it is not already selected.

Now you need to select what to print. To print the complete workbook, select the Entire workbook option button. To print the active worksheet, select the Active sheet(s) option button. To print the selected cells on the active sheet, click the Selection option button.

▶ **3.** Click the **Entire workbook** option button.

▶ **4.** Make sure **1** appears in the Number of copies list box, since you only need to print one copy of the workbook. Figure 1-33 shows the Print dialog box.

Print dialog box ◀ **Figure 1-33**

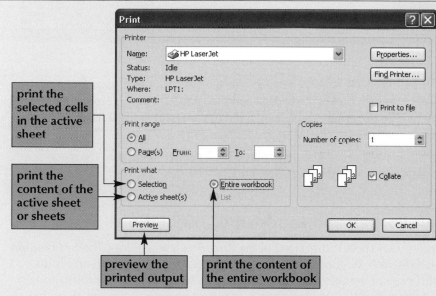

print the selected cells in the active sheet

print the content of the active sheet or sheets

preview the printed output

print the content of the entire workbook

Next you will preview the worksheet to ensure that it looks correct before printing it.

To preview the workbook before printing it:

▶ **1.** Click the **Preview** button in the Print dialog box. Excel displays a preview of the first full page of the worksheet, in this case the Documentation sheet, as it will appear printed. As you can see from the status bar in Figure 1-34, this is the first of three pages.

Trouble? If the status bar on your screen indicates that there are just two pages, you can still complete the steps.

Figure 1-34 | **Print Preview window**

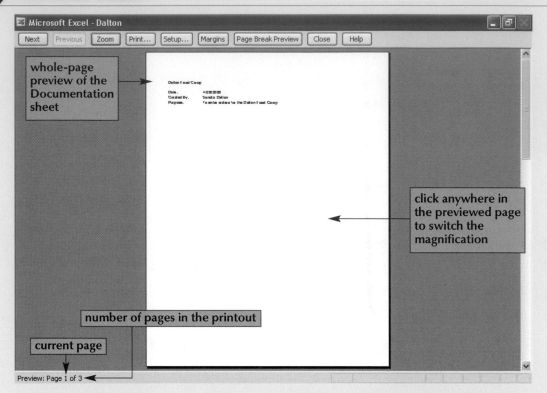

2. Click the **Next** button on the Print Preview toolbar to move to the next page in the pre-view. On this page you see part of the Orders worksheet, but it is difficult to read because the text is so small. To better see the content of the printed page, you can click the preview page to switch between a magnified view and a whole-page view.

3. Click anywhere within the previewed page with the 🔍 pointer to increase the magnifica-tion, and click again to reduce the magnification.

Working with Portrait and Landscape Orientation

Not all of the Orders worksheet is displayed in the Print Preview window. The last column in the sheet, which displays the total amount of each order, has been cut off and is dis-played on the third page of the printout. Naturally Sandra wants all of the information on a single sheet, but the problem is that the page is not wide enough to display all of this information. One way of solving this problem is to change the orientation of the page. There are two types of page orientations: portrait and landscape. In **portrait orientation** the page is taller than it is wide. In **landscape orientation** the page is wider than it is tall. In many cases, you will want to print your worksheets in landscape orientation. You'll choose this option for the Orders worksheet.

To print in landscape orientation:

1. Click the **Setup** button on the Print Preview toolbar. The Page Setup dialog box opens.

2. Verify that the Page tab is selected in the dialog box, and then click the **Landscape** option button. See Figure 1-35.

Print Setup dialog box ◀ **Figure 1-35**

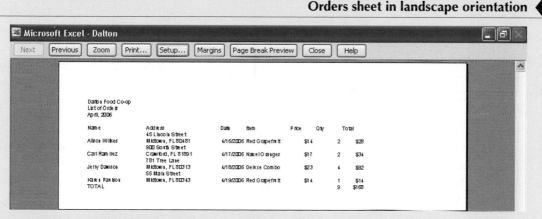

3. Click the **OK** button to close the Page Setup dialog box.

4. If necessary, click anywhere within the previewed page to switch the magnification back to a whole-page view. As shown in Figure 1-36, the entire Orders worksheet is now displayed on the second (and last) page of this printout.

Orders sheet in landscape orientation ◀ **Figure 1-36**

5. Click the **Print** button on the Print Preview toolbar to print the workbook and close the Print Preview window.

Note that the Documentation sheet is printed in portrait orientation, whereas the Orders worksheet is printed in landscape orientation. Changing the orientation only affects the worksheet currently displayed in the Print Preview window; it does not apply to other sheets in the workbook.

Printing the Worksheet Formulas

Sandra examines the printout and notices that none of the formulas are displayed. This is to be expected since most of the time you're only interested in the final results and not the formulas used to calculate those results. In some cases, you will want to view the formulas used in developing your workbook. This is particularly useful in situations where the results were not what you expected, and you want to examine the formulas to see if a mistake has been made. To switch to **Formula view** in your workbook, you can press the keyboard shortcut Ctrl + grave accent (`). Try this now for the Orders worksheet.

To view the worksheet formulas:

▶ **1.** With the Orders worksheet active, press the **Ctrl + `** (grave accent) keys and then scroll the worksheet to the left so columns F and G are visible. (Make sure you press the grave accent key (`) and not the single quotation mark key ('). The grave accent key is usually located above the Tab key on your keyboard.) Excel displays the formulas in columns F and G. See Figure 1-37.

Figure 1-37 | **Viewing the worksheet formulas**

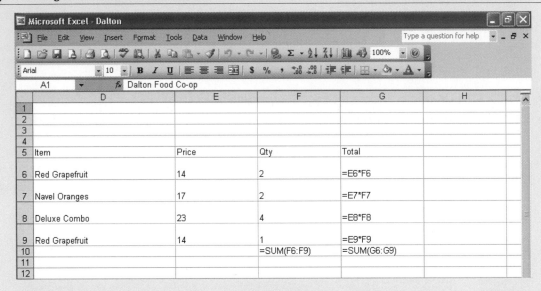

Trouble? If the Formula Auditing toolbar appears, close the toolbar.

Note that the column widths have been changed. Excel does this automatically to ensure that the entire formula can be displayed within each cell. These changed column widths will not affect the normal view of your worksheet as long as you don't change the column widths while in Formula view.

Sandra asks you to print a copy of the worksheet with the formulas displayed. First, you'll preview the worksheet.

▶ **2.** Click the **Print Preview** button on the Standard toolbar. Excel displays a preview of the Orders worksheet in Formula view. Not all of the contents of the worksheet in this view are displayed on a single page. To fit the printout to a single page, you will change the setup of the page using the Page Setup dialog box.

▶ **3.** Click the **Setup** button on the Print Preview toolbar. The Page Setup dialog box opens.

▶ **4.** Click the **Fit to** option button to fit the Orders worksheet on one page, and then click the **OK** button. The Formula view of the Orders worksheet should now fit on a single page.

▶ **5.** Click the **Print** button on the Print Preview toolbar to print the worksheet and close the Print Preview window.

Trouble? If the Print Preview window closes and the Print dialog box opens, click the OK button to print the worksheet.

As you may have noticed while you were working in Print Preview and the Page Setup dialog box, there are a lot of options for choosing what to print and how to print. You'll examine more of these options in Tutorial 3. For now, you can switch the Orders worksheet back to Normal view and save and then close the file.

To complete your work:

▶ 1. Press the **Ctrl +`** (grave accent) keys to switch the worksheet back to Normal view. The keyboard shortcut Ctrl + ` (grave accent) works as a toggle, so you can display or hide the formulas by pressing this combination of keys.

▶ 2. Save your changes to the Dalton workbook, and then close it.

You give Sandra the hard copy of the Dalton workbook. If she needs to add new information to the workbook or if she needs you to make further changes to the structure of the workbook, she'll contact you.

Session 1.2 Quick Check

Review

1. Describe the two types of cell ranges in Excel.
2. How do you write the cell reference for the rectangular group of cells that extends from cell A5 through cell F8?
3. The _____ button provides a quick way to enter the SUM function.
4. When you insert a new row into a worksheet, the existing rows are shifted

   _____.

5. When you insert a new column into a worksheet, the existing columns are shifted

   _____.

6. How do you change the name of a worksheet?
7. How does clearing a cell differ from deleting a cell?
8. What keyboard shortcut do you press to display the worksheet formulas?

Tutorial Summary

Review

In this tutorial, you learned the basics of spreadsheets and Excel. You learned about the major components of the Excel window. You also learned how to navigate within a worksheet and between worksheets in an Excel workbook. You learned how to enter text, dates, values, and formulas into a worksheet and were introduced to functions using the AutoSum button. Within the workbook, you practiced selecting and moving cell ranges. You saw how to insert new rows and columns into a workbook and how to modify the size of a column or row. You learned how to create new worksheets, rename them, and move them around the workbook. You learned how to check the spelling in a workbook, and finally, you learned how to print the contents of a workbook in different orientations and how to print the formulas in that workbook.

Key Terms

active cell	edit mode	sheet
adjacent range	formula	sheet tab
argument	Formula bar	Spell Checker
arithmetic operator	Formula view	spreadsheet
AutoComplete	function	SUM function
AutoSum	landscape orientation	tab scrolling buttons
cell	Name box	value
cell range	nonadjacent range	what-if analysis
cell reference	order of precedence	workbook
clear	portrait orientation	workbook window
column	range	worksheet
delete	range reference	worksheet window
documentation sheet	row	

Practice

Practice the skills you learned in the tutorial using the same case scenario.

Review Assignments

There are no Data Files needed for the Review Assignments.

Sandra has another set of orders she wants you to enter into a new Excel workbook. The data is shown in Figure 1-38.

Figure 1-38

Name	Address	Date	Item	Price	Qty
Wendy Battle	313 Oak Street Midtown, FL 80481 (833) 555-1284	5/1/2006	Deluxe Combo	$23	2
Eugene Burch	25 Fourth Street Cabot, FL 81121 (833) 555-3331	5/1/2006	Red Grapefruit	$14	4
Nicole Sweeny	312 Olive Street Midtown, FL 81241 (833) 555-9811	5/3/2006	Deluxe Combo	$23	1
Amy Yang	315 Maple Street Midtown, FL 80440 (833) 555-3881	5/4/2006	Navel Oranges	$17	3

Note that Sandra has added the phone numbers of the customers to her data. She wants the phone numbers entered into the customer address cell, but on a different line within that cell. To complete this task:

1. Start Excel and open a blank workbook. In the range A1:F5, enter the labels and data from Figure 1-38. Make sure that the address information is inserted with the street address on the first line; the city, state, and ZIP code on the second line; and the phone number on the third line.
2. In cell G1, enter the label "Total."
3. In the cells below G1, enter formulas to calculate the total amount of each order.
4. In cell A6, enter the label "TOTAL."

5. In cell F6, use the AutoSum button to calculate the total quantity of items ordered, and in cell G6, use the AutoSum button to calculate the total revenue generated by these orders.

6. Move sales data from the range A1:G6 to the range A5:G10.

7. In cell A1, enter the text "Dalton Food Co-op." In cell A2, enter the text "List of Orders." In cell A3, enter the text "May, 2006."

8. Change the width of columns A and B to 20 characters (or 145 pixels) each. Change the width of column D to 15 characters (or 110 pixels). Change the width of column G to 10 characters (or 75 pixels).

9. Select all of the cells in the worksheet, and then reduce the amount of empty space in the rows by reducing the row height to the height of the data contained in the rows.

10. Change the name of the worksheet to "Orders".

11. Create a worksheet named "Documentation" at the beginning of the workbook and, in the Documentation sheet, enter the following:
    - Cell A1: Dalton Food Co-op
    - Cell A3: Date:
    - Cell B3: *current date*
    - Cell A4: Created By:
    - Cell B4: *your name*
    - Cell A5: Purpose:
    - Cell B5: To enter May orders for the Dalton Food Co-op

12. Increase the width of column A in the Documentation worksheet to 20 characters.

13. Check the spelling on both worksheets, correcting any errors found.

14. Delete any empty worksheets from the workbook.

15. Print the contents of the workbook with the Documentation sheet in portrait orientation and the Orders worksheet in landscape orientation.

16. Display the formulas in the Orders worksheet. Preview the worksheet before printing it, and set up the worksheet to print as a single page.

17. Save the workbook as **Dalton2** in the Tutorial.01\Review folder included with your Data Files.

18. Insert the following new order in the Orders worksheet directly below Amy Yang's order:
    - Name: Chad Reynolds
    - Address: 100 School Lane
                 Midtown, FL 80411
                 (833) 555-4425
    - Date: 5/5/2006
    - Item: Navel Oranges
    - Price: $17
    - Qty: 2

19. Remove Amy Yang's order from the worksheet, and change the quantity ordered by Eugene Burch from 4 to 3.

20. Check the spelling in the Orders worksheet again, correcting any errors found.

21. Print the contents and formulas of the Orders worksheet again.

22. Save the workbook as **Dalton3** in the Tutorial.01\Review folder, and then close the workbook.

Apply

Use the skills you have learned to create a cash flow analysis worksheet for a working couple.

Case Problem 1

Data File needed for this Case Problem: CFlow1.xls

Madison Federal Lisa Wu is a financial consultant at Madison Federal. She is working on a financial plan for Tom and Carolyn Watkins. Lisa has a cash flow analysis for the couple, and she wants you to record this information for her. Here are the relevant financial figures:

Receipts
- Employment Income: 95,000
- Other Income: 5,000

Disbursements
- Insurance: 940
- Savings/Retirement: 8,400
- Mortgage Payments: 18,000
- Children's Tuition: 10,000
- Groceries: 14,000
- Utilities: 6,000
- Other: 15,000
- Taxes: 16,300

Lisa wants you to calculate the total receipts and total disbursements and then calculate the cash surplus (receipts minus disbursements) in an Excel workbook that she has already started. To complete this task:

1. Open the **CFlow1** workbook located in the Tutorial.01\Cases folder included with your Data Files, and then save the workbook as **CFlow2** in the same folder.
2. Move the contents of the range A1:C16 to the range A5:C20.
3. Insert the text "Tom and Carolyn Watkins" in cell A1. In cell A2, insert the text "Cash Flow Analysis." In cell A3, insert the text "For the year 2006."
4. Increase the width of column A to 130 pixels, the width of column B to 160 pixels, and the width of column C to 130 pixels.
5. Insert the financial numbers listed earlier into the appropriate cells in column C.
6. Use the AutoSum button to calculate the total receipts and total disbursements, placing these values in cells C8 and C18, respectively.
7. Insert a formula to calculate the surplus in cell C20 (total receipts minus total disbursements).
8. Rename Sheet1 as "Cash Flow."
9. Insert a worksheet at the beginning of the workbook named "Documentation," and then enter the following information on the sheet:
   - Cell A1:   Cash Flow Report
   - Cell A3:   Date:
   - Cell B3:   *current date*
   - Cell A4:   Created By:
   - Cell B4:   *your name*
   - Cell A5:   Purpose:
   - Cell B5:   Cash flow analysis for Tom and Carolyn Watkins
10. Increase the width of column A in the Documentation worksheet to 20 characters.
11. Delete any empty sheets in the workbook.
12. Use the Spell Checker to correct any spelling errors in the workbook.
13. Print the contents of the entire workbook in portrait orientation, and then save your changes to the workbook.

14. Change the couple's taxes to 18,500, and then print the Cash Flow worksheet with the recalculated values.
15. Save the workbook as **CFlow3** in the Tutorial.01\Cases folder, and then close the workbook.

Case Problem 2

Apply

Use the skills you have learned to create a balance sheet for a financial services company.

Data File needed for this Case Problem: Balance1.xls

EMS Industries   Lee Evans is an agent at New Haven Financial Services. His job is to maintain financial information on investments for client companies. He has the balance sheet data for a company named EMS Industries in an Excel workbook and needs your help in finishing the workbook layout and contents. To complete this task:

1. Open the **Balance1** workbook located in the Tutorial.01\Cases folder included with your Data Files, and then save the workbook as **Balance2** in the same folder.
2. Select the range A1:C4, and then insert four new rows into the worksheet, shifting the selected cells down.
3. Enter the text "EMS Industries" in cell A1 and "Balance Sheet" in cell A2. In cell A3, enter the date "4/30/2006".
4. Increase the width of column A to 110 pixels.

Explore

5. Move the contents of the range A22:C32 to the range E5:G15, and then move the range A34:C38 to the range E20:G24.
6. Change the width of column B to 150 pixels, the width of column D to 20 pixels, and the width of column F to 240 pixels.
7. Use the AutoSum button to calculate the total current assets in cell C12; to calculate the total property, plant, and equipment assets in cell C18; to calculate the total current liabilities in cell G9; and to calculate the total long-term liabilities (only one value) in cell G13.
8. In cell C20, insert a formula to calculate the total of the current assets (cell C12) plus the noncurrent assets (cell C18). In cell G15, insert a formula to calculate the total of the current liabilities (cell G9) plus the long-term liabilities (cell G13).
9. In cell G23, enter a formula to calculate the total shareholders' equity, which is equal to the value of the common stock (cell G21) plus the value of retained earnings (cell G22). In cell G24, calculate the value of the total liabilities (cell G15) plus the shareholders' equity (cell G23).
10. Rename Sheet1 as "Balance Sheet," and then delete Sheet2 and Sheet3.
11. Insert a worksheet named "Documentation" at the front of the workbook, and then enter the following information into the sheet:
    - Cell A1:   Balance Sheet
    - Cell A3:   Company:
    - Cell B3:   EMS Industries
    - Cell A4:   Date:
    - Cell B4:   *current date*
    - Cell A5:   Recorded By:
    - Cell B5:   *your name*
    - Cell A6:   Purpose:
    - Cell B6:   Balance Sheet
12. Increase the width of column A in the Documentation worksheet to 20 characters.
13. Use the Spell Checker to correct any spelling mistakes in the workbook.
14. Print the entire contents of the workbook in landscape orientation.
15. Save your changes to the workbook, and then close it.

Challenge

Challenge yourself by going beyond what you've learned to create a worksheet that calculates the weighted scores of four possible locations for a new shoe factory.

Case Problem 3

Data File needed for this Case Problem: Site1.xls

Kips Shoes Kips Shoes is planning to build a new factory. The company has narrowed the site down to four possible cities. Each city has been graded on a 1-to-10 scale for four categories: the size of the local market, the quality of the labor pool, the local tax base, and the local operating expenses. Each of these four factors is given a weight, with the most important factor given the highest weight. After the sites are analyzed, the scores for each factor will be multiplied by their weights, and then a total weighted score will be calculated.

Gwen Sanchez, the senior planning manager overseeing this project, has entered the weights and the scores for each city into an Excel workbook. She needs you to finish the workbook by inserting the formulas to calculate the weighted scores and the total overall score for each city. To complete this task:

1. Open the **Site1** workbook located in the Tutorial.01\Cases folder included with your Data Files, and then save the workbook as **Site2** in the same folder.
2. Switch to the Site Analysis sheet.
3. In cell B14, calculate the weighted Market Size score for Waukegan by inserting a formula that multiplies the value in cell B7 by the weight value in cell G7.
4. Insert formulas to calculate the weighted scores for the rest of the cells in the range B14:E17.

Explore

5. Select the range B18:E18, and then click the AutoSum button to calculate the sum of the weighted scores for all four of the cities. Note that you can apply the AutoSum button to more than one cell at a time. Which city has the highest weighted score?
6. Switch to the Documentation sheet, and enter your name and the date in the appropriate locations on the sheet.
7. Spell check the workbook, print the entire workbook in portrait orientation, and then save your changes to the workbook.

Explore

8. Gwen has another set of weighted scores she wants you to try. However, she doesn't want you to enter the new values in the Site Analysis worksheet, so you need to make a copy of the worksheet. To learn how to copy a worksheet, open the Excel Help task pane, and then enter "copy a worksheet" in the Search for text box. Scroll the list of topics in the Search Results task pane to locate the topic "Move or copy sheets." Open the topic, read the information about copying a sheet, and then close the Microsoft Excel Help window and the Search Results task pane.

Explore

9. Using what you learned in Step 8, create a copy of the Site Analysis worksheet, placing the new worksheet at the end of the workbook. Rename the new sheet "Site Analysis 2".
10. In the Site Analysis 2 worksheet, change the weighted scores of Market Size to 0.2 and Labor Pool to 0.4. Which city has the highest weighted score now?
11. Print the contents of the Site Analysis 2 worksheet.
12. Save the workbook as **Site3** in the Tutorial.01\Cases folder, and then close the workbook.

Create

Use Figure 1-39, which shows the "end results," to create a workbook containing monthly budget figures over a three-month period for a college student.

Case Problem 4

There are no Data Files needed for this Case Problem.

Monthly Budget Alice Drake is a first-year student at MidWest University and has a part-time job in the admissions department. Her college-related expenses, such as tuition, books, and fees, are covered through grants and scholarships, so the money Alice makes goes towards her personal expenses. Being on her own for the first time, Alice is finding it difficult to keep within a budget. She has asked you to look at her finances and help her figure out how her money is being spent. Figure 1-39 shows the worksheet that you will create to help Alice analyze her budget.

Figure 1-39

enter formulas to calculate the ending cash balance and the net cash flows

use the AutoSum button to calculate these totals

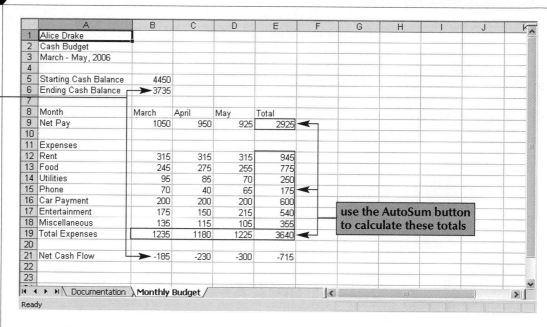

To complete this task:

1. Start Excel and save a new workbook with the name **Budget** in the Tutorial.01\Cases folder included with your Data Files.
2. On the Sheet1 worksheet, enter the labels and values as indicated in Figure 1-39. Note that the cells in which totals will be calculated have been marked. Do not enter the values shown; you will enter appropriate formulas next.
3. Using the AutoSum button, calculate the values for the total net pay, the total monthly expenses, and the total of each expense for the three months.
4. Enter formulas to calculate the net cash flow for each month and for all three months.
5. Enter a formula to calculate the ending cash balance, which is based on the value of the starting cash balance minus the total net cash flow over the three months. (*Hint:* Because two negatives make a positive, you need to *add* the total net cash flow to the starting cash balance.)
6. Rename Sheet1 as "Monthly Budget."
7. Create a worksheet named "Documentation" at the front of the workbook containing your name, the date, and the purpose of the workbook.
8. Delete any blank worksheets in the workbook.
9. Check the spelling on both worksheets, correcting any errors found.
10. Print the entire workbook in portrait orientation.
11. Save your changes to the workbook, and then close it.

Research

Use the Internet to find and work with data related to the topics presented in this tutorial.

Internet Assignments

The purpose of the Internet Assignments is to challenge you to find information on the Internet that you can use to work effectively with this software. The actual assignments are updated and maintained on the Course Technology Web site. Log on to the Internet and use your Web browser to go to the Student Online Companion for New Perspectives Office 2003 at **www.course.com/np/office2003**. Click the Internet Assignments link, and then navigate to the assignments for this tutorial.

SAM Assessment and Training

If you have a SAM user profile, you may have access to hands-on instruction, practice, and assessment of the skills covered in this tutorial. Log in to your SAM account and go to your assignments page to see what your instructor has assigned.

Reinforce

Lab Assignments

The New Perspectives Labs are designed to help you master some of the key concepts and skills presented in this text. The steps for completing this Lab are located on the Course Technology Web site. Log on to the Internet and use your Web browser to go to the Student Online Companion for New Perspectives Office 2003 at **www.course.com/np/office2003**. Click the Lab Assignments link, and then navigate to the assignments for this tutorial.

Review

Quick Check Answers

Session 1.1

1. cell
2. D2
3. Ctrl + Home
4. click the Sheet2 tab
5. a. value
   b. text
   c. value
   d. text (there is no equal sign indicating a formula)
   e. text
   f. formula
   g. text
6. Press the Alt + Enter keys to enter text on a new line within a cell.
7. =E5/E6

Session 1.2

1. An adjacent cell range is a rectangular block of cells. A non-adjacent cell range consists of two or more separate adjacent ranges.
2. A5:F8
3. AutoSum
4. down
5. to the right
6. Double-click the sheet tab and then type the new name to replace the highlighted sheet tab name.
7. Clearing a cell deletes the cell's contents but does not affect the position of other cells in the workbook. Deleting a cell removes the cell from the worksheet, and other cells are shifted in the direction of the deleted cell.
8. Ctrl + ` (grave accent)

Objectives

Session 2.1
- Learn about the syntax of an Excel function
- Use the SUM, AVERAGE, and MAX functions
- Copy and paste formulas
- Work with relative, absolute, and mixed references
- Change the magnification of the workbook window
- Insert a function using the Insert Function dialog box
- Use Auto Fill to insert formulas and complete a series
- Insert the current date using a Date function

Session 2.2 (Optional)
- Work with Financial functions
- Work with Logical functions

Working with Formulas and Functions

Developing a Family Budget

Case

Tyler Family Budget

As a newly married couple, Amanda and Joseph Tyler are trying to balance career, school, and family life. Amanda works full time as a legal assistant, and Joseph is in a graduate program at a nearby university. He recently was hired as a teaching assistant. In the summer, he is able to take on other jobs that bring additional income to the family. The couple also just moved into a new apartment. Although Joseph's and Amanda's salaries for the past year were greater than the years before, the couple seemed to have less cash on hand. This financial shortage has prompted them to take a closer look at their finances and figure out how to best manage them.

Because Amanda has agreed to take the lead role in the management of the family finances, she has set up an Excel workbook. Amanda has entered their salary amounts, which are their only income, and she has identified and entered several expenses that the family pays on a monthly basis, such as the rent and Joseph's tuition. She wants to calculate how much money they bring in and how much money they spend. She also wants to figure out their average monthly expenses and identify their greatest financial burden.

Amanda has asked for your help in completing the workbook. She wants you to insert formulas to perform the calculations she needs to get a better overall picture of the family's finances, which, in turn, should help the couple manage their money more effectively. Because the values entered cover a 12-month span, you will be able to copy and paste the formulas from one month to another and fill in series of data, such as the months of the year, rather than retyping formulas or entering each month individually. Finally, Amanda also wants the current date in her workbook, which you can enter using one of Excel's Date functions.

Student Data Files

▼Tutorial.02

▽ Tutorial folder	▽ Review folder	▽ Cases folder
Budget1.xls	Family1.xls	Sonic1.xls
		Soup1.xls
		Stock1.xls

Once she has a better handle on the family's finances, Amanda might want to evaluate whether buying a house would be possible in the near future, especially in light of the low interest rates that are available.

Session 2.1

Working with Excel Functions

In her budget worksheet, Amanda has already entered the couple's take-home salaries (that is, the amount of money in their paychecks minus taxes and other work-related deductions) and their expenses from the past year. You'll begin by opening her workbook so you can see what Amanda has done so far.

To open Amanda's workbook:

▶ 1. Start Excel and then open the **Budget1** workbook located in the Tutorial.02\Tutorial folder included with your Data Files.

▶ 2. On the Documentation sheet, enter *your name* in cell B3 and the *current date* in cell B4.

▶ 3. Save the workbook as **Budget2** in the Tutorial.02\Tutorial folder, and then click the **Budget** tab to make this sheet the active worksheet. See Figure 2-1. Amanda has recorded the couple's take-home salaries as income and has listed a variety of expenses in columns for each month. January's income and expenses are shown in column B, February's income and expenses are shown in column C, and so forth.

Figure 2-1	Budget worksheet

Microsoft Excel - Budget2

A1   fx Tyler Family Budget: 1/1/2006 - 12/31/2006

	A	B	C	D	E	F	G	H	I	J	K
1	Tyler Family Budget!	1/1/2006 - 12/31/2006									
2											
3	MONTHLY TOTALS										
4		1/1/2006	2/1/2006	3/1/2006	4/1/2006	5/1/2006	6/1/2006	7/1/2006	8/1/2006	9/1/2006	10/1/2006	1
5	Income										
6	Amanda	2,400	2,400	2,400	2,400	2,400	2,400	2,400	2,400	2,400	2,400
7	Joseph	850	850	850	850	850	1,650	1,650	1,650	850	850
8	Total										
9											
10	Expenses										
11	Rent	850	850	850	850	850	850	850	850	850	850
12	Food	607	657	613	655	644	761	699	672	683	609
13	Utilities	225	210	200	175	150	130	145	165	175	175
14	Phone	58	63	63	63	59	59	64	63	64	58
15	Loan Payments	150	150	150	150	150	150	150	150	150	150
16	Car Payments	175	175	175	175	175	175	175	175	175	175
17	Insurance	50	50	50	50	50	50	50	50	50	50
18	Miscellaneous	140	191	171	135	171	272	146	182	144	140
19	Entertainment	192	160	172	166	185	310	155	164	132	150
20	Tuition	2,000	0	0	0	0	0	0	2,200	0	0
21	Books	520	0	0	0	0	0	0	572	0	0
22	Total										
23											

Documentation \ **Budget**

Ready

Amanda would like the worksheet to calculate the family's total income and expenses for each month. She would also like to see a year-end summary that displays the family's total income and expenses for the entire year. This summary should also display the average income and expenses so that Amanda can get a picture of what a typical month looks like for her family. Amanda realizes that some expenses increase and decrease during certain months, so she would like to calculate the minimum and maximum values for each expense category, which will give her an idea of the range of these values throughout the year. All of this information will help Amanda and Joseph budget for the upcoming year.

To perform these calculations, you'll have to add several formulas to the workbook. As discussed in the previous tutorial, formulas are one of the most useful features in Excel because they enable you to calculate values based on data entered into the workbook. For more complex calculations, you can enter formulas that contain one or more functions. Recall that a function is a predefined formula that performs calculations using specific values. Each Excel function has a name and syntax. The **syntax** is the rule specifying how the function should be written. The general syntax of all Excel functions is

FUNCTION(argument1, argument2, ...)

where *FUNCTION* is the name of the Excel function and *argument1, argument2,* and so forth are **arguments** specifying the numbers, text, or cell references used by the function to calculate a value. An argument can also be an **optional argument** that is not necessary for the function to calculate a value. If an optional argument is not included, Excel assumes a default value for it. Each argument entered in a function is separated by a comma. The convention used in this text shows optional arguments within square brackets along with the argument's default value, as follows:

FUNCTION(argument1, [argument2=value2])

where *argument2* is an optional argument and *value2* is the default value for this argument. As you learn more about individual functions, you will also learn which arguments are required and which are optional.

Another convention followed in this text is to write function names in uppercase letters, but Excel recognizes the function names entered in either uppercase or lowercase letters, converting the lowercase letters to uppercase automatically.

There are 350 different Excel functions organized into the following 10 categories:

- Database functions
- Date and Time functions
- Engineering functions
- Financial functions
- Information functions
- Logical functions
- Lookup and Reference functions
- Math and Trigonometry functions
- Statistical functions
- Text and Data functions

You can learn about each function using Excel's online Help. Figure 2-2 describes some of the more important Math and Statistical functions that you may often use in your workbooks.

Figure 2-2 **Math and Statistical functions**

Function	Description
AVERAGE(*number1*, [*number2, number3*, ...])	Calculates the average of a collection of numbers, where *number1, number2*, and so forth are numeric values or cell references
COUNT(*value1*, [*value2, value3*, ...])	Calculates the total number of values, where *value1, value2*, and so forth are numeric values, text entries, or cell references
MAX(*number1*, [*number2, number3*, ...])	Calculates the maximum of a collection of numbers, where *number1, number2*, and so forth are either numeric values or cell references
MEDIAN(*number1*, [*number2, number3*, ...])	Calculates the median, or the number in the middle, of a collection of numbers, where *number1, number2*, and so forth are either numeric values or cell references
MIN(*number1*, [*number2, number3*, ...])	Calculates the minimum of a collection of numbers, where *number1, number2*, and so forth are either numeric values or cell references
ROUND(*number, num_digits*)	Rounds a number to a specified number of digits, where *number* is the number you want to round and *num_digits* specifies the number of digits to which you want to round the number
SUM(*number1*, [*number2, number3*, ...])	Calculates the sum of a collection of numbers, where *number1, number2*, and so forth are either numeric values or cell references

For example, the **AVERAGE function** calculates the average value of a collection of numbers. The syntax of this function is AVERAGE(*number1*, [*number2*, ...]). When you enter the arguments *(number1, number2)*, you can enter these numbers directly into the function, as in AVERAGE(3, 2, 5, 8), or you can enter the references to the worksheet cells that contain those numbers, as in AVERAGE(A1:A4). You can also enter a function as part of a larger formula. For example, the formula =*MAX(A1:A100)/100* calculates the maximum value in the cell range A1:A100 and then divides that number by 100. You can include, or "nest," one function within another. For example, in the formula =*ROUND(AVERAGE(A1:A100),1)*, the first argument in the ROUND function uses the value calculated by the AVERAGE function; the second argument is a constant. The result is a formula that calculates the average value of the numbers in the range A1:A100, rounding that value to the first decimal place.

In the previous tutorial, you calculated totals using the AutoSum button on the Standard toolbar. Although using the AutoSum feature is a quick and convenient way to calculate a value, it is only one way to perform this calculation in Excel. To determine the totals Amanda wants, you can also use the **SUM function**, which calculates the sum of a collection of numbers. The syntax of the SUM function is SUM(*number1*, [*number2*, ...]), which is similar to that of the AVERAGE function.

You'll use the SUM function now to begin calculating the values Amanda needs, starting with the values for the month of January.

To calculate the total income and expenses for January using the SUM function:

1. Click cell **B8** on the Budget worksheet, type **=SUM(B6:B7)** and then press the **Enter** key. Excel displays the value 3,250 in cell B8, indicating that the total income for the month of January is $3,250.

   You can also enter the cell range for a function by selecting the cell range rather than typing it. You'll use this method to determine the total expenses for January.

2. Click cell **B22** and then type **=SUM(** to begin the function.

3. Select the range **B11:B21** using your mouse. As you drag to select the range, its cell reference is automatically entered into the SUM function, as shown in Figure 2-3.

Entering the SUM function **Figure 2-3**

4. Press the **Enter** key to complete the formula. Note that you didn't have to type the closing parenthesis. When you press the Enter key, the closing parenthesis is inserted automatically. The value 4,967 is displayed in cell B22, indicating that the total expenses for January are $4,967.

Amanda wants to know how much money is left over at the end of each month or, in other words, the family's *net income* each month. To determine this amount, you need to enter a formula that subtracts the total monthly expenses from the total monthly income. You'll begin by calculating the net income for the month of January.

To calculate the net income for the first month:

1. Click cell **A24**, type **Net Income**, and then press the **Tab** key to move to cell B24, where you will enter the formula.

2. Type **=B8-B22** and then press the **Enter** key. Excel displays the value –1,717, which indicates that the family's net income for the month of January is a negative $1,717. Amanda and Joseph's expenses are greater than their income for that month.

Now that you've entered the formulas to calculate the total income, total expenses, and net income for January, you need to enter the same formulas for the other 11 months of the year. Entering the formulas for each of the remaining months individually would be time-consuming, but there is a quicker way.

Copying and Pasting Formulas

To use the same formula in different cells on the worksheet, you can copy the formula and paste it to a new location or locations. The cell (or range of cells) that contains the formula you copy is referred to as the **source cell** (or **source range**). The new location is the **destination cell** (or **destination range**). When you paste your selection, Excel automatically adjusts the cell references contained in the formulas. For example, if you copy cell B8, which contains the formula *=SUM(B6:B7)*, and paste the contents of the copied cell into cell C8 (the destination cell), Excel automatically changes the formula in cell C8 to *=SUM(C6:C7)*.

In effect, Excel recognizes that the intent of the function is to calculate the sum of the values in the two cells above the active cell. The new location does not even have to be in the same row as the copied cell. If you copy the formula in cell B8 to cell C10, the pasted formula would be *=SUM(C8:C9)*. You can copy the formula in one cell to a whole range of cells, and Excel will correctly adjust the cell references in the formula for each cell in the range.

Reference Window	**Copying and Pasting a Cell or Range**

- Select the cell or range that you want to copy, and then click the Copy button on the Standard toolbar.
- Select the cell or range into which you want to copy the selection, and then click the Paste button on the Standard toolbar.

Next, you'll copy the formula in cell B8 to the range C8:M8 to calculate the total income for the remaining months.

To copy and paste the formula from cell B8 to the range C8:M8:

1. Click cell **B8** on the Budget worksheet, and then click the **Copy** button on the Standard toolbar. Note that the copied cell has a moving border. This border is a visual reminder that the range has been copied and is ready to be pasted.

2. Select the range **C8:M8**, and then click the **Paste** button on the Standard toolbar. Excel copies the formula in cell B8 into each of the cells in the range C8:M8, changing the cell references to match the location of each cell in the range. See Figure 2-4. Note that when you paste a selection, Excel automatically displays the Paste Options button. This button provides options that give you control over the paste process. You will learn more about this button in the next tutorial.

pasted formulas

Trouble? If your screen does not match the one shown in the figure, you may have scrolled the worksheet further to the right so column B is no longer visible. You can click the left scroll button on the horizontal scroll bar to reposition the worksheet in the workbook window to better match the one in the figure.

3. Press the **Ctrl + `** (grave accent) keys to display the formulas in the range B8:M8. Notice that the cell references in each formula refer to the income values for that particular month.

4. Press the **Ctrl + `** (grave accent) keys to return to Normal view.

You are not limited to copying a single formula from one cell. You can also copy a range of formulas. When you copy a range of cells, each of which contains a formula, and then paste the selection into a new location, Excel pastes the formulas in each cell to their corresponding locations in the new cell range. You don't have to select a range that is the same size as the range being copied. You just need to select the first, or upper leftmost, cell in the destination range, and Excel will paste the selection in a range that accommodates all the cells. Any existing text or values in the destination range will be overwritten. So, be sure you paste the selection in an area of the worksheet that can accommodate the selection without deleting existing data.

Next, you need to copy the formulas for January's total expenses and net income, which are in cells B22 and B24, to the ranges C22:M22 and C24:M24. Then Amanda will be able to see each month's total expenses and net income values. Although there is no formula in cell B23, you will select the range B22:B24 and paste the selection to range C22:M24, simplifying the process. No values will appear in row 23.

To copy and paste the formulas in the range B22:B24 to the range C22:M24:

1. Scroll the worksheet to the left, if necessary, so column B is visible, select the range **B22:B24**, and then click the **Copy** button on the Standard toolbar.

   Trouble? If the Clipboard task pane opens, close it. You will not need to use it in this tutorial.

2. Select the range **C22:M24**, and then click the **Paste** button on the Standard toolbar. Figure 2-5 shows the total expenses and net income values for each month in the Budget worksheet. Note that Excel has duplicated the two formulas from the first month in each succeeding month.

Figure 2-5   **Copying and pasting a cell range**

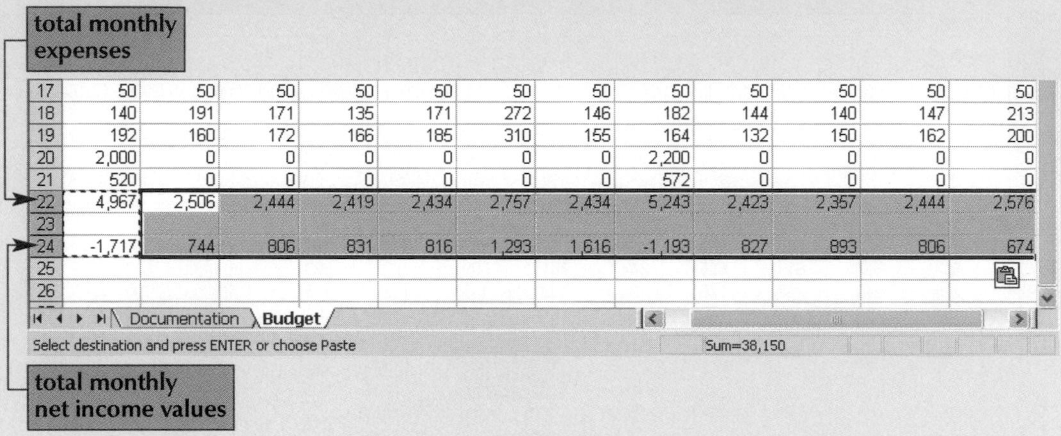

total monthly expenses

17	50	50	50	50	50	50	50	50	50	50	50	50
18	140	191	171	135	171	272	146	182	144	140	147	213
19	192	160	172	166	185	310	155	164	132	150	162	200
20	2,000	0	0	0	0	0	2,200	0	0	0	0	0
21	520	0	0	0	0	0	572	0	0	0	0	0
22	4,967	2,506	2,444	2,419	2,434	2,757	2,434	5,243	2,423	2,357	2,444	2,576
23												
24	-1,717	744	806	831	816	1,293	1,616	-1,193	827	893	806	674
25												
26												

◄ ► ►│ \ Documentation \ **Budget** /

Select destination and press ENTER or choose Paste   Sum=38,150

total monthly net income values

3. Press the **Esc** key to remove the moving border from the selected range.

As you can see, Excel's ability to adjust cell references when copying and pasting formulas makes it easy to create columns or rows of formulas that share a common structure.

Using Relative and Absolute References

The type of cell reference that you just worked with is called a relative reference. A **relative reference** is a cell reference that changes when it is copied and pasted in a new location. Excel interprets the reference *relative* to the position of the active cell. For example, when you copied the formula *=SUM(B6:B7)* from the source cell, B8, and pasted it in the destination range, C8:M8, Excel adjusted the cell references in each pasted formula relative to the new location of the formula itself. The formula in cell C8 became *=SUM(C6:C7)*, the formula in cell D8 became *=SUM(D6:D7)*, and so on.

A second type of cell reference is an absolute reference. An **absolute reference** is a cell reference that doesn't change when it is copied. Excel does not adjust the cell reference because the cell reference points to a fixed, or *absolute,* location in the worksheet, and it remains fixed when the copied formula is pasted. In Excel, an absolute reference appears with a dollar sign ($) before each column and row designation. For example, $B$8 is an absolute reference, and when it is used in a formula, Excel will always point to the cell located at the intersection of column B and row 8.

Figure 2-6 provides an example in which an absolute reference is necessary to a formula. In this example, a sales worksheet records the units sold for each region as well as the overall total. If you want to calculate the percent of units sold for each region, you divide the units sold for each region by the overall total. If you use only relative references, copying the formula from the first region to the second will produce an incorrect result, because Excel shifts the location of the total sales cell down one row. To correct this problem, you use an absolute cell reference, fixing the location of the total sales cell at cell B8. In the example, this means changing the formula in cell C4 from *=B4/B8* to *=B4/$B$8*.

Using relative and absolute references | **Figure 2-6**

Formulas Using Relative References

	A	B	C	D
1	Sales			
2				
3	Regions	Units Sold	Percent	
4	Region 1	2,238	=B4/B8	
5	Region 2	1,321		
6	Region 3	3,093		
7	Region 4	1,905		
8	Total	8,557		
9				
10				

	A	B	C	D
1	Sales			
2				
3	Regions	Units Sold	Percent	
4	Region 1	2,238	0.26154026	
5	Region 2	1,321	=B5/B9	
6	Region 3	3,093		
7	Region 4	1,905		
8	Total	8,557		
9				
10				

When the formula is copied, the relative reference to the cell (B8) is shifted down and now points to an incorrect cell (B9).

Formulas Using Absolute References

	A	B	C	D
1	Sales			
2				
3	Regions	Units Sold	Percent	
4	Region 1	2,238	=B4/$B$8	
5	Region 2	1,321		
6	Region 3	3,093		
7	Region 4	1,905		
8	Total	8,557		
9				
10				

	A	B	C	D
1	Sales			
2				
3	Regions	Units Sold	Percent	
4	Region 1	2,238	0.26154026	
5	Region 2	1,321	=B5/$B$8	
6	Region 3	3,093		
7	Region 4	1,905		
8	Total	8,557		
9				
10				

When the formula is copied, the absolute reference to the cell ($B$8) continues to point to that cell.

Another type of reference supported by Excel is the mixed reference. A **mixed reference** contains both relative and absolute cell references. A mixed reference for cell B8 is either $B8 or B$8. In the case of the mixed reference $B8, the column portion of the reference remains fixed, but the row number adjusts as the formula is copied to a new location. In the B$8 reference, the row number remains fixed, whereas the column portion adjusts to each new cell location.

As you enter a formula that requires an absolute reference or a mixed reference, you can type the dollar sign for the column and row references as needed. If you have already entered a formula and need to change the type of cell reference used, you can switch to edit mode and then press the **F4** key. As you press this function key, Excel cycles through the different references for the cell in the formula at the location of the insertion point. Pressing the F4 key changes a relative reference to an absolute reference, then to a mixed reference for the row, then to a mixed reference for the column, and then back to a relative reference.

In Amanda's family budget, monthly expenses vary greatly throughout the year. For example, tuition is a major expense, and that bill must be paid once in January and once in August. Amanda knows that the family has more entertainment and miscellaneous expenses during the month of December than at other times. The family's monthly income also fluctuates as Joseph brings in more income during the summer months than at other times. Amanda would like her budget worksheet to keep a running total of the family's net income as it progresses through the year. For example, she knows that the family will start the year with less money because of the tuition bill in January. Amanda wonders how many months pass before they recover from that major expense and begin saving money again.

One way to calculate the running total is to add the net income values of consecutive months. For example, to figure out how much money the family has saved or lost after two months, you add the net income for January to the net income for February, using the formula =SUM(B24:C24). To figure out the total net income for the first three months, you use the formula =SUM(B24:D24); through the first four months the formula will be =SUM(B24:E24), and so on.

The starting point of the range in the formula needs to be fixed at the cell that contains the net income for January, cell B24. To be sure that the formula points to cell B24, you need to use the absolute reference $B$24. The ending cell of the range will shift as you copy the formula to the other months in the worksheet. You need to use a relative reference for the ending cell in the range so that Excel will adjust the reference as the formula is copied. The formula for the running total through the first two months will be =SUM($B$24:C24). When you paste this formula to the other months of the year, Excel will adjust the cell range to calculate the total for all of the months up to that point.

To calculate the running total using an absolute reference to cell B24:

1. Click cell **A25**, type **Running Total**, and then press the **Tab** key twice to move to column C.

2. Type **=SUM(B24:C24)** in cell C25, and then press the **Enter** key. Excel displays the value –973, showing that the family's expenses exceed their income by $973 through the first two months of the year.

   Now you'll change the formula to use an absolute reference for cell B24 by selecting it in the formula and pressing the F4 key.

3. Double-click cell **C25** to switch to edit mode, and then double-click **B24** within the formula to select the cell reference.

4. Press the **F4** key to change the cell reference from B24 to $B$24. See Figure 2-7.

Figure 2-7 ▶ **Entering an absolute reference**

17	Insurance	50	50	50	50	50	50	50	50	50	50
18	Miscellaneous	140	191	171	135	171	272	146	182	144	140
19	Entertainment	192	160	172	166	185	310	155	164	132	150
20	Tuition	2,000	0	0	0	0	0	0	2,200	0	0
21	Books	520	0	0	0	0	0	0	572	0	0
22	Total	4,967	2,506	2,444	2,419	2,434	2,757	2,434	5,243	2,423	2,357
23											
24	Net Income	-1,717	744	806	831	816	1,293	1,616	-1,193	827	893
25	Running Total		=SUM($B$24:C24)								
26			SUM(**number1**, [number2], …)								
27											
28					**absolute reference entered by pressing the F4 key**						
29											

Documentation \ Budget /

Edit

Trouble? If you pressed the F4 key too many times and passed the absolute reference, continue pressing the F4 key to cycle through the options until $B$24 is displayed in the formula.

5. Press the **Enter** key when the correct reference is displayed. Excel displays the value –973.

   Now you can copy this formula to the remaining months of the year.

6. Click cell **C25**, and then click the **Copy** button on the Standard toolbar. The moving border indicates that cell C25 has been copied.

7. Select the range **D25:M25**, and then click the **Paste** button on the Standard toolbar. Excel copies the formula to the remaining cells, as shown in Figure 2-8. The amount shown for each month represents the cash on hand that the family accumulated during the year, up to and including that month. So, for example, at the end of the year, after paying all expenses, they have a total of $6,396.

Running total of the family's net income **Figure 2-8**

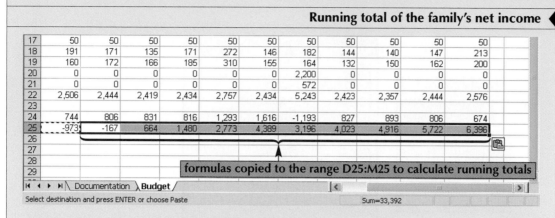

17	50	50	50	50	50	50	50	50	50	50	50
18	191	171	135	171	272	146	182	144	140	147	213
19	160	172	166	185	310	155	164	132	150	162	200
20	0	0	0	0	0	0	2,200	0	0	0	0
21	0	0	0	0	0	0	572	0	0	0	0
22	2,506	2,444	2,419	2,434	2,757	2,434	5,243	2,423	2,357	2,444	2,576
23											
24	744	806	831	816	1,293	1,616	-1,193	827	893	806	674
25	-973	-167	664	1,480	2,773	4,389	3,196	4,023	4,916	5,722	6,396
26											
27											
28											
29											

formulas copied to the range D25:M25 to calculate running totals

Documentation \ **Budget** /

Select destination and press ENTER or choose Paste   Sum=33,392

8. Press the **Ctrl +** ` (grave accent) keys to examine the pasted formulas in the range D25:M25. The use of absolute and relative references ensures the integrity of the formula copied in each cell used to calculate the running net income total.

9. Press the **Ctrl +** ` (grave accent) keys to return to Normal view.

Working with Other Paste Options

So far you've used the Paste button to paste formulas from a source cell or range to a destination cell or range. When Excel pastes the contents of a selected cell or range, it also pastes any formatting applied to the source cell (you'll learn about formatting in the next tutorial). If you want more control over how Excel pastes the data from the source cell, you can click the list arrow next to the Paste button and choose one of the available paste options. Figure 2-9 describes each of these options.

Paste options **Figure 2-9**

Option	Description
Formulas	Pastes the formula(s), but not the formatting, of the source cell range
Values	Pastes the value(s), but not the formula(s) or formatting, of the source cell range
No Borders	Pastes the formula(s) and formatting of the source cell range, but not the format of the cell range's borders
Transpose	Pastes the formula(s) and formatting of the source cell range, except changes the orientation so that rows in the source cell range become columns, and columns become rows
Paste Link	Pastes a link to the cell(s) in the source cell range, including the formatting used
Paste Special	Opens a dialog box displaying more paste options

For example, if you want to paste the value calculated by the formula in a cell but not the formula itself, you use the Values option. This is useful in situations in which you want to "freeze" a calculated value and remove the risk of it being changed by inadvertently changing another value in the worksheet. For even more control over the paste feature, you can select the Paste Special option. When you select this option, the Paste Special dialog box opens, as shown in Figure 2-10.

Figure 2-10   **Paste Special dialog box**

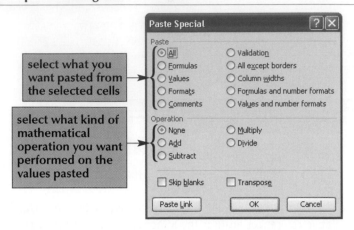

select what you want pasted from the selected cells

select what kind of mathematical operation you want performed on the values pasted

Using this dialog box, you can not only specify exactly which parts of the source cell or range—formulas, values, or formats—you want to paste, but also specify a mathematical operation you want performed as part of the paste action. For example, you can copy the value of one cell and add that value to cells in the destination range.

Another method that gives you control over the paste process is provided by the Paste Options button, which appears each time you paste a selection. By clicking this icon, you can choose from a variety of options that determine how the pasted data should be formatted. You'll explore this feature more in the next tutorial.

Changing the Magnification of a Worksheet

As you learned in Tutorial 1, an Excel worksheet can have 256 columns and more than 65,000 rows of data. You also learned that you can freeze columns and rows, so as you scroll through the data in the worksheet, the column and row headings remain visible. The number of columns and rows displayed in the workbook window depends on the zoom magnification set for the worksheet. The default zoom magnification setting is 100%. You can change this setting using the Zoom command on the View menu or the Zoom button on the Standard toolbar. Changing the zoom magnification setting allows you to see more or less of the worksheet at one time. If you decrease the magnification, you will see more of the data in the worksheet, but the data will be smaller and may be more difficult to read. If you increase the magnification, you will see less of the data in the worksheet, but the data will be larger and easier to read.

Reference Window	**Changing the Zoom Magnification of the Workbook Window**

- Click View on the menu bar, and then click Zoom.
- Click the option button for the percent magnification you want to apply, and then click the OK button.

or

- Click the Zoom list arrow on the Standard toolbar, and then click the percent option you want to apply.

You can change the magnification of the workbook window from 10% up to 400% or enter a percent not offered, for example, 65%, to further customize the display of your workbook window. You can also select a zoom magnification specific to the content of your worksheet. To do this, you select the worksheet's content and then choose the Selection option in the Zoom dialog box or on the Zoom list. Excel displays the content of the selection at a magnification that fills the entire workbook window.

Before continuing, Amanda wants to review the work done so far. Try changing the magnification so more of the worksheet is displayed at one time.

To change the zoom setting for the workbook window:

1. Press the **Ctrl + Home** keys to make cell A1 the active cell.

2. Click **View** on the menu bar, and then click **Zoom** to open the Zoom dialog box.

3. Click the **75%** option button in the list of options, and then click the **OK** button. At this setting, all the data in the worksheet is displayed in the workbook window, as shown in Figure 2-11.

Budget worksheet at 75 percent magnification **Figure 2-11**

indicates the current zoom magnification setting

	A	B	C	D	E	F	G	H	I	J	K	L
1	Tyler Family Budget: 1/1/2006 - 12/31/2006											
2												
3	MONTHLY TOTALS											
4		1/1/2006	2/1/2006	3/1/2006	4/1/2006	5/1/2006	6/1/2006	7/1/2006	8/1/2006	9/1/2006	10/1/2006	11/1/2006	12/1/2006
5	Income											
6	Amanda	2,400	2,400	2,400	2,400	2,400	2,400	2,400	2,400	2,400	2,400	2,400	2,400
7	Joseph	850	850	850	850	850	1,650	1,650	1,650	850	850	850	850
8	Total	3,250	3,250	3,250	3,250	3,250	4,050	4,050	4,050	3,250	3,250	3,250	3,250
9													
10	Expenses											
11	Rent	850	850	850	850	850	850	850	850	850	850	850	850
12	Food	607	657	613	655	644	761	699	672	683	609	642	606
13	Utilities	225	210	200	175	150	130	145	185	175	176	190	220
14	Phone	58	63	63	63	59	59	64	63	64	58	78	112
15	Loan Payments	150	150	150	150	150	150	150	150	150	150	150	150
16	Car Payments	175	175	175	175	175	175	175	175	175	175	175	175
17	Insurance	50	50	50	50	50	50	50	50	50	50	50	50
18	Miscellaneous	140	191	171	135	171	272	146	182	144	140	147	213
19	Entertainment	192	160	172	166	185	310	155	164	132	150	162	200
20	Tuition	2,000	0	0	0	0	0	0	2,200	0	0	0	0
21	Books	520	0	0	0	0	0	0	572	0	0	0	0
22	Total	4,967	2,506	2,444	2,419	2,434	2,757	2,434	5,243	2,423	2,357	2,444	2,576
23													
24	Net Income	-1,717	744	806	831	816	1,293	1,616	-1,193	827	893	806	674
25	Running Total		-973	-167	664	1,480	2,773	4,389	3,196	4,023	4,916	5,722	6,396
26													
27													

More of the worksheet is visible; however, reading the individual cell values is more difficult, so you will change the magnification back to 100%.

4. Click the **Zoom** list arrow [100% ▾] on the Standard toolbar, and then click **100%** to return to this higher magnification. Although the overall appearance of your screen may differ from the figures in this text, the data is not affected.

From examining the running totals, Amanda has learned several important facts. One of the family's largest expenses is Joseph's tuition, which is paid in January and August. She has also learned that the family does not recover from this January expense and show a positive overall net income until the month of April, when the total savings amount for the year up to that point is $664. Therefore, with their current income and expenses, it takes four months to "catch up" with the tuition expenditure in January, which leaves the family short on cash during February and March. The good news is that the total net income at the end of 12 months is $6,396, which represents the amount of money the family is able to save for the entire year.

Amanda now wants to know the family's total income and its total yearly expenses. You'll place these calculations in a table below the monthly figures. First, you will copy the income and expense categories to a new cell range.

To copy the income and expense categories:

► 1. Click cell **A27**, type **YEAR-END SUMMARY**, and then press the **Enter** key.

► 2. Copy the range **A5:A24** and paste it into the range **A29:A48**. If you want to remove the selection border from the copied range, you can press the Esc key. The selection border will disappear as soon as you select another range.

Now you will enter the formula to calculate the total income for the family over the entire year.

► 3. Click cell **B28**, type **Total**, and then press the **Enter** key twice. You will enter the formula to calculate Amanda's salary for the year.

► 4. Type **=SUM(B6:M6)** in cell B30, and then press the **Enter** key. The amount 28,800 appears in the cell.

Now you will copy this formula to calculate Joseph's yearly income, the couple's combined income, and the yearly totals for the expense categories.

► 5. Click cell **B30** to select this cell again, and then click the **Copy** button 🗐 on the Standard toolbar.

► 6. Select the range **B31:B32**, press and hold the **Ctrl** key, select the range **B35:B46**, click cell **B48**, and then release the mouse button and the Ctrl key. The nonadjacent range B31:B32;B35:B46;B48 should now be selected.

► 7. Click the **Paste** button 🗐 on the Standard toolbar. As shown in Figure 2-12, the total values for all income and expense categories should now be pasted in the worksheet.

Figure 2-12	Year-end totals for income and expenses

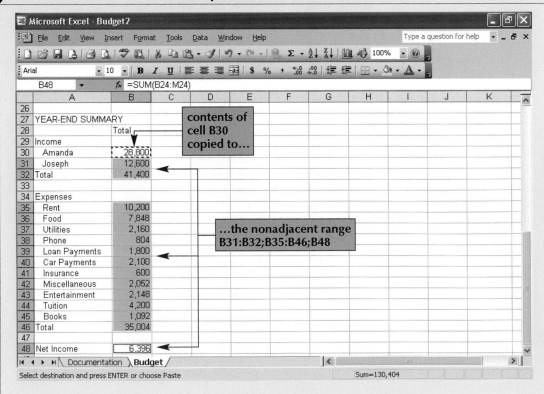

From these calculations, Amanda can quickly see that her family's yearly income is $41,400, whereas their yearly expenses total $35,004. Their largest expense is rent—a total of $10,200 per year.

Using the Insert Function Dialog Box

It's easier for Amanda to plan a budget if she knows approximately how much the family makes and spends each month. So your next task is to add a column that calculates the monthly averages for each of the income and expense categories. Rather than typing the function directly into the cell, you may find it helpful to use the Insert Function button on the Formula bar. Clicking this button displays a dialog box from which you can choose the function you want to enter. Once you choose a function, another dialog box opens, which displays the function's syntax. In this way, Excel makes it easy for you to avoid making mistakes. Try this now by entering the AVERAGE function using the Insert Function dialog box.

To insert the AVERAGE function:

▶ **1.** Click cell **C28**, type **Average**, and then press the **Enter** key.

▶ **2.** Click cell **C30** and then click the **Insert Function** button f_x on the Formula bar. The Insert Function dialog box opens. See Figure 2-13.

Insert Function dialog box ◀ **Figure 2-13**

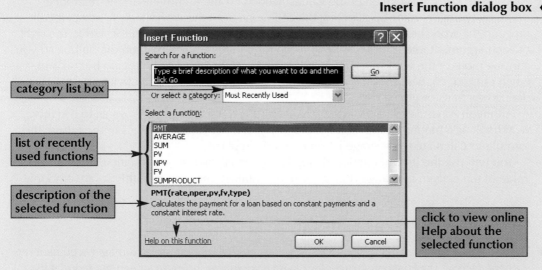

The Insert Function dialog box shows a list of the most recently used functions. As you can see from Figure 2-13, one of these is the AVERAGE function. However, your list may be different and might not include the AVERAGE function. You can display a different function list using the category list box. Try this now to display a list of the Statistical functions supported by Excel.

▶ **3.** Click the **Or select a category** list arrow, and then click **Statistical**. Excel displays a list of Statistical functions. See Figure 2-14.

Figure 2-14 **Excel's Statistical functions**

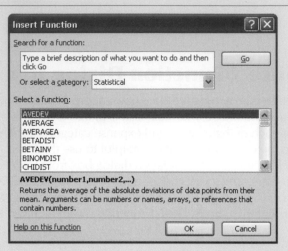

4. Click **AVERAGE** in the list, and then click the **OK** button. The Function Arguments dialog box opens.

The Function Arguments dialog box provides the syntax of the selected function in an easy-to-use form. You can enter the values needed for the arguments in the reference boxes by typing them or by selecting the cell range from the worksheet. To select a cell range in the worksheet, you can click the Collapse Dialog Box button located to the right of each argument reference. Clicking this button reduces the size of the dialog box so you can see more of the worksheet. The Collapse Dialog Box button is a toggle button and, when clicked, changes to the Expand Dialog box button, which you click to restore the dialog box to its original size.

Although Amanda's salary did not change during the past year, she wants to use this workbook as a model for the next couple of years. If her salary changes in the future, the formula to calculate the average income will be in place.

You will use the Insert Function dialog box to enter the formula to calculate the average value of the cells in the range B6:M6, which contains Amanda's monthly salary amount.

To insert values into the AVERAGE function:

1. Click the **Collapse Dialog Box** button located to the right of the Number1 argument reference box. The Function Arguments dialog box reduces in size to let you see more of the worksheet, and the Collapse Dialog Box button changes to the Expand Dialog Box button.

Trouble? If the collapsed dialog box is still in the way of the range you need to select, drag the dialog box to another location on the worksheet.

2. Select the range **B6:M6** on the worksheet, and then click the **Expand Dialog Box** button to restore the Function Arguments dialog box to its original size, as shown in Figure 2-15.

Function Arguments dialog box ◄ **Figure 2-15**

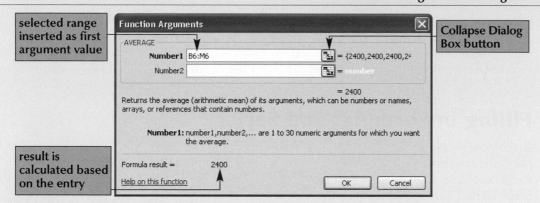

selected range inserted as first argument value

Collapse Dialog Box button

result is calculated based on the entry

3. Click the **OK** button. The value 2,400 appears in C30.

Now you will copy the formula to calculate the average of other income and expense categories.

To copy the AVERAGE function into the remaining cells:

1. Click cell **C30**, if necessary, and then click the **Copy** button 🔄 on the Standard toolbar.

2. Select the nonadjacent range **C31:C32;C35:C46;C48**, and then click the **Paste** button 🔄 on the Standard toolbar. Figure 2-16 shows the monthly averages in Amanda's budget.

Year-end average values ◄ **Figure 2-16**

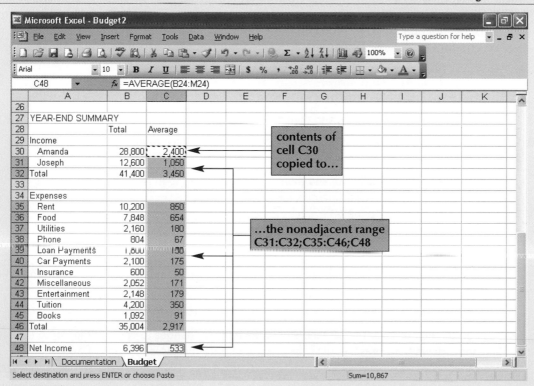

contents of cell C30 copied to...

...the nonadjacent range C31:C32;C35:C46;C48

On average, the couple makes $3,450 per month and spends $2,917. Their net income is about $533 a month on average; this is the amount that Amanda can expect the family to save. It is obvious that expenses for some months will be higher than expected. Amanda wonders how much higher? She would like to calculate the maximum and minimum amounts for each of the income and expense categories. She knows that this will give her a better picture of the range of values for her family's income and expenses.

Filling in Formulas and Series

Up to now you've used the Copy and Paste buttons to enter the same formula into multiple cells. Another approach you can use is to fill in the values. You may have noticed a small black square in the lower-right corner of a selected cell or cell range. That small black square is called the **fill handle**. This Excel tool enables you to copy the contents of the selected cells simply by dragging the fill handle over another adjacent cell or range of cells rather than going through the two-step process of clicking the Copy and Paste buttons. This technique is also referred to as **Auto Fill**.

Reference Window

Copying Formulas Using the Fill Handle

- Select the cell or range that contains the formula or formulas you want to copy.
- Drag the fill handle in the direction you want to copy the formula(s), and then release the mouse button.
- To select a specific fill option, click the Auto Fill Options button, and then select the option you want to apply to the selected range.

To calculate the maximum and minimum amounts for each of the income and expense categories, you will enter the **MIN** and **MAX functions**, which have a similar syntax as the AVERAGE and SUM functions. Once you enter the formulas using the MIN and MAX functions for Amanda's income, you can use Auto Fill to fill in the formulas for Joseph's income and for the expense categories.

To calculate the year-end minimum and maximum amounts:

1. Click cell **D28**, type **Minimum**, and then press the **Tab** key.

2. Type **Maximum** in cell E28, and then press the **Enter** key twice to move back to column D where you will enter the formula to calculate minimum values.

3. Type **=MIN(B6:M6)** in cell D30, and then press the **Tab** key to move to column E where you will enter the formula to calculate maximum values.

4. Type **=MAX(B6:M6)** in cell E30, and then press the **Enter** key. Excel displays the value 2,400 in both cell D30 and cell E30 because Amanda's monthly salary is $2,400 and does not vary throughout the year.

   You will use the fill handle to copy the formulas with the MIN and MAX functions into the remaining income and expense categories.

5. Select the range **D30:E30**. The fill handle appears in the lower-right corner of the selection.

6. Position the pointer over the fill handle until the pointer changes to ✛, and then drag the fill handle down the worksheet until the selection border encloses the range **D30:E48**.

7. Release the mouse button. The Auto Fill Options button appears, and by default Excel copies the formulas and formats found in the source range, D30:E30, into the destination range. Note that rows 33, 34, and 47 contain zeros. This is because those rows correspond to empty cells in the monthly table. You can delete the MIN and MAX functions in those cells.

8. Select the nonadjacent range **D33:E34;D47:E47**, and then press the **Delete** key to clear the contents of the selected cells. Figure 2-17 shows the minimum and maximum values for each income and expense category.

Year-end minimum and maximum values ◀ **Figure 2-17**

These calculations provide Amanda with an idea of the range of possible values in her budget. From these figures she can see that the maximum amount the family earned in a single month was $4,050 (cell E32), while the maximum amount the family spent in a single month was $5,243 (cell E46). How frugal can the family be? Based on her calculations, the lowest amount the family spent in a given month was $2,357 (cell D46). Amanda has also discovered that the most the family was able to save in a month was $1,616 (cell E48), while their largest deficit was $1,717—which occurred in the month of January, when a tuition payment was due. If the average values in column C give Amanda a picture of what a "typical" month looks like, the values in columns D and E give her an idea of the extremes in the family budget.

If you have a large selection to fill, you may find it difficult to use the fill handle feature of Auto Fill. If you don't want to use the fill handle, you can select the cell range that you want to fill and then use the Fill command on the Edit menu. Excel provides a list of Fill commands that you can use to fill in the selected range.

Auto Fill Options

When you use Auto Fill with formulas, Excel copies not only the formulas but also the formatting applied to the copied cell or range. However, there may be times when you only want the values in a cell copied, or maybe just the formatting. You can control what Excel does when you use the fill handle to copy formulas. When you release the mouse button, a button appears at the lower-right corner of the cell range. This is the Auto Fill Options button. Clicking this button provides a list of available options that you can choose to specify how Excel should handle the pasted selection.

The Auto Fill default option is to copy both the formulas and the formats of selected cells into the cell range. To copy only the formulas or just the formats, you can choose one of the other Auto Fill options, as shown in Figure 2-18.

| Figure 2-18 | Auto Fill options |

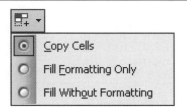

Filling a Series

The Auto Fill feature can also be used to continue a series of values, dates, or text based on an established pattern. As shown in Figure 2-19, to create a list of sequential numbers, you enter the first few numbers of the sequence and then drag the fill handle, completing the sequence. In this case, a list of numbers from 1 to 10 is quickly generated.

| Figure 2-19 | Using Auto Fill to complete a series of numbers |

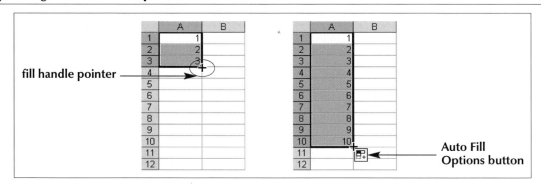

The series does not have to be numeric. It can also contain text and dates. Figure 2-20 shows a few examples of other series that can be completed using the Auto Fill feature.

Type	Initial Selection	Extended Series
Values	1, 2, 3	4, 5, 6, ...
	2, 4, 6	8, 10, 12, ...
Dates and Times	Jan	Feb, Mar, Apr, ...
	January	February, March, April, ...
	Jan, Apr	Jul, Oct, Jan, ...
	15-Jan, 15-Feb	15-Mar, 15-Apr, 15-May, ...
	12/30/2005	12/31/2005, 1/1/2006, 1/2/2006, ...
	12/31/2005, 1/31/2006	2/28/2006, 3/31/2006, 4/30/2006, ...
	Mon	Tue, Wed, Thu, ...
	Monday	Tuesday, Wednesday, Thursday, ...
	11:00 AM	12:00 PM, 1:00 PM, 2:00 PM, ...
Patterned Text	1st period	2nd period, 3rd period, 4th period, ...
	Region 1	Region 2, Region 3, Region 4, ...
	Quarter 3	Quarter 4, Quarter 1, Quarter 2, ...
	Qtr3	Qtr4, Qtr1, Qtr2, ...

Amanda would like to replace dates in the Budget worksheet with the abbreviations of each month. Rather than directly typing this text, you will insert the abbreviations using the fill handle.

To fill in the abbreviations for the months of the year:

1. Press the **Ctrl + Home** keys to make the columns on the left and the top rows visible.

2. Click cell **B4**, type **Jan**, and then click the **Enter** button ☑ on the Formula bar. Because "Jan" is a commonly used abbreviation for January, Excel will recognize it as a month without your having to type in "Feb" for the next month in the series.

3. Position the pointer over the fill handle in the lower-right corner of cell B4 until the pointer changes to **+**.

4. Drag the fill handle over the range **B4:M4**, and then release the mouse button. Excel fills in the abbreviation for each month in the range of cells, as shown in Figure 2-21. As you drag the fill handle, ScreenTips for the month abbreviations appear.

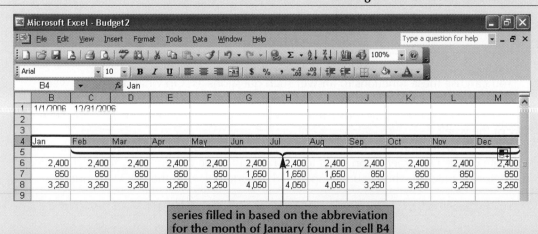

series filled in based on the abbreviation for the month of January found in cell B4

Excel provides other techniques for automatically filling in values and text. You can even create your own customized fill series. You can use Excel's online Help to explore other Auto Fill options.

Working with Date Functions

Entering the current date in a worksheet might not always address a date-related issue or need. If you want the current date to always appear in your workbook, versus the date you may have entered when you created the workbook, you can use a Date function rather than re-entering the current date each time you open the workbook. The **Date functions** provided by Excel store and calculate dates as numeric values, representing the number of days since January 1, 1900. For example, when you enter the date 1/1/2008 into a worksheet cell, you are actually entering the value 39448, because that date is 39,448 days after January 1, 1900. This method of storing dates allows you to work with dates using the same formulas you would use to work with any value. If you want to determine the number of days between two dates, you simply subtract one date from the other.

Excel automatically updates the values returned by the TODAY() and NOW() functions whenever you reopen the workbook. The **TODAY() function** displays the current date based on your computer's internal clock; the **NOW() function** displays both the date and time. If you want a permanent date (reflecting when the workbook was initially created, for example), enter the date directly into the cell without using either function.

If you have additional tasks to perform with a date or time, you can use one of the functions listed in Figure 2-22.

Figure 2-22 ▷ **Date and Time functions**

Function	Description
DATE(*year, month, day*)	Creates a date value for the date represented by the *year*, *month*, and *day* arguments
DAY(*date*)	Extracts the day of the month from the *date* value
MONTH(*date*)	Extracts the month number from the *date* value, where 1=January, 2=February, and so forth
YEAR(*date*)	Extracts the year number from the *date* value
WEEKDAY(*date*, [*return_type*])	Calculates the day of the week from the *date* value, where 1=Sunday, 2=Monday, and so forth. To choose a different numbering scheme, set the optional *return_type* value to "1" (1=Sunday, 2=Monday, ...), "2" (1=Monday, 2=Tuesday, ...), or "3" (0=Monday, 1=Tuesday, ...).
NOW()	Displays the current date and time
TODAY()	Displays the current date

You can use these functions to answer such questions as: On what day of the week does 1/1/2008 fall? You can calculate the day of the week with the **WEEKDAY function** as =*WEEKDAY(1/1/2008)*. This formula returns the value 7, which is Saturday—the seventh day of the week.

Because Amanda intends to use this worksheet as a model for future budgets, she wants the date on the Documentation sheet to always display the current date. You will replace the date you entered when you first opened the workbook with the TODAY() function.

To enter the TODAY() function on the Documentation sheet:

▸ **1.** Switch to the Documentation sheet.

▸ **2.** Click cell **B4**, type **=TODAY()**, and then click the **Enter** button ✔ on the Formula bar. Note that there are no arguments in the TODAY() function, but you still have to include the opening and closing parentheses, and there are no spaces between the parentheses. Excel displays the current date as shown in Figure 2-23.

Inserting the current date ◀ **Figure 2-23**

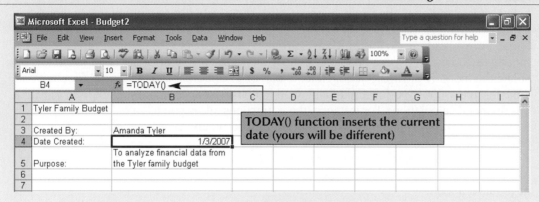

You have completed your work on the Budget2 workbook.

▸ **3.** Save your changes to the workbook, and then close it.

Using Math and Statistical functions, you have been able to calculate the monthly and end-of-year values Amanda requested. With these values in place, Amanda has a better picture of the family's finances, and she is more confident about how she will manage the family budget in the year to come.

Session 2.1 Quick Check

Review

1. What is the function you enter to calculate the minimum value in the range B1:B50?
2. Cell A10 contains the formula =A1+B1. When you copy the content of cell A10 and paste it into cell B11, what formula is inserted into the destination cell?
3. Cell A10 contains the formula =$A$1+B1. When you copy the content of cell A10 and paste it into cell B11, what formula is inserted into the destination cell?
4. Express the reference to cell A1 as (a) a relative reference, (b) an absolute reference, and (c) a mixed reference (both possibilities).
5. List the steps you use in Excel to create a series of odd numbers from 1 to 99 in column A of your worksheet.
6. To display the current date in a workbook each time you reopen it, you enter the _____ function in the cell where you want the date to appear.

(**Note:** This session presents topics related to Financial functions and Logical functions. This session *is optional and may be skipped* without loss of continuity of the instruction.)

Working with Financial Functions

After reviewing the figures calculated in the Budget worksheet, Amanda thinks she has a better understanding of the family finances. Now she would like to determine whether the family could afford the monthly payments required to purchase a house if they were to take a loan from a bank. To do this, she wants to create a worksheet containing a "typical" month's income and expenses, and then she wants to use an Excel Financial function to calculate the monthly payments required for a loan of $175,000. Excel's **Financial functions** are the same as those widely used in the world of business and accounting to perform various financial calculations. For instance, these functions allow you to calculate the depreciation of an asset, determine the amount of interest paid on an investment, compute the present value of an investment, and so on. Although she is not a business or financial professional, Amanda's question is a financial one: Given the family budget, how great a loan payment can they afford if they want to buy a home? There are four principal factors involved in negotiating a loan:

- The size of the loan
- The length of time in which the loan must be repaid
- The interest rate charged by the lending institution
- The amount of money to be paid to the lending institution in periodic installments, called *payment periods*. (For most home loans, payments are due monthly, so the payment period is a month.)

To be sure, this is a simplified treatment of loans. Often other issues are involved, such as whether payments are due at the beginning of the payment period or at the end. For the purposes of this exercise, the above are the major factors on which Amanda will concentrate for now. Once you know any three of these factors, you can use Excel to calculate the value of the remaining fourth. Amanda is interested in a loan with the following conditions:

- The size of the loan is equal to $175,000.
- The length of time to repay the loan is equal to 30 years.
- The annual interest rate is equal to 5.5%.

She wants to calculate the fourth value—the monthly payment required by the lending institution to pay back the loan. To answer this question, you'll add a new worksheet to her workbook in which she can analyze various loan possibilities.

To create the Loan Analysis worksheet:

▶ **1.** If you took a break after the last session, make sure that Excel is running and that the Budget2 workbook is open.

▶ **2.** Insert a new worksheet at the end of the workbook named **Loan Analysis**, and then save the workbook as **Budget3** in the Tutorial.02\Tutorial folder included with your Data Files.

▶ **3.** Click cell **A1**, type **LOAN ANALYSIS**, and then press the **Enter** key.

Now you need to copy the labels and the average values from the Budget worksheet, which you completed in the previous session.

4. Switch to the Budget worksheet, select the nonadjacent range **A29:A48;C29:C48**, and then click the **Copy** button on the Standard toolbar.

5. Switch to the Loan Analysis worksheet, and then click cell **A3** to make it the active cell.

   Rather than pasting the formulas into this worksheet, you will simply paste the values.

6. Click the **Paste** list arrow on the Standard toolbar, and then click **Values** in the list of paste options. Excel pastes the labels from column A in the Budget worksheet into column A on the Loan Analysis worksheet and also pastes the average values from column C in the Budget worksheet into column B in the current worksheet. See Figure 2-24.

Pasting the income and expense categories and the average values | **Figure 2-24**

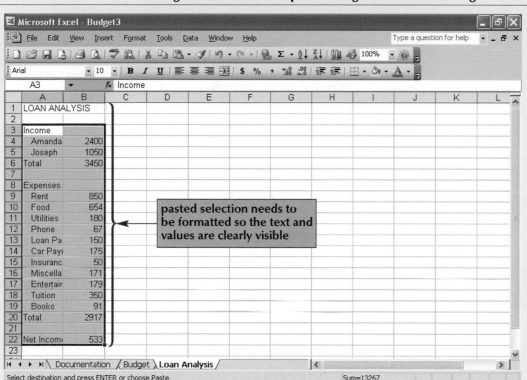

Excel pastes the cells as an adjacent range, not as a nonadjacent range. The result is that the values pasted from column C are shifted to the left into column B—right next to the labels in column A. These are the values you will need; their new location is not an issue. You will have to make some minor changes to the data, but first you need to increase the width of the columns so the values are easier to read. Then you will insert the formulas back into cells B6, B20, and B22 to calculate the total income, total expenses, and net income for a typical month.

To modify the layout of the worksheet and replace some of the values with formulas:

1. Click cell **A1** to remove the selection highlight from the pasted range.

2. Increase the width of column A to **18** characters (**131** pixels) and the width of column B to **10** characters (**75** pixels).

> 3. Click cell **B6**, click the **AutoSum** button Σ on the Standard toolbar, and then press the **Enter** key. Excel inserts the formula *=SUM(B4:B5)* into cell B6 to calculate the total average monthly income.
>
> 4. Click cell **B20**, click the **AutoSum** button Σ on the Standard toolbar, and then press the **Enter** key. Excel inserts the formula *=SUM(B9:B19)* into cell B20 to calculate the total average monthly expenses.
>
> 5. Click cell **B22**, type **=B6-B20** to calculate the average monthly net income, and then press the **Enter** key.

Now that you've entered the average monthly income and expense values for Amanda's budget and have widened the columns, you can enter the conditions for the loan. When you enter the amount of the loan, you will enter it as a negative value rather than as a positive value. The reason that you enter it as a negative value is because the loan is the amount owed to the lending institution; therefore, it is an expense. As you'll see later, Excel's Financial functions require loans to be entered as negative values because they represent negative cash flow. You will enter the labels and the conditions in columns D and E.

To enter the conditions of the loan in the worksheet:

> 1. Click cell **D3**, type **Loan Conditions**, and then press the **Enter** key to move to the next row where you will enter the Loan Amount label and the loan amount as a negative value.
>
> 2. Type **Loan Amount** in cell D4, press the **Tab** key, and then enter **-175,000** in cell E4.
>
>   Next you will enter the length of the loan in years.
>
> 3. Type **Length of Loan** in cell D5, press the **Tab** key, and then enter **30** in cell E5.
>
>   Now you will enter the annual interest rate, which is 5.5%.
>
> 4. Type **Annual Interest Rate** in cell D6, press the **Tab** key, and then enter **5.5%** in cell E6. Note that Excel may enter a zero, which doesn't change the value of the percentage.
>
>   Next, you will enter the conditions under which the loan is to be repaid. In this case, you will assume that payments are due monthly.
>
> 5. Click cell **D8**, type **Payment Conditions**, and then press the **Enter** key.
>
>   You will enter the number of payments to be made each year, which is 12.
>
> 6. Type **Payments per Year** in cell D9, press the **Tab** key, type **12** in cell E9, and then press the **Enter** key.
>
>   Next you will enter the formula to calculate the total number of payments required to pay back the loan, which is the length of the loan (found in cell E5) multiplied by the payments per year (found in cell E9).
>
> 7. Type **Total Payments** in cell D10, press the **Tab** key, type **=E5*E9** in cell E10, and then press the **Enter** key.
>
> 8. Type **Payment Amount** in cell D11, and then press the **Tab** key.
>
>   Before you continue, you will widen the columns so information is clearly visible.
>
> 9. Increase the width of column D to **18** characters (**131** pixels) and the width of column E to **10** characters (**75** pixels). Figure 2-25 shows the Loan Analysis worksheet with the values, loan conditions, and payment conditions entered.

Entering conditions for the loan and the monthly payments ◄ **Figure 2-25**

Paying off this loan will require 12 payments per year for 30 years, or 360 total payments. But how much will Amanda have to pay each month? To answer that question, you can use one of Excel's Financial functions.

Using the PMT Function

The monthly payment required to pay off a loan can be determined using the **PMT function**. The syntax of the PMT function is

=PMT(*rate, nper, pv,* [*fv=0*], [*type=0*])

where *rate* is the interest rate per payment period (determined by dividing the annual interest rate by the number of payment periods in a year), *nper* is the total number of payments, and *pv* is the present value of the future payments that will be made. In the case of a loan, the *pv* argument must be entered as a negative number. There are two optional parameters in this function: *fv* and *type*. The *fv* parameter indicates the future value of the loan and has a default value of 0. A future value of 0 means that the loan is paid off completely. The *type* parameter specifies whether payments are due at the beginning of the period (*type=1*) or at the end (*type=0*). The default value of the *type* parameter is 0.

Note that you can also use the PMT function for investments in which a specified amount of money is saved each month at a specified interest rate. In that case, the value of the *pv* argument would be positive since it represents an investment (a positive cash flow) rather than a loan (a negative cash flow).

Because the PMT function, like many Excel functions, has several required arguments, in addition to some optional arguments, you might not always remember all of the function's arguments and the order in which they should be entered. To make your task easier, you'll use the Insert Function dialog box to determine the payment amount for the loan Amanda is considering.

To select the PMT function using the Insert Function dialog box:

▶ 1. With E11 as the active cell, click the **Insert Function** button f_x on the Formula bar. The Insert Function dialog box opens.

To locate the PMT function, you'll enter a text description of this function in the Search for a function text box.

▶ 2. Type **loan payment** in the Search for a function text box, and then click the **Go** button. Excel displays a list of functions related to loan payments. See Figure 2-26.

Figure 2-26 ▶ Searching for functions related to loan payments

enter a description of the function you want to use

click to search for a function

functions related to loan payments

▶ 3. Verify that **PMT** is selected in the list of functions, read the description provided in the lower portion of the dialog box, and then click the **OK** button. The Function Arguments dialog box for the PMT function opens, as shown in Figure 2-27.

Figure 2-27 ▶ Function Arguments dialog box for the PMT function

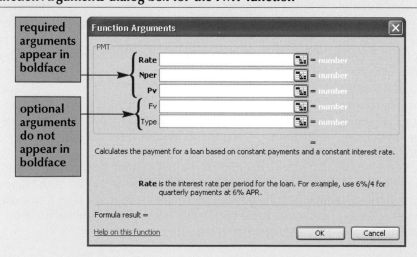

required arguments appear in boldface

optional arguments do not appear in boldface

Note that, in the Function Arguments dialog box, required arguments are displayed in a boldfaced font, whereas optional arguments are not. Neither the Fv nor Type argument is displayed in a bold font. You will use this dialog box to enter values for the PMT function's arguments. The first argument that you will enter is for the rate, which is determined by dividing the annual interest rate by the number of payment periods in a year.

To enter values for the PMT function:

1. Click the **Collapse Dialog Box** button located to the right of the Rate box.

2. Click cell **E6** to enter the cell reference for the annual interest rate.

   To determine the rate, you will divide the value in cell E6 by the number of payment periods in a year (cell E9).

3. Type **/** (the division sign), and then click cell **E9** to enter the cell reference.

4. Click the **Expand Dialog Box** button to restore the Function Arguments dialog box. The expression E6/E9 should now appear in the Rate box.

   Next you will enter the value for the second argument, the *nper* argument, which is the total number of payments that need to be made for the 30-year loan. This number is displayed in cell E10.

5. Click in the **Nper** box, and then enter **E10** either by typing it directly into the reference box or by selecting the cell from the workbook.

   Finally, you will enter the *pv* (present value) argument. In the case of a loan, the present value is the amount of the loan Amanda's family is seeking. This value is stored in cell E4.

6. Click in the **Pv** box, and then enter **E4** using the method you prefer. Figure 2-28 shows the completed Function Arguments dialog box and illustrates how this dialog box relates to the function that will be inserted into cell E11.

Entering the PMT function | Figure 2-28

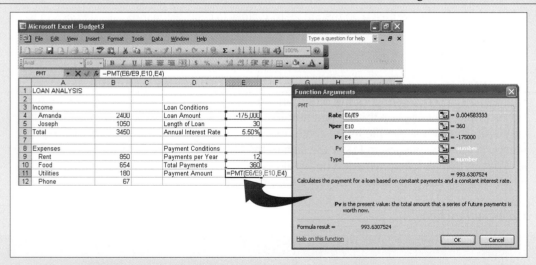

7. Click the **OK** button. Excel displays the value $993.63 in cell E11. Therefore, the required monthly payment is $993.63 for a loan of $175,000 at a 5.5% annual interest rate for 30 years.

   To see how this would affect Amanda's family budget, you will enter this information into the Expenses portion of the worksheet.

8. Click cell **A9**, type **House Payment** to replace the word "Rent," and then press the **Tab** key.

   Now you will enter a formula in cell B9 so the value House Payment is equal to the value Payment Amount.

9. Type **=E11** in cell B9, and then press the **Enter** key. The average total monthly expenses are recalculated.

If Amanda and Joseph were to buy a home with a $175,000 mortgage under the loan conditions specified in this workbook, their average monthly expenses would increase from $2,917 to $3,060.63 (cell B20), and the amount of money they could save each month would drop from $533 to about $389 (cell B22). By replacing the rent expense with the monthly home loan payment, Amanda can quickly gauge the effects of the loan on the family budget. Because the differences don't seem too unreasonable, Amanda now wants you to increase the size of the loan to $250,000, but keep all of the other factors constant.

To explore a what-if analysis for the mortgage:

▶ **1.** Click cell **E4**, type **-250,000** as the new loan amount, being sure to enter this as a negative value, and then press the **Enter** key. Under this scenario, the monthly payment increases to about $1,419 and the family's monthly expenses increase to about $3,486, which is more than they make in a typical month. Obviously a loan of this size is more than they can afford.

▶ **2.** Click the **Undo** button ⟲ on the Standard toolbar to restore the worksheet to its previous condition.

This time Amanda wants to know what would happen if the interest rate changed. To determine the difference between the low interest rate of 5.5% and a higher one, you will change the interest rate to 6.5%.

▶ **3.** Click cell **E6**, type **6.5%**, and then press the **Enter** key. Excel calculates the monthly payment to be about $1,106. Amanda can see that if the interest rate increases by 1%, then the monthly payment increases by about $113. She wants you to change the interest rate back to 5.5%.

▶ **4.** Click the **Undo** button ⟲ on the Standard toolbar to change the interest rate back to its previous value.

The PMT function is just one of the many Financial functions supported by Excel. Figure 2-29 describes some of the other functions that can be used for mortgage analysis. For example, you can use the PV function to calculate the size of the loan that Amanda could afford given a specific interest rate, monthly payment, and total number of payments. If Amanda wanted to know the size of the loan she could afford by using the $850 rent payment as a loan payment, you would enter the formula =PV(5.5%/12,360,850), which would return the value –$149,703.50, or a total loan of almost $150,000.

Figure 2-29 ▶ **Financial functions**

Function	Description
PMT(*rate*, *nper*, *pv*, [*fv*=0], [*type*=0])	Calculates the payments required each period on a loan or investment, where *rate* is the interest rate per period, *nper* is the total number of periods, *pv* is the present value or principal of the loan, *fv* is the future value of the loan, and *type* indicates whether payments should be made at the end of the period (0) or the beginning (1)
PV(*rate*, *nper*, *pmt*, [*fv*=0], [*type*=0])	Calculates the present value of a loan or investment based on periodic, constant payments
NPER(*rate*, *pmt*, *pv*, [*fv*=0], [*type*=0])	Calculates the number of periods required to pay off a loan or investment
RATE(*nper*, *pmt*, *pv*, [, *fv*=0], [*type*=0])	Calculates the interest rate of a loan or investment based on periodic, constant payments

You can use the other functions described in Figure 2-29 to calculate the interest rate and the total number of payment periods. Once again, if you know three of the conditions for the loan, there is an Excel function that you can use to calculate the value of the fourth.

From the calculations you have performed, Amanda now knows that a monthly mortgage payment of $993 is required to pay off a $175,000 loan in 30 years at 5.5% interest. This leaves the family with a net income of about $390 per month. The question remains whether Amanda feels that the mortgage is affordable. Amanda knows that she and Joseph will have to purchase a second car soon, that there are other expenses on the horizon, and that a new house will, no doubt, bring with it additional expenses that she may not have considered yet, such as property taxes. To prepare for those new future expenses, Amanda wants the family's net income to exceed their expenses by about $5,000 per year.

Does her current budget, with a home loan payment of $993 per month, meet that requirement? To find out, you will enter the amount of money Amanda feels that the family needs to save each year and a formula to calculate if they can achieve this goal.

To calculate the family's yearly net income:

1. Click cell **D13**, type **Is the loan affordable?** and then press the **Enter** key.

   You will enter the amount Amanda wants the family to save each year.

2. Type **Required Savings** in cell D14, press the **Tab** key, type **5,000** in cell E14, and then press the **Enter** key.

   Next, you'll enter the formula to calculate how much the family saved in one year using the average monthly net income multiplied by 12 months.

3. Type **Calculated Savings** in cell D15, press the **Tab** key, type **=B22*12** in cell E15, and then press the **Enter** key. See Figure 2-30. Note that the value in cell E15 shows five places to the right of the decimal. You'll learn how to specify the number of decimal places in Tutorial 3.

Calculating the yearly savings   **Figure 2-30**

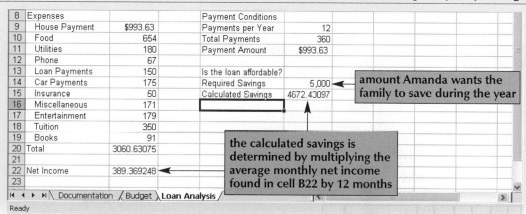

Under the proposed loan and assuming only the current expenses, the family could save about $4,672 per year, which is less than Amanda had hoped. So, Amanda would need to look at getting a smaller loan or hope that interest rates decrease in the future.

Amanda appreciates the type of information the worksheet provides, but she is concerned about getting lost in all of the numbers. She would like the worksheet to display a simple text message: "Yes" if the loan is affordable given the conditions she has set for the budget and "No" if otherwise. To add such a feature to the worksheet, you'll need to use a Logical function.

Working with Logical Functions

A **Logical function** is a function that tests, or evaluates, whether a condition in the workbook is true or false. The condition is usually entered as an expression. For example, the expression A1=10 would be true if cell A1 contains the value 10; otherwise, the expression is false.

Using the IF Function

The most commonly used Logical function is the **IF function**, which has the following syntax:

=IF(*logical_test*, *value_if_true*, [*value_if_false*])

where *logical_test* is an expression that is either true or false, *value_if_true* is the value displayed in the cell if the logical test is true, and *value_if_false* is the value displayed if the logical test is false. Note that the *value_if_false* argument is optional, though in most cases you will use it so that the function covers both possibilities.

For example, the formula *=IF(A1=10, 20, 30)* tests whether the value in cell A1 is equal to 10. If the expression A1=10 is true, the function displays the value 20 in the cell containing the function; otherwise, the cell displays the value 30. You can also construct logical tests that involve text values. The formula *=IF(A1="Retail", B1, B2)* tests whether cell A1 contains the text "Retail"; if it does, the function returns the value of cell B1; otherwise, it returns the value of cell B2.

Expressions in the logical test always include a comparison operator. A **comparison operator** indicates the relationship between two values. Figure 2-31 describes the comparison operators supported by Excel.

Figure 2-31	Comparison operators

Operator	Example	Description
=	A1 = B1	Tests whether the value in cell A1 *is equal to* the value in cell B1
>	A1 > B1	Tests whether the value in cell A1 *is greater than* the value in cell B1
<	A1 < B1	Tests whether the value in cell A1 *is less than* the value in cell B1
>=	A1 >= B1	Tests whether the value in cell A1 *is greater than or equal to* the value in cell B1
<=	A1 <= B1	Tests whether the value in cell A1 *is less than or equal to* the value in cell B1
<>	A1 <> B1	Tests whether the value in cell A1 *is not equal to* the value in cell B1

You'll use the IF function to display a text message in the worksheet indicating whether a $175,000 loan is affordable. In this case, the logical expression will test whether the value in cell E14 (the required savings) is less than the value in cell E15 (the calculated savings). The expression is E14 < E15. If this expression is true, then the loan is affordable for Amanda's family; otherwise, it is not. You will now enter the formula that includes the IF function *=IF(E14 < E15, "Yes", "No")*.

To insert the IF function to evaluate whether the loan is affordable:

1. Click cell **D16**, type **Conclusion**, and then press the **Tab** key.

2. In cell E16, type **=IF(E14<E15,"Yes","No")** and then press the **Enter** key. The text "No" appears in cell E16, indicating that the value in cell E14 is not less than the value in cell E15, and, therefore, the conditions of the mortgage are not acceptable to Amanda.

   Amanda asks you to reduce the size of the loan to $165,000 to see whether this amount changes the conclusion about the mortgage's affordability.

3. Click cell **E4**, type **-165,000** as the new loan amount, and then press the **Enter** key. As shown in Figure 2-32, the monthly payment drops to about $936 and the net yearly savings rise to about $5,354. Cell E16 displays the text string "Yes," indicating that this loan does satisfy Amanda's conditions for affordability.

Inserting a Logical function   **Figure 2-32**

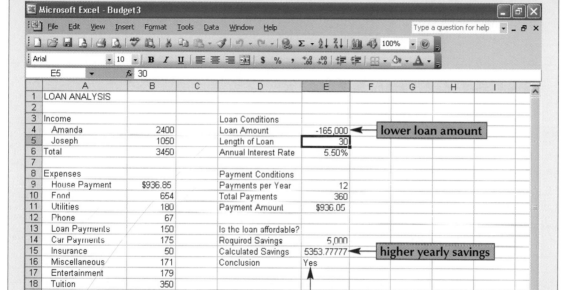

Now Amanda knows that buying a house is something that her family budget can support in the near future if she and Joseph manage their budget well. You will now save and close the Budget3 workbook.

4. Save your changes to the workbook, and then close it.

Excel has several other Logical functions that you can use to create more complicated tests. Figure 2-33 describes the syntax of each of these functions.

Figure 2-33   **Logical functions**

Function	Description
IF(*logical_test*, *value_if_true*, [*value_if_false*])	Returns the value *value_if_true* if the *logical_test* expression is true and *value_if_false* if otherwise
AND(*logical1*, [*logical2*, *logical3*, ...])	Returns the value TRUE if all *logical* expressions in the function are true and FALSE if otherwise
OR(*logical1*, [*logical2*, *logical3*, ...])	Returns the value TRUE if any *logical* expression in the function is true and FALSE if otherwise
FALSE()	Returns the value FALSE
TRUE()	Returns the value TRUE
NOT(*logical*)	Returns the value FALSE if the *logical* expression is true and the value TRUE if the *logical* expression is false

Amanda's budget workbook contains much of the information that she and Joseph can use to build a more stable financial picture for themselves in the future.

Review

Session 2.2 Quick Check

1. What are the four principal factors in a loan?
2. If you were to take a five-year loan for $10,000 at 7% annual interest rate, with monthly payments, what formula would you enter to calculate the monthly payment on the loan?
3. To calculate the present value of a loan based on a set, monthly payment, you could use the _____ function.
4. What formula would you use to display the text string "Yes" if the value in cell A1 is greater than the value in cell B1 and "No" if otherwise?
5. To change a logical expression from FALSE to TRUE or from TRUE to FALSE, use the _____ function.

Review

Tutorial Summary

In Session 2.1, you learned about the general syntax used by all Excel functions, and you learned about some of the Math and Statistical functions supported by Excel. You used the SUM function in a formula to calculate income and expenses for the month of January. You then learned how to copy and paste these formulas into other cells in the worksheet to calculate total figures for every month of the year. You learned the difference between the three types of cell references—relative, absolute, and mixed—and then you used an absolute reference to calculate a running total of the net income. You learned about the AVERAGE, MIN, and MAX functions, and then used them to summarize the entire year's budget figures. Once you entered the formulas that used these functions, you learned how to copy and paste the formulas using the Auto Fill feature. You also learned how to change the magnification of the workbook window so you can see more or less of the data in a worksheet. Finally, you used the TODAY() function to display the current date in the Documentation sheet.

In Session 2.2, you learned about the PMT function, which is a Financial function supported by Excel. You used the PMT function to calculate the monthly payment required to pay off a specified mortgage. You also learned about one of Excel's most commonly used Logical functions, the IF function. You used the IF function to display a text string indicating whether a loan was affordable.

Key Terms

Session 2.1	MAX function	TODAY() function
absolute reference	MIN function	WEEKDAY function
argument	mixed reference	*Session 2.2*
Auto Fill	NOW() function	comparison operator
AVERAGE function	optional argument	Financial function
Date function	relative reference	IF function
destination cell	source cell	Logical function
destination range	source range	PMT function
F4 key	SUM function	
fill handle	syntax	

Practice

Practice the skills you learned in Session 2.1 using the same case scenario.

Review Assignments

Data File needed for the Review Assignments: Family1.xls

Amanda appreciates the work you did on her family budget. Her friends Ken and Ava Giles have examined the workbook you created and have asked you to create a similar workbook for their budget.

Once you have completed a budget worksheet for the Giles family, they may want you to help them determine if they can afford to purchase their dream house in the country. The mortgage would be substantially higher than the family's current mortgage, but with Ava now working full time, the couple feels that they may be able to afford the higher mortgage. They would like you to create a workbook that will help them to determine if purchasing the house is possible.

To complete this task:

1. Open the **Family1** workbook located in the Tutorial.02\Review folder included with your Data Files, and then save the workbook as **Family2** in the same folder.
2. In the Documentation sheet, enter your name in cell B3, and then enter the current date in cell B4 using the TODAY() function.
3. Switch to the Budget worksheet, and then enter the formulas in the ranges C7:N7 and C14:N14 to calculate the total income and expenses, respectively, for each month. (*Hint*: Enter the formula in cells C7 and C14 first, and then copy and paste the formulas to the other cells in the ranges.)
4. In the range C16:N16, enter a formula to calculate the family's net income. (*Hint*: Enter the formula in cell C16 first, and then copy and paste the formula to the other cells in the range.)
5. In the range D17:N17, enter a formula using the SUM function to calculate the running total for net income from February through December. (*Hint*: Use an absolute reference for the appropriate cell reference.)
6. In the range C4:N4, use Auto Fill to fill in the month names January, February, March, and so forth.

Practice the skills you learned in Session 2.2 using the same case scenario.

7. In the range C21:F23, enter a formula to calculate the total, average, minimum, and maximum values of the two incomes.
8. In the range C25:F30, enter a formula to calculate the total, average, minimum, and maximum values of each expense category.
9. In the range C32:F32, enter a formula to calculate the total, average, minimum, and maximum values for net income.
10. Print the contents of the Budget worksheet, and save the changes you have made. If you are not continuing with the remaining steps, close the workbook.

    (**Note:** The following steps are *optional*. You should attempt them only if you have completed **Session 2.2** in the tutorial.)

11. Save the workbook as **Family3** to the Tutorial.02\Review folder.
12. Add a worksheet named "Loan Analysis" to the end of the workbook, and then enter the text "Loan Analysis" in cell A1 of the worksheet.
13. Switch to the Budget worksheet, copy the nonadjacent range A21:B32;D21:D32, switch to the Loan Analysis worksheet, and then paste the values, but not the formulas, into range A3:C14, using the Paste Special option. Increase the width of columns A and C to 12 characters (89 pixels) each, and column B to 15 characters (110 pixels). Edit the entries in cells C5, C12, and C14 so they contain formulas that calculate the total income, total expense, and net income.
14. Enter the following labels in the cells as indicated:
    - Cell E3: Loan Conditions
    - Cell E4: Loan Amount
    - Cell E5: Length of Loan
    - Cell E6: Annual Interest Rate
    - Cell E8: Payment Conditions
    - Cell E9: Payments per Year
    - Cell E10: Total Payments
    - Cell E11: Payment Amount
15. Widen column E to 21 characters (152 pixels).
16. In the range F4:F9, enter values for the following loan and payment conditions:
    - Loan Amount = –300,000
    - Years = 15
    - Annual Interest Rate = 6%
    - Payments per Year = 12
17. In cell F10, enter a formula to calculate the total number of payments. In cell F11, enter a formula using the PMT function to calculate the monthly loan payment.
18. In cell C8, enter the formula to make the mortgage expense equal to the result of the calculation in cell F11.
19. Enter the following labels in the cells as indicated:
    - Cell E13: Is the loan affordable?
    - Cell E14: Minimum Loan Payment
    - Cell E15: Conclusion
20. The family does not want a monthly loan payment greater than $2,500. Enter this value into cell F14, and then in cell F15 enter a formula using the IF function to display the text string "Yes" if the monthly payment is less than or equal to the value you entered in cell F14, and "No" if otherwise. Is the loan affordable under the loan conditions you have entered?
21. Print the contents of the Loan Analysis worksheet.

22. Change the loan from a 15-year loan to a 20-year loan. What effect does this have on the monthly loan payment and the conclusion about the affordability of the loan? Print the contents of the revised Loan Analysis worksheet.
23. Save your changes to the workbook, and then close it.

Apply

Apply the lessons you learned in Session 2.1 by creating a worksheet that analyzes the performance of a stock.

Case Problem 1

Data File needed for this Case Problem: Stock1.xls

Hardin Financial   Carol Gilson works at Hardin Financial compiling reports on different stocks for portfolios managed by the company. Carol would like to use Excel to create a summary report for a particular stock, Point Electronics (PEC). She has entered the stock's performance for the past 50 days of trading and needs to summarize these values over the last 5 days, 10 days, and 50 days. She has asked you to help her complete the workbook. To complete this task:

1. Open the **Stock1** workbook located in the Tutorial.02\Cases folder included with your Data Files, and then save the file as **Stock2** in the same folder.
2. In the Documentation sheet, enter your name and enter the current date using the TODAY() function.
3. Switch to the Stock History worksheet, and in the range E3:E52 enter the numbers 50 through 1 in descending order using Auto Fill.
4. Column F needs to contain the opening value of the PEC stock. The opening value of the stock is equal to the closing value of the stock on the previous day. For example, the value in cell F3 should equal the value in cell I4. Enter the formula for the opening value for Day 50, and then use Auto Fill to fill in the opening values of the stock in the range F4:F51. (*Note:* The closing value for Day 1 has already been entered in cell F52 for you.)
5. In cell C4, enter a formula that calculates the highest value of the stock in the last 5 days (Day 46 through 50) using the values in column H.
6. In cell C5, enter a formula to calculate the lowest value of the stock in the same time period using the values in column G.
7. In cell C6, enter a formula to calculate the range (the difference between the maximum and minimum) of the stock's value in that time period.
8. In cell C7, enter a formula to display the stock's average closing value in the 5-day period.
9. Repeat Steps 5 through 8 for the 10-day statistics, placing the maximum, minimum, range, and average closing values in the range C9:C12.
10. Repeat Steps 5 through 8 for the 50-day statistics, placing the maximum, minimum, range, and average closing values in the range C14:C17.

Explore

11. Select range A1:C20, and then print just the selection.
12. Save your changes to the workbook, and then close it.

Create

Using what you learned in Session 2.1, create a workbook that summarizes regional sales information.

Case Problem 2

There are no Data Files needed for this Case Problem.

Maxwell Scientific Lisa Dunn manages orders for Maxwell Scientific, a mail-order company that sells science kits and education products to schools and educators. Lisa has asked you to help her with some projects. To begin, Lisa wants you to enter sales information for three different Maxwell Scientific products by region in an Excel workbook. After you enter the sales data, you need to enter formulas to calculate total, average, minimum, and maximum sales for each product and each region, and then for all the models and regions. You will also need to calculate the percentage of sales for each product.

To complete this task:

1. Open a new blank workbook and save it as **Maxwell1** in the Tutorial.02\Cases folder included with your Data Files.
2. Rename the first sheet in the workbook "Documentation," and then enter your name, the current date, and the purpose of the project in this sheet.
3. Rename the second worksheet "Sales Summary," and then enter the sales data shown in Figure 2-34.

Figure 2-34

| Region | Units Sold | | |
	Night Disks	Planet Cards	Solar Mobiles
Region 1	2305	1483	824
Region 2	1281	1782	1005
Region 3	1885	2285	721
Region 4	2100	2108	1287

4. For each product, enter formulas to calculate the total sales for all regions, the average sales per region, and the maximum and minimum sales over all the regions.
5. For each product, enter a formula that uses absolute cell references to calculate the percentage of units sold per region.
6. Summarize the sales for all three of these Maxwell Scientific products by calculating the total, average, maximum, and minimum units sold for all products in all regions.
7. Calculate the percent of units sold for all products in each region.
8. Print the Sales Summary worksheet, and save your changes to the workbook. If you are not continuing with the remaining steps, close the workbook.

   (**Note:** The following steps are *optional*. You should attempt them only if you completed **Session 2.2** in the tutorial.)

Using what you learned in Session 2.2, create another worksheet that determines discount prices and shipping expenses.

9. Rename the third worksheet "Orders," and then save the workbook as **Maxwell2** in the Tutorial.02\Cases folder. Lisa has asked you to help her with another project. She wants you, using the Orders worksheet, to calculate the cost of each order and the total cost of all customer orders. Maxwell Scientific offers a 5% discount if customers order more than 50 units of a particular product. Also, customers can choose between two shipping options: standard shipping for a cost of $4.95, and express shipping for a cost of $9.95. You need to include both of these factors when calculating the cost of the order. Figure 2-35 shows a preview of the worksheet you'll create.

Figure 2-35

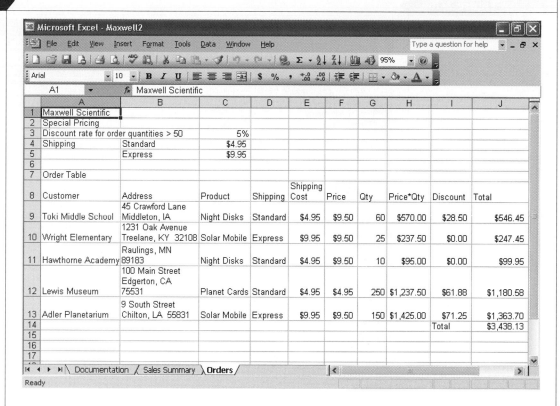

10. Enter formulas to calculate the total amount of each order and the total amount of all the customer orders. Use IF functions to calculate the shipping cost and discount for each order.

11. Preview the completed Orders worksheet, and then print it.

12. Save your changes to the Maxwell2 workbook.

13. Maxwell Scientific is considering changing its bulk discount rate from 5% to 8%. It is also looking at changing standard shipping charges to $5.50 and express shipping to $10.95. Lisa wants you to make these changes in the Orders worksheet. Change the discount rate and the shipping charges. What effect does the changes have on the current orders?

14. Print the revised Orders worksheet.

15. Save the workbook as **Maxwell3** in Tutorial.02\Cases folder, and then close the workbook.

Challenge

Go beyond what you learned in Session 2.2 to use the IF function as you create a payroll worksheet.

Case Problem 3

Data File needed for this Case Problem: Sonic1.xls

Sonic Sounds Jeff Gwydion manages the payroll at Sonic Sounds. He has asked you for help in setting up an Excel worksheet to store payroll information. The payroll contains three elements: each employee's salary, 401(k) contribution, and health insurance cost. The company's 401(k) contribution is 3% of an employee's salary for those who have worked for the company at least one year; otherwise, the company's contribution is zero. Sonic Sounds also supports two health insurance plans: Premier and Standard. The cost of the Premier plan is $6,500, and the cost of the Standard plan is $5,500. The workbook has already been set up for you. Your job is to enter the formulas to calculate the 401(k) contributions and health insurance costs for each employee. Figure 2-36 shows the worksheet as it will appear at the end of this exercise.

Figure 2-36

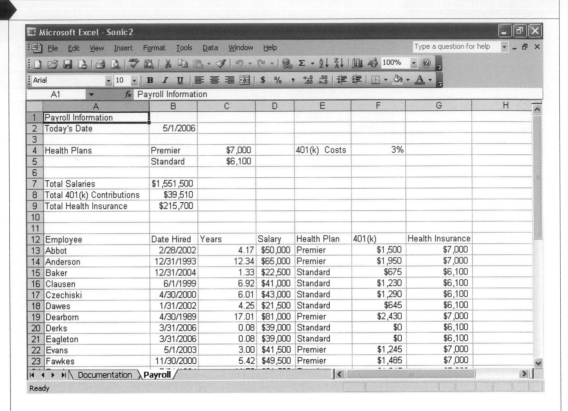

To complete this task:

1. Open the **Sonic1** workbook located in the Tutorial.02\Cases folder included with your Data Files, and then save the workbook as **Sonic2** in the same folder.
2. In the Documentation sheet, enter your name and then enter the date using the TODAY() function.
3. Switch to the Payroll worksheet. In cell C13, enter a formula to calculate the number of years the first employee has worked at Sonic Sounds. Use an absolute reference for cell B2. Divide the difference by 365. (*Hint*: You need to subtract the date the employee was hired from the current date, which is in cell B2, and then divide the difference by the number of days in a year. For the purposes of this exercise, do not try to account for leap years.)
4. Use Auto Fill to calculate the number of years the remaining employees in the table have worked for the company.

Explore

5. In the range F13:F45, insert a formula to calculate the 401(k) contributions for each employee. The formula should determine that if the number of years employed is greater than or equal to 1, then the contribution is equal to the contribution percentage in cell F4 multiplied by the employee's salary; otherwise, the contribution is zero.

Explore

6. In the range G13:G45, enter a formula to calculate the health insurance cost for each employee by testing whether the name of the employee's plan is equal to the name of the health plan in cell B4. If it is, then the cost of the health plan is equal to the value of cell C4; otherwise, the cost is equal to the value of cell C5.

7. In the range B7:B9, enter the formulas to calculate the total salaries, 401(k) contributions, and health insurance costs.
8. Print the contents of the Payroll worksheet.
9. Rework the analysis, assuming that the cost of the Premier plan has risen to $7,000 and the cost of the Standard plan has risen to $6,100.
10. Print the revised Payroll worksheet.
11. Save your changes to the workbook, and then close it.

Challenge

Go beyond what you learned in Session 2.2. Use the PMT, PPMT, and IPMT functions to create a payment schedule for a small business.

Case Problem 4

Data File needed for this Case Problem: Soup1.xls

The Soup Shop Ken Novak is the owner of a diner in Upton, Ohio, named The Soup Shop. Business has been very good lately, so Ken is considering taking out a loan to cover the cost of upgrading and expanding the diner. Ken wants your help in creating an Excel workbook that provides detailed information about the loan. He would like the workbook to calculate the monthly payment needed for a five-year, $125,000 loan at 6.5% interest. Ken believes that the expansion will increase business, so he also wants to know how much he would save on interest payments by paying off the loan after one, two, three, or four years.

To do this type of calculation, you need to know what part of each monthly payment is used to reduce the size of the loan (also referred to as payments toward the principal) and what part is used for paying interest on the loan. Excel provides two functions to calculate these values, both of which are similar to the PMT function used to calculate the total monthly payment. To calculate how much of a monthly payment is used to pay off the principal, you use the PPMT function, which has the following syntax:

=PPMT(*rate, period, nper, pv* [*,fv=0*] [*,type=0*])

where *rate* is the interest rate period, *period* is the payment period you want to examine (such as the first period, the second period, and so forth), *nper* is the total number of payment periods, *pv* is the amount of the loan, *fv* is the future value of the loan (assumed to be zero), and *type* indicates whether the payment is due at the beginning (*type*=1) or at the end (*type*=0) of the month. The function to calculate how much of the monthly payment is used for paying the interest is the IPMT function, which has a similar syntax:

=IPMT(*rate, period, nper, pv* [*,fv=0*] [*,type=0*])

As with the PMT function, the value of the *pv* argument should be negative when you are working with loans—as you are in this case.

Ken wants you to use these two functions to create a payment schedule that indicates for each of the 60 months of the loan, how much of the monthly payment is being used to pay off the loan and how much is being used to pay interest on the loan. You can then use this schedule to discover how much Ken could save in interest charges by paying off the loan early. Figure 2-37 shows the worksheet as it will appear at the end of this exercise.

Figure 2-37

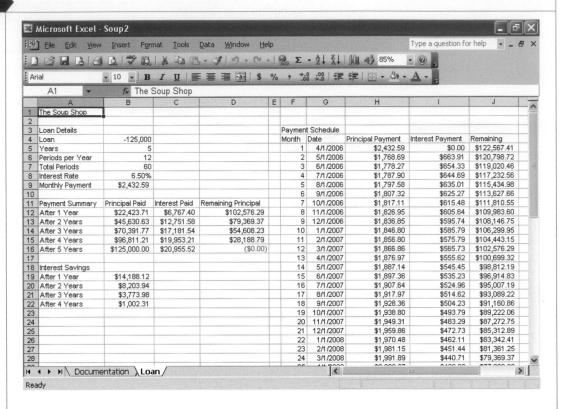

To complete this task:

1. Open the **Soup1** workbook located in the Tutorial.02\Cases folder included with your Data Files, and then save the workbook as **Soup2** in the same folder.
2. Enter your name and the current date in the Documentation sheet.
3. Switch to the Loan worksheet, and then in the range B4:B8, enter the following loan details:
   - Loan Amount = –125,000
   - Years = 5
   - Periods per Year = 12
   - Interest Rate = 6.5% (annually)
   In cell B7, enter a formula to calculate the total number of payment periods.
4. In cell B9, enter a formula using the PMT function to calculate the total monthly payment required to pay off the loan. Assume that payments are made at the beginning of each period, *not* at the end, which is the default. (*Hint*: Use the *fv* and *type* arguments.)
5. In the range F5:F64, enter the numbers 1 through 60 using Auto Fill. Each number indicates the payment period in the payment schedule.
6. Ken would like his payment schedule to include the dates on which the payments are due. In cell G5, enter the date 4/1/2006. This is the due date for the first payment. In cell G6, enter the date 5/1/2006. This is the due date for the second payment. Use the Auto Fill to enter the rest of the due dates into the range G7:G64.

Explore

7. In cell H5, enter a formula using the PPMT function to calculate the amount of the first month's payment devoted to reducing the principal of the loan. The details of the loan should reference the appropriate cells in the B4:B8 range of the worksheet using absolute references. The period number should reference the value in cell F5 using a relative reference. Be sure to indicate in the function that the payments are made at the beginning, not the end, of the month.

Explore

Explore

8. In cell I5, enter a formula using the IPMT function to calculate the amount of the first month's payment that is used for paying the interest on the loan.

9. In cell J5, enter a formula that calculates the amount of the principal remaining to be paid. Ken would like this expressed as a positive value. To calculate this value, construct a formula that is equal to the *negative* of the value in cell B4 (the amount of the loan) minus the running total of the principal payments. To calculate a running total of the principal payments, use the formula =SUM($H$5:H5). Note that this formula uses both an absolute reference and a relative reference, much like the running total example in the tutorial.

10. Using Auto Fill, copy the formulas in the range H5:J5 to the range H5:J64. (*Hint*: The value displayed in cell J64 should be $0.00, indicating that the loan is completely paid off. Also, the interest payment for the last month should be $13.11.)

11. In cell B12, enter a formula to calculate the total amount of payments made to the principal in the first 12 months of the schedule. In cell C12, enter a formula to calculate the total amount of the interest payments. In cell D12, enter a formula to calculate the amount of the remaining principal. Once again, Ken wants this expressed as a positive value, so the formula must subtract the value in cell B12 from the *negative* of the value in cell B4.

12. Repeat Step 11 for the range B13:D13, calculating the totals for the first 24 months. In the range B14:D14, calculate the totals for the first 36 months. In the range B15:D15, calculate the 48-month totals. In the range B16:D16, calculate the 60-month totals.

13. In the range B19:B22, enter a formula to calculate the amount of money Ken would save in interest payments if he paid off the loan after one year, two years, three years, and four years.

Explore

14. Preview the worksheet before printing it. Open the Page Setup dialog box, change the page orientation of the worksheet to landscape orientation, and then select the option so the worksheet will print on one page. Preview the worksheet again and then print it.

15. Save your changes to the workbook and then close it.

Research

Use the Internet to find and work with data related to the topics presented in this tutorial.

Internet Assignments

The purpose of the Internet Assignments is to challenge you to find information on the Internet that you can use to work effectively with this software. The actual assignments are updated and maintained on the Course Technology Web site. Log on to the Internet and use your Web browser to go to the Student Online Companion for New Perspectives Office 2003 at **www.course.com/np/office2003**. Click the Internet Assignments link, and then navigate to the assignments for this tutorial.

Assess

SAM Assessment and Training

If you have a SAM user profile, you may have access to hands-on instruction, practice, and assessment of the skills covered in this tutorial. Log in to your SAM account and go to your assignments page to see what your instructor has assigned.

Quick Check Answers

Session 2.1

1. =MIN(B1:B50)
2. =B2+C2
3. =$A$1+C2
4. (a) A1 (b) $A$1 (c) $A1 and A$1
5. Enter the values 1 and 3 in the first two rows of column A. Select the two cells and then drag the fill handle down over the range A1:A99, completing the series.
6. TODAY()

Session 2.2

1. the loan amount, the interest rate, the number of payment periods, and the payment due each period
2. =PMT(7%/12,5*12,10000)
3. PV
4. =IF(A1>B1, "Yes", "No")
5. NOT

Objectives

Session 3.1
- Format data using the Comma, Currency, and Percent styles
- Copy and paste formats using the Format Painter
- Modify and apply number formatting styles
- Change font type, style, size, and color
- Change alignment of cell contents
- Apply borders and background colors and patterns

Session 3.2
- Merge a range of cells into a single cell
- Hide rows, columns, and worksheets
- Add a background image to a worksheet
- Format worksheet tabs
- Clear and replace formats
- Create and apply styles
- Apply an AutoFormat
- Set up a worksheet for printing
- Add headers and footers to printouts

Developing a Professional-Looking Worksheet

Formatting a Sales Report

Case

NewGeneration Monitors

NewGeneration Monitors is a computer equipment company that specializes in computer monitors. Joan Sanchez, sales manager, has been entering sales data for three of the company's monitors into an Excel workbook. She plans on including the sales data in a report to be presented later in the week. Joan has made no attempt to change or enhance the presentation of this data. She has simply entered the numbers. She needs you to transform her raw figures into a presentable report.

To create a professional-looking document, you will learn how to work with Excel's formatting tools to modify the appearance of the data in each cell, the cell itself, and the entire worksheet. You will also learn how to format printouts, create headers and footers, and control which parts of the worksheet are printed on which pages.

Student Data Files

▼ **Tutorial.03**

▽ **Tutorial folder**
Back.jpg
Sales1.xls

▽ **Review folder**
Region1.xls

▽ **Cases folder**
Blades1.xls
Running1.xls
WBus1.xls

Session 3.1

Formatting Worksheet Data

The data for Joan's sales report has already been stored in an Excel workbook. Before going further, you will open the workbook and save it with a new filename.

To open the Sales report workbook:

1. Start Excel and then open the **Sales1** workbook located in the Tutorial.03\Tutorial folder included with your Data Files.

2. On the Documentation worksheet, enter *your name* in cell B3, and enter the *current date* in cell B4.

3. Save the workbook as **Sales2** in the Tutorial.03\Tutorial folder.

4. Click the **Sales** tab to display the unformatted worksheet, shown in Figure 3-1.

Figure 3-1	The unformatted Sales worksheet

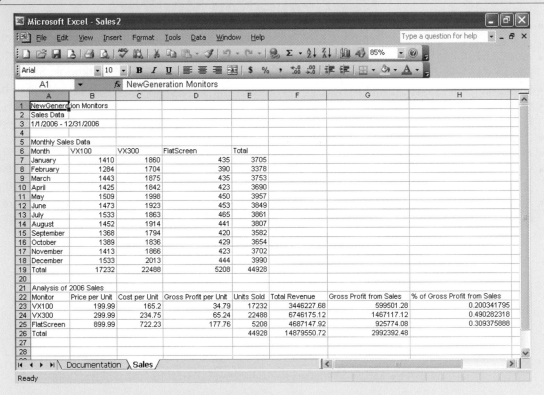

The Sales worksheet contains two tables. The table in the upper portion of the worksheet displays the monthly sales figures for three of NewGeneration's monitors: the VX100, the VX300, and the FlatScreen. The other table presents an analysis of these sales figures. Although the data in the worksheet is accurate and complete, the numbers are not as easy to read as they could be, which also makes interpreting the data more difficult. To help improve the readability of the data presented in a worksheet, you can change its appearance by formatting it.

Formatting is the process of changing the appearance of your workbook. A properly formatted workbook can be easier to read, appear more professional, and help draw attention to the important points you want to make. Formatting only changes the appearance of the data; it does not affect the data itself. For example, if a cell contains the value 0.124168, and you format the cell to display only up to the thousandths digit (so the value appears as 0.124), the cell still contains the precise value, even though you cannot see it displayed in the worksheet.

Unless you specify different formatting, Excel automatically displays numbers in the worksheet cells using the **General number format**, which, for the most part, formats numbers just the way you enter them. There are some exceptions to this approach. For example, if the cell is not wide enough to show the entire number, the General number format rounds numbers that contain decimals and uses scientific notation for large numbers.

If you don't want to use the General number format, you can choose from a wide variety of number formats. Formats can be applied using either the Formatting toolbar or the Format menu. Formats can also be copied from one cell to another, giving you the ability to apply a common format to different cells in your worksheet.

Using the Formatting Toolbar

The Formatting toolbar is one of the fastest ways to format a worksheet. By clicking a single button on the Formatting toolbar, you can increase or decrease the number of decimal places displayed in a selected range of cells, and display a value as currency with a dollar sign or a percentage with a percent sign. You also can use the Formatting toolbar to change the font type (for example, Times New Roman or Arial), style (such as bold), color, or size.

When Joan entered the monthly sales figures for the three monitors, she was concerned with entering the figures as accurately and as efficiently as possible and wasn't concerned with the appearance of the numbers in the worksheet. She entered the sales figures without including a comma to separate the thousands from the hundreds and so forth. Now, to make the numbers easier to read, Joan wants all the values to appear with commas, and for the figures that are whole numbers, she doesn't want any zeros after the decimal point (also referred to as "trailing zeros"). She believes that these changes will make the worksheet easier to read.

To insert commas in the figures in Joan's worksheet, you will apply the Comma style using its button on the Formatting toolbar. By default, Excel automatically adds two decimal places to the numbers that you have formatted with the Comma style. You will then need to use the Decrease Decimal button on the Formatting toolbar to change the number of decimal places displayed in a number.

To apply the Comma style and remove the trailing zeros:

▶ 1. Select the range **B7:E19** in the Sales worksheet.

▶ 2. Click the **Comma Style** button 🟦 on the Formatting toolbar. Excel adds the comma separator to each of the values in the table and displays the values with two digits to the right of the decimal point.

   Trouble? If you do not see the Comma Style button 🟦 on the Formatting toolbar, click the Toolbar Options button 🟦 on the Formatting toolbar, point to Add or Remove Buttons, point to Formatting, and then click 🟦 on the menu of available buttons.

   Because Joan wants whole numbers displayed without trailing zeros, you will remove any that are displayed.

▶ 3. Click the **Decrease Decimal** button 🟦 on the Formatting toolbar twice to remove the zeros. Figure 3-2 shows the worksheet with the formatting changes you have made so far.

Figure 3-2 Applying the Comma style

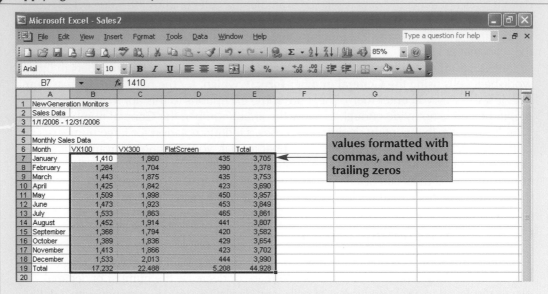

Joan wants the price and production cost of each monitor as well as last year's total sales and gross profit displayed using dollar signs, commas, and two decimal places. A quick and easy way to format the values with these attributes is to use the Currency style, which is available as a button on the Formatting toolbar. When you apply the Currency style, Excel adds a dollar sign and comma separator to the value and displays two decimal places. Try applying the Currency style to the total sales and profit values.

To apply the Currency style:

1. Select the nonadjacent range **B23:D25;F23:G26**.

   Trouble? To select a nonadjacent range, select the first range, press and hold the Ctrl key, and then select the next range.

2. Click the **Currency Style** button $ on the Formatting toolbar. As shown in Figure 3-3, Excel adds the dollar signs and commas, and keeps two decimal places to display the values as currency. Also note that the alignment of the dollar signs is along the left edge of the cell and the decimal points are aligned vertically.

Figure 3-3 Applying the Currency style

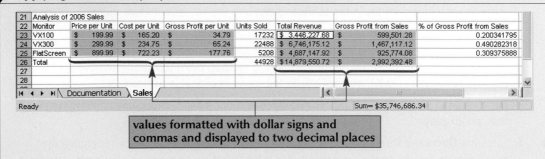

Finally, the range H23:H25 displays the percentage that each monitor contributes to the overall profit from sales. Joan wants these values displayed with a percent sign and two decimal places. To format a value as a percent, you can apply the Percent style. By default, Excel does not display any decimal places with the Percent style; therefore, you will need to increase the number of decimal places displayed.

To apply the Percent style and increase the number of decimal places:

▶ **1.** Select the range **H23:H25**.

▶ **2.** Click the **Percent Style** button % on the Formatting toolbar. The values appear with percent signs and without zeros.

▶ **3.** Click the **Increase Decimal** button   on the Formatting toolbar twice to display the percentages to two decimal places. Figure 3-4 shows the values in column H formatted with percent signs and to two decimal places.

Applying the Percent style ◀ **Figure 3-4**

	A	B	C	D	E	F	G	H
21	Analysis of 2006 Sales							
22	Monitor	Price per Unit	Cost per Unit	Gross Profit per Unit	Units Sold	Total Revenue	Gross Profit from Sales	% of Gross Profit from Sales
23	VX100	$ 199.99	$ 165.20	$ 34.79	17232	$ 3,446,227.68	$ 599,501.28	20.03%
24	VX300	$ 299.99	$ 234.75	$ 65.24	22488	$ 6,746,175.12	$ 1,467,117.12	49.03%
25	FlatScreen	$ 899.99	$ 722.23	$ 177.76	5208	$ 4,687,147.92	$ 925,774.08	30.94%
26	Total				44928	$14,879,550.72	$ 2,992,392.48	
27								
28								

◄ ◄ ► ►◄ Documentation \ Sales / |◄   ►|

Ready   Sum=100.00%

values formatted with percent signs and displayed to two decimal places

By displaying the percentages, you can quickly see that one monitor, the VX300, accounts for almost half of the profit from monitor sales.

Copying Formats

As you look over the sales figures, you see that one area of the worksheet still needs to be formatted. The Units Sold column in the range E23:E26 still does not display the comma separator you used with the sales figures. To fix a formatting problem like this one, you can use the Format Painter button located on the Standard toolbar. When you use the **Format Painter** option, you "paint" a format from one cell to another cell or to a range of cells. This is a fast and efficient way of copying a format from one cell to another.

Copying Formatting Using the Format Painter   Reference Window

- Select the cell or range whose formatting you want to apply to other cells.
- To apply the formatting to one cell or an adjacent range of cells, click the Format Painter button on the Standard toolbar, and then click the destination cell or drag the Format Painter pointer over the adjacent range.
- To apply the formatting to nonadjacent ranges, double-click the Format Painter button on the Standard toolbar, and then drag the Format Painter pointer over the first range and then over the other ranges you want to format.

You will use the Format Painter button to copy the format used in the sales figures and to paste that format into the range E23:E26.

To copy the formatting to the range E23:E26 using the Format Painter button:

1. Select cell **B7**, which contains the formatting that you want to copy. You do not have to copy the entire range, because the range is formatted in the same way.

2. Click the **Format Painter** button [icon] on the Standard toolbar. As you move the pointer over the worksheet area, the pointer changes to [icon].

3. Drag the pointer over the range **E23:E26** to apply the modified Comma style format to the sales figures.

Another approach is to use the fill handle discussed in Tutorial 2 to fill in the format (not the values) from one cell to another. To use this approach, you have click the Auto Fill Options button and select the Fill Formatting option. This technique only works when the cell or cells that you want to format are adjacent to the cell containing the format you want to copy. You can also use the Paste Special command from the Copy and Paste buttons to paste only the format of a selected group of cells into a new range of cells. This technique was also discussed in Tutorial 2. One of the advantages of the Format Painter button is that it does what these two methods do, but it does so in fewer steps. However, you should use the approach with which you feel most comfortable.

The Format Painter button and the buttons on the Formatting toolbar are fast and easy ways to copy and apply cell formats, but on occasion you will need more control over your formatting choices than is provided by these toolbar buttons. In those cases, you will need to use the Format Cells dialog box.

Using the Format Cells Dialog Box

Joan agrees that formatting the values has made the worksheet easier to read, but she has a few other suggestions. She does not like the way the currency values are displayed with the dollar signs placed at the left edge of the cell, leaving a large blank space between the dollar sign and the numbers, which is characteristic of values that use an accounting format. She would rather see the dollar sign placed directly to the left of the dollar amounts, which would eliminate the blank space.

The convenience of the Formatting toolbar's one-click access to many of the formatting tasks you will want to perform does have its limits. As you can see in the worksheet, when you use the Formatting toolbar, you cannot specify how the format is applied. To make the change that Joan suggests, you will open the Format Cells dialog box, which gives you more control over the formatting by providing categories of formats from which you can choose and modify to suit your needs.

To open the Format Cells dialog box:

► **1.** Select the nonadjacent range **B23:D25;F23:G26**.

► **2.** Click **Format** on the menu bar, and then click **Cells**. The Format Cells dialog box opens, as shown in Figure 3-5. In addition to the General format category, there are 11 number format categories from which to choose.

Format Cells dialog box ◄ **Figure 3-5**

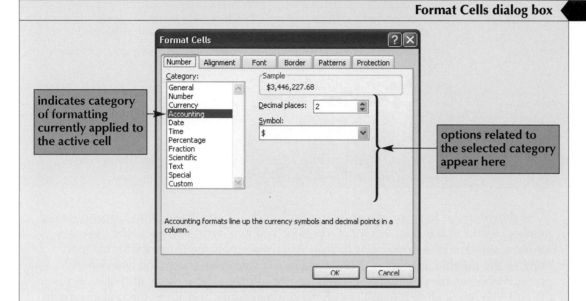

The Format Cells dialog box contains the following six tabs, each dedicated to a different set of format properties. You can apply the options available in this dialog box to any cell or range of cells that you select. The six tabs are:

- **Number:** Provides options for formatting the appearance of numbers, including dates and numbers treated as text (for example, telephone numbers)
- **Alignment:** Provides options for controlling how data is aligned within a cell
- **Font:** Provides options for selecting font types, sizes, and styles and other formatting attributes, such as underlining and colors
- **Border:** Provides options for adding borders around cells
- **Patterns:** Provides options for creating and applying background colors and patterns to cells
- **Protection:** Provides options for locking or hiding cells to prevent other users from modifying their contents

Excel supports several categories of number formats, ranging from Accounting, which you applied using the Currency Style button, to Scientific, which might be used for recording engineering data. Figure 3-6 describes the number format categories.

Figure 3-6 | Number format categories

Category	Description
General	Default format that displays numbers as they are entered
Number	Used for a general display of numbers, with options for the formatting of negative numbers and the number of decimal places
Accounting	Used for displaying monetary values with dollar signs aligned at the left edge of the cell, the decimal points aligned vertically, and comma separators inserted
Currency	Used for displaying monetary values with dollar signs aligned next to leftmost digit and comma separators inserted (decimal points are not aligned)
Date, Time	Used for displaying date and time values
Percentage	Used for displaying decimal values as percentages
Fraction, Scientific	Used for displaying values as fractions or in scientific notation
Text	Used for displaying values as text strings
Special	Used for displaying ZIP codes, phone numbers, and social security numbers
Custom	Used for displaying numbers used in coding or specialized designs

As shown in the Format Cells dialog box in Figure 3-5, the Accounting format displays numbers with a dollar sign, a comma separator, and two decimal places. The Currency format is similar to the Accounting format. When you apply the Currency format to a number, the number appears with a dollar sign, a comma separator, and two decimal places. However, the difference between the two formats is how these attributes appear in the cell. The Accounting format lines up the decimal points and aligns the dollar signs at the left edge of the cell border (creating blank spaces between the dollar signs and the values, as you saw earlier). The Currency format aligns the dollar sign closer to the number, which removes the blank spaces. Joan prefers the Currency format, so you will apply this format to the nonadjacent range that you already selected.

To modify and apply the Currency format:

▶ 1. On the Number tab, click **Currency** in the Category list box. The Format Cells dialog box displays the options available for customizing the Currency category and provides a preview of the selected format. As shown in the Negative numbers list box, Excel displays negative currency values either with a minus sign (-) or with a combination of a red font and parentheses. Joan wants negative currency values to be displayed with a minus sign, which is one of the variations of the Currency format available to you.

▶ 2. Click the first entry in the Negative numbers list box, and then click the **OK** button. Excel changes the format of the currency values, removing the blank spaces between the dollar signs and the values and changing the alignment of the decimal points.

By using the Format Cells dialog box, you can control the formatting to ensure that text and values are displayed the way you want them to be.

Changing Font Type, Size, Style, and Color

A **font** is a set of characters that use the same typeface, style, and size. A **typeface** is the specific design of a set of printed characters, including letters, numbers, punctuation marks, and symbols. Some of the more commonly used fonts are Arial, Times Roman, and Courier. Each font can be displayed using one of the following **font styles**: regular, *italic*, **bold**, or ***bold italic***. Fonts can also be displayed with special effects, such as ~~strikeout~~, underline, and color.

Fonts can also be rendered in different sizes. **Font sizes** are measured using points. A **point** is a unit of measurement used in printing and is equal to approximately 1/72 of an inch. By default, Excel displays characters using a 10-point Arial font in a regular style. To change the font used in a selected cell, you either click the appropriate buttons on the Formatting toolbar or select options in the Format Cells dialog box.

In the logo that the company uses on all its correspondence and advertising materials, the name "NewGeneration Monitors" appears in a large Times New Roman font, which is a serif font. Characters that are designed as **serif fonts** have small lines stemming from and at an angle to the upper and lower ends of the character. **Sans serif fonts** do not include the small lines. A serif font is considered easier to read than a sans serif font. Joan wants the title in cell A1 to reflect this company-wide format, so you will format the title accordingly.

To change the font and font size of the title:

▶ **1.** Click cell **A1** to make it the active cell.

▶ **2.** Click the **Font** list arrow Arial ▾ on the Formatting toolbar, scroll down the list of available fonts, and then click **Times New Roman**.

 Trouble? If you do not have the Times New Roman font installed on your computer, choose a different Times Roman font or choose MS Serif or another serif font in the list.

▶ **3.** Click the **Font Size** list arrow 10 ▾ on the Formatting toolbar, and then click **18**. Figure 3-7 shows the revised format for the title in cell A1.

Changing the font and font size ◄ **Figure 3-7**

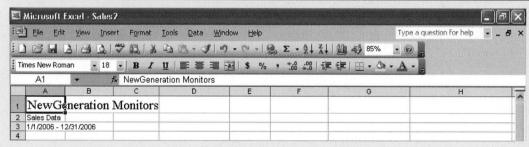

Joan wants the column titles of both tables displayed in bold font and the word "Total" in both tables displayed in italics. To make these modifications, you will again use the Formatting toolbar.

To apply the bold and italic styles:

▶ **1.** Select the nonadjacent range **A6:E6;A22:H22**.

▶ **2.** Click the **Bold** button B on the Formatting toolbar. The titles in the two tables now appear in a boldface font.

 Trouble? Some of the title text may appear truncated within their cells. You'll fix this problem shortly.

3. Select the nonadjacent range **A19;A26**.

4. Click the **Italic** button *I* on the Formatting toolbar. The word "Total" in cells A19 and A26 is now italicized.

Joan points out that NewGeneration's logo usually appears in a red font. Color is another one of Excel's formatting tools and can dramatically enhance the presentation of your data if you have a color printer. Excel provides a palette of 40 different colors. If the color you want is not listed, you can modify Excel's color configuration to create a different color palette. Excel's default color settings will work for most situations, so in this case you will not modify Excel's color settings. You will apply a red color to the name of the company and the two subtitles, which describe the contents of this worksheet.

To change the font color of the title to red:

1. Select the range **A1:A3**.

2. Click the **Font Color** list arrow **A ·** on the Formatting toolbar to display a color palette, and then position the pointer over the Red square (third row, first column from the left) on the palette, as shown in Figure 3-8.

Figure 3-8	Choosing a font color

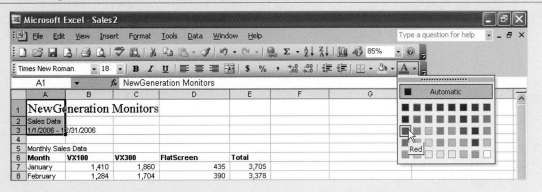

3. Click the **Red** square to change the color of the font in the selected cells to red. See Figure 3-9.

Figure 3-9	Changing the font color of a cell

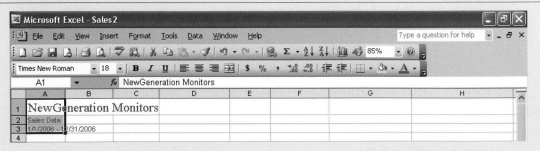

Aligning Cell Contents

When you enter numbers and formulas into a cell, Excel automatically aligns them with the cell's right edge and bottom border. Text entries are aligned with the left edge and bottom border. The default Excel alignment does not always create the most readable worksheets. As a general rule, you should center column titles, and format columns of numbers so that the decimal places are lined up within a column. You can change horizontal alignment using the alignment tools on the Formatting toolbar or the options on the Alignment tab in the Format Cells dialog box.

Next, you will center the column titles above the values in each column in the two tables.

To center the column titles:

▶ **1.** Select the nonadjacent range **B6:E6;B22:H22**.

▶ **2.** Click the **Center** button ▤ on the Formatting toolbar. Excel centers the text in the selected cells in each column.

The Formatting toolbar also provides the Align Left button and the Align Right button so that you can left-align and right-align cell contents. If you want to align cell contents vertically, you have to open the Format Cells dialog box and choose the vertical alignment options on the Alignment tab.

Another alignment option available in the Format Cells dialog box is to center text across a range of cells. Joan wants the text in the cell range A1:A3 to be centered at the top of the worksheet across the first eight columns of the worksheet. This time you will open the Format Cells dialog box to make this formatting change.

To center the titles and subtitles across the first eight columns of the worksheet:

▶ **1.** Select the range **A1:H3**.

▶ **2.** Click **Format** on the menu bar, and then click **Cells** to open the Format Cells dialog box.

▶ **3.** Click the **Alignment** tab.

▶ **4.** Click the **Horizontal** list arrow in the Text alignment pane, click **Center Across Selection**, and then click the **OK** button. See Figure 3-10.

Centering text within and across columns ◀ **Figure 3-10**

text is centered across the first eight columns of the worksheet

The text in these cells is centered horizontally across the selection. Note that centering the text does not affect the location. The title and subtitles are still placed in cells A1 through A3. In general, you should only use this approach for text that is in the leftmost column of the selection, and there should be no text in any other column. If you had text in column B in the previous set of steps, then that text would have been centered across columns B through H, and the text in column A would have remained where it was.

Indenting and Wrapping Text

Sometimes you will want a cell's contents offset, or indented, a few spaces from the cell's edge. This is particularly true for text entries that are aligned with the left edge of the cell. Indenting is often used for cell entries that are considered "subsections" of your worksheet. Joan wants you to indent the names of the months in the range A7:A18 and the monitor titles in the range A23:A25. You will indent the text using one of the indent buttons on the Formatting toolbar.

To indent the months and monitor titles:

1. Select the nonadjacent range **A7:A18;A23:A25**.
2. Click the **Increase Indent** button on the Formatting toolbar. Excel shifts the contents of the selected cells to the right. See Figure 3-11.

Figure 3-11 **Indenting text within cells**

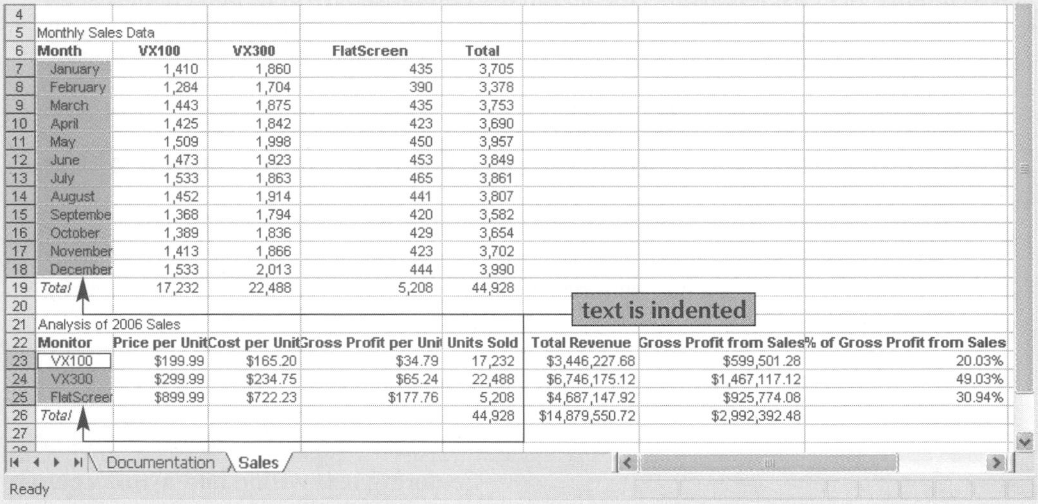

4								
5	Monthly Sales Data							
6	**Month**	**VX100**	**VX300**	**FlatScreen**	**Total**			
7	January	1,410	1,860	435	3,705			
8	February	1,284	1,704	390	3,378			
9	March	1,443	1,875	435	3,753			
10	April	1,425	1,842	423	3,690			
11	May	1,509	1,998	450	3,957			
12	June	1,473	1,923	453	3,849			
13	July	1,533	1,863	465	3,861			
14	August	1,452	1,914	441	3,807			
15	Septembe	1,368	1,794	420	3,582			
16	October	1,389	1,836	429	3,654			
17	November	1,413	1,866	423	3,702			
18	December	1,533	2,013	444	3,990			
19	*Total*	17,232	22,488	5,208	44,928			
20								
21	Analysis of 2006 Sales							
22	**Monitor**	**Price per Unit**	**Cost per Unit**	**Gross Profit per Unit**	**Units Sold**	**Total Revenue**	**Gross Profit from Sales**	**% of Gross Profit from Sales**
23	VX100	$199.99	$165.20	$34.79	17,232	$3,446,227.68	$599,501.28	20.03%
24	VX300	$299.99	$234.75	$65.24	22,488	$6,746,175.12	$1,467,117.12	49.03%
25	FlatScreen	$899.99	$722.23	$177.76	5,208	$4,687,147.92	$925,774.08	30.94%
26	*Total*				44,928	$14,879,550.72	$2,992,392.48	
27								

Clicking the Increase Indent button increases the amount of indentation by roughly one character. To decrease or remove an indentation, click the Decrease Indent button or modify the Indent value using the Format Cells dialog box.

If you enter text that is too wide for a cell, Excel either extends the text into the adjoining cells (if the cells are empty) or truncates the display of the text (if the adjoining cells contain text or values). To avoid cutting off the display of text in a cell, you can widen the columns, or place the text on several lines using the method you learned in Tutorial 1 (pressing the Alt key to move to a second line with a cell). You can also have Excel wrap the text within the cell for you. To wrap text within a cell, you click the Wrap text check box on the Alignment tab of the Format Cells dialog box.

Joan notes that some of the column titles in the second table are long. For example, the "Cost per Unit" label in cell C22 is much longer than the values below it. This formatting has caused some of the columns to be wider than they need to be. Another problem is that the text for some cells has been truncated because the columns are not wide enough. Joan suggests that you wrap the text within the column titles and then change the width of the columns where necessary. To make this change, you will use the Format Cells dialog box.

To have Excel automatically wrap text within a cell:

1. Select the range **A22:H22**.

2. Click **Format** on the menu bar, and then click **Cells** to open the Format Cells dialog box.

3. Make sure that the Alignment tab is selected, select the **Wrap text** check box in the Text control pane, and then click the **OK** button. The text in many of the selected cells now appears on two rows within the cells.

4. Change the width of columns **A** and **D** to about **12** characters (**89** pixels) each, columns **B** and **C** to about **10** characters (**75** pixels) each, columns **F** and **G** to about **13** characters (**96** pixels) each, and column **H** to about **17** characters (**124** pixels) each. See Figure 3-12.

Wrapping text and resizing the worksheet columns | Figure 3-12

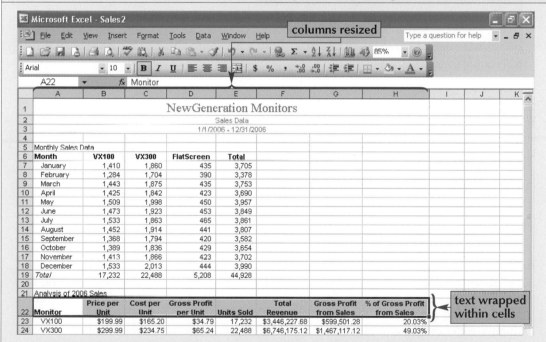

Trouble? If your screen does not match Figure 3-12, resize the columns so the values are easy to read. If some of the text is still hidden, you may need to resize the height of row 22 by dragging the bottom row border down (see Tutorial 1 for a description of resizing rows and columns).

Other Formatting Options

Excel supports even more formatting options than have been discussed so far. For example, instead of wrapping the text, you can have Excel shrink it to fit the size of the cell. If you reduce the cell later on, Excel will automatically resize the text to match. You can also rotate the contents of the cell, displaying the cell entry at almost any angle (see Figure 3-13). Joan does not need to use either of these options in her workbook, but they might be useful later for another project.

Figure 3-13 **Rotating text within a cell**

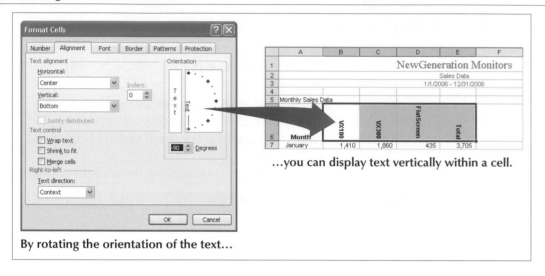

By rotating the orientation of the text…

…you can display text vertically within a cell.

Working with Cell Borders and Backgrounds

Up to now, all the formatting you have done has been applied to the contents of a cell. Excel also provides a range of tools to format the cells themselves. Specifically, you can add borders to cells and color a cell's background.

Adding a Cell Border

As you may have noticed from the printouts of other worksheets, the gridlines that appear in the worksheet window are not normally displayed on the pages that you print. **Gridlines** provide a visual cue for the layout of the cells in a worksheet. Although you can choose to print the gridlines using the Page Setup dialog box, you might want to display borders around individual cells in a worksheet. This would be particularly useful when you have different sections or tables in a worksheet, as in the Sales worksheet.

You can add a border to a cell using either the Borders button on the Formatting toolbar or the options on the Border tab in the Format Cells dialog box. The Borders button allows you to create borders quickly, whereas the Format Cells dialog box lets you further refine your choices. For example, you can specify the style, thickness, and color using the options available in the Format Cells dialog box.

Joan wants you to place a border around each cell in the two tables in the worksheet. You'll select the appropriate border style from the list of available options on the Borders palette.

To create a grid of cell borders in the two tables:

1. Select the nonadjacent range **A6:E19;A22:H26**.

2. Click the **Borders** list arrow on the Formatting toolbar, then move the pointer over the gallery of borders to highlight the All Borders option as shown in Figure 3-14.

Border options ◄ **Figure 3-14**

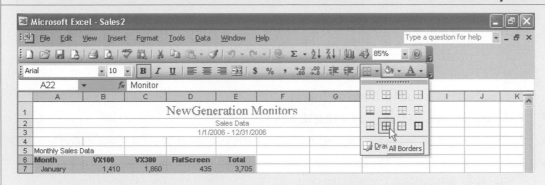

3. Click the **All Borders** option (third row, second column from the left) in the borders gallery. A thin border appears around each cell in the selected range.

4. Click any cell to deselect the range and to see the applied border.

You can also place a border around the entire range itself (and not the individual cells) by selecting a different border style. Try this by creating a thick border around the cell range.

To create a thick border around a selected range:

1. Select the nonadjacent range **A6:E19;A22:H26** again.

2. Click the **Borders** list arrow on the Formatting toolbar, and then click the **Thick Box Border** option (third row, fourth column from the left) in the borders gallery.

3. Click any cell to deselect the range so you can see the thick border applied to the tables. The interior borders should be unchanged.

If you want a more interactive way of drawing borders on your worksheet, you can use the Draw Borders button, which is another option on the borders gallery. To see how this option works, you will add a thick black line under the column titles in both of the tables.

To draw borders using the Draw Borders button:

1. Click the **Borders** list arrow on the Formatting toolbar, and then click the **Draw Borders** button at the bottom of the borders gallery. The pointer changes to ✏, and a floating Borders toolbar opens with four tools. The Draw Border button (currently selected) on the Borders toolbar draws a border line on the worksheet; the Erase Border button erases border lines; the Line Style button specifies the style of the border line; and the Line Color button specifies the line color.

2. Click the **Line Style** list arrow to display a list of line style options, and then click the **thick line** option (the ninth from the top) in the list.

3. Click and drag the pointer over the lower border of the range **A6:E6**. The lower border thickens, matching the top border in thickness.

4. Click and drag the pointer over the lower border of the range **A22:H22**. The lower border thickens.

5. Click the **Close** button ✖ on the floating Borders toolbar to close it.

Finally, you will add a double line above the Total row in each table. You will add the line using the options in the Format Cells dialog box.

To create the double border lines:

1. Select the nonadjacent range **A18:E18;A25:H25**.

2. Click **Format** on the menu bar, and then click **Cells** to open the Format Cells dialog box.

3. Click the **Border** tab. The Border tab displays a diagram showing what borders, if any, are currently surrounding the selected cells.

   The bottom border is currently a single thin line. You want to change this to a double line.

4. Click the **double line** style in the Style list box located on the right side of the tab, and then click the **bottom border** in the border diagram to apply the double-line style. The bottom border changes to a double line. See Figure 3-15.

Figure 3-15 ▶ **Border tab in the Format Cells dialog box**

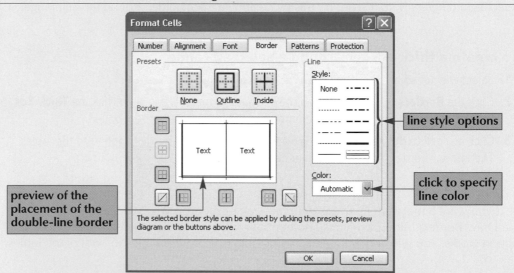

5. Click the **OK** button to close the dialog box, and then click cell **A1** to deselect the ranges. Figure 3-16 shows all of the border styles you've applied to the two tables.

You can also specify a color for the cell borders by using the Color list box located on the Border tab (see Figure 3-15). Joan does not need to change the border colors, but she would like you to change the background color for the column title cells. When you copy the formatting of a cell, any border that you have applied is also copied.

Applying Background Colors and Patterns

Patterns and color can be used to turn a plain worksheet full of numbers and labels into a powerful presentation of information that captures your attention and adds visual emphasis to the different sections of the worksheet. If you have a color printer or a color projection device, you might want to take advantage of Excel's color tools. By default, worksheet cells are not filled with any color (the white you see in your worksheet is not a fill color for the cells). To change the background color in a worksheet, you can use the Fill Color button on the Formatting toolbar, or you can use the Format Cells dialog box, which also provides patterns that you can apply to the background. When choosing to apply color to a worksheet, you must always give consideration to the availability of a color printer. Also, if you plan to print a worksheet as an overhead, black print on a clear overhead transparency is easier to read than other colors.

Joan wants to change the background color of the worksheet. When she prints her report later in the week, she will be using the company's color laser printer. Therefore, she would like you to explore using background color in the column titles for the two sales tables. She suggests that you try formatting the column titles with a light-yellow background.

To apply a fill color to the column titles:

▶ 1. Select the nonadjacent range **A6:E6;A22:H22**.

▶ 2. Click the **Fill Color** button list arrow 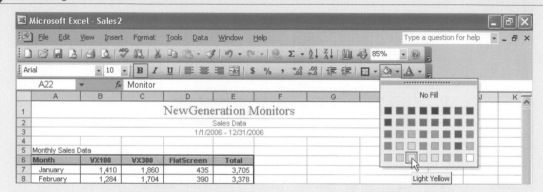 on the Formatting toolbar. The color palette appears.

▶ 3. Position the pointer over the **Light Yellow** square (fifth row, third column from the left) on the color palette, as shown in Figure 3-17.

Figure 3-17 ▶	Selecting a fill color

▶ 4. Click the **Light Yellow** square to apply the color to the selected range, and then click any cell to deselect the range and to see the applied color. The column titles now have light-yellow backgrounds.

Joan would also like to investigate whether you can apply a pattern to the fill background. Excel supports 18 different fill patterns. To create and apply a fill pattern, you have to open the Format Cells dialog box.

To apply a fill pattern to the column titles:

▶ 1. Select the nonadjacent range **A6:E6;A22:H22**.

▶ 2. Click **Format** on the menu bar, click **Cells** to open the Format Cells dialog box, and then click the **Patterns** tab to display the options provided.

▶ 3. Click the **Pattern** list arrow to display a gallery of patterns and a palette of colors that you can apply to the selected pattern. The default pattern color is black. First, you will choose a crosshatch pattern, which is a pattern using crossed diagonal lines.

▶ 4. Click the **50% Gray** pattern (first row, third column) in the pattern gallery, as shown in Figure 3-18.

Selecting a fill pattern ◄ Figure 3-18

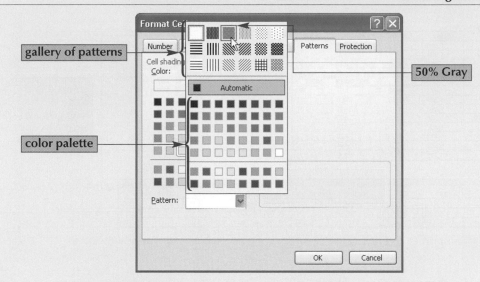

▶ **5.** Click the **OK** button, and then click any cell to deselect the ranges and to see the pattern.

The background pattern you have chosen overwhelms the text in these column titles. You can improve the appearance by changing the color of the pattern itself from black to a light orange.

To change the pattern color:

▶ **1.** Select the range **A6:E6;A22:H22**. The default (or automatic) color of a selected pattern is black, but you want to choose a brighter and lighter color for the pattern.

▶ **2.** Click **Format** on the menu bar, and then click **Cells** to open the Format Cells dialog box again. The Patterns tab should be displayed automatically because it is the last set of options you used.

▶ **3.** Click the **Pattern** list arrow to display the gallery of patterns and the color palette.

▶ **4.** Click the **Light Orange** square (third row, second column) in the color palette, click the **OK** button to close the dialog box, and then click cell **A1** to deselect the range and to see the color applied to the pattern. See Figure 3-19. The column titles now appear in a light-orange patterned background. The pattern and the color do not overwhelm the column titles.

Figure 3-19 **Cells with formatted backgrounds**

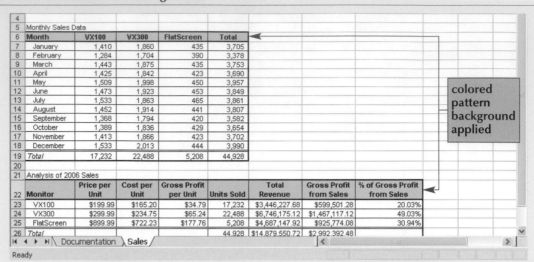

5. Save your changes to the workbook.

Joan is pleased with the progress you have made. In the next session, you will explore other formatting features.

Review

Session 3.1 Quick Check

1. Describe two ways of applying the Currency style to cells in your worksheet.
2. If the number 0.05765 has been entered into a cell, what will Excel display if you:
    a. format the number using the Percent style with one decimal place?
    b. format the number using the Currency style with two decimal places and a dollar sign?
3. Which two buttons can you use to copy a format from one cell range to another?
4. A long text string in one of your worksheet cells has been truncated. List three ways to correct this problem.
5. How do you center the contents of a single cell across a range of cells?
6. Describe three ways of creating a cell border.
7. How would you apply a colored background pattern to a selected cell range?

Session 3.2

Formatting the Worksheet

In the previous session, you formatted individual cells within the worksheet. Excel also provides tools for formatting the columns and rows in a worksheet. You will explore some of these tools as you continue to work on Joan's sales report.

Merging Cells into One Cell

Joan has several other formatting changes that she would like you to make to the Sales worksheet. She wants you to format the titles for the two tables in her report so that they are centered in a bold font above the tables. You could do this by centering the cell title across a cell range, as you did for the title in the last session. Another way is to merge several cells into one cell and then center the contents of that single cell. Merging a range of cells into a single cell removes all of the selected cells from the worksheet, except the cell in the upper-left corner of the range. Any content in the other cells of the range is deleted. To merge a range of cells into a single cell, you can use the Merge cells check box on the Alignment tab in the Format Cells dialog box or click the Merge and Center button on the Formatting toolbar.

To merge and center the cell ranges containing the table titles:

1. If you took a break after the previous session, make sure that Excel is running and that the Sales2 workbook is open.

2. In the Sales worksheet, select the range **A5:E5**.

3. Click the **Merge and Center** button 🔳 on the Formatting toolbar. The cells in the range A5:E5 are merged into a single cell whose cell reference is A5. The text in the merged cell is centered as well.

4. Click the **Bold** button 🅱 on the Formatting toolbar.

5. Select the range **A21:H21**, click the **Merge and Center** button 🔳 on the Formatting toolbar, and then click the **Bold** button 🅱 on the Formatting toolbar.

6. Click cell **A1** to deselect the range. Figure 3-20 shows the merged and centered table titles.

Merging and centering cells ◄ | **Figure 3-20**

	Month	VX100	VX300	FlatScreen	Total			
4								
5			Monthly Sales Data					
6	Month	VX100	VX300	FlatScreen	Total			
7	January	1,410	1,860	435	3,705			
8	February	1,284	1,704	390	3,378			
9	March	1,443	1,875	435	3,753			
10	April	1,425	1,842	423	3,690			
11	May	1,509	1,998	450	3,957			
12	June	1,473	1,923	453	3,849			cells merged and centered
13	July	1,533	1,863	465	3,861			
14	August	1,452	1,914	441	3,807			
15	September	1,368	1,794	420	3,582			
16	October	1,389	1,836	429	3,654			
17	November	1,413	1,866	423	3,702			
18	December	1,533	2,013	444	3,990			
19	Total	17,232	22,488	5,208	44,928			
20								
21				Analysis of 2006 Sales				

	Monitor	Price per Unit	Cost per Unit	Gross Profit per Unit	Units Sold	Total Revenue	Gross Profit from Sales	% of Gross Profit from Sales
22	Monitor	Price per Unit	Cost per Unit	Gross Profit per Unit	Units Sold	Total Revenue	Gross Profit from Sales	% of Gross Profit from Sales
23	VX100	$199.99	$165.20	$34.79	17,232	$3,446,227.68	$599,501.28	20.03%
24	VX300	$299.99	$234.75	$65.24	22,488	$6,746,175.12	$1,467,117.12	49.03%
25	FlatScreen	$899.99	$722.23	$177.76	5,208	$4,687,147.92	$925,774.08	30.94%
26	Total				44,928	$14,879,550.72	$2,992,392.48	

◄ ► ►│\ Documentation \ Sales /

Ready

To split a merged cell back into individual cells, regardless of the method you used to merge the cells, you select the merged cell and then click the Merge and Center button again. You can also merge and unmerge cells using the Alignment tab in the Format Cells dialog box.

Hiding Rows, Columns and Worksheets

Sometimes Joan does not need to view the monthly sales for the three monitors. She does not want to remove this information from the worksheet, but she would like the option of temporarily hiding that information. Excel provides this capability. Hiding a row or column does not affect the data stored there, nor does it affect any other cell that might have a formula referencing a cell in the hidden row or column. Hiding part of your worksheet is a good way of temporarily concealing nonessential information, allowing you to concentrate on the more important data contained in your worksheet. To hide a row or column, first you must select the row(s) or column(s) you want to hide. You can then use the Row or Column option on the Format menu or right-click the selection to open its shortcut menu.

You will hide the monthly sales figures in the first table in the worksheet.

To hide the monthly sales figures:

1. Select the headings for rows **7** through **18**.

2. Right-click the selection, and then click **Hide** on the shortcut menu. Excel hides rows 7 through 18. Note that the total sales figures in the range B19:E19 are not affected by hiding the monthly sales figures. See Figure 3-21.

Figure 3-21 ▶ **Hiding worksheet rows**

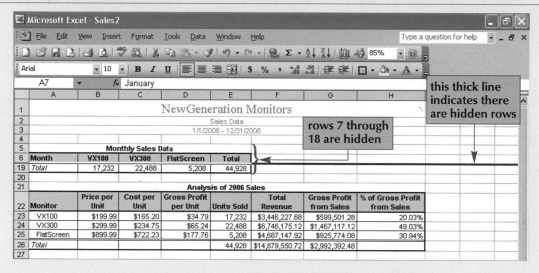

To unhide a hidden row or column, you must select the headings of the rows or columns that border the hidden area; then you can use the right-click method or the Row or Column command on the Format menu to choose the Unhide option. You will let Joan know that it is easy to hide any row or column that she does not want to view. But for now you will redisplay the hidden sales figures.

To unhide the monthly sales figures:

1. Select the row headings for rows **6** and **19**.

2. Right-click the selection, and then click **Unhide** on the shortcut menu. Excel redisplays rows 7 through 18.

3. Click cell **A1** to deselect the rows.

Hiding and unhiding a column follows the same process, except that you select the worksheet column headings rather than the row headings. For example, to hide column B, you select the column heading B. To unhide the column, you must select columns A and C.

On other occasions Joan would like to hide an entire worksheet. This could occur in situations where a worksheet contains detailed information and she only wants to display the summary figures from another sheet. To show how to hide an entire worksheet, you should suggest that she hide the documentation sheet located at the front of the workbook.

To hide the Documentation sheet:

▶ **1.** Click the **Documentation** sheet tab to make it the active sheet.

▶ **2.** Click **Format** on the menu bar, point to **Sheet**, and then click **Hide**.

The Documentation sheet disappears from the workbook. It is still present in the workbook, it is just hidden at this point. Excel maintains a list of the hidden worksheets in the current workbook, so you can always select one of those sheets to be redisplayed. Do this now to unhide the Documentation sheet.

To unhide the Documentation sheet:

▶ **1.** Click **Format** on the menu bar, point to **Sheet**, and then click **Unhide**. Excel displays the Unhide dialog box, listing all hidden worksheets in the workbook.

▶ **2.** Verify that **Documentation** is selected in the list of hidden worksheets, and click the **OK** button.

The Documentation sheet should be redisplayed in the workbook and made the active sheet.

▶ **3.** Click the **Sales** sheet tab to return to the Sales worksheet.

Adding a Background Image

In the previous session you learned how to create a background color for individual cells within the worksheet. Excel also allows you to use an image file as a background for a worksheet. The image from the file is tiled repeatedly until the images fill up the entire worksheet. Images can be used to give the background a textured appearance, like that of granite, wood, or fibered paper. The background image does not affect the format or content of any cell in the worksheet, and if you have already defined a background color for a cell, Excel displays the color on top, hiding that portion of the image.

Adding a Background Image to the Worksheet

Reference Window

- Click Format on the menu bar, point to Sheet, and then click Background.
- Locate the image file that you want tiled over the worksheet background.
- Click the Insert button.

If you add a background and then decide against it, you can remove the background image by clicking Format on the menu bar, pointing to Sheet, and then clicking Delete Background. The image will automatically be removed.

Joan wants you to experiment with using a background image for the Sales worksheet. You will add the image file that she has selected.

To add a background image to the worksheet:

1. Click **Format** on the menu bar, point to **Sheet**, and then click **Background**. The Sheet Background dialog box opens.

2. Navigate to the Tutorial.03\Tutorial folder, click the **Back** image file, and then click the **Insert** button. The Back image file is applied repeatedly to, or is "tiled over," the worksheet, creating a textured background for the Sales sheet. Notice that the tiling is hidden in the cells that already contain a background color. To make the sales figures easier to read, you'll change the background color of those cells to white.

3. Select the nonadjacent range **A7:E19;A23:H26**.

4. Click the **Fill Color** list arrow ![fill color icon] on the Formatting toolbar, click the **White** square (lower-right corner) in the color palette, and then click cell **A1** to deselect the range, making the background image easier to see. Figure 3-22 shows the Sales worksheet with the formatted background.

| Figure 3-22 | Inserting a background image |

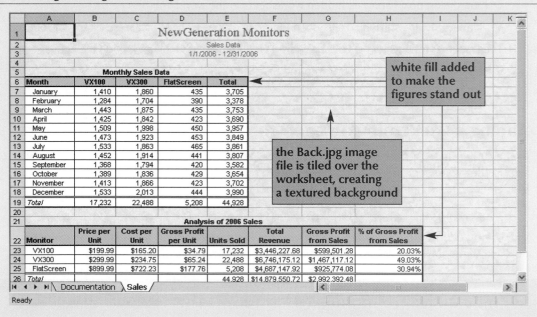

Note that you cannot apply a background image to all of the sheets in a workbook at the same time. If you want to apply the same background to several sheets, you must format each sheet separately.

Formatting Sheet Tabs

In addition to the sheet background, you can also format the background color of worksheet tabs. This color is only visible when the worksheet is not the active sheet in the workbook. By default, the tab of the active sheet in a workbook is white. If you change the color of a tab, the tab changes to white with a narrow colored stripe at the bottom of the tab when the sheet is active. You can use tab colors to better organize the various sheets in your workbook. For example, worksheets that contain sales information could be formatted with blue tabs, whereas sheets that describe the company's cash flow or budget could be formatted with green tabs. To explore how to color worksheet tabs, you will change the tab color of the Sales worksheet to light orange.

To change the tab color:

1. Right-click the **Sales** tab, and then click **Tab Color** on the shortcut menu. The Format Tab Color dialog box opens.

2. Click the **Light Orange** square (third row, second column from the left) in the color palette, and then click the **OK** button. Because the Sales sheet is the active worksheet, the tab is white with a light-orange horizontal stripe at the bottom of the tab.

3. Switch to the Documentation sheet so you can see the light-orange color of the Sales sheet tab, and then switch to the Sales sheet again.

Clearing and Replacing Formats

Sometimes you might want to change or remove some of the formatting from your workbooks. As you experiment with different formats, you can use the Undo button on the Standard toolbar to remove formatting choices that did not work out as well as you expected. Another choice is to clear the formatting from the selected cells, returning the cells to their previous format. To see how this option works, you will remove the formatting from the company name in cell A1 on the Sales worksheet.

To clear the formatting from cell A1:

1. Make sure cell **A1** is selected.

2. Click **Edit** on the menu bar, point to **Clear**, and then click **Formats**. Excel removes the formatting that was applied to the text and removes the formatting that merged the cells and then centered the text across the range.

3. Click the **Undo** button 🔄 on the Standard toolbar to undo your action, restoring the formats you cleared.

Sometimes you will want to make a formatting change that applies to several different cells. If those cells are scattered throughout the workbook, you may find it time consuming to search for and replace the formats for each individual cell. If the cells share a common format that you want to change, you can use the Find and Replace command to locate the formats and modify them.

Reference Window | Finding and Replacing a Format

- Click Edit on the menu bar, and then click Replace.
- Click the Options >> button, if necessary, to display the format choices.
- Click the top Format list arrow, and then click Format.
- Specify the format you want to find in the Find Format dialog box, and then click the OK button.
- Click the bottom Format list arrow, and then click Format.
- Enter the new format, which will replace the old format, and then click the OK button.
- Click the Replace All button to replace all occurrences of the old format; click the Replace button to replace the currently selected cell containing the old format; or click the Find Next button to find the next occurrence of the old format before replacing it.
- Click the Close button.

In the Sales worksheet, the table titles and column titles are displayed in a bold font. After seeing how the use of color has made the worksheet come alive, Joan wants you to change the titles to a boldface blue. Rather than selecting the cells that contain the table and column titles and formatting them, you will replace all occurrences of the boldface text with blue boldface text.

To find and replace formats:

▶ 1. Click **Edit** on the menu bar, and then click **Replace**. The Find and Replace dialog box opens. You can use this dialog box to find and replace the contents of cells. In this case, you will use it only for finding and replacing formats, leaving the contents of the cells unchanged.

▶ 2. Click the **Options >>** button to display additional find and replace options. See Figure 3-23. The dialog box expands to display options that allow you to find and replace cell formats. It also includes options to determine whether to search within the active sheet or the entire workbook. Currently no format options have been set.

Figure 3-23 ▶ **Find and Replace dialog box**

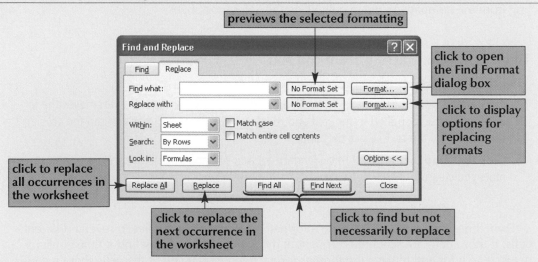

Trouble? If the button on your workbook appears as Options <<, the additional options are already displayed, and you do not need to click any buttons.

▶ 3. Click the top **Format** button to open the Find Format dialog box. Here is where you specify the format you want to search for. In this case, you are searching for cells that contain boldface text.

4. Click the **Font** tab, and then click **Bold** in the Font style list box. See Figure 3-24.

Find Format dialog box ◄ **Figure 3-24**

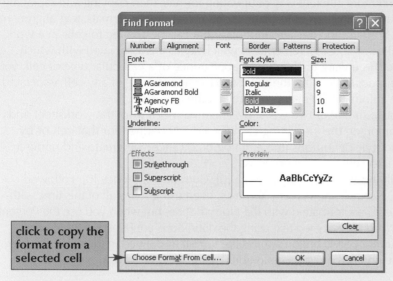

click to copy the format from a selected cell

5. Click the **OK** button.

Next, you will specify the new format that you want to use to replace the boldface text. In this case, you will specify blue boldface text.

6. Click the bottom **Format** button to open the Replace Format dialog box again, and then click **Bold** in the Font style list box.

7. Click the **Color** list box, click the **Blue** square (second row, sixth column from the left) in the color palette, and then click the **OK** button.

8. Click the **Replace All** button to replace all boldface text in the worksheet with blue boldface text. Excel indicates that it has completed its search and made 15 replacements.

9. Click the **OK** button, and then click the **Close** button to close the Find and Replace dialog box. See Figure 3-25. The boldface text has been replaced with blue boldface text.

Sales worksheet with blue boldface text ◄ **Figure 3-25**

bold formatting found and replaced with bold blue formatting

	Month	VX100	VX300	FlatScreen	Total
5		Monthly Sales Data			
6	Month	VX100	VX300	FlatScreen	Total
7	January	1,410	1,860	435	3,705
8	February	1,284	1,704	390	3,378
9	March	1,443	1,875	435	3,753
10	April	1,425	1,842	423	3,690
11	May	1,509	1,998	450	3,957
12	June	1,473	1,923	453	3,849
13	July	1,533	1,863	465	3,861
14	August	1,452	1,914	441	3,807
15	September	1,368	1,794	420	3,582
16	October	1,389	1,836	429	3,654
17	November	1,413	1,868	423	3,702
18	December	1,533	2,013	444	3,990
19	Total	17,232	22,488	5,208	44,928

	Monitor	Price per Unit	Cost per Unit	Gross Profit per Unit	Units Sold	Total Revenue	Gross Profit from Sales	% of Gross Profit from Sales
21		Analysis of 2006 Sales						
23	VX100	$199.99	$165.20	$34.79	17,232	$3,446,227.68	$599,501.28	20.03%
24	VX300	$299.99	$234.75	$65.24	22,488	$6,746,175.12	$1,467,117.12	49.03%
25	FlatScreen	$899.99	$722.23	$177.76	5,208	$4,687,147.92	$925,774.08	30.94%
26	Total				44,928	$14,879,550.72	$2,992,392.48	

Documentation \ Sales

Ready

Using Styles

If you have several cells that employ the same format, you can create a style for those cells. This can be a faster and more efficient way of updating formats than copying and replacing formats. A **style** is a saved collection of formatting options—number formats, text alignment, font sizes and colors, borders, and background fills—that can be applied to cells in a worksheet. When you apply a style, Excel remembers which styles are associated with which cells in the workbook. If you want to change the appearance of a particular type of cell, you need only modify the specifications for the style, and the appearance of any cell associated with that style will be automatically changed to reflect the new style.

You can create a style in one of two ways: by selecting a cell from the worksheet and basing the style definition on the formatting choices already defined for that cell or by manually entering the style definitions into a dialog box. Once you create and name a style, you can apply it to cells in the workbook.

Excel has eight built-in styles: Comma, Comma [0], Currency, Currency [0], Followed Hyperlink, Hyperlink, Normal, and Percent. You have been using styles all of this time without knowing it. Most cells are formatted with the Normal style, but when you use the Percent Style button, Excel formats the selected text using the definitions contained in the Percent style. Similarly, the Currency Style button applies the format as defined in the Currency style. As you'll see, you can modify these style definitions or create some of your own.

Creating a Style

Joan wants you to further modify the appearance of the worksheet by changing the background color of the months in the first table and the monitor names in the second table to yellow. Rather than applying new formatting to the cells, you will create a new style called "Category" and then apply the new style to the category columns of the tables in the worksheet. You will create the style using the format already applied to cell A7 as a basis.

To create a style using a formatted cell:

1. Click cell **A7** to select it. The format applied to this cell becomes the basis of the new style that you want to create.

2. Click **Format** on the menu bar, and then click **Style**. The Style dialog box opens. All of the formatting options associated with the style of the active cell are listed. For example, the font is 10-point Arial. The check boxes indicate whether these various formatting categories are part of the style definition. If you deselect one of the formatting categories, such as Border, then that category will not be part of the style definition.

   To create a new style for this cell, you simply type a different name into the list box.

3. Type **Category** in the Style name list box, as shown in Figure 3-26. At this point, cell A7 is no longer formatted using the Normal style; rather it is formatted using the Category style you just created.

Now you will modify the properties of this style.

4. Click the **Border** check box to deselect it. Category style will not include any border format options.

Next, you will modify the pattern of the style.

5. Click the **Modify** button to open the Format Cells dialog box, and then click the **Patterns** tab.

6. Click the **Yellow** square (fourth row, third column from the left) in the color palette, and then click the **OK** button to close the Format Cells dialog box and redisplay the Style dialog box.

If you click the OK button in the Style dialog box, the style definition changes and is applied to the active cell and the Style dialog box closes. If you click the Add button in the dialog box, the style change is saved and applied, but the Style dialog box remains open for further style changes.

7. Click the **OK** button to save the new style and apply it to the background color of cell A7.

Now you need to apply this style to other cells in the workbook.

Applying a Style

To apply a style to cells in a worksheet, you first select the cells you want associated with the style and then open the Style dialog box.

To apply the Category style:

1. Select the nonadjacent range **A8:A18;A23:A25**.

2. Click **Format** on the menu bar, and then click **Style**. The Style dialog box opens.

3. Click the **Style name** list arrow, and then click **Category**. The formatting options change to reflect the associated options for the selected style.

4. Click the **OK** button to close the dialog box and apply the Category style to the selected range, and then click cell **A1** to deselect the cells. A yellow background color is applied to all of the month and monitor cells in the two tables.

The yellow background appears a bit too strong. You decide to change it to a light-yellow background. Since all the month and monitor cells are now associated with the Category style, you need only modify the definition of the Category style to make this change.

To modify the Category style:

▶ 1. Click **Format** on the menu bar, and then click **Style**.

▶ 2. Click the **Style name** list arrow, and then click **Category**. The options in the Style dialog box change to reflect the selected Category style.

▶ 3. Click the **Modify** button to open the Format Cells dialog box, and then click the **Patterns** tab, if necessary.

▶ 4. Click the **Light Yellow** square (fifth row, third column from the left) in the color palette, and then click the **OK** button.

▶ 5. Click the **Add** button in the Style dialog box. Excel changes the background color of all the cells associated with the Category style.

   Trouble? If you clicked the OK button instead of the Add button, the Category style would have been applied to the active cell as well as the ranges formatted with the Category style. Click the Undo on the Standard toolbar to undo the application of the Category style to cell A2, and then skip Step 6.

▶ 6. Click the **Close** button. See Figure 3-27. The updated Category style is applied to the ranges using that format.

Figure 3-27 ▶ **Category style in the Sales worksheet**

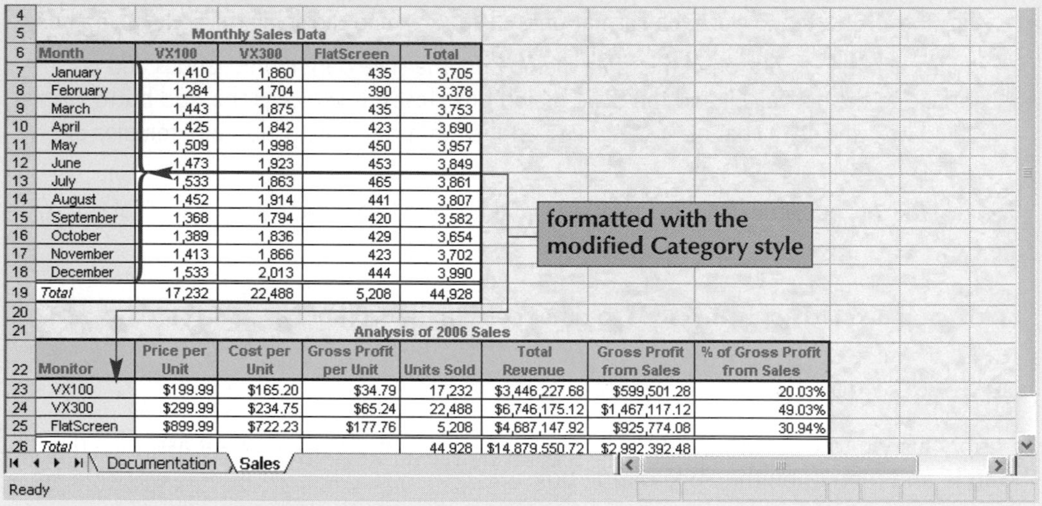

The Category style becomes part of the Sales2 workbook, but it is not available to other workbooks. However, you can copy styles from one workbook to another. Copying styles allows you to create a collection of workbooks that share a common look and feel.

To copy styles from one workbook to another, open the workbook containing your customized styles, and then open the workbook into which you want to copy the styles. Open the Styles dialog box, click the Merge button, and select the first workbook. All of the styles in that workbook will be copied into the second workbook for use on that workbook's contents. Note that if you make changes to the style definitions later on, you will have to copy them again. Excel will not automatically update styles across workbooks.

Using AutoFormat

Excel's **AutoFormat** feature provides a gallery of 17 predefined formats that you can select and apply to your worksheet cells. Rather than spending time testing different combinations of fonts, colors, and borders, you can apply an existing format to your worksheet.

You have done a lot of work already formatting the data in the Sales worksheet to give it a more professional and polished look, but you decide to see how the formatting you have done compares to one of Excel's AutoFormat designs.

You'll apply an AutoFormat design to the sales figures table so that you can compare a predefined format to the format you have worked on.

To apply an AutoFormat design to the table:

1. Select the range **A5:E19**.

2. Click **Format** on the menu bar, and then click **AutoFormat**. The AutoFormat dialog box opens. See Figure 3-28. The dialog box displays a preview of how each format will appear when applied to cells in a worksheet.

AutoFormat gallery | **Figure 3-28**

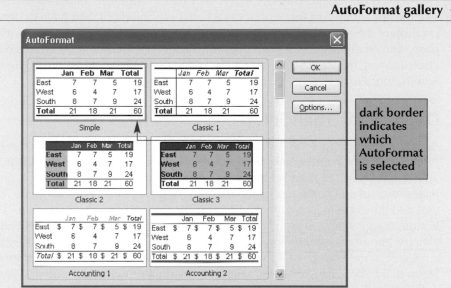

3. Click **Classic 3** in the list of available designs, click the **OK** button, and then click cell **A1** to remove the highlighting from the table. Figure 3-29 shows the appearance of the Classic 3 design to the cells containing the monthly sales data.

Applying an AutoFormat | **Figure 3-29**

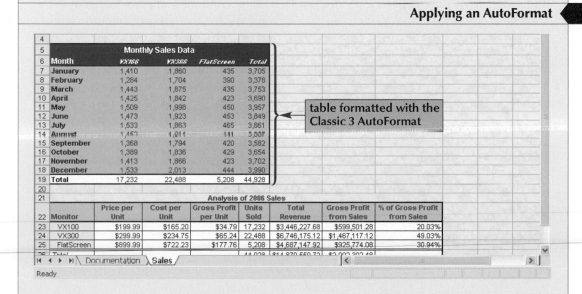

The colors and contrast of the AutoFormat design do not complement the background, so you will revert to the format you created.

▶ **4.** Click the **Undo** button 🔄 on the Standard toolbar to remove the AutoFormat design.

Although you will not use AutoFormat in this case, you can see how an AutoFormat design can be a starting point. You could start with an AutoFormat design and then make modifications to the worksheet to fit your own needs.

Formatting the Printed Worksheet

You have settled on an appearance for the Sales worksheet—at least the appearance that is displayed on your screen. But that is only half of your job. Joan also wants you to format the appearance of this worksheet when it is printed out. You have to decide on the position of the report on the page, the size of the page margins, the orientation of the page, and whether the page will have any headers or footers. You can make many of these choices using the Page Setup dialog box, which you can open from the File menu or from within Print Preview.

Defining the Page Setup

As you learned in Tutorial 1, you can use the Page Setup dialog box to change the page orientation, which determines if the page is wider than it is tall or taller than it is wide. You can also use the Page Setup dialog box to control how a worksheet is placed on a page. You can adjust the size of the **margins**, which are the spaces between the page content and the edges of the page. You can center the worksheet text between the top and bottom margins (horizontally) or between the right and left margins (vertically). You can also use the Page Setup dialog box to display text that will appear in the area at the top of a page or at the bottom of a page for each page of a worksheet. You can open the Page Setup dialog box using the File menu or using the Print Preview toolbar. Working from within Print Preview can be helpful. Each time you close a dialog box in which you have made a change or selected an option, you will see how that action impacts the worksheet before printing it.

By default, Excel places a one-inch margin above and below the report and a ¾-inch margin to the left and right. Excel also aligns column A in a worksheet at the left margin and row 1 at the top margin. Depending on how many columns and rows there are in the worksheet, you might want to increase or decrease the page margins or center the worksheet between the left and right margins or between the top and bottom margins.

You will increase the margin size for the Sales worksheet to one inch all around. You will also center the worksheet between the right and left margins.

To change the margins and positioning of the worksheet:

▶ 1. Click the **Print Preview** button 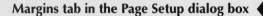 on the Standard toolbar. The Print Preview window opens, displaying the worksheet as it will appear on the printed page.

▶ 2. Click the **Setup** button on the Print Preview toolbar, and then click the **Margins** tab. The Margins tab, as shown in Figure 3-30, provides a diagram that shows you the placement of the worksheet on the page. In addition to adjusting the sizes of the margins, you can also adjust the positioning of the worksheet on the printout.

Margins tab in the Page Setup dialog box ◀ **Figure 3-30**

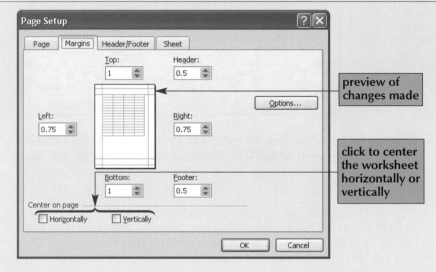

▶ 3. Click the **Left** up arrow to set the size of the left margin to **1** inch, and then click the **Right** up arrow to increase the size of the right margin to **1** inch.

▶ 4. Click the **Horizontally** check box, and then click the **OK** button to close the Page Setup dialog box and return to Print Preview.

Note that this printout does not fit on a single page. As indicated in the status line located in the lower-left corner of the Print Preview window, the worksheet covers two pages instead of one; two columns of the bottom table have been moved to the second page. You could try to reduce the left and right margins, so the worksheet fits on a single page, but as you learned in Tutorial 1, you also can change the page orientation to landscape, making the worksheet page wider than it is tall. This will accommodate all the columns of the bottom table so all the data will fit on the same page.

To change the page orientation:

▶ 1. Click the **Setup** button on the Print Preview toolbar to open the Page Setup dialog box again.

▶ 2. Click the **Page** tab and then click the **Landscape** option button, as shown in Figure 3-31.

Figure 3-31   **Changing the page orientation**

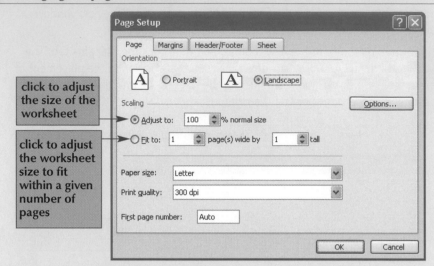

click to adjust the size of the worksheet

click to adjust the worksheet size to fit within a given number of pages

3. Click the **OK** button to close the dialog box and return to the Print Preview window. The preview of the printed worksheet in landscape orientation shows that the report will fit on a single page.

The Page tab in the Page Setup dialog box contains other useful formatting features. You can reduce or increase the size of the worksheet on the printed page. The default size is 100 percent. You can also have Excel automatically reduce the size of the report to fit within a specified number of pages.

Working with Headers and Footers

Joan wants you to add a header and footer to the report. A **header** is text printed in the top margin of every worksheet page. A **footer** is text printed at the bottom of every page. Headers and footers can add important information to your printouts. For example, you can create a header that displays your name and the date the report was created. If the report covers multiple pages, you can use a footer to display the page number and the total number of pages. You use the Page Setup dialog box to add headers and footers to a worksheet.

Excel tries to anticipate headers and footers that you might want to include in your worksheet. Clicking the Header or Footer list arrow displays a list of possible headers or footers (the list is the same for both). For example, the "Page 1" entry inserts the page number of the worksheet prefaced by the word "Page" in the header; the "Page 1 of ?" displays the page number and the total number of pages. Other entries in the list include the name of the worksheet or workbook.

If you want to use a header or footer not available in the lists, you click the Custom Header or Custom Footer button and create your own header and footer. The Header dialog box and the Footer dialog box are similar. Each dialog box is divided into three sections: left, center, and right. If you want to enter information such as the filename or the date into the header or footer, you can either type the text or click one of the format buttons located above the three section boxes. Figure 3-32 describes the format buttons and the corresponding format codes.

Header/Footer formatting buttons | **Figure 3-32**

Button	Name	Formatting Code	Action
A	Font	None	Sets font, text style, and font size
	Page Number	&[Page]	Inserts page number
	Total Pages	&[Pages]	Inserts total number of pages
	Date	&[Date]	Inserts current date
	Time	&[Time]	Inserts current time
	File Path	&[Path]&[File]	Inserts path and filename
	Filename	&[File]	Inserts filename
	Tab Name	&[Tab]	Inserts name of active worksheet
	Insert Picture	&[Picture]	Inserts an image file
	Format Picture	None	Opens the Format Picture dialog box

Joan wants a header that displays the filename at the left margin and today's date at the right margin. She wants a footer that displays the name of the workbook author, with the text aligned at the right margin of the footer. You'll create the header and footer now.

To add a custom header and footer to the workbook:

1. Click the **Setup** button on the Print Preview toolbar, and then click the **Header/Footer** tab. The Header/Footer dialog box opens.

2. Click the **Custom Header** button. The Header dialog box opens. See Figure 3-33.

Header dialog box | **Figure 3-33**

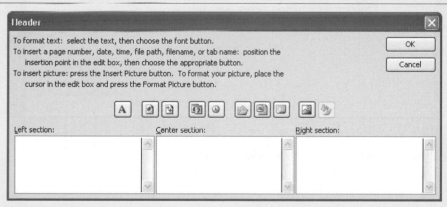

3. In the Left section box, type **Filename:** and then press the **spacebar**.

4. Click the **Filename** button to insert the format code. The formatting code for the name of the file "&[File]" appears after the text that you entered.

5. Click the **Right section** box, and then click the **Date** button. Excel inserts the &[Date] format code into the section box.

6. Click the **OK** button to close the Header dialog box, and then click the **Custom Footer** button to open the Footer dialog box, which duplicates the layout of the Header dialog box. Now you will create a footer that centers the page number and the total number of pages at the bottom of the printout.

7. Click the **Center section** box, type **Page**, press the **spacebar**, click the **Page Number** button 🔢, press the **spacebar**, type **of**, press the **spacebar**, and then click the **Total Pages** button 🔢. The text and codes in the Center section should appear as "Page &[Page] of &[Pages]"—which, if the worksheet was divided into five pages, would appear as "Page 1 of 5."

   Next, you will enter the workbook author in the right section of the footer.

8. Click the **Right section** box, type **Prepared by:**, press the **spacebar**, and then type your name.

9. Click the **OK** button to return to the Page Setup dialog box, which provides a preview of the custom header and footer that you created, and then click the **OK** button to return to Print Preview. As shown in Figure 3-34, the worksheet now is displayed with the new header and footer.

Figure 3-34 | **Preview of the custom header and footer**

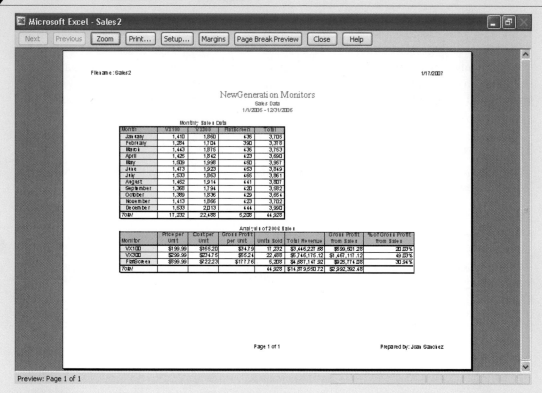

10. Click the **Close** button on the Print Preview toolbar.

Note that a header or footer is added only for the printed worksheet—not the entire workbook. You can define different headers and footers for each sheet in your workbook.

Working with the Print Area and Page Breaks

When you displayed the worksheet in the Print Preview window, how did Excel know which parts of the active worksheet you were going to print? The default action is to print all parts of the active worksheet that contain text, formulas, or values, which will not always be what you want. If you want to print only a part of the worksheet, you can define a **print area** that contains the content you want to print. To define a print area, you must first select the cells you want to print, and then select the Print Area command on the File menu.

A print area can include an adjacent range or nonadjacent ranges. You can also hide rows or columns in the worksheet in order to print nonadjacent ranges. For her report, Joan might decide against printing the sales analysis information. To remove those cells from the printout, you will define a print area that excludes the cells for the second table.

To define the print area:

1. Select the range **A1:H19**.

2. Click **File** on the menu bar, point to **Print Area**, and then click **Set Print Area**. Excel places a dotted black line around the selected cells of the print area. This is a visual indicator of what parts of the worksheet will be printed.

3. Click the **Print Preview** button 🔍 on the Standard toolbar. The Print Preview window displays only the first table. The second table has been removed from the printout because it is not in the defined print area.

4. Click the **Close** button on the Print Preview toolbar.

Another way to preview the print areas in your worksheet is through **page break preview**, which displays a view of the worksheet as it is divided up into pages. Anything outside of the print area is grayed out. Try previewing the contents of the Sales worksheet using page break preview.

To switch to page break preview:

1. Click cell **A1** to remove the selection.

2. Click **View** on the menu bar, and then click **Page Break Preview**. The workbook window adjusts to display the worksheet with any page break inserted in it and the Welcome to Page Break Preview dialog box, as shown in Figure 3-35. The dialog box serves to remind you that you can adjust the page breaks. A page number appears as a watermark on each page to be printed out. Notice that the second table is grayed out because it is not part of the printed area of the worksheet.

Figure 3-35   **Using Page Break Preview**

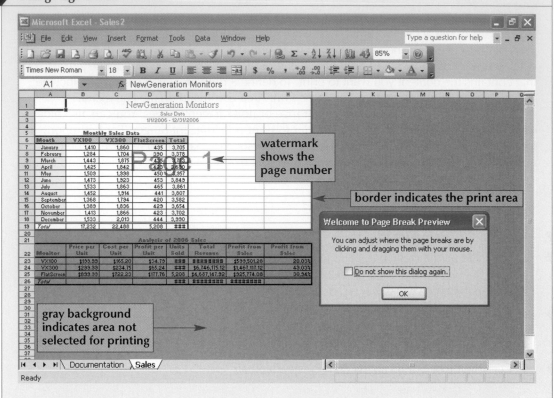

3. Click the **OK** button to close the dialog box before you change the dimensions of the printed area to include the other table.

4. Position the pointer at the bottom border of the print area (located at row 19) until the pointer changes to ↕, and then click the border and drag it down to row **26**. The print area has now been expanded to the cell range A1:H26.

   Trouble? If you are unsure of the location of the bottom border, click row 19 to make the border easier to see, and then repeat Step 3.

5. Click **View** on the menu bar, and then click **Normal** to switch back to Normal view.

Another approach that Joan might take is to place the two tables on separate pages. You can do this for her by inserting a **page break**, which forces Excel to place a portion of a worksheet on a new page. Before you insert a page break, you need to indicate where in the worksheet you want the break to occur. If you select a cell in the worksheet, the page break will be placed directly above and to the left of the cell. Selecting a row or a column places the page break directly above the row or directly to the left of the column. You will place a page break directly above row 20, which will separate the first sales table from the second.

To insert a page break:

1. Click row **20**, click **Insert** on the menu bar, and then click **Page Break**. Another black dotted line appears—this time above row 20, indicating there is a page break at this point in the print area.

▶ **2.** Click cell **A1** to remove the selection, click **View** on the menu bar, click **Page Break Preview**, and then click the **OK** button to close the Welcome to Page Break Preview dialog box. As shown in Figure 3-36, the second table will now appear on page 2 of the printout.

Inserting a page break ◀ **Figure 3-36**

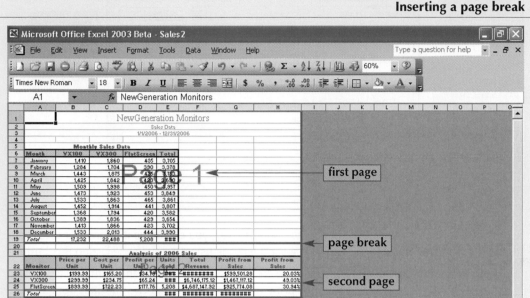

▶ **3.** Click **View** on the menu bar, and then click **Normal** to return to Normal view.

As Joan reviews the preview of the worksheet, she notices that the name of the company, "NewGeneration Monitors," and the two subtitles appear on the first page, but not on the second. That is not surprising because the range that includes the titles and subtitles is limited to the first page of the printout. However, Joan would like to have this information repeated on the second page.

You can repeat information, such as the company name, by specifying which cells in the print area should be repeated on each page. This is particularly useful in long tables that extend over many pages. In such cases, you can have the column titles repeated for each page of the printout.

To set rows or columns to repeat on each page, you will open the Page Setup dialog box from the worksheet window.

To repeat the first three rows on each page:

▶ **1.** Click **File** on the menu bar, click **Page Setup**, and then click the **Sheet** tab. The Sheet tab displays options you can use to control how the worksheet is printed. Note that the print area you have defined is already entered into the Print area box. Because Joan wants the first three rows of the worksheet to be repeated on each printed page, you will have to select them.

▶ **2.** Click the **Rows to repeat at top** box, move your pointer over to the worksheet, and then click and drag over the range **A1:A3**. A flashing border appears around the first three rows in the worksheet. This is a visual indicator that the contents of the first three rows will be repeated on all pages of the printout. In the Rows to repeat at top box, the cell reference $1:$3 appears. See Figure 3-37.

Figure 3-37 | **Sheet tab of the Page Setup dialog box**

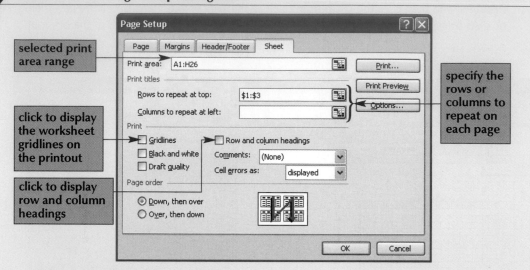

Trouble? If the Page Setup dialog box is in the way, you can move it to another location in the workbook window, or you can select the range using the Collapse Dialog Box button.

▶ 3. Click the **Print Preview** button, and then click the **Next** button on the Print Preview toolbar to display the second page of the printout. Now the title and two subtitles appear on this page as well. See Figure 3-38.

Figure 3-38 | **Second page of the printout**

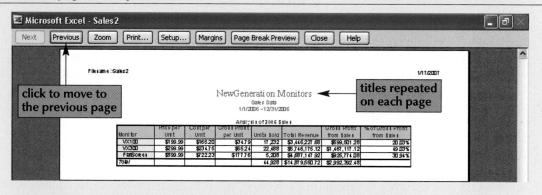

▶ 4. Click the **Print** button on the Print Preview toolbar, make sure the settings in the Print dialog box are correct, and then click the **OK** button.

For now, your work is done. When you save the workbook, your printing options are saved along with the file, so you will not have to re-create the print format in the future.

▶ 5. Save your changes to the workbook, and then close it.

Note that the Sheet tab also provides other options, such as the ability to print the worksheet's gridlines or row and column headings. You can also have Excel print the worksheet in black and white or draft quality. If there are multiple pages in the printout, you can indicate whether the pages should be ordered going down the worksheet first and then across, or across first and then down.

You show the final version of the workbook and the printout to Joan. She is very happy with the way in which you have formatted her report. She will spend some time going over the printout and will get back to you with any further changes she wants you to make.

Review

Session 3.2 Quick Check

1. Describe two ways of merging a range of cells into one.
2. How do you clear a format from a cell without affecting the underlying data?
3. How do you add a background image to the active worksheet?
4. To control the amount of space between the content on a page and its edges, you can adjust the page's _____.
5. By default, Excel prints what part of the active worksheet?
6. How do you define a print area? How do you remove a print area?
7. How do you insert a page break into your worksheet?

Review

Tutorial Summary

In this tutorial, you learned how to use Excel's formatting tools to design your worksheet. You saw how to quickly format cells using the buttons on the Formatting toolbar, and you learned how the Format Cells dialog box can give you even more control over the appearance of your worksheet. You saw how to create and edit cell borders using the Borders button and the Draw Borders button. You also learned how to change cell backgrounds using colors and patterns and external graphic files. The tutorial also demonstrated how to apply the formats in one cell range to another through the use of the Format and Replace dialog box and through styles. Finally, you learned how to format the appearance of your printed worksheet through the use of customized headers, footers, and print areas.

Key Terms

AutoFormat	General number format	point
font	gridline	print area
font size	header	sans serif font
font style	margin	serif font
footer	page break	style
Format Painter	page break preview	typeface
formatting		

Practice

Review Assignments

Practice the skills you learned in the tutorial using the same case scenario.

Data File needed for the Review Assignments: Region1.xls

Joan Sanchez has another report that she wants to format. The report displays regional sales for the three monitor brands you worked on earlier. As before, Joan wants to work on the overall appearance of the worksheet so the printout of the report is polished and professional looking. Figure 3-39 shows a preview of the worksheet you'll create for Joan.

Figure 3-39

	A	B	C	D	E	F	G
1		*NewGeneration Monitors*					
2		Regional Sales Report					
3		1/1/2006 - 12/31/2006					
4							
5	**Sales by Region**						
6	**Region**	**VX100**	**VX300**	**Flatscreen**	**Total**		
7	Northeast	1,723	2,248	520	4,491		
8	East	3,446	4,497	1,041	8,984		
9	Southeast	2,067	2,698	624	5,389		
10	Midwest	1,723	2,248	520	4,491		
11	Southwest	1,378	1,799	416	3,593		
12	West	4,308	5,622	1,302	11,232		
13	Canada	1,378	1,799	416	3,593		
14	Europe	861	1,124	260	2,245		
15	Asia	348	453	109	910		
16	**Total**	17,232	22,488	5,208	44,928		
17							
18	**Regional Analysis**						
19			**Region**	**Units Sold**	**Total Sales**	**Profit from Sales**	**% of Profit**
20		VX100	Domestic	14,645	$ 2,928,853	$ 509,499	17.03%
21			Foreign	2,587	$ 517,374	$ 90,001	3.01%
22			Total	17,232	$ 3,446,227	$ 599,500	20.03%
23		VX300	Domestic	19,112	$ 5,733,408	$ 1,246,866	41.67%
24			Foreign	3,376	$ 1,012,766	$ 220,250	7.36%
25			Total	22,488	$ 6,746,174	$ 1,467,116	49.03%
26		Flatscreen	Domestic	4,423	$ 3,980,655	$ 786,232	26.27%
27			Foreign	785	$ 706,492	$ 139,541	4.66%
28			Total	5,208	$ 4,687,147	$ 925,773	30.94%
29		Total	Domestic	38,180	$12,642,918	$ 2,542,598	84.97%
30			Foreign	6,748	$ 2,236,632	$ 449,793	15.03%
31			Total	44,928	$14,879,550	$ 2,992,391	100.00%
32							

To format the report:

1. Open the **Region1** workbook located in the Tutorial.03\Review folder included with your Data Files.
2. Enter your name and the current date in the Documentation sheet, and then save the workbook as **Region2** in the Tutorial.03\Review folder.
3. Switch to the Regional Sales worksheet.
4. Format the text in cell A1 with a 20-point, italicized, red, Times New Roman font. Format the text in cells A2 and A3 with a red font. Select the range A1:F3, and center the text across the selection. Do not merge the cells.
5. Select the range A5:E16, and then apply the List 2 format from the AutoFormat gallery.
6. Change the format of all values in the Sales by Region table to display a comma separator, but no decimal places. Resize column E to about 14 characters.
7. Change the format of the Units Sold values in the second table to display a comma separator, but no decimal places.
8. Indent the region names in the range A7:A15 by one character.
9. Display the text in cell A18 in bold.
10. Change the format of the values in the Total Sales and Profit from Sales columns to display a dollar sign on the left edge of the cell and no decimal places.
11. Change the format of the values in the % of Profit column to display a percent sign and two decimal places.
12. Allow the text in the range B19:F19 to wrap to a second line of text. Bold and center the text within each cell.

13. Merge and center the cells in the range A20:A22, and change the vertical text alignment to center. (*Hint*: Use the correct Text alignment option in the Format Cells dialog box to vertically align the text; see Figure 3-13.) Apply this format to the cells in the following ranges: A23:A25, A26:A28, and A29:A31.

14. Change the background color of the cells in the range A19:F19;A20:A31 to Sea Green (third row, fourth column of the color palette). Change the font color to white.

15. Change the background color of the cells in the range B20:F31 to white. Change the background color of the cells in the range B22:F22;B25:F25;B28:F28;B31:F31 to Light Green (fifth row, fourth column of the color palette).

16. Apply a thin black border to each of the cells in the range A19:F31.

17. Place a double line on the bottom border of the cells in the range B22:F22;B25:F25;B28:F28.

18. Set the print area as the range A1:F31. Insert a page break above row 18. Repeat the first three rows of the worksheet on every page of any printouts you produce from this worksheet.

19. Set up the page to print in portrait orientation with one-inch margins on all sides. Center the contents of the worksheet horizontally on the page.

20. Add a footer with the following text in the Left section box of the footer (with the date on a separate line): "Filename: *the name of the file*" and "Date: *current date*," and then the following text in the Right section box of the footer: "Prepared by: *your name*." In the Center section, place the text "Page *page_number* of *total_pages*" where *page_number* is the number of the page and *total_pages* is the total number of pages in the printout.

21. Add a header with the text "Regional Sales Report" displayed in the Center section using a 14-point Times New Roman font with a double underline. (*Hint*: Select the text in the Center section, and then click the Font button in the Footer dialog box to open the Format Cells dialog box.)

22. Preview the two-page worksheet, and then print it.

23. Save your changes to the workbook and then close it.

Case Problem 1

Apply

Use the skills you learned in this tutorial to format a worksheet that presents an annual sales report.

Data File needed for this Case Problem: Running1.xls

Jenson Sportswear Quarterly Sales Carol Roberts is the national sales manager for Jenson Sportswear, Inc., a company that sells sportswear to major department stores. She has been using an Excel worksheet to track the results of her staff's sales incentive program. She has asked you to format the worksheet so that it looks professional. She also wants a printout before she presents the worksheet at the next sales meeting. To complete this task:

1. Open the **Running1** workbook located in the Tutorial.03\Cases folder included with your Data Files, and then save the file as **Running2** in the same folder.

2. In the Documentation sheet, enter your name and the current date. Format the date so that it appears as *Weekday, Month Day, Year* where *Weekday* is the day of the week, *Month Day* is the name of the month and the day, and *Year* is a four-digit year.

Explore

3. Switch to the Sales worksheet, and then enter the formulas to calculate the following results:
   a. the totals for each product
   b. the quarterly subtotals for the Shoes and Shirts departments
   c. the totals for each quarter and the grand total

4. Using Figure 3-40 as a guide, format the worksheet with the following attributes:

Figure 3-40

	A	B	C	D	E	F
1		Jenson Sportswear, Inc.				
2		Sales Report				
3		1/1/2006 - 12/31/2006				
4						
5			Quarterly Sales by Product			
6	Shoes	Qtr1	Qtr2	Qtr3	Qtr4	Total
7	Running	2,250	2,550	2,650	2,800	10,250
8	Tennis	2,800	1,500	2,300	2,450	9,050
9	Basketball	1,250	1,400	1,550	1,550	5,750
10	Subtotal	6,300	5,450	6,500	6,800	25,050
11						
12	Shirts	Qtr1	Qtr2	Qtr3	Qtr4	Total
13	Tee	1,000	1,150	1,250	1,150	4,550
14	Polo	2,100	2,200	2,300	2,400	9,000
15	Sweat	250	250	275	300	1,075
16	Subtotal	3,350	3,600	3,825	3,850	14,625
17						
18	Grand Total	9,650	9,050	10,325	10,650	39,675

5. Create a style named "Subtotal" that is based on the font, border, and pattern formats found in the cell ranges B10:F10 and B16:F16.
6. Use the Page Setup dialog box to center the table both horizontally and vertically on the printed page and to change the page orientation to landscape.
7. Add the filename, your name, and the date on separate lines in the Right section box of the footer.
8. Preview the sales report and then print it.
9. Save your changes to the workbook and then close it.

Apply

Use the skills you have learned in this tutorial to format a revenue report for women-owned businesses.

Case Problem 2

Data File needed for this Case Problem: WBus1.xls

Wisconsin Department of Revenue Ted Crawford works for the Wisconsin Department of Revenue. Recently he compiled a list of the top 50 women-owned businesses in the state. He would like your help in formatting the report, in regard to both how it appears in the worksheet window and how it appears on the printed page. A preview of the worksheet you'll create is shown in Figure 3-41.

Figure 3-41

	A	B	C	D	E	F	G
1		Wisconsin's top 50 women-owned businesses					
2	Rank	Name	Sales	Employees	Year Founded	Line	
3	1	Jockey International	$ 450,000,000	500	1930	Manufacturing Clothing	
4	2	Astronautics	$ 425,000,000	1,400	1959	Manufacturing Flight & Electronic Equip.	
5	3	Pleasant Company	$ 74,000,000	280	1986	Mail Order Books, Dolls & Accessories	
6	4	Dawes Transport	$ 52,000,000	163	1981	Trucking	
7	5	East Capitol Drive Foods Inc.	$ 45,800,000	285	1984	Grocery Stores	
8	6	TSR Inc.	$ 40,000,000	140	1986	Manufacturing Toys & Games	
9	7	Ricom Electronics	$ 34,000,000	52	1982	Mail Order Consumer Electronics	
10	8	Rollette Oil Co.	$ 32,300,000	46	1960	Gasoline Service Stations	
11	9	Mainline Industrial Distributors	$ 31,000,000	125	1964	Industrial Equipment	
12	10	Mueller Graphics	$ 27,100,000	48	1982	Printing Equip. & Supplies	
13	11	Nor-Lake Inc.	$ 26,000,000	208	1947	Refrigeration & Heating Equip.	
14	12	V & J Foods	$ 25,000,000	1,200	1984	Restaurant	
15	13	Fuchs Holding Corporation	$ 24,000,000	103	1955	Trucking Firm	
16	14	O'Connor Oil Corporation	$ 18,600,000	110	1961	Petroleum Bulk Stations	
17	15	A. D. Schinner Co.	$ 17,000,000	34	1910	Distributor Packaging Products	
18	16	Pro-Track Corporation	$ 15,000,000	51	1982	Distributor Footwear	
19	17	Racine Travel Service Inc.	$ 15,000,000	36	1979	Travel Agencies	
20	18	Runzheimer International, Ltd.	$ 14,000,000	165	1933	Info-Management Consultant	
21	19	Triangle Wholesale	$ 14,000,000	55	1981	Distributor Liquor & Beer	

To complete this task:

1. Open the **WBus1** workbook located in the Tutorial.03\Cases folder included with your Data Files, and then save the file as **WBus2** in the same folder.
2. Enter your name and the current date in the Documentation sheet, and then switch to the Business Data worksheet.
3. Change the font in cell A1 to a boldface font that is 14 points in size. Merge and center the title across the range A1:F1.
4. Display the text in the range A2:F2 in bold, and then center the text in the range C2:F2. Place a double line on the bottom border of the range A2:F2.
5. Display the sales information in the Accounting format with no decimal places. Increase the width of the column, if necessary.
6. Display the employees' data using a comma separator with no decimal places.
7. Change the background color of the cells in the range A3:F3 to light green, and then change the background color of the cells in A4:F4 to white.
8. Use the Format Painter to apply the format found in the cell range A3:F4 to the cell range A5:F52.
9. Set up the worksheet page so it prints in landscape orientation with a bottom margin of 1.5 inches. Also, center the contents of the worksheet horizontally on the page.
10. Set the print area as the cell range A1:F52, and then repeat the first two rows of the worksheet in the printouts.

Explore

11. Remove the existing header and footer from the printed page. (*Hint*: Choose (none) from the list of available header and footer text to remove the previous header and footer text.) Insert a customized footer that displays the following text on three separate lines in the Right section box of the footer:
    Compiled by: *your name*
    current date
    Page *page number* of *total number of pages*

Explore

12. Fit the worksheet on a printout that is one page wide and two pages tall.
13. Preview the worksheet, and then print it.
14. Save your changes to the workbook, and then close it.

Case Problem 3

Data File needed for this Case Problem: Blades1.xls

Sales Report at Davis Blades   Andrew Malki is a financial officer at Davis Blades, a leading manufacturer of roller blades. He has recently finished entering data for the yearly sales report. Andrew has asked you to help him with the design of the main table in the report. A preview of the format you will apply is shown in Figure 3-42.

Challenge

Using Figure 3-42 as your guide, challenge yourself by experimenting with more formatting techniques to enhance a worksheet presenting regional sales figures.

Figure 3-42

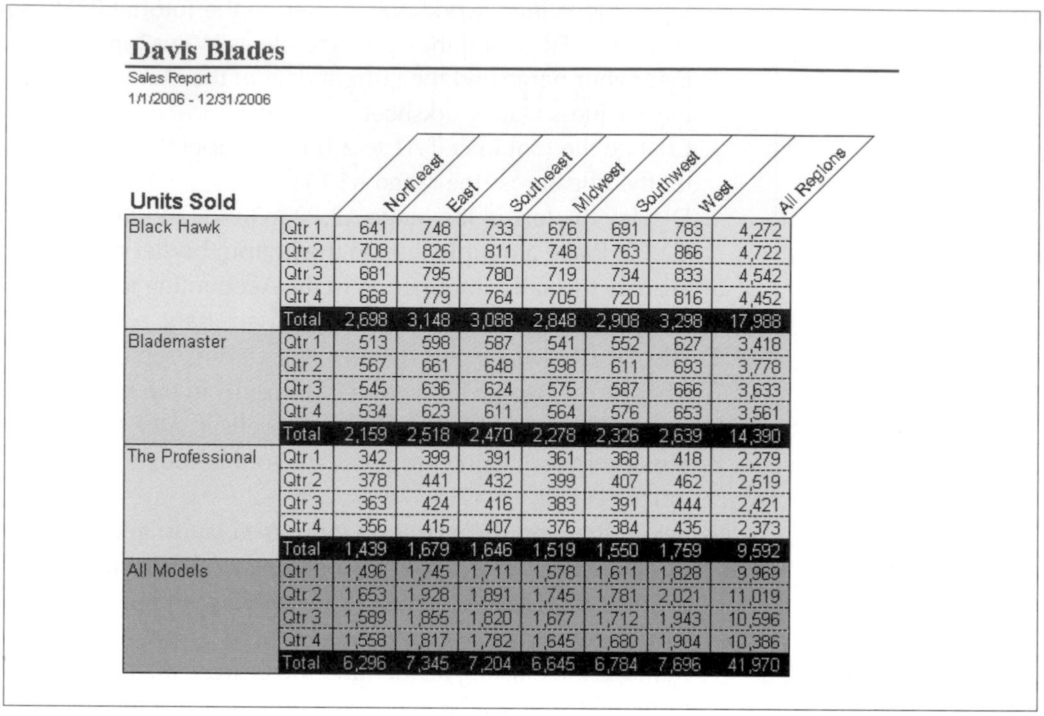

Davis Blades
Sales Report
1/1/2006 - 12/31/2006

Units Sold		Northeast	East	Southeast	Midwest	Southwest	West	All Regions
Black Hawk	Qtr 1	641	748	733	676	691	783	4,272
	Qtr 2	708	826	811	748	763	866	4,722
	Qtr 3	681	795	780	719	734	833	4,542
	Qtr 4	668	779	764	705	720	816	4,452
	Total	2,698	3,148	3,088	2,848	2,908	3,298	17,988
Blademaster	Qtr 1	513	598	587	541	552	627	3,418
	Qtr 2	567	661	648	598	611	693	3,778
	Qtr 3	545	636	624	575	587	666	3,633
	Qtr 4	534	623	611	564	576	653	3,561
	Total	2,159	2,518	2,470	2,278	2,326	2,639	14,390
The Professional	Qtr 1	342	399	391	361	368	418	2,279
	Qtr 2	378	441	432	399	407	462	2,519
	Qtr 3	363	424	416	383	391	444	2,421
	Qtr 4	356	415	407	376	384	435	2,373
	Total	1,439	1,679	1,646	1,519	1,550	1,759	9,592
All Models	Qtr 1	1,496	1,745	1,711	1,578	1,611	1,828	9,969
	Qtr 2	1,653	1,928	1,891	1,745	1,781	2,021	11,019
	Qtr 3	1,589	1,855	1,820	1,677	1,712	1,943	10,596
	Qtr 4	1,558	1,817	1,782	1,645	1,680	1,904	10,386
	Total	6,296	7,345	7,204	6,645	6,784	7,696	41,970

To complete this task:

1. Open the **Blades1** workbook located in the Tutorial.03\Cases folder included with your Data Files, and then save the file as **Blades2** in the same folder.
2. Enter your name and the current date in the Documentation sheet, and then switch to the Sales worksheet.
3. Change the font of the title in cell A1 to a 16–point, dark blue, boldface, Times New Roman font. Change the subtitles in cells A2 and A3 to an 8-point, blue font. Reduce the height of row 2 and row 3 to 12 characters.
4. Add a solid black bottom border to the range A1:K1.
5. Format the text in cell A5 in a 12-point, blue, Arial font. Vertically align the text in this cell with the bottom of the cell.

Explore

6. Merge the cells in the range A6:A10, and align the contents of the cell vertically at the top of the cell. Repeat this for the following ranges: A11:A15, A16:A20, and A21:A25.
7. Change the background color of the cell range A6:I10 to light yellow. Change the background color of the range A11:I15 to light green. Change the background color of the range A16:I20 to light turquoise. Change the background color of the range A21:I25 to pale blue.
8. Reverse the color scheme for the subtotal values in the range B10:I10, so that instead of black on light yellow, the font color is light yellow on a black background. Reverse the subtotal values for the other products in the table.
9. Apply the borders, as shown in Figure 3-42, to the cells in the range A6:I25.

Explore

10. Rotate the column titles in the range C5:I5 by 45 degrees. Align the contents of each cell along the bottom-right corner of the cell. Change the background color of these cells to white, and then add a border to each cell.

Explore

11. Open the Options dialog box from the Tools menu. Deselect the Row & column headings and Gridlines options to remove the row and column headings and grid-lines from the Sales worksheet window.

12. Set the print area as the range A1:K25.
13. Leave the page orientation as portrait, but center the worksheet horizontally on the page.
14. Create a custom footer with the text "Filename: *the name of the file*" left-aligned and with the text "Prepared by: *your name*" and "*the current date*" right-aligned, with your name and date on separate lines.
15. Preview the worksheet and then print it.
16. Save your changes to the workbook and then close it.

Create

Using Figure 3-43 as a guide, test your knowledge of formatting by creating your own design for a payroll worksheet.

Case Problem 4

There are no Data Files needed for this Case Problem.

Oritz Marine Services Vince DiOrio is an information systems major at a local college. He works three days a week at a nearby marina, Oritz Marine Services, to help pay for his tuition. Vince works in the business office, and his responsibilities range from making coffee to keeping the company's books.

Recently, Jim Oritz, the owner of the marina, asked Vince if he could help computerize the payroll for the employees. He explained that the employees work a different number of hours each week at different rates of pay. Jim now does the payroll manually, and finds it time consuming. Moreover, whenever he makes an error, he is annoyed at having to take the additional time to correct it. Jim is hoping that Vince can help him.

Vince immediately agrees to help. He tells Jim that he knows how to use Excel and that he can build a worksheet that will save him time and reduce errors. Jim and Vince meet to review the present payroll process and discuss the desired outcome of the payroll spreadsheet. Figure 3-43 displays the type of information that Jim records in the spreadsheet.

Figure 3-43

Employee	Hours	Pay Rate	Gross Pay	Federal Withholding	State Withholding	Total Deductions	Net Pay
Bramble	16	9.50					
Cortez	30	10.50					
DiOrio	25	12.50					
Fulton	20	9.50					
Juarez	25	12.00					
Smiken	10	9.00					
Smith	30	13.50					
Total							

To complete this task:

1. Create a new workbook named **Payroll1**, and save it in the Tutorial.03\Cases folder included with your Data Files.
2. Name two worksheets "Documentation" and "Payroll," and then delete the third sheet.
3. On the Documentation sheet, include the name of the company, your name as the author of the workbook, the date the workbook is being created, and a brief description of the purpose of the workbook.
4. On the Payroll worksheet, enter the payroll table shown in Figure 3-43.

5. Enter the formulas to calculate total hours, gross pay, federal withholding tax, state withholding tax, total deductions, and net pay, using the following information:
   a. Gross pay is equal to the number of hours multiplied by the pay rate.
   b. Federal withholding tax is equal to 15% of the gross pay.
   c. State withholding tax is equal to 4% of the gross pay.
   d. Total deductions are the sum of federal and state withholdings.
   e. Net pay is equal to the difference between the gross pay and the total amount of deductions.
6. Format the appearance of the payroll table using the techniques you learned in this tutorial. The appearance of the payroll table is up to you; however, do not use an AutoFormat design to format the table.
7. Format the printed page, setting the print area and inserting an appropriate header and footer. Only a few employees are entered into the table at present. However, after Jim Oritz approves your layout, many additional employees will be added, which will cause the report to cover multiple pages. Format your printout so that the worksheet title and column titles appear on every page.
8. Preview your worksheet, and then print it. Save your changes.
9. Add the following new employees to the worksheet. The employee list should be in alphabetical order, so these new employees should be inserted at the appropriate places in the sheet:

Name	Hours	Pay Rate
Carls	20	10.50
Lopez	35	11.50
Nelson	20	9.50

10. Preview the revised worksheet, and then print it.
11. Save this revised workbook as **Payroll2** in the Tutorial.03\Cases folder, and then close the workbook.

Research

Use the Internet to find and work with data related to the topics presented in this tutorial.

Internet Assignments

The purpose of the Internet Assignments is to challenge you to find information on the Internet that you can use to work effectively with this software. The actual assignments are updated and maintained on the Course Technology Web site. Log on to the Internet and use your Web browser to go to the Student Online Companion for New Perspectives Office 2003 at **www.course.com/np/office2003**. Click the Internet Assignments link, and then navigate to the assignments for this tutorial.

Assess

SAM Assessment and Training

If you have a SAM user profile, you may have access to hands-on instruction, practice, and assessment of the skills covered in this tutorial. Log in to your SAM account and go to your assignments page to see what your instructor has assigned.

Review

Quick Check Answers

Session 3.1

1. Click the Currency Style button on the Formatting toolbar; or click Format on the menu bar, click Cells, click the Number tab, and then select Currency from the Category list box.
2. a. 5.8%
   b. $0.06
3. Format Painter button and Copy button
4. Increase the width of the column; decrease the font size of the text; or select the Shrink to fit check box or the Wrap text check box on the Alignment tab in the Format Cells dialog box.
5. Select the range, click Cells on the Format menu, click the Alignment tab, and then select Center Across Selection in the Horizontal list box.
6. Use the Borders button on the Formatting toolbar; use the Draw Borders button in the Border gallery; or click Cells on the Format menu, click the Border tab, and then choose the border options in the dialog box.
7. Click Cells on the Format menu, click the Patterns tab, click the Pattern list arrow, and then select the pattern type and color.

Session 3.2

1. Select the cells and either click the Merge and Center button on the Formatting toolbar; or click Cells on the Format menu, click the Alignment tab, and then click the Merge cells check box.
2. Select the cell, click Edit on the menu bar, point to Clear, and then click Formats.
3. Click Format on the menu bar, point to Sheet, and then click Background. Locate and select an image file to use for the background, and then click the Insert button.
4. margins
5. Excel prints all parts of the active worksheet that contain text, formulas, or values.
6. To define a print area, select a range in the worksheet, click File on the menu bar, point to Print Area, and then click Set Print Area. To remove a print area, point to Print Area on the File menu, and then click Clear Print Area.
7. Select the first cell below the row at which you want to insert the page break, and then select Page Break on the Insert menu.

Objectives

Working with Charts and Graphics

Charting Sales Data

Case

Vega Telescopes

Alicia Kendall is a sales manager at Vega Telescopes, one of the leading manufacturers of telescopes and optics. She has been asked to present information on last year's sales for four of Vega's most popular telescopes: the 6- and 8-inch BrightStar and the 12- and 16-inch NightVision. Her presentation will be part of a sales conference that will be held next week in Charlotte, North Carolina.

As part of her presentation, Alicia would like to include a report that shows the sales figures for each model in the United States, Europe, and Asia. She knows that this kind of information is often best understood when presented visually, that is, in a graphical or pictorial form. She would like to use a column chart to show the sales data and a pie chart to show how each model contributes to Vega's overall sales of these four popular telescope models. Alicia is especially interested in making the charts visually appealing, and she wants to draw attention to the top-selling telescope model. She also will need printouts of the charts.

Alicia has asked you to help her create charts that will clearly and effectively present the sales data. Your task is to format the charts and individual chart components to enhance the presentation of the data, which will help Alicia explain and highlight the data at the sales conference. You will also add a drawing object that points out the top-selling telescope, and you will print the completed charts.

Student Data Files

▼ **Tutorial.04**

▽ **Tutorial folder**	▽ **Review folder**	▽ **Cases folder**
Space.jpg	VegaUSA1.xls	CIC1.xls
Vega1.xls		Powder1.xls
		Pixal1.xls

Session 4.1

Excel Charts

Alicia's sales data has already been entered into a workbook for you. You will begin by opening the workbook so you can examine the sales data.

To open Alicia's workbook:

▶ **1.** Start Excel and then open the **Vega1** workbook located in the Tutorial.04\Tutorial folder included with your Data Files.

▶ **2.** Enter *your name* and the *current date* in the Documentation sheet.

▶ **3.** Save the workbook as **Vega2** to the Tutorial folder, and then switch to the Sales worksheet to view the sales data as shown in Figure 4-1.

| Figure 4-1 | Sales worksheet for Vega Telescopes |

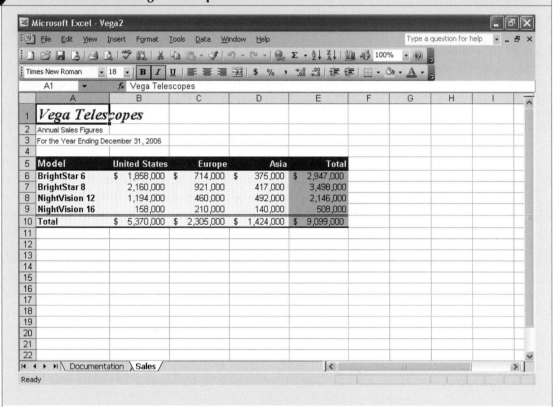

The Sales worksheet shows the annual sales, in U.S. dollars, for each of the four Vega telescope models. The sales data is broken down by world regions. As Alicia has explained, she wants two charts. The first chart should show the sales for each telescope in each region represented by columns, in which the height of the column represents the sales volume for each model. The second should be a pie chart that interprets how the total sales of each telescope model relate to overall sales. Sketches of the charts Alicia wants to create are shown in Figure 4-2.

Sketch of column and pie charts ◄ **Figure 4-2**

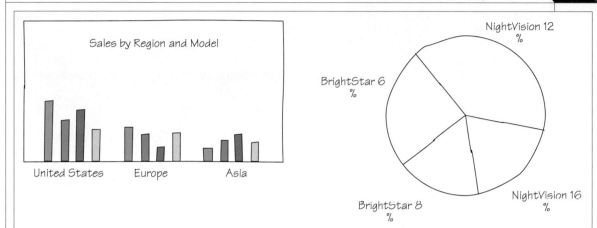

Charts, also known as graphs, provide a visual representation of the workbook data. Using charts, one can often see trends in the data that are more difficult to detect by viewing the raw numbers in a table. A chart can also be used to highlight items of interest, such as a region with low sales or an unexpectedly good sales month. Excel makes it easy to create charts through the use of the **Chart Wizard**, a series of dialog boxes that prompt you for information about the chart you want to create. This includes information such as the chart type, the cell range that the chart is based on, and features that the chart will contain. You will use the Chart Wizard to create the first chart that Alicia sketched for you—the column chart of the sales figures broken down by region and telescope model.

Creating a Chart Using the Chart Wizard

The Chart Wizard is a series of four dialog boxes, and each one is a step in the process of creating your chart. At each point in the process, you provide more detailed information about the chart you want Excel to create. Figure 4-3 describes the four steps in the Chart Wizard.

Tasks performed in each step of the Chart Wizard ◄ **Figure 4-3**

Dialog Box	Task Options
Chart Type	Select from list of available chart types and corresponding sub-types, or choose to customize a chart type
Chart Source Data	Specify the cells that contain the data on which the chart will be based and the cells that contain the labels that will appear in the chart
Chart Options	Change the appearance of the chart by selecting the options that affect titles, axes, gridlines, legends, data labels, and data tables
Chart Location	Specify where the chart will be placed: embedded as an object in the worksheet containing the data or on a separate worksheet, also called a chart sheet

You can stop the Chart Wizard at any time, and Excel will complete the remaining dialog boxes for you using the default specifications for the chart you have chosen.

Reference Window

Creating a Chart Using the Chart Wizard

- Select the data you want to chart.
- Click the Chart Wizard button on the Standard toolbar.
- In the first step of the Chart Wizard, select the chart type and sub-type, and then click the Next button.
- In the second step, make any modifications or additions to the chart's data source, and then click the Next button.
- In the third step, make any modifications to the chart's appearance, and then click the Next button.
- In the fourth step, specify the location for the chart, and then click the Finish button.

Before starting the Chart Wizard, you can select the cell range that contains the data that will be used in the chart. If you don't select a cell range, the Chart Wizard will "guess" at the cell range. If the selected range isn't correct, you can select the correct cell range as you work with the Chart Wizard. To create the first chart that Alicia wants, you'll select the data in the cell range A5:D9. The range needs to include both the labels and the sales figures for each telescope model. You will not include the total sales within each region.

To start the Chart Wizard:

1. Select the range **A5:D9**.

2. Click the **Chart Wizard** button on the Standard toolbar. The first step of the Chart Wizard is shown in Figure 4-4.

Figure 4-4 Step 1 of the Chart Wizard

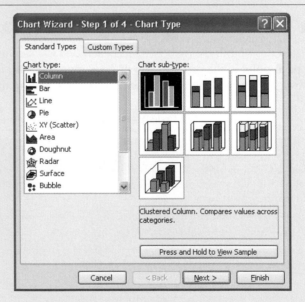

Choosing a Chart Type

The first step of the Chart Wizard provides the chart types, from which you choose the one that you feel will best display the data you want to plot. Excel supports 14 types of charts, ranging from the column chart, similar to the one shown in Alicia's first sketch, to stock market charts that can be used to record the daily behavior of stocks. Figure 4-5 provides information about some of the chart types. The charts are useful in different situations. When you want to compare the values from different categories (such as the sales of different telescope models), you will want to use a column, bar, or line chart. If you want to compare the values of individual categories to a whole collection of categories, you will want to use either a pie chart or a doughnut chart. If your data doesn't contain categories and you want to compare one set of numeric values with another, you will probably want to create an XY Scatter (scatter) chart or a bubble chart. Finally, for stock market data, you can use an Excel stock chart.

Excel chart types | **Figure 4-5**

Icon	Chart Type	Description
	Column	Compares values from different categories. Values are indicated by the height of the columns.
	Bar	Compares values from different categories. Values are indicated by the length of the bars.
	Line	Compares values from different categories. Values are indicated by the height of the line. Often used to show trends and changes over time.
	Pie	Compares relative values of different categories to the whole. Values are indicated by the size of the pie slices.
	XY (scatter)	Shows the patterns or relationship between two or more sets of numeric values. Often used in scientific studies and statistical analyses.
	Area	Similar to the line chart, except that areas under the lines are filled with colors indicating the different categories.
	Doughnut	Similar to the pie chart, except that it can display multiple sets of data.
	Radar	Compares a collection of values from several different data sets.
	Surface	Compares three sets of values in a three-dimensional chart.
	Bubble	Similar to the XY (scatter) chart, except the size of the data marker is determined by a third numeric value.
	Cylinder, Cone, Pyramid	Similar to the column chart, except that cylinders, cones, and pyramids are used in place of columns.

Each chart type has its own collection of sub-types that provide an alternative format for the chart's appearance. For example, the column chart type has seven different sub-types, including the clustered column and the stacked column. There are also 3-D, or three-dimensional, sub-types.

Finally, Excel also supports 20 additional "custom" chart types with additional formatting options. Some of the custom charts actually combine the properties of two or more of the main chart types. You can also create your own customized chart designs and add them to the custom chart list.

Alicia wants you to create a column chart for the sales data, in which values are arranged into separate columns. To see whether the chart you are creating is the right one, you will click the button in the first dialog box that lets you preview the chart before continuing with the Chart Wizard.

To select the chart type and preview it:

▶ 1. Verify that the **Column** chart type is selected in the Chart type list box and that the first sub-type, **Clustered Column**, is also selected.

▶ 2. Press the **Press and Hold to View Sample** button, but do not release the mouse button. A preview of the selected chart is displayed, as shown in Figure 4-6.

| Figure 4-6 | Preview of the clustered column chart |

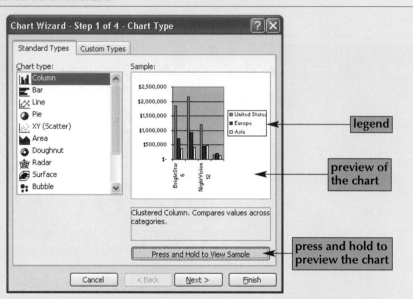

The Chart Wizard has assigned a different colored column to represent the sales values within each region. The legend on the right identifies the regions. The blue columns represent the United States, the maroon columns represent Europe, and the yellow columns represent Asia. Though the size of the Sample pane prevents you from viewing much of the chart's detail, you can see that the columns are clustered into groups; each group represents a different model. The first cluster represents sales for the BrightStar 6 telescope. The second cluster represents sales for the BrightStar 8 and so forth. Because this is the chart type that Alicia wants you to create, you can continue to the next step of the Chart Wizard.

▶ 3. Release the mouse button, and then click the **Next** button to go to step 2 of the Chart Wizard.

Choosing a Data Source

In the second step of the Chart Wizard, shown in Figure 4-7, you specify the **data source** for the chart, indicating the cell range that contains the chart's data. Excel organizes the data source into a collection of **data series**, where each data series is a range of data values that is plotted as a unit on the chart. In the case of this column chart, each data series contains the sales values of each sales region. A data series consists of **data values**, which are plotted on the chart's vertical axis, or **y-axis**. On the horizontal axis, or **x-axis**, are the data series' **category values**, or **x values**. In this chart, the data values are the sales values and the category values are the names of the different telescope models.

Specifying the data source   **Figure 4-7**

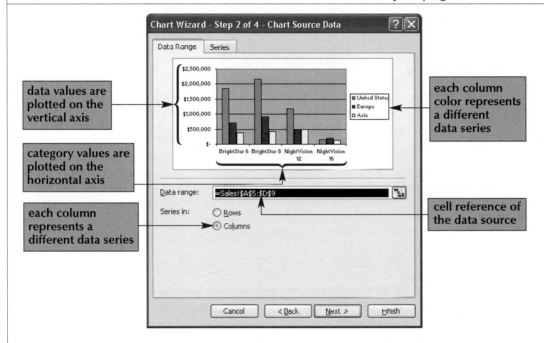

In this case, the Chart Wizard has organized the data source by columns, so that the leftmost column contains the category values and the subsequent columns each contain a different data series. The first row of the data contains the labels that identify each data series. In general, if the data spans more rows than columns, then the Chart Wizard interprets the data series by columns; otherwise, the Chart Wizard interprets the data series by rows.

In Alicia's sketch, she has indicated that she wants the name of the region to be the category value, which means that each telescope model represents a different data series. Therefore, you need to ensure that the Chart Wizard organizes the data source by rows and not columns. The first row will contain the category values, and each subsequent row will contain a data series. The first column will then contain the labels of each series.

To organize the data source by rows:

▶ 1. Click the **Rows** option button. Excel changes the orientation of the data source. The category values now represent the three regions rather than the four telescope models. See Figure 4-8.

Figure 4-8   Changing the orientation of the data source

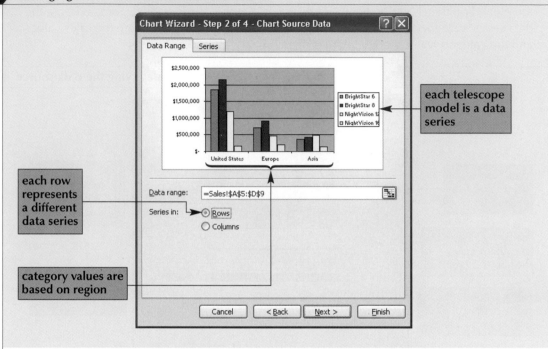

You can further define the data range using the Series tab. From this tab, you can add or remove individual data series from the chart or change the category values. Although it is recommended that you select the data series before starting the Chart Wizard, it is not necessary because you can define all of the data series and chart values using the Series tab. However, selecting the data series first does save time. You will switch to the Series tab so you can view its options.

To view the Series tab:

▶ **1.** Click the **Series** tab. The Series tab lists all of the data series used in the chart and the corresponding cell references for the cell that contains the name of the data series, the cells that contain the values for the data series, and the cells the contain the category labels. Note that the cell references include the name of the sheet from which the values are selected. See Figure 4-9.

Series tab ◀ **Figure 4-9**

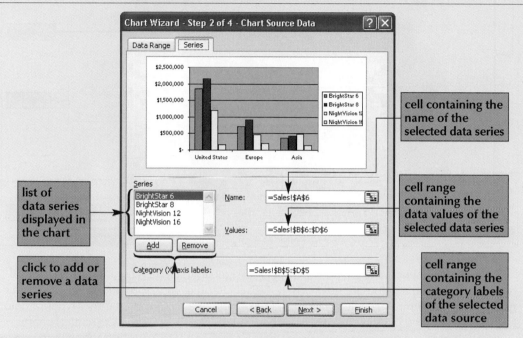

You do not have to make any changes in the data series at this point, so you will continue in the Chart Wizard.

▶ **2.** Click the **Next** button to go to step 3 of the Chart Wizard.

Choosing Chart Options

The third step of the Chart Wizard provides the options that you can use to control the appearance of the chart. To better understand the options available to you, first you'll explore the terminology that Excel uses with respect to charts. Figure 4-10 shows the elements of a typical Excel chart.

Figure 4-10 ▶ **Excel chart elements**

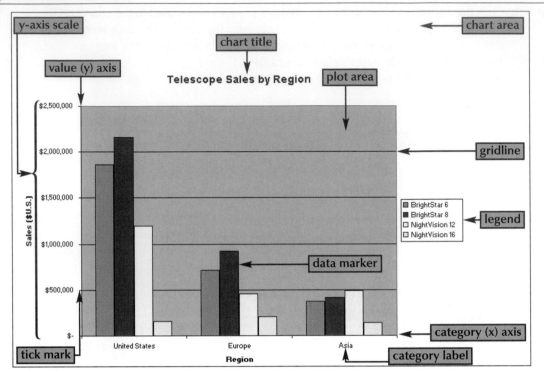

The basic element of the chart is the **plot area**, a rectangular area containing a graphical representation of the values in the data series. Each graphical representation is called a **data marker**. Each column in a column chart is an example of a data marker. Other types of data markers include the pie slices used in pie charts and the points used in XY (scatter) charts.

Most charts have two axes that border the plot area: an x-axis (or horizontal axis) and a y-axis (or vertical axis). As mentioned earlier, values from the data series are plotted along the y-axis, whereas the category labels are plotted along the x-axis. Each axis can have a title that describes the values or labels displayed on the axis. In Figure 4-10, the x-axis title is "Region" and the y-axis title is "Sales ($U.S.)."

The range of values that spans along an axis is called a **scale**. Excel automatically chooses a scale to match the range of values in the data series. In the chart shown in Figure 4-10, the scale of the y-axis ranges from $0 to $2,500,000. Next to the values on the scales are **tick marks**, which act like the division lines on a ruler, making it easier to read the scale. Your charts might also contain **gridlines**, which extend the tick marks across the plot area. Excel divides gridlines into two types. **Major gridlines** are the lines that extend the tick marks across the plot area; **minor gridlines** are the lines that divide the space between the major gridlines.

If your chart contains more than one data series, the chart will usually have a **legend** identifying the format of the data marker used for each series. Above the plot area, you can add a **chart title** to describe the contents of the plot area and the data series. The entire chart and all of the elements discussed so far are contained in the **chart area**.

You can format these various chart elements in the third step of the Chart Wizard. You can also format these features later on, after the chart has been created. As shown in Figure 4-11, step 3 of the Chart Wizard contains six tabs: Titles, Axes, Gridlines, Legend, Data Labels, and Data Table. Each tab provides tools for formatting different elements of your chart.

Step 3 of the Chart Wizard ◄ **Figure 4-11**

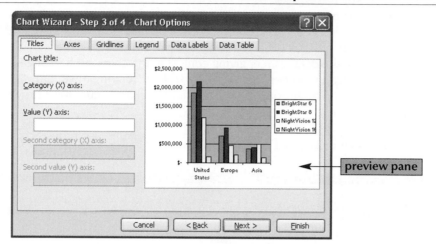

preview pane

Alicia wants you to add descriptive titles to the chart and to each of the axes. She also wants you to remove the gridlines because they are not necessary in such a simple, straightforward chart. Using the Titles and Gridlines tabs, you will make these changes now.

To insert titles into the chart:

1. Make sure that the **Titles** tab is active.

2. Click the **Chart title** text box, type **Telescope Sales by Region**, and then press the **Tab** key. The preview pane updates the chart image to reflect the addition of the chart title to the chart area.

3. Type **Region** in the Category (X) axis text box, and then press the **Tab** key.

4. Type **Sales ($U.S.)** in the Value (Y) axis text box, and then press the **Tab** key. The preview pane shows all of the new titles you entered into the chart.

5. Click the **Gridlines** tab.

6. Click the **Major gridlines** check box for the Value (Y) axis to remove the major gridlines from the chart.

7. Click the **Next** button to move to the last Chart Wizard dialog box, shown in Figure 4-12.

Step 4 of the Chart Wizard ◄ **Figure 4-12**

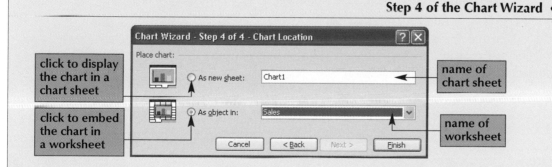

click to display the chart in a chart sheet

name of chart sheet

click to embed the chart in a worksheet

name of worksheet

Choosing the Chart Location

In the final step of the Chart Wizard, you choose a location for the chart. You can either create an embedded chart or a chart sheet. An **embedded chart** is a chart that is displayed within a worksheet. The advantage of creating an embedded chart is that you can place the chart alongside the data source, giving context to the chart. A **chart sheet** is a new sheet that is automatically inserted into the workbook, occupying the entire workbook window and thus providing more space and details for the chart. Figure 4-13 provides examples of each type of chart.

Figure 4-13 ▶ **Example of an embedded chart and a chart sheet**

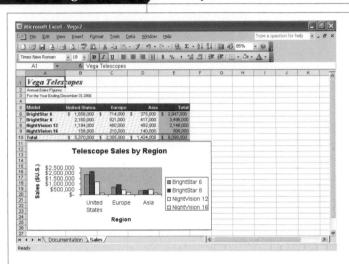
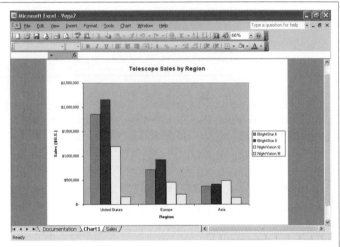

embedded chart in the Sales worksheet   chart sheet named "Chart1"

For this first chart, you'll embed the chart in the Sales worksheet.

To embed the clustered column chart in the Sales worksheet:

▶ **1.** Make sure that the **As object in** option button is selected and that **Sales** is selected in the adjacent list box.

▶ **2.** Click the **Finish** button. Excel creates the column chart with the specifications you selected and embeds the chart in the Sales worksheet, as shown in Figure 4-14.

Embedded column chart | **Figure 4-14**

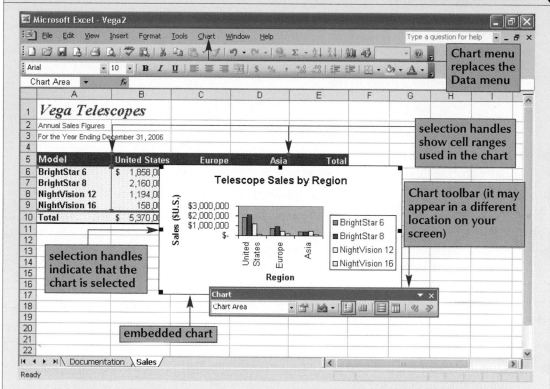

Trouble? If the Chart toolbar is not visible, it may have been closed during a previous Excel session. Click View on the menu bar, point to Toolbars, and then click Chart to redisplay the toolbar.

When the Chart Wizard creates the embedded chart, the chart appears with selection handles around it. The selection handles indicate that the chart is an **active chart** and is ready for additional formatting. The Chart toolbar also appears when the chart is selected. (Note that the Chart toolbar doesn't always appear when a chart is selected if the toolbar was closed in an earlier Excel session.) Another change that occurs is the Chart menu replaces the Data menu on Excel's menu bar. You will also find that certain Excel commands are not available to you when a chart is the active object in the workbook window. When a chart is not active, the default Excel menus return and the Chart toolbar disappears.

Try switching between the chart and the worksheet.

To switch between the embedded chart and the worksheet:

1. Click anywhere in the worksheet outside of the chart to deselect it. The Chart toolbar disappears and the Data menu replaces the Chart menu on the menu bar. There are no selection handles around the chart.

2. Move the pointer over a blank area of the chart so that the pointer changes to ⌖ and the ScreenTip "Chart Area" displays in the chart, and then click in the empty chart area. The Chart toolbar and the Chart menu reappear, and the selection handles appear around the chart.

   Trouble? If you clicked one of the chart's elements, you made that element active rather than the entire chart. Click a blank area in the chart to select the entire embedded chart.

Moving and Resizing an Embedded Chart

The Chart Wizard has a default size and location for embedded charts, which might not match what you want in your worksheet. In this case, the new chart is covering some of the data in the Sales worksheet and the chart titles seem to overwhelm the plot area. You will move the chart so you can see all of the sales data, and then you will make the chart a little larger to make it easier to read.

To move and resize the embedded chart:

1. Verify that the embedded chart is still selected, and then move the pointer over a blank area of the chart so that the pointer changes to ⌖ and the ScreenTip "Chart Area" displays.

2. Drag the embedded chart so that the upper-left corner of the chart aligns with the upper-left corner of cell A11. Note that as you drag the chart with the pointer, an outline of the chart area appears, which you can use as a guideline.

3. Release the mouse button when the chart is positioned correctly. The chart moves to a new location in the worksheet.

   To resize the chart, you drag a selection handle in the direction that you want the chart resized. To keep the proportions of the chart the same, press and hold the Shift key as you drag one of the corner selection handles.

4. Move your pointer over the lower-right selection handle until the pointer changes to ⤡.

5. Drag the lower-right corner of the embedded chart until that corner is aligned with the lower-right corner of cell F26.

6. Release the mouse button when the chart is resized, and then, if necessary, scroll the worksheet so the chart is visible. Figure 4-15 shows the chart, repositioned and resized.

Figure 4-15 ▶ **Embedded chart moved and resized**

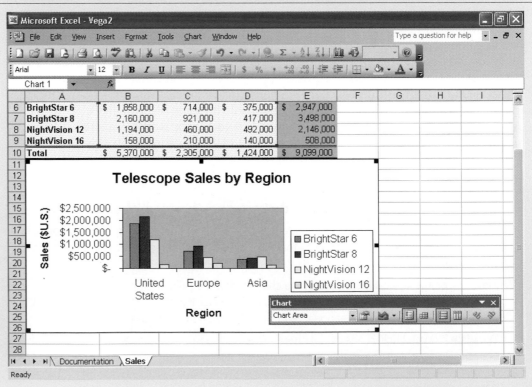

Updating a Chart

Every chart you create is connected to its data source. As a result, if you change values in the data source, Excel automatically updates the chart to reflect the change. This is true for category labels as well as for data values.

Alicia sees two changes that she would like you to make to the Sales worksheet. First, the European sales amount for the BrightStar 6 model should be $914,000, not $714,000. She also wants to change the label "United States" to "USA." You'll make these changes and observe how the embedded chart is automatically updated.

To update the column chart:

1. Scroll the worksheet so both the chart and the sales data are visible.

2. Click cell **C6**, type **914000**, and then press the **Enter** key. The data marker corresponding to European sales for the BrightStar 6 changes to reflect the new sales value.

3. Click cell **B5**, type **USA**, and then press the **Enter** key. The x-axis reflects the change to the category name.

Creating a Pie Chart

The second chart that Alicia sketched (shown in Figure 4-2) is a pie chart that shows the relative contribution of each telescope model to the total sales. In a pie chart, the size of each slice is determined by the relative value of a single data point to the sum of all values in the data series. Unlike the column chart you just created, a pie chart has only one data series, which is the total sales for each model from all regions.

To create the pie chart:

1. Select the nonadjacent range **A6:A9;E6:E9**, and then click the **Chart Wizard** button [icon] on the Standard toolbar. The first step of the Chart Wizard opens.

2. Click **Pie** in the Chart type list box, make sure that the first chart sub-type **Pie** is selected, and then click the **Next** button.

   Because you already selected the data series for the chart, which appears in columns, you do not have to make any changes, so you can bypass the second step of the Chart Wizard.

3. Click the **Next** button to move to the third step of the Chart Wizard. You will enter the chart title that Alicia wants in this dialog box.

4. Make sure that the **Titles** tab is active, click the **Chart title** text box, and then type **Total Telescope Sales**.

   Next you will add data labels to the chart that display the percentage of sales for each model.

5. Click the **Data Labels** tab, and then click the **Percentage** check box. The preview of the charts reflects the options you have chosen. See Figure 4-16.

Figure 4-16 Displaying percentage labels in a pie chart

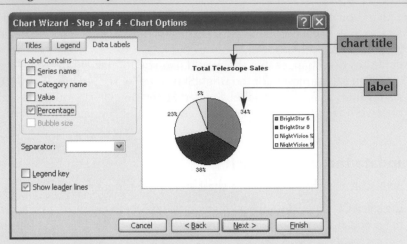

6. Click the **Next** button to display the final step of the Chart Wizard. You will place the pie chart in its own chart sheet and name the sheet "Pie Chart of Sales."

7. Click the **As new sheet** option button, and then type **Pie Chart of Sales** in the adjacent list box. The text you type in the text box will appear on the tab of the chart sheet.

8. Click the **Finish** button. Figure 4-17 shows the completed pie chart displayed on a chart sheet, which has been inserted before the Sales sheet. Note that the zoom magnification of the chart sheet on your screen might differ, depending on the settings and resolution of your monitor.

Figure 4-17 Pie chart of total telescope sales

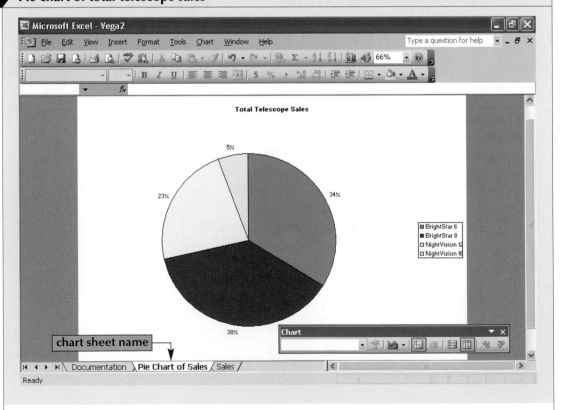

After reviewing the pie chart, Alicia has a few questions about the chart's appearance. She wonders why the slices are organized the way they are and whether the arrangement of the pie slices can be changed. The slices are arranged in a counterclockwise direction following the order that they appeared in the table. The first entry is for the BrightStar 6 telescope, the next is for the BrightStar 8, and so forth. Alicia asks whether it would be possible to move the placement of the BrightStar 6 telescope.

Rotating the Pie Chart

You cannot change the order in which the slices are arranged in the pie chart without changing their order in the data series, but you can rotate the chart. This is done by breaking the chart into 360-degree increments, starting from the top of the pie. Using this approach, the first slice starts at 0 degrees—a value that you can change. Based on Alicia's suggestion, you will change the starting point to 180 degrees, so that the first slice appears at the bottom of the pie chart.

To rotate the pie chart:

1. Double-click the pie chart to open the Format Data Series dialog box, and then click the **Options** tab.

2. Double-click the value in the Angle of first slice text box, and then click the **Degrees** up arrow to increase the angle of first slice value to **180**. As you click the up arrow, the pie chart in the preview pane rotates accordingly, as shown in Figure 4-18.

Rotating the pie chart 180 degrees   **Figure 4-18**

3. Click the **OK** button to close the dialog box.

Alicia tells you that the company is particularly interested in the sales performance of the BrightStar 6 telescope, because the company is considering replacing this scope with a six-inch version of the NightVision. Alicia has seen pie charts in which a single slice is removed from the others to give it greater emphasis. She wants the slice for the BrightStar 6 removed from the other slices to draw attention to this telescope.

Exploding a Slice of a Pie Chart

This method of emphasizing a particular pie slice over others is called separating or "exploding" the slice. An exploded slice is more distinctive because it is not connected to the other slices in the pie and it appears to be bigger. Excel allows you to explode any or all of the slices in the pie. A pie chart with one or more pie slices separated from the whole is referred to as an exploded pie chart.

Reference Window

Creating an Exploded Pie Chart

To explode one pie slice from a pie chart:
- Click the pie chart to select it, and then click the pie slice you want to explode.
- Drag the selected pie slice away from the rest of the pie, and then release the mouse button.

To explode all the pie slices in a pie chart:
- Click the pie chart to select it.
- Drag any pie slice to explode all the slices an equal distance apart, and then release the mouse button.

Next, you'll separate the BrightStar 6 telescope pie slice from the rest of the pie.

To explode the slice for the BrightStar 6 telescope:

1. Make sure that the pie chart is still selected, and then click the pie slice representing the total sales for the BrightStar 6. When you position the pointer over the pie slice, a ScreenTip appears with the corresponding worksheet cell information.

2. Drag the pie slice down and to the left. As you drag the pie slice, an outline marks your progress.

3. Release the mouse button, moving the slice into its new position. See Figure 4-19 for the location of the exploded pie slice.

Exploding a pie slice   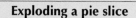 Figure 4-19

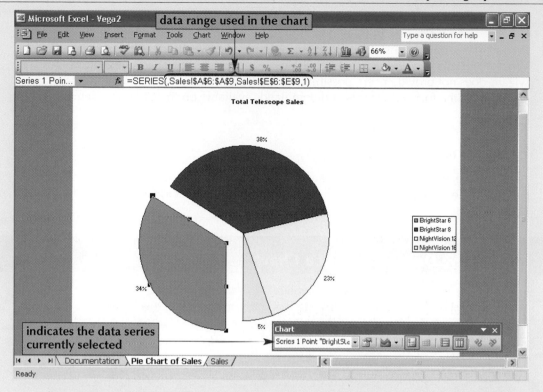

You have created the two charts that Alicia wanted, so you can save your work and then close the workbook and Excel.

4. Save your changes to the workbook, and then close it.

Rotating the pie and exploding a pie slice are both examples of formatting the appearance of an Excel chart after it has been created with the Chart Wizard. In the next session, you will learn about the other tools available that you can use to format the charts that you create.

Session 4.1 Quick Check

Review

1. What is the difference between a chart type and a chart sub-type?
2. Which chart would you most likely use to track the daily values of a stock?
3. What is a data series?
4. What is the difference between the plot area and the chart area?
5. What are gridlines?
6. Describe the two types of chart locations.
7. A chart that shows the relative contribution of each data value to the whole is called a(n) _____ chart.
8. A pie chart in which all slices are separated from one another is called a(n) _____ chart.

Modifying a Chart

In the last session, you used the Chart Wizard to create two charts. Although the Chart Wizard presents you with a variety of choices concerning your chart's appearance, the wizard does not provide every possibility. To make further modifications to your charts, you can use the formatting tools and commands available on the Chart toolbar and the Chart menu.

Editing the Data Source

After you create a chart, you can change the data that is used in the chart. You might need to change the data if you selected the wrong data or if you decide to display a different data series.

Reference Window	**Editing the Data Source of a Chart**

- Select the chart whose data source you want to edit.
- Click Chart on the menu bar, click Source Data, and then click the Series tab.
- To remove a data series, select the data series in the Series list box, and click the Remove button.
- To add a data series, click the Add button, and then select the cell references for the new data series.
- To revise a data series, select the data series in the Series list box, click the reference box for the data series, and then select a new cell reference.
- Click the OK button.

Alicia can see from the charts that 16-inch telescopes comprise a small portion of Vega's sales. For this reason, she wants you to remove the NightVision 16 from the two charts you created. You will begin by removing the NightVision 16 data series from the column chart.

To remove the NightVision 16 data series from the column chart:

1. If you took a break after the previous session, make sure that Excel is running and the Vega2 workbook is open.

2. Switch to the Sales worksheet, and then click the embedded column chart to select it.

3. Click **Chart** on the menu bar, and then click **Source Data**. The Source Data dialog box opens. Note that this dialog box is identical to the second dialog box in the Chart Wizard.

4. Click the **Series** tab, click **NightVision 16** in the Series list box, and then click the **Remove** button. The preview of the chart reflects the change you have made. See Figure 4-20.

Removing the NightVision 16 from the column chart ◄ **Figure 4-20**

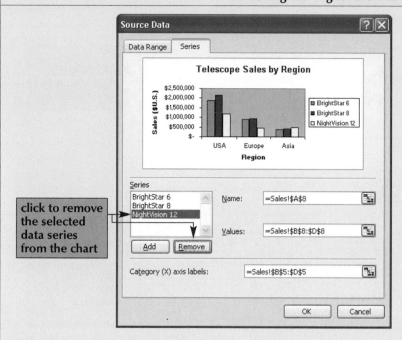

click to remove the selected data series from the chart

5. Click the **OK** button. The NightVision 16 sales data is no longer represented in the column chart.

Removing the NightVision 16 pie slice from the pie chart presents a slightly different challenge. Unlike the column chart (which has multiple data series), the pie chart has only one data series. To remove the NightVision 16 from the pie chart, you will have to change the cell reference of the chart's data source to exclude the NightVision 16 row.

To remove the NightVision 16 from the pie chart:

1. Switch to the Pie Chart of Sales worksheet.

2. Click **Chart** on the menu bar, click **Source Data** to open the Source Data dialog box, and then verify that the Series tab is selected. From this dialog box, you can see that the values for the data series are found in the cell range E6:E9 on the Sales worksheet and the category labels come from the range A6:A9 on the same sheet. You have to change these cell references to remove the NightVision 16 telescope from the chart.

3. Click the **Collapse Dialog Box** button for the Values reference box, select the range **E6:E8**, and then click the **Expand Dialog Box** button to redisplay the Source Data dialog box with the new value range.

4. Click the **Collapse Dialog Box** button for the Category Labels reference box, select the range **A6:A8**, and then click the **Expand Dialog Box** button to redisplay the Source Data dialog box. As shown in Figure 4-21, the preview pane displays the new pie chart with the NightVision 16 telescope excluded.

Figure 4-21 Removing the NightVision 16 from the pie chart

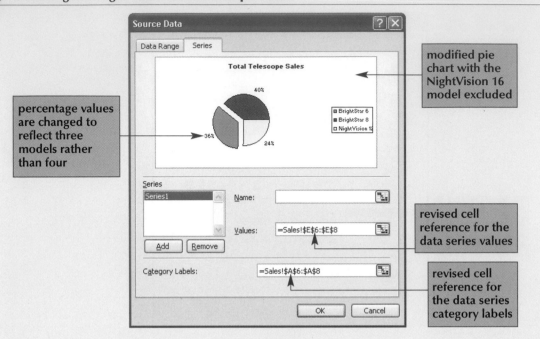

percentage values are changed to reflect three models rather than four

modified pie chart with the NightVision 16 model excluded

revised cell reference for the data series values

revised cell reference for the data series category labels

5. Click the **OK** button to save your changes to the chart.

Note that when you removed the NightVision 16 from the data series, the percentages in the pie chart changed as well to reflect a total sales figure based on only three models rather than four.

Changing the Chart Location

Alicia has decided that she prefers the chart sheet to the embedded chart. She wants you to move the embedded column chart on the Sales worksheet to a chart sheet. Rather than re-creating the chart using the Chart Wizard, you will use the Location command on the Chart menu. You will move the embedded chart to a chart sheet, which you will name "Column Chart of Sales."

To change the location of the embedded column chart:

1. Switch to the Sales worksheet, and then, if necessary, click the embedded column chart to select it.

2. Click **Chart** on the menu bar, and then click **Location**. The Chart Location dialog box opens. The dialog box is identical to the fourth dialog box in the Chart Wizard.

3. Click the **As new sheet** option button, type **Column Chart of Sales** as the name of the chart sheet, and then click the **OK** button. The column chart moves into its own chart sheet.

Changing Chart Options

As mentioned, the dialog boxes to change the chart's data source and location look identical to the dialog boxes for steps 2 and 4 of the Chart Wizard. Dialog boxes for the remaining two Chart Wizard steps are also available through commands on the Chart menu. Recall that the third step of the Chart Wizard allowed you to format the chart's appearance by adding or removing chart titles, gridlines, legends, and labels.

Alicia wants to revisit some of the chart options selected earlier. After seeing that the percent labels in the pie chart provided useful information, she wants you to add labels to the column chart displaying the actual sales values for each column. You will use the Chart Options dialog box to make this change.

To revise the chart options for the column chart:

1. Click **Chart** on the menu bar, and then click **Chart Options**. The Chart Options dialog box opens. Note that the dialog box is identical to step 3 of the Chart Wizard.

2. Click the **Data Labels** tab.

3. Click the **Value** check box, and then click the **OK** button. The sales figures for each model now appear above the corresponding column. See Figure 4-22. The values appear to be a little crowded, and you will change this next.

Adding labels to the columns | **Figure 4-22**

Alicia has a few changes that she wants you to make to the chart labels. You cannot make these changes by modifying the chart options. Instead, you have to format the individual elements within the chart.

Formatting Chart Elements

So far, all of the formatting that you have done has applied to the chart as a whole. You can also select and format individual chart elements, such as the chart title, legend, and axes. To select an individual chart element, you either click on the element or select the element's name from a drop-down list on the Chart toolbar. You can then use buttons on the Formatting toolbar or open a dialog box to modify the element's appearance. You can also double-click a chart element to both select it and open a dialog box or right-click the chart element and select a format from a shortcut dialog box.

In some cases, a chart element will be composed of several elements. For example, a data series will have several data markers. If you click on one data marker, you select all of the markers in the series. If you click that marker again, the selection is confined to that specific marker, removing the selection from other markers in the series. In this way, you can format all of the elements at once or confine your formatting to a specific element.

You'll have a chance to try these selection and formatting techniques in the steps that follow.

Formatting Chart Text

Alicia wants you to change the alignment of the data labels that appear above the columns. She feels that the labels would look better if you changed their alignment from horizontal to vertical. She would also like the labels to appear within and at the bottom of the columns themselves, so she suggests that you change the color of the data labels as well. You will make these changes by double-clicking the data label to open the Format Data Labels dialog box.

To format the data labels:

1. Double-click the data label **$1,858,000**, located above the first column in the chart. The Format Data Labels dialog box opens. The Format Data Labels dialog box has four tabs. You use the Font and Number tabs to change font-related options for text and values and to apply number formats to values as you did in the previous tutorial. You use the Patterns tab to change the fill color, patterns, and borders around labels. You use the Alignment tab to change the alignment of the text in the label.

   The $1,858,000 label is part of the set of labels for the BrightStar 6 data series. By double-clicking the first data label, you've selected all of the labels for this particular series. Any changes you make in this dialog box will apply to all of the labels for the BrightStar 6 sales data (but not for the labels in the other data series).

2. Click the **Font** tab, click the **Color** list box, and then click the **Yellow** square (fourth row, third column from the left) in the color palette.

   Trouble? If you are working with a black-and-white printer, select the White font color, located in the bottom-right corner of the color palette.

3. Click the **Alignment** tab.

4. In the Orientation section, change the value in the Degrees box to **90**. The text changes to a vertical orientation with an angle of 90 degrees.

5. Click the **Label Position** list arrow, and then select **Inside Base** to display the values label inside and at the base of each column in the chart. See Figure 4-23.

Changing the orientation of the data labels **Figure 4-23**

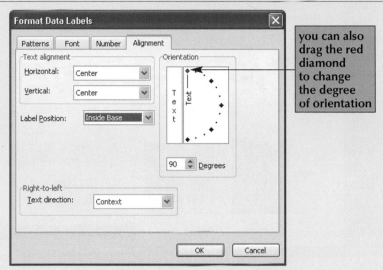

6. Click the **OK** button. The labels for the BrightStar 6 data series have been rotated 90 degrees and now appear in a yellow font at the base of the columns.

Next you'll make a similar change to the labels for the BrightStar 8 data series. Rather than double clicking the label, you'll use the shortcut menu.

7. Right-click the **$2,160,000** label above the second column in the chart, click **Format Data Labels** from the shortcut menu, and then repeat Steps 2 through 6 to change the label to a white font rotated 90 degrees and displayed at the inside base of each column.

Finally, you'll select the data labels for the NightVision 12 data series using the Chart toolbar.

8. Click the **Chart Objects** list arrow [   ] on the Chart toolbar, scroll down the list of options, click **"NightVision 12" Data Labels** to select this chart element, and then click the **Format Data Labels** button 📰 on the Chart toolbar.

9. Repeat Steps 3 through 6 to rotate the label to **90** degrees and display it at the inside base of each column. You don't have to change the color of the font.

10. Click the **OK** button to save your changes. Figure 4-24 shows the revised labels for all of the data series in the chart.

Figure 4-24 Revised data labels

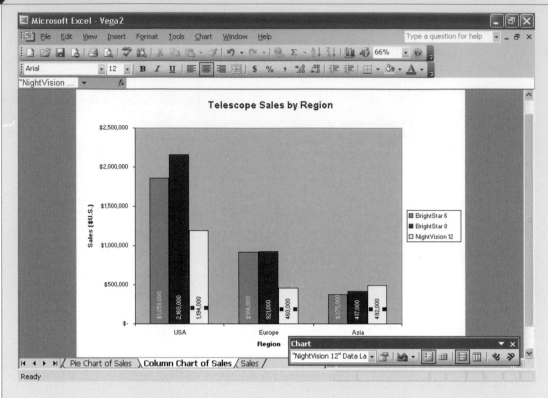

Next, Alicia wants you to add some additional text to the chart.

Inserting Unattached Text

Excel classifies chart text in three categories: label text, attached text, and unattached text. Label text includes the category names, the tick mark labels (which you've just worked with), and the legend text. Label text often is linked to cells in the worksheet. Attached text includes the chart title and the axes titles. Although the text appears in a predefined position, you can edit and move it. Unlike label text, attached text is not linked to any cells in the worksheet. Finally, unattached text is any additional text that you want to include in the chart. Unattached text can be positioned anywhere within the chart area and formatted with the same tools you use to format label and attached text.

To add unattached text to a chart, you type the text in the Formula bar. Excel automatically creates a text box for the text entry and places the text box in the chart area. You can then resize the text box and move it to another location in the chart area. You can format the text using the Format Text Box dialog box.

Inserting Unattached Text into a Chart

- Select the chart.
- In the Formula bar, type the text that you want to include in the chart.
- To resize the new unattached text box, click and drag one of the text box's selection handles.
- To move the unattached text box, click the border of the text box, and drag the text box to a new location in the chart area.
- To format the unattached text, select the text box and click the appropriate formatting buttons on the Formatting toolbar; or double-click the border of the text box to open the Format Text Box dialog box, use the options provided on the dialog box tabs, and then click the OK button.

Alicia wants you to add the text "Vega Sales from the Last Fiscal Year" to the upper-right corner of the plot area, and she wants the text to be ivory in color.

To add unattached text to the chart:

1. Click the column chart to select it, click in the Formula bar above the chart, type **Vega Sales from the Last Fiscal Year**, and then press the **Enter** key. Excel places a text box containing the new unattached text in the middle of the chart area. The text box is selected so you can modify its appearance.

2. Click the **Font Color** list arrow ![A] on the Formatting toolbar, and then click the **Ivory** square (sixth row, third column from the left) in the color palette.

3. Move the pointer over the edge of the unattached text box until the pointer changes to ↖, drag the text box to the upper-right corner of the plot area, and then release the mouse button. The text should now be placed in the upper-right corner of the plot.

You can double-click an unattached text box at any time to open the Format Text Box dialog box, in which you can change the font format, alignment, and color. You can also create a border around the text. Try this now by creating a yellow border.

To create a border for the text box:

1. Verify that the text box is still selected, and then double-click the border of the selected text box to open the Format Text Box dialog box.

   Trouble? If you double-clicked the text in the text box, the Format Text Box dialog box did not open. Try double-clicking the border of the text box again.

2. Click the **Colors and Lines** tab.

3. Click the **Color** list box in the Line section, click the **Ivory** square (sixth row, third column) in the color palette, and then click the **OK** button.

4. Click outside the chart to deselect it. Figure 4-25 shows the text box with the ivory border.

Figure 4-25   **Adding unattached text to a chart**

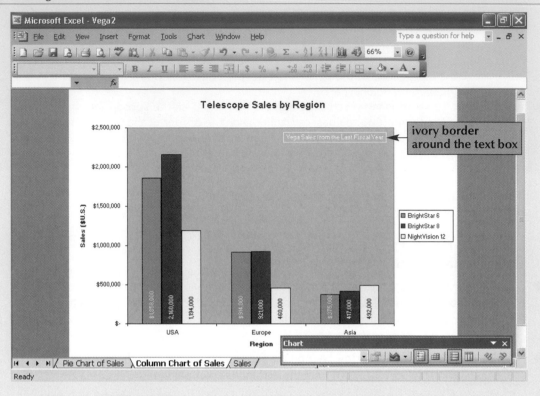

Now that you have formatted the chart labels and added unattached text, you can turn to some of the other features of Excel charts that need modifying.

Working with Colors and Fills

The formatted data labels and the unattached text help to clarify the sales data, but Alicia feels that the column chart lacks visual appeal. Alicia has seen objects filled with a variety of colors that gradually blend from one color to another. She wonders if you can do the same thing for the columns in the column chart. One idea she has is to make the columns appear more like tubes, such as telescope tubes.

When you want to fill a column (or area) in a chart with a pattern or color, you are actually modifying the appearance of the data marker in the chart. You will concentrate only on the fill color used in the data marker. Other data markers have other patterns that you can modify. For example, in an XY (scatter) chart, the data markers are points that appear in the plot. You can specify the color of those data points, their size, whether a line will connect the data points and, if so, the color, thickness, and style of that line.

You will format the data markers in the column chart beginning with the column that represents the BrightStar 6 telescope.

To format the fill color of the chart columns:

1. Double-click the first column on the left in the chart to open the Format Data Series dialog box for that data series. You can use the options available on the different dialog box tabs to control one or more aspects of the selected data marker. For example, you use the options provided on the Patterns tab to control the border style that appears around the column as well as the interior appearance of the column. Currently, the column is format-ted with a black border and filled with a pale-blue color.

2. Click the **Fill Effects** button to open the Fill Effects dialog box. The tabs in this dialog box provide a full range of options that you can use to create sophisticated and lush colors and patterns.

3. Make sure the **Gradient** tab is displayed in the dialog box.

You use the options on the Gradient tab to create fill effects that blend together different and varying amounts of color. Three color options are:

- **One color:** To create a blend that uses different shades of one color
- **Two colors:** To create a blend from one color into another
- **Preset:** To apply a predefined blend style, including Early Sunset, Nightfall, Ocean, Rainbow, and Chrome

You can also specify the direction of the blending effect, choosing from horizontal, vertical, diagonal up, diagonal down, from corner, and from center. For the selected column in the current chart, you will create a blend fill effect using a single color starting from a dark shade of the pale-blue color. You will use a vertical shading style to give the color dimension.

To create the fill effect:

1. Click the **One color** option button on the Gradient tab, and then drag the scroll box to the **Dark** end of the shading scale. Note that as you change the shading scale, the images in the Variants section reflect the degree of shading.

2. Click the **Vertical** option button in the Shading styles section. Now the images in the Variants section show the varying degrees of shading vertically.

3. Click the bottom-right Variants box, which shows the darker edges of the shading on the left and right edges of the object, as shown in Figure 4-26.

Specifying a fill effect   **Figure 4-26**

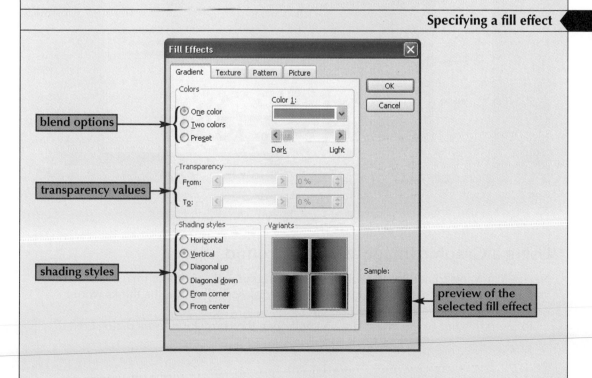

4. Click the **OK** button twice to close the dialog boxes and redisplay the chart. Excel displays the first column series with a dark-blue color on the left and right side of the column, giving it the illusion of appearing as a tube.

   Next you will create a similar blend for the other columns.

5. Double-click the second column from the left in the chart to open the Format Data Series dialog box.

6. Click the **Fill Effects** button to open the Fill Effects dialog box.

7. Click the **One color** option button, drag the scroll box to the **Dark** end of the shading scale, make sure the **Vertical** option button is selected, select the bottom-right Variants option, and then click the **OK** button twice.

8. Double-click the third column, and then repeat Steps 6 and 7 to create a one-color fill effect that goes from the dark end of the ivory scale to the light end.

9. Click outside the chart area. Figure 4-27 shows the revised column chart with blends for each of the three data series.

Figure 4-27 | **Columns with the applied fill effects**

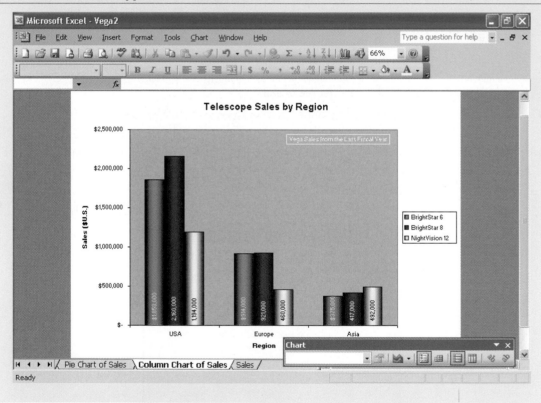

Using a Graphic Image as a Background

Next Alicia wants to replace the solid gray background with a graphic image. She has a graphic file that shows an image from the Hubble telescope, which she thinks would work well with the theme of telescope sales.

To insert this image into the chart, you will open the Format Plot Area dialog box.

To fill the plot area with an image:

▶ 1. Click the **Chart Objects** list arrow [   ] on the Chart toolbar, click **Plot Area**, and then click the **Format Plot Area** button 🖻 on the Chart toolbar. The Format Plot Area dialog box opens.

▶ 2. Click the **Fill Effects** button on the Patterns tab to open the Fill Effects dialog box.

▶ 3. Click the **Picture** tab, and then click the **Select Picture** button. The Select Picture dialog box opens.

▶ 4. Navigate to the Tutorial.04\Tutorial folder, select the **Space** file, and then click the **Insert** button. The image appears in the Fill Effects dialog box.

▶ 5. Click the **OK** button twice to close the dialog boxes, and then click outside the chart area. Figure 4-28 shows the revised column chart with the new background image.

Chart with space background image ◄ **Figure 4-28**

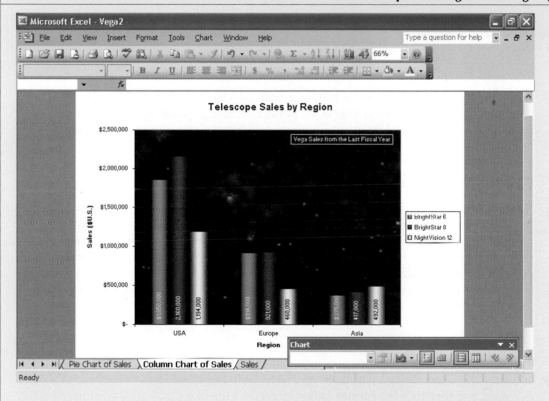

Graphic images can be applied to other elements in the chart. For example, you can replace the data markers in the chart with graphic images. To do this, select the data markers and open the Fill Effects dialog box that you used to create a background image for the chart. Select the image file that you want to use in place of the data marker. If you are working with a column chart, you can also choose to either stack or stretch the chosen image to the height of the column. Figure 4-29 shows the effect of these two options on the appearance of the column chart.

Figure 4-29 **Replacing columns with graphics**

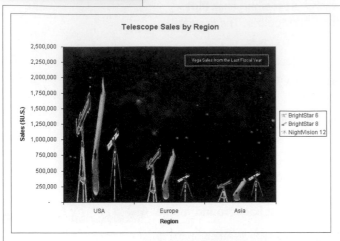

the Stretch option stretches the graphic
over the height of the column

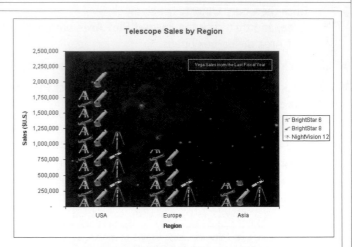

the Stack option stacks the graphic
up to the height of the column

Excel provides several ways of adding special effects to your charts, and you must be careful not to overdo it. Some effects, however interesting, can actually make your charts more difficult to read and interpret. Remember also that some of your effects may look good in color, but will not transfer well to a black-and-white printout.

Changing the Axis Scale

Alicia might want you to make one other change to the column chart. She knows that the scale used by the chart is automatically set by Excel. Excel uses the data that you have plotted and determines an appropriate scale for the y-axis, usually designed to cover a range of reasonable values. Alicia wants you to examine the scale that Excel set for this chart to see if a change is warranted. She also thinks that expressing the sales in terms of dollars on the chart is a bit unwieldy for sales of this magnitude. She would rather have the sales expressed in terms of thousands of dollars.

To view the y-axis scale:

1. Click the **Chart Objects** list arrow [   ] on the Chart toolbar, click **Value Axis**, and then click the **Format Axis** button 🖻 on the Chart toolbar. The Format Axis dialog box opens. You can use this dialog box to format the scale's appearance and to change the range and increments used in the scale.

2. Click the **Scale** tab. See Figure 4-30.

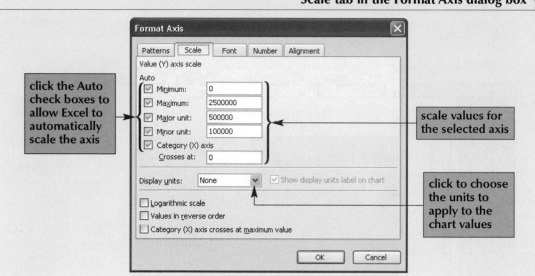

click the Auto check boxes to allow Excel to automatically scale the axis

scale values for the selected axis

click to choose the units to apply to the chart values

There are four values that comprise the scale: the minimum, maximum, major unit, and minor unit. The minimum and maximum values are the smallest and largest tick marks that appear on the axis. The major unit is the increment between the scale's **major tick marks**. The chart also has a second set of tick marks, called **minor tick marks**, that may or may not be displayed. The difference between major and minor tick marks is that axis values appear next to major tick marks, whereas no values appear next to minor tick marks.

In the current chart, the scale that Excel displayed ranges from 0 to 2,500,000 in increments of 500,000. The minor tick mark increment is 100,000, but these tick marks are not displayed on the axes. Alicia wants to reduce the increment value to 250,000 in order to show more detail on the chart. Then she wants to change the display units from none to thousands.

To revise the y-axis scale:

1. Double-click the current entry in the Major unit box, and then type **250000**. Note that when you manually change a scale value its Auto check box is automatically deselected.

2. Click the **Display units** list arrow, and then select **Thousands** in the list.

3. Make sure that the **Show display units label on chart** check box is selected, and then click the **OK** button. Figure 4-31 shows the revised y-axis scale.

Figure 4-31 ▶ Revised scale for the y-axis

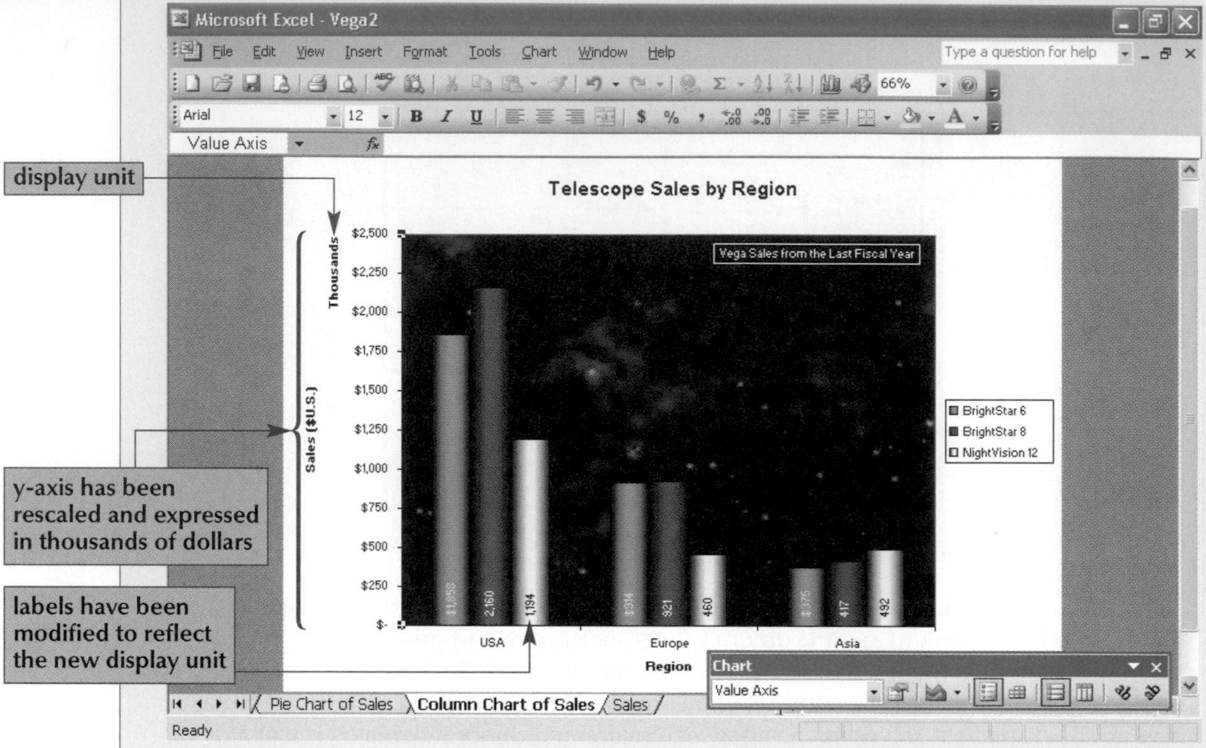

In this chart, $2,500,000 is displayed as $2,500. Because you have changed the display units in this way, you need to include information about the new value. Excel does this for you by adding the text "Thousands" to the value axis. Also note that the label values for each column now use the thousands display unit, so the Asian sales for the BrightStar 6 are displayed as $375 rather than $375,000.

Pleased with the latest version of the column chart, Alicia now wants you to go back to the pie chart and make some modifications there.

Working with Three-Dimensional Charts

Many of the Excel charts can be displayed either as two-dimensional "flat" charts or as charts that appear in three dimensions. Alicia wants you to change the pie chart to a three-dimensional pie chart. To do this, you have to change the chart type.

To change the pie chart to 3-D:

▶ **1.** Switch to the Pie Chart of Sales chart sheet.

▶ **2.** Click **Chart** on the menu bar, and then click **Chart Type**. The Chart Type dialog box opens.

▶ **3.** Click the second chart sub-type in the top row, as shown in Figure 4-32.

Changing to a 3-D pie chart | **Figure 4-32**

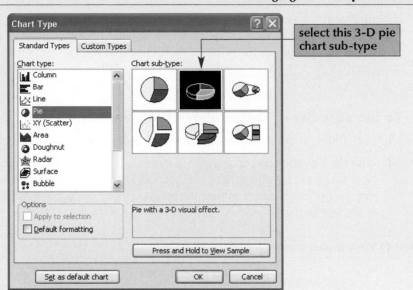

4. Click the **OK** button. Excel displays the pie chart in three dimensions. Note that Excel has retained the rotation you applied to the chart in the last session, and the BrightStar 6 slice is still exploded. See Figure 4-33.

3-D pie chart | **Figure 4-33**

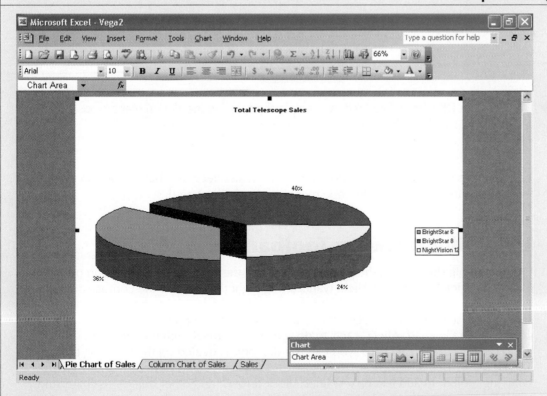

In a 3-D chart, you have several options to modify the 3-D effect. One of these is **elevation**, which is the illusion that you're looking at the 3-D chart from either above or below the chart. Another of these is **perspective**, which is the illusion that some parts of the 3-D chart are farther away from you than others. Finally, you can rotate a 3-D chart to bring different parts of the chart to the forefront. In a pie chart, you can change the elevation and rotation, but not the perspective.

Alicia likes the 3-D view of the pie chart but feels that the angle of the pie is too low. She wants you to change the angle of the pie so that the viewer is looking "down" on the chart more.

To increase the elevation above the pie chart:

▶ 1. Click **Chart** on the menu bar, and then click **3-D View**. The 3-D View dialog box opens.

▶ 2. Click the **Elevation** up button twice to increase the elevation to **25** degrees. See Figure 4-34. Note that there are also buttons that you can use to rotate the pie chart. Clicking one of the rotation buttons is similar to the rotation setting that you applied to the pie chart at the end of the first session.

| Figure 4-34 | 3-D View dialog box |

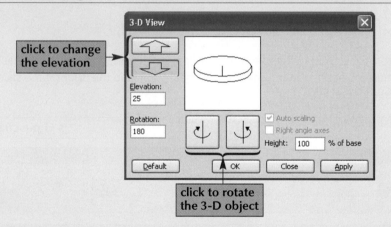

▶ 3. Click the **OK** button. Excel redraws the pie chart, giving the illusion that the observer is at an elevation above the chart.

The charts you have created present the sales data effectively, but Alicia also wants to be sure that the top-selling telescope model is clearly illustrated.

Using the Drawing Toolbar

One of the big stories from the past fiscal year was the successful introduction of the NightVision telescopes, and Alicia wants to highlight the fact that the company had in excess of $1,800,000 in sales of the NightVision 12. She has seen charts that contain shapes, like starbursts and block arrows, that give added emphasis to details and facts contained in the chart. Alicia wants to do something similar with the pie chart.

To create a graphical shape, you can use the tools provided on the Drawing toolbar. The Drawing toolbar is a common feature of all Office 2003 products. You can use the Drawing toolbar to add text boxes, lines, block arrows, and other objects to charts and worksheets. In Excel, an **object** is any entity that can be manipulated. A chart is an Excel object, as are its elements. Next, you will learn how to use the Drawing toolbar to create and format one type of object, an AutoShape.

Displaying the Drawing Toolbar

Depending on your Excel configuration, the Drawing toolbar may or may not be displayed in the Excel window when you start Excel. (The default is to not show the toolbar.) As with all toolbars, you can choose to display or hide the Drawing toolbar. Although you can display the Drawing toolbar using the View menu, you will display the toolbar by clicking the Drawing button on the Standard toolbar.

To display the Drawing toolbar:

▶ 1. Click the **Drawing** button 🔲 on the Standard toolbar. The Drawing toolbar appears in the workbook window.

▶ 2. If necessary, drag the Drawing toolbar to the bottom of the worksheet window, and then release the mouse button. The Drawing toolbar should now be anchored to the bottom of the window.

Now you will use the Drawing toolbar to add a drawing object to the pie chart.

Working with AutoShapes

The Drawing toolbar contains a list of predefined shapes called **AutoShapes**. These AutoShapes can be simple squares or circles or more complicated objects such as flow chart objects and block arrows. Once you insert an AutoShape into a chart or worksheet, you can resize and move it, like any other object. You can modify the fill color of an AutoShape, change the border style, and even insert text.

Reference Window

Inserting an AutoShape

- Click the AutoShapes list arrow on the Drawing toolbar.
- Point to the AutoShape category that you want to use, and then click the AutoShape that you want to create.
- Position the crosshair pointer over the location for the AutoShape in the chart or worksheet, and then drag the pointer over the area where you want the shape to appear. To draw an AutoShape in the same proportion as the shape on the palette, press and hold the Shift key as you drag the pointer to draw the shape.
- Release the mouse button.
- To resize an AutoShape, click the shape to select it, and then drag one of the nine selection handles.
- To rotate an AutoShape, click the green rotation handle that is connected to the shape, and drag the handle to rotate the shape.
- To change the shape of the AutoShape, click the yellow diamond tool, and then drag the tool to change the shape.

You will now add a multi-pointed star to the pie chart to highlight the success of the NightVision 12 telescope.

To add a multi-pointed AutoShape star to the pie chart:

▶ 1. Click the **AutoShapes** list arrow on the Drawing toolbar, point to **Stars and Banners**, and then click the **16-Point Star** AutoShape (second row, second column from the left) on the AutoShapes palette. A ScreenTip appears when you position the pointer over an AutoShape on the palette so you will know which shape you are selecting.

▶ 2. Move the pointer to the upper-right corner of the chart area, about one inch to the right of the chart title. As you move the pointer over the worksheet, the pointer shape changes to ┼.

To draw an AutoShape in the same proportion as the shape on the palette, you must press and hold the Shift key as you drag the pointer to draw the shape.

▶ 3. Press and hold the **Shift** key, and then click and drag the pointer down and to the right about one and one-half inches. Note that pressing the Shift key allows you to create a perfect 16-point star; otherwise, the shape might be lopsided.

▶ 4. Release the mouse button. A 16-point star appears in the upper-right corner of the chart area. See Figure 4-35.

Figure 4-35 ▶ Adding an AutoShape to the pie chart

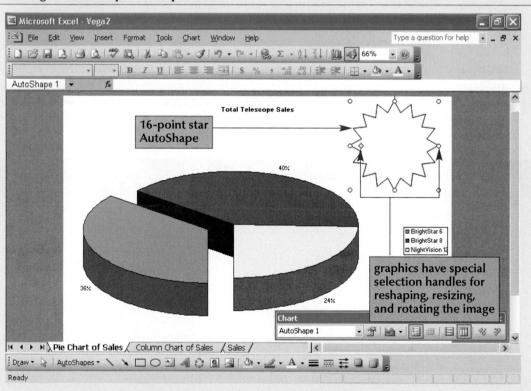

Trouble? If the AutoShape on your screen does not match the size and shape of the AutoShape shown in the figure, you can resize the object again by pressing and holding the Shift key as you drag a selection handle. Or click the Undo button ⟲ on the Standard toolbar to delete the object, and then repeat Steps 1 through 4 to redraw the AutoShape, being sure to press and hold the Shift key to draw the object proportionally.

You probably noticed that the selection handles of the AutoShape appear as open circles and that there is also a diamond tool. You can use the diamond tool to change the shape of the AutoShape. For example, you can change the size of the jagged points of the star by dragging the diamond tool either toward the center of the star (to increase the size of the points) or away from the center (to decrease the size of the points). You may have also noticed a green selection handle that is attached to the AutoShape through a vertical line. This is a rotation handle. By clicking and dragging this handle, you can rotate the AutoShape.

Formatting an AutoShape

In addition to modifying the shape, size, and rotation of an AutoShape, you can add text to it. To add text to an AutoShape, you first select it and then start typing the desired text. The text will automatically be placed within the boundaries of the shape.

Inserting Text into an AutoShape

- Click the border of the AutoShape to select the object.
- Type the text you want to appear in the AutoShape.
- Select the text within the AutoShape.
- Format the text using the options on the Formatting toolbar.
- Click outside of the shape to deselect it.

To highlight the success of the NightVision 12, you will add the text that Alicia wants to the AutoShape star.

To insert text into the AutoShape:

1. Make sure that the 16-point star is still selected.
2. Type **NightVision 12 Sales Exceed $1.8 Million!**
3. Click **Format** on the menu bar, click **AutoShape** to open the Format AutoShape dialog box, and then click the **Alignment** tab.

   Trouble? If there is no Alignment tab in the dialog box that opens, close the dialog box. Click the AutoShape again, making sure that the object, and not just its frame, is selected. Then repeat Step 3.
4. Click the **Horizontal** list arrow, and then click **Center**.
5. Click the **Vertical** list arrow, click **Center**, and then click the **OK** button.

   Trouble? If the text does not wrap logically within the boundaries of the AutoShape, resize the star to better accommodate the text.

The star with text adds value to the overall appearance of the chart. However, the star could use some background color to make it more visually interesting. In keeping with the other colors you have been using in the charts, you will format the AutoShape by adding a yellow background.

To change the background color of the AutoShape:

1. Make sure the 16-point star is still selected.
2. Click the **Fill Color** list arrow ⬛ ▾ on the Drawing toolbar, and then click the **Ivory** square (sixth row, third column) in the color palette.

   Trouble? If the background color does not change to ivory, you may have selected the text in the star rather than the star itself. Click the Undo button ↺ on the Standard toolbar, and then repeat Steps 1 and 2, being sure to select the AutoShape.

The AutoShape definitely looks better with the ivory background. You decide to try one more thing: if adding a shadow effect to the star will be too much or will add depth to the object. To add a shadow effect to an object, you can choose one of the available shadow effects provided on the Drawing toolbar.

To add a drop shadow to the AutoShape:

1. Make sure the 16-point star is still selected.
2. Click the **Shadow Style** button on the Drawing toolbar to display the gallery of shadow options.
3. Click **Shadow Style 6** (second row, second column from the left) in the shadow gallery, and then click outside the star to deselect it.

   As a final step, Alicia feels that the pie chart is a little too far to the left. You will move it down and to the right to center it better.
4. Click the **Chart Objects** list arrow on the Chart toolbar, and then click **Plot Area**.
5. Click on the gray selection border around the plot area, drag the border down and to the right, and then click outside the chart area. Figure 4-36 shows the revised pie chart with the formatted AutoShape and the relocated pie.

| **Figure 4-36** | **Drop shadow added to the 16-point star AutoShape** |

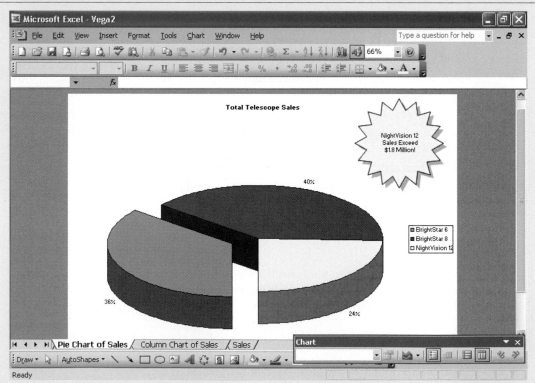

Alicia doesn't want any other changes to be made, so you will hide the Drawing toolbar, which will increase the workspace on your screen.

6. Click the **Drawing** button on the Formatting toolbar. The Drawing toolbar closes.

Printing Your Charts

Now that you have completed your work on the two charts for Alicia, you will make hard copies of them. Printing a chart sheet is similar to printing a worksheet. As when printing a worksheet, you should preview the printout before sending the worksheet to the printer. From the Print Preview window, you can add headers and footers and control the page layout, just as you do for printing the contents of your worksheets. You also have the added option of resizing the chart to fit within the confines of a single printed page.

To print both charts at the same time, you will select both chart sheets, open Print Preview, and then set up each chart to print on its own page.

To set up the two charts for printing:

1. Make sure the Pie Chart of Sales worksheet is the current sheet.
2. Press and hold the **Shift** key, and then click the **Column Chart of Sales** tab. Both chart sheets are selected.
3. Click the **Print Preview** button 🔍 on the Standard toolbar. The Print Preview window opens, showing the pie chart on the first of two pages.
4. Click the **Setup** button on the Print Preview toolbar to open the Page Setup dialog box. The Page Setup options are similar to the options for printing a worksheet, except that a new dialog box tab, Chart, appears.
5. Click the **Chart** tab. See Figure 4-37.

Chart tab in the Page Setup dialog box ◄ **Figure 4-37**

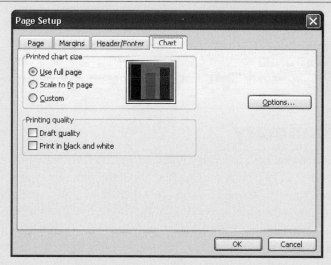

Excel provides three choices for defining the size of a chart printout. These are:

- **Use full page:** The chart is resized to fit the full page, extending to fit the full width and height of the page. The proportions of the chart may change since it is extended in all directions to fit the page. This is the default option.
- **Scale to fit page:** The chart is resized until one of the edges reaches a page margin. The chart expands in both dimensions (width and height) proportionally until one dimension fills the space between the margins.
- **Custom:** The dimensions of the printed chart are specified on the chart sheet using the Zoom tool.

You will use the Scale to fit page option because you do not want to have the charts resized disproportionately.

To set the size of the charts:

▶ **1.** Click the **Scale to fit page** option button, and then click the **OK** button. The Use full page option and the Scale to fit page option will often result in charts that are close in the same size. You may not see much difference in the chart size in the Print Preview window.

▶ **2.** Click the **Next** button to preview the column chart printout.

▶ **3.** Click the **Setup** button, click the **Scale to fit page** option button on the Chart tab, and then click the **OK** button.

▶ **4.** Click the **Print** button to open the Print dialog box, make any necessary changes, and then click the **OK** button to send both chart sheets to the printer.

For now, there are no other changes to be made. Alicia will use the printouts of the charts at the meeting next week.

▶ **5.** Save your changes to the workbook and then close it

Alicia is pleased with the results and will get back to you with any other tasks she might need you to do before the sales meeting next week.

Review

Session 4.2 Quick Check

1. How would you remove a data series from a column chart?
2. How would you change the location (either embedded or as a chart sheet) of a chart?
3. What is the difference between label text, attached text, and unattached text?
4. What is the difference between major tick marks and minor tick marks?
5. How would you change a column chart into a 3-D column chart?
6. What is an AutoShape?
7. Describe the three options for sizing a chart on the printed page.

Review

Tutorial Summary

In this tutorial, you learned how to work with charts in Excel. You saw how to use Excel's Chart Wizard to create a basic chart and learned about the different types of charts that can be created by Excel. You also learned how to embed charts within a worksheet or place them on their own chart sheet in the workbook. You used Excel's editing tools to modify the chart's appearance by inserting additional text, changing font and background colors and images, rotating the chart in three dimensions, and changing the scale of the chart. This tutorial also introduced you to the Drawing toolbar, which you used to create an AutoShape, placing that shape on a chart to provide additional emphasis on key points. Finally, you learned about the different options Excel provides for printing your completed charts.

Key Terms

active chart	chart title	embedded chart
attached text	Chart Wizard	exploded pie chart
AutoShape	data marker	gridline
category values	data series	horizontal axis
chart	data source	label text
chart area	data value	legend
chart sheet	elevation	major gridline

major tick mark	plot area	vertical axis
minor gridline	scale	x-axis
minor tick mark	tick mark	x value
object	unattached text	y-axis
perspective		

Practice

Practice the skills you learned in the tutorial using the same case scenario.

Review Assignments

Data File needed for the Review Assignments: VegaUSA1.xls

Alicia has another workbook that shows the monthly United States sales for the three major telescope models. She wants you to create a column chart showing the monthly United States sales figures and a pie chart showing the total sales figures for each telescope model. To complete this task:

1. Open the **VegaUSA1** workbook located in the Tutorial.04\Review folder included with your Data Files, and then save the workbook as **VegaUSA2** to the same folder.
2. Enter your name and the current date in the Documentation sheet, and then switch to the Monthly Sales worksheet.
3. Select the range A6:D18, and then start the Chart Wizard.
4. Use the Chart Wizard to create a column chart, using the first chart sub-type. Specify "United States Telescope Sales" as the chart title, "Month" as the x-axis title, and "Sales ($U.S.)" as the y-axis title. Place the chart on a chart sheet named "Monthly Sales Chart."
5. Format the x-axis labels, changing the alignment to 90 degrees.
6. Change the scale of the y-axis using thousands as the display unit.
7. Change the background color of the plot area to white. Apply a horizontal blending effect to each column's fill color.
8. Place the chart legend at the bottom of the chart. (*Hint*: Open the Format Legend dialog box and select the Bottom option on the Placement tab.)
9. Use the Drawing toolbar to create an 8-point star located in the upper-left corner of the chart area.
10. Insert the text "NightVision 12 sales remained high in Autumn!" into the 8-point star you just created. Center the text both horizontally and vertically.
11. Change the fill color of the 8-point star to ivory, and apply Shadow Style 1 to the shape.
12. Return to the Monthly Sales worksheet, select the nonadjacent range B6:D6;B19:D19, and use the Chart Wizard to create a 3-D pie chart of the data. Assign the chart the title "Pie Chart of Total Sales" and display the sales values next to the pie slices. Place the pie chart in a chart sheet named "Pie Chart of Total Sales."
13. Apply the Late Sunset fill effect to the pie chart's chart area.
14. Select both charts, and then open the Print Preview window.
15. Use the Setup dialog box to scale both charts to fit their respective pages and to add a footer to the charts displaying your name and the date in the lower-right corner of the page. Print the charts.
16. Save your changes to the workbook and then close it.

Apply

Use the skills you have learned to create a worksheet displaying a 3-D column chart.

Case Problem 1

Data File needed for this Case Problem: CIC1.xls

Cast Iron Concepts Andrea Puest, the regional sales manager of Cast Iron Concepts (CIC), a distributor of cast-iron stoves, is required to present a report of the company's first-quarter sales for the states of New Hampshire, Vermont, and Maine. Her sales data covers four major models: Star Windsor, Box Windsor, West Windsor, and Circle Windsor. The Circle Windsor is CIC's latest entry in the cast-iron stove market.

Andrea will make a presentation of her sales figures next month and has asked for your help in creating a chart showing the sales results. She wants to create a 3-D column chart, with each column representing the sales for a particular model and state. To complete this task:

1. Open the **CIC1** workbook located in the Tutorial.04\Cases folder included with your Data Files, and then save the file as **CIC2** to the same folder.
2. Enter your name and the current date in the Documentation sheet, and then switch to the Sales worksheet.
3. Select the range A5:D9, and then start the Chart Wizard.
4. Use the Chart Wizard to create an embedded 3-D column chart that compares values across categories and across series. The data series in the chart should be organized by columns, not rows. Specify "Windsor Stove Sales" as the chart title. Do not specify titles for the axes. Do not include a legend.
5. Move the embedded chart so that the upper-left corner of the chart is located in cell A11, and then resize the chart so that it covers the range A11:E32.
6. Change the font of the chart title to a 14-point, bold, dark-blue Arial font.
7. Add the subtitle "1/1/2006 - 3/31/2006" as unattached text to the chart. Format the text in an 8-point, bold, dark-blue Arial font and place it under the chart's main title.
8. Change the color of the chart area to tan.

Explore

9. Change the 3-D view of the chart so that its elevation equals 10 degrees, its rotation equals 120 degrees, and its perspective equals 15.
10. Change the font of the y-axis (also called the "series axis") labels (the names of the states) to an 8-point regular Arial font.
11. Change the font of the x-axis labels (the model names) to an 8-point regular Arial font, displayed at a –90 degree angle.

Explore

12. Select the walls of the 3-D plot, and change the wall color to white.
13. Center the contents of the worksheet horizontally on the page, and then add a header that displays your name and the date in the upper-right corner of the worksheet.
14. Preview and then print the worksheet.
15. Save your changes to the workbook, and then close it.

Challenge

Broaden your knowledge and challenge your skills by exploring how to use Excel to create a Pareto quality control chart.

Case Problem 2

Data File needed for this Case Problem: Powder1.xls

Dantalia Baby Powder   Kemp Wilson is a quality control engineer for Dantalia Baby Powder. Part of the company's manufacturing process involves a machine called a "filler," which pours a specified amount of powder into bottles. Sometimes the heads on the filler become partially clogged, causing the bottles to be under-filled. If that happens, the bottles must be rejected. On each assembly line, there are a certain number of bottles rejected during each shift.

Kemp's job is to monitor the number of defective bottles and locate the fillers that may have clogged filler heads. One of the tools he uses to do this is a Pareto chart. A Pareto chart is a column chart in which each column represents the total number of defects assigned to different parts of the production process. In this case, the columns would represent the 24 different fillers in the assembly line. The columns are sorted so that the part that caused the most defects is displayed first, the second-most is displayed second, and so forth. Superimposed on the columns is a line that displays the cumulative percentage of defects for all of the parts. Thus, by viewing the cumulative percentages, you can determine, for example, what percentages of the total defects are due to the three worst parts. In this way, Kemp can isolate the problem filler heads and report how much they contribute to the total defects.

Kemp has a worksheet listing the number of defects per filler head from a recent shift. The data is already sorted going from the filler head with the most defects to the one with the fewest. The cumulative percent values have also been calculated already. Kemp wants you to create a Pareto chart based on this data. To complete this task:

1. Open the **Powder1** workbook located in the Tutorial.04\Cases folder included with your Data Files, and then save the file as **Powder2** to the same folder.
2. Enter your name and the current date in the Documentation sheet, and then switch to the Quality Control Data worksheet.
3. Select the range A5:C29, and then start the Chart Wizard.

Explore

4. Use the Chart Wizard to create a custom chart, selecting the Line – Column on 2 Axes option in the Custom Types list box. Specify "Filler Head Under Fills" as the chart title. Specify "Filler Head" as the x-axis title, "Count of Under Fills" as the y-axis title, and "Cumulative Percentage" as the second y-axis title. Do not include a legend. Place the chart on a chart sheet named "Pareto Chart."
5. Change the alignment of the x-axis labels to an angle of 90 degrees.
6. Change the alignment of the second y-axis title to –90 degrees.

Explore
Explore

7. Change the scale of the second y-axis so that the values range from 0 to 1.0.
8. Select the data series that displays the number of defects for each filler head, and add data labels that display the number of defects above each column. Do *not* display labels above the lines that represent the cumulative percentages. (*Hint*: Use the Data Labels tab in the Format Data Series dialog box.)

Explore

9. From the Format Data Series dialog box for the chart's columns, use the Options tab to reduce the gap separating the columns to 0 pixels.
10. Change the fill color of the chart columns and the plot area to white.
11. Examine the Pareto chart, and determine approximately what percentage of the total number of defects can be attributed to the three worst filler heads.
12. Add a header to the Pareto Chart sheet that displays the name of the worksheet in the center and your name and the date on the right of the page, and then print the Pareto chart.
13. Save your changes to the workbook, and then close it.

Case Problem 3

Challenge

Go beyond what you've learned in the tutorial by exploring how to use Excel to chart stock market data.

Data File needed for this Case Problem: Pixal1.xls

Charting Stock Activity You work with Lee Whyte, a stock analyst who plans to publish a Web site on stocks. One component of the Web site will be a five-week record of the activity of various key stocks. Lee has asked for your help in setting up an Excel workbook to keep a running record of the trading volume, open, high, low, and close values of some of the stocks he's tracking.

Lee wants you to create a stock market chart of the activity of Pixal Inc. stock as a sample. The last six weeks of the stock's performance have been saved in a workbook. He wants you to create a chart sheet for the data that has been entered. To complete this task:

1. Open the **Pixal1** workbook located in the Tutorial.04\Cases folder included with your Data Files, and then save the file as **Pixal2** to the same folder.
2. Enter your name and the current date in the Documentation sheet, and then switch to the Pixal Data worksheet.
3. Select the range B6:G36, and then start the Chart Wizard.

4. Use the Chart Wizard to create a stock chart using the Volume-Open-High-Low-Close sub-type. Specify "Pixal Inc." as the chart title. Specify "Date" as the x-axis title, "Volume (mil)" as the y-axis title, and "Price" as the second y-axis title. Remove the gridlines and do not include a legend. Place the chart in a chart sheet named "Pixal Chart."

5. Change the scale of the first y-axis so that the scale ranges from 0 to 5 with a major unit of 0.5.

6. Change the scale of the second y-axis so that the scale ranges from 15 to 21 with a major unit of 1.

7. Change the alignment of the second y-axis title to –90 degrees.

Explore ▶ 8. Change the scale of the x-axis so that the major unit occurs every seven days.

9. Double-click the column data series that displays the volume of shares traded and, using the Options tab, reduce the gap between adjacent columns to 0 pixels.

10. Change the fill color of the plot area to light yellow.

11. Change the font size of the chart title to 16 points.

Explore ▶ 12. In the upper-right corner of the plot area, insert the Rounded Rectangular Callout AutoShape from the Drawing toolbar. Enter the following quote into the AutoShape:
"Pixal Inc. is experiencing a tough first quarter" – Stock Reviews
Format the text in a bold, red, 14-point font. Resize the AutoShape if necessary.

13. Add the Shadow Style 6 drop shadow to the AutoShape.

14. Add your name and the date to the right section of the header. Scale the chart to fit the page in landscape orientation.

15. Save the changes, and then print the chart sheet.

Explore ▶ 16. Lee has a new week's worth of data for the Pixal worksheet. Enter the data shown in Figure 4-38 to the table of stock activity, and then modify that chart's data source to include the new data values for each data series.

Figure 4-38 ▶

Date	Volume (mil)	Open	High	Low	Close
2/17/2006	0.35	16.30	16.95	16.75	16.85
2/18/2006	0.45	16.85	17.20	17.05	17.15
2/19/2006	0.52	17.15	17.45	17.25	17.25
2/20/2006	0.40	17.25	17.35	16.95	17.25
2/21/2006	0.38	17.25	17.55	16.75	16.95

17. Save your changes to a new workbook named **Pixal3** in the Cases folder, and then reprint the chart sheet with the new data values. Close the workbook.

Create

Test your knowledge of charts by creating a workbook with an XY (scatter) chart that presents data from a cancer research study.

Case Problem 4

There are no Data Files needed for this Case Problem.

Relating Cancer Rates to Temperature A 1965 study analyzed the relationship between the mean annual temperature in 16 regions in Great Britain and the annual mortality rates in those regions for a certain type of breast cancer. Lynn Watson is working on a symposium on the history of breast cancer research and has asked you to chart the data from this historic study. Figure 4-39 shows a preview of the workbook and chart that you'll create.

Figure 4-39

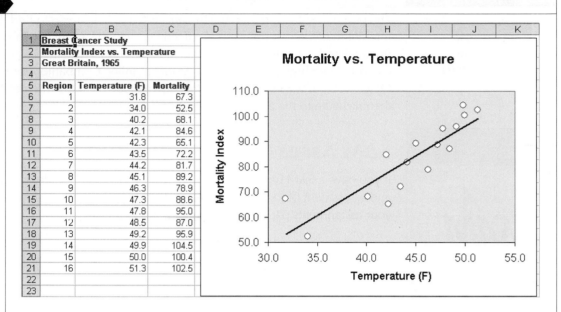

To complete this task:

1. Create a new workbook and save it as **BCancer** in the Tutorial.04\Cases folder included with your Data Files. The workbook should contain a Documentation sheet displaying your name, the date, and the purpose of the workbook. Name one of the other work-sheets "Breast Cancer Data," and then add the titles and data shown in Figure 4-39.

Explore

2. Use the Chart Wizard to create an embedded XY (scatter) chart with no data points connected. Specify "Mortality vs. Temperature" as the chart title. Specify "Temperature (F)" as the title of the x-axis and "Mortality Index" as the title of the y-axis. Remove the gridlines. Do not include a legend. The scatter chart should be embedded on the Breast Cancer Data worksheet.

3. Change the scale of the x-axis to cover the temperature range 30 to 55 degrees Fahrenheit.

4. Change the scale of the y-axis to cover the mortality index range 50 to 110.

Explore

5. Double-click one of the data points in the chart to open the Format Data Series dialog box, and make the following changes to the appearance of the data points:
   - Change the marker style to a circle that is 7 points in size.
   - Change the background color of the circle to white.
   - Change the foreground color of the circle to red.

Explore

6. Open the Add Trendline dialog box from the Chart menu, and select the Linear trend line option on the Type tab. The purpose of the linear trend line is to display whether a linear relationship exists between the 16 regions' mean annual temperature and their annual mortality index. Does it appear that such a relationship exists? What does a high mean annual temperature imply about the annual mortality index?

7. Change the fill color of the plot area to light yellow.

8. Set up the worksheet to print in landscape orientation, centered horizontally and vertically on the page. Enter your name and the date in the right section of the page's header. Print the chart.

9. Save your changes to the workbook and close it.

Research

Use the Internet to find and work with data related to the topics presented in this tutorial.

Internet Assignments

The purpose of the Internet Assignments is to challenge you to find information on the Internet that you can use to work effectively with this software. The actual assignments are updated and maintained on the Course Technology Web site. Log on to the Internet and use your Web browser to go to the Student Online Companion for New Perspectives Office 2003 at **www.course.com/np/office2003**. Click the Internet Assignments link, and then navigate to the assignments for this tutorial.

Assess

SAM Assessment and Training

If you have a SAM user profile, you may have access to hands-on instruction, practice, and assessment of the skills covered in this tutorial. Log in to your SAM account and go to your assignments page to see what your instructor has assigned.

Review

Quick Check Answers

Session 4.1

1. A chart type is one of the 14 styles of charts supported by Excel. Each chart type has various alternate formats, called chart sub-types.
2. stock chart
3. A data series is a range of data values that is plotted on a chart.
4. The plot area contains the actual data values that are plotted in the chart, as well as any background colors or images for that plot. The chart area contains the plot area and any other element (such as titles and legend boxes) that may be included in the chart.
5. Gridlines are lines that extend out from the tick marks on either axis into the plot area.
6. embedded charts, which are placed within a worksheet, and chart sheets, which contain only the chart itself
7. pie
8. exploded pie

Session 4.2

1. Click Chart on the menu bar, click Source Data, click the Series tab, select the data series in the Series list box, and then click the Remove button.
2. Click Chart on the menu bar, click Location, and then select a new location.
3. Label text is text that consists of category names, tick mark labels, and legend text. Attached text is text that is attached to other elements of the chart, such as the chart title or axes titles. Unattached text is additional text that is unassociated with any particular element of the chart.
4. Major tick marks are tick marks that appear on the axis alongside the axis values. Minor tick marks do not appear alongside any axis value, but instead are used to provide a finer gradation between major tick marks.
5. Click Chart on the menu bar, click Chart Type, and then select one of the 3-D chart sub-types for the column chart.
6. An AutoShape is a predefined shape available on the Drawing toolbar. You can add an AutoShape to any worksheet or chart. You can change the size or shape of an AutoShape, and you can change its fill color.
7. Use full page, in which the chart is resized to fit the full size of the printed page (the proportions of the chart may change in the resizing); Scale to fit page, in which the chart is resized to fit the page but retains its proportions; and Custom, in which the dimensions of the printed chart are specified in the chart sheet.

New Perspectives on

Microsoft® Office Excel 2003

Read This Before You Begin: Tutorials 5-8

To the Student

Data Files

To complete the Level II Excel Tutorials (Tutorials 5 through 8) plus Appendices A and B, you need the starting student Data Files. Your instructor will either provide you with these Data Files or ask you to obtain them yourself.

The Level II Excel tutorials and Appendices A and B require the folders shown in the next column to complete the Tutorials, Review Assignments, and Case Problems. You will need to copy these folders from a file server, a standalone computer, or the Web to the drive and folder where you will be storing your Data Files. Your instructor will tell you which computer, drive letter, and folder(s) contain the files you need. You can also download the files by going to www.course.com; see the inside back or front cover for more information on downloading the files, or ask your instructor or technical support person for assistance.

If you are storing your Data Files on floppy disks, you will need **six** blank, formatted, high-density disks for these tutorials. Label your disks as shown, and place on them the folders indicated.

▼ **Excel 2003 Level II: Data Disk 1**
Tutorial.05 folder

▼ **Excel 2003 Level II: Data Disk 2**
Tutorial.06 folder

▼ **Excel 2003 Level II: Data Disk 3**
Tutorial.07\Tutorial folder
Tutorial.07\Review folder

▼ **Excel 2003 Level II: Data Disk 4**
Tutorial.07\Cases folder

▼ **Excel 2003 Level II: Data Disk 5**
Tutorial.08 folder

▼ **Excel 2003 Level II: Data Disk 6**
Appendix.A folder
Appendix.B folder

When you begin a tutorial, refer to the Student Data Files section at the bottom of the tutorial opener page, which indicates which folders and files you need for the tutorial. Each end-of-tutorial exercise also indicates the files you need to complete that exercise

To the Instructor

The Data Files are available on the Instructor Resources CD for this title. Follow the instructions in the Help file on the CD to install the programs to your network or standalone computer. See the "To the Student" section above for information on how to set up the Data Files that accompany this text.

You are granted a license to copy the Data Files to any computer or computer network used by students who have purchased this book.

System Requirements

If you are going to work through this book using your own computer, you need:

• **Computer System** Microsoft Windows 2000, Windows XP or higher must be installed on your computer. These tutorials assume a typical installation of Microsoft Excel 2003.

• **Data Files** You will not be able to complete the tutorials or exercises in this book using your own computer until you have the necessary starting Data Files.

Objectives

Working with Excel Lists

Tracking Vehicle Data

Case

Ardmoor University

Linda Pell was recently hired as Coordinator of Facilities, a new position, at Ardmoor University. One of her first assignments is to get a handle on the fleet of vehicles owned by the institution. In the past, the Property department was responsible for keeping these records, but it was more interested in repairing the vehicles than in doing the record keeping. As a result, the administration really has no idea which department has been assigned what vehicles, how much each vehicle is being used, which vehicles are insured, and so on.

To track the information on the fleet of vehicles, Linda set up an Excel list. She recorded information such as the vehicle identification number, type of car, model year, purchase price, department to which a vehicle was assigned, maintenance cost, and other pieces of information. Linda has asked that you help her maintain this database of information so she can provide up-to-date and accurate information to the administration about the university's vehicles.

Your job is to use Excel to manage Linda's list of vehicle data. You will work with the data in Linda's list using list range features available in Excel 2003. You will sort the data using a variety of methods, and you will maintain the data using the insert row list range feature and a data form. You will also use the data form to search for information that meets certain criteria. You will filter the information to display only data that meets certain criteria. You will also apply conditional formatting to a range of cells to highlight specific values in the range. You will compute filtered subtotals using the total row list range feature and calculate totals and subtotals using the Subtotals command. You will display various levels of subtotals using the Outline buttons. Finally, you will summarize the list of data using a PivotTable and PivotChart.

Student Data Files

▼Tutorial.05

▽ Tutorial folder	▽ Review folder	▽ Cases folder
Vehicle1.xls	VehicleR.xls	Faculty1.xls
		Gourmet1.xls
		Receive1.xls
		Teahouse.xls

Introduction to Lists

One of the more common uses of a worksheet is to manage lists of data, such as client lists, phone lists, and transaction lists. Excel provides you with the tools to manage such tasks. Using Excel, you can store and update data, sort data, search for and retrieve data, summarize and compare data, and create reports.

In Excel a **list** is a collection of similar data stored in a structured manner: in rows and columns. Figure 5-1 shows a portion of Linda's vehicles list. Within an Excel list, each column represents a **field** that describes some attribute or characteristic of a person, place, or thing. In this list, a vehicle's identification number, the department that is responsible for the vehicle, and the purchase price of the vehicle are examples of fields. When related fields are grouped together in a row, they form a **record**, a collection of fields that describes a person, place, or thing. For example, the data for each vehicle—ID number, model year, make, vehicle type, department to which the vehicle is assigned, odometer reading, purchase price, and annual maintenance cost—represents a record. A collection of related records makes up an Excel list.

Figure 5-1   Portions of the vehicles list

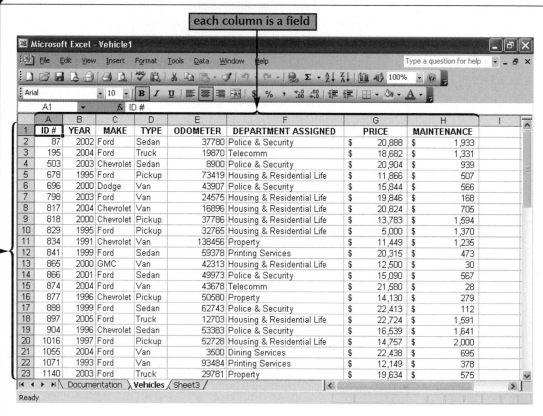

Planning and Creating a List

Before you create a list, you should do some planning. As you spend time thinking about how you will use the list, consider the types of reports, queries, and searches you might need. This process can help you determine the kind of information to include for each record and the contents of each field. As with most projects, the planning that you do before you create your list will help you avoid redesigning the list later.

To create the vehicles list, Linda first determined her information requirements. Linda plans to use the list to keep track of which departments have been assigned vehicles, how much it's costing to maintain each vehicle, and the mileage of each vehicle (to aid in maintenance and replacement decisions), among other uses. As a way of documenting the information requirements of the vehicles list, she developed a **data definition table**, which is a table that describes the fields she plans to maintain for each vehicle. Figure 5-2 shows the data definition table Linda developed to define her data requirements. She used this table as a guide in creating the vehicles list.

Data definition table for the vehicles list ⟩ **Figure 5-2**

Field Name	Description
ID #	Vehicle's identification number
YEAR	Model year of the vehicle
MAKE	Manufacturer of the vehicle (Chevrolet, Dodge, Ford, GMC)
TYPE	Category of the vehicle (Pickup, Sedan, Truck, Van)
ODOMETER	Latest reading of the odometer
DEPARTMENT ASSIGNED	Department responsible for the vehicle
PRICE	Purchase price of the vehicle
MAINTENANCE	Annual maintenance cost for the vehicle

Once you determine the design of your list, you can create the list in a worksheet. You can use a blank worksheet or a workbook that already contains data. When creating a list in Excel, use the following guidelines:

- The top row of the list should contain a **field name**, a unique label describing the contents of the data in the rows below it. This row of field names is sometimes referred to as the **header row**. Although the header row often begins in row 1, the header row can begin in any row.
- Field names can contain up to 255 characters. Usually a short name is easier to understand and remember. Short field names also enable you to display more fields on the screen at one time.
- Formatting (such as bold, color, and font size) the field names makes it easier for users to identify the row header; in some situations, formatting is used by Excel to distinguish between the data in the list and the header row.
- Each column should contain the same kind of information for each row in the list.
- The list should be separated from any other information in the same worksheet by *at least* one blank row and one blank column. Separating the list from the other parts of the worksheet enables Excel to automatically determine the range of the list by identifying the blank row and column. For the same reason, you should avoid rows and columns that are entirely blank within the list. Note there can be cells within a list that are empty; an entire row or column cannot be.

Now you will open the workbook that Linda created that contains the vehicles list.

To open the Vehicle1 workbook:

▶ 1. Start Excel and then open the **Vehicle1** workbook located in the Tutorial.05\Tutorial folder included with your Data Files.

▶ 2. On the Documentation sheet, enter the *current date* and *your name*, and then save the workbook as **Vehicle2** in the Tutorial.05\Tutorial folder.

▶ 3. Switch to the Vehicles sheet. This worksheet (which is the same worksheet as the one shown in Figure 5-1) contains the list of vehicles. Currently there are 71 vehicles. Each vehicle record is stored as a separate row (rows 2 through 72). There are eight fields (columns A through H) for each record. Notice that the field names are boldface to make it easier to distinguish the field names from the data in the list.

To view the current information, you will scroll through the list of vehicles.

▶ 4. Scroll down to the bottom of the list (row 72). As the list scrolls, notice that the column headings are no longer visible.

▶ 5. Press the **Ctrl + Home** keys to return to cell A1.

You want to be able to keep the column headings on the screen as you scroll the vehicles list. Not being able to see the column headings makes it difficult to know what the data in each column represents.

Freezing Rows and Columns

You can select rows and columns to remain visible on your screen as you scroll around the worksheet. *Freezing* a row or column lets you keep headings on the screen as you work with the data in a large worksheet. To freeze a row or column, you select the cell below and to the right of the row(s) or column(s) you want to freeze. For example, if you want to keep just the top row of column headings displayed on the screen, you click cell A2 (first column, second row), and then you select the Freeze Panes option on the Window menu. As you scroll down the list, the first row will remain on the screen so the column headings are visible, making it easier for you to understand the data in each record. Because the Freeze Panes option is a toggle, once you freeze the rows or columns, the option on the Window menu changes to Unfreeze Panes.

You will freeze the first row, which contains the column headings, and the ID # column so that they remain on the screen as you scroll the list.

To freeze the first row and column in the worksheet:

▶ 1. Click cell **B2** to make it the active cell.

▶ 2. Click **Window** on the menu bar, and then click **Freeze Panes** to freeze the rows above row 2 and the columns to the left of column B. Excel displays dark horizontal and vertical lines to indicate which rows and columns are frozen.

Now you will scroll the worksheet again—this time with the column headings remaining on the screen.

▶ 3. Scroll down to move to the bottom of the list (row 72). This time notice that the column headings remain visible as the list scrolls. See Figure 5-3.

Column headings remain visible as the list scrolls

Figure 5-3

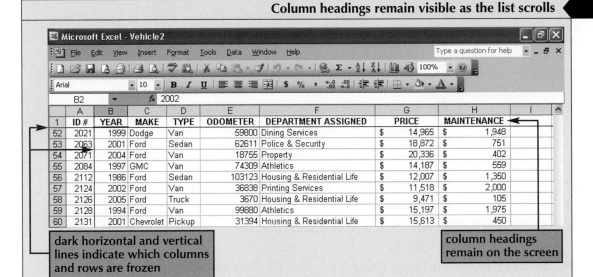

	A	B	C	D	E	F	G	H	I
1	ID #	YEAR	MAKE	TYPE	ODOMETER	DEPARTMENT ASSIGNED	PRICE	MAINTENANCE	
52	2021	1999	Dodge	Van	59800	Dining Services	$ 14,965	$ 1,948	
53	2063	2001	Ford	Sedan	62611	Police & Security	$ 18,872	$ 751	
54	2071	2004	Ford	Van	18755	Property	$ 20,336	$ 402	
55	2084	1997	GMC	Van	74309	Athletics	$ 14,187	$ 559	
56	2112	1986	Ford	Sedan	103123	Housing & Residential Life	$ 12,007	$ 1,350	
57	2124	2002	Ford	Van	36838	Printing Services	$ 11,518	$ 2,000	
58	2126	2005	Ford	Truck	3670	Housing & Residential Life	$ 9,471	$ 105	
59	2128	1994	Ford	Van	99880	Athletics	$ 15,197	$ 1,975	
60	2131	2001	Chevrolet	Pickup	31394	Housing & Residential Life	$ 15,613	$ 450	

dark horizontal and vertical lines indicate which columns and rows are frozen

column headings remain on the screen

4. Click the **scroll right arrow**. As the list scrolls to the right, notice that the ID # column (that is, column A) remains visible.

5. Press the **Ctrl + Home** keys to return to cell B2. Notice that pressing the key combination Ctrl + Home no longer returns you to cell A1—instead, it returns you to the cell directly below and to the right of the frozen row and column.

As you review the worksheet, you notice that the value "Telecomm" in the DEPARTMENT ASSIGNED column of the vehicles list reflects the abbreviated name. You want to change the name to "Telecommunications" instead of "Telecomm" before any reports are prepared.

Using Find and Replace

To find every occurrence of a character string or value in a large worksheet, you can use the Find and Replace commands. The Find command locates a value or character string, and the Replace command overwrites values or character strings.

Now you will change every DEPARTMENT ASSIGNED field that contains the value "Telecomm" to "Telecommunications."

To replace the value "Telecomm" with "Telecommunications" in the DEPARTMENT ASSIGNED field:

1. Select the entire column **F** (DEPARTMENT ASSIGNED).

2. Click **Edit** on the menu bar, and then click **Replace** to open the Find and Replace dialog box. See Figure 5-4.

Figure 5-4 ▶ Find and Replace dialog box

> **3.** Type **Telecomm** in the Find what list box, and then press the **Tab** key.
>
> **4.** Type **Telecommunications** in the Replace with list box.
>
> **5.** Click the **Replace All** button to replace all matches. A message informs you that five replacements were made.
>
> **6.** Click the **OK** button in the message box, click the **Close** button in the Find and Replace dialog box, and then click any cell in the worksheet. See Figure 5-5. Notice that the Telecomm entries have been changed to Telecommunications.

Figure 5-5 ▶ Telecommunications replaces Telecomm

full name of department displayed

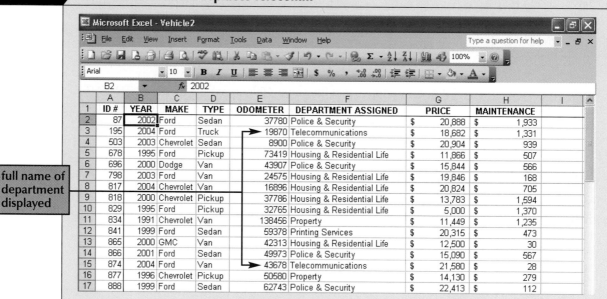

> **7.** Scroll to view the other occurrences of the replacement text, and then press the **Ctrl + Home** keys to return to the top of the worksheet.

With the name of the Telecommunications department correct, you can now continue working with the data.

Creating a List Range

In Excel 2003, lists can now be maintained as a **list range**, which consist of rows and columns contained within a list frame. When you designate a range as a list, Excel provides features designed to make it easy to manage and analyze groups of related data in an Excel worksheet. You can manage and analyze the data in the list range independent of data outside the list. For example, using only the data contained within the list, you can filter columns, add a row for totals, and even create a PivotTable report.

Excel displays several visual elements to help you work with a list range efficiently and effectively:

- The dark blue list border outlines the range of cells that makes up a list, indicating that data inside the frame is part of the list and data outside the frame is not.
- AutoFilter arrows are automatically added in the header row of a list as soon as the list is created, enabling you to quickly filter or sort the data.
- An insert row is displayed whenever a list range is active. The **insert row** consists of a blank row displayed directly below the last row of data. It also displays a blue asterisk (*) inside the leftmost cell. Typing values in this row will automatically add data to the list.
- A total row can be added to a list immediately below the insert row whenever the list range is active. The **total row** provides you with the opportunity to calculate totals (sum, average, count, and so on) for all columns in the list.
- The List toolbar gives you quick access to the tools you need to set up, modify, and manage your list.

When you create a list range, you are able to:

- Create one or more lists on a single worksheet
- Perform tasks such as sorting and filtering data
- Add data validation to ensure data integrity
- Format cells in a list the same way you format cells in a worksheet
- Add conditional formatting to the list

You will create a list range using the vehicles data in the Vehicles worksheet.

To create a list range:

1. Click any cell within the list of vehicles.

2. Click **Data** on the menu bar, point to **List**, and then click **Create List** to open the Create List dialog box. See Figure 5-6. The range reference of the list is displayed and the My list has headers check box is selected. Note that the My list has headers option is selected automatically because Excel recognized the formatting of the column heading and distinguished those values from the data in the list.

Create List dialog box ◄ **Figure 5-6**

3. Click the **OK** button to accept the settings in the dialog box and to create the list range.

4. Click any cell within the list range to view the visual elements that help identify the list range. See Figure 5-7. A blue border frames the list; AutoFilter arrows appear in the header row; the insert row appears at the bottom of the list range (row 73); and the List toolbar is docked on the right side of the worksheet window.

Figure 5-7 **List range created for the vehicles list**

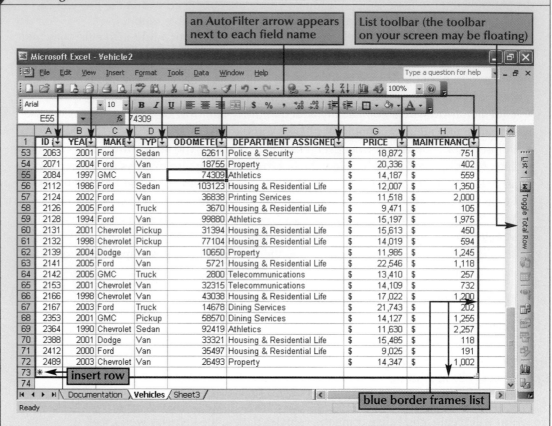

an AutoFilter arrow appears next to each field name

List toolbar (the toolbar on your screen may be floating)

blue border frames list

insert row

Trouble? The List toolbar on your screen might not be docked along the edge of the worksheet window. You can let it float, or drag the toolbar to the right side of the worksheet to dock it, as shown in the figure.

Trouble? If the insert row is not visible (row 73), scroll down to bring it into view.

► **5.** Click any cell outside the list range, and note that the list range becomes inactive. The border is dimmed, the AutoFilter arrows and List toolbar disappear, and the insert row is hidden.

► **6.** Click any cell inside the list to activate the list range. When the list range is active, the visual elements associated with the list range reappear.

► **7.** Press the **Ctrl + Home** keys to make cell B2 the active cell.

Sorting Data

When you enter a new record into a list, the new record is usually placed at the bottom of the list. To rearrange the records in a list, you can sort the records based on the data in one or more of the fields (columns). The fields you use to order your data are called **sort fields**, or **sort keys**. For example, to prepare a list of vehicles by department, you sort the data using the values in the DEPARTMENT ASSIGNED field. DEPARTMENT ASSIGNED becomes the sort field. Because DEPARTMENT ASSIGNED is the first sort field, and in this case the only sort field, it is also the **primary sort field**.

Before you complete the sort, you need to decide whether you want to put the list in ascending or descending order. **Ascending order** arranges labels alphabetically from A to Z and numbers from smallest to largest. **Descending order** arranges labels in reverse alphabetical order from Z to A and numbers from largest to smallest. In both ascending and descending order, any blank fields are placed at the bottom of the list.

In preparation for her meetings this week, Linda wants a list of vehicles sorted by the departments to which the vehicles are assigned so she can answer questions from department managers about their inventory of vehicles. She asks you to prepare a list of vehicles arranged by department.

Sorting a List Using Sort Buttons on the Standard Toolbar

To sort data in an Excel worksheet, you can use the Sort Ascending and Sort Descending buttons on the Standard toolbar, the AutoFilter Sort options, or the Sort commands on the Data menu. An easy way to sort data when there is only one sort field is to use the Sort Ascending or Sort Descending button on the Standard toolbar.

For the quick reference list of vehicles, Linda wants you to sort the list by DEPARTMENT ASSIGNED in ascending order. You will generate the alphabetized list of vehicles by departments for Linda now.

To sort the list of vehicles using the Sort Ascending button:

1. Click any cell in the DEPARTMENT ASSIGNED column. You do not have to select the entire vehicles list, which consists of range A1:H72. Excel automatically determines the range of the list when you click any cell inside the list range.

2. Click the **Sort Ascending** button [🔼] on the Standard toolbar. The data is sorted in ascending order by DEPARTMENT ASSIGNED. See Figure 5-8.

Vehicles list sorted by DEPARTMENT ASSIGNED | Figure 5-8

	A	B	C	D	E	F	G	H	I
1	ID	YEAR	MAKE	TYP	ODOMETER	DEPARTMENT ASSIGNED	PRICE	MAINTENANCE	
2	1415	1997	GMC	Van	89006	Athletics	$ 16,748	$ 755	
3	1462	1997	GMC	Van	82091	Athletics	$ 20,882	$ 980	
4	2084	1997	GMC	Van	74309	Athletics	$ 14,187	$ 559	
5	2128	1994	Ford	Van	99880	Athletics	$ 15,197	$ 1,975	
6	2364	1990	Chevrolet	Sedan	92419	Athletics	$ 11,630	$ 2,257	
7	1055	2004	Ford	Van	3500	Dining Services	$ 22,438	$ 695	
8	1602	1999	GMC	Van	35860	Dining Services	$ 16,356	$ 1,826	
9	1949	2004	Chevrolet	Van	34474	Dining Services	$ 18,712	$ 1,025	
10	2021	1999	Dodge	Van	59800	Dining Services	$ 14,965	$ 1,948	
11	2167	2003	Ford	Truck	14678	Dining Services	$ 21,743	$ 202	
12	2353	2001	CMC	Pickup	50570	Dining Services	$ 14,127	$ 1,255	
13	678	1995	Ford	Pickup	73419	Housing & Residential Life	$ 11,866	$ 507	
14	798	2003	Ford	Van	24575	Housing & Residential Life	$ 19,846	$ 168	
15	817	2004	Chevrolet	Van	16896	Housing & Residential Life	$ 20,824	$ 705	
16	818	2000	Chevrolet	Pickup	37788	Housing & Residential Life	$ 13,783	$ 1,594	
17	829	1995	Ford	Pickup	32765	Housing & Residential Life	$ 5,000	$ 1,370	
18	865	2000	GMC	Van	42313	Housing & Residential Life	$ 12,500	$ 30	
19	897	2005	Ford	Truck	12703	Housing & Residential Life	$ 22,724	$ 1,591	
20	1016	1997	Ford	Pickup	52728	Housing & Residential Life	$ 11,767	$ 2,000	
21	1167	2000	Ford	Truck	39292	Housing & Residential Life	$ 15,366	$ 3,491	
22	1196	1998	Chevrolet	Van	53560	Housing & Residential Life	$ 12,493	$ 1,299	
23	1375	1999	Ford	Pickup	45608	Housing & Residential Life	$ 15,866	$ 72	

departments in alphabetical order

Trouble? If you clicked in the wrong column or if the data is sorted in the wrong order, click the Undo button [↩] on the Standard toolbar to return the list to its original order, and then repeat Steps 1 and 2.

Linda also needs a list of vehicles sorted in descending order by price, from the highest value to the lowest.

Sorting a List Using the AutoFilter Sort Options

You can also sort a list using the **AutoFilter** sort options. When you create a list range, AutoFilter arrows appear beside each column heading. To select an AutoFilter option, you click the AutoFilter arrow for the column by which you want to sort. One of the benefits of this method is that you can sort the list by the field whose AutoFilter arrow you clicked without having clicked in the column itself first. You will use the AutoFilter arrow to sort the list by price with the highest price displayed first in the list.

To sort the list by price in descending order using the AutoFilter:

1. Click the **PRICE** column AutoFilter arrow in cell G1 to display a list of items you can use to sort or filter the data (scroll up if necessary to view the AutoFilter sort options). See Figure 5-9.

Figure 5-9   Sorting the vehicles list using AutoFilter sort options

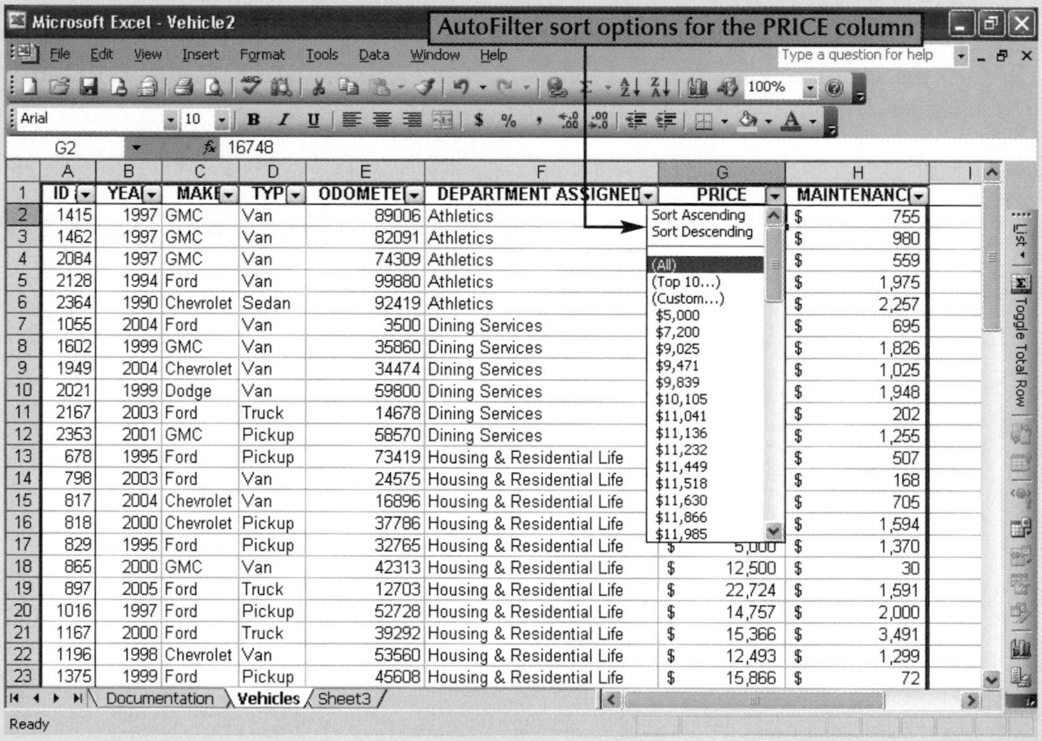

2. Click the **Sort Descending** item. The data is sorted in descending order by the price of the vehicle. See Figure 5-10.

Sorting a List Using the Sort Commands

Sometimes sorting by one sort field results in a tie—a tie occurs when more than one record has the same value for a field. For example, if you were to sort the vehicles list using the TYPE field, all vehicles with the same type would be grouped together. To break a tie, you can sort the list using multiple fields. For example, you can sort the vehicles list by type and then by year within each type. In this case, you specify the TYPE field as the primary sort field and the YEAR field as the **secondary sort field**.

Sorting a List Using More Than One Sort Field

Reference Window

- Click any cell within the list, click Data on the menu bar, and then click Sort.
- Click the Header row or No header row option button to indicate whether Excel should include the first row in the sort.
- Click the Sort by list arrow, select the column heading that you want to specify as the primary sort field, and then click the appropriate option button to specify the sort order.
- To sort by a second column, click the first Then by list arrow, select the column heading that you want to specify as the secondary sort field, and then click the appropriate sort order option button.
- To sort by a third column, click the second Then by list arrow, select the column heading that you want to specify as the tertiary sort field, and then click the appropriate sort order option button.
- Click the OK button.

Linda needs another list of vehicles. This time she wants the vehicles sorted by type and within type by model year, with new vehicles displayed before older ones. She wants vehicle type in alphabetical order and then by year in descending order within each type. This arrangement of the records will make finding information about the age of each type of vehicle much easier. To generate this list, you need to sort the data using two columns: TYPE as the primary sort field and YEAR as the secondary sort field. When you have more than one sort field, you must use the Sort command on the Data menu to specify the columns you want to sort.

Now you will sort the vehicles list by the type of vehicle in ascending order, and within type by the model year in descending order.

To sort the records using the Sort command:

1. Make sure the active cell is within the list.

2. Click **Data** on the menu bar, and then click **Sort**. The Sort dialog box opens, as shown in Figure 5-11. Note that all the rows and columns in the list, except for the first row (that is, the header row), are automatically selected.

Figure 5-11   Sort dialog box

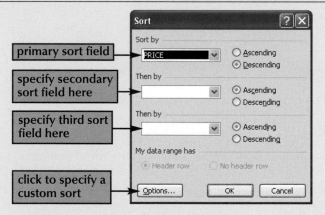

3. Click the **Sort by** list arrow to display the list of column headings, click **TYPE**, and then make sure the **Ascending** option button is selected.

Now you will specify the secondary sort field.

4. Click the first **Then by** list arrow, click **YEAR**, and then click the **Descending** option button.

5. Click the **OK** button to sort the records by type and within type by year. See Figure 5-12.

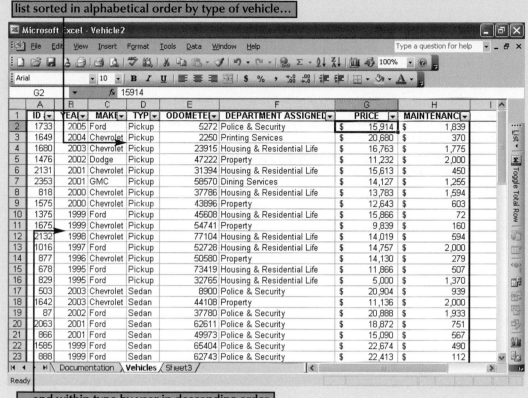

Vehicles list sorted by type and within type by year

Figure 5-12

list sorted in alphabetical order by type of vehicle...

...and within type by year in descending order

6. Scroll the list to view the data sorted by the type of vehicle and within type by the model year. For each vehicle type, the newer vehicles are displayed before the older ones.

This sorted list makes finding information about the age of each type of vehicle much easier.

Maintaining a List

Linda has several changes regarding vehicle status that need to be reflected in the list. First, Dining Services has purchased a new truck, and the Police & Security department has purchased a new patrol car; both vehicles need to be added to the vehicles list. Second, Linda just received the latest odometer reading for the vehicle with ID # 2142. This vehicle's record must be updated to reflect the new information. Finally, one of the older pickup trucks used by the Housing & Residential Life department is being scrapped because of its high mileage and high annual maintenance cost; the record for this vehicle, with ID # 678, needs to be deleted from the vehicles list. Linda asks you to update the vehicles list to reflect these changes.

Using the Insert Row to Add a Record

You can add records to a list using the insert row of a list range. The insert row is the blank row immediately following the last record in the list range. When your list is relatively short, using the insert row to enter a record into the list is a quick and convenient way to update your information.

You will add the new truck assigned to the Dining Services department using the insert row at the bottom of the list range.

To add a record using the insert row of a list range:

1. Scroll to the insert row, which is row 73, and then click cell **A73**.

2. Type **2520** in the ID # text box, and then press the **Tab** key to move to the YEAR column. Excel adds the row to the list range and inserts a new insert row at the bottom of the list range.

   Trouble? If you pressed the Enter key instead of the Tab key, scroll to row 73 and continue entering the data in Step 3.

3. Type **2006**, **GMC**, **Truck**, **73**, **Dining Services**, **18225**, and **75** in the cells for YEAR, MAKE, TYPE, ODOMETER, DEPARTMENT, PRICE, and MAINTENANCE, pressing the Tab key to move from cell to cell. See Figure 5-13.

Figure 5-13 | New record to be added to vehicles list

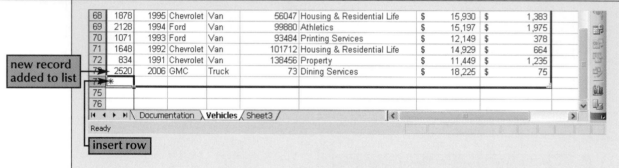

Using a Data Form to Add a Record

You can also maintain a list in Excel by using a data form. A **data form** is a dialog box in which you can add, find, edit, and delete records in a list. A data form displays one record at a time, as opposed to the table of rows and columns you see in the worksheet. You might find that using the data form is a better method than the insert row method if the record contains a large number of fields.

| Reference Window | **Adding a Record Using a Data Form** |

- Click any cell in the list.
- Click Data on the menu bar, and then click Form.
- Click the New button to display a blank form in which to enter a new record.
- Type the values for the new record, pressing the Tab key to move from field to field.
- Press the Enter key to add the record.
- When finished adding records, click the Close button.

You will update the vehicles list using the data form to enter the information on the new patrol car for the Police & Security department.

To add the new record using the data form:

1. Make sure the active cell is within the list.

2. Click **Data** on the menu bar, and then click **Form** to display the Vehicles data form. See Figure 5-14. The first record in the list appears in the Vehicles data form. Notice that Excel uses the worksheet name, Vehicles, as the title of the data form. The labels that appear on the left side of the data form are taken from the header row of the vehicles list. In the upper-right corner of the form, there is information on how many records there are in the list and which record is currently selected.

Vehicles data form ◄ **Figure 5-14**

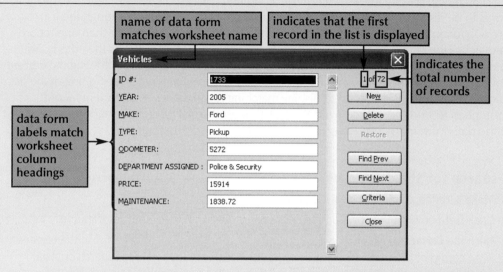

3. Click the **New** button to display a blank data form. Notice that the label "New Record" appears in the upper-right corner of the data form.

Now you will enter the values for the new record in the text boxes next to each label.

4. Type **2525** in the ID # text box, and then press the **Tab** key to move to the YEAR text box.

   Trouble? If you pressed the Enter key instead of the Tab key, a blank data form appears. To return to the record that you were entering, click the Find Prev button, click in the YEAR text box, and then continue with Step 5.

5. Type **2005** in the YEAR text box, press the **Tab** key to move to the MAKE text box, and then type **Chevrolet**.

6. Press the **Tab** key to move to the TYPE text box, and then enter the following data, pressing the Tab key after you enter each value:

   TYPE: **Sedan**
   ODOMETER: **1203**
   DEPARTMENT ASSIGNED: **Police & Security**
   PRICE: **22400**
   MAINTENANCE: **76**

   You do not have any more new records to add now, so you will close the data form and return to the worksheet.

7. Click the **Close** button to update the list and close the data form, and then scroll down to the bottom of the list to view the new record that has been automatically added. A new insert row always appears.

8. Press the **Ctrl + Home** keys to return to cell B2.

You have entered the new vehicles in the vehicles list, and you are ready to make the other changes to the vehicles list. You need to update the odometer reading for the vehicle with ID # 2142, and you need to delete the record for the vehicle with ID # 3544. Although you can manually scroll through the list to find a specific record, with larger lists of data this method is slow and prone to error. A quicker and more accurate way to find a record is to use the data form's search capabilities. You will use this method to update the vehicle's odometer reading and to delete the pickup truck no longer in use.

Using a Data Form to Search for a Record

You can use the data form to search for a specific record or group of records. When you initiate a search, you specify the **search criteria**, conditions placed on fields that define the records to be displayed. Excel starts from the current record and moves through the list, searching for any records that match the search criteria. If Excel finds more than one record that matches the search criteria, Excel displays the first record that matches the criteria. You can use the Find Next button in the data form to display the next record following the current record that matches the search criteria. If you do not start a search at the beginning of the list, you can use the Find Prev button to display matching records above the current record.

You need to find the vehicle with ID # 2142 to update its odometer reading. You will use the data form to find and update this record.

To search for the record of vehicle 2142 using the data form:

▶ 1. Make sure the active cell is within the list.

▶ 2. Click **Data** on the menu bar, and then click **Form** to display the Vehicles data form.

▶ 3. Click the **Criteria** button to display a blank data form. The label "Criteria" in the upper-right corner of the data form indicates that the form is ready to accept search criteria, which in this case is vehicle ID # 2142.

▶ 4. Type **2142** in the ID # text box. You can enter multiple criteria to narrow the scope of your search. When you enter multiple criteria, only records that match all the criteria that you have entered will be displayed. There is only one specification that the record must match, so you do not have to enter anything else.

▶ 5. Click the **Find Next** button to display the next record in the list that meets the specified criteria. The record that you are searching for is ID # 2142. See Figure 5-15. If there were more than one vehicle with the same ID # and the current record was not the one you were interested in, you could click the Find Next button again to display the next record meeting the search criteria. If no records meet the search criteria, no message is displayed; instead, the data form simply displays the current record.

Figure 5-15 ▶ **Record for vehicle with ID # 2142 found**

Now you will update this record.

6. Double-click in the **ODOMETER** text box to select the current value, type **3456**, and then click the **Close** button to complete the update and return to the vehicles list.

7. Scroll the list to find the vehicle with ID # 2142. Note that the odometer reading for this vehicle now displays 3456.

Now you need to complete the final update to the list by deleting the pickup truck record assigned to Housing & Residential Life.

Using a Data Form to Delete a Record

To delete a record, you first need to locate it. You can use the data form to search the list to find and then delete the record.

Deleting a Record Using a Data Form

Reference Window

- Click any cell in the list.
- Click Data on the menu bar, and then click Form.
- Locate and display the record you want to delete.
- Click the Delete button, and then click the OK button to confirm the deletion.

The record ID # for the pickup truck assigned to Housing & Residential Life, which you need to delete, is 678. You will use the data form to find and delete this record.

To search for and delete the pickup truck record:

1. Make sure the active cell is within the list.

2. Click **Data** on the menu bar, and then click **Form** to display the Vehicles data form.

3. Click the **Criteria** button, type **678** in the ID # text box, and then click the **Find Next** button. The record for a 1995 Ford pickup truck record assigned to Housing & Residential Life is displayed.

4. Click the **Delete** button. A message box appears, warning you that the displayed record will be permanently deleted from the list.

5. Click the **OK** button to confirm the record deletion. The vehicle with ID # 678 has been deleted from the list, and the next record in the list is displayed in the data form. Note that the next record shows another pickup truck assigned to Housing & Residential Life, but the ID # is different.

6. Click the **Close** button to close the data form and return to the worksheet. The vehicles list is now updated.

7. Save the changes you have made to the workbook, and then close it.

You can also delete a record directly from the list range. First, you need to select the entire row that you want to delete, and then right-click the selected row and click Delete on the shortcut menu or click Delete on the Edit menu. When you use one of these methods, you are not asked to confirm the deletion, so make sure you have selected the correct row.

You have now provided Linda with a current and updated list of all vehicles, sorted by type and within type by year. Next, you will use the vehicles list to retrieve specific information on only some of the vehicles. To find the information that you need, you will create a customized list, which is limited to the information you need, by filtering the vehicles list to show just the necessary information. You will do this in Session 5.2.

Review

Session 5.1 Quick Check

1. In Excel, a(n) _____ is a collection of similar data stored in a structured manner.
2. What does the Freeze Panes option on the Window menu do? Why is this feature helpful?
3. Identify three visual elements that indicate a list range has been created.
4. The fields that you use to order your data are called _____ or _____.
5. You have a list of college students. First name, last name, major, current year (that is, freshman, sophomore, and so on), and year of graduation are the fields used in the list. Explain how to order the list of students so that those with the same major appear together in alphabetical order by the student's last name.
6. To locate a record quickly, you can use the _____ associated with the list.
7. You have a list of 250 employees. Social Security number, first name, last name, and address are fields you track for each employee. Explain how to find Jin Shinu's record using the data form.
8. A(n) _____ sort key is a field used to arrange records in a list.
9. If you sort the vehicles list from the most recent purchase date to the oldest purchase date, you have sorted the vehicles in _____ order.

Session 5.2

Filtering a List Using AutoFilters

Linda received a letter indicating that there might be a recall of certain Ford vans manufactured between 2000 and 2003. To be prepared for any such recall and the associated upgrades, Linda needs information on these vehicles so that she can alert the Property department.

To get a list of Ford vans whose model year is between 2000 and 2003, you could scan the entire vehicles list. However, with large lists, locating specific data can be difficult and time-consuming. Sorting can help because you group the data; however, you're still working with the entire list. You could use a data form, but if you use a data form to find records that meet specified criteria, you will only display one record at a time. A better solution is to have Excel find the specific records you want and display only these records in the worksheet. This process of displaying a subset of data in the list that meets the criteria you specified is called **filtering** the data. Filtering doesn't rearrange the data as sorting does. When you filter a list of data, all records that do not meet your criteria are temporarily hidden from view.

You saw the AutoFilter arrows appear when you first created the list range. You can use an AutoFilter arrow to select the criteria you want to use to filter the data.

Filtering a List Using AutoFilter

- Click any cell in the list.
- Click Data on the menu bar, point to Filter, and then click AutoFilter to insert list arrows next to each column heading in the list.
- Click the AutoFilter arrow in the column that contains the data you want to filter.
- Click the specific criteria by which you want to filter the data in the list.

Using an AutoFilter, you will create the list of Ford vans that may be recalled. Remember, by filtering the list you will be hiding some of the records.

To filter the vehicles list using an AutoFilter:

1. If you took a break after the last session, make sure Excel is running, the Vehicle2 workbook is open, and the Vehicles worksheet is displayed.

2. Click any cell within the vehicles list to activate the list range.

3. Click the **MAKE** AutoFilter arrow in cell C1 to display a list of criteria you can use to filter the data. See Figure 5-16. Besides the unique values—Chevrolet, Dodge, Ford, GMC—in the list of items for the MAKE column, there are five other items that appear and can be applied to every column. The first two items are the sort options you used earlier in the tutorial. The other three items—ALL, Top 10, and Custom—are related to filtering tasks.

Filtering options for the MAKE field | **Figure 5-16**

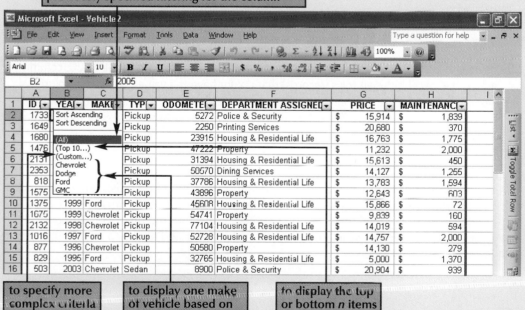

to display all items in the column, removing any previously specified filtering for the column

to specify more complex criteria

to display one make of vehicle based on a value in the column

to display the top or bottom *n* items

Trouble? If the AutoFilter arrows are not visible in the header row, click Data on the menu bar, point to Filter, and then click AutoFilter.

Now you will select your criterion for filtering the data

4. Click **Ford** to display only Ford vehicles. See Figure 5-17. In the status bar, Excel displays the number of records found, out of the total records in the list. There are 30 records found.

Figure 5-17 ▶ **Vehicles list displaying only Ford vehicles**

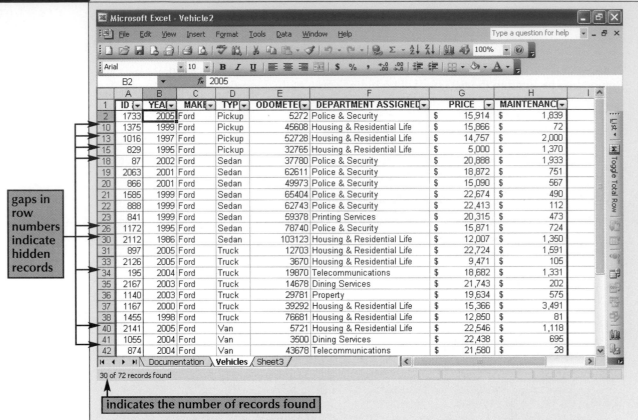

gaps in row numbers indicate hidden records

indicates the number of records found

5. Review the list to verify that only records with a value equal to Ford in the MAKE column are visible. Excel hides all rows (records) that do not have the value Ford in this column. Notice the gaps in the row numbers in the worksheet, and the blue color of the row numbers of the filtered records. The color of the filter arrow next to the MAKE column changes to blue to let you know that this column has been used to filter the list.

If you need to further restrict the records that appear in the filtered list, you can select entries from the lists of criteria for the other columns. Linda wants to display only Ford vans, rather than all Ford vehicles. To add another criterion to the filter, you will click the arrow for the TYPE column, which contains the value you need to use to further filter the data to display just Ford vans.

To add another criterion by which to filter the vehicles list:

▸ **1.** Click the **TYPE** AutoFilter arrow in cell D1.

▸ **2.** Click **Van** to display Ford vans. See Figure 5-18.

Vehicles list showing only Ford vans ◂ **Figure 5-18**

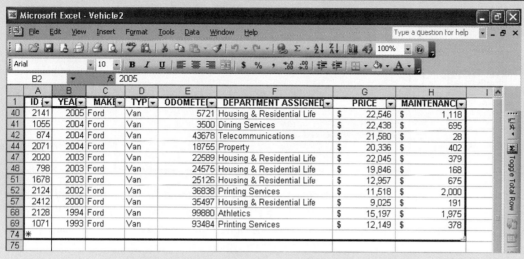

If you wanted to remove the filter from the TYPE field, you would click the TYPE column list arrow again and then click All to remove the filter from this field. All Ford vehicles would be displayed in the list again.

Using Custom AutoFilters to Specify More Complex Criteria

Although you can often find the information you need by selecting a single item from a list of values in the AutoFilter list, there are times when you need to specify a custom set of criteria to find certain records. **Custom AutoFilters** allow you to specify relationships other than those that are "equal to" the criteria specified in the filter records. For example, you filtered records by type; that is, the values in the TYPE field were equal to the specified criterion, which was Ford. But the type of vehicle is only part of the information that you need. The recall specified that the vehicles were manufactured between 2000 and 2003. Therefore, you need to complete the search by filtering for vehicles manufactured between 2000 and 2003.

To complete the search, you need to develop a custom set of criteria. You will create this set of criteria to retrieve these records using the Custom AutoFilter dialog box.

To use a custom AutoFilter to filter the vehicles list:

▶ 1. Click the **YEAR** AutoFilter arrow, and then click **Custom**. The Custom AutoFilter dialog box opens. See Figure 5-19.

Figure 5-19 **Custom AutoFilter dialog box**

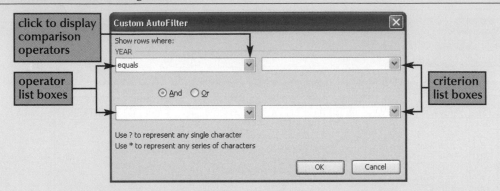

You use the operator list box, which is the first list box in the dialog box, to specify a comparison operator that you need to use for the filter by selecting an operator from the list. You use the criteria list box, the list box to the right of the operator list box, to specify the field value that you want to use for the filter by typing the value or selecting an item from the list. You can select the And or Or option button if you want to display rows that meet two conditions for the field. You select And to display rows that meet both criteria. You select Or to display rows that meet either criterion.

▶ 2. Click the first operator list arrow, and then click **is greater than or equal to**.

▶ 3. Click in the first criteria list box, and then type **2000** as the first value.

▶ 4. If necessary, click the **And** option button. The And option indicates that both conditions will need to be met.

▶ 5. Click the second operator list arrow, and then scroll down the list and click **is less than or equal to**.

▶ 6. Click in the second criteria list box, and then type **2003**.

▶ 7. Click the **OK** button to display the filtered list consisting of all Ford vans manufactured between 2000 and 2003. See Figure 5-20. The status bar indicates that 5 of 72 records were found.

Figure 5-20 **Filtered list showing Ford vans with model years between 2000 and 2003**

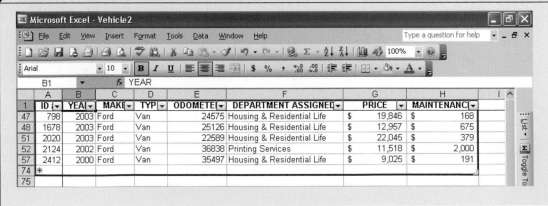

You have completed your task. You will restore the entire list of vehicles.

To show all records from the filtered list:

1. Click **Data** on the menu bar, point to **Filter**, and then click **Show All** to display all the records in the list and remove all the filters. All the records are displayed.

If you wanted to remove the AutoFilter arrows from the header row, you would select AutoFilter instead of Show All from the Filter submenu.

Linda wants to be able to quickly identify "high mileage" vehicles as she views the vehicles lists and asks you to apply Excel's conditional formatting feature to the ODOMETER field.

Using Conditional Formatting

Excel's **conditional formatting** is formatting that appears in a cell only when data in the cell meets conditions that you specify or is the result of a formula. One use of conditional formatting is to easily identify critical highs or lows in a report. For example, cells representing sales that do not meet projections can be formatted in bold or with a red background. Or, in our case, if certain vehicles have high maintenance costs, the value can be displayed in red. You can specify up to three conditions to categorize the value of a cell or the formula that produces the value. You specify the formatting (font, font style, font color, border, and so on) that will be applied to the cell if the condition is true.

Reference Window

Applying Conditional Formatting to Cells

- Select the cells to which you want to apply conditional formatting.
- Click Format on the menu bar, and then click Conditional Formatting.
- Specify the condition on which to apply formatting using the Condition 1 boxes.
- Click the Format button.
- Select the font style, font color, underlining, borders, shading, or patterns that you want to apply if that condition is met, and then click the OK button.
- To specify another condition, click the Add >> button, and enter the necessary specifications for the condition and its formatting.
- Click the OK button.

Linda wants to determine the best time to trade in vehicles that have higher mileage. She wants to format high-mileage vehicles using two categories—those with over 100,000 miles and those with between 80,000 and 100,000 miles—so she can easily spot them. To highlight these two categories of vehicles, you want to apply a light turquoise background to any cell in the ODOMETER field containing a value exceeding 100,000 and a light yellow background for any vehicles with an odometer reading between 80,000 and 100,000. You will specify the conditional formatting and apply it to the ODOMETER field.

To apply conditional formatting to the ODOMETER field:

1. Select the range **E2:E73**. This is the range to which you will apply the conditional formatting.

2. Click **Format** on the menu bar, and then click **Conditional Formatting**. The Conditional Formatting dialog box opens. See Figure 5-21.

Figure 5-21

Figure 5-21 | Conditional Formatting dialog box

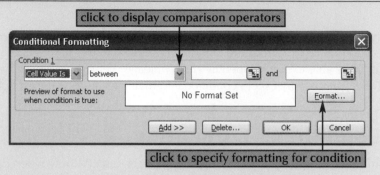

First, you will specify the condition that will be applied to the range of odometer readings.

3. Make sure that **Cell Value Is** appears in the first Condition 1 box.

   Next, you will choose the comparison operator that will compare the cell value to the condition you specify.

4. Click the list arrow in the second box to display a list of comparison operators, and then click **greater than**. Notice that the number of boxes changes to reflect the comparison operator you selected.

   Now you will enter the value for the condition that the values in the ODOMETER field must meet.

5. Click in the third box for Condition 1, and then type **100000**. The condition is defined.

   Next, you will specify the formatting to be applied to the cell or range if the condition is true.

6. Click the **Format** button to open the Format Cells dialog box.

7. Click the **Patterns** tab, and then click the **light turquoise** color square (fifth row, fifth column from the left) in the color palette.

8. Click the **OK** button to return to the Conditional Formatting dialog box. Notice that light turquoise shading appears in the Preview box.

   Now you will specify the second condition.

9. Click the **Add >>** button to display the boxes that you can use to specify the criteria for a second condition.

10. Repeat Steps 3 to 8 to specify vehicles driven *between* **80,000** and **100,000** miles and apply a light yellow background (fifth row, third column from the left) to the records that meet the second condition. If you had a third condition to specify (a maximum of three can be entered), you would click the Add >> button again and return to Steps 3 to 8.

11. Click the **OK** button to apply the conditional formatting to the selected cells, and then click any cell to deselect the range.

12. Scroll the list so you can see where the conditional formatting has been applied. See Figure 5-22. Notice that the background color of several cells in the range is now light turquoise, and others are light yellow.

Vehicles list with conditional formatting applied

Figure 5-22

records that meet the conditions specified

Note that if the value of the cell changes and no longer meets the specified condition(s), Excel does not display the conditional formats associated with that cell. Likewise, if the value of the cell changes and now the specified condition is met, then Excel applies the format associated with the condition to the cell. In all cases, the conditional formats remain applied to the cells until you *remove* conditional formatting specifications, even when none of the conditions is met and the specified cell formats are not displayed. To remove a conditional format, you must select the range of cells to which the conditional formatting has been applied, and then open the Conditional Formatting dialog box. In the dialog box, you click the Delete button to open the Delete Conditional Format dialog box, in which you clear the check box of the condition(s) that you want to delete. Click the OK button twice to remove the formatting from the selected cells. Even though you applied conditional formatting to cells in an Excel list, it is important to know that you can apply conditional formatting to any cells in an Excel worksheet, not just in an Excel list.

Using the Total Row to Calculate Totals in a List

The manager of the physical plant is considering outsourcing the maintenance of trucks because the department has had difficulty hiring and retaining good maintenance mechanics. The manager asked Linda for the average annual maintenance cost of all trucks in the university's fleet of vehicles that were manufactured beginning in 2000. The list range can be used to calculate summary statistics (such as sums, averages, counts, maximums, and minimums) on a filtered list. To quickly calculate a total and display a total row in a list, you can click the Toggle Total Row button on the List toolbar. As the name indicates, you can click this button again to hide the total row. Once the total row is displayed, you can select a subtotal function to calculate the values you need.

In order to calculate the average maintenance cost for trucks manufactured starting in the year 2000, you will first filter the list to display trucks manufactured in 2000 or later.

To calculate summary statistics on a filtered list:

1. Click the **Type** AutoFilter arrow, and then click **Truck** to display only trucks. The rows that are not trucks are hidden and the list range border frames the remaining rows.

   Now you will remove any truck models manufactured before 2000 from the filtered list.

2. Click the **Year** AutoFilter arrow, and then click **Custom** in the AutoFilter list. The Custom AutoFilter dialog box opens.

3. Select **is greater than or equal to** in the comparison box, enter **2000** in the box at the right, and then click the **OK** button. Eight trucks remain in the filtered list.

   Now you will add a total row to calculate the average maintenance cost.

4. Click the **Toggle Total Row** button on the List toolbar. A total row is added below the insert row, the word "Total" is displayed in the leftmost cell, and the sum of the values in the rightmost column is displayed in the total row.

5. Select cell **H75**, as shown in Figure 5-23.

Figure 5-23	Filtered vehicles list after the total row is displayed

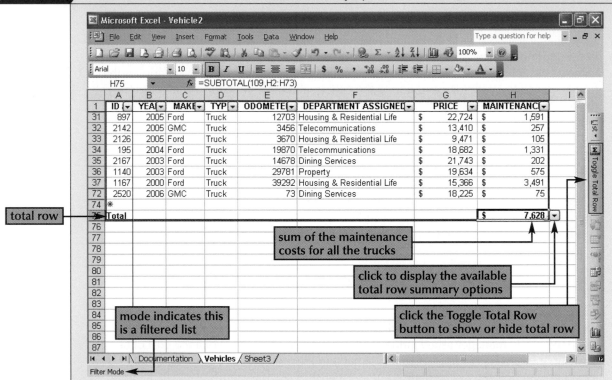

6. Click the list arrow next to cell H75 to display a list of subtotal functions. See Figure 5-24. The Sum function is the default.

Total row displays options for calculating totals | **Figure 5-24**

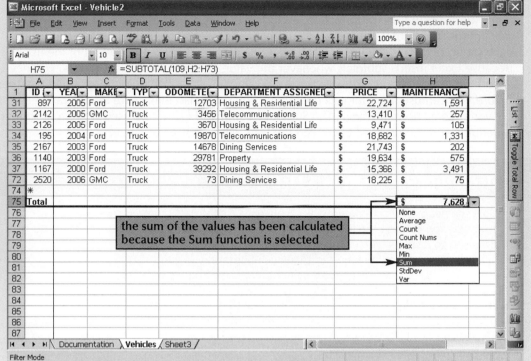

7. Click **Average** in the list to calculate the average annual maintenance cost for the eight trucks. The average total of $953 is displayed.

Linda has the information that she requested. You will, therefore, show all the records in the list and remove the total row from the worksheet.

To remove the total row from the list range:

1. Click **Data** on the menu bar, point to **Filter**, and then click **Show All** to restore all records to the list.

2. Click the **Toggle Total Row** button on the List toolbar, and then scroll down to the bottom of the list. The total row is removed from the list range.

The budget director has also asked Linda for a report displaying the data for all vehicles sorted by department, followed by the total amount each department has spent for its vehicles. Linda decides to use Excel's Subtotals command to satisfy this information request.

Although Linda could use the total row feature of the list range to calculate the expected results, this method requires filtering, totaling, and printing the data separately for each department. A faster way to provide the information that Linda needs is to use the Subtotals command.

Inserting Subtotals into a List

Excel can summarize data in a list by inserting subtotals. The Subtotals command offers many kinds of summary information, including counts, sums, averages, minimums, and maximums. The Subtotals command automatically inserts a subtotal line into the list for each group of data in the list. A grand total line is also added to the bottom of the list. Because Excel inserts subtotals whenever the value in a specified field changes, you need to sort the list so that records with the same value in a specified field are grouped together *before* you can use the Subtotals command. You must also make sure the list range is converted to a "normal" range. The Subtotals command cannot be used while a list range is defined, so first you need to convert the list range to a normal range.

Reference Window	Calculating Subtotals in a List

- Sort the list by the column for which you want a subtotal.
- If necessary, convert the list range to a normal range by clicking Data on the menu bar, pointing to List, clicking Convert to Range, and then clicking the Yes button.
- Click Data on the menu bar, and then click Subtotals.
- In the At each change in list box, select the column that contains the group you want to subtotal.
- In the Use function list box, select the function that you want to use to summarize the data.
- In the Add subtotal to list box, select the column that contains the values you want to summarize.
- To calculate a second category of subtotals, repeat the steps above, but remove the check from the Replace current subtotals check box.
- Click the OK button.

To supply Linda with the information she has requested, you will generate a list of vehicles, sorted by department, with a subtotal calculated for the PRICE field and insert a subtotal after each departmental grouping.

To calculate subtotals using the Subtotals command:

1. If the list is not sorted by department, click the **DEPARTMENT ASSIGNED** AutoFilter arrow, and then click **Sort Ascending** in the list.

2. Click **Data** on the menu bar, point to **List**, and then click **Convert to Range**. A message box appears, asking if you want to convert the list to a normal range. See Figure 5-25.

Figure 5-25	Converting a list to a normal range

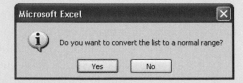

3. Click the **Yes** button. The AutoFilter arrows, List toolbar, and list border are no longer displayed.

▶ **4.** Click **Data** on the menu bar, and then click **Subtotals** to open the Subtotal dialog box. See Figure 5-26.

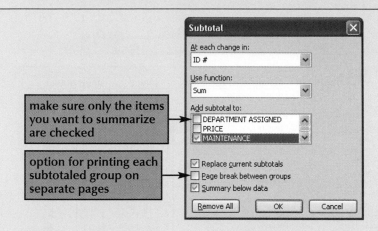

make sure only the items you want to summarize are checked

option for printing each subtotaled group on separate pages

▶ **5.** Click the **At each change in** list arrow, and then click **DEPARTMENT ASSIGNED** to select the column where the subtotals will be inserted.

▶ **6.** If necessary, click the **Use function** list arrow and click **Sum**. The Use function list provides several options for subtotaling data, including counts, averages, minimums, and maximums.

Now you will specify the PRICE field, which is the field to be subtotaled.

▶ **7.** In the Add subtotal to list box, scroll the list and select the **PRICE** check box, and, if necessary, remove the check from the **MAINTENANCE** check box and any other checked option. If you're preparing a new subtotal and want to replace existing subtotals in the list, select the Replace current subtotals check box; otherwise, new subtotals will be displayed on a separate row above the existing subtotal. Since there currently are no subtotals in the list, whether you select this option or not will make no difference.

▶ **8.** Make sure the **Summary below data** check box is selected so that the subtotals appear below the related data; otherwise, Excel places the subtotals above the first entry in each group and places the grand total at the top of the column just below the row of column headings.

▶ **9.** Click the **OK** button to insert subtotals into the list. Rows that display subtotals for the PRICE column have been inserted throughout the list, showing the totals for each department. Note that a series of Outline buttons now appears to the left of the worksheet. These buttons allow you to display or hide the detail rows within each subtotal while the Subtotals feature is active.

Trouble? If necessary, increase the column width so you can view the subtotal values.

▶ **10.** Scroll through the list to see all the subtotals, moving to the bottom of the list to view the grand total, as shown in Figure 5-27.

Figure 5-27 ▶ **Vehicles list with subtotals**

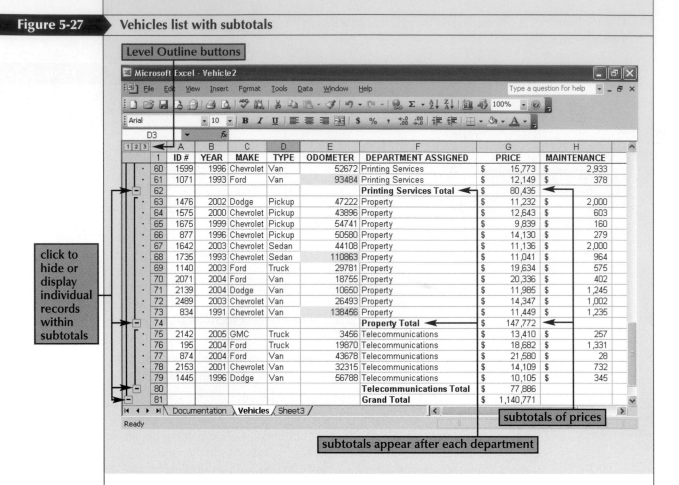

The subtotals are useful, but Linda asks if there is a way to isolate the different subtotal sections so that she can focus on them individually.

Using the Subtotals Outline View

In addition to displaying subtotals, the Subtotals feature "outlines" your worksheet so you can control the level of detail that is displayed. The three Outline buttons displayed at the top of the outline area, as shown in Figure 5-27, allow you to show or hide different levels of detail in your worksheet. By default, the highest level is active, in this case Level 3. Level 3 displays the most detail—the individual vehicle records, the subtotals, and the grand total. If you click the Level 2 Outline button, Excel displays the subtotals and the grand total, but not the individual records. If you click the Level 1 Outline button, Excel displays only the grand total.

You will use the Outline buttons to prepare a report for Linda that includes only subtotals and the grand total.

To use the Outline buttons to hide records:

1. Click the **Level 2 Outline** button. See Figure 5-28. Notice that the worksheet hides the individual vehicle records and shows only the subtotals for each department and the grand total.

Subtotals after Level 2 Outline button is selected　　**Figure 5-28**

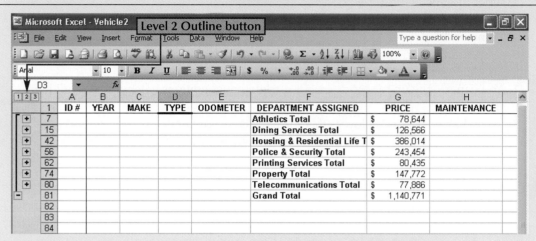

Trouble? If necessary, scroll up the window to see the complete Level 2 list.

2. Click the **Level 3 Outline** button to show all the records again.

Now that you have prepared the list with subtotals, you will remove the subtotals from the list so that you can perform other list-related tasks in the next session.

To remove the subtotals from the list:

1. Click **Data** on the menu bar, and then click **Subtotals** to open the Subtotal dialog box.

2. Click the **Remove All** button to remove the subtotals from the list. When the subtotals are removed, only the records in the list are displayed. You have supplied Linda with the information she needs for her meeting with the budget director to review financial plans for the next fiscal cycle.

3. Click **Data** on the menu bar, point to **List**, and then click **Create List** to open the Create List dialog box.

4. Click the **OK** button to create the list range, and then click any cell in the list. Notice that the list range is now active.

5. Save your changes to the workbook and then close it.

Now Linda needs to generate some information for a meeting with the budget director to review financial plans for the next fiscal cycle. You will work with the vehicles list in the next session to gather the information she needs for that meeting.

Review

Session 5.2 Quick Check

1. Explain the relationship between the Sort and Subtotals commands.
2. If you have a list of 500 employees and want to calculate the average salary of employees in the Marketing department, you can use the _____ and _____ of a list range.
3. Explain how you can display a list of marketing majors with a GPA of 3.0 or greater from a list of 300 students.
4. Once subtotals are displayed, you can use the _____ button to control the amount of detail displayed.
5. True or False: The Count function is a valid subtotal function when using the Subtotals command.
6. _____ enables formatting to appear only when the data in a cell meets a condition you specify.
7. You can specify up to _____ different conditions when using conditional formatting.
8. If you have a list of employees that includes fields for gender and salary, among others, explain how you could determine the average salary for females using the Toggle Total Row button on the List toolbar.

Session 5.3

Creating and Using PivotTables to Summarize a List

An Excel list can contain a wealth of information, but because of the large amounts of detailed data, it is often difficult to form a clear overall view of the information. You can use a PivotTable to help organize the data into a meaningful summary. A **PivotTable** report is an interactive table that enables you to group and summarize an Excel list into a concise, tabular format for easier reporting and analysis. A PivotTable summarizes data into different categories using functions such as COUNT, SUM, AVERAGE, MAX, and MIN. You can also summarize the list by creating a PivotChart. A **PivotChart** report contains the same elements as a regular chart but also contains fields and items that can be added to, rotated, or removed to display different views of your data. A PivotChart report must be associated with a PivotTable report in the same workbook. When you create a PivotChart report, Excel automatically creates an associated PivotTable report. If you have an existing PivotTable report, you can use it to create the PivotChart report, which will reflect the view of that table.

To generate a PivotTable report, you need to specify which fields you want to summarize. Salaries, sales, and costs are examples of fields that are often summarized for reports. In PivotTable terminology, these fields are known as **data fields**. In addition to data fields, a PivotTable uses **category fields** to group values such as department, model, year, and vehicle type. Category fields appear in PivotTables as rows, columns, or pages, and they are referred to as **column fields**, **row fields**, and **page fields**. Figure 5-29 shows an example of a PivotTable.

Sample PivotTable | **Figure 5-29**

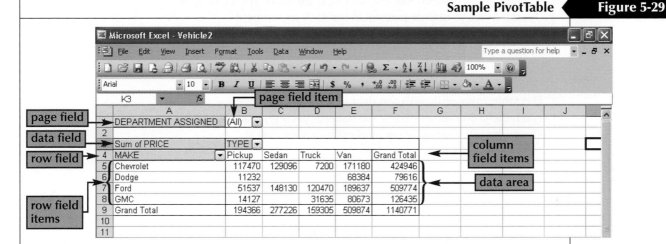

One advantage of PivotTables is that you can easily rearrange, hide, and display different category fields in the PivotTable to provide alternative views of the data. The ability to "pivot" your table—for example, change column headings to row positions and vice versa—gives the PivotTable its name and makes it a powerful analytical tool.

At budget time, Linda meets with the head of the Property department to discuss the department's budget for the upcoming fiscal year. The Property department is responsible for vehicle maintenance and has a budget for upcoming maintenance expenses for all the vehicles owned by the university. Linda needs a report showing the average annual maintenance cost by type of vehicle and by department.

Although the Total Row of the list range and the Subtotals command on the menu can be used to analyze data, the best approach to generating the information that Linda needs is to create a PivotTable. A useful first step in creating a PivotTable is to plan it and sketch its layout. Use your plan and sketch, shown in Figures 5-30 and 5-31, to help you produce the PivotTable you want to create.

| **Figure 5-30** | **PivotTable plan for calculating average annual maintenance costs** |

My Goal
Create a table that compares average maintenance costs for each department by type of vehicle

What results do I want to see?
Average departmental maintenance cost for each type of vehicle
Overall average maintenance cost for each department
Overall average maintenance cost for each type of vehicle
Overall average maintenance cost for each vehicle

What information do I need?
The table rows will show the data for each department.
The table columns will show the data for each type of vehicle.
The table will summarize annual maintenance cost.

What calculation method will I use?
The annual maintenance cost will be averaged.

| **Figure 5-31** | **Sketch of table to compare average annual maintenance costs** |

Average Maintenance Cost by Department and Type of Vehicle

Department	Pickup	Sedan	Truck	Van	Total
Athletics					
Dining Services					
Housing & Residential Life					
Police & Security					
Printing Services					
Property					
Telecommunications					
Total					

Now you are ready to create a PivotTable summarizing the average annual maintenance cost of the different types of vehicles by department.

Creating a PivotTable

To create the PivotTable that will provide Linda with the information she needs, you will use Excel's PivotTable and PivotChart Wizard to guide you through a three-step process. Although the PivotTable and PivotChart Wizard will prompt you for the information necessary to create the table, the preliminary plan and sketch you created will be helpful in achieving the layout Linda wants.

Most often when creating a PivotTable, you begin with a list stored in a worksheet, although a PivotTable can also be created using data stored in an external database file, such as one in Access. In this case, you will use the vehicles list to create the PivotTable.

To create a PivotTable using the vehicles list:

1. If you took a break after the last session, make sure Excel is running and that the Vehicle2 workbook is open.

2. Switch to the Vehicles worksheet if necessary, and then make sure the list range is active.

3. Click **Data** on the menu bar, and then click **PivotTable and PivotChart Report** to display the first step in the PivotTable and PivotChart Wizard, as shown in Figure 5-32.

Step 1 of the PivotTable and PivotChart Wizard | **Figure 5-32**

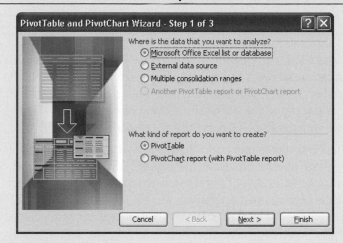

In this step, you specify the kind of report you want to display—either a PivotTable or a PivotChart along with a PivotTable. You also indicate where the data for the PivotTable can be found. You can select from an Excel list, an external data source (such as an Access database file), multiple consolidation ranges, or another PivotTable. To develop the average annual maintenance cost PivotTable, you will use the list range in the Vehicles worksheet.

4. Make sure the **Microsoft Excel list or database** and **PivotTable** options are selected, and then click the **Next** button to display the next step in the PivotTable and PivotChart Wizard. See Figure 5-33. In this step, you need to identify the location of the data you are going to summarize in the PivotTable. Because the active cell is located within the list range in this case, the wizard automatically selects the range $A$1:$H$73 as the source of data for the PivotTable.

Step 2 of the PivotTable and PivotChart Wizard | **Figure 5-33**

Trouble? If the Range box displays "Database" instead of $A$1:$H$73 as the source of the data, select the range A1:H73 or type A1:H73 to identify the correct source of the data.

5. Click the **Next** button to display the last step in the PivotTable and PivotChart Wizard. See Figure 5-34.

Figure 5-34 ▶ **Step 3 of the PivotTable and PivotChart Wizard**

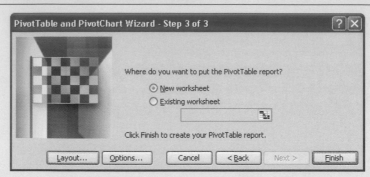

In this step, you need to decide where to place the PivotTable—either in a new worksheet or in an existing worksheet. You also have the opportunity to complete the layout of the PivotTable within the wizard by selecting the Layout button; otherwise, you can complete the PivotTable directly on the worksheet. You will place the PivotTable in a new worksheet and then work with the PivotTable directly on the worksheet.

6. Make sure the **New worksheet** option button is selected, and then click the **Finish** button to create the PivotTable report layout. See Figure 5-35. A new worksheet, Sheet1, appears to the left of the Vehicles sheet. Sheet1 contains a blank PivotTable report layout, a diagram containing blue outlined drop areas. You use this diagram and the PivotTable Field List box to complete the PivotTable. The PivotTable Field List box includes the names of each field in your Excel list.

Figure 5-35 ▶ **PivotTable report layout diagram with drop areas**

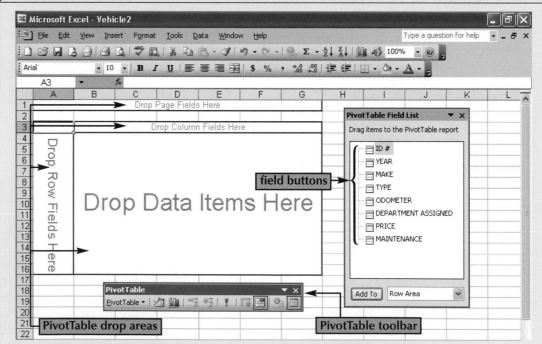

Trouble? The PivotTable toolbar and PivotTable Field List box might not appear in the same location as shown in Figure 5-35. If necessary, move the PivotTable toolbar and PivotTable Field List box so they are visible on your screen and more accessible.

The worksheet also includes the PivotTable toolbar. Figure 5-36 describes the tools available on this toolbar.

Buttons available on PivotTable toolbar   **Figure 5-36**

Button	Name	Function
PivotTable ▾	PivotTable	Displays a shortcut menu of all PivotTable commands
	Format Report	Displays a list of preformatted styles for PivotTable reports
	Chart Wizard	Creates a chart of the PivotTable report on a chart sheet
	Hide Detail	Hides the detail lines for a selected field in a PivotTable
	Show Detail	Shows the detail lines for a selected field in a PivotTable
	Refresh Data	Updates the contents of a PivotTable based on changes made to the source data
	Include Hidden Items in Totals	Calculates the totals, including hidden items
	Always Display Items	Includes all items, displayed or hidden, in calculated totals and subtotals
	Field Settings	Opens the PivotTable Field dialog box so you can modify options for the selected field
	Show/Hide Field List	Displays the PivotTable Field List on the worksheet, or hides it when you no longer need it

Now you are ready to lay out the PivotTable report directly on the worksheet.

Laying Out a PivotTable Directly on a Worksheet

Using the blank PivotTable report layout diagram, you specify which fields will appear as column, row, and page category fields in the PivotTable and which fields contain the data you want to summarize. At this point in the creation of the PivotTable, the fields are represented by a set of fields in the PivotTable Field List. You create the PivotTable by dragging the fields with the data you want from the PivotTable Field List to any of the four areas of the diagram: Drop Row Fields Here, Drop Column Fields Here, Drop Page Fields Here, or Drop Data Items Here.

Laying Out a PivotTable on a Worksheet   Reference Window

- Click and drag the fields you want to display in rows to the area of the PivotTable diagram labeled Drop Row Fields Here.
- Click and drag the fields you want to display in columns to the area of the PivotTable diagram labeled Drop Column Fields Here.
- Click and drag the fields you want to display in pages to the area of the PivotTable diagram labeled Drop Page Fields Here.
- Click and drag the fields that contain the data you want to summarize to the area of the PivotTable diagram labeled Drop Data Items Here.

You need to calculate average annual maintenance cost by department for each type of vehicle. In the PivotTable, you want the values in the DEPARTMENT ASSIGNED field to appear as row labels, the values in the TYPE field to appear as column headings, and the data in the MAINTENANCE field to be summarized.

You will now lay out the PivotTable on the worksheet.

To lay out a PivotTable on a worksheet:

▶ **1.** From the PivotTable Field List, click and drag the **DEPARTMENT ASSIGNED** field to the area on the PivotTable diagram labeled Drop Row Fields Here, and then release the mouse button when the field is positioned correctly. When you release the mouse button, the DEPARTMENT ASSIGNED field button appears in the PivotTable report along with a row label for each unique value in the DEPARTMENT ASSIGNED field. See Figure 5-37.

Figure 5-37	PivotTable with DEPARTMENT ASSIGNED field as a row field

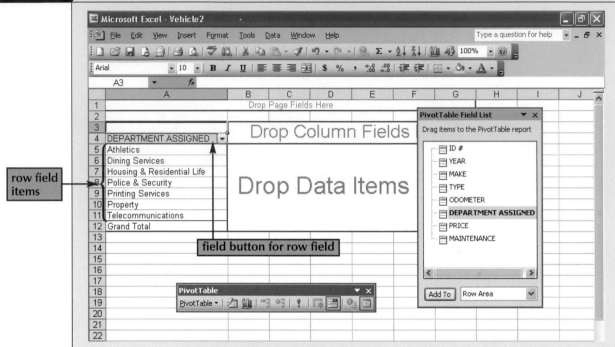

Trouble? If you moved the wrong field into the PivotTable diagram, you can remove the field by dragging its field button anywhere outside the diagram or by clicking the Undo button ↺ on the Standard toolbar. Then repeat Step 1.

▶ **2.** Drag the **TYPE** field from the PivotTable Field List to the area of the diagram labeled Drop Column Fields Here. When you release the mouse button, the TYPE field button appears in the diagram, and each unique value in the TYPE field appears as a column heading.

▶ **3.** Drag the **MAINTENANCE** field from the PivotTable Field List to the area of the diagram labeled Drop Data Items Here. When you release the mouse button, the Sum of MAINTENANCE field button appears above the DEPARTMENT ASSIGNED field button to indicate the type of summary function; the report contains the total annual maintenance costs for each department for each vehicle type. See Figure 5-38.

PivotTable showing sum of the annual maintenance costs Figure 5-38

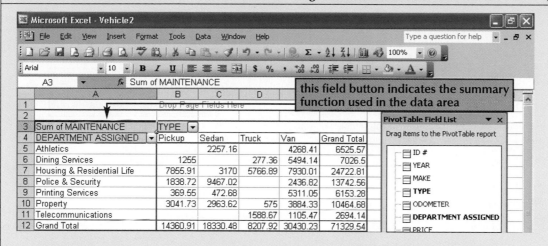

> **Trouble?** If the wrong function appears in the diagram, don't worry. You will learn how to change the function next.

By default, the PivotTable report uses the Sum function for calculations involving numeric values placed in the Drop Data Items Here area and the COUNT function for nonnumeric values. If you want to calculate a different summary function, such as average, maximum, or minimum, you click the Field Settings button on the PivotTable toolbar, and then you select the summary function from a list of available functions in the PivotTable Field dialog box.

Linda wants to compare average annual maintenance costs by department and vehicle type. You will change the summary function from Sum to Average.

To calculate the average annual maintenance costs by department and type of vehicle:

1. Click a cell within the PivotTable report, and then click the **Field Settings** button 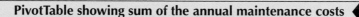 on the PivotTable toolbar. The PivotTable Field dialog box opens. See Figure 5-39.

PivotTable Field dialog box Figure 5-39

2. Click **Average** in the Summarize by list box, and then click the **OK** button to return to the PivotTable report. See Figure 5-40. Notice that the summary field button now displays "Average of MAINTENANCE" and that the data in the PivotTable report has been recalculated to show the average cost of maintenance by department for each type of vehicle.

Figure 5-40   **PivotTable showing the average of the annual maintenance costs**

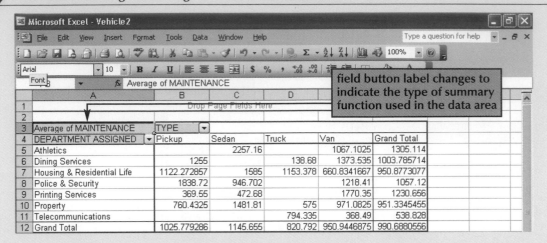

Trouble? If some of the values in the report are displayed with several decimal places, don't worry about formatting at this time.

3. Rename the worksheet **AvgMaintCost**.

You can also change the type of summary information in a PivotTable by double-clicking the field button that appears inside the PivotTable.

The PivotTable in Figure 5-40 shows the average annual maintenance cost of each vehicle by department and type. Although the data in a PivotTable might look like data in any other worksheet, you cannot directly enter or change data in the PivotTable because the PivotTable is linked to the source data. Any changes that affect the PivotTable must first be made to the Excel list. Later in the tutorial you will change a vehicle's department and learn how to reflect that change in the PivotTable.

Changing the Layout of a PivotTable

Although you cannot change the values inside a PivotTable, there are many ways to change the layout, formatting, and computational options of a PivotTable. For example, once a PivotTable is created, you have numerous ways of rearranging, adding, and removing fields.

Formatting Numbers in a PivotTable

Linda feels that the numbers in the PivotTable are too difficult to read. You can apply standard formatting to the cells in the PivotTable just as you would to any cell in a worksheet. You can also select from a list of over 20 AutoFormats that apply predefined fonts, colors, and borders to your PivotTable. You will try formatting the PivotTable using an AutoFormat.

To apply an AutoFormat to PivotTable values:

1. Make sure the active cell is within the PivotTable, and then click the **Format Report** button 🖼 on the PivotTable toolbar to open the AutoFormat dialog box.

2. Scroll down the list of AutoFormats until Table 4 is displayed, click the **Table 4** AutoFormat, and then click the **OK** button. The AutoFormat is applied to the PivotTable.

To make the appearance of the numbers more consistent, you will apply the Currency number format to the numbers in the PivotTable.

3. Click the **Currency Style** button $ on the Formatting toolbar.

   Trouble? If you deselected the PivotTable after applying the AutoFormat, select the range B5:F12 and then repeat Step 3.

4. Click any cell to deselect the range, and view the newly formatted PivotTable. See Figure 5-41.

PivotTable with an AutoFormat applied | **Figure 5-41**

	A	B	C	D	E	F
3	Average of MAINTENANCE	TYPE				
4	DEPARTMENT ASSIGNED	Pickup	Sedan	Truck	Van	Grand Total
5	Athletics		$ 2,257.16		$ 1,067.10	$ 1,305.11
6	Dining Services	$ 1,255.00		$ 138.68	$ 1,373.54	$ 1,003.79
7	Housing & Residential Life	$ 1,122.27	$ 1,585.00	$ 1,153.38	$ 660.83	$ 950.88
8	Police & Security	$ 1,838.72	$ 946.70		$ 1,218.41	$ 1,057.12
9	Printing Services	$ 369.55	$ 472.68		$ 1,770.35	$ 1,230.66
10	Property	$ 760.43	$ 1,481.81	$ 575.00	$ 971.08	$ 951.33
11	Telecommunications			$ 794.34	$ 368.49	$ 538.83
12	Grand Total	$ 1,025.78	$ 1,145.66	$ 820.79	$ 950.94	$ 990.69

With the AutoFormat applied and the numbers formatted as currency, the data in the PivotTable is much easier to interpret.

Modifying the Layout of a PivotTable

Recall that the benefit of a PivotTable is that it summarizes large amounts of data into a readable format. Once you have created the table, you can also choose to view the same data in different ways. At the top of the PivotTable's row and column areas are field buttons that enable you to change, or pivot, the view of the data by dragging these buttons to different locations in the PivotTable.

Linda reviews the tabular format of the PivotTable you have created and decides it might be more useful if the information in the PivotTable displayed the vehicle type as the row classifications under the departments. To change the presentation of the data, you will reposition the column headings for the TYPE field as row labels.

To move the TYPE column field to a row field in the PivotTable:

1. Click and drag the **TYPE** field button down and position it immediately below the list arrow for the DEPARTMENT ASSIGNED field button, then release the mouse button. The PivotTable is reordered so that the TYPE field is treated as a row field instead of a column field. See Figure 5-42.

Figure 5-42 ▶ **PivotTable rearranged with TYPE as a row field**

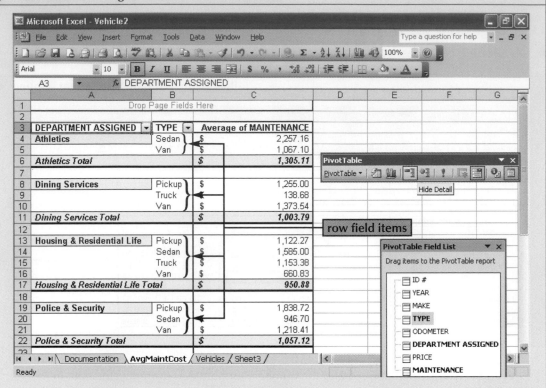

Trouble? If the TYPE field button appears to the left of the DEPARTMENT ASSIGNED field button, click the Undo button [image] on the Standard toolbar, and then repeat Step 1. When you drag the TYPE field button, drag the button into the blank area directly under the list arrow for the DEPARTMENT ASSIGNED field button. If you drag the button much further to the left, you will change the order of the fields.

After viewing the PivotTable in the new arrangement, Linda decides she prefers the original layout so you will undo the change that you made.

▶ **2.** Click the **Undo** button [image] on the Standard toolbar. The PivotTable again looks like Figure 5-41.

Sorting Items Within a PivotTable

Linda wants you to rearrange the PivotTable so that it displays the vehicle type with the highest average annual maintenance cost first. To complete this task, you will sort the data that is already laid out in the PivotTable.

To sort the PivotTable to display the highest average maintenance cost first:

1. Click cell **F5** to select the cell that contains the field you want to sort.

2. Click the **Sort Descending** button on the Standard toolbar. See Figure 5-43. The average annual departmental maintenance costs are now sorted from most costly to least costly.

PivotTable sorted by the grand total averages in descending order　　Figure 5-43

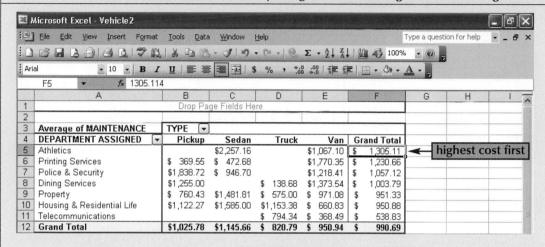

Adding a Field to a PivotTable

You can expand a PivotTable by adding columns, rows, and page fields and by adding data fields; this creates a more informative table. For example, Linda believes that a more accurate comparison of average maintenance costs would include the MAKE field. Adding this field to the PivotTable would enable you to calculate the average maintenance cost based on an additional breakdown—one that categorizes the vehicles in each department by the make as well as by type. Linda wants the additional information because it will be useful in her discussion with the budget director, and she wants you to add the field to the PivotTable. You will add the MAKE field to the PivotTable.

To add the MAKE field to the PivotTable:

1. From the PivotTable Field List, click and drag the **MAKE** field up and position it immediately below the list arrow for the DEPARTMENT ASSIGNED field button.

2. Release the mouse button. Excel adds the MAKE field button and redisplays the PivotTable. See Figure 5-44. The PivotTable now displays the MAKE subcategories for each department.

Figure 5-44 ▶ **PivotTable with MAKE field added as a row field**

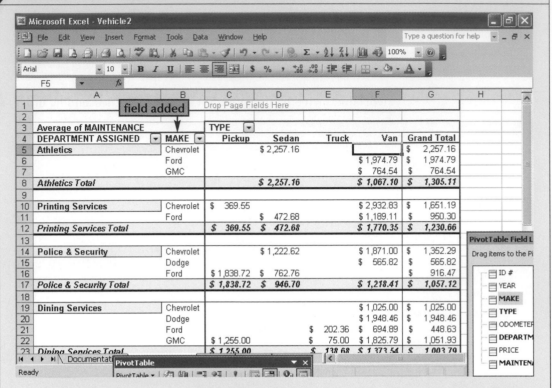

Trouble? If the MAKE field button appears to the left of the DEPARTMENT ASSIGNED field button, drag the DEPARTMENT ASSIGNED field button over the MAKE field button. When you release the mouse button, the field buttons should be in the correct positions.

Trouble? If the PivotTable toolbar and PivotTable Field List are in the way, drag them to a different location on your screen.

Linda doesn't like the look of the report with the MAKE field added; the report looks too busy and is difficult to read. She asks you if there is another way to use the MAKE field information in the report, but in a way that adds value to the report and doesn't overwhelm the reader.

Adding a Page View of a PivotTable

You can drag a field to the Drop Page Field area to create a page view of the PivotTable report. A **page view** allows you to filter the PivotTable so it displays summarized data for either a single field item or all field items. For example, creating a page view for the MAKE field allows you to display average annual maintenance costs for Fords, Chevrolets, or any other make.

You will try adding a page view for the MAKE field to see if using this information adds value to the report.

To display a page view of the average annual maintenance costs:

1. Click and drag the **MAKE** field button to the area labeled Drop Page Fields Here. See Figure 5-45. Notice that the item All appears as the page field item. This item indicates that the PivotTable report displays all the summarized data associated with the MAKE field.

Page view displaying all summarized data

Figure 5-45

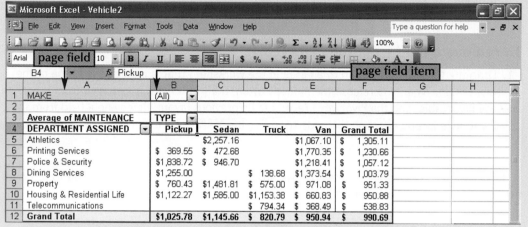

Now you will display the summarized data that applies only to Ford vehicles.

2. Click the item list arrow for the **MAKE** field button. A list of field items for the MAKE field is displayed.

3. Click **Ford** in the list, click the **OK** button, and then click a cell in the PivotTable to remove the highlighting if necessary. The PivotTable automatically changes to display the average annual maintenance costs for the summarized data associated with Ford vehicles. See Figure 5-46.

Page view displaying summarized data for Ford vehicles

Figure 5-46

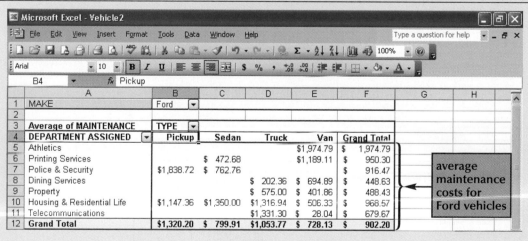

Removing a Field from a PivotTable

If you decide you want to remove a field from a PivotTable, just drag the field button outside the PivotTable. Linda reviews the PivotTable showing the data arranged by vehicle type, department, and make. Although Linda thinks this is important information, she feels the additional breakdown is not needed to show the difference in average annual maintenance costs between departments and vehicles, so she wants you to remove this data. You will remove the MAKE field from the PivotTable.

To remove a field from the PivotTable:

1. Drag the **MAKE** field button to an area in the worksheet that is outside the range of the PivotTable. When you release the mouse button, the MAKE field is removed from the PivotTable, and the PivotTable reverts to its previous layout. Removing a field from the PivotTable has no effect on the underlying list; the MAKE field is still in the vehicles list.

Linda wants to focus the analysis on sedans, vans, and pickups. She asks you to remove trucks from the PivotTable report.

Hiding Field Items on a PivotTable

You can hide row or column field items in the PivotTable by clicking the list arrow for the field button that represents the data you want to hide and then clearing the check box for each item you want to hide. To show hidden items, you click the list arrow for the field button and select the check box for the item you want to show. Now you will hide the Truck item from the PivotTable.

To hide the Truck item on the PivotTable:

1. Click the list arrow for the **TYPE** field button to display the list of items in the TYPE field. See Figure 5-47.

Figure 5-47 List of field items for the TYPE field

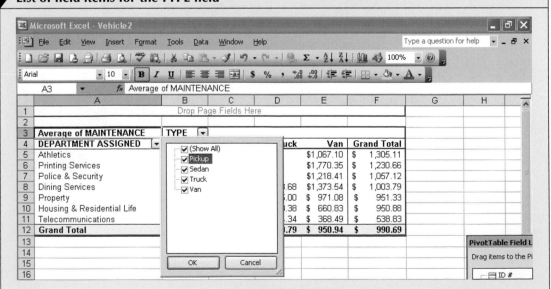

2. Click the **Truck** check box to deselect the item. Note that the Show All option is automatically deselected as well.

3. Click the **OK** button. See Figure 5-48.

PivotTable with the Truck item hidden ◄ **Figure 5-48**

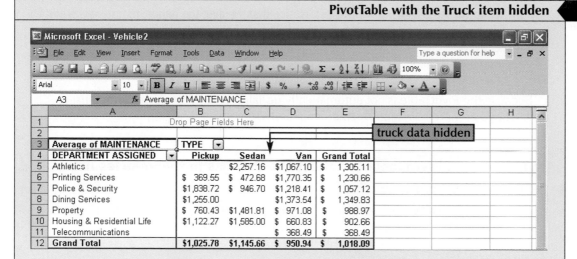

Now the report contains the vehicle data Linda wants to review. Although the item is hidden, you can show the item again by clicking the field button and checking the check box for the hidden item.

Linda has just told you that the vehicle with ID # 818, a vehicle assigned to the Housing & Residential Life department, will be reassigned to Dining Services. You want to update the PivotTable before you print a copy of it for Linda.

Refreshing a PivotTable

Recall that you cannot directly change the data in the PivotTable. In order to change the data in the PivotTable, you must make the changes to the original Excel list first, and then you need to update the PivotTable. To update, or "refresh," the PivotTable so that it reflects the current state of the vehicles list, you use the Refresh Data command.

You need to update the record for vehicle 818 in the vehicles list. Making this change will affect the PivotTable because the average annual maintenance cost for vehicles assigned to Dining Services (which is currently $1,349.83) and to Housing & Residential Life (which is currently $902.66) will change. You will update the vehicle information in the Excel list, and then check to see if the changes are reflected in the PivotTable.

To update the vehicles list:

1. Switch to the Vehicles worksheet, and then click cell **A2**.

2. Click **Edit** on the menu bar, and then click **Find** to open the Find and Replace dialog box.

3. Type **818** in the Find what list box, and then click the **Find Next** button. Depending on the location of the Find and Replace dialog box on your screen, you may be able to see that row 16 is highlighted.

4. Click the **Close** button to close the dialog box. Cell A16 is selected, which is the location of the record for vehicle 818.

> **5.** Press the **Tab** key to move to the DEPARTMENT ASSIGNED column in row 16, and then change the vehicle's assigned department to **Dining Services**.
>
> Now you'll return to the PivotTable to see whether there is any change in the average annual maintenance cost.
>
> **6.** Switch to the AvgMaintCost worksheet. Notice that the average annual maintenance costs for Dining Services and Housing & Residential Life remain at $1,349.83 and $902.66, respectively.

Because the PivotTable is not automatically updated when data in the source list is updated, you will refresh the PivotTable manually.

To refresh the PivotTable to reflect the changes in the vehicles list:

> **1.** Click any cell within the PivotTable.
>
> **2.** Click the **Refresh Data** button ![] on the PivotTable toolbar to update the PivotTable. See Figure 5-49. The new average annual maintenance cost for Dining Services increases to $1,390.52 and Housing & Residential Life decreases to $868.10.

Figure 5-49 ▶ **PivotTable after being refreshed**

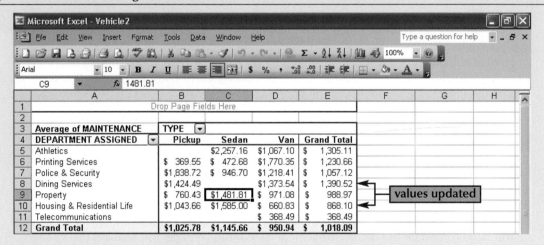

The PivotTable shows the average annual maintenance cost by vehicle type and department.

Creating a PivotChart

Linda thinks a chart can more effectively convey the summary information of the PivotTable. She asks you to create a clustered column chart. You can create a PivotChart using the PivotTable and PivotChart Wizard, or you can first create a PivotTable and then click the Chart Wizard button on the PivotTable toolbar to create a PivotChart. The second approach takes a single mouse click. Since you already have created a PivotTable, you will use the single mouse click approach.

To create the PivotChart based on the PivotTable:

▶ **1.** Click any cell inside the PivotTable, and then click the **Chart Wizard** button 📊 on the PivotTable toolbar. A stacked-column chart, PivotTable Field List, PivotTable toolbar, and Chart toolbar all appear in a new chart sheet. See Figure 5-50.

Stacked-column PivotChart linked to PivotTable ◀ **Figure 5-50**

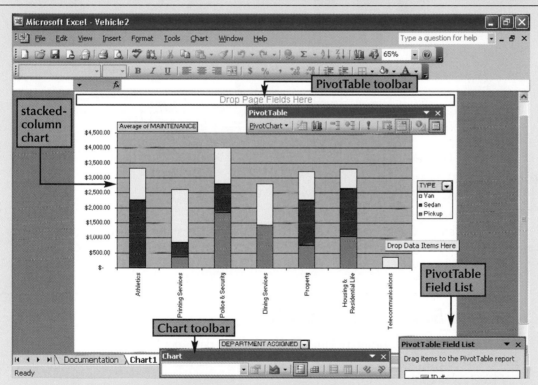

Next you will change the chart type to a clustered-column chart.

▶ **2.** Click the **Chart Wizard** button 📊 on the PivotTable toolbar again, this time to open the Chart Wizard Step 1 of 4 dialog box. The default chart type is the column chart.

▶ **3.** Click the **Clustered Column** sub-type, and then click the **Finish** button. A clustered-column chart appears. See Figure 5-51. The chart fields have many of the same properties as PivotTable fields. You can use the filter arrows to filter chart items, select a button to rename a field, and double-click a data button to change the summary function.

Figure 5-51 Clustered-column PivotChart

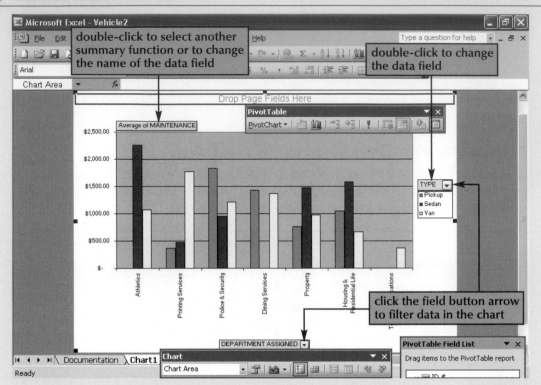

You have completed your work on the Vehicle2 workbook, so you can save your changes.

4. Save your changes to the workbook and then close it.

Linda is pleased with the PivotTable and PivotChart. Both show the average annual maintenance cost by department and vehicle type, which will be important information for her upcoming budget meeting.

Review

Session 5.3 Quick Check

1. What is the default summary function for numeric data in a PivotTable?

2. When creating a PivotTable, you use the _____ to layout the fields in the PivotTable report.

3. After the data in a list has been updated, you have to _____ the PivotTable in order to see an updated version of it.

4. Fields such as region, state, country, and ZIP code are most likely to appear as _____ in a PivotTable.

5. Fields such as revenue, costs, and profits are most likely to appear as _____ in a PivotTable.

6. Assume that you have a list of college students, and in the list there is a code for males and females, and there is a field identifying the student's major. Which tool, AutoFilter or PivotTable, would you use in each of the following situations:
   a. You want a list of all females majoring in history.
   b. You want the number of males and females in each major at your institution.

Review

Tutorial Summary

In this tutorial, you learned how to manage a list of vehicle data. You also learned how to create a list range, sort data, and then enter, edit, and delete data in the list using a list range and data form. You also used the data form to search for information that meets certain criteria. You filtered a list to display only data that meets certain criteria. You applied conditional formatting to a range of cells to highlight specific values in the range. You inserted subtotals and viewed them. Finally, you learned how to summarize a list using a PivotTable and PivotChart.

Key Terms

ascending order	field	PivotTable
AutoFilter	field name	primary sort field
category field	filter	record
column field	header row	row field
conditional formatting	insert row	search criteria
custom AutoFilter	list	secondary sort field
data definition table	list range	sort field
data field	page field	sort key
data form	page view	total row
descending order	PivotChart	

Practice

Practice the skills you learned in the tutorial to answer additional questions about the list of vehicles.

Review Assignments

Data File needed for the Review Assignments: VehicleR.xls

Linda has another vehicle that needs to be entered in the vehicles list. To further understand the information in the workbook, she wants to know which type of vehicle has been purchased the most often and which types of vehicle each department uses the most often. She also wants to analyze the age of the vehicles in the fleet. She also wants a PivotTable report that will show the average purchase cost by make, type, and department assigned. Linda has asked you to gather the information she needs for further analysis of the university's fleet. To complete this task:

1. Open the **VehicleR** workbook located in the Tutorial.05\Review folder included with your Data Files, and then save the workbook as **VehicleData** in the same folder.
2. On the Documentation sheet, enter the date and your name, and then switch to the Vehicles worksheet.
3. Freeze the column headings so they remain on the screen as you scroll the list.
4. Create a list range for the vehicles list.

5. Add the following information for the latest vehicle assigned to the Athletics department:

   ID #: 2500 ODOMETER: 225

   YEAR: 2006 DEPARTMENT ASSIGNED: Athletics

   MAKE: GMC PRICE: 28000

   TYPE: Van MAINTENANCE: 50

6. You need to determine how many Ford vehicles there are in the list. Explain the steps you would take using sorting to get your answer. Explain the steps you would take using filtering to get your answer.

7. Sort the vehicles list by make, within make by type, and within type by year (newest vehicles first). Print the sorted list.

8. Use AutoFilter to produce a list of the vehicles with odometer readings above 100,000 in descending order. Print the filtered list, and then display all vehicles.

9. Use conditional formatting to highlight vehicles with a model year before 1995, formatting the YEAR field with a light blue font color and a bold font style. Print the vehicles list with the conditional formatting applied.

10. Using a list range, calculate the average maintenance cost for all sedans driven more than 100,000 miles. Print the filtered list with the total row, and then display all vehicles.

11. Use the Subtotals command to count how many vehicles there are of each type, displaying the count in the ID # column. Print only the subtotals, and then remove all subtotals after printing the report.

12. Create a PivotTable to show the average purchase price of vehicles by make and type. Place your PivotTable in a new worksheet. Format your PivotTable to produce an attractive report. Rename the PivotTable sheet using an appropriate name. Include your name in the custom footer, and then print the PivotTable.

13. Modify the PivotTable in Step 13 to include DEPARTMENT ASSIGNED as a page field, and then print the modified PivotTable. Explain how the page field can be used.

14. Save and close the workbook.

Case Problem 1

Data File needed for this Case Problem: Teahouse.xls

Tea House Distribution Arnold Taymore, sales manager for Tea House Distribution, is getting ready for its semiannual sales meeting at the company's headquarters. At this meeting, Arnold plans to present summary data on the product line. The data that he has accumulated consists of revenues by product, by month, and by region for the last six months. Help him summarize and analyze the data. To complete this task:

1. Open the **Teahouse** workbook located in the Tutorial.05\Cases folder included with your Data Files, and then save the workbook as **TeahouseSummary** in the same folder.

2. Enter the date and your name in the Documentation sheet, and then switch to the Tea Data worksheet.

3. Improve the formatting of the revenue field so it is clear that this field deals with dollars.

4. Freeze the column headings so they remain on the screen as you scroll the worksheet.

5. Use conditional formatting to display revenue above $54,000 using a formatting that you feel will best highlight the results. Print the list.

6. Sort the tea list by region and within region by product. Insert subtotals for revenue generated by region. Include your name in a custom footer, and then print the information for each region. Make sure column headings appear on each page of the printed report. After printing, remove the subtotals.

7. Using the list range, filter the list to display revenue during May and June in the West region. (*Hint:* Think about the criteria you need to use to display rows from May and June.) Sort the results (highest revenue first). Calculate the total revenue for the filtered list. Print the results. After printing the results, remove the total revenue and show all records.

8. Create a PivotTable that displays total revenue by month and region. Place your PivotTable in a new worksheet. Format the PivotTable. Rename the PivotTable worksheet "RevenueByMonthAndRegion." Print the PivotTable.

9. Modify the PivotTable to display revenue generated by Wild Berry Tea by month and region.

10. Save and close the workbook.

Case Problem 2

Apply

Apply the skills you learned in the tutorial to compile and summarize reports from a list of faculty data.

Data File needed for this Case Problem: Faculty1.xls

Eastern State College   Michelle Long is the dean of the College of Business Administration at Eastern State College. The College of Business Administration has three academic departments: Management, Marketing, and Accounting. Each faculty member holds an academic rank, such as professor or associate professor. Most faculty members are hired as instructors or assistant professors. After a period of time, the faculty member might be promoted to associate professor and then to full professor. Faculty salaries usually reflect the faculty member's rank and length of service in the department.

The dean frequently asks you to locate and summarize information about the College of Business Administration faculty. This week she has several important budget and staffing meetings to attend for which she will need to produce detailed and specific information on her faculty. She asks for your help to compile the necessary data. She has created an Excel workbook that contains a worksheet with the name, academic rank, department, hire date, salary, and sex of each faculty member in the College of Business Administration. She asks you to use the worksheet to create several reports that will organize the information to produce the specific output she requires for each meeting. To complete this task:

1. Open the **Faculty1** workbook located in the Tutorial.05\Cases folder included with your Data Files, and then save the workbook as **Faculty2** in the same folder.

2. Enter the date and your name in the Documentation sheet, and then switch to the Faculty Data worksheet.

3. Complete the worksheet by calculating the matching retirement dollar amount for each faculty member (column I). Note that not all of the faculty members participate in the plan (column H). For any faculty member who is participating in the retirement plan, the institution will contribute (match) 3% (cell I1) of the faculty member's salary, placing the contribution in the retirement fund. If the faculty member is not participating, enter a zero in the appropriate cell of column I.

4. Freeze the column headings and the First and Last Name row labels so they remain on the screen as you scroll the faculty list.

5. Use the Find and Replace command to change all faculty members with the rank Full Prof to Full.

6. Create a list range and display only the accounting faculty with the rank Full hired after 1990. Print the list with the highest salary displayed first. When finished printing, display all the faculty records.

Explore

7. Sort the data so the faculty is sorted by rank in the following order: Full, Associate, Assistant, and Instructor. Print the sorted worksheet. (*Hint*: Use the Custom Lists tab found in the Options dialog box, which you can access from the Options command on the Tools menu.)

8. The institution is studying an early retirement program. To make it easier to identify eligible faculty, apply conditional formatting, with a color of your choice, to highlight all faculty hired before 1985.

9. Use the Subtotals command to compute the total salary in each department. Print the faculty list with subtotals. In the printout, omit row 1, make sure all fields for a faculty member are displayed on one page (the printout will require more than one page), and make sure field names appear on every page. When finished printing, remove the subtotals.

10. Create a PivotTable to compute the average salary by gender and rank. Place the PivotTable in a new worksheet. Format the PivotTable to improve its appearance. Give a descriptive name to the new worksheet. Print the PivotTable.

11. Use the PivotTable in Step 10 to develop a PivotChart. Choose an appropriate type of chart. Print the PivotChart.

Explore

12. Using the results from Step 10 and the drill-down feature of PivotTables, display all data on female full professors in a separate worksheet. (*Hint*: Use the Help system to look up the topic "Change the amount of detail displayed in a PivotTable report.") Print the worksheet.

13. Save and close the workbook.

Create

Apply filtering, conditional formatting, and subtotaling to a PivotTable to analyze a list of government contracts.

Case Problem 3

Data File needed for this Case Problem: Receive1.xls

Outstanding Accounts Receivable   Marcus Choy is an accountant for a company that provides research services to various government agencies and private corporations. The credit manager has asked Marcus to prepare an accounts receivable report for all government customers. The credit manager needs this report so he can follow up on overdue accounts.

The information that Marcus needs to prepare the report has been saved in an Excel workbook. In the workbook, the records are organized in an Excel list, which includes the following fields:

Field	Description
Customer #	Number assigned to each customer
Invoice #	Number assigned to each bill, increasing the number by 1
Date Billed	Date bill is mailed
Balance	Amount owed
Agency Name	Government agency funding the research
PI	Principal investigator who has major responsibility for the research
Days Outstanding	Number of days since Date Billed
Over 120 Days Old	Message "Follow Up" displays when payment is overdue; otherwise, cell is blank

To complete this task:

1. Open the **Receive1** workbook located in the Tutorial.05\Cases folder included with your Data Files, and then save the workbook as **Receive2** in the same folder
2. Enter the date and your name in the Documentation sheet, and then switch to the Amount Owed worksheet.
3. Complete the worksheet by calculating the number of days that the invoice has remained unpaid (column G) by subtracting the date that the invoice was sent (column C) from the current date. Use the date in cell B1 as the current date. Format the Days Outstanding column using the Number format (no decimal places). In column H, use an IF function to place the words "Follow Up" in the cell for any invoice that is overdue by more than 120 days; otherwise, leave the cell blank.
4. Create a list range for the Amount Owed list.
5. Freeze the Customer # and Invoice # columns so they remain on the screen as you scroll the Amount Owed list.
6. Sort the list by the PI, Agency Name, and Balance columns. Print the results.
7. Display only the invoices to NASA that have an amount due (Balance) over $25,000. Print the results by date billed, with the earliest date displayed first. Display all the records when finished printing.
8. Apply one set of formatting to all invoices that have been outstanding for more than 120 days and a second formatting to invoices outstanding between 90 and 120 days. Apply the format of your choice to the Days Outstanding column. Print the results.

Explore 9. Use the Subtotals command to display the total balance owed by agency and principal investigator within each agency group. Print the report with only the subtotals included. After printing the report, remove the subtotals. (*Hint*: Use Help to learn about inserting nested subtotals.)

10. Create a PivotTable that summarizes the total owed (Balance) by each agency. Place the PivotTable in a new worksheet. Format the PivotTable. Give a descriptive name to the new worksheet. Print the PivotTable.
11. Modify the PivotTable in Step 10 to summarize the average owed (Balance) by agency and principal investigator. Print the PivotTable.

Explore 12. Using Figure 5-52 as a guide, create a PivotTable on a new worksheet that shows the amount outstanding by month billed and agency. (*Hint*: Use Help to learn about grouping items in PivotTables.) Click the Yes button in the message box that opens regarding how to save memory.

Figure 5-52

	A	B	C	D	E	F	G	H
1								
2								
3	Total Owed	Agency Name ▾						
4	Date Billed ▾	Army	EPA	Interior	NASA	Grand Total		
5	Jan	$ 473.13			$ 167,345.66	$ 167,818.79		
6	Mar	$ 5,538.84		$ 25,562.21	$ 7,460.00	$ 38,561.05		
7	Apr	$ 37,812.64	$ 67,767.38	$ 20,419.48	$ 33,453.83	$ 159,453.33		
8	May			$ 5,572.73	$ 5,588.14	$ 11,160.87		
9	Jun	$ 48,028.86	$ 22,291.96	$ 46,702.17	$ 621,038.64	$ 738,061.63		
10	Grand Total	$ 91,853.47	$ 90,059.34	$ 98,256.59	$ 834,886.27	$ 1,115,055.67		
11								
12								

13. Save and close the workbook.

Case Problem 4

Data File needed for this Case Problem: Gourmet1.xls

E-Gourmet Express Jerry Mayer is operations manager at E-Gourmet Express, an Internet startup company. The company sells gourmet food products to specialty food stores around the world. E-Gourmet sells a wide range of premium beverages, bakery goods, spices, desserts, and gourmet meat items through the use of a Web storefront. E-Gourmet Express guarantees shipments within 48 hours.

The company has been in operation a little over a year, and Jerry wants to analyze where it stands. Jerry downloaded a portion of the company's sales data and stored it in an Excel file. He wants to summarize sales by country, product categories, products, months, and the like. He asks for your help with the analysis. To complete this task:

1. Open the **Gourmet1** workbook located in the Tutorial.05\Cases folder included with your Data Files, and then save the workbook as **Gourmet2** in the same folder.
2. Insert a new worksheet. Enter the company name, your name, the date, and a purpose statement in the worksheet, and then rename the sheet "Documentation."
3. Switch to the CustSales worksheet.
4. Freeze the panes so that the column headings and the CompanyName, Country, and OrderDate row values remain on the screen as you scroll the customer sales list.
5. Calculate the total sales for each item sold, placing the value in the Total column (column L). Use the following formula: Quantity multiplied by UnitPrice multiplied by an adjustment plus Freight. The adjustment is calculated using the formula "1 – Discount %," or the value of 1 minus the value in the Discount % field. (*Hint*: Remember to use parentheses to indicate the order of precedence needed to calculate the adjustment first.)
6. Create a list range and then display all beverages ordered between January 1 and March 15. Sort the list by company name and within company name by order date (with the most recent order date displayed first). Print these records. Use landscape orientation. Be sure the company name, country, and order date appear on the second page. After printing the results, display all records.

Explore

7. Sort the worksheet by country, within country by category, within category by product name, and within product name by order date. (*Hint*: Use Help to learn how to sort a list with more than three sort keys.) Print the sorted worksheet omitting sales rep, shipper, unit price, quantity, discount, and freight from the printout. Remember to display all fields after printing this report.
8. Apply conditional formatting to the Product Name column to highlight the Tofu and Chai products. Choose different formatting for each product.
9. Create a PivotTable that summarizes the total sales by country, by category, and then by sales rep. Place the PivotTable in a new worksheet. Give a descriptive name to the new worksheet. You decide on the formatting and layout of the PivotTable. Print the PivotTable.
10. Create a PivotTable in a new worksheet that filters total sales by country with a breakdown by company name and category. Format the PivotTable. Rename the new worksheet. Print the results for Brazil.

Explore

11. Create a PivotTable that summarizes the total amount of orders (column L) by quarter. Place the PivotTable in a new worksheet. Give a descriptive name to the new worksheet. You decide on the formatting and layout of the PivotTable. (*Hint*: Use Help to learn how to group items in a PivotTable.)

Explore

Explore

12. Modify Step 11 to include a PivotChart of the total amount of orders by quarter. Choose an appropriate chart type. Print the PivotChart.
13. Use advanced filters to filter "in-place" all orders for beverages sold after 4/1/06 by sales rep Davis. Copy these orders to a separate worksheet and rename the sheet. Print these orders. Show all orders when you have completed the question. (*Hint*: Use Help to learn to filter a list using advanced criteria.)
14. Use database functions to calculate total and average orders for beverages sold after 4/1/06 by sales rep Davis. Place the labels "# of Orders" and "Average Orders" in cells O1 and O2, respectively. Using the database functions, calculate the summary results for the orders that meet the criteria and place the results in cells P1 and P2. Format the results and print only the summary in the range O1:P2. (*Hint*: Use Help to learn about database functions.)
15. Save and close the workbook.

Research

Use the Internet to find and work with data related to the topics presented in this tutorial.

Internet Assignments

The purpose of the Internet Assignments is to challenge you to find information on the Internet that you can use to work effectively with this software. The actual assignments are updated and maintained on the Course Technology Web site. Log on to the Internet and use your Web browser to go to the Student Online Companion for New Perspectives Office 2003 at **www.course.com/np/office2003**. Click the Internet Assignments link, and then navigate to the assignments for this tutorial.

Assess

SAM Assessment and Training

If you have a SAM user profile, you may have access to hands-on instruction, practice, and assessment of the skills covered in this tutorial. Log in to your SAM account and go to your assignments page to see what your instructor has assigned.

Review

Quick Check Answers

Session 5.1

1. list
2. The Freeze Panes option allows you to keep, or freeze, rows and columns so that they don't scroll off the screen as you move around the worksheet. Freezing the rows and columns, which often contain headings, on the screen makes understanding the data in each record easier.
3. A dark blue border appears around the list, AutoFilter arrows appear in the header row, an insert row is displayed below the last row of data in the list, and a list toolbar is displayed.
4. sort fields, sort keys
5. sort by major and then, within major, sort by last name
6. data form
7. Assuming that you have the fields FirstName and LastName as part of the employee list, you would click the Criteria button in the Data Form dialog box. In the FirstName field text box, type "Jin"; in the LastName field text box, type "Shinu." Click the Find Next button to display the record in the data form.

8. primary (sort field or sort key)

9. descending

Session 5.2

1. In order to have Excel calculate subtotals correctly, you must first sort the data because the subtotals are inserted whenever the value in the specified field changes.

2. AutoFilter, total row

3. Use the AutoFilter feature. Click the Major AutoFilter arrow, and then click Marketing. For the GPA field, click Custom in the list of filtering options. Enter the greater than (>) comparison operator and the constant 3.0 to specify the condition for a GPA greater than 3.0.

4. Level Outline

5. True

6. Conditional formatting

7. three

8. Click the AutoFilter arrow in the gender column, and select the female option to display only female employees. Click the Toggle Total Row button on the List toolbar to insert a total row at the bottom of the list, click the arrow that appears to the right of the total for the column with the salaries, and then click Average in the list of subtotal functions.

Session 5.3

1. Sum

2. PivotTable Field List box

3. refresh

4. rows, columns, page fields, or category fields

5. data items

6. a. AutoFilter
   b. PivotTable

Objectives

Session 6.1
- Create and print a worksheet group
- Format and edit multiple worksheets at the same time
- Create cell references to other worksheets
- Consolidate information from multiple worksheets using 3-D references

Session 6.2
- Create a workbook template
- Learn how to store and access a template
- Change the default template and the default folder and file location

Session 6.3
- Create a link to data in another workbook
- Create a workbook reference using the point-and-click method
- Learn how to edit links
- Create a lookup table and use Lookup functions
- Create and use an Excel workspace

Working with Multiple Worksheets and Workbooks

Tracking Cash Flow

Case

Lakeland Boychoir

The Lakeland Boychoir is a nonprofit performing choir for boys ages 8 through 14 who live in and around the city of Lakeland, Nebraska. The choir of almost 60 boys performs several concerts throughout the year for the people of central and western Nebraska. The choir also tours the Midwest and participates in several regional and national competitions.

Because of its nonprofit status, the choir relies heavily on volunteer support, particularly from parents. Joy Ling is one such parent. She has two children in the choir, and she also acts as the choir's treasurer. Joy wants to use Excel for the choir's budget information so it can be printed in the choir's annual financial report given to its members and supporters.

Joy has asked you to help her with a cash flow report that will show the monthly inflows and outflows of cash for the past year. She has already entered each month's values on separate worksheets, but she needs your assistance in making all the sheets work together. She wants to be able to summarize all the information in the 12 sheets into a single sheet. Joy realizes that this will be a yearly task, so she also wants to be able to access the financial information from a previous year's workbook and use that information as the basis of the current year's workbook.

Student Data Files

▼ Tutorial.06

▽ Tutorial folder	▽ Review folder	▽ Cases folder
LBC1.xls	CList.xls	Bike1.xls
LBC2003.xls	Contrib1.xls	Bike2.xls
LBC2004.xls		Bike3.xls
LBC2005.xls		Grade1.xls
LBCSum1.xls		Refrig1.xls

Using Multiple Worksheets

One of the most useful ways to organize your workbook data is to place that data in several worksheets. Using multiple worksheets makes it easier to group and summarize your data. For example, a company with branches located in different geographic regions can place sales information for each region on separate worksheets. Rather than scrolling through a single large and complicated worksheet that contains data for all regions, employees can view regional sales information for a specific region by clicking a sheet in the workbook.

You can also use multiple worksheets to place the most important or summarized data first. Supervisors only interested in the bottom line can view the first worksheet containing summary data without going through the details available on separate worksheets. Others, of course, may be interested in viewing the backup documentation and combing through the individual worksheets that follow the summarized worksheet. In the case of the Lakeland Boychoir, Joy Ling has created separate worksheets that display the cash flow for each month of the 2006 season. She has already entered the data in an Excel workbook. You will open Joy's workbook and review the current information.

To open the Lakeland Boychoir workbook:

▶ 1. Start Excel and open the **LBC1** workbook located in the Tutorial.06\Tutorial folder included with your Data Files.

▶ 2. On the Documentation sheet, enter *your name* and the *current date*, and then save the workbook as **LBC2006** in the Tutorial.06\Tutorial folder.

▶ 3. Switch to the January worksheet to view the cash flow figures for the first month of the year. See Figure 6-1.

Figure 6-1   **January worksheet for the Lakeland Boychoir**

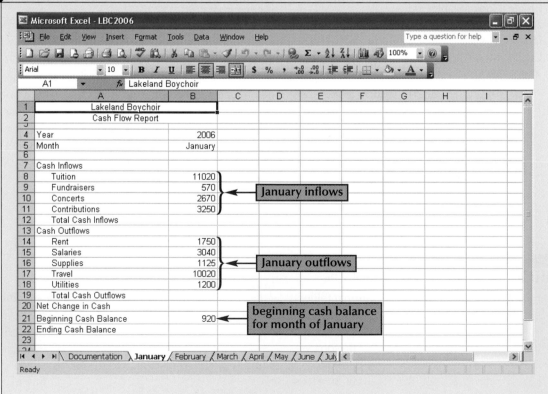

Joy hasn't entered any formulas in the workbook yet, so your first task will be to enter the formulas. The formulas that you enter will need to calculate the total inflows entered in the range B8:B11, the total outflows entered in the range B14:B18, net change in cash in cell B20 (total cash inflows minus total cash outflows), and the ending cash balance (the beginning cash balance plus net change in cash), which will appear in cell B22.

Joy wants you to add these formulas to all 12 worksheets. Rather than laboriously retyping the commands in each sheet, you can enter them all at once by creating a worksheet group.

Grouping Worksheets

A **worksheet group** is a collection of two or more selected worksheets. Once you group a collection of worksheets, any changes you make to one worksheet are applied to all sheets in the group. Like cell ranges, the collection can contain adjacent or nonadjacent sheets. To select adjacent worksheets, you click the sheet tab of the first sheet in the group, press and hold the Shift key, and then click the sheet tab of the last sheet in the group. To select nonadjacent worksheets, you click a sheet tab of one of the worksheets, and then press and hold the Ctrl key as you click the sheet tabs of the other worksheets you want included in the group.

Reference Window

Grouping and Ungrouping Worksheets

- To select an adjacent group, click the sheet tab of the first worksheet in the group, press and hold the Shift key, and then click the sheet tab of the last sheet in the group.
- To select a nonadjacent group, click the sheet tab of one of the sheets in the group, press and hold the Ctrl key, and then click the sheet tabs of the remaining members of the group.
- To ungroup the sheets, either click the sheet tab of a worksheet not in the group, or right-click the sheet tab of one of the sheets in the group, and then select Ungroup Sheets on the shortcut menu.

Entering Formulas in a Worksheet Group

In the choir workbook, you'll select an adjacent range of worksheets: the January sheet through the December sheet.

To group the choir worksheets:

1. Make sure that the January worksheet is still selected.
2. Click the **Last Sheet** button ▶| to display the last tab in the workbook (December).
3. Press and hold the **Shift** key, click the **December** tab, and then release the Shift key. See Figure 6-2. The worksheet tabs for January through December are highlighted, indicating that they are all selected, and the caption "[Group]" appears in the Excel title bar, indicating that a worksheet group has been selected in the workbook.

Worksheets grouped | **Figure 6-2**

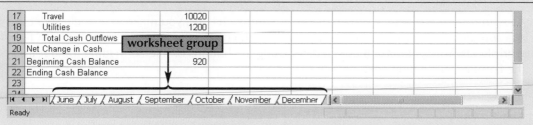

4. Click the **First Sheet** button ⏮ to return to the first sheet in the worksheet group, which is January.

With the monthly sheets grouped together, you will now enter the formulas to calculate the total inflows, total outflows, net change in cash, and ending cash balance in one sheet, and the formulas will be entered in all the sheets in the group.

To enter the same formulas in all the sheets in the worksheet group:

1. Click cell **B12** and then enter **=SUM(B8:B11)** to calculate the total cash inflow amount.

   Next you will enter the formula to calculate the total cash outflow amount.

2. Click cell **B19** and then enter **=SUM(B14:B18)**.

   Now you will enter the formula to calculate the net change in cash, which is the difference between the total cash inflow and total cash outflow amounts.

3. If necessary, click cell **B20** and then enter **=B12-B19**. The net change in cash during January is 375.

   Finally, you will enter the formula to calculate the ending cash balance, which is the sum of the beginning cash balance and the net change value.

4. Click cell **B22** and then enter **=B21+B20**. The ending cash balance (cell B22) for January should be 1,295. As you entered formulas into the January worksheet, the same formulas were added to the rest of the sheets in the group.

5. Click the **February** tab. The ending cash balance for February is 505.

6. Click cell **B22** and observe that the formula is the same as the formula in the January worksheet. Note that the beginning cash balance in cell B21 has been set to zero. This beginning cash balance doesn't take into account the cash that will carry over from January into February. You'll learn shortly how to carry over values from the previous month.

7. Click the **Last Sheet** button ⏭ to display the last tab in the workbook, click the **December** tab, and then observe that the formula is the same as the formula in the January and February worksheets, and the ending cash balance for December is 9,210.

8. Click the **First Sheet** button ⏮, and then click the **January** tab to redisplay the January cash figures.

Remember that when you enter or edit cells in a worksheet group, the changes you make to one sheet are automatically applied to the other sheets in the group. For example, if you delete a value from one cell, the value in that cell on all the sheets in the group is also deleted. Thus, you should be cautious when editing the contents of a sheet when it is part of the group.

Formatting a Worksheet Group

As with inserting formulas and text, any formatting changes you make to a single sheet in a group are applied to all sheets. Joy wants you to change the appearance of the cash flow worksheets. You will make these changes using the buttons on the Formatting toolbar and the Format Cells dialog box.

To apply the same formatting to all sheets in the worksheet group:

1. Bold the text in the nonadjacent range **A1:A2;A4:A22**.

2. Fill the nonadjacent range **A7:B11;A13:B18;A20:B20** with the **Gray-25%** color, and then enclose the same nonadjacent range using the **Thick Box Border** option.

3. Underline the text in cells **A7** and **A13**.

4. Apply the Number format to the range **B8:B22** so the values appear with a comma and no decimal places.

5. Click cell **A1** to view the formatting changes, as shown in Figure 6-3.

Applying formatting to a worksheet group | **Figure 6-3**

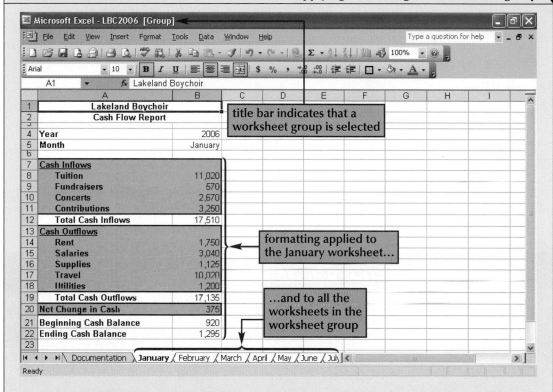

6. Click the other sheet tabs in the group to verify that the formatted changes you've made to the January sheet have been applied to the rest of the sheets in the group, and then click the **First Sheet** button ◄.

Now that you've applied a common set of formulas and formats to the monthly worksheets, you can ungroup the selected sheets. To remove a worksheet group, you can click a sheet tab of a sheet not in the group, or you can right-click the sheet tab of a selected sheet and then click Ungroup Sheets on the shortcut menu that appears. You will ungroup the sheets now.

To ungroup the monthly worksheets:

1. Right-click the **January** tab. A shortcut menu appears.

2. Click **Ungroup Sheets** on the shortcut menu. Only the January tab should be highlighted now, and the word "[Group]" no longer appears in the title bar.

All the formulas in the individual worksheets have been entered except a formula to carry the cash balance over from one month to another. You'll do this next using a formula that references a cell on another worksheet in the same workbook.

Referencing Cells and Ranges in Other Worksheets

Often the best way to organize a workbook is to store the data in multiple worksheets. By using multiple worksheets, you will be able to find, manage, and summarize the information quickly and more efficiently. When you use multiple worksheets for related data, you may often need to reference a cell or range in one of the other worksheets.

To reference a cell or range in a different worksheet, precede the cell or range reference with the worksheet name followed by an exclamation mark. For example, to develop a formula in the Budget worksheet that references cell D10 in the Sales worksheet, you would enter the formula

=Sales!D10

where *Sales* references the worksheet and *D10* references the cell in that worksheet. The exclamation point (!) separates the sheet reference from the cell reference. If the worksheet name contains spaces, you must enclose the sheet name in single quotation marks. For example, if a sheet were named Sales Data, then you would enter the reference as *'Sales Data'!D10*. You can use these references to create formulas that reference cells in different locations in different worksheets. For example, to add total sales from two worksheets—cell B10 of the Domestic worksheet and cell B8 of the International worksheet—you would enter the formula *=Domestic!B10 + International!B8*.

Reference Window

Entering a Formula That References Another Worksheet

- Click the cell where you want to enter the formula.
- Type = and then begin entering the formula.
- To insert a reference from another worksheet, click the tab for the worksheet.
- Click the cell you want to reference.
- Continue building the formula by typing the arithmetic operator and repeating the previous two steps.
- When the formula is complete, press the Enter key.

For each month, Joy wants you to enter a formula in cell B5 that displays the beginning cash balance for the month. The beginning cash balance comes from the ending cash balance of the previous month. The formula that you enter on a current month's worksheet must reference the cell on the previous month's worksheet that contains the ending cash balance for that month.

In the choir workbook, the beginning cash balance for each month after January is based on the ending cash balance found in the previous month's worksheet. Formulas from one worksheet reference data from another worksheet. For February, this amount is equal to the value of cell B22 in the January worksheet. The reference in the February worksheet is *=January!B22*. You will enter a reference to this cell now in the February worksheet.

To insert the cell reference to the January worksheet in the February worksheet:

▸ **1.** Click the **February** tab, and then click cell **B21**.

▸ **2.** Type **=** but do *not* press the Enter key.

Next you will display the worksheet that contains the first cell reference that you want to insert in the formula.

▸ **3.** Click the **January** tab, click cell **B22**, and then click the **Enter** button ✓ on the Formula bar. The February sheet is redisplayed, as shown in Figure 6-4. As indicated in the Formula bar for the February worksheet, Excel automatically inserted the formula *=January!B22* in cell B21. The beginning cash balance for February changes to 1,295, and the ending cash balance changes to 1,800.

February worksheet with reference to January worksheet ◂ **Figure 6-4**

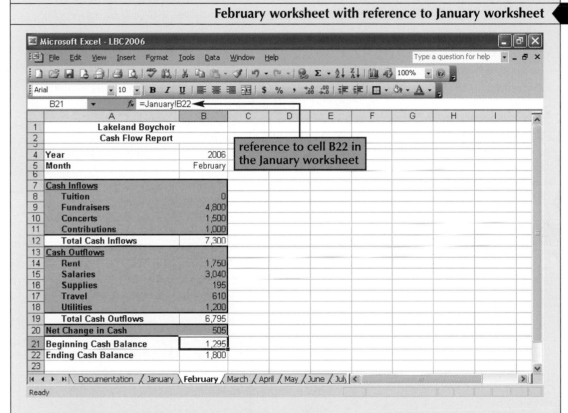

Trouble? If a Microsoft Excel message box appears, indicating that Excel cannot calculate the formula correctly, the worksheets are probably still grouped (that is, the "[Group]" caption appears in the title bar). Click the Cancel button to close the message box, and then click the Undo button ↺ on the Standard toolbar. Right-click any of the sheet tabs, click Ungroup Sheets on the shortcut menu, and then repeat Steps 1 through 3.

▸ **4.** Repeat Steps 1 through 3 for the remaining 10 months of the year to calculate each month's beginning cash balance based on the previous month's ending cash balance. At the end of 2006, the ending cash balance for the entire year is 1,620.

Trouble? If the ending cash balance on your screen is different, check the formulas you entered into cell B21 for each of the monthly worksheets in the workbook. The value should always be equal to the value of cell B22 for the previous month.

Next, Joy wants you to add a new worksheet that contains a summary of the inflows and outflows for the entire year.

Consolidating Data from Multiple Worksheets Using a 3-D Reference

When two or more worksheets have identical row and column layouts, you can consolidate those worksheets in another worksheet using formulas containing 3-D references. A **3-D reference** is a reference that refers to the *same* cell or range of cells on multiple worksheets in the same workbook. The reference specifies not only the rows and columns of a cell range, but also the range of worksheet names on which the cells appear. The general format of a 3-D cell reference is

WorksheetRange!CellRange

where *WorksheetRange* is the range of worksheets specified with a colon between the first and last sheet in the range followed by an exclamation mark (!), and *CellRange* is the same cell or range of cells within those sheets. For example, the formula *=SUM(Sheet1:Sheet4!B21)* adds the values in cell B21 on the worksheets between Sheet1 and Sheet4. If worksheets named "Sheet1," "Sheet2," "Sheet3," and "Sheet4" are included in the workbook, the worksheet range Sheet1:Sheet4 references all four worksheets. Although "Sheet2" and "Sheet3" aren't mentioned in this 3-D reference, the worksheets are included as long as they are positioned within the starting and ending names in the reference. Figure 6-5 shows a formula in one worksheet using a 3-D reference to sum values in multiple worksheets.

Figure 6-5 ▶ **Three dimensions of a workbook**

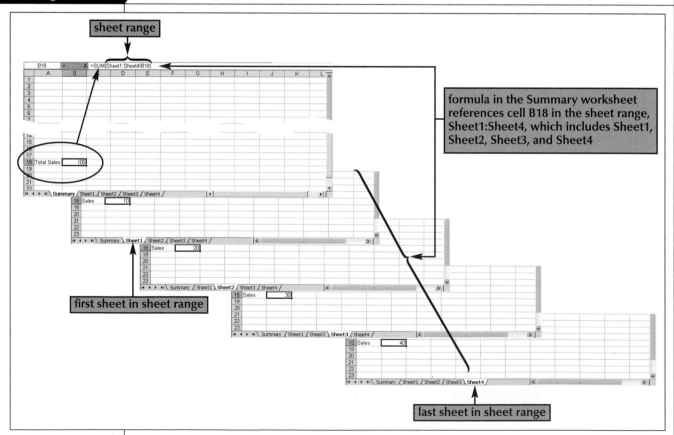

sheet range

formula in the Summary worksheet references cell B18 in the sheet range, Sheet1:Sheet4, which includes Sheet1, Sheet2, Sheet3, and Sheet4

first sheet in sheet range

last sheet in sheet range

A note of caution: A 3-D cell reference based on a worksheet group may become inaccurate if you move the position of the worksheets outside the range of adjacent worksheets or remove one of the worksheets from the workbook. For example, in the example described above, if Sheet3 were moved so it follows Sheet4, then the sheet range *Sheet1:Sheet4* would only include Sheet1, Sheet2, and Sheet4. On the other hand, you *can* rename worksheets, and the 3-D reference will be automatically updated to reflect the change.

You enter a 3-D reference either by typing the reference directly into the cell or by using your mouse to select the appropriate worksheet cells in the workbook. If you use the mouse, you must first select the sheet range, followed by the cell range.

Entering a Formula That Contains a 3-D Reference

Reference Window

- Click the cell where you want to enter the formula.
- Type = to begin the formula, type the name of the function, and then type (to indicate the beginning of the argument.
- Click the tab for the first worksheet in the group, press and hold the Shift key, and then click the tab for the last worksheet in the group.
- Select the cell or range of cells to be referenced, and then click the Enter button on the Formula bar.

In the choir workbook, you'll use 3-D references in a new worksheet named "Annual" to sum each of the cash flow values for the entire year (January through December).

To insert the Annual worksheet:

1. Click the **First Sheet** button ⏮, right-click the **January** tab, and then click **Insert** on the shortcut menu. The Insert dialog box opens.

2. On the General tab, click the **Worksheet** icon, if necessary, and then click the **OK** button. Excel inserts a new worksheet to the left of the January sheet.

3. Double-click the new sheet tab, type **Annual** as the new sheet name, and then press the **Enter** key.

The Annual worksheet needs to have the same format and structure as the monthly worksheets on which you've been working. To ensure consistency among the worksheets, you can copy the format from the January worksheet to the Annual worksheet.

Copying Information Across Worksheets

To copy information from one worksheet to another sheet (or worksheet group), you can use the Copy and Paste commands. However, when you establish a group of worksheets, the Across Worksheets command on the Fill submenu on the Edit menu becomes available. You can use this command to copy formulas, values, and formats from one worksheet to another. You will try this now using the January and Annual worksheets.

To copy the values and formats from the January worksheet across the worksheet group:

▶ 1. Click the **January** tab, press and hold the **Shift** key, click the **Annual** tab, and then release the Shift key. The Annual tab is highlighted, and the word "[Group]" appears in the title bar. Note also that the January worksheet is still the active sheet.

▶ 2. Select the range **A1:B22** on the January worksheet.

▶ 3. Click **Edit** on the menu, point to **Fill**, and then click **Across Worksheets**. The Fill Across Worksheets dialog box opens, as shown in Figure 6-6. You can choose to copy only the contents of the selected cells, the formats, or both. In this case, you will choose both, which is the default.

Figure 6-6	Fill Across Worksheets dialog box

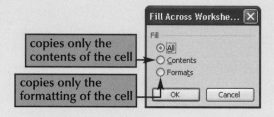

copies only the contents of the cell

copies only the formatting of the cell

▶ 4. Make sure that the **All** option button is selected, and then click the **OK** button.

▶ 5. Right-click the **January** tab, and click **Ungroup Sheets** on the shortcut menu. The worksheets are no longer grouped.

▶ 6. Click the **Annual** tab. The contents and formats have been copied to the worksheet, although the widths of the columns have not been adjusted.

You will adjust the width of the columns so all of the cell entries are visible.

▶ 7. Increase the width of column A to **29** characters (**208** pixels) and the width of column B to **10** characters (**75** pixels), and then click any cell to view the copied selection.

You next need to revise the contents of the Annual worksheet so that it displays the total cash inflows and outflows for the entire year.

Summing Values Across Worksheets

To calculate the annual cash inflows and outflows, you'll insert a formula that includes a 3-D reference to the group of worksheets, January through December. You will begin by entering a formula to sum the amount of tuition paid for the year.

To enter the formula that includes the 3-D cell reference:

1. In the Annual sheet, click cell **B8** and then type **=SUM(** to begin the formula. Do *not* press the Enter key. Note that a ScreenTip with the SUM function and its arguments appears.

2. Click the **January** tab, click the **Last Sheet** button ▶│, press and hold the **Shift** key, click the **December** tab, and then release the Shift key.

3. In the December worksheet, click cell **B8** and then click the **Enter** button ✓ on the Formula bar. See Figure 6-7. The Annual worksheet is redisplayed, and the completed formula *=SUM(January:December!B8)* appears in cell B8. The total tuition received for the year is 27,020.

Formula bar displaying the 3-D reference ◄ **Figure 6-7**

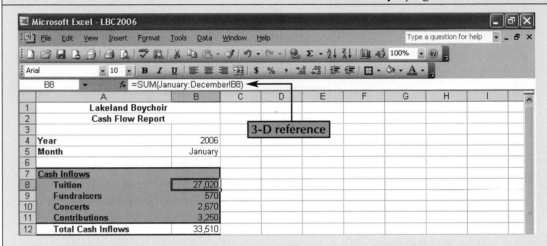

You will copy the formula that uses the SUM function to the other inflow cells.

4. If necessary, click cell **B8**, drag the fill handle down over the range **B9:B11**, and then release the mouse button. Excel fills in the rest of the cash inflow totals for the entire year, and the Auto Fill Options button appears.

5. Click the **Auto Fill Options** button 🖳 and then click the **Fill Without Formatting** option button. The total cash inflow is 106,830.

6. Click cell **B14**, and then, using the same method described in Steps 1 to 3, enter the formula **=SUM(January:December!B14)** in the cell. The total paid for rent during the year is 22,500.

   You will copy the formula to the other cash outflow cells.

7. If necessary, click cell **B14**, drag the fill handle down over the range **B15:B18**, click the **Auto Fill Options** button 🖳, and then click the **Fill Without Formatting** option button. Excel fills in the total outflows for the year. The choir paid a total of 106,130 during the year. Note that the ending cash balance for the entire year in cell B22 is equal to the ending cash balance in the month of December, and it should be 1,620.

8. Click cell **B5** on the Annual worksheet, and then change the cell content to **All Months**. See Figure 6-8.

Figure 6-8 **Complete Annual worksheet**

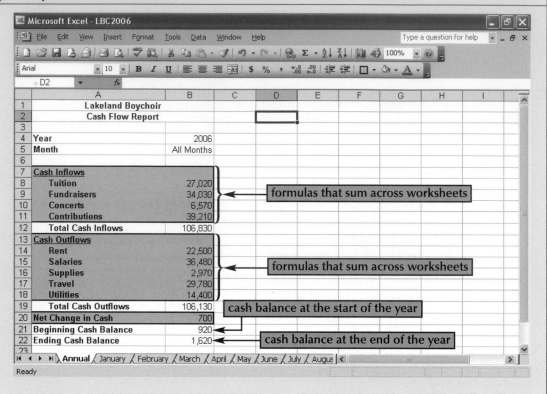

Joy realizes that there's an error in the information she gave you. It turns out that she was not aware of an additional payment of $1,000 in travel for January. One of the benefits of consolidating data using 3-D reference formulas, like any other formula, is that, if you change the value in one worksheet, the formula will automatically show the result of the change. You will change the Travel value for January now.

To change a value in the January worksheet:

▶ **1.** Before switching to the January worksheet, note that the payments for Travel in cell B17 total 29,780 for the year.

▶ **2.** Switch to the January worksheet, click cell **B17**, and then change the value to **11020**. The ending cash balance for January is now 295.

Now you will examine the impact this change has on the annual cash flow.

▶ **3.** Switch to the Annual worksheet. The total travel is now 30,780. The ending cash balance has dropped to 620, and the total outflows have increased to 107,130.

To verify that the worksheet is operating properly, you will compare the ending cash balance for the year with the ending cash balance for December.

▶ **4.** Switch to the December sheet to view the ending cash balance for December, which should be 620 as well, and then redisplay the Annual worksheet.

Now that you've completed filling in the values for the Annual worksheet, you can print the entire contents of the workbook for Joy to include in her report.

Printing Worksheet Groups

You can set up the page layout and print area for all of the worksheets in the choir workbook by selecting a worksheet group and then accessing the Page Setup dialog box. You will set up the worksheet group to print in portrait orientation with the name of the worksheet in the header and your name and the date in the footer.

To print the cash flow sheets with a customized header and footer:

▸ **1.** Select the worksheets from the **Annual** sheet through the **December** sheet.

▸ **2.** Click **File** on the menu bar, and then click **Page Setup**. The Page Setup dialog box opens.

▸ **3.** On the Page tab, verify that the **Portrait** option button is selected, click the **Margins** tab, and then click the **Horizontally** check box to center the output horizontally on the page.

▸ **4.** Click the **Header/Footer** tab, click the **Custom Header** button, click in the Center section box, click the **Tab Name** button 🗐, and then click the **OK** button. A preview of the header appears in the upper portion of the dialog box.

▸ **5.** Click the **Custom Footer** button, type *your name* and the *current date* on separate lines in the Right section box, and then click the **OK** button.

▸ **6.** Click the **Print Preview** button, and then scroll through the pages to verify that Excel has applied the same page layout to each sheet. See Figure 6-9.

Print preview of the worksheet group ◂ **Figure 6-9**

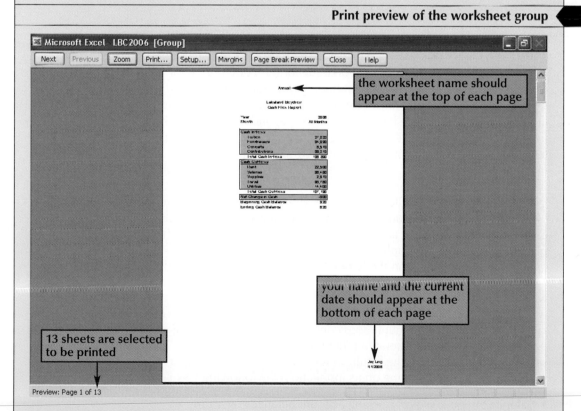

7. Click the **Close** button to close the Print Preview window without printing all the sheets, unless you are instructed to print the sheets.

8. Switch to the Documentation sheet so that the next time this workbook is opened the Documentation sheet is the first sheet to appear.

9. Save your changes to the workbook and close it.

Joy wants to apply the same format to financial data from previous years that she has stored in other workbooks. In the next session, you'll learn how to create workbooks that follow a customized format.

Review

Session 6.1 Quick Check

1. What is a worksheet group?
2. How do you select an adjacent and a nonadjacent worksheet group? How do you deselect a worksheet group?
3. What is the 3-D cell reference to cell A10 on the Summary Data worksheet?
4. What is the 3-D cell reference to cell A10 on the worksheets Summary 1, Summary 2, and Summary 3 (assuming that these sheets occupy an adjacent range in the workbook)?
5. How do you copy the contents and format from a range in one worksheet to the rest of the worksheets in a worksheet group?
6. How do you apply the same printing page layout to all the sheets in your workbook?

Session 6.2

Using Templates

In the last session, you created a workbook for the 2006 budget of the Lakeland Boychoir. Joy now wants to use the same workbook format for the financial data from previous years stored in her other workbooks. One approach to accomplish this goal is to open the LBC2006 workbook, save it under a new name, and then replace the 2006 values with figures from one of the previous years. Joy is reluctant to use that approach because mistakes could easily be introduced, or in a worse case, previous year's figures could be inadvertently overwritten. A better alternative is to have a workbook that you can open with the labels, formats, and formulas already built into it.

Such a document is called a **template**. When you open a template, Excel opens a copy of the workbook that includes text (row and column labels), formatting, and formulas. You can make any changes or additions you want to the workbook without affecting the template file. The original template retains its formatting and formulas, and the next time you open a workbook based on the template, those original settings will still be present.

Excel has several templates that are automatically installed on your hard disk. In fact, when you start Excel and see the blank workbook called Book1, you are actually using a workbook based on a template known as the **default template**. The default template contains no text or formulas, but it does contain the default formatting you start out with in every new workbook: General number format, Arial 10-point font, labels aligned to the left side of a cell, values and the results of formulas aligned to the right side of a cell, etc. Excel may also include (depending on its installation) the following task-specific templates:

- **Balance Sheet:** Used for tracking account balances over time
- **Expense Statement:** Used for creating an expense report
- **Loan Amortization:** Used for tracking the costs of loans and mortgages

- **Sales Invoice:** Used for creating a sales invoice
- **Timecard:** Used for creating an online time card to track employees' work hours

Using these templates saves you from "reinventing the wheel." You can also download additional templates from the Microsoft Office Templates Web page (a link on the New Workbook task pane) or from third-party vendors.

Creating a Workbook Based on a Template

To see how templates work, you'll create a new workbook based on one of the built-in Excel templates.

Create a Workbook Based on a Template

- Click File on the menu bar, and then click New.
- Click the On my computer link in the New Workbook task pane.
- Click the Spreadsheet Solutions tab, click the icon representing the template you want to use, and then click the OK button.
- Save the workbook with a new filename.

You'll open the Excel Balance Sheet template.

To create a workbook based on a built-in template:

1. If you took a break at the end of the last session, make sure Excel is running.

   Trouble? If the LBC2006 workbook is still open, close it now, saving any changes you made.

2. Click **File** on the menu bar, and then click **New** to display the New Workbook task pane.

3. In the Templates section, click the **On my computer** link to open the Templates dialog box, and then click the **Spreadsheet Solutions** tab. See Figure 6-10.

Spreadsheet Solutions tab in the Templates dialog box **Figure 6-10**

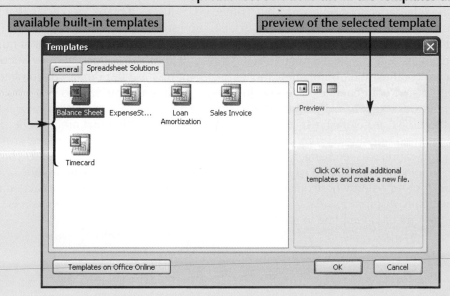

4. Click the **Timecard** icon, and then click the **OK** button. If this is the first time the Timecard template has been accessed on your computer, Excel might need to install some template components, which takes only a few seconds. See Figure 6-11 for the workbook based on the Timecard template.

Figure 6-11 Timecard template

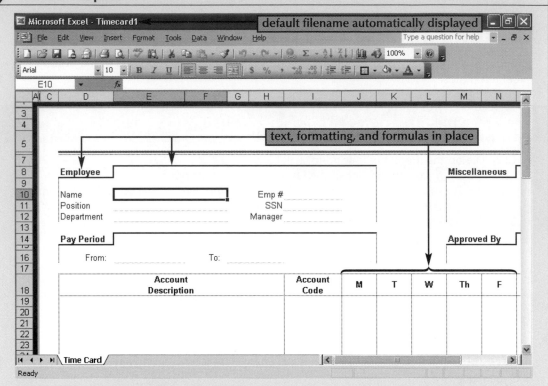

5. To see more of the layout of the worksheet components, click the right scroll arrow on the horizontal scroll bar.

Figure 6-11 displays a workbook based on the Timecard template. Notice that the name in the title bar is not "Timecard," but "Timecard1." Just as a blank workbook that you open is named sequentially, "Book1," "Book2," and so forth, a workbook based on a specific template always displays the name of the template followed by a sequential number. Any changes or additions that you make to this workbook only affect the new document you are creating and do not affect the template, in this case the Timecard template. If you want to save your changes, you save the workbook in the same way as you would save any new workbook based on the default template.

As for the Time Card worksheet, observe the labels and formatting that are present immediately upon opening the Timecard template. Most cells in the worksheet are protected, so you cannot make changes to these cells; other cells are not protected, so you can enter data in these cells; and still other cells contain formulas (cells with a pale-yellow background color) where calculations for total hours worked by day and account are automatically displayed as data is entered. You'll enter some data in the worksheet based on the Timecard template to see how it works.

To explore a workbook based on the Timecard template:

1. Click cell **D10**. You are prevented from making cell D10 the active cell. Most cells in this worksheet are protected so you cannot accidentally alter the value in the cell.

2. Click cell **E10**, type **Jay Finch**, and then press the **Enter** key. This cell is not protected, so you were able to enter a value.

3. Click cell **D19**, type **Job 101**, and then press the **Tab** key twice to move to column J so you can enter the hours for Monday and Tuesday.

4. Type **8** in cell J19, press the **Tab** key, and then enter **3** in cell K19.

5. Click cell **D20**, type **Job 102**, press the **Tab** key to move to column K, type **5** in cell K20, and then press the **Enter** key.

6. Scroll to the right to display column Q, and notice that the total hours worked for each account are automatically summed.

7. Scroll down to row 36, and notice that the total hours worked each day and for the week have been computed.

   Having seen how to create a workbook based on a template, you will close the Timecard1 workbook without saving it.

8. Close the workbook and click the **No** button when prompted to save the changes.

Now that you know the purpose of a template and have opened one of the built-in Excel templates, you can see how useful templates can be. Having completed the workbook according to Joy's specifications, you now have the basis for a template that can be used for similar projects. Instead of using one of Excel's built-in templates, you can save the LBC2006 workbook as a template file, and then Joy can create new workbooks based on that template.

Creating and Saving a Custom Workbook Template

To create a template from an existing workbook, you need to be sure that all the formulas work as intended, numbers and text are entered correctly, and the worksheet is formatted appropriately. Next, you need to remove the values and text that will change each time you create a workbook using your customized template. Be careful not to delete the formulas. You may find it helpful to replace variable data values with zeros, which will help you recognize the cells in which to enter the new data. Sometimes a different background color is applied to cells that accept data. Finally, you need to save this workbook in an Excel template file format using the Save As dialog box.

Saving a Workbook as a Template

Reference Window

- Prepare the workbook by entering the values, text, and formulas that you need, by applying any formatting you want, and by replacing data values with zeros.
- Click File on the menu bar, and then click Save As.
- Click the Save as type list arrow, and then select Template.
- Click the Save button.

To save the LBC2006 workbook as a custom workbook template, you'll reopen the workbook and replace the data values in the worksheets with zeros, keeping all of the formulas intact. After completing these modifications, you will save the workbook as a template.

To replace the data values in the choir workbook:

1. Open the **LBC2006** workbook located in the Tutorial.06\Tutorial folder.

2. Group the sheets from **January** through **December** (do *not* select the Annual worksheet), and then redisplay the January worksheet.

3. Replace the data values in cells **B4** and **B21** with zeros.

   Trouble? If a dash appears in cell B21 instead of a zero, you used the Comma Style and Decrease Decimal buttons on the Formatting toolbar and not the Format Cells dialog box to apply the Number format as instructed in the first session. Before continuing, ungroup the sheets, group the worksheets Annual through December, select the nonadjacent range B21;B8:B11;B14:B18 on one of the sheets, open the Format Cells dialog box, and then apply a modified Number format so the values appear with a comma and no decimal places. Deselect the range and then ungroup the worksheets. Repeat Steps 2 and 3.

4. Replace the inflow data values in the range **B8:B11** with zeros, and then replace the outflow data values in the range **B14:B18** with zeros.

5. Click cell **A1** on the January worksheet so cell A1 will always be the active cell on each worksheet.

6. Switch to the Annual sheet, replace the data values in cells **B4** and **B21** with zeros, and then click cell **A1**. See Figure 6-12.

Figure 6-12   **Worksheet with formatting and formulas but no data**

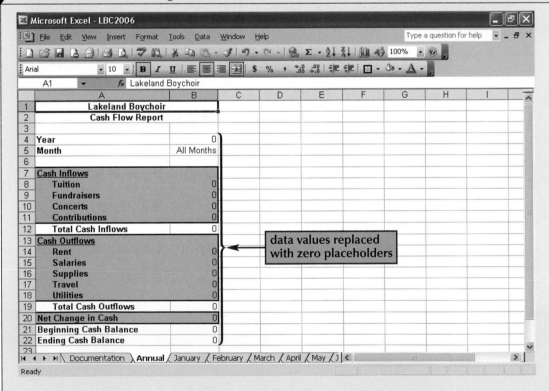

7. Switch to the Documentation sheet, and then delete the date in cell B3 and your name in cell B4.

Now you'll save the workbook in template format.

To save the workbook as a template:

▶ 1. Click **File** on the menu bar, and then click **Save As**. The Save As dialog box opens.

▶ 2. Type **LBC Cash Flow** in the File name list box.

▶ 3. Click the **Save as type** list arrow, and then click **Template** in the list. When you select the Template file type, Excel automatically opens a folder named "Templates" in which all template files are stored. Excel automatically looks for template files in this particular folder, but you might not have access to your computer network's Templates folder; therefore, you should save the template file with your Data Files.

▶ 4. Using the Save in list box, navigate to the Tutorial.06\Tutorial folder, and then click the **Save** button. Now Joy has a template file she can use to create workbooks for the cash flow information for the other years. By basing these new workbooks on the template file, she will not run the risk of accidentally changing her workbook containing the 2006 data.

▶ 5. Close the LBC Cash Flow workbook template.

All template files have an .xlt extension. This extension differentiates template files from workbook files that have the .xls extension. Once you've saved a workbook in template format, you can make the template accessible to other users. To do this, you have to understand a bit more about how Excel stores template files.

Using the Templates Folder

To use a template like the one you just created, the template file typically is placed in the Templates folder. The location of this folder will vary from user to user, but the path is often C:\Documents and Settings*user_name*\Application Data\Microsoft\Templates where *user_name* is the name of the user account. In some cases, such as on a computer network, you will have to check with the network administrator to determine the location of the Templates folder.

Once a file has been stored in the Templates folder (either by saving it to that folder directly via the Save As dialog box or by moving the file to the folder using Windows Explorer), the template file becomes an icon on the General tab in the Templates dialog box. Figure 6-13 shows how the General tab would look with an icon for the LBC Cash Flow template on it. You can create subfolders in the Templates folder to organize your templates. Subfolders of the Templates folder appear as tabs in the Templates dialog box.

Templates dialog box with the LBC Cash Flow template icon ◄ **Figure 6-13**

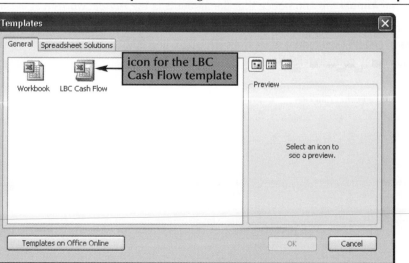

Using the LBC Cash Flow Template

You are not limited to storing a template in the Templates folder. You can store it in any folder. If you don't save the template to the Templates folder, the New Workbook task pane enables you to create a new workbook much like creating a workbook based on a template found in the Templates folder.

You will try this method with the LBC Cash Flow workbook template.

To create a workbook based on the LBC Cash Flow template:

▶ 1. Click **File** on the menu bar, and then click **New**. The New Workbook task pane opens. See Figure 6-14.

Figure 6-14 ▶ **Basing a new workbook on an existing file**

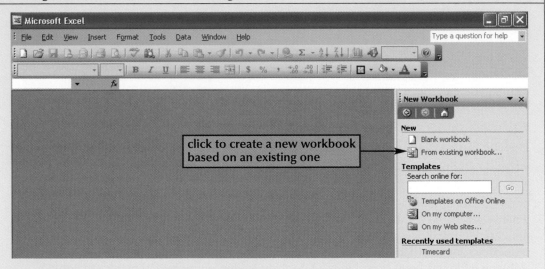

▶ 2. Click **From existing workbook** in the New section of the task pane. The New from Existing Workbook dialog box opens, with all types of Excel files displayed in the list box.

▶ 3. Select the **LBC Cash Flow** template from the Tutorial.06\Tutorial folder, and then click the **Create New** button. Excel opens a copy of the LBC Cash Flow workbook. The filename in the title bar is "LBC Cash Flow1," indicating that it is the first copy of the LBC Cash Flow workbook created during this Excel session.

▶ 4. Click the **Annual** tab and notice that the amounts in the Annual worksheet are all zeros.

▶ 5. Switch to the January sheet, click cell **B8**, type **12000**, press the **Enter** key, and then type **1000** in cell B9. See Figure 6-15. Cells B12, B20, and B22 have automatically been updated because they contain formulas.

New workbook based on LBC Cash Flow template   Figure 6-15

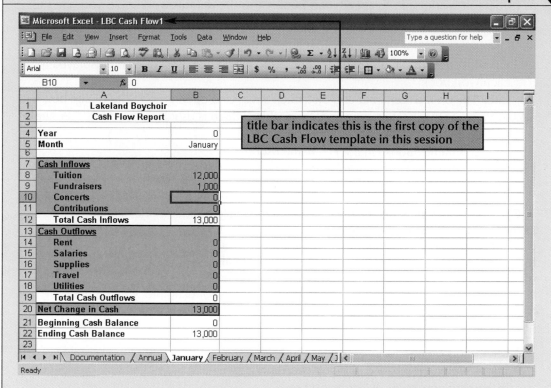

6. Switch to the Annual sheet. Note that totals appear in cells B8, B9, B12, B20, and B22 as a result of the formulas contained in this worksheet.

7. Close the workbook, but do not save it.

The task pane option of creating a new workbook works much like creating a work-book based on a template found in the Templates folder. The advantage of this option is that you are not limited to storing a workbook file in the Templates folder. This option also protects the original workbook from being inadvertently altered.

Editing a Template

If you need to change labels, formatting, or formulas in a template, you open the template file from the Template folder or whatever folder in which it's been stored. You use the Open command on the File menu, rather then the New command so that you can edit the template file itself. After making changes to the template, you save it. When you open the template to create a new workbook, the changes will appear.

Changing the Default Workbook Template

As you know, each time you start Excel, a new blank workbook is displayed in the workbook window and the default filename appears in the title bar as "Book1." The blank workbook that is displayed is based on the default Excel workbook template. If you want to use a template that you created as the default template for all your Excel workbooks, you need to save the template file with the name Book.xlt in the XLStart folder. If the XLStart folder contains a file named Book.xlt, Excel will use the Book.xlt as its default workbook. To specify the Book.xlt as the default workbook, you need to complete the following steps:

1. Display a new blank workbook in the Excel workbook window.
2. Specify fonts, font sizes, styles, borders, colors, and text that you want displayed in each workbook.
3. Click File on the menu bar and then click Save As to open the Save As dialog box.
4. Navigate to the location of your XLStart folder, which is usually located in C:\Program Files\Microsoft Office\Office2003\XLStart\ folder.
5. Enter the name "Book" in the File name list box.
6. Click the Save as type list arrow, and then click Template.
7. Click the Save button.

Once you have specified the Book.xlt file in the XLStart folder as the default template, Excel will base all new workbooks on it.

You can also specify an alternate startup folder. An alternate startup folder is a folder that contains workbooks you want to open automatically when you start Excel and templates that you want to be available when you create new workbooks. You can use Windows Explorer to create the alternate startup folder. For example, you might create a folder named "Spreadsheets." To specify an alternate startup directory, you need to complete the following steps:

1. Click Tools on the menu bar and then click Options to open the Options dialog box.
2. Click the General tab, and then enter the path, such as C:\My Documents\Spreadsheets\, in the At startup, open all files in text box.
3. Click the OK button.

Organizing Folders and Files

The files that you create using the programs in the Office 2003 suite are by default saved in the My Documents folder. As you create more and more files, you might find it helpful to create subfolders in which to save project or task-related files. For example, you might create a folder named "Budgets" for your Excel files. To ensure that your workbooks are automatically saved in this folder, you need to follow these steps:

1. Click Tools on the menu bar, and then click Options to open the Options dialog box.
2. Click the General tab, and then enter the path, such as C:\My Documents\Budgets\, for the default file location where you want to save files.
3. Click the OK button.

As you work on different projects, you may find if necessary to change the name of a folder or file. To rename a folder or file, you can use Windows Explorer, or you can change the name of a folder or file from within Excel itself, by following these steps:

1. Click File on the menu bar, and then click Open to display the Open dialog box.
2. Using the Look in list arrow, navigate to the location that contains the folder or file that you want to rename. The folder or file must be displayed in the list box in the middle portion of the Open dialog box and not in the Look in list box at the top of the dialog box.
3. Right-click the folder or file you want to rename, and then click Rename on the short-cut menu. The folder or file name is selected.
4. Type the new name and then press the Enter key.

A note of caution: Because you are probably working in a classroom or lab, you should not change any default folder or file unless instructed to.

In the next session, you will use the LBC Cash Flow template for the cash flow reports that Joy wants for the previous years of the choir, and use data located in different workbooks.

Session 6.2 Quick Check

Review

1. What is a template?
2. What is an advantage of using a template over simply using the original workbook file?
3. What is the default workbook template?
4. How do you save a file as a template?
5. Where are customized template files stored by default in Excel? Can you store a template file that you create anywhere else?
6. How do you place a template into a separate tab in the Templates dialog box?
7. How do you create a workbook based on another file without creating a template?

Session 6.3

Using Data from Multiple Workbooks

Joy has completed the process of entering data from other years into Excel. She has created three additional workbooks, named LBC2003, LBC2004, and LBC2005, which contain monthly cash flow statements for the years 2003, 2004, and 2005, respectively.

When you created the LBC2006 workbook in the first session, you had to insert a formula that would carry the ending cash balance from one month to the beginning cash balance of the next month. Joy wants you to do something similar with her other cash flow workbooks. She wants each year's beginning cash balance to be based on the ending cash balance for the previous year. The previous year's cash flow statements for 2006 are located in the LBC2005 workbook (the previous year's workbook). You will open the LBC2006 and LBC2005 workbooks now.

To open the two workbooks:

1. If you took a break at the end of the last session, make sure Excel is running.
2. Open the **LBC2006** workbook located in the Tutorial.06\Tutorial folder, and then open the **LBC2005** workbook located in the same folder. You can tell that both workbook files are opened from the program buttons on the taskbar, but only one of the workbooks is visible. You can switch between the workbooks using the Window menu or by clicking the program button displaying the workbook name on the taskbar. You will use the Window menu method first.
3. Click **Window** on the menu bar. A list of open workbooks appears at the bottom of the menu.
4. Click **LBC2006** to switch to the LBC2006 workbook.

Because you need to reference data located in one workbook while in another workbook, you have to create a link between the two workbooks. A **link** is a connection between two files allowing information to be transferred from one file to the other. When two files are linked together, one workbook is called the **source file** because it contains the information, and the other workbook is called the **destination file** because it receives the information. In this case, as illustrated in Figure 6-16, LBC2005 is the source file because this workbook contains the ending cash balance data for the year 2005, and LBC2006 is the destination file because this workbook will receive that ending cash balance data to determine the beginning cash balance for 2006.

Figure 6-16   ▶   **Source and destination files**

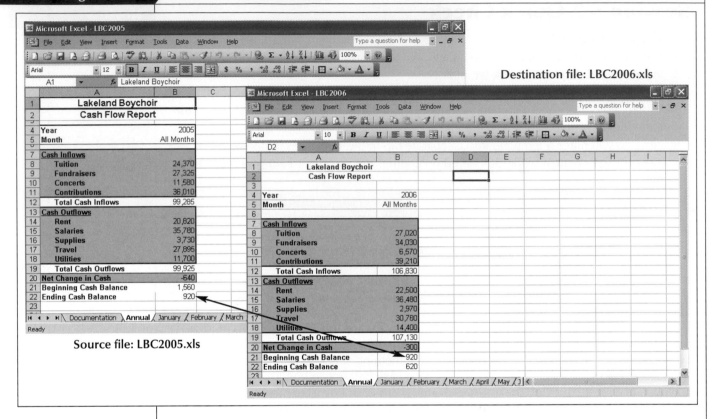

Source file: LBC2005.xls

Destination file: LBC2006.xls

To create this link, you have to insert a formula in the LBC2006 workbook that points to a specific cell or range in the LBC2005 workbook. Because the formula will contain a reference that refers to a cell on a sheet in another workbook, that reference is called an **external reference**. The general form of an external reference is

[WorkbookName]SheetReference!CellRange

where *WorkbookName* is the filename of the workbook (including the file extension) enclosed in square brackets and where *SheetReference* and *CellRange* are worksheets and cells in the workbook, respectively. For example, if you were to create a formula in one workbook to reference cell B21 on the Summary worksheet of the Sales.xls workbook, you would create the formula *=[Sales.xls]Summary!B21.*

If the workbook name or sheet name contains one or more spaces, you must enclose the entire workbook name and sheet name reference in single quotation marks. For example, if you want to reference cell B21 on the Summary worksheet of the US Sales.xls workbook, you would enter the formula *='[US Sales.xls]Summary'!B21.*

If the two workbooks are located in the same folder, you do not need to include the location information in the workbook reference. However, if one of the workbooks is in a different folder, then you will have to modify the workbook reference to include the complete location (always called the path). For example, if the current location of the active workbook is C:\My Documents, and the US Sales workbook is stored in C:\My Documents\Domestic Sales, then to reference cells in the US Sales workbook, the complete reference is *='C:\My Documents\Domestic Sales\[US Sales.xls]Summary'!21.*

Managing Multiple Workbooks

Excel provides a number of commands that you can use to help manage your workbook window if you need to move between opened workbooks. Although you can click the program button on the taskbar that appears for each workbook that you open, you can also have all the opened workbooks displayed on your screen at the same time. The Windows menu provides several commands that enable you to deal with open workbooks in an organized and succinct way.

If you have multiple workbooks opened, you can choose to arrange them in different ways. To arrange multiple workbooks that you have opened, you follow these steps:

1. Click Windows on the menu bar, and then click Arrange to open the Arrange Windows dialog box.
2. Select the option that you want to use for arranging your workbooks: tiled, horizontal, vertical, or cascade.
3. When arranging multiple workbooks, be sure that the Windows of the active workbook option in not checked.
4. Click the OK button.

To undo the arrangement, you click the Maximize button on each of the windows to redisplay the workbook on the screen.

You can also hide a workbook without having to close it. You might want to hide a workbook if you are focusing on another workbook or workbooks, but still need access to the hidden one. To hide a workbook, you follow these steps:

1. Make the workbook that you want to hide the active workbook.
2. Click Windows on the menu bar, and then click Hide. The workbook is no longer displayed in the Excel window, nor is its program button displayed on the taskbar.

When you are ready to redisplay the workbook, you need to open the Unhide workbook dialog box. To unhide a workbook, you follow these steps:

1. Click Windows on the menu bar, and then click Unhide. This command appears on the Window menu only when a workbook has been hidden. The Unhide dialog box opens with a list of workbooks that have been hidden.
2. Click the name of the workbook you want to redisplay.

How you manage opened workbooks will depend on how you like to work and the tasks that you want to accomplish.

Now you need to replace the beginning cash balance value in the LBC2006 workbook with a reference to the ending cash balance in the LBC2005 workbook. Although you can enter linked formulas by typing them, you will use the same point-and-click method you used in creating the 3-D cell references in the first session to switch between the source files and dependent files.

To create the workbook reference:

1. Switch to the Annual sheet in the LBC2006 workbook, click cell **B21**, and then type **=** (do *not* press the Enter key).
2. Switch to the LBC2005 workbook, click the **Annual** tab, click cell **B22**, and then click the **Enter** button ✓ on the Formula bar. The Annual sheet in the LBC2006 workbook redisplays with cell B21 as the active cell. The formula *=[LBC2005.xls]Annual!$B$22* appears in the Formula bar of the workbook.

Now you will change the beginning cash balance formula in the January worksheet so that the cell is also linked to the corresponding cell in the LBC2005 workbook.

▶ 3. Click the **January** tab in the LBC2006 workbook, click cell **B21**, and then type **=** (do *not* press the Enter key). This time you will switch to the LBC2005 workbook by clicking its program button on the taskbar.

▶ 4. Click the **LBC2005** program button on the taskbar, switch to the Annual sheet, click cell **B22**, and then click the **Enter** button ☑ on the Formula bar. The formula in cell B21 in the January worksheet in the LBC2006 workbook should be *=[LBC2005.xls]Annual!$B$22*.

Creating the link between the two workbooks will help Joy more efficiently analyze the data. However, she wonders what will happen if she changes a value in the LBC2005 workbook. How soon will that change be reflected in the beginning cash flow value in 2006? To answer Joy's question, you need to look further at the concept of linking.

Working with Linked Workbooks

When two workbooks are linked, it's important that the data in the destination file accurately reflects the contents of the source file. To do this, the link must be periodically updated. Excel updates a link in the following circumstances:

- Excel will prompt you to update the link with the source file when you initially open the destination file.
- If both the destination and source files are open, Excel will update the link automatically whenever a value in the source file is changed.
- If only the destination file is open, you can manually update the link at any time during your Excel session without opening the source file.

You currently have both the source and destination files open. You will show Joy what would happen if a value in the LBC2005 workbook were changed.

To change a value in the 2005 cash flow workbook:

▶ 1. Switch to the LBC2005 workbook, and then click the **January** tab.

To illustrate the effect of changing a value in a linked workbook, you will increase the value of the January fundraisers by 1,000 to 1,360. This change should increase the starting 2006 cash balance as well, from 920 to 1,920.

▶ 2. Click cell **B9**, type **1360**, press the **Enter** key, and then switch to the Annual sheet. The ending cash balance for 2005 has changed to 1,920.

Now you'll check the beginning cash balance for 2006, which should match the ending cash balance for 2005.

▶ 3. Switch to the LBC2006 workbook, and then click the **Annual** tab. The value in cell B21 has changed to 1,920, reflecting the new value you entered into the LBC2005 workbook.

▶ 4. Switch to the LBC2005 workbook, save your changes, and then close the workbook.

Being able to change values in linked workbooks will save time and ensure consistency across the workbooks.

Editing Workbook References

Joy now wants you to create a summary workbook that will contain a table showing the annual cash flows over the past four years. A formatted workbook has already been created for you. Your job will be to add the appropriate formulas to the workbook. First you will open the summary workbook and view its contents.

To create the summary workbook:

1. Click **File** on the menu bar, click **Open**, and then open the **LBCSum1** workbook located in the Tutorial.06\Tutorial folder.

2. Enter *your name* and the *current date* on the Documentation sheet, and then save the workbook as **LBCSum2** in the Tutorial.06\Tutorial folder.

3. Click the **Summary** tab. Figure 6-17 shows the contents of the Summary worksheet.

Summary worksheet ◄ **Figure 6-17**

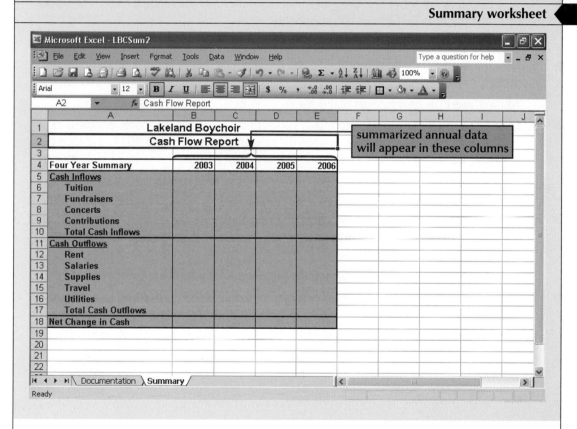

There are four columns in the table in which to enter the annual cash inflows and outflows for the past four years. Your job is to link the contents of this table to four different annual workbooks. You'll start by linking the last column of the table to the annual values in the LBC2006 workbook.

To link the LBCSum2 workbook to the LBC2006 workbook:

▶ 1. Click cell **E6** on the Summary sheet in the LBCSum2 workbook, and then type **=** (do *not* press the Enter key).

▶ 2. Switch to the LBC2006 workbook and, if necessary, switch to the Annual worksheet.

▶ 3. Double-click cell **B8** in the Annual worksheet of the LBC2006 workbook. By default, Excel uses an absolute cell reference when linking to a different workbook. You have to change the absolute reference to a mixed reference because you are going to fill in the rest of the values in the table using the fill handle. You will change the column reference to an absolute reference so it will stay the same.

▶ 4. Change the cell reference from $B$8 to the mixed reference **$B8**, and then click the **Enter** button ☑ on the Formula bar. The figure 27,020 appears in cell E6 on the Summary sheet and the formula =[LBC2006.xls]Annual!$B8 appears on the Formula bar.

You will now copy the formula.

▶ 5. With cell E6 as the active cell, drag the fill handle down over the range **E7:E10**. The values fill in and the Auto Fill Options button appears.

Because you want just the formula copied, you will use an Auto Fill option.

▶ 6. Click the **Auto Fill Options** button 🔛, and then click the **Fill Without Formatting** option button.

You will insert the next formula to link the rent values.

▶ 7. Click **E12**, type **=** (to begin the formula), switch to the LBC2006 workbook, double-click cell **B14** in the Annual worksheet, change the reference from $B$14 to **$B14**, and then click the **Enter** button ☑ on the Formula bar. The total rent paid for the year, 22,500, appears in cell E12.

You will now copy the formula.

▶ 8. With cell E12 as the active cell, drag the fill handle down over the range **E13:E17** to fill in the values, click the **Auto Fill Options** button 🔛, and then click the **Fill Without Formatting** option button.

Now you will enter the formula to compute the change in cash flow for the year.

▶ 9. Click cell **E18**, type **=E10-E17**, and then press the **Enter** key. Figure 6-18 shows the cash flows for 2006.

Cash flows for 2006 **Figure 6-18**

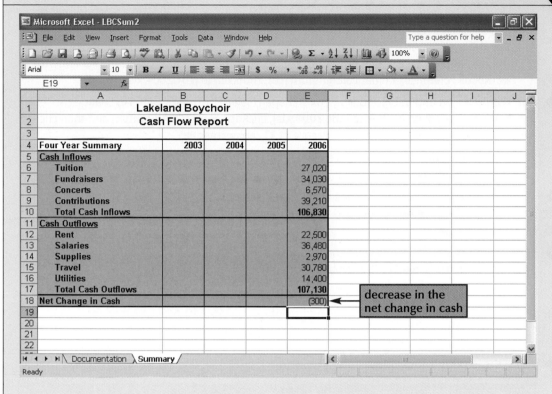

Now that you have linked the column values for 2006, you can link the remaining column values. You can't use the fill handle or Auto Fill options to fill across different workbooks. Instead, you'll copy the formulas from column E into the remaining columns, and then replace the workbook references with new references by pointing to the other workbooks.

To enter the remaining values:

1. Select the range **E6:E18**, and then click the **Copy** button on the Standard toolbar.

2. Select the range **B6:D18**, and then click the **Paste** button on the Standard toolbar. The formulas with the correct formatting, but with the values for 2006, are now copied to the other columns. To update workbook references in each column for the correct year, you will use Excel's Find and Replace feature.

3. Select the range **D6:D18**, click **Edit** on the menu bar, and then click **Replace**. The Find and Replace dialog box opens.

4. Type **[LBC2006.xls]** in the Find what list box, press the **Tab** key, and then type **[LBC2005.xls]** in the Replace with list box. See Figure 6-19.

Find and Replace dialog box **Figure 6-19**

5. Click the **Replace All** button to replace all LBC2006.xls workbook references with LBC2005.xls workbook references in the selected range, and then click the **OK** button to acknowledge that Excel replaced 11 occurrences.

   You will continue to make a similar replacement for the other year. You don't have to close the Find and Replace dialog box yet. You can select the next column and then change the workbook references in that column from [LBC2006.xls] to [LBC2004.xls].

6. With the Find and Replace dialog box still open, select the range **C6:C18**, change the text in the Replace with list box to **[LBC2004.xls]**, click the **Replace All** button, and then click the **OK** button to confirm the occurrence of 11 replacements.

   Trouble? If the Find and Replace dialog box covers column B, move the dialog box to another location in the workbook window.

7. Select the range **B6:B18**, change the text in the Replace with list box to **[LBC2003.xls]**, click the **Replace All** button, and then click the **OK** button to confirm the occurrence of 11 replacements.

8. Click the **Close** button to close the Find and Replace dialog box, and then press the **Esc** key to remove the blinking selection border around the range E6:E18.

   To make the cash inflow and outflow subtotal rows stand out, you will apply a white fill color.

9. Apply the **White** fill color to the nonadjacent range **A10:E10;A17:E17**, and then click cell **A1**. Figure 6-20 shows the revised summary table.

Figure 6-20	Annual cash flows for 2003–2006

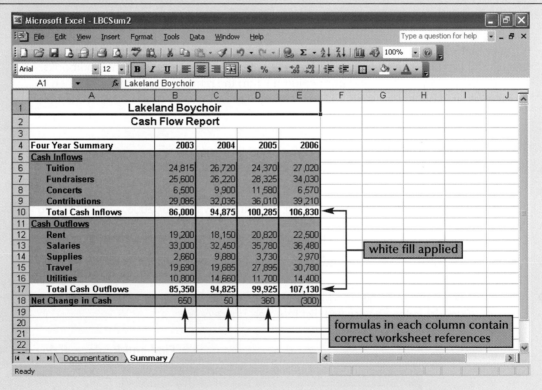

Each of the values in the table is linked to a cell in one of the cash flow workbooks. For example, the total rent in cell B12 comes from a cell in the Annual worksheet of the LBC2003 workbook. By examining the table, Joy can quickly see that both inflows and outflows for the choir have increased by about $20,000 over the past four years; therefore, making ends meet is a continuing struggle for the group.

Working with a List of Links

Joy wonders how one would know what links are present in a workbook without viewing the contents of each cell. One way would be to use Excel's Find feature and search through the workbook for cell references containing the text string *.xls]* because this text string implies a workbook reference.

Another way is to view a list of links in the Edit Links dialog box. You will show Joy how this works with the current workbook.

To view the list of linked workbooks:

▶ **1.** Click **Edit** on the menu bar, and then click **Links**. The Edit Links dialog box opens, as shown in Figure 6-21.

Edit Links dialog box   **Figure 6-21**

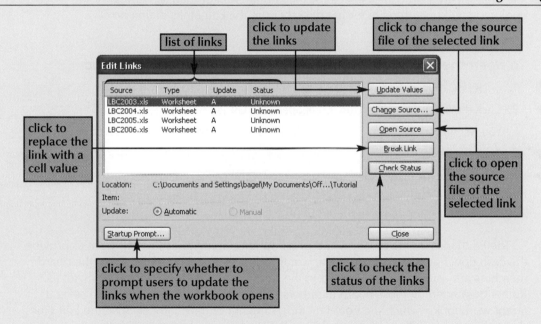

The Edit Links dialog box lists all of the links in the current workbook. Currently there are four links pointing to the four cash flow workbooks: LBC2003.xls, LBC2004.xls, LBC2005.xls, and LBC2006.xls. The list also indicates the type of each source file. In this case, the type is an Excel worksheet. The third column indicates how values are updated from the source file. The letter "A" indicates that these links are updated automatically either when you initially open the workbook or when you have both the source and the destination file open at the same time. A letter "M" indicates that the link has to be updated manually by the user. The final column gives the status of the link, indicating whether Excel has been able to successfully access the link and update the values from the source document. Currently the status of all four links is unknown because Excel has not attempted to update the links in this session.

Joy wants to know how to update all of the links in the workbook. You can do that by selecting the links in the list and then clicking the Update Values button. Try this now.

To update the links in the summary workbook:

▶ 1. If necessary, click **LBC2003.xls** in the list of links, press and hold the **Shift** key, click **LBC2006.xls**, and then release the Shift Key. Excel selects all of the links in the list.

   Trouble? If the list of links is not selected, the workbooks might not be listed in the same order as shown in Figure 6-21. To select all the workbook links, click the first workbook in the list, press and hold the Shift key, and then click the last workbook in the list. All the links should be selected.

▶ 2. Click the **Update Values** button. The status column changes to indicate the current status of each linked workbook. Excel displays the text "OK" for the status of the first three links, indicating that those links are acting correctly and have been updated in this session. The LBC2006 link displays the text "Source is open," indicating that the source file is currently open. Any changes you make in the LBC2006 file will be automatically reflected in the summary workbook.

Joy wants to view the January 2005 cash flow figures. She wants to examine how much the choir received in contributions for that month. Rather than searching for the workbook, you will open the file for her directly from the Edit Links dialog box.

To open the LBC2005 workbook from the Edit Links dialog box:

▶ 1. Click **LBC2005.xls** in the list of links.

▶ 2. Click the **Open Source** button. Excel opens the LBC2005 workbook.

   You will now examine in more detail the 2005 figures for the Lakeland Boychoir.

▶ 3. Click the **January** tab, which shows that the January contributions were 2,270.

▶ 4. Close the LBC2005 workbook. The LBCSum2 workbook is redisplayed and the Edit Links dialog box is closed.

The Edit Links dialog box provides other options. Sometimes Joy will want to provide the cash flow figures to other members of the choir board. Joy tells you that the board members are usually only interested in the summary figures—not the monthly totals. Rather than handing those board members a workbook that contains links to several different workbooks (which the board members might not have), Joy can use the Edit Links dialog box to break those links, replacing the workbook references with the most recent values obtained from the source file. Note that if you do break a link, you cannot undo that action. To restore the link, you have to retype the workbook references.

Using Lookup Tables

Joy likes using the summary table to review budget figures from previous years, but she wonders if there is a way to retrieve that information without having to open the LBCSum2 workbook. Joy would like to have the ability within the LBC2006 workbook to type in the budget category and the year and to have Excel report the value without opening up any additional workbooks.

To do this in Excel, you need a lookup table. A **lookup table** is a table that organizes values that you want to retrieve into different categories. The categories for the lookup table, called **compare values**, are usually located in the table's first row or column. To retrieve a particular value from the table, you need a **lookup value**, which is matched against the compare values. When the lookup value matches a particular compare value, a value from an appropriate column (or row) in the table is returned.

You can use the layout of the data on the Annual sheet in the LBC2006 workbook as a lookup table. For example, Joy wants to know the travel outflows for 2004. The lookup value is "Travel" and the compare values come from the first column of the summary table. To retrieve the payments for travel during 2004, she moves down the first column until she finds the word "Travel" and then moves to the third column to view the answer, which is 19,685, as shown in Figure 6-22.

Using the summary data as a lookup table   **Figure 6-22**

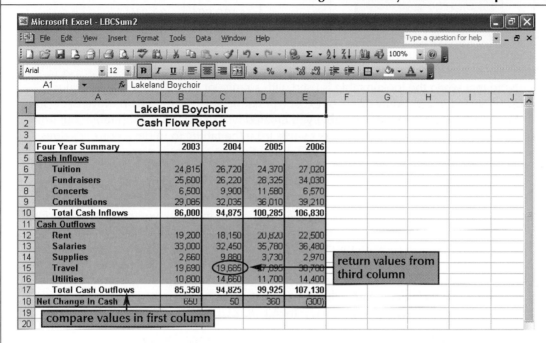

The categories in the first row or column of a lookup table can also represent a range of values. Figure 6-23 shows a sample table of tax rates for different income categories.

Tax rates for different income ranges   **Figure 6-23**

Income Range	Tax Rate
$0–$26,250	15.0%
$26,251–$63,550	28.0%
$63,551–$132,600	31.9%
$132,601–$288,350	36.0%
$288,351–higher	39.6%

Figure 6-24 shows the tax rates for different income ranges. In the tax rate table, you would not be looking for an exact match for the lookup value. Instead, you would want to test whether the lookup value falls within a range of values. To do this, the compare values represent the upper end of the range for each category. You go through the compare values until you locate the largest compare value that is still less than the lookup value. At that point, you would move across the table to retrieve the appropriate value. In the example, a person with an income of $45,000 would fall into the 28% tax bracket.

Figure 6-24   **A lookup table for a range of values**

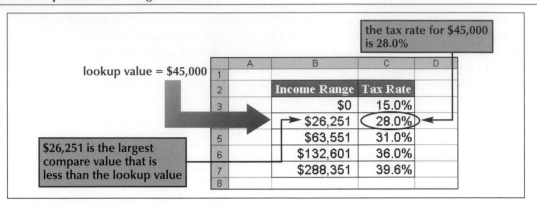

Note that when the lookup table is used with a range of values, the compare values *must* be sorted in ascending order, or Excel will not be able to correctly retrieve the results.

You've seen that the summary table you created will work as a lookup table, but how do you use Excel to retrieve the correct value from the table? To retrieve correct values from a table, you use one of Excel's Lookup functions.

Using Lookup Functions

Excel has several **Lookup functions**. For the purposes of the work you need to do for Joy, you need to learn about two Lookup functions: VLOOKUP and HLOOKUP. The **VLOOKUP** (or vertical lookup) **function** is used for lookup tables in which the compare values are placed in the table's first column. The **HLOOKUP** (or horizontal lookup) **function** is used when the compare values are placed in the table's first row. The summary table you created places the compare values in the first column, so you would use the VLOOKUP function. The general form of the VLOOKUP function is

VLOOKUP(*lookup_value, table_array, col_index_num, [range_lookup]*)

where *lookup_value* is the lookup value you want to send to the table, *table_array* is the cell reference of the table, *col_index_num* is the number of the column in the lookup table containing the value you want to retrieve, and *range_lookup* indicates whether the compare values constitute a range of values or an exact match. If you're using a range of values (as you would in the tax rate table), set the *range_lookup* value to TRUE; if you want *lookup_value* to exactly match a value in the first column of *table_array*, the *range_lookup* value should be set to FALSE. The *range_lookup* argument is optional, so if you omit a *range_lookup* value, Excel will assume that the value is TRUE.

For example, in the tax rate table shown earlier in Figure 6-24, the formula =VLOOKUP(45000, B2:C7, 2, TRUE) returns the value "28%." Note that the value of the *col_index_num* parameter is 2 because the tax rate values appear in the second column of the lookup table.

Similarly, to determine the travel payments for 2004 from the summary table shown earlier in Figure 6-22, you could use the formula *=VLOOKUP("Travel", A6:E18,3,FALSE)*. You use FALSE for the *range_lookup* argument because you want the lookup value to exactly match a value in the first column of the Annual sheet in the LBC2006 workbook.

Now that you've seen how the VLOOKUP function works, you can add the lookup capability to the LBC2006 workbook. First, you will enter the labels to identify the information found in the cells in the range.

To set up the lookup section:

1. Switch to the LBC2006 workbook and, if necessary, click the **Annual** tab.
2. Click cell **D7**, type **Lookup Previous Year's Values**, and then press the **Enter** key.
3. Enter **Category** in cell D8, enter **Column** in cell D9, and then enter **Value** in cell D10.

   Next, you will add the lookup value—an inflow or outflow category.
4. Click cell **E8**, type **Travel**, and then press the **Enter** key.

   Finally, you will enter the column number in the four-year summary table that identifies the column where the data for the year 2004 is found (third column in the Summary table).
5. Type **3** in cell E9, and then press the **Enter** key. See Figure 6-25.

Setting up the lookup section   **Figure 6-25**

Now you will enter the VLOOKUP function that will look up the values in the summary table.

To insert the VLOOKUP function:

1. With cell E10 as the active cell, click **Insert** on the menu bar, and then click **Function**. The Insert Function dialog box opens.
2. Click **Lookup & Reference** in the Or select a category list box.
3. Scroll to the bottom of the list of functions, and then double-click **VLOOKUP**. The Function Arguments dialog box opens.

   The Lookup_value parameter is equal to the value you entered into cell E8 of the current worksheet.
4. Enter **E8** in the Lookup_value reference box, and then press the **Tab** key to move the insertion point to the Table_array reference box. The Table_array parameter is equal to the range containing the summary table located in the LBCSum2 workbook.
5. Switch to the LBCSum2 workbook, select the range **A6:E18** on the Summary sheet, and then press the **Tab** key.

   The next parameter you must enter is Col_index_num. This parameter indicates the column number in the lookup table. For the year 2003, the value would be column 2. For the year 2004, the value would be column 3, and so forth. The column value is entered in cell E9.

▶ 6. Click cell **E9**, and then press the **Tab** key. You may find that you want to enter the column letter of the column where the data to be retrieved is stored, rather than the value that represents the column. For example, for the year 2003, you might want to enter column letter B as the column index number; however, Excel expects the value of 2, indicating the second column in the summary table.

▶ 7. Type **FALSE** in the Range_lookup parameter box because you are not using range values as compare values in the lookup table. See Figure 6-26 for the completed Function Arguments dialog box.

Figure 6-26 ▶ **Arguments for the VLOOKUP function**

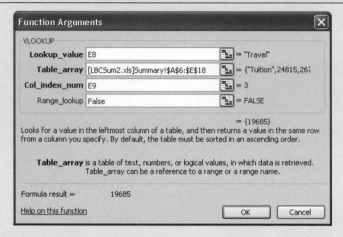

▶ 8. Click the **OK** button to close the dialog box. The value 19,685 appears in cell E10, indicating that the travel payments in the year 2004 were $19,685.

You will test this lookup feature with another value. For example, what were the total contributions for the year 2005?

To view other values:

▶ 1. Click cell **E8**, type **Contributions**, and then press the **Enter** key.

You will now enter the column number from the four-year summary table where the data for 2005 is found.

▶ 2. Type **4** in cell E9, and then press the **Enter** key. Excel displays the value 36,010 in cell E10, indicating that the total contributions for the year 2005 were $36,010.

The lookup feature provides an easy method for viewing information from previous years. However, Joy finds entering the column index number confusing; she wants to enter the year in cell E9 to indicate the year for which she is searching. The column index number can be entered as an integer, as you did above. You can also enter an expression; in this case, the year minus 2001. For example, if you are searching for data in 2003, then 2003 minus 2001 equals 2, which points to the second column in the summary table. If you are searching for data in 2004, then 2004 minus 2001 equals 3, which is the correct column index number in the summary table for 2004 data. You will modify the VLOOKUP function by using the expression *E9–2001* as the column index number.

To modify the VLOOKUP formula:

1. Click cell **D9**, and then type **Year** as the label for the lookup results.

2. Click cell **E10**, and then click the **Insert Function** button 𝑓𝑥 on the Formula bar to open the Function Arguments dialog box.

   You will modify the entry in the Column_index_num reference box.

3. Click in the Col_index_num reference box, type **E9-2001**, and then click the **OK** button. The Value# error appears in cell E10 because you need to change the value in cell E9 to the year 2005, which you will do next.

4. Click cell **E9**, and then enter **2005** as the year. The value 36,010 is displayed for contributions in the year 2005.

Before you go further, you will format the values in the lookup section of the Annual worksheet.

To format the lookup section:

1. Bold the text in the range **D7:D10**.

2. Fill the range **D7:G10** with the **Gray-25%** color, and then enclose the same range with the **Thick Box Border** option.

3. Format the value in cell **E10** so the numbers appear with a comma and no decimal places, and then click any cell to see the formatting applied. See Figure 6-27.

Formatted lookup section ◄ **Figure 6-27**

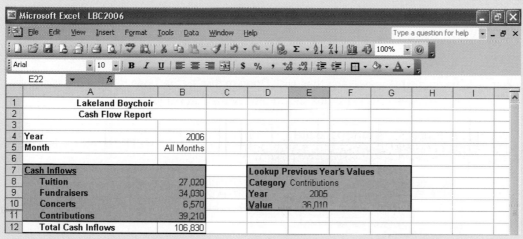

4. Click cell **A1** and save your changes to the workbook.

Creating an Excel Workspace

Joy now has five different workbooks containing budget data for the choir. Most of the time she'll only need to access one workbook at a time, but there will be occasions when she'll want to be able to access all of the workbooks. It would be great help if Joy could open all those workbooks at once. Being able to open all the workbooks will save time, but more importantly, it will save Joy the trouble of remembering all the filenames and folder locations.

To have the ability to open multiple workbooks at one time, you need to create a workspace. A **workspace** is an Excel file that saves information about all of the currently opened workbooks, such as their locations, their window sizes, and their screen positions. The workspace does not contain the workbooks themselves—only information about them. To work with that set of workbooks, you only have to open the workspace file and Excel will then open the workbooks. You will create a workspace file for Joy now.

To create the choir workspace file:

1. Open the **LBC2003**, **LBC2004**, and **LBC2005** workbooks located in the Tutorial.06\Tutorial folder. You now have five files open.

   Trouble? If you closed the LBC2006 and the LBCSum2 workbooks, be sure you open them as well. All five workbooks should be open.

2. Switch to the LBCSum2 workbook.

3. Click **File** on the menu bar, and then click **Save Workspace**. The Save Workspace dialog box opens.

4. Type **Choir Files** in the File name list box, verify that **Workspaces** is selected in the Save as type list box and that the Tutorial.06\Tutorial appears in the Save in list box, and then click the **Save** button. Excel prompts you to save your changes to the various open workbook files. You will save changes to all the open workbooks.

5. Click the **Yes To All** button. The Choir Files workspace is saved with your Data Files.

Now that you've created the workspace file, you will test to make sure it opens all five choir workbooks.

To test the Choir Files workspace:

1. Close all five of the choir workbooks.

2. Click **File** on the menu bar, and then click **Open** to display the Open dialog box, as shown in Figure 6-28. The Look in list box should display the Tutorial folder.

Figure 6-28   **Opening the Choir Files workspace file**

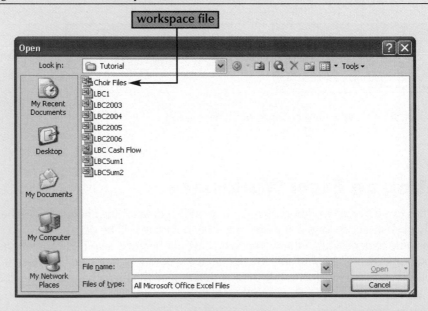

3. Click **Choir Files** in the list of files, click the **Open** button, and then click the **Update** button when you are prompted to update any links contained in these files. The five choir workbooks are all opened.

   The work you have done will make managing multiple workbooks easier for Joy.

4. Close all of the choir workbooks without saving any changes.

You have been able to work with multiple worksheets and workbooks, summarizing data and linking values. Joy will be able to work with these workbooks efficiently using the workspace file you created.

Session 6.3 Quick Check

Review

1. What is the workbook reference for the A1:A10 cell range on the Sales Info worksheet in the Product Report workbook located in the Reports folder on drive D?
2. What is a source file? What is a destination file?
3. Name three ways of updating a link in a workbook.
4. How would you view a list of links to other workbooks in your current workbook?
5. Define lookup table, lookup value, and compare value.
6. What are two of the functions that Excel uses to retrieve values from a lookup table?
7. What is the range_lookup parameter? What does a value of TRUE mean for the range_lookup parameter?
8. What is a workspace file? Explain how workspace files can help you organize your work.

Tutorial Summary

Review

In this tutorial, you worked with multiple worksheets and workbooks. You learned how to create a worksheet group and then edit multiple worksheets at the same time. You learned how to consolidate information on multiple worksheets using 3-D references. You also learned how to set up grouped worksheets for printing.

You learned about built-in Excel templates. You learned how to use a template as the basis of a new worksheet. You also learned how to create a customized template from a worksheet you created. You learned where Excel stores its templates and how you can access templates that are built-in or customized.

You learned about linking workbooks to one another. You learned to create a lookup table using the Excel VLOOKUP function. Finally, you learned about Excel workspaces and how to create and use them when you need to work with multiple workbooks that are related to one project or goal.

Key Terms

3-D reference	HLOOKUP function	source file
compare value	link	template
default template	Lookup function	VLOOKUP function
destination file	lookup table	worksheet group
external reference	lookup value	workspace

Practice

Practice the skills you learned in this tutorial to answer additional questions about the Lakeland Boychoir contributions workbook.

Review Assignments

Data Files needed for the Review Assignments: Contrib1.xls, CList.xls

Joy Ling has approached you with another workbook project. She wants you to create a workbook that displays monthly contributions for the year. The workbook should contain a separate worksheet for each month of the year, showing the total contributions for that month and for the year up through that month.

Each contributor has been assigned an ID number. Joy has a separate workbook that contains the contributor's name, address, and phone number, as well as whether the contribution came from a personal, business, or governmental source. Rather than repeating this information in the new workbook, Joy has only included the contributor's ID number. She wants you to insert the remaining information using Excel's lookup feature. When you're finished working with the file, she wants you to create a template so that she can use the workbook in future years. To complete this task:

1. Open the **Contrib1** workbook located in the Tutorial.06\Review folder included with your Data Files, and then save the workbook as **Contrib2006** in the same folder.
2. Enter your name and the current date in the Documentation sheet, and review the sheets in the workbook.
3. Create a worksheet group that contains the January through December worksheets.
4. In the worksheet group, insert a formula in cell B5 to display the sum of the contributions in column E.
5. Ungroup the worksheets, and then insert a formula in cell B6 that displays the total contributions for the current month plus the total of all previous months for the year. (*Hint*: Enter the formula using a cell reference in cell B6 to the previous month's contributions, cell B5, plus the contributions of the current month.)
6. Open the **CList** workbook located in the Tutorial.06\Review folder. This workbook contains the list of choir contributors in the range A2:E44 of the Contributors worksheet.
7. Switch to the Contrib2006 workbook, and then regroup the monthly worksheets. In cell F3, insert the VLOOKUP function, where the lookup value is the contributor ID found in cell D3, the lookup table is located in the range A2:E44 in the Contributors worksheet of the CList workbook, the column index number is 2, and the range_lookup value is FALSE.
8. Insert the VLOOKUP function for the rest of the values in row 3, making sure that you use the correct column index number: For column G, the column index number is 3; for column H, the column index number is 4; for column I, the column index number is 5. (*Hint*: Use the mixed reference $D3 to refer to the lookup value so that you can copy the VLOOKUP formula to the right.)
9. Use the fill handle to fill in the VLOOKUP formulas from row 3 into the range F3:I25. (*Note*: You will see the result #N/A for those rows in which no contribution ID has been entered.)
10. Format the range D2:I25 using the List 1 AutoFormat. Format the entries in the range H3:H25 so that the text is wrapped within the cell. Reduce the width of column H to 22 characters. Format the values in the nonadjacent range B5:B6;E3:E25 so the numbers appear with a comma but no decimal places. Increase the width of column E to 9 characters.

11. Format each page in the workbook so that each worksheet is displayed in landscape orientation with the sheet fitted to a single page. Display the name of the workbook and the name of the worksheet on separate lines in the upper-right corner of the header. Display your name and the date on separate lines in the lower-right corner of the footer. Preview the worksheets, and then print the contents of the January and February worksheets.

12. Ungroup the worksheets, switch to the Documentation sheet, and then save your changes.

13. Regroup the monthly worksheets, clear all contributor ID values and contribution values in the range D3:E25, and then delete the year value in cell B3. Click cell A1, and then ungroup the worksheets. Return to the Documentation sheet, and make cell A1 the active cell.

14. Save the workbook as an Excel template with the name **Contribution Record** to the Tutorial.06\Review folder.

15. Close all the workbooks and the template file.

Case Problem 1

Data File needed for this Case Problem: Refrig1.xls

Consolidating Refrigerator Sales   Freezing Point makes six brands of refrigerators. The company tracks sales information from its four sales regions—North, South, East, and West—in an Excel workbook. Your supervisor, Jayne Mitchell, has asked you to format the workbook and to create a summary worksheet that calculates the total sales totals for all four regions. To complete this task:

1. Open the **Refrig1** workbook located in the Tutorial.06\Cases folder included with your Data Files, and then save the workbook as **Refrig2** in the same folder.

2. Enter your name and the current date in the Documentation sheet, and then insert a new blank worksheet named "Total Sales" after the Documentation sheet.

3. Complete the four regional worksheets by inserting formulas to total sales by quarter and by product.

4. Copy the row titles and column titles from the East worksheet into the Total Sales worksheet.

5. In the range B3:F9 of the Total Sales worksheet, insert the formulas that sum the sales in the corresponding cells of the North through East worksheets.

6. Format the numbers in the five sales worksheets so you have a more attractive workbook.

7. Set up the five sales worksheets to center the worksheet data horizontally on the page. Insert the name of the sheet centered in the header, and *your name* and the *current date* placed on separate lines in the right section of the footer.

8. Preview the worksheets, and then print the entire workbook.

9. Save your changes to the workbook.

10. Remove the sales data, but not the formulas from the workbook.

11. Return to cell A1 of the Documentation sheet, and then save the workbook as an Excel template with the name **Refrigerator Sales Form** to the Tutorial.06\Cases folder.

12. Close the workbook template.

Case Problem 2

Data File needed for this Case Problem: Grade1.xls

Creating a Grading Workbook at MidWest University You're an assistant to Professor David Templeton, who teaches Math 220 at MidWest University. He's asked you to help him develop a grading workbook. His course has three sections, and he wants to enter the grades for each section in a separate worksheet. The workbook should track three sets of grades: the first and second exams and the final exam. The workbook should also calculate an overall final score, which is equal to 25% of the first exam score, plus 25% of the second exam, plus 50% of the final exam. Finally, the workbook should display a final grade based on the overall score. Professor Templeton plans to assign grades according to the following range of points:

```
 0 to 49 = F
50 to 59 = D
60 to 74 = C
75 to 89 = B
90 to 100 = A
```

A set of exam scores has already been entered for you. Your job will be to calculate an overall score and grade for each student in each session. You should also format the worksheets and the output. Finally, Professor Templeton will want to use this workbook again, so he will want you to create a template based on your work. To complete this task:

1. Open the **Grade1** workbook located in the Tutorial.06\Cases folder included with your Data Files, and then save the workbook as **Grade2** in the same folder.
2. Enter your name and the current date in the Documentation sheet, and then insert a worksheet named "Grading Criteria" after the Documentation sheet.
3. On the Grading Criteria worksheet, enter the text "Exam Average" in cell A1 and the text "Grade" in cell B1.
4. In the range A2:B6, create a lookup table for the range of grades specified by Professor Templeton. (*Hint*: Each letter grade should be matched up with the lowest score possible for that grade.)
5. Insert a formula in column E of each worksheet to calculate the overall score for each student based on the results of the three exams. Remember to include the weight of each exam in the calculation of the overall student average.
6. In column F, insert a formula to calculate the final letter grade for each student based on the grade table you entered in the Grading Criteria worksheet.
7. Format the section worksheets to improve their appearance.
8. Define the page setup for the three section worksheets so that each worksheet is centered horizontally on the page, with the name of the section centered in the header, and your name and the date on the separate lines in the right section of the footer. Print the grades for the three sections.

9. Save your changes to the workbook.

Explore

10. Enter the following labels and values in the Grading Criteria worksheet:

    Cell   Value
    A9   Exam Type
    B9   Weight
    A10   Exam1
    B10   25%
    A11   Exam2
    B11   25%
    A12   Final
    B12   50%

11. Modify the formula in column E of each section worksheet so the weight applied to each exam in computing the overall student score is based on data obtained from the range B10:B12 in the Grading Criteria worksheet. Change the weight for Exam1 from 25% to 15%, and the Final from 50% to 60%.

12. Print the revised section sheets, and then save the workbook.

13. Clear all the data values from the section worksheets and then save the workbook as an Excel template named **Grading Template** to the Tutorial.06\Cases folder.

14. Close the template workbook file.

Apply

Using group worksheets, 3-D references, external references, and workspaces, create a workbook that summarizes data for a bike manufacturer with multiple locations.

Case Problem 3

Data Files needed for this Case Problem: Bike1.xls, Bike2.xls, Bike3.xls

Projected Income Statement for Tour Bikes   You work at Tour Bikes, an up-and-coming manufacturer of touring bikes. Your supervisor, Ken Delaney, has asked you to prepare the annual projected income statement for the company. You've been given workbooks from three regions of the country. Each workbook has quarterly projected income statements for three of the company's bikes: Tour, Tour XL, and Cross Country. Ken wants you to summarize each workbook for him, reporting the annual totals for sales in a new worksheet. Once you have added this information to each workbook, he wants you to consolidate the information from the three regional workbooks, reporting in a single workbook the same information for each company. To complete this task:

1. Open each of the regional sales workbooks (**Bike1**, **Bike2**, and **Bike3**) located in the Tutorial.06\Cases folder included with your Data Files. Then save Bike1 as **North**, Bike2 as **South**, and Bike3 as **Southwest** in the same folder.

2. On the Documentation sheet in each regional sales workbook, enter the name of the workbook, your name, and the date.

3. Each regional workbook contains a Documentation sheet and a Summary sheet. Use the Summary sheet to compute Sales (row 6 in each quarterly sheet) for each bike model for each quarter. Include totals for all bikes and quarters.

4. Format the Summary sheet using any format you choose, and the save the changes you have made to the workbooks.

5. Create a new workbook, and save it as **Tour Bikes Report** in the Tutorial.06\Cases folder.

6. Rename the first sheet "Documentation," and then enter your name and the date in the sheet.

7. Switch to the second sheet, and then use Figure 6-29 as a guide to enter the text shown. Enter the formulas that summarize the sales over all regions by quarters and products. Include totals for all products and quarters as well. Name the worksheet SummaryByQtrAndProduct.

Figure 6-29

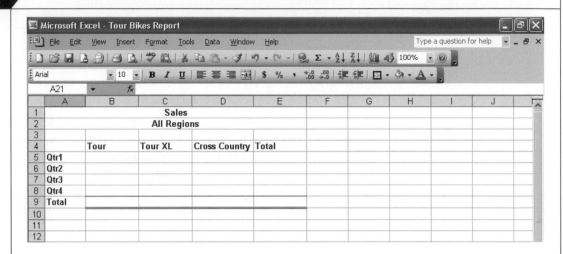

8. Switch to the third sheet and then use Figure 6-30 as a guide to enter the text shown. Enter the formulas that summarize the sales of all products by quarters and regions. Include totals for regions and quarters as well. Name the worksheet SummaryByQtrAndRegion.

Figure 6-30

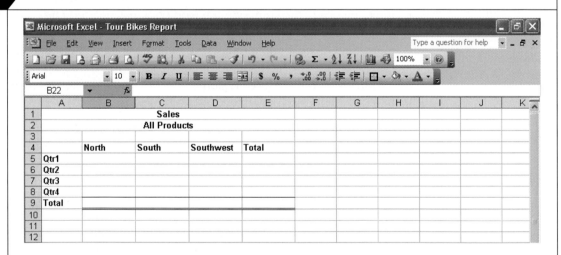

9. Format the worksheets with any format you choose.
10. Print the two summary worksheets with your name and the date on separate lines in the right section of the footer, and then save your changes to the workbook.
11. Create a workspace for the four workbooks, and then save it as **Tour Bike Files** in the Tutorial.06\Cases folder.
12. Save all the workbooks, and then close them.

Create

Figures 6-31 and 6-32 show the "end results." Use Lookup functions to create currency conversion worksheets.

Case Problem 4

There are no Data Files needed for this Case Problem.

Convenient Currency Conversion Tourists from the U.S. often want to obtain funds in the local currency of the country to which they are traveling before leaving the U.S. To serve this need at the regional Sky Blue Airport, Convenient Currency Exchange (CCE) set up a small shop that provides currency exchange services for a small fee. CCE's owner has asked you to run this part of her business and to establish an Excel spreadsheet to simplify the calculation process.

Figure 6-31 shows the final worksheet you will create. It includes the currency conversion data in the range D1:F17, the transaction data in the range A4:B6, and the results of currency exchange calculation in the range A7:B8.

Figure 6-31

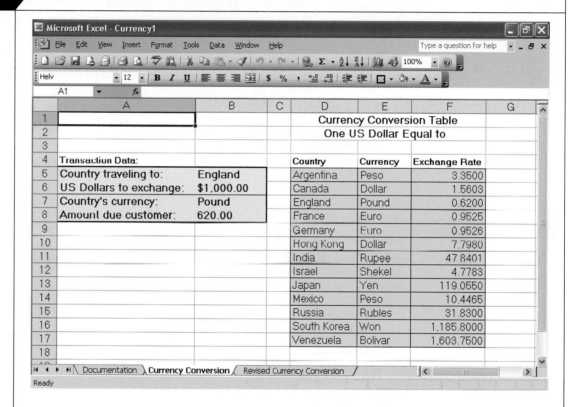

To complete this task:

1. Create a new workbook, and then save it as **Currency1** in the Tutorial.06\Cases folder provided with your Data Files.
2. Rename the first sheet "Documentation" and then enter *your name* and the current date.
3. Rename Sheet2 "Currency Conversion," and then, using Figure 6-31 as a guide, do the following:
   a. Enter the currency labels and data in the range D1:F17 and the labels in the range A4:A8.
   b. Use a Lookup function in cell B7 to display the type of currency for a country when a CCE clerk enters in cell B5 the name of the country to which a customer is traveling. For example, in Figure 6-31, when the CCE employee enters the country "England" in cell B5, the foreign currency, which is the Pound, appears in cell B7.

   c. Use a Lookup function in cell B8 to determine the amount of foreign currency due a customer. This is calculated by multiplying the country's exchange rate by the amount of U.S. dollars being exchanged. For example, when a CCE employee enters "England" in cell B5, "Pound" appears in cell B7. When the employee then enters in cell B6 the amount of U.S. currency to be exchanged (for example, $1,000), the worksheet calculates the amount of foreign currency the customer is due and displays this amount in cell B8.

4. Print the worksheet on one page with your name in the footer and the sheet name in the header.

5. Enter another transaction in cells B5 and B6 for a customer traveling to Japan who wants to convert $125. Enter the transaction data, and then print just the results that appear in the range A4:B8 (do not include the currency conversion table in the printout).

Explore

6. Figure 6-32 shows a modification of the original worksheet. Rename Sheet3 "Revised Currency Conversion" and develop the modified currency conversion worksheet. CCE charges a 3% administrative fee, with a $4 minimum fee, per transaction. Expand the Transaction Data section to display the administrative fee (the amount of U.S. dollars exchanged multiplied by 3%) and adjust the formula that computes the amount due a customer (the amount of money exchanged minus the administrative fee multiplied by the conversion rate for the country). The administrative fee for the data in Figure 6-32 is $30 (based on the calculation *1000 * 3%*), and the amount due the customer is 601.40 pounds (based on the calculation *1000 - 3% * .62*). Remember, the formula you develop to calculate the administrative fee must include a minimum fee. For example, if a customer exchanges $100, the administrative fee would be the minimum fee of $4, not $3. (*Hint*: The lookup formula in the Revised Currency Conversion worksheet references the currency conversion table in the Currency Conversion worksheet.)

Figure 6-32

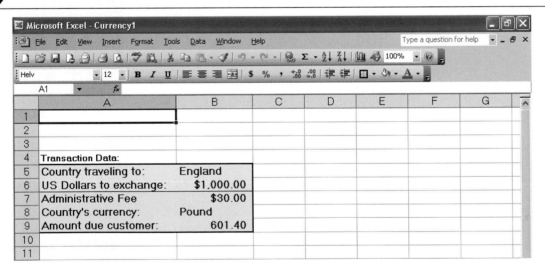

7. Enter the data from Step 5 in the Revised Currency Conversion worksheet, and then print the worksheet.

8. Save and close the workbook.

Research

Go to the Web to find information you can use to create effective spreadsheets.

Internet Assignments

The purpose of the Internet Assignments is to challenge you to find information on the Internet that you can use to work effectively with this software. The actual assignments are updated and maintained on the Course Technology Web site. Log on to the Internet and use your Web browser to go to the Student Online Companion for New Perspectives Office 2003 at **www.course.com/np/office2003**. Click the Internet Assignments link, and then navigate to the assignments for this tutorial.

Assess

SAM Assessment and Training

If you have a SAM user profile, you may have access to hands-on instruction, practice, and assessment of the skills covered in this tutorial. Log in to your SAM account and go to your assignments page to see what your instructor has assigned.

Review

Quick Check Answers

Session 6.1

1. A worksheet group is a collection of worksheets that have been selected for editing and formatting.
2. To select an adjacent group of worksheets, click the first sheet tab, press and hold the Shift key, and then click the sheet tab of the last sheet in the range. To select a nonadjacent group of worksheets, click the sheet tab of one of the sheets in the group, press and hold the Ctrl key, and then click the sheet tabs of the remaining members of the group. Deselect a worksheet group by either clicking the sheet tab of a worksheet not in the group or right-clicking one of the sheet tabs in the group and clicking Ungroup Sheets on the shortcut menu.
3. 'Summary Data'!A10
4. 'Summary 1:Summary 3'!A10
5. Create a worksheet group consisting of the range of worksheets. In the first worksheet in the group, select the text and formulas you want to copy, click Edit on the menu bar, point to Fill, and then click Across Worksheets. Next, select whether you want to copy the contents, formulas, or both, and then click the OK button.
6. Select a worksheet group that consists of all sheets in the workbook, click File on the menu bar, and then click Page Layout.

Session 6.2

1. A template is a workbook that contains specific content and formatting that you can use as a model for other similar workbooks.
2. A user can modify the contents of a workbook based on a template without changing the template file itself. The next time a new workbook is created based on a template, the workbook opens with all the original properties intact.

3. The template used in creating the blank workbook that you first see when starting a new Excel session. This template contains no text or formulas, but it does contain the default General number format.

4. Click File on the menu bar, click Save As, click the Save as type list arrow, click Template, type a filename for the template, and then click the Save button.

5. Templates folder (usually located in C:\Document and Settings*user_name*\Application Data\Microsoft\Templates). Yes, you can store a template anywhere.

6. Create a subfolder in the Templates folder, and then move the template file into the subfolder.

7. Click the From existing workbook option in the New section of the New Workbook task pane.

Session 6.3

1. 'D:\Reports\[Product Report]Sales Info'!A1:A10

2. The source file is the file that contains the values to be linked. The destination file displays the value placed in the source file.

3. a) When you initially open the workbook, Excel prompts you to update the link; b) if both the destination and source files are open, Excel will update the link automatically; and c) if only the destination file is open, click Edit on the menu bar, click Links, and then click the Update Link button to manually update the link.

4. Click Edit on the menu bar, and then click Links.

5. A lookup table is a table in which rows and columns of information are organized into separate categories. The lookup value is the value that indicates the category in which you are looking. The categories for the lookup table are usually located in the table's first row or column and are called compare values.

6. VLOOKUP and HLOOKUP

7. The range_lookup value is a parameter in the VLOOKUP and HLOOKUP functions that tells Excel where to look for an exact match in a lookup table. A value of TRUE means that Excel does not have to find an exact match.

8. A workspace file is a file containing information about all of the currently opened workbooks, including their locations, window sizes, and screen positions. By opening a workspace file, you open all workbooks defined in the workspace. Using a workspace helps you organize projects that might involve several workbooks.

Objectives

Working with Excel's Editing and Web Tools

Collaborating on a Workbook and Web Page

Case

Digital Products

Digital Products is a company specializing in digital video editing software and hardware. Each year, the company publishes a financial report for its stockholders. The company also publishes the report on the World Wide Web for the general public. Kevin Whyte and his team are responsible for creating and publishing this year's report.

In the process of developing the report, different employees will review and edit the workbook's content, thus creating several drafts of the workbook. Kevin has asked for your help to manage the development of this workbook from its initial draft to its final form. Because stockholders will see this report, Kevin is acutely aware that the workbook should contain no errors. Once the report is finalized, the workbook will be printed in a booklet.

Kevin also wants to have a summary of the report converted into a form that can be published on the company's Web site, making it available to a larger community. Kevin has asked for your assistance in creating that file as well.

In this tutorial, you will use Excel's auditing tools to ensure the workbook is error free. You will also review the comments and edits made by other users on the workbook and incorporate their suggestions into the final document. Finally, you will convert the workbook into a format for publishing on the Web.

Student Data Files

▼ **Tutorial.07**

▽ **Tutorial folder**
DPrpt1.xls
DPrpt3.xls
DPrpt5.xls
Karen1.xls
Meeting.htm

▽ **Review folder**
Project1.xls
Project3.xls
Stkhldrs.htm

▽ **Cases folder**
Budget1.xls
CHome.htm
Cutler1.xls
CWorld1.xls
Erdahl.xls
Hung.xls
NewPrice.xls
Nolan.xls
StuStat1.xls

Splitting a Worksheet into Panes

Kevin has created a rough draft of the report containing the initial figures, formulas, and text. He now wants you to check the accuracy of the values and the formulas in his workbook. You will begin by opening the financial report workbook so you can review its data.

To open the workbook:

1. Start Excel and open the **DPrpt1** workbook located in the Tutorial.07\Tutorial folder included with your Data Files.

2. Enter the *current date* and *your name* in the Documentation sheet, and then save the workbook as **DPrpt2** in the Tutorial.07\Tutorial folder.

3. Switch to the Balance Sheet worksheet.

The DPrpt2 workbook contains four other worksheets besides the Documentation sheet. These are labeled:

- **Balance Sheet**: contains the company's balance sheets for the past three years
- **Financial Data**: contains an overview of selected financial figures
- **Income Statement**: contains the company's income statements for the past three years
- **Cash Flows**: contains the company's cash flow over the past three years

Kevin suspects that there may be some discrepancies between the assets and liabilities of the statement in the Balance Sheet worksheet. He wants to review the Total Assets and the Total Liabilities and Stockholders' Equity sections of the balance sheet. To do this, he suggests that you split the worksheet so that the different parts of the worksheet can be viewed at the same time.

You can split a worksheet horizontally and vertically into panes so that up to four separate areas of the worksheet can be viewed at the same time. To divide the workbook window into four separate panes, you can use the Split command on the Window menu. To divide the workbook window into two panes, vertically or horizontally, you can use the split box at the top of the vertical scroll bar or at the right end of the horizontal scroll bar. When the workbook is split into panes, each pane has its own scroll bar so different parts of a worksheet can be scrolled independently. You will split the worksheet so the assets are in one pane and the liabilities in another.

To split the Balance Sheet worksheet into two panes:

1. Move the pointer over the split box at the top of the vertical scroll bar until the point changes to ÷.

2. Click and then drag the pointer down to row 10. As you drag the pointer down, a thick gray bar appears across the worksheet.

3. Release the mouse button to separate the worksheet into two panes. A solid split bar now appears across the worksheet.

4. Click any cell in the top pane, and then, using the scroll bar for that pane, scroll down until row 21 is the last row displayed in the pane.

5. Press the **F6** key to make the bottom pane the active pane, and then, using the scroll bar for the bottom pane, scroll down until row 34 is the last row displayed in the bottom pane, as shown in Figure 7-1. By splitting the worksheet and scrolling the panes, you can view the Total Assets and the Total Liabilities and Stockholders' Equity sections of the balance sheet together.

Balance Sheet worksheet split into two panes ◄ **Figure 7-1**

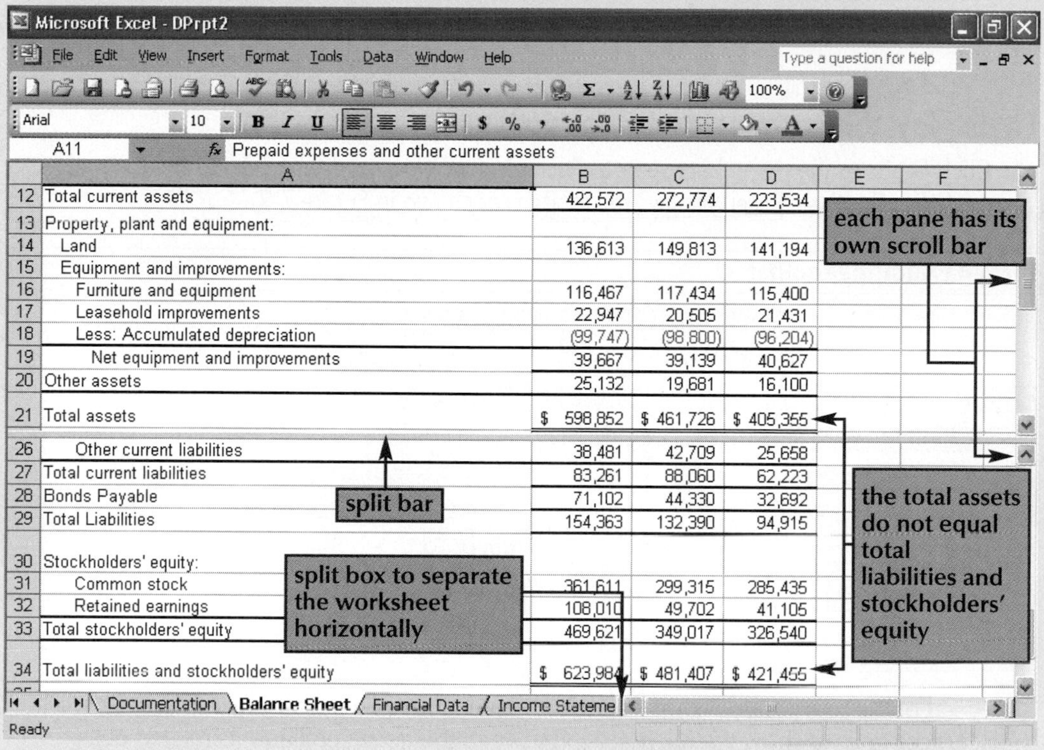

You can now see that the value of the total assets does not equal the total liabilities and equities, so you can remove the split before continuing. If you have separated the worksheet into four panes, you can double-click one of the solid split bars to remove one pane at a time. To remove all the panes regardless of how many, you can select the Remove Split command on the Window menu. Since there are only two panes, you will use the double-click method.

To remove the split in the Balance Sheet worksheet:

1. Double-click any part of the split bar that divides the panes. The split bar is removed.

Auditing Formulas

Errors in a workbook can occur in several different forms, such as in a formula that has been entered incorrectly, causing Excel to return an error value. Perhaps more difficult to detect is an Excel formula that appears to have been entered correctly because a value appears in the cell, but it is not correct because a wrong formula was used. For example, Kevin noticed that the total assets displayed in the range B21:D21 in the Balance Sheet worksheet are lower than what he expected and do not equal the total liabilities and stockholders' equity (range B34:D34). He thinks that the wrong formula might have been used and asks you to check it out. One way of checking the accuracy of the formulas is by using Excel's **audit** feature, which enables you to review the structure and behavior of the formulas in your worksheet.

The Formula Auditing toolbar contains tools that graphically display the relationship between formulas used in various mathematical operations. You will use one of these tools to examine the formula that calculates the company's total assets. First, you will display the Formula Auditing toolbar.

To display the Formula Auditing toolbar:

1. Click **Tools** on the menu bar, point to **Formula Auditing**, and then click **Show Formula Auditing Toolbar**. Excel displays the toolbar, as shown in Figure 7-2.

| Figure 7-2 | Formula Auditing toolbar |

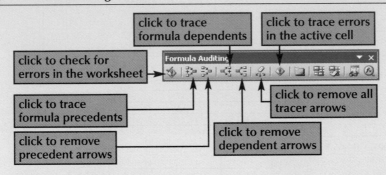

Several of the tools on the Formula Auditing toolbar display tracer arrows on your worksheet. **Tracer arrows** show the relationship between the active cell and its related cells. Tracer arrows are blue when pointing from a cell that provides data to another cell, and red when the cell contains an error value. There are two types of tracer arrows: one that displays precedent cells and one that displays dependent cells. **Precedent cells** are the cells that are referred to in the formula of the active cell. They provide the values used in the formula of the active cell. For example, if cell C15 contains the formula $=C13 + C14$, then cells C13 and C14 are precedent cells to cell C15, because they provide the values used in the formulas. **Dependent cells** are cells that use the value in the active cell in their formulas. For example, if cell B4 is the active cell, cell C20 contains the formula $=B4$, and cell C25 contains the formula $=B4 * B5$, then cells C20 and C25 are dependent on cell B4.

| Reference Window | **Tracing Precedent and Dependent Cells** |

- Select the cell that contains the formula that you want to trace.
- Click the Trace Precedents button to display tracer arrows pointing to the formula's precedent cells.
- Click the Trace Dependents button to display tracer arrows pointing to cells dependent on the formula's value.

Tracing Precedent Cells

To check the accuracy of the total assets displayed in the cell range B21:D21, you can start by tracing the cells that are used in the formula in cell B21. The value in cell B21 should be based on the total current assets in row 12, the land in row 14, the net computer equipment and improvements in row 19, and other assets in row 20. But is it? You will trace the precedent cells used in the formulas that calculated the value of the total assets (B21:D21).

To trace the precedent cells for the range B21:D21:

1. Click cell **B21**.

2. Click the **Trace Precedents** button on the Formula Auditing toolbar. Excel displays tracer arrows that point from the precedent cells to the active cell.

3. Click cell **C21** and then click the **Trace Precedents** button on the Formula Auditing toolbar to display the tracer arrows that point from the precedent cells to cell C21, the active cell. Note that the tracer arrows for cell B21 are still displayed.

4. Click cell **D21** and then click the **Trace Precedents** button on the Formula Auditing toolbar to display the tracer arrows that point from the precedent cells to cell D21.

5. Click cell **B21** to make it the active cell again. Figure 7-3 shows the tracer arrows for all three cells.

Precedent tracer arrows   **Figure 7-3**

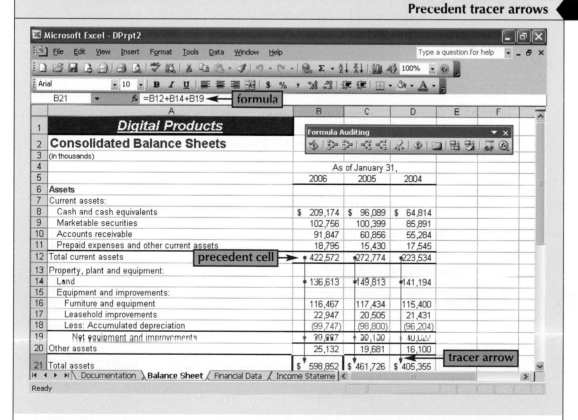

The formula in cell B21 is *=B12+B14+B19*. As shown in Figure 7-3, the precedent cells for the formula in cell B21 are indicated by small solid blue circles, such as the one displayed in cell B12. All the precedent cells are connected by a blue tracer arrow that points to cell B21. As you view the tracer arrows, you will note that the values in row 20 (Other assets) are *not* included as precedent cells. This omission may account for the fact that the total assets are lower than Kevin expected. You will add those cells to the formulas in the range B21:D21.

To revise the formulas in range B21:D21:

1. With cell B21 still selected, click in the Formula bar, change the formula to **=B12+B14+B19+B20**, and then press the **Enter** key. The tracer arrows disappear and the value of the total assets shown in cell B21 increases to 623,984. This value is more in line with Kevin's expectations.

2. Scroll to display cell B34 and verify that total assets equal the total liabilities and stockholders' equity. Now that you have verified the values, you will remove the tracer arrows.

3. Click the **Remove All Arrows** button 🔏 on the Formula Auditing toolbar to remove all the tracer arrows on the worksheet.

   You will copy the revised formula to the other total asset cells for the other years.

4. Scroll up the worksheet so the upper portion of the worksheet is visible, click cell **B21**, and then drag the fill handle over the range **C21:D21**. The value of the total assets in cell C21 increases to $481,407, and the value in cell D21 increases to $421,455.

Tracer arrows are particularly helpful in more complicated formulas involving several ranges and multiple worksheets. In these cases, formula errors might not be easily detected by examining the formula itself. Sometimes a graphical view is more helpful, such as tracer lines and arrows, which can guide you to the possible source of an error.

Tracing Dependent Cells

Other locations in this workbook might rely on the total assets values in the range B21:D21. Now that you've modified the formula, you're interested in seeing how this might have affected other cells in the workbook. To find out, you will trace the dependent cells for cell B21.

To trace the dependent cells:

1. Click cell **B21** and then click the **Trace Dependents** button 🔂 on the Formula Auditing toolbar. A tracer arrow appears pointing from cell B21 to a worksheet icon. See Figure 7-4. This worksheet icon means that a cell on a different worksheet is dependent on cell B21.

Figure 7-4 ▶ **Dependent tracer arrows**

To determine the dependent cell, you will open the Go To dialog box, which you can do by double-clicking the tracer arrow.

2. Move the pointer over the tracer arrow until the pointer changes to ↘, and then double-click the **tracer arrow**. The Go To dialog box opens, as shown in Figure 7-5.

Go To dialog box ◄ **Figure 7-5**

3. Click **'[DPrpt2.xls]Financial Data'!$B$14** in the Go to list box, and then click the **OK** button. Cell B14 in the Financial Data worksheet is displayed, as shown in Figure 7-6. Notice that the Formula bar displays 'Balance Sheet'!B21, indicating that in the Balance Sheet worksheet, cell B14 is dependent on the value in cell B21 in the Balance Sheet worksheet.

Display the worksheet that contains the dependent cell ◄ **Figure 7-6**

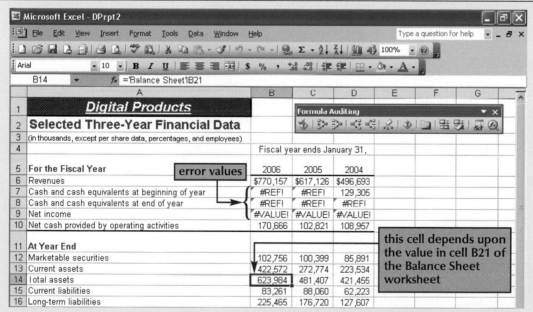

Trouble? If the message "Reference is not valid" appears, click the OK button, and then repeat Step 3, being sure to click '[DPrpt2.xls]Financial Data'!$B$14 in the Go to list box.

You've located the cell in the workbook that depends on the total assets value (cell B14); however, in doing so, you notice that the Financial Data worksheet seems to have several problems. Many of the cells display the #REF! or #VALUE! error value. What do these error values mean, and how do you fix them?

Tracing and Fixing Errors

When Excel cannot properly evaluate a formula (do the calculations) entered in a cell, an **error value** is displayed in the cell. An error value begins with a number sign (#) followed by an error name. This error value indicates the type of error encountered by Excel. Figure 7-7 provides descriptions of several of the error values that might appear in your workbooks.

Figure 7-7 ▶ **Excel error values**

Error Values	Source of Error
#DIV/0!	The formula or function contains a number divided by zero.
#NAME?	Excel doesn't recognize text in the formula or function, such as when the name of an Excel function has been misspelled.
#N/A	A value is not available to a function or formula, which can occur when an invalid value is specified in the VLOOKUP function.
#NULL!	A formula or function requires that two cell ranges intersect, but they don't.
#NUM!	Invalid numbers are used in a formula or function, such as entering text in a function that requires a numeric value.
#REF!	A cell reference used in a formula or function is no longer valid, which can occur when cells used by the function have been deleted from the worksheet.
#VALUE!	The wrong type of argument has been used in a function or formula. This can occur when you supply a range of values to a function that requires a single value.

Notice the green triangles in the upper-left corner of many of the worksheet cells in the Financial Data worksheet. These **error indicators** are another way Excel indicates that an error or potential error in the formula of a cell exists. If you select a cell that displays an error indicator, an Error Alert button appears. Excel also attempts to provide additional information about the source of the error. For example, Excel might indicate that you've attempted to divide a number by zero or that the formula is attempting to reference a cell that has been deleted. You can view this additional information by clicking the cell that contains the error.

You will explore the error that Excel has found in cell B7.

To view error information:

▶ 1. Click cell **B7** to display the Error Alert button ◈, which appears to the left of the cell.

▶ 2. Move the mouse over the Error Alert button to display a ScreenTip that provides a possible explanation for the error.

▶ 3. Click the **Error Alert** button ◈ to display a list of options that will help you resolve the problem.

▶ 4. Click **Help on this error**. The Microsoft Excel Help window opens with information relating to the #REF! error value. See Figure 7-8. The Help window also provides some possible solutions for correcting the error.

Help on the #REF! error   Figure 7-8

5. Close the Help window.

Sometimes a single error may affect many other cells if these cells contain formulas that reference the cell in error. That may be the reason you see the error value #REF! in cell B7. One possible source of the error in cell B7 is that a cell that was being used by a formula somewhere in the worksheet has been deleted. When that happens, Excel returns the #REF! error value, and the error will propagate down through any workbook cells that are dependent upon the formula. What you need to do then is trace the error value in cell B7 back to its source, so you can correct the cell with the error and eliminate all error values in all cells that are dependent on the problem cell. You can do that by repeatedly clicking the Trace Precedents button on the Formula Auditing toolbar as you move through the formula's precedents, but a much faster way is to use the Trace Error button on the same toolbar.

Tracing Errors

Reference Window

- Click the cell displaying an error value.
- Click the Trace Error button on the Formula Auditing toolbar.
- Follow the tracer arrows back to the source of the error.
- Correct the source of the error.

You will trace the source of the error in cell B7 now.

To locate the source of the error in cell B7:

1. Verify that cell **B7** is still the active cell and that the Formula Auditing toolbar is still visible.

2. Click the **Trace Error** button on the Formula Auditing toolbar. A tracer arrow appears, pointing from cell B7 to a worksheet icon, which means that the source of this error value lies on a different worksheet.

3. Double-click the tracer arrow with the ▷ pointer to open the Go To dialog box, click **'[DPrpt2.xls]Cash Flows'!$B$37** in the Go to list box, and then click the **OK** button. Cell B37 in the Cash Flows worksheet is displayed.

Trouble? If the Go To dialog box does not open, click cell B7 again, hover the pointer over the tracer arrow until the pointer changes to ▷, and then double-click the tracer arrow.

4. Click the **Trace Error** button ⬦ on the Formula Auditing toolbar. A series of red tracer arrows appear, tracing the error from cell B37 to cells C38, C37, D38, D35, and then finally to cell D33. See Figure 7-9. The red arrows indicate cells that contain error values.

| Figure 7-9 | Tracing the #REF! error |

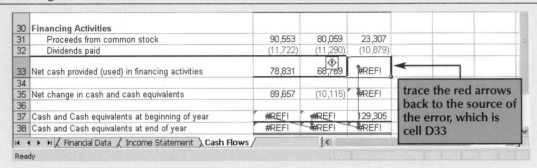

5. Click each cell on the path of the tracer arrows to examine the formula in the Formula bar. Only the formula in cell D33 appears unusual.

Apparently the source of the error lies in cell D33 of the Cash Flows worksheet. The formula in the cell is =SUM(#REF!), which indicates that the SUM function is attempting to use worksheet cells that were probably deleted at some point in the creation of the worksheet. Cell D33 should display the total net cash of the company's financing activities, which should be equal to the sum of the values in range D31:D32.

You will modify the formula so that it references these cells.

To correct the error value:

1. If necessary, click cell **D33**, click in the Formula bar, change the formula in cell D33 to **=SUM(D31:D32)**, and then press the **Enter** key. The error value #REF! disappears and is replaced with the value (12,428). Also, the red tracer arrows turn blue because the cell no longer is causing an error.

2. Click the **Remove All Arrows** button 🔏 on the Formula Auditing toolbar to remove the tracer arrows from the worksheet.

Now you will check to see whether the error values from the Financial Data worksheet have been fixed.

3. Click the **Financial Data** tab. The #REF! error value in cell B7 has been replaced with the value 49,473. Although there are other error values in the worksheet, you can remove the tracer arrows that you just used to identify the source of the #REF! error value.

4. Click the **Remove All Arrows** button 🔏 on the Formula Auditing toolbar to remove the tracer arrows from the worksheet.

The next type of error you see in the Financial Data worksheet is the #VALUE! error value, which occurs in the ranges B9:D9 and B23:D23. This type of error occurs when an improper value is used as an argument in a formula. For example, a formula might call for a numeric value, but a text string is used instead. As before, you'll trace the error to its roots in the workbook.

To trace the #VALUE! error value:

1. Click cell **B9** in the Financial Data worksheet, and then click the **Trace Error** button on the Formula Auditing toolbar. The source of the error is on another worksheet, as indicated by the worksheet icon.

2. Double-click the tracer arrow with the pointer, click **'[DPrpt2.xls]Income Statement'!$B$17** in the Go to list box, and then click the **OK** button. Cell B17 in the Income Statement worksheet is displayed.

3. Click the **Trace Error** button on the Formula Auditing toolbar. Excel traces the error to cell B13. See Figure 7-10.

Tracing the #Value! error | **Figure 7-10**

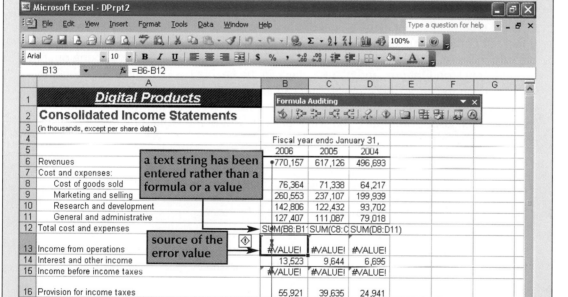

Cell B13 displays the income from operations for Digital Products, which is calculated by subtracting the total costs and expenses in cell B12 from the net revenues in cell B6. Since the equal sign (=) was omitted before the SUM function name, Excel is treating the contents of the cell as a label instead of a formula. You will correct this mistake now.

4. Click cell **B12**, change the formula to **=SUM(B8:B11)**, and then click the **Enter** button on the Formula bar. The red tracer arrows turn blue.

5. Drag the fill handle for cell B12 to the right over the range **C12:D12**. The #VALUE! error values are removed from all of the cells in the Income Statement worksheet.

▶ **6.** Switch to the Financial Data worksheet. All error values have been removed from the Financial Data worksheet.

▶ **7.** Click the **Remove All Arrows** button in each worksheet.

Not all mistakes in formulas result in error values. As you saw earlier, an incorrect formula can be entered that returns a value—just the wrong value. Most of the time, mistakes such as these are difficult to detect; however, you can use the Error Checking button on the Formula Auditing toolbar to assist you. This option flags the cell (or cells) in which there might be a **suspect formula**, or in which a mistake in the formula has been made.

Reference Window	**Locating Suspect Formulas**

- Switch to the worksheet that you want to search for suspect formulas.
- Click the Error Checking button on the Formula Auditing toolbar.
- Use the options presented in the Error Checking dialog box to correct the suspect formula, or click the Next button to move on to the next suspect formula.
- Click the OK button.

Excel labels cells containing suspect formulas with a green triangle located in the cell's upper-left corner. If you do not see cells with green triangles in their upper-left corner, background error checking may be turned off. To turn background error checking on, click on Tools, click on Options, and place a check in the Enable background error checking check box on the Error Checking tab. You can also search for these cells using the Error Checking button on the Formula Auditing toolbar. To ensure that the worksheet does not include other suspect formulas, you will search the rest of the workbook for errors using the Error Checking button.

To search for errors in the workbook:

▶ **1.** Make sure the Financial Data worksheet is the active sheet.

▶ **2.** Click the **Error Checking** button 🔖 on the Formula Auditing toolbar. An Excel message box appears, indicating that the error check is complete for the entire sheet. No more errors have been detected on the Financial Data worksheet.

▶ **3.** Click the **OK** button.

▶ **4.** Click the **Income Statement** tab, click the **Error Checking** button 🔖 on the Formula Auditing toolbar, and then click the **OK** button when the Excel message dialog box appears indicating that no errors have been found.

▶ **5.** Click the **Cash Flows** tab, click cell **A1**, and then click the **Error Checking** button 🔖 on the Formula Auditing toolbar. The Error Checking dialog box opens, as shown in Figure 7-11. This dialog box displays information relating to a possible error in cell B19, which calculates the total net cash provided by the operating activities.

Trouble? If the dialog box on your screen does not look like the one in the figure, click the Resume button and then scroll to row 1.

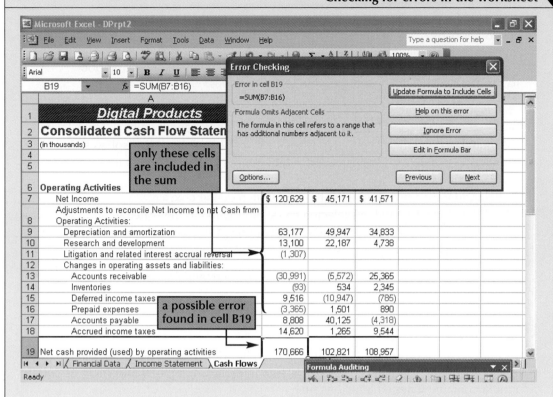

What is the problem? The formula in cell B19 applies the SUM function to the range B7:B16 and ignores the values in the range B17:B18. When the SUM function is applied to a range that has additional numbers adjacent to it, Excel will flag the formula as a possible error. In this case, the SUM function should be applied to *all* the operating Income values in the range B7:B18. Rather than retyping the formula yourself, you can have Excel update the formula automatically.

To correct the error in the SUM function:

▶ **1.** Click the **Update Formula to Include Cells** button in the Error Checking dialog box. Excel updates the formula, changing it to =SUM(B7:B18). Excel has identified other suspect formulas.

▶ **2.** Click the **Update Formula to Include Cells** button for cell C19. The formula is updated and Excel displays the next suspect formula.

▶ **3.** Click the **Update Formula to Include Cells** button for cell D19. The formula is updated and there are no other suspect formulas found.

▶ **4.** Click the **OK** button to close the message box and the dialog box, and then examine the formulas in cell C19 and D19 by clicking each of them. The formulas in the cells are *=SUM(C7:C18)* and *=SUM(D7:D18)*, respectively.

You've completed your editing of the rough draft of Digital Products' financial report, so you will close the Formula Auditing toolbar and the workbook.

▶ **5.** Click the **Close** button ⊠ to close the Formula Auditing toolbar.

▶ **6.** Save and close the workbook.

Using the Watch Window

At times, you want to watch cells and their formulas as you make changes to precedent cells in other parts of a worksheet or on another worksheet. Instead of returning to the location of the formula to see the results of a change in a precedent cell, you can use the watch window, which provides you with a view of any cell in an open workbook.

To use the Watch Window you need follow these steps:

1. Select the cells you want to watch.
2. Click Tools on the menu bar, point to Formula Auditing, and then click Show Watch Window to open the Watch Window dialog box. This dialog box displays the workbook, sheet, cell location, named range, current value, and formula for every cell added to the watch list.
3. Click Add Watch button to open the Add Watch dialog box.
4. Click Add button to add the selected cell's information to the watch window.
5. Change the value of a cell that the watch window uses as a precedent and the value in the Watch Window changes.

To delete an item in the Watch Window, select the item and click the Delete Watch button. When finished, close the Watch Window.

Evaluating a Complex Formula

Sometimes a complex formula is not working and it is difficult to tell what's going on. The evaluation Formula feature evaluates part of a formula in the current cell. This is useful in a formula containing nested functions such as:

=IF(C2="F",5000,IF(C2="I",4000,0))

To use the Evaluate Formula feature, you must follow these steps:

1. Select the cell you want to evaluate. Only one cell can be evaluated at a time.
2. Click Tools on the menu bar, point to Formula Auditing, and then click Evaluate formula to display the Evaluate formula dialog box. The formula to be evaluated is displayed.
3. Click the Evaluate button to examine the value of the underlined reference. The result of the evaluation is shown in italics.
4. Continue to click the Evaluate button until each part of the formula has been evaluated.
5. To see the evaluation again, click the Restart button, or, to end the evaluation, click the Close button.

By using tracer arrows and the error checking features, you located and resolved the errors in your workbook. Kevin will share the workbook with other employees in his group to get their feedback. In the next session, you'll work with Kevin to set up this workbook so others can collaborate on it.

Review

Session 7.1 Quick Check

1. What are precedent cells? What are dependent cells?
2. What would cause Excel to display the #NAME? error value in a cell?
3. What is the fastest way of locating the source of a #REF! error value in a formula?
4. What does a red tracer arrow mean?
5. How does Excel indicate cells whose formulas are "suspect," but which do not necessarily return an error value?

Session 7.2

Adding Comments to a Workbook

In the last session, you and Kevin completed your edit of the initial draft of Digital Products' financial report. You're now ready to share this document over the company network with three other members of your group: Anjali Mahanez, Brad Vukovich, and Sally Breen. A fourth member of your group, Karen Ziegler, is currently at an overseas conference and will not be back for a week. You'll e-mail a copy of the document to her after you receive feedback from the other members.

Kevin is concerned that the scope of the report is not broad enough. Currently the report only covers the last three years, but he has seen other reports in which a five-year history is reported. He wants you to add a comment to the workbook, asking the other members of his group whether the scope of the report should be expanded.

An Excel **comment** is a text box that is attached to a specific cell in a worksheet. In a collaborative document, comments from several different users could be attached to the same cell; therefore, the comment box will typically include the name of the user along with the text of the comment.

Inserting a Comment

Reference Window

- Click the cell to which you want to attach a comment.
- Right-click the cell and then click Insert Comment on the shortcut menu (or click Insert and then click Comment).
- Type your comment into the comment box.

You'll add Kevin's comment to cell B6 of the Documentation sheet in the DPrpt2 workbook.

To attach a comment to cell B6:

1. If you took a break at the end of the previous session, make sure Excel is running and the DPrpt2 workbook is open, and then switch to the Documentation sheet.

2. Right-click cell **B6** and then click **Insert Comment** on the shortcut menu. Excel opens a text box to the right of cell B6. Your user name should appear in bold at the top of the box. A small red triangle appears in the upper-right corner of the cell.

   Trouble? Depending on your Excel configuration, the user name might be yours, or the network administrator or technical support person may have set it to a different name.

3. Type **Should we increase the scope of this report to cover the previous five years?** in the text box. Selection handles appear around the comment box. Using the selection handles, you can increase the size of the box or move it to a new location on the worksheet. In its current location, the comment box obscures part of the information in cell B6. Try moving the text box further to the right and down.

4. Move the pointer over the border of the comment box until the pointer changes to ⁺⬩, press and hold the mouse button, and then drag the comment down a couple of rows and to the right a little.

5. Release the mouse button. Figure 7-12 shows the current location of the comment box. Note that an arrow points from the text box to cell B6, which contains the comment.

Figure 7-12 ▶ Inserting a comment into a cell

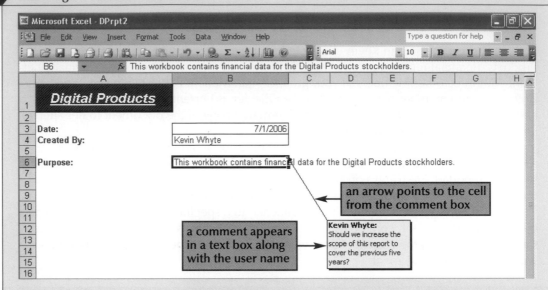

Trouble? If you clicked outside of cell B6, the comment box may have disappeared. You'll learn how to hide and unhide comments next.

Comments can be distracting in a worksheet. To reduce the distraction, you can hide a comment. The comment box then will only appear when you hover the pointer over the cell containing the comment. The presence of a hidden comment will be indicated by a small red triangle located in the upper-right corner of the cell.

To hide and then redisplay the comment in cell B6:

1. Right-click cell **B6** and then click **Hide Comment** on the shortcut menu. The comment disappears; however, the small red triangle remains in the upper-right corner of the cell.

   Trouble? If the Hide Comment command does not appear on the shortcut menu, your version of Excel is already set up to hide comments automatically. If this is the case, click cell B6 and continue with the next step.

2. Hover the pointer over cell B6 to display its comment.

3. Move the pointer away from cell B6. The comment disappears.

4. To redisplay the comment, right-click cell **B6** and then click **Show/Hide Comments** on the shortcut menu. The comment remains on the screen.

By default, a comment box appears with a yellow background, and the font used is Arial. To format the comment box, you can click it to select it, and then double-click the selection border to open the Format Comment dialog box, which contains various formatting options. You can also open the Format Comment dialog box by right-clicking the comment box and selecting Format Comment, or by selecting the comment box, clicking Format on the menu bar, and then clicking Comment.

You can choose whether or not to have comments appear on the worksheet printout. By default, comments are not printed, but you can change that by opening the Page Setup dialog box for the active worksheet and then clicking the Sheet tab. On the Sheet tab, you can click the Comments list arrow and then choose from one of three printing options:

- **None**: suppresses the display of comments on the printout
- **At end of sheet**: prints all of the comments on a separate sheet at the end of the printout of the worksheet
- **As displayed on sheet**: prints all comments on the printout as they appear in the workbook window

At this point, Kevin does not need to print the comment that you added to the Documentation sheet, but he'll remember this information for future tasks. Now that you've added Kevin's comment to the worksheet, you are ready to share the workbook with the other members of the group.

Creating a Shared Workbook

If you want to allow several users to view and modify a workbook while you have it open, you need to share the workbook. A **shared workbook** is a workbook that can be edited simultaneously by more than one user. Excel allows for simultaneous editing, which can occur if the workbook has been placed in a network folder accessible to several network users. Editing could also be done sequentially, in which case several users can access the workbook in turn and make changes.

Reference Window

Sharing a Workbook

- Click Tools on the menu bar, and then click Share Workbook.
- Click the Allow changes by more than one user at the same time check box.
- Click the OK button.

Using a shared workbook is similar to using any workbook. You can enter numbers and text, edit cells, move data around a worksheet, insert new rows and columns, and perform other tasks. In a shared workbook, however, some Excel features aren't available. For example, you cannot delete worksheets or cell ranges. You also cannot insert a block of cells, or merge or split cells. Nor can you use the Drawing toolbar or insert or change charts.

Sharing a Workbook

Because the data displayed in the workbook comes from various sources, Kevin wants to make sure the information is correct and that nothing has been omitted or misrepresented. By sharing the workbook with other members of his group, Kevin will be able to gather feedback that might affect the information contained in the workbook.

To begin sharing the workbook:

1. Click **Tools** on the menu bar, and then click **Share Workbook**. The Share Workbook dialog box opens. See Figure 7-13.

Figure 7-13 | **Share Workbook dialog box**

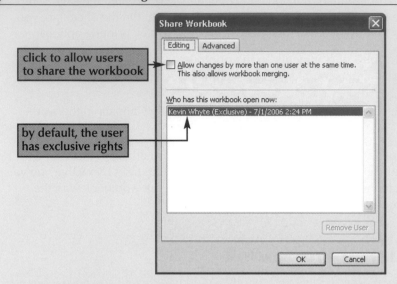

click to allow users to share the workbook

by default, the user has exclusive rights

2. Click the **Allow changes by more than one user at the same time** check box to allow other members of the group simultaneous access to this workbook.

3. Click the **OK** button. A message box appears, indicating that the workbook will be saved in order to change its status to a shared document.

4. Click the **OK** button to save and share the workbook. The workbook is saved on the network. Note that the text "[Shared]" appears in the title bar.

Kevin notifies the other members of his group that the workbook is available on the network for review. He will monitor their access to the document by opening the same Share Workbook dialog box that he used to save the workbook as a shared workbook. For example, when Kevin selects the Share Workbook option on the Tools menu a second time, he might see a dialog box similar to the one shown in Figure 7-14.

Figure 7-14 | **Shared workbook with two users**

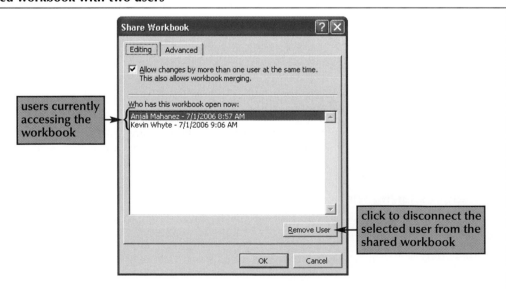

users currently accessing the workbook

click to disconnect the selected user from the shared workbook

Apparently, Anjali has already responded to Kevin's message and has opened the workbook. So now, two employees are working simultaneously on the financial report: Kevin and Anjali. If both Kevin and Anjali have the workbook open at the same time, how does Excel manage the changes they might make?

Resolving Conflicts

As long as each person makes changes to different cells, Excel will automatically integrate these saved changes into the shared workbook and notify the users of the change. Consider the situation shown in Figure 7-15, in which Anjali edits the content of cell B8. She then saves and closes the document. Afterward, Kevin saves his changes to the shared workbook. The action of saving the shared document forces Excel to display any changes made by other users and to attach a comment to the modified cells (in this case, cell B8). Note that Excel will automatically remove this comment the next time Kevin opens the workbook.

Modifying a shared workbook ◀ **Figure 7-15**

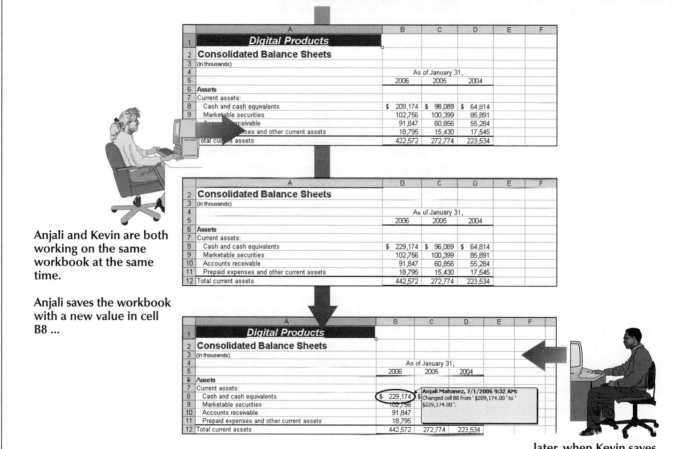

Anjali and Kevin are both working on the same workbook at the same time.

Anjali saves the workbook with a new value in cell B8 ...

... later, when Kevin saves the workbook, Excel displays a comment in cell B8, notifying him of the change.

A conflict can occur when users try to save different changes to the same cell. As shown in Figure 7-16, both Anjali and Kevin have the workbook open at the same time and are editing the contents of cell B8. Anjali saves her changes first. When Kevin tries to save his work, Excel notices a conflict in the value of cell B8 and displays the Resolve Conflicts dialog box. From this dialog box, Kevin can choose which edit to accept. If there are several conflicting cells, Kevin can go through the list, accepting some of Anjali's edits and rejecting others, or he can accept (or reject) them all at once.

Figure 7-16 **Resolving a conflict in a shared workbook**

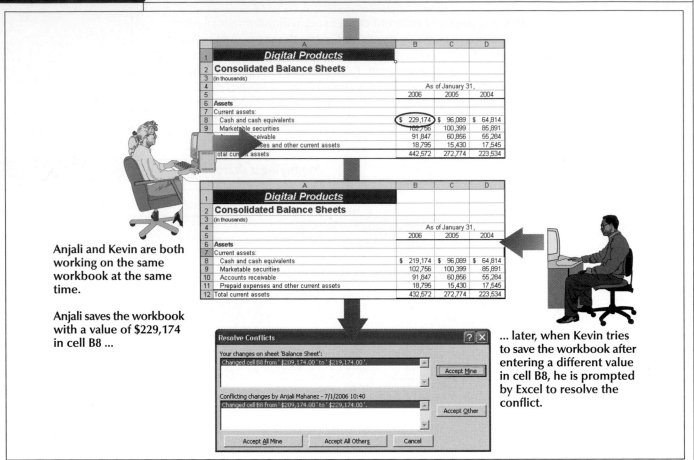

Anjali and Kevin are both working on the same workbook at the same time.

Anjali saves the workbook with a value of $229,174 in cell B8 ...

... later, when Kevin tries to save the workbook after entering a different value in cell B8, he is prompted by Excel to resolve the conflict.

All users have equal authority in deciding which changes are kept and which are discarded. The last user to save the document sees the Resolve Conflicts dialog box. However, rejected changes are stored in a **tracking log** to allow users to go back and retrieve erroneously rejected changes. This feature is particularly useful when a large group is editing a document and more control over the final content is needed. In this financial report project, Kevin is the final authority, so he will need to review the tracking log before signing off on the report.

At this point, Kevin has no further work to do on the financial report. You can close his document and await feedback from his colleagues.

To save your changes:

1. Click cell **A1** in the Documentation sheet.

2. Save your changes to the workbook, and then close it.

Tracking Changes

A few days have passed. The other members of Kevin's group have had time to examine the contents of the workbook; they've inserted their own comments and made their own edits. Kevin returns to you with a new version of the workbook.

A shared workbook allows several people to edit a workbook simultaneously and track the changes that have been made to the workbook. For example, if the people in a workgroup each handle several projects and need to know each other's status, the group could use a list in a shared workbook where each person enters and updates a row of information for each project. When working with a shared workbook, you can examine all the changes that have been saved in a workbook since the workbook has been shared, as well as set criteria for which changes you want to view. Excel allows you to view changes on the screen; you can also view the changes on a separate history worksheet. As you review the changes made in a workbook, you can accept or reject the changes by looking at each change one-by-one or by accepting all changes in total.

Kevin needs your help in reviewing and reconciling their edits. You will open the new version of the workbook, which has been saved as DPrpt3.

To open the DPrpt3 workbook:

1. Open the **DPrpt3** workbook located in the Tutorial.07\Tutorial folder included with your Data Files.

2. Enter the *current date* and *your name* in the Documentation sheet.

3. Save the workbook as **DPrpt4** in the Tutorial.07\Tutorial folder.

Before reviewing the changes that have been made to the document, you'll first review your colleagues' comments.

Reviewing and Deleting Comments

To review all of the comments in a workbook, you can use the Reviewing toolbar, which contains buttons that allow you to move to the next or previous comment in the workbook, as well as to edit or delete the currently selected comment.

You will display the Reviewing toolbar so you and Kevin can review the comments that the others have made.

To view your colleagues' comments:

1. Click **View** on the menu bar, point to **Toolbars**, and then click **Reviewing**. The Reviewing toolbar is displayed.

    Trouble? The location of the Reviewing toolbar on your screen might be different. Drag the toolbar to anchor it above the Formula bar, or drag the toolbar to a blank area in the workbook window.

2. Click the **Next Comment** button 🖳 on the Reviewing toolbar. Excel selects the first comment on the Documentation sheet, as shown in Figure 7-17.

Figure 7-17 ▶ **View other users' comments**

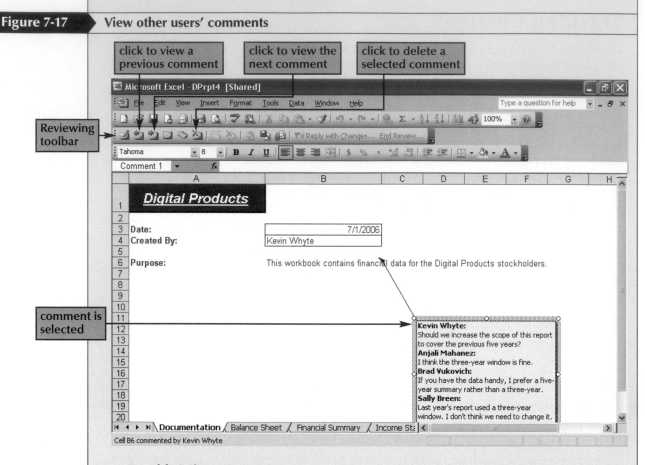

Trouble? If you clicked the comment box with your mouse, your user name appears in the box and Excel waits for you to enter your own comments. If this happens, click cell B7 to deselect the comment box.

Recall that Kevin asked you to insert a comment questioning whether the scope of the report should be expanded to cover the last five years. In the first comment, Kevin sees the response to his query. Anjali and Sally think that the three-year report is fine, whereas Brad would prefer a five-year report if the data is easily available.

You will continue to review the comments.

To continue reviewing the comments:

▶ **1.** Click the **Next Comment** button 🖾 on the Reviewing toolbar. Excel jumps to the comment attached to cell A20. Anjali has a question about whether the number of employees reported on the worksheet includes part-time employees. Brad has replied to Anjali's query.

▶ **2.** Click the **Next Comment** button 🖾 to continue, and then read each comment. When you reach the end of the comments, a message box appears, indicating that you have reached the end of the workbook.

▶ **3.** Click the **OK** button to return to the first comment in the workbook.

After reviewing all of the comments, Kevin wants to remove them from the workbook because he no longer needs them. He has decided to leave the report coverage at three years. He can review the edits made by the other users without having to read their comments again. You will delete the comments now.

To delete the comments:

1. Click the **Delete Comment** button 🖾 on the Reviewing toolbar to delete the selected comment.

2. Click the **Next Comment** button 🖾 on the Reviewing toolbar to go to the next comment in the workbook.

3. Click the **Delete Comment** button 🖾 on the Reviewing toolbar to delete the second comment.

4. Continue through the rest of the workbook, deleting the remaining comments. Note that when all the comments have been deleted from the workbook, the Next Comment button and the Delete Comment button are no longer available on the Reviewing toolbar.

5. Close the Reviewing toolbar when you're finished.

   Trouble? If the Reviewing toolbar is floating, click its Close button. If the toolbar is anchored, click View on the menu bar, point to Toolbars, and then click Reviewing.

From reading the comments, Kevin has learned that the other users in his group have been editing the contents of some of the cells, deleting others, and moving and renaming worksheets. Although his colleagues have noted these changes in their comments, they might not have documented all the changes they made. To ensure consistency and accuracy, Kevin needs to be able to review everything his colleagues have done in the workbook.

Reviewing Changes

As noted earlier, Excel stores changes to a shared workbook in a tracking log. By default, the log will store changes in the workbook entered over the previous 30 days. Not all changes are tracked, however. Excel will not track changed sheet names, inserted or deleted worksheets, and format changes.

To review the changes that are tracked, you can have Excel highlight them using the Track Changes feature. When Track Changes is enabled, the changes made to a worksheet are displayed in a text box alongside the cell, indicating what change was made, who made it, and when.

Tracking Changes to Cells

Reference Window

- Open a shared workbook.
- Click Tools on the menu bar, point to Track Changes, and then click Highlight Changes.
- Click the list arrow for the When check box, and select the timeframe of the changes that you want to track.
- Click the list arrow for the Who check box, and then select whose changes you want to view.
- Click the Where reference box and specify where in the workbook you want to review the changes.
- Click the Highlight changes on screen check box to display the changed cells in the worksheet.
- Click the List changes on a new sheet check box to display a list of changed cells on a separate worksheet.
- Click the OK button.

To display all the changes that have been made to this shared workbook, you will turn on the Track Changes feature.

To highlight the changes in the shared workbook:

1. Click **Tools** on the menu bar, point to **Track Changes**, and then click **Highlight Changes**. The Highlight Changes dialog box opens.

   From this dialog box, you can select a time interval for the changes you want highlighted. You can choose to highlight: (1) changes created since the last time you saved the workbook, (2) all changes, (3) changes that you haven't reviewed yet, or (4) changes since a specified date. You can also review changes from a specified user or changes made in a specified section of the workbook. In this case, you'll review all the changes made by everyone but yourself.

2. Click the **When** list arrow, and then click **All**.

3. Click the **Who** list arrow, and then click **Everyone but Me**. Note that clicking the list arrow automatically selects the Who check box. Note that the Everyone but Me option refers to all users who have edited this document other than the user who currently has it open.

4. Verify that the **Highlight changes on screen** check box is selected and that the **List changes on a new sheet** check box is *not* selected. The completed dialog box appears in Figure 7-18.

Figure 7-18	Highlighting changes

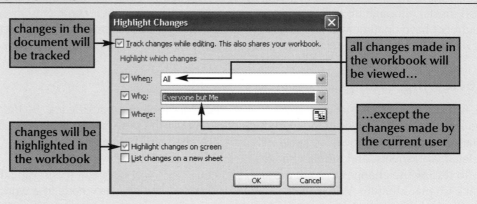

changes in the document will be tracked

all changes made in the workbook will be viewed...

changes will be highlighted in the workbook

...except the changes made by the current user

5. Click the **OK** button.

Excel highlights the locations in the workbook that have been modified. Each cell that has been changed is displayed with a colored border. When you hover the pointer over the cell, a description of the change is displayed.

You will review all the changes beginning with the changes made to the Financial Summary sheet.

To review the changes made by other users:

1. Click the **Financial Summary** tab.

2. Hover the pointer over cell A12. A comment appears, describing the change. See Figure 7-19.

Changes in the workbook ◄ **Figure 7-19**

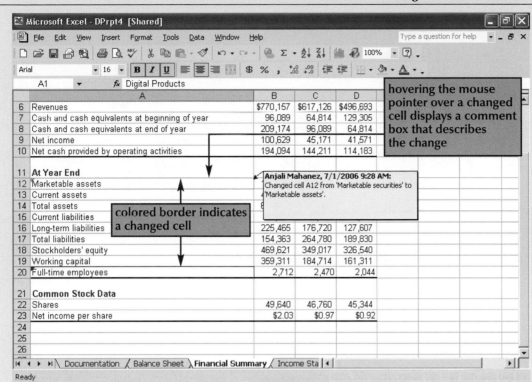

Examining all the sheets in a workbook to look for changes might be a tiresome process, especially in large workbooks that contain many worksheets. Kevin asks whether there is a way of viewing the contents of the tracking log itself rather than having to switch to each sheet to look for the changes.

To make the process of reviewing changes in a workbook easier and more efficient, you will display the contents of the tracking log.

To show the contents of the tracking log:

► **1.** Click **Tools** on the menu bar, point to **Track Changes**, and then click **Highlight Changes**. The Highlight Changes dialog box opens.

► **2.** Click the **List changes on a new sheet** check box to select it, and then click the **OK** button. The contents of the tracking log appear in a new worksheet named "History," as shown in Figure 7-20. The History worksheet displays each change in the order it was entered, along with the date and time it was made, who made the change, where it was made, and what kind of change it is. From viewing the contents of this sheet, Kevin can tell at a glance what kinds of modifications have been made in the workbook.

Figure 7-20 **History list describing the changes made to the workbook**

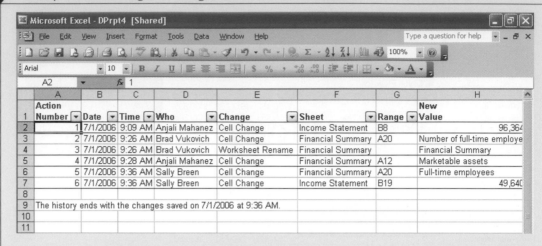

3. Review the different columns in the History worksheet.

Note that the History sheet will only exist for the current Excel session. Once the workbook is closed, even if changes are saved, the History sheet will not appear the next time the workbook is opened.

Accepting and Rejecting Changes

After examining the contents of the History sheet, Kevin sees some changes that he might want to keep. Although he could reverse the changes by editing the workbook, he prefers to simply reject those changes that he doesn't approve. Using the Accept or Reject Changes option of the Track Changes feature can save Kevin time and help him to maintain accuracy.

Reference Window | **Accepting and Rejecting Changes to Cells**

- Open a shared workbook.
- Click Tools on the menu bar, point to Track Changes, and then click Accept or Reject Changes.
- Click the list arrow for the When check box, and then select the timeframe of the changes that you want to review.
- Click the list arrow for the Who check box, and then select the person whose changes you want to review.
- Click the Where reference box and specify where in the workbook you want to review the changes.
- Click the OK button.

You will review the changes, accepting or rejecting them as needed.

To accept and reject changes to the workbook:

▶ **1.** Click **Tools** on the menu bar, point to **Track Changes**, and then click **Accept or Reject Changes**. The Select Changes to Accept or Reject dialog box opens. See Figure 7-21.

Reviewing changes ◀ **Figure 7-21**

You'll select those changes that have not yet been reviewed and limit the changes to only those created by users other than you.

▶ **2.** Verify that your dialog box looks like the one shown in Figure 7-21, and then click the **OK** button. The Accept or Reject Changes dialog box opens, indicating that others made six changes to this workbook, as shown in Figure 7-22.

Accept or Reject Changes dialog box ◀ **Figure 7-22**

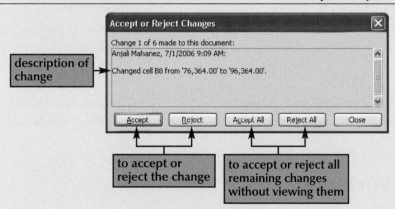

Anjali Mahanez made the first modification by changing the value of cell B8 in the Income Statement worksheet from $76,364 to $96,364. Kevin contacts Anjali and learns that the value for the cost of goods sold in 2006 originally entered into the cell was incorrect. He wants to accept her edit, which you will do next.

▶ **3.** Click the **Accept** button. The next edit is displayed. The contents of cell A20 in the Financial Summary worksheet were edited twice, as shown in Figure 7-23. The original text was "Number of employees" (employed at the company). After some discussion, it was determined that the values in the report referred only to full-time employees. Brad changed the label, and then Sally Breen edited his change. At this point, you have to choose one of the three versions. You'll choose Sally's edit.

Figure 7-23 ▶ **Choosing among several changes**

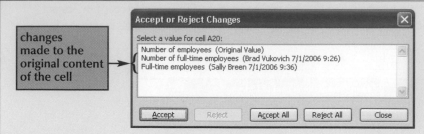

4. Click **Full-time employees** from the list of values for cell A20, and then click the **Accept** button.

Brad also changed the name of the worksheet from "Financial Data" to "Financial Summary." Kevin recalls from reviewing the comments earlier that Brad thought this was a more descriptive title for the sheet, so you will accept the edit.

5. Click the **Accept** button. Excel displays the next edit. The information in the dialog box shows that Anjali has changed the label in cell A12 of the Financial Summary worksheet from "Marketable securities" to "Marketable assets." Kevin disagrees. The first label was the correct one, so you will reject that edit.

6. Click the **Reject** button.

Sally has changed the number of outstanding shares. You'll accept her change.

7. Click the **Accept** button.

8. Save the approved changes made to the workbook, and then close the workbook.

You and Kevin have finished editing the work of three of his colleagues. A fourth colleague, Karen Ziegler, is away at a conference. To get her feedback, Kevin wants you to send the workbook to her via e-mail.

Mailing a Workbook

To send a workbook via e-mail, you use the Send To submenu located on the File menu, as shown in Figure 7-24. Excel supports several different e-mail commands. The Mail Recipient command enables you to send the workbook either as an attachment to your e-mail message or as part of the body of the e-mail message. The Mail Recipient (as Attachment) command sends the workbook only as an attachment to the message. Also, you can use the e-mail button on the Standard toolbar to send an entire workbook as an attachment to an e-mail message or send the current sheet as the body of an e-mail message.

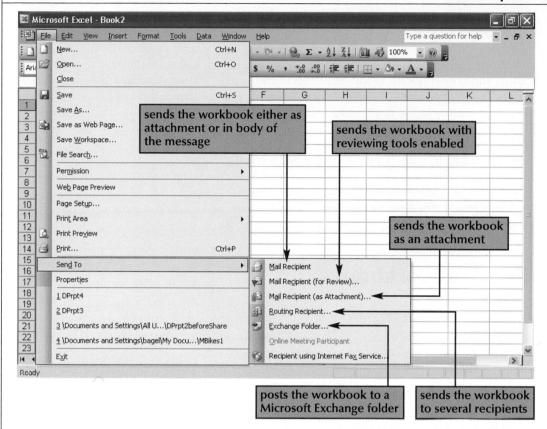

To send an attached workbook, you need an e-mail program that supports the **Message Application Programming Interface**, or **MAPI**, which is a set of standards that allows documents, such as Excel workbooks, to be attached to an e-mail message. Most e-mail programs are MAPI-compliant, although some older ones are not.

If you want to send the workbook in the body of an e-mail message, your recipients need to be using Microsoft Outlook 2000 or a later version. For Outlook 97 or earlier versions, you can still send the workbook in the body of the message, but the formatting will be lost.

Mailing a Workbook for Review

If you want your recipients to review and comment on the workbook, you can use the Mail Recipient (for Review) command on the Send To submenu. This command acts like a wizard by prompting you to turn on Excel's Track Changes feature and by helping you to merge any changes made by the workbook's recipients to your workbook. When you choose the Mail Recipient (for Review) command, you must send the entire workbook as an attachment; you cannot send a portion of the workbook, nor can a section of the workbook be inserted directly into the body of the message.

Routing a Workbook

When you send a workbook through e-mail to a group of recipients, each user gets a separate copy of the workbook. If you want those users to work on the same copy of the file, you must route the e-mail message using the Routing Recipient command on the Send To submenu.

Routing causes Excel to attach the file and a routing slip to the e-mail message. The routing slip contains a list of the recipients of the message. When one recipient is finished with the message (and the attached workbook), the edited workbook then is sent to the next person listed in the routing slip. After the last recipient makes changes to the workbook, the message with the attached workbook is returned to the originator of the message. A recipient can be added at any time during the routing cycle by editing the routing slip. For routing to work, all recipients must be running Microsoft Outlook.

You discuss these various e-mail options with Kevin. He decides that in the future he may use some of these techniques, particularly routing, to collaborate with other employees in his group. For now, he only needs to send the workbook to one employee. Kevin sends a mail message to Karen Ziegler with a copy of the workbook as an attached file.

Merging Workbooks

Since sending the workbook to Karen, Kevin has received a copy of the file containing Karen's edits. He now has two copies of the workbook: Karen's and the one he has created based on the edits of Brad, Anjali, and Sally. Kevin wants to merge the two copies into a single workbook. In order for two workbooks to be merged into one, the following requirements must be met:

- The two workbooks must be copies of the same file, which must be a shared workbook.
- The two workbooks must have different filenames.
- The two workbooks must either have the same password or not be password-protected at all.
- The Track Changes feature must be turned on for both workbooks from the time the copy is first made.
- The tracking history must be kept from the time the copy is first made.

To merge two workbooks, you must first open the workbook into which you want the changes merged. Next, you select the Compare and Merge Workbook command on the Tools menu, and then you open the other workbook (or workbooks) containing the changes you want to incorporate into your file.

Reference Window	**Merging Workbooks**

- Open the workbook into which you want to merge the files.
- Click Tools on the menu bar, and then click Compare and Merge Workbooks.
- Select the workbooks that you want to merge into the active file.
- Click the OK button.

Having accepted and rejected the edits made by three of the group members, Kevin has saved the workbook as "DPrpt5." This is the workbook that Kevin sent to Karen. Karen's changes to that particular workbook have been stored in a file named "Karen1," which Kevin has received. You will merge the two workbooks.

To merge two workbooks:

1. Open the **DPrpt5** workbook located in the Tutorial.07\Tutorial folder included with your Data Files, enter the current date and your name in the Documentation sheet, and then save the workbook as **DPrpt6** in the same folder.

2. Click **Tools** on the menu bar, and then click **Compare and Merge Workbooks**. The Select Files to Merge Into Current Workbook dialog box opens.

3. If necessary, navigate to the Tutorial.07\Tutorial folder, select the **Karen1** workbook, and then click the **OK** button. The content of the Karen1 workbook is merged into the DPrpt6 workbook. Note that the word "[Shared]" appears in the title bar, confirming that you are still working in the DPrpt6 workbook and that the comment that you now see has been added to the workbook. The comment was made by Karen.

4. If necessary, hover the mouse pointer over cell A1 to see Karen's comment, as shown in Figure 7-25. Karen explains that she only made minor changes in the report, so you will delete it because you do not have to act on it.

Merging workbooks   **Figure 7-25**

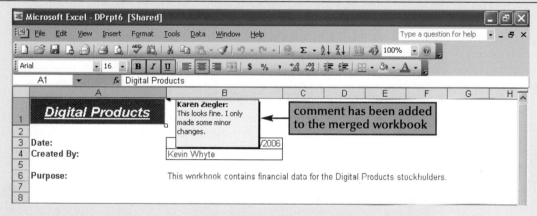

5. Right-click cell **A1** and then click **Delete Comment** on the shortcut menu.

Next, you want to review the changes that have been incorporated into the workbook. Since you've already reviewed changes from other employees, you'll only review those changes made by Karen Ziegler.

To accept or reject the changes in the merged workbook:

1. Click **Tools** on the menu bar, point to **Track Changes**, and then click **Accept or Reject Changes**. The Select Changes to Accept or Reject dialog box opens.

2. Verify that the **Not yet reviewed** option appears in the list box for the When check box.

3. Click the **Who** list arrow, scroll down the list (if necessary), click **Karen Ziegler**, and then click the **OK** button. The Accept or Reject Changes dialog box opens and indicates that there are three changes, with the first change made by Karen displayed. The first change listed is in cell B4, in which Karen changed the entry from "Fiscal year ends January 31" to "Fiscal year ending January 31"; you will accept this change.

4. Click the **Accept** button to accept the change, and then review the remaining changes and accept each of them.

Kevin appreciates the ease of the merge feature. One of the advantages of merging workbooks is that each user works on a separate copy, protecting the original from mistakes until the workbooks are finally merged.

Online Meetings and Web Discussions

Excel supports two other ways of collaborating on a workbook: online meetings and Web discussions. To run an online meeting, you need to have access to Windows NetMeeting, a program that allows users to meet over a network to work on issues in real time. The advantage of an online meeting is that the users in a group can discuss the contents of a workbook and make changes together, receiving instant feedback.

You can either host the online meeting or be invited to participate in one. All participants must have NetMeeting, but only one person needs to have access to the workbook. During the meeting, the contents of the workbook appear on a screen. Although only one user can have control at a time, each user can gain control of the document and make changes that are viewed instantly by the other meeting participants.

In a Web discussion, users can insert comments into a document that is opened by a **Web browser** (an application that is used to view Web pages). The comments appear in the document, but they are actually stored, not in the document itself, but in a **discussion server**. The discussions are "threaded," which means that the comments are organized by the initial comments and then by the replies to those comments, followed by subsequent replies. Users cannot modify the contents of the document itself. To run a Web discussion, all participants must be running Microsoft Internet Explorer 4.01 or higher. Also, the system or network administrator must set up a discussion server to store the discussion.

You've completed your work incorporating the comments from Kevin's colleagues. The current version of the file represents the final draft, so you can remove the sharing feature from the workbook and then save and close it.

To remove shared mode from the workbook:

1. Click **Tools** on the menu bar, and then click **Share Workbook**. The Share Workbook dialog box opens.

2. Click the **Allow changes by more than one user at the same time** check box to deselect it.

3. Click the **OK** button. A message appears, indicating that this action removes sharing from the workbook. In addition, the change history is erased, and users who are editing the workbook at the same time cannot save their changes.

   The word "[Shared]" no longer appears in the title bar.

4. Save the changes you have made to the DPrpt6 workbook.

Now that Kevin has a final version of the workbook, the tables in the report will be printed in a booklet for stockholders. In the next session, you'll learn how to publish a portion of this report on the company's Web site.

Review

Session 7.2 Quick Check

1. What is a shared workbook, and how can you tell whether a workbook is being shared?
2. How does Excel resolve a conflict between two users editing the same cell at the same time?

3. Name two ways of displaying changes made by other users to a shared workbook.
4. For how many days are changes made to a shared workbook typically recorded?
5. What is routing? What are some requirements for routing a workbook through several users?
6. What five requirements must be met before two workbooks can be merged?

Session 7.3

Working with the Web

During the first two sessions, you worked with Kevin on creating a final draft of the financial report workbook. Now that it's finished, Kevin wants you to store the summary on the company's Web page for the stockholders to view. Before doing that, you want to review some of the underlying concepts of the Web and how it developed.

One of most important uses of computers is to share and disseminate information. Computers linked together to share files and hardware resources form a structure called a **network** or a **local area network (LAN)**. Networks are so useful and economical that many networks are linked together to create even more extended networks. The most far-reaching and popular of these extended networks is the **Internet**. Originally developed in the late 1960s, the Internet now encompasses the globe, involving millions of mainframes, personal computers, and computer workstations supplied by governments, universities, businesses, and private users.

Introducing the World Wide Web

The original tools to access and navigate the Internet were often too difficult for all but the most experienced computer users, which somewhat limited the usefulness of the Internet. This limitation changed in 1989 when Timothy Berners-Lee and other researchers at the CERN nuclear facility in Geneva, Switzerland, developed a way of sharing network information through the use of hypertext documents. A **hypertext document** is an electronic file containing elements called **links**, or **hyperlinks**, that provide access to other hypertext documents. Rather than memorizing arcane commands, the user can jump from one hypertext document to another by activating a link (usually by clicking it with a mouse).

Hypertext documents were just what the Internet needed to become a more universal and important information source. Within a few years, many Internet resources were available in hypertext form. The collection of these hypertext documents is collectively called the **World Wide Web**. With the development of the World Wide Web, the Internet exploded in popularity, extending beyond the confines of academia into governments and the private sector.

Understanding Web Pages, Browsers, and HTML

On the World Wide Web, or Web for short, each hypertext document is referred to as a **Web page**. A collection of Web pages is called a **Web site**. Larger Web sites used for universities or businesses can contain hundreds of Web pages. Web sites are stored on computers called **Web servers**. To view a Web page, a user must have a software program called a **Web browser**, which retrieves the hypertext file from the Web server and then displays the document on the user's computer.

Web pages need to be readable by all operating systems and computer models. For this reason, Web pages are formatted in a common language called **Hypertext Markup Language**, or **HTML**. No one company owns or manages HTML; rather, HTML was developed by a consortium of Web developers and software companies. Through the years, HTML has gone through several versions, improving the Web page developer's ability to create sophisticated and exciting page layouts and features.

The companies that produce Web browsers have also added additional features to HTML. Although the consortium might ultimately adopt these extensions, often certain features are viewable by only one browser and not by others. An additional source of confusion is that a particular feature might be available in one version of a browser, but not in an earlier version. Trying to accommodate different browsers and browser versions is one of the major tasks of a Web author. The two major browsers are Netscape Navigator and Internet Explorer (developed by Microsoft). As you'll see later, you can configure Excel to support a specific browser or browser version when converting workbooks into Web pages.

Creating Web Pages in Excel

Microsoft provides tools to convert Excel workbooks into Web pages that can be placed on the Web to be viewed by others. Excel allows you to create two types of Web pages: noninteractive and interactive. In a **noninteractive Web page**, users can scroll through the contents of an Excel workbook and switch between worksheets, but they cannot make any changes to the data or formatting displayed on the Web page. When you save a workbook as a noninteractive workbook, Excel converts the contents of the workbook into HTML format. Noninteractive pages are supported by versions of Netscape and Internet Explorer 3.0 and higher, although there might be some minor discrepancies in how each browser displays the page.

When you publish an interactive workbook on a Web page, the result is an HTML file that contains a special **spreadsheet component** that allows users to interact with a workbook through a Web browser. This **interactive Web page** enables users to switch between worksheets using a sheet selector, enter or edit data, format values, and change formulas on each sheet on the Web page. However, any change users make on the Web page does not affect the original workbook, nor do changes last from one browser session to another. Figure 7-26 shows examples of both kinds of Web page.

Figure 7-26	Noninteractive and interactive Web pages

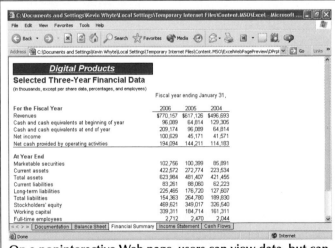

On a noninteractive Web page, users can view data, but can not edit or format it.

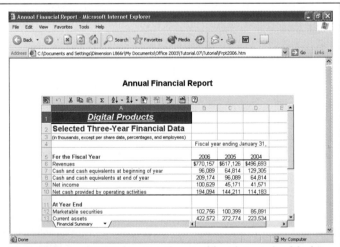

On an interactive Web page, the workbook is embedded in the page as a spreadsheet component that the user can edit and format.

You can save an Excel workbook, a worksheet, or an item of a worksheet as a Web page and make it available to viewers via the Internet or an intranet. For example, Kevin wants to make the Financial Report worksheet available to shareholders; however, he does not want to give shareholders the ability to edit the data, so he needs you to create a noninteractive Web page of a single worksheet.

Publishing a Noninteractive Workbook on a Web Page

To create the noninteractive Web page, you'll use the Excel workbook that you created in the last session. Before creating the page, you can preview the Web page. Previewing a Web page enables you to view the workbook in a Web browser before committing your work to an HTML file. Because you're planning to save an entire workbook as a noninteractive Web page, you will preview the page first without publishing it by clicking Web Page Preview on the file menu.

To preview the Web page:

1. If you took a break after the last session, make sure Excel is running and the DPrpt6 workbook is open.

2. Click **File** on the menu bar, and then click **Web Page Preview**. Excel opens your Web browser and displays a version of the Excel workbook in HTML format. The tab scrolling buttons and the sheet tabs have been replaced with symbols and boxes. By clicking these symbols and boxes, you can navigate through the contents of the workbook.

   Trouble? If your default Web browser is Netscape, you might not be able to work with many of the features of the Web page version of this workbook.

3. Hover the pointer over the **Financial Summary** box at the bottom of the Web page. The box changes from gray to white, and information about the file appears in the browser's address bar and status bar.

4. Click the **Financial Summary** box. The browser displays the contents of the Financial Summary worksheet. See Figure 7-27.

Previewing a noninteractive Web page ◄ **Figure 7-27**

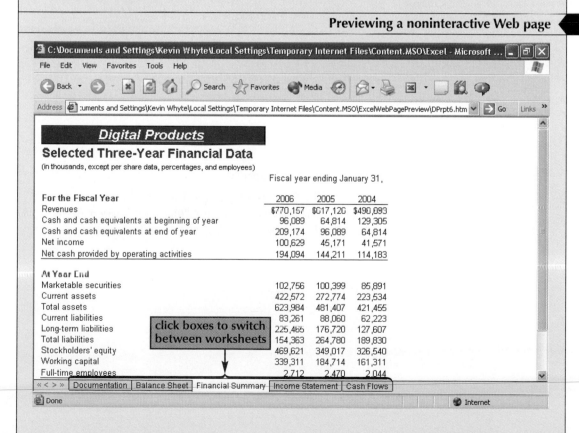

> **5.** Click the **Balance Sheet** box to display the Balance Sheet worksheet in the browser, and then click the other boxes in the report to view the remaining Web pages.

> **6.** Close your Web browser to return to the DPrpt6 workbook.

Now that you've previewed a noninteractive Web page based on an Excel workbook, you can start the process of actually creating the Web page for use on the Web.

Choosing Between a Noninteractive and Interactive Web Page

The process of creating a Web page based on a workbook involves opening the Save As dialog box. In this dialog box, you choose to save the workbook as a noninteractive or interactive Web page. You also use this dialog box to specify what you want to publish; that is, you can choose to publish the entire workbook or a portion of it. You can also enter a title for the Web page and select other publishing-related options.

Reference Window	**Saving a Workbook as a Web Page**

- Click File on the menu bar, and then click Save as Web Page.
- Click the Add interactivity check box to create an interactive Web page. Leave the check box unselected to create a noninteractive page.
- Click the Publish button.
- Click the Choose list box, and select which portions of the workbook you want to publish as a Web page.
- Click the Change button to change the title of the Web page.
- Click the Browse button to specify a filename and location for the Web page.
- Click the AutoRepublish every time this workbook is saved check box to automatically republish the Web page each time you save the workbook.
- Click the Open published web page in browser check box to automatically open the Web page in your Web browser.
- Click the Publish button.

You will open the Save As dialog box, and then choose the noninteractive format for the Web page.

To start creating a noninteractive workbook:

> **1.** Click **File** on the menu bar, and then click **Save as Web Page**. The Save As dialog box opens. See Figure 7-28. Note that there is a Web page named "Meeting" located in the Tutorial.07\Tutorial folder included with your Data Files. You will use this file shortly.

Saving a workbook as a Web page | Figure 7-28

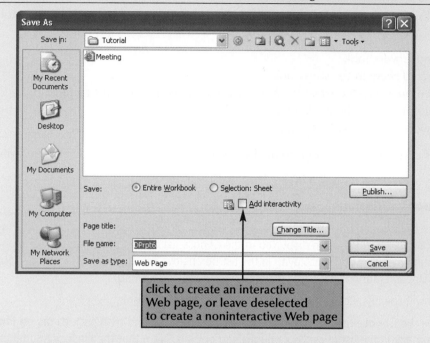

click to create an interactive
Web page, or leave deselected
to create a noninteractive Web page

Because you are creating a noninteractive Web page, you will verify that the interactivity option is deselected.

▶ **2.** Make sure that the **Add interactivity** check box is *not* selected.

Setting the Page Title

Web pages will usually have a page title that appears in the title bar of the Web browser. (If a page title is missing, the browser will display the page's filename.)

Kevin wants the Web page title to clearly indicate to the stockholders the nature of the report.

To specify the page title:

▶ **1.** Click the **Change Title** button. The Set Page Title dialog box opens.

▶ **2.** Type **Annual Financial Report** in the Page title text box, and then click the **OK** button. Note that the page title you just typed now appears above the File name list box in the Save As dialog box.

The next step in setting up the page for publishing on the Web is to choose which elements of the workbook to publish.

Setting the Publishing Options

Excel allows you to specify which elements to publish. You can choose from the following set of choices:

- The entire workbook
- A selected sheet in the workbook
- An item on a selected sheet, such as an embedded chart or pivot table
- A range of cells in the workbook
- A previously published selection from the workbook

In this case, Kevin only wants to publish the contents of the Financial Summary worksheet.

To select the Financial Summary worksheet for publishing:

▶ 1. Click the **Publish** button. The Publish as Web Page dialog box opens with the Items on Documentation option displayed in the Choose list box and the Sheet, All contents of Documentation option displayed in the list box below, indicating that the entire contents of the Documentation sheet are currently selected for publishing.

You will specify just the Financial Summary sheet for publishing.

▶ 2. Click the **Choose** list arrow at the top of the dialog box, and then click **Items on Financial Summary** in the list of available publishing options. Note that the Financial Summary sheet becomes the active sheet in the Excel window.

The Web development team at Digital Products needs to have a filename for the Web page so the team can create links to the Web page from other Digital Products Web pages. The default filename for a Web page is "Page.htm," but Kevin has already been told that, for consistency in naming company-related Web pages, he should name the file "Frpt2006.htm." The extension .htm refers to an HTML file. You will change the filename now.

To specify a filename for the HTML file:

▶ 1. Click the **Browse** button. The Publish As dialog box opens.

▶ 2. Verify that the Tutorial.07\Tutorial folder is selected, type **Frpt2006** in the File name list box, and then click the **OK** button.

Finally, Kevin knows that he might be updating this particular workbook in the future. He would like the Web page to be updated automatically so that it always matches any changes made to the source workbook. You can do this by enabling the **AutoRepublish** feature, which republishes the Web page automatically whenever the workbook is saved.

To turn on the AutoRepublish feature:

▶ 1. Click the **AutoRepublish every time this workbook is saved** check box in the Publish as Web Page dialog box.

Rather than hunting around for the Web page after you publish it, you will have Excel launch your Web browser automatically.

▶ 2. If necessary, click the **Open published web page in browser** check box to select it. Figure 7-29 shows the completed dialog box. You're now ready to publish the Web page.

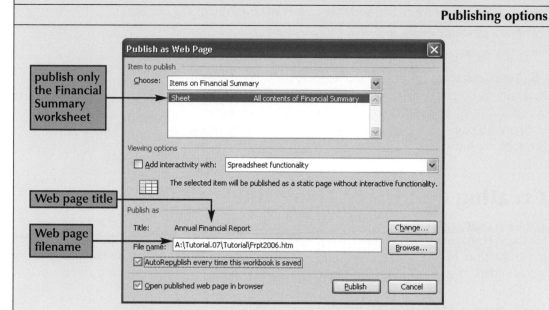

publish only the Financial Summary worksheet →

Web page title →

Web page filename →

3. Click the **Publish** button. The Web page based on the contents of the Financial Summary worksheet is opened in your browser. Figure 7-30 shows the contents of the Web page. Note that the page title "Annual Financial Report" appears in the browser's title bar and above the worksheet.

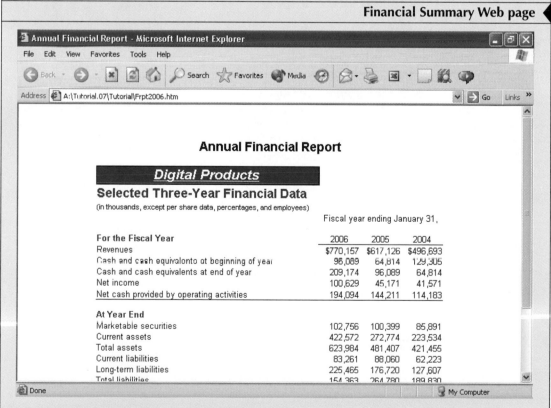

4. Scroll to the bottom of the Web page. Note that, unlike the previous version of the Web page you opened earlier, this Web page does not display symbols or boxes. There are no symbols or boxes because this is a single worksheet, not an entire workbook.

Kevin wants a hard copy of the Web page, so you will print a copy now.

5. Click **File** on the menu bar, and then click **Print**. The Print dialog box opens.

6. Make sure the settings are correct for your printer.

7. Click the **Print** button.

8. Close your browser window, and return to the DPrpt6 workbook.

The Web page will provide a concise summary of the financial status of Digital Products for the stockholders.

Creating and Using Hyperlinks

The Web page you just created will be placed on the company's Web server, but in order for the Web page to function effectively, the Web site team wants Kevin to include a hyperlink from his Web page to a Web page that announces the details of the annual stockholders' meeting.

Inserting a Hyperlink

Excel allows you to insert hyperlinks directly into your workbook files. The hyperlinks can point to other workbooks or documents, to sites on the Web, or to specific cells within the workbook.

Reference Window	**Inserting a Hyperlink**

- Select the text, graphic, or cell in which you want to insert the hyperlink.
- Click Insert on the menu bar, and then click Hyperlink.
- To link to a file or Web page, click Existing File or Web Page in the Link to list, and then select the file or Web page from the Look in list box.
- To link to a location in the current workbook, click Place in This Document in the Link to list, and then select the worksheet, cell, or range in the current workbook.
- To link to a new document, click Create New Document in the Link to list, and then specify the filename and path of the new document.
- To link to an e-mail address, click E-mail Address in the Link to list, and then enter the e-mail address of the recipient and a subject line for the e-mail message.

To link the financial summary Web page to the Web page that announces the annual stockholders' meeting, you'll insert a link that points to the file "Meeting.htm."

To insert a hyperlink into the workbook:

1. Scroll down the Financial Summary worksheet, and then click cell **A26**.

2. Type **View Meeting Details** and then press the **Enter** key.

3. Select the range **A26:D26** and then click the **Merge and Center** button ⊞ on the Formatting toolbar.

4. Click **Insert** on the menu bar, and then click **Hyperlink**. The Insert Hyperlink dialog box opens. You use this dialog box to select the target for the hyperlink. See Figure 7-31.

Inserting a hyperlink — **Figure 7-31**

Trouble? If either the Existing File or Web Page option or the Current Folder option is not selected, select it before continuing.

5. Click **Meeting** in the list of files, click the **OK** button, and then click cell **E26**. As shown in Figure 7-32, the text "View Meeting Details" appears in an underlined blue font, indicating that the cell functions as a hyperlink.

Hyperlink to the Meeting.htm file — **Figure 7-32**

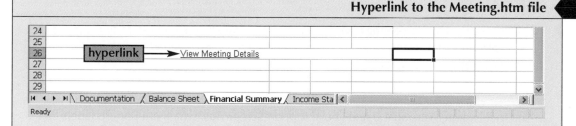

Editing and Using a Hyperlink

You will test the hyperlink that you just created by clicking the cell that contains the link, cell A26.

To test the hyperlink:

▶ **1.** Move the pointer over cell A26 until the pointer changes to 🖑, and then click cell **A26**. The Meeting.htm file opens in your browser. See Figure 7-33.

Figure 7-33 ▶ **Meeting.htm Web page**

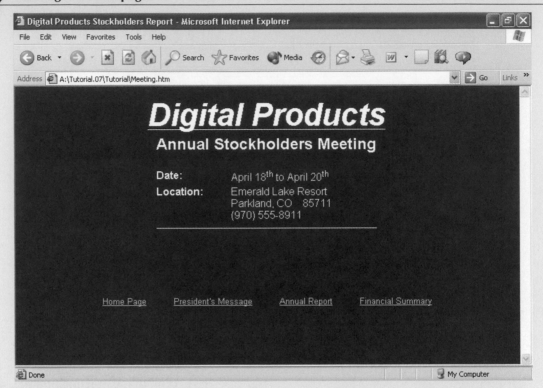

▶ **2.** Click the **Back** button on the navigation bar in your Web browser to return to Excel and the DPrpt6 workbook. Notice that the color of the hyperlink has changed, indicating that you have linked to the target file.

Internet Explorer version 4.0 and above support **ScreenTips**, which are pop-up labels that appear whenever a user hovers the pointer over a hyperlink. ScreenTips provide additional information about the target of the link. The default ScreenTip is the folder location and file-name of the target of the link, but Kevin doesn't think that this is very helpful. The company has a style for its Web site that uses a more descriptive ScreenTip. Kevin wants you to change the ScreenTip for the link you just created to "View details on the stockholders' meeting."

Because you've already created the hyperlink, to make this change you'll have to edit the link's properties.

To edit the hyperlink:

▶ **1.** Right-click cell **A26** in the Financial Summary worksheet, and then click **Edit Hyperlink** on the shortcut menu. The Edit Hyperlink dialog box opens.

▶ **2.** Click the **ScreenTip** button in the upper-right corner of the dialog box. The Set Hyperlink ScreenTip dialog box opens.

▶ **3.** Type **View details on the stockholders' meeting** in the ScreenTip text box, and then click the **OK** button.

4. Click the **OK** button to close the Edit Hyperlink dialog box.

5. Hover the pointer over cell A26, and confirm that the ScreenTip you created appears just below the cell.

Kevin agrees that the ScreenTip is a useful addition to the Web page and workbook.

Setting Excel's Web Options

You can fine-tune the process of converting Excel workbooks into Web pages by modifying Excel's Web options. Using the Web Options dialog box, you can specify the level of support for different browsers that Excel will provide. You can also control how Excel creates the HTML and graphics files that make up your Web site. Some of these options are only for advanced Web page authors, but they do provide an additional level of control if you need it.

You will open the Web Options dialog box to view the options available.

To view Excel's Web options:

1. Click **Tools** on the menu bar, and then click **Options**. The Options dialog box opens.

2. Click the **General** tab, and then click the **Web Options** button. The Web Options dialog box opens. This dialog box divides the various Web-related options into six categories: General, Browsers, Files, Pictures, Encoding, and Fonts.

   Kevin is interested in how he might control Excel's support for different browsers and browser versions, so you will review the options on the Browsers tab.

3. Click the **Browsers** tab. Excel provides support for different browsers, as shown in Figure 7-34. You will specify a target browser for the Web pages you are creating.

Browsers tab in the Web Options dialog box ◄ **Figure 7-34**

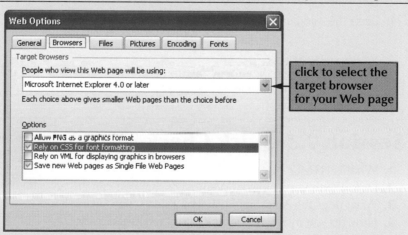

4. Click the **People who view this Web page will be using** list arrow to view a list of browser support options. Excel can create Web pages for Netscape and Internet Explorer 3.0 or later, or 4.0 or later. You can also limit the support to only Internet Explorer versions 4.0, 5.0, or 6.0 or later.

At this point, Kevin does not want you to modify any of the Web options, so you will leave this dialog box unchanged.

5. Click the **Cancel** button twice to close the dialog boxes.

Saving a Workbook as an XML File

Kevin received a request from the director of IT (Information Technology) for a copy of the Financial Summary worksheet (DPrpt6). Digital Product's data is currently stored in different computer systems in a variety of formats, making it difficult to share information across the company. The IT team is working on a project to combine data from these various sources, and they have asked you to save the workbook in an XML spreadsheet format.

Extensible Markup Language (XML) was developed in 1998 to facilitate data transfer between computers and systems. XML provides a method for transferring structured data between a variety of applications and computer systems. You will learn more about XML in a later tutorial, but for now you will need to create the XML file as requested by the IT department, and then close the workbook.

To save a workbook as an XML spreadsheet file:

1. Click **File** on the menu bar, and then click **Save As** to open the Save As dialog box.

2. Click the **Save as type** list arrow, click **XML Spreadsheet**, click the **Save** button, and then click the **Yes** button to acknowledge that the custom views will not be saved with the file.

3. Click the **Enable the AutoRepublish feature** option button, and then click the **OK** button. The XML spreadsheet file is created.

4. Close the workbook.

Kevin will complete the process by uploading the Web page you created to the company's Web site at a later time.

Review

Session 7.3 Quick Check

1. What is HTML?
2. Describe the two types of Web pages that you can create using Excel.
3. What does the AutoRepublish feature do when saving a workbook as a Web page?
4. How do you insert a hyperlink into a worksheet cell?
5. What is a ScreenTip?
6. How do you edit a cell's hyperlink?

Tutorial Summary

In this tutorial, you split a worksheet into panes and used Excel's auditing tools to check the workbook for errors. You saw how tracer arrows can graphically display a formula's dependent and precedent cells. When formulas contained an error, you learned how to trace the error back to its source so you could correct the error.

You learned how to attach and edit comments in worksheet cells and share a workbook with many users simultaneously. You saw how Excel resolves conflicts among users editing the same workbook by tracking and reviewing changes made by these users.

Finally, you learned how to convert the workbook into a format for publishing interactive and noninteractive pages on the Web, save workbooks in XML format, and add hyperlinks to your worksheet.

Key Terms

audit	Hypertext Markup	route
AutoRepublish	Language (HTML)	ScreenTip
comment	interactive Web page	shared workbook
dependent cell	Internet	spreadsheet component
discussion server	link	suspect formula
error indicator	local area network (LAN)	tracer arrow
error value	Message Application	tracking log
Extensible Markup	Programming	Web browser
Language (XML)	Interface (MAPI)	Web page
hyperlink	network	Web server
hypertext document	noninteractive Web page	Web site
	precedent cell	World Wide Web

Practice

Get hands-on practice of the skills you learned in the tutorial to answer additional questions about the Financial Summary workbook.

Review Assignments

Data Files needed for the Review Assignments: Project1.xls, Project3.xls, and Stkhldrs.htm

Kevin has been asked to include a projected income statement and projected cash flow statement for the next year in the financial report. He has a set of initial figures, but he'll need to discuss his projections with some of the other members of his group. He has asked you to help him use Excel's auditing and reviewing tools to create the report. Once the report is finished, Kevin needs to publish it on the company's Web site for the stockholders to view.

To complete this task:

1. Open the **Project1** workbook located in the Tutorial.07\Review folder included with your Data Files, and then save the workbook as **Project2** in the same folder.
2. Enter the current date and your name in the Documentation sheet. Switch to the Projected Cash Flow worksheet. Display the Formula Auditing toolbar.
3. The cash and cash equivalents at the beginning of the projected year (2007) should equal the cash and cash equivalents at the end of the current year (2006). Display the precedent tracer arrows for cell B5 in the Projected Cash Flow worksheet to see if this is the case. Print the tracer arrow or arrows for the cell. If necessary, correct any mistake(s) you find.

4. The net income value in cell B9 of the Projected Cash Flow worksheet shows the #REF! error value. Use tracer arrows to locate the original source of this error. Fix the source of the problem. Remove all tracer arrows and close the Formula Auditing toolbar.

5. Kevin has projected net revenues for the company at $840,000. He is not sure whether this is a reasonable figure. Attach the following comment to cell B5 of the Projected Income worksheet: "Do you think that $840,000 is a reasonable estimate for next year's revenue?" Hide the comment.

6. Save your changes to the Project2 workbook and share the workbook, allowing changes by more than one user at the same time. Close the **Project2** workbook, saving your changes.

7. Open the **Project3** workbook located in the Tutorial.07\Review folder, enter the current date and your name in the Documentation sheet, and then save the workbook as **Project4** in the same folder.

8. Review the changes made in the workbook by Anjali Mahanez, Brad Vukovich, and Sally Breen. Accept all of Brad's changes and reject the others.

9. Change the properties of the comment in cell B5 of the Projected Income worksheet, so that the comment is always visible. Move the comment below row 17.

10. Change the page setup of the Projected Income worksheet so that the comments are printed at the end of the sheet, and then print the contents of the Projected Income worksheet.

11. Remove sharing from the Project4 workbook, and then save your changes.

12. In cell B1 of the Projected Cash Flow worksheet, insert the text "Return to Annual Report Page." Format the text in a 10-point black regular Arial font. Create a hyperlink linking cell B1 to the **Stkhldrs.htm** file. Add a hyperlink ScreenTip with the text "Return to Annual Report."

13. Test the hyperlink in cell B1 to verify that it opens the Stkhldrs.htm file when the hyperlink is clicked. Close your browser window.

14. Save the workbook and then save the Projected Cash Flow worksheet as a noninteractive Web page with the name **Project**. Set the title of the page to "2007 Projections." Enable the AutoRepublish feature.

15. Open the **Project.htm** page in your Web browser. Test the hyperlink "Return to Annual Report Page" you created in Step 12.

16. Print the Web page and close your browser.

17. Save and close the workbook, and enable the AutoRepublish option when prompted.

Apply

Apply the skills you learned to create 3-D cell references and hyperlinks, insert comments, and print worksheet formulas for a university's institutional research office workbook.

Case Problem 1

Data File needed for this Case Problem: StuStat1.xls

Office of Institutional Research   You are an intern in the University of New Mesa's Office of Institutional Research. Ellen Ryan, your supervisor, has asked you to help complete the compilation of the annual student fact book. Data on each major at the institution has been entered in separate worksheets of the StuStat1 workbook.

To complete this task:

1. Open the workbook **StuStat1** located in the Tutorial.07\Cases folder included with your Data Files, and then save the workbook as **StuStat2** in the same folder.

2. Enter your name and the current date in the Documentation sheet, and then review all the worksheets in the workbook.

3. Add a new worksheet and place it in front of the Accounting worksheet. Name the sheet "Summary." Figure 7-35 previews the worksheet you'll create that displays a

count of males and females for all students in the junior and senior class. Develop the formulas to generate this table. (*Hint*: Use 3-D references to quickly summarize the individual worksheets.)

Figure 7-35

	A	B	C	D	E	F	G	H
1								
2			All Students				Majors	
3			Count			Accounting	General Business	
4		Class	Female	Male		Art	Journalism	
5		Junior	656	495		Biology	Management	
6		Senior	510	361		Chemical Engineering	Marketing	
7						Civil Engineering	Physical Education	
8						Communications	Political Science	
9						Elementary Education	Psychology	
10						English	Secondary Education	
11						Finance	Theatre	
12								

4. In the cell in which you entered the title "All Students," add the comment "Counts are based on full-time students—12 or more credits." Set the comment so it is only visible when your mouse hovers over the cell.

5. Print the formulas, not the values, used in the Summary worksheet. Before printing, expand the cells so the entire formula is displayed in its cell. The printed output should include row and column headings (Column A, B, C... and Rows 1, 2, 3...). After printing is completed, display the values.

6. You want a way to quickly jump to each worksheet from the Summary worksheet. Enter "Majors" in cell F2, and then enter the name of each worksheet in the range F3:G11. Use this list to create hyperlinks to the corresponding worksheets. For example, if the user clicks Accounting, then the Accounting sheet becomes the active sheet. (*Hint*: Use the Place in This Document option in the Insert Hyperlink dialog box.) Test the hyperlinks.

7. In cell B8 of the Summary worksheet, type the name of your institution and then insert a hyperlink from this label to your institution's Web page. Add a ScreenTip of your choosing to this hyperlink. Test the hyperlink.

8. Print only the range B2:D6 in the Summary worksheet with the comments at the end of the sheet. Save the changes you have made to the workbook.

9. Save the entire workbook as a noninteractive Web page with the filename StudentCount. Enter "Number of Upper Division Students" as the page title. Do not use the AutoRepublish feature on any of these Web pages.

10. Open the **StudentCount.htm** file in your Web browser. Test the Summary sheet tab to verify that it displays the information from the Summary worksheet. Close the Web browser.

11. Save and close the workbook.

Apply

Apply the skills you learned to merge data from several shared workbooks, create a chart, convert worksheets to publish on a Web site, and split a worksheet into panes.

Case Problem 2

Data Files needed for this Case Problem: Cutler1.xls, Erdahl.xls, Hung.xls, and Nolan.xls

Forecasting a Budget for the Town of Cutler   You work for the town of Cutler. It's time for the four-year budget forecast, and Alice Day, town treasurer, mailed a workbook to various department heads to get their budget projections. Ed Erdahl is responsible for all expenditures except capital expenditure projects. May Hung is responsible for capital expenditure projects, and Amy Nolan is responsible for forecasting revenues. Alice has received back three workbooks and needs your help in merging the workbooks. She also wants to place the budget forecasts on the town's Web site to allow for greater input from the community. Alice has asked your assistance in setting up the Web page.

To complete this task:

1. Open the **Cutler1** workbook located in the Tutorial.07\Cases folder included with your Data Files, and then save the workbook as **Cutler2** in the same folder.
2. Enter the current date and your name in the Documentation sheet, and then review all the worksheets in the workbook.
3. Merge the **Cutler2** workbook with the **Erdahl**, **Hung**, and **Nolan** workbooks, which are located in the Tutorial.07\Cases folder.
4. Turn off sharing for the workbook.
5. Freeze the column heading on the Expenditures and Revenues worksheets so the information is easier to follow as you scroll through the rows of the worksheets.
6. The town is projected to run a deficit from 2005 through 2007. Highlight this fact by adding the following comment to cell A1 of the Expenditures worksheet: "Please note that after 2004 the town of Cutler will be running a deficit of over two million dollars by 2006." Set the comment so that it is always visible.

Explore

7. Using Figure 7-36 as a guide, create a pie chart of revenue for 2007. (*Hint*: Use the Fill Effects options to format the plot area.)

Figure 7-36

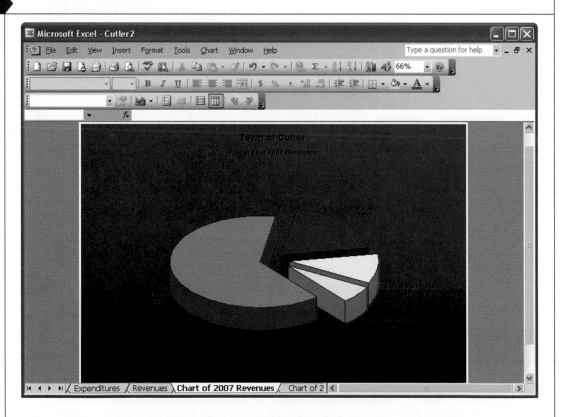

8. Save the workbook as a noninteractive Web page with the filename **Cutler** in the Tutorial.07\Cases folder. Specify "Cutler Budget 2004-2007" as the page title. Do not enable the AutoRepublish option.

9. Open the **Cutler** Web page file in your Web browser. Go to the Expenditures sheet, and hover the pointer over the upper-left corner of the Web page. Can you see the comment that you inserted into the workbook?

10. Close the Web browser and return to Excel. Print a copy of the Cutler2 workbook.

11. Split the Revenues worksheet into two panes at row 20. In the bottom pane display row 50, Total Revenue, and use the top pane to view all revenue items.

12. Save and close the workbook.

Case Problem 3

Data File needed for this Case Problem: Budget1.xls

Hardwood Furniture   Hardwood Furniture manufactures and sells furniture. Mahan Nuh is a budget analyst for the company and has been working on a master budget workbook for one of its lines of furniture. Before completing the work, Mahan became ill and has taken a leave of absence from the company. You have been asked to complete the master budget.

The Master Budget workbook consists of five worksheets. The Income Statement worksheet gets data from four supporting worksheets: Sales, Cost of Goods Sold, Selling, and Administrative. Comments that explain the formulas in each worksheet have been inserted into the five worksheets.

To complete this task:

1. Open the workbook **Budget1** located in the Tutorial.07\Cases folder included with your Data Files, and then save the workbook as **Budget2** in the same folder.

2. Enter your name and the current date in the Documentation sheet.

3. Examine each worksheet and review the comments to better understand the calculations underlying the master budget.

4. Use the Trace Error button on the Formula Auditing toolbar to find the source of the #Value! error value that appears in cell D7 of the Income Statement worksheet. Correct any mistakes that you discover.

5. Once the #Value! error values are removed, display the precedent tracer arrows for cells B10, C10, and D10 in the Income Statement worksheet. Print the Income Statement worksheet with tracer arrows. Do you see anything suspicious about the formulas? (*Hint*: Review the comments explaining the computation of net income before taxes.) Correct any errors you find. When finished, remove all tracer arrows.

6. In cell A15 of the Income Statement worksheet, enter the label "If you have questions you can reach me at" and then type your e-mail address in cell B15. Wrap the text in cell A15 so you can view all the text without increasing the width of column A. Print the worksheet.

7. Insert the comment "Assumes the company goes ahead with a planned 5% price increase" into cell B18 of the Sales worksheet. Display the comment. Print the worksheet with comments printed at the end.

8. Modify the comment in cell A10 of the Selling Expense worksheet so that the second sentence is removed. Show the comment on the page. Print the worksheet with the comment displayed on the printed sheet.

9. Save the changes you have made to the workbook, and then save the workbook as an XML spreadsheet with the name **BudgetXML** in the Tuorial.07\Cases folder. Close the workbook.

Explore

10. Start Notepad and then open the **BudgetXML** file you created in Step 9. Find and print the XML code that pertains to the Sales worksheet. Close the file and Notepad.

11. Switch to Excel and save the entire workbook as a noninteractive Web Page with the filename **MasterBudget**. Specify "Quarterly Forecast" as the page title. Do not turn on the AutoRepublish feature. Close the workbook.

12. Start your Web browser and then open the **MasterBudget** Web page file you created in Step 11. Test the boxes at the bottom of the browser to move to each page. Close your browser.

13. Save and close the workbook.

Challenge

Go beyond what you've learned in this tutorial to merge workbooks, accept and reject changes from other users, develop a table lookup, set up an interactive Web page, and save the workbook as an XML file.

Case Problem 4

Data Files needed for this Case Problem: CHome.htm, CWorld1.xls, and NewPrice.xls

Creating a Product Lookup Web Page for C-World   C-World is an online computer supply store. You're working with Paul Robinson and his assistant to set up a Web page for the modem product line. Paul has created a shared workbook that contains a list of the modems sold by the company. Paul's assistant, Roy Manon, is updating the document with a new list of prices. Paul needs your help to combine the changes made by Mary into a single workbook. Paul also wants to create a hyperlink to C-World's home page. Once the changes have been reviewed and the hyperlink created, Paul wants to publish the workbook on the company's Web site. He wants you to help him create an interactive Web page that displays the modem product line using a VLOOKUP function.

To complete this task:

1. Open the **CWorld1** workbook located in the Tutorial.07\Cases folder included with your Data Files, and then save the workbook as **CWorld2** in the same folder.

2. Enter the current date and your name in the Documentation sheet.

3. Merge the **CWorld2** workbook with the **NewPrice** workbook located in the Tutorial.07\Cases folder.

4. Display all of the changes made by Roy on a separate worksheet, and then print the History worksheet.

5. In looking over the list of price changes made by Roy, Paul notices that a mistake has been made in cell E13; the original price is correct. Review all of Roy's changes, accepting all of the changes *except* the one made to cell E13.

6. Turn off workbook sharing for the CWorld2 workbook.

7. Figure 7-37 displays the contents of a new worksheet Paul would like you to create. Paul wants to be able to enter a product ID in cell B5 and have the type, model, shipping information, and price displayed in cells C7, C8, C9, and C10, respectively. Use the VLOOKUP function to complete this task. Name the worksheet "Product Lookup."

Figure 7-37

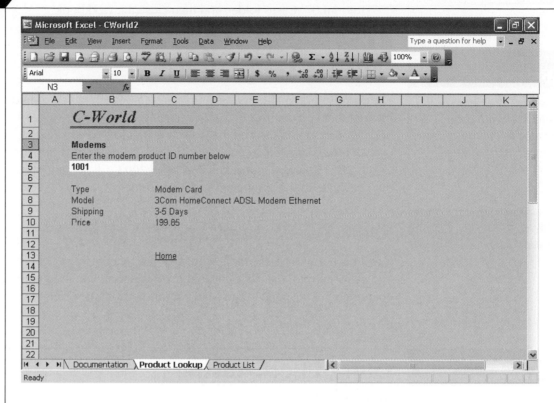

8. To test the formulas you entered in the Product Lookup worksheet, enter the product ID "1064" in cell B5. Do the correct values display in the other cells? Print the Product Lookup worksheet.

Explore

9. Clear the value in cell B5. The error value #N/A is displayed in the range C7:C10. Modify the VLOOKUP formulas so the cells in the range C7:C10 are empty instead of displaying #N/A when no product ID or an incorrect product ID is entered in cell B5. (*Hint*: Use Help to find information on the IS and ISERROR functions.) Enter the product ID "9999" in cell B5. Print the Product Lookup worksheet.

10. Create a hyperlink to C-World's home page. Enter the text "Home" into cell B13 in the Product Lookup worksheet. Create a hyperlink pointing to the CHome Web page, which is the **CHome.htm** file, and then change the ScreenTip for the cell to "Go to the C-World home page."

11. Test the hyperlink to make sure it works correctly, and then save the workbook.

Explore

12. Save the entire workbook as an interactive Web page with the filename **Modems** in the Tutorial.07\Cases folder. Specify "Modems at C-World" as the page title, and turn on the AutoRepublish feature.

Explore

13. Start your Web browser and then open the **Modems** Web Page file you created in Step 12. Test the interactive feature of the Web page by clicking cell B5 on the Product Lookup sheet in the spreadsheet component and typing "1081" for the product ID number. Which item is displayed in the table? (*Note:* You have to be running Internet Explorer version 4.0 or higher to use the spreadsheet component.)

14. Print the contents of the Web page, and then close the Web browser.

15. Save the workbook as an XML spreadsheet with the filename **CWorldXML** in the Tutorial.07\Cases folder, and then close the workbook.
16. Open the XML file in Excel, and then close it.

Internet Assignments

The purpose of the Internet Assignments is to challenge you to find information on the Internet that you can use to work effectively with this software. The actual assignments are updated and maintained on the Course Technology Web site. Log on to the Internet and use your Web browser to go to the Student Online Companion for New Perspectives Office 2003 at **www.course.com/np/office2003**. Click the Internet Assignments link, and then navigate to the assignments for this tutorial.

SAM Assessment and Training

If you have a SAM user profile, you may have access to hands-on instruction, practice, and assessment of the skills covered in this tutorial. Log in to your SAM account and go to your assignments page to see what your instructor has assigned.

Quick Check Answers

Session 7.1

1. Precedent cells are those cells used in the formula of the active cell. Dependent cells are cells that use the value of the active cell in their formulas.
2. When unrecognized text appears in a formula or function (for example, when the name of an Excel function has been misspelled), Excel displays the #NAME? error value.
3. Select the cell containing the formula, and then click the Trace Error button in the Formula Auditing toolbar.
4. Red tracer arrows indicate cells that contain error values.
5. Excel labels cells containing suspect formulas with a green triangle located in the cell's upper-left corner.

Session 7.2

1. A shared workbook is a workbook that can be edited by more than one user. Shared workbooks have the word "[Shared]" displayed in the Excel title bar alongside the name of the workbook.
2. As long as each person makes changes to different cells, Excel will automatically integrate these changes into the shared workbook and notify the users of the change. If there is a conflict, Excel will display the Resolve Conflicts dialog box to the person who last attempts to save the workbook.
3. alongside each edited cell in a pop-up comment box or listed in a separate worksheet
4. the previous 30 days

5. Routing causes the workbook to move through a collection of users listed on a routing slip. When one recipient is finished with the workbook, it is then sent to the next person listed in the routing slip. For routing to work, all recipients must be running Microsoft Outlook.

6. The two workbooks must be copies of the same shared workbook. The workbooks must have different filenames. The workbooks must either have the same password or not be password-protected at all. The Track Changes feature must be turned on for both workbooks from the time the copy is first made. The tracking history must be kept from the time the copy is first made.

Session 7.3

1. HTML stands for Hypertext Markup Language. It is a language that is used to format Web pages.

2. You can use Excel to create interactive Web pages in which you can enter and edit data. You can use Excel to create noninteractive Web pages that you can use to view the contents of a workbook.

3. When you enable the AutoRepublish feature, each time you attempt to save the workbook, Excel will prompt you to indicate whether you want to publish the new version of the Web page you created earlier.

4. Click the cell in which you want to insert the hyperlink, click Insert on the menu bar, and then click Hyperlink.

5. A ScreenTip is a pop-up label that provides information about the target of a hyperlink. A ScreenTip appears when you hover the mouse pointer over a hyperlink.

6. To edit a cell's hyperlink, right-click the cell, and then click Edit Hyperlink on the shortcut menu. Make the necessary changes to the hyperlink in the Edit Hyperlink dialog box, and then click the OK button.

Objectives

Session 8.1
- Create validation rules for data entry
- Learn to protect the contents of worksheets and workbooks

Session 8.2
- Create and use names

Session 8.3
- Learn about macro viruses and Excel's security features
- Create a macro using the macro recorder
- Edit and print a macro using the Visual Basic Editor
- Assign a macro to a keyboard shortcut and a button

Developing an Excel Application

Creating a Stock Reporter

Case

Harris & Burton

Harris & Burton is a financial planning and investment firm located in Elkhorn, Indiana. Founded by Diane Harris and Kevin Burton, the company provides financial services to a large clientele mostly located in Indiana and Kentucky.

Nigel Turner is one of the financial planners employed by Harris & Burton. Nigel wants to create an Excel workbook that reports the activity of selected stocks. The report will contain a chart displaying the high, low, opening, and closing values of a stock, as well as the volume of shares traded. He wants the ability to quickly switch between reports of a stock's performance in the last 30, 60, and 90 days. He also wants to be able to insert the latest stock values into the report. Eventually, Nigel will be sharing this workbook with other people in the company, so he wants the workbook to be easy to work with.

Although many of these tasks can be accomplished using Excel in a traditional way, Nigel realizes that some people in the company are not always comfortable using Excel. Ideally, he would like a customized interface for this report that does not rely exclusively on Excel menus and toolbars. Nigel has asked for your help in creating an Excel application that will provide the necessary stock-related information.

Student Data Files

▼**Tutorial.08**

▽ **Tutorial folder**

Stock1.xls

▽ **Review folder**

Chart1.xls

▽ **Cases folder**

HWSales1.xls
MBikes1.xls
Popcorn1.xls

Planning an Excel Application

An Excel application transforms data into information that forms the basis for decision making. Applications typically include the following:

- Reports and charts designed to aid understanding and produce insights
- A means to enter and edit data, often controlling the type of values that are allowed to be entered and where a user can enter data
- An interface to assist the user in using the system, ranging from special buttons that assist in executing specific tasks to changing the entire Excel interface with custom-designed menus, toolbars, and commands
- Clearly written instructions and documentation for the user

Nigel has an Excel application in mind for his workbook. He has recorded the last 90 days worth of information on a particular stock, and he has generated a chart and a table of statistics describing the stock's performance. He wants you to create an Excel application that allows him to more easily enter new data and to view his data in different ways. You will begin by opening Nigel's workbook so you can review its data.

To open Nigel's workbook:

1. Start Excel and open the **Stock1** workbook located in the Tutorial.08\Tutorial folder included with your Data Files.

2. Enter the *current date* and *your name* in the Documentation sheet, and then save the workbook as **Stock2** in the Tutorial.08\Tutorial folder.

3. Review the contents of the workbook, and then display the Reporter worksheet.

Aside from the Documentation sheet, there are two worksheets in the Stock2 workbook: Reporter and History Log. The Reporter worksheet displays a chart and table of statistics describing the performance of Maxwell Sports Inc., one of the stocks in Nigel's portfolio. The stock market data itself is stored in the range A1:F91 of the History Log worksheet, with the most recent values reported at the top of the table. Nigel has recorded information on the stock's daily high, low, opening, and closing values, as well as the volume of shares traded in millions.

Nigel describes the type of customized interface he wants you to create, shown in Figure 8-1. He wants to have the ability to view the stock history over the last 30, 60, or 90 days. To do this, he wants to be able to switch between reports by clicking one of three buttons located to the right of the stock history chart. As he receives the latest stock values, he wants to be able to enter those values into a range of cells at the bottom of the worksheet, and then, by clicking a button, transfer those values into the History Log sheet. Thus, clicking one of four buttons will do most of the work in this application, and there is little need for users to work with Excel's extensive system of menus and commands.

Nigel's plan for the Excel application **Figure 8-1**

click to view 30-, 60-, 90-day chart and statistics

click to insert latest stock values into the History Log and to update the chart and statistics

user enters latest stock values here

Nigel plans to share this application with other employees at the company. He's concerned that other users might unwittingly change essential parts of the workbook, perhaps erasing an important value or formula. Therefore, Nigel wants you to control what values users can enter into the workbook, and also control where they can enter those values.

You'll start work on Nigel's application by creating a series of validation checks, designed to prevent users from inserting erroneous data values.

Validating Data Entry

One way to ensure that correct data is entered into a cell or range is to use the Excel **data validation** feature, which enables you to define a set of rules that guide data entry for a specific range of cells. To implement data validation you create a **validation rule** that defines the parameters by which data is entered into a cell. You can specify the type of data (whole numbers, dates, time, or text) as well as a range of acceptable values (for instance, integers between 1 and 100). To assist the user in data entry, you can also display an input message specifying the type of data that can be entered into a cell. You can also have Excel display an error-specific message if the value entered by the user fails the validation check, preventing the erroneous value from being stored.

Specifying a Data Type and Acceptable Values

Nigel wants to assist users so that they enter the correct values in the designated range of the Reporter worksheet. He has three validation rules he wants you to add to the workbook. These are:

- The new date value in cell B23 must be later than the previous ending date value stored in cell K14.
- The new opening value in cell D23 must be equal to the previous ending value stored in cell K16.

- The new closing value in cell G23 must fall between the high and low values in cells E23 and F23.

Creating a Validation Rule

- Click Data on the menu bar, and then click Validation.
- Click the Settings tab.
- From the Allow list box, select the type of data allowed in the cell.
- Enter the validation rule using the available input boxes.
- Click the OK button.

You will define the validation rules now.

To specify data types and the ranges of acceptable values:

▶ 1. Scroll down the Reporter worksheet, and then click cell **B23**. This is the first cell for which you will enter a validation rule.

▶ 2. Click **Data** on the menu bar, and then click **Validation**. The Data Validation dialog box opens. There are three tabs: Settings, Input Message, and Error Alert. You use the Settings tab to enter the validation rules for the active cell.

Users will need to enter a date in cell B23 that is after the date of the previous stock value entered. This date, identified as the ending date, is displayed in cell K14 of the Reporter worksheet. First, you will select the type of data allowed in the cell.

▶ 3. Make sure that the Settings tab is displayed, click the **Allow** list arrow, and then click **Date**. The Data Validation dialog box expands to display the options that are specific to the date setting you have selected.

Now you will specify the criteria for the validation.

▶ 4. Click the **Data** list arrow, and then click **greater than**. Note that the dialog box changes again to reflect the criteria selected.

Now you will specify the cell that contains the date that is after, or "greater than," the date that needs to be entered in cell B23.

▶ 5. Press the **Tab** key to move to the Start date box, and then click cell **K14**. See Figure 8-2. The formula =K14 appears in the Start date box.

Figure 8-2 ▶ **Setting validation criteria**

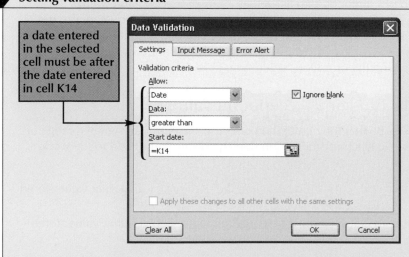

Trouble? If necessary, move the Data Validation dialog box in order to see cell K14. You may need to move the Data Validation dialog box to different positions in the workbook window as you select cells on the worksheet.

6. Click the **OK** button.

Next, you will enter the validation rule for cell D23, whose opening value must be equal to the value in cell K16 (which is the previous ending value).

7. Click cell **D23**, click **Data** on the menu bar, and then click **Validation** to open the Data Validation dialog box.

8. Click the **Allow** list arrow, and then click **Decimal**. The dialog box expands to display the available decimal-related options, which include a Minimum box and a Maximum box.

9. Click the **Data** list arrow, and then click **equal to**. The dialog box changes again because there is no need to specify minimum and maximum values. The data in this cell will be equal to one value.

10. Press the **Tab** key to move to the Value box, click cell **K16** to enter the formula =K16, and then click the **OK** button.

Finally, you will enter the validation rule for cell G23, whose closing value should lie between the values in cell F23 (the low value) and cell E23 (the high value).

11. Click cell **G23**, click **Data** on the menu bar, and then click **Validation** to open the Data Validation dialog box once again.

12. Click the **Allow** list arrow, and then click **Decimal** to display the decimal-related options.

13. Make sure **between** is selected in the Data list box, press the **Tab** key to move to the Minimum box, and then click cell **F23** to enter the formula =F23, which is the cell that contains the low, or minimum, stock value.

14. Press the **Tab** key to move to the Maximum box, click cell **E23** to enter the formula =E23 (which is the cell that contains the high, or maximum, stock value), and then click the **OK** button.

The options in the Allow list box dictate the types of values for which you can specify criteria. As you just saw, the Data Validation dialog box changes depending on the option you choose in the Allow list. Figure 8-3 provides the list of options and their descriptions.

Options in the Allow list box ◀ **Figure 8-3**

Allow	Description
Any Value	Any value can be entered into the cell.
Whole Number	The cell will accept only integers. A validation rule can further specify the range of acceptable integers.
Decimal	The cell will accept any type of numeric value. A validation rule can further specify the range of acceptable values.
List	The cell will accept only values from a list. The list can be taken from a range of cells in the worksheet, or the list of values can be entered directly into the dialog box, with the values separated by commas.
Date	The cell will accept only dates. A validation rule can further specify the range of acceptable dates.
Time	The cell will accept only times. A validation rule can further specify the range of acceptable times.
Text Length	The cell will accept only text of a specified number of characters.
Custom	The validation rule will be based on an Excel logical formula.

An important point to remember is that the validation rules that you just entered only apply during data entry. If a cell already has an erroneous value in it when you create these validation rules, Excel will not notify you of the problem.

Specifying an Input Message

One way of reducing the chance of data-entry error is to display an input message when a user clicks on the cell, before a value is entered. The **input message** can provide additional information about the type of data allowed for the cell. Input messages appear as ScreenTips next to the cell when the cell is selected. Sometimes when you build a worksheet for other users, you may decide to add an input message to a cell even if you don't validate the data in that cell.

Nigel wants you to add an input message for the volume (cell C23), high (cell E23), and low (cell F23) values even though no validation of this data occurs. In this case, the validation criteria in the Settings tab, by default, allow any value to be entered. In addition, you will create input messages for the cells Date (cell B23), Open (cell D23), and Close (cell G23).

To create input messages for the cells:

1. Click cell **B23**, click **Data** on the menu bar, and then click **Validation**. The Data Validation dialog box opens.

2. Click the **Input Message** tab.

3. Verify that the **Show input message when cell is selected** check box is selected.

4. Click in the Title text box and type **Date**, press the **Tab** key, and then type **Enter the date the stocks were traded.** in the Input message text box, as shown in Figure 8-4.

Specifying an input message for the date value

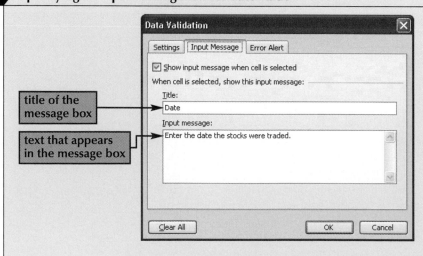

5. Click the **OK** button. The input message you created appears next to cell B23. See Figure 8-5.

Displaying the date input message | **Figure 8-5**

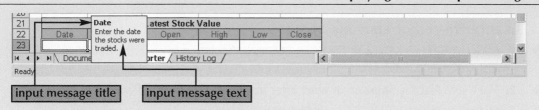

input message title   input message text

6. Press the **Tab** key to move to cell C23. Note that the input message disappears when cell B23 is no longer the active cell.

7. Click **Data** on the menu bar, click **Validation** to open the Data Validation dialog box, click in the Title text box, and then type **Volume**.

8. Press the **Tab** key to move to the Input message text box, type **Enter the volume of shares traded (in millions)**, and then click the **OK** button. The input message for cell C23 is displayed.

9. Press the **Tab** key to move to cell D23, and then enter the following input messages for the remaining cells in the range:

Cell D23: Title: **Open** Input message: **Enter the opening value of the stock.**
Cell E23: Title: **High** Input message: **Enter the highest value of the stock.**
Cell F23: Title: **Low** Input message: **Enter the lowest value of the stock.**
Cell G23: Title: **Close** Input message: **Enter the closing value of the stock.**

Trouble? If you make a mistake entering the input message, click the cell again, open the Data Validation dialog box, and then reenter the text correctly.

The input messages you've entered will make the worksheet easier to work with and will help minimize the chance of an employee entering an incorrect stock value.

Specifying an Error Alert Style and Message

Nigel would still like Excel to display an error alert if data is entered that violates any of the three validation rules you specified earlier. Excel supports three types of error alerts, labeled as Stop, Warning, and Information. The style of the error alert determines what choices the user is presented with when an invalid entry is detected. The most serious is the Stop alert, which prevents you from storing the data in the cell. Next in severity is the Warning alert, which, by default, prevents you from storing the data in the cell, unless you override the rejection and decide to continue using the data. The least severe is the Information alert, which, by default, accepts the data value entered, but allows you to cancel the data entry if you choose.

Creating an Error Alert Message | Reference Window

- Click Data on the menu bar, click Validation, and then click the Error Alert tab.
- Make sure that the Show error alert after invalid data is entered check box is checked.
- Select an alert style.
- Enter the title and text for the error alert message.
- Click the OK button.

You will create an error alert message that will display a Stop alert when a user attempts to violate any of the validation rules defined earlier.

To enter the error alert messages:

1. Click cell **B23**, click **Data** on the menu bar, click **Validation** to open the Data Validation dialog box, and then click the **Error Alert** tab.

2. Make sure that the **Show error alert after invalid data is entered** check box is checked.

3. Make sure **Stop** is displayed in the Style list box.

4. Click in the Title text box, and then type **Invalid Date**. This text will appear as the title in the alert message box.

5. Press the **Tab** key and then type **The date must be after the previous ending date shown in cell K14.** in the Error message list box, as shown in Figure 8-6.

| Figure 8-6 | Error alert message |

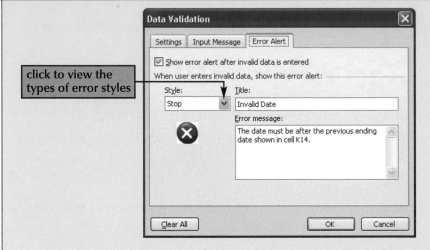

6. Click the **OK** button, and then press the **Tab** key to move to cell D23 so you can enter the error alert message for the validation rule you created for the stock's opening value.

7. Open the Data Validation dialog box, type **Invalid Open Value** in the Title text box, press the **Tab** key, type **The open value must be equal to the previous ending value shown in cell K16.** in the Error message text box, and then click the **OK** button.

Finally, you will enter the error alert message for the validation rule for the closing stock value.

8. Click cell **G23**, open the Data Validation dialog box, type **Invalid Close Value** in the Title text box, press the **Tab** key, type **The close value must lie between the high value (cell E23) and the low value (cell F23).** in the Error message list box, and then click the **OK** button.

Nigel has some new stock data to enter in the range B23:G23. You will test the validation feature you've just created by initially entering incorrect values that violate the validation rules.

To test the data validation rules:

1. Click cell **B23**. The input message that you entered appears as a ScreenTip, indicating the type of data allowed in the cell.

   You will enter a date to test the validation rule for the Date field.

2. Type **5/17/2006** and then press the **Tab** key. The Invalid Date message box opens, informing you that the date you entered must be after the date shown in cell K14 (in this case, that date is 5/17/2006).

3. Click the **Retry** button, type **5/18/2006** in cell B23, and then press the **Tab** key. Excel allows the new data to be stored in the cell. Notice the input message for volume is displayed.

   You will now enter the value for the volume.

4. Type **0.55** in cell C23, and then press the **Tab** key. The value is accepted because there is no validation criteria assigned to this cell.

   Next, you will enter the opening value.

5. Type **38.5** in cell D23, and then press the **Tab** key. The Invalid Open Value message box opens, indicating that the opening value must be equal to the value in cell K16 (the ending value from the previous day).

6. Click the **Retry** button, type **38**, and then press the **Tab** key. This time, the value you entered meets the criteria.

7. Type **39.5** in cell E23, and then press the **Tab** key. The data is accepted without a validation check because no validation criteria have been specified for this cell.

   Next, you will enter the low values.

8. Type **36** in cell F23, and then press the **Tab** key. The data is accepted because the value you entered meets the criteria specified for this cell.

   Finally, you will enter the closing value.

9. Type **40** in cell G23, and then press the **Tab** key. The Invalid Close Value message box appears, indicating that the closing value is not between the stock's high and low values for that day (the high is 39.50 and the low is 36).

10. Click the **Retry** button, type **39**, and then press the **Tab** key. Excel accepts the new stock data.

Circling Invalid Data

To find errors in values you already entered in a worksheeet, you can use the Circle Invalid Data button on the Formula Auditing toolbar. Clicking this button finds and circles cells that are outside the limits of the validation criteria. When you fix an error, the circle around the cell is removed.

To display circles around invalid data, you must follow these steps:

1. Click the Circle Invalid Data button on the Auditing toolbar. Circles appear around cells that currently contain invalid data.

2. To remove the circle from a single cell, enter valid data in the cell.

3. To hide all circles, click the Clear Validation Circles button on the Formula Auditing toolbar.

Nigel can see how validation rules will reduce the probability of incorrect data being entered. Another way to reduce data-entry "errors" is limiting access to certain parts of the workbook.

Protecting a Worksheet and Workbook

When you **protect** a workbook, you control the ability users have to make changes to the file. For example, you can prevent users from changing formulas in a worksheet, or you can keep users from deleting worksheets or inserting new ones. You can even keep users from viewing the formulas used in the workbook.

Nigel wants to protect the contents of the Reporter and History Log worksheets, granting user access to the range where new stock prices are entered (B23:G23), while preventing users from editing the contents of any other cells on the Reporter worksheet. How can he protect some cells in the worksheet, but not others?

Locking and Unlocking Cells

Every cell in a workbook has a **locked property** that determines whether or not changes can be made to that cell. The locked property has no impact as long as the worksheet is unprotected; however, once you protect a worksheet, the locked property is enabled and controls whether or not the cell can be edited. You leave cells unlocked by turning the locked property off. By default, the locked property is turned on for each cell, and worksheet protection is turned off.

If you don't "unlock" cells in a worksheet *before* protecting the worksheet, then all the cells in the worksheet will be locked, and you won't be able to make changes in the worksheet. There will be, however, situations where you will want to protect the worksheet, but not protect every cell in it. For example, you might want to protect the formulas and formatting so they can't be changed, but you want to leave other cells unprotected so data can be entered in them.

To protect some—but not all—cells in a worksheet, you implement protection by following a two-step process. First, you select the cells in which data can be entered and then you turn off their locked property. Once you have "unlocked" the selected cells, you activate the locked property for the remaining cells by protecting the sheet. Figure 8-7 describes the relationship between the locked property and the Protect Sheet command.

Figure 8-7   ▶   **Effect of the Protect Sheet command on the locked property of a cell**

Protect Sheet	Locked Property ON	Locked Property OFF
Activated	Cell is protected; no data can be entered	Cell is not protected; data can be entered
Not activated	Cell is not protected; data can be entered	Cell is not protected; data can be entered

In the Reporter worksheet, you want to enter data in the range B23:G23 while preventing data from being entered in any other cell in the worksheet. You must, then, unlock the cells in the range B23:G23 before you begin to enter the data.

To unlock the cells:

▶ 1. Select the range **B23:G23** in the Reporter worksheet. This is the range of values that you need to unlock before you protect the worksheet.

▶ 2. Click **Format** on the menu bar, and then click **Cells**. The Format Cells dialog box opens.

▶ 3. Click the **Protection** tab, and then deselect the **Locked** check box, as shown in Figure 8-8.

Unlocking the selected cells ◄ **Figure 8-8**

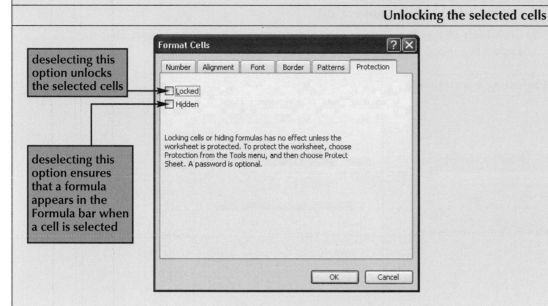

deselecting this option unlocks the selected cells

deselecting this option ensures that a formula appears in the Formula bar when a cell is selected

▶ **4.** Click the **OK** button.

With the Locked check box deselected, the cells are no longer locked, and you can now proceed to protect the worksheet.

Protecting a Worksheet

As part of the process of protecting a worksheet, you specify which actions are still available to users once the sheet is protected. For example, you can allow users to insert new rows or columns into the sheet or to delete rows and columns. You can limit the user to selecting only unlocked cells or allow the user to select any cell in the sheet. The choices you make will be active as long as the worksheet is protected.

A protected sheet can always be unprotected, but you can also require users to enter a password before the protection is removed. Unless you are working on confidential material, it's probably best to not specify a password.

Protecting a Worksheet   Reference Window

- Unlock the cell or range of cells that you don't want to protect. Click Format on the menu bar, click Cells, click the Protection tab, and then deselect the Locked check box.
- Click Tools on the menu bar, point to Protection, and then click Protect Sheet.
- Enter a password (optional).
- Select all of the actions that you will allow users to do even if the sheet is protected.
- Click the OK button.

(*Note of caution*: Be sure to keep the password in a safe place, because if you forget the password, there will be no way of removing the worksheet protection. A common cause for password frustration is not realizing that passwords are case sensitive.)

Nigel wants to protect the Reporter and History Log worksheets, but he doesn't want a password specified. You will enable worksheet protection that will allow users to select any cell in those sheets, but only the unlocked cells will be available for data entry.

To enable worksheet protection:

1. Click **Tools** on the menu bar, point to **Protection**, and then click **Protect Sheet**. The Protect Sheet dialog box opens, as shown in Figure 8-9.

Figure 8-9   **Protecting a worksheet**

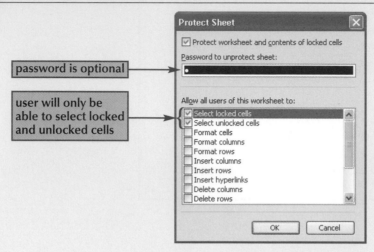

You will leave the Password text box blank. Below the Password text box is a list of actions that you can allow users to perform even if the sheet is protected. By default, users are only allowed to select locked and unlocked cells. This allows users to select all cells in the worksheet, but to enter or edit values only in unlocked cells. This is all that Nigel wants his users to be able to do; therefore, you will close the dialog box without making any changes.

2. Click the **OK** button. The Protect Sheet dialog box closes.

   Nigel wants to see what would happen if someone tried to edit one of the cells in the Reporter sheet. You will try changing the ending value in cell K16 to 40.

3. Click cell **K16** and then try to type **40**. As soon as you press any key on the keyboard, Excel displays a message box, indicating that the cell is protected and cannot be modified.

4. Click the **OK** button to close the message box.

   You have already provided users access to the range B23:G23; therefore, the range is not protected, so you can change the high price in cell E23.

5. Click cell **E23**, type **40**, and then press the **Tab** key. The change is allowed because editing is allowed in cells B23:G23. A user can enter and edit values in these cells. Although users can select any cell in the worksheet, they cannot make an entry in any other cell.

   Now you will protect all cells in the History Log worksheet.

6. Switch to the History Log worksheet.

7. Click **Tools** on the menu bar, point to **Protection**, click **Protect Sheet** to open the Protect Sheet dialog box, and then click the **OK** button to accept the default set of user actions.

   You will test to see what would happen if someone tried to edit one of the cells in the History Log sheet.

8. Click cell **A1** and press any letter on your keyboard. Excel displays a message box, indicating that the cell is protected and cannot be modified. All the cells in this worksheet are protected because no cells have been *unlocked*.

9. Click the **OK** button to close the dialog box.

Protecting a Workbook

The contents of the two sheets, with the exception of the range B23:G23, can't be changed, but Nigel wonders whether the protection extends to the sheets themselves. Can someone rename or even delete a protected worksheet? The answer is "yes"; worksheet protection only applies to the contents of the sheet, not to the sheet itself. To keep the worksheets themselves from being modified, you will have to protect the workbook.

You can protect the structure and the windows of the workbook. Protecting the structure prohibits users from renaming, deleting, hiding, or inserting worksheets. Protecting the windows prohibits users from moving, resizing, closing, or hiding parts of the Excel window. The default is to protect only the structure of the workbook, not the windows used to display it.

Protecting a Workbook

- Click Tools on the menu bar, point to Protection, and then click Protect Workbook.
- Enter a password (optional).
- Click the check boxes to indicate whether you want to protect the workbook's structure, windows, or both.
- Click the OK button.

Nigel doesn't want users to be able to change the structure of the workbook, so you will set protection for the workbook structure, but not the window.

To enable workbook protection:

▶ **1.** Click **Tools** on the menu bar, point to **Protection**, and then click **Protect Workbook**. The Protect Workbook dialog box opens, as shown in Figure 8-10.

Protecting a workbook   **Figure 8-10**

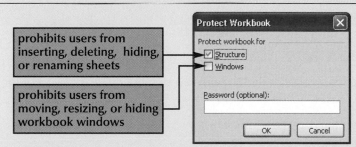

prohibits users from inserting, deleting, hiding, or renaming sheets

prohibits users from moving, resizing, or hiding workbook windows

▶ **2.** Make sure the **Structure** check box is selected, and then click the **OK** button to protect the workbook, without specifying a password.

▶ **3.** Right-click the **History Log** tab to display a shortcut menu. Note that the Insert, Delete, Rename, Move or Copy, and Tab Color commands are all grayed out, indicating that the options that modify the worksheets are no longer available.

▶ **4.** Press the **Esc** key to close the shortcut menu.

Unprotecting a Worksheet

Nigel is pleased with the different levels of protection that can be applied to the worksheet. At this point, you still have a lot of editing to do, so you'll turn off worksheet protection for now. Later on, when you've completed your modifications, you'll turn worksheet protection back on.

To disable worksheet protection:

▶ 1. Click **Tools** on the menu bar, point to **Protection**, and then click **Unprotect Sheet**. Protection is removed from the History Log worksheet.

▶ 2. Switch to the Reporter worksheet, click **Tools** on the menu bar, point to **Protection**, and then click **Unprotect Sheet** to remove protection from this worksheet.

You've completed your work to protect Nigel's application from errors in data entry and edits, so you will save your work.

▶ 3. Save your changes to the workbook.

The two worksheets in the Stock2 workbook are now unprotected. You do not have to unprotect the workbook, since Nigel does not foresee a need to insert, delete, or rename the sheets at this time.

In the next session, you'll start working on the main feature of the application—the ability to switch between a 30-, 60-, and 90-day stock report.

Review

Session 8.1 Quick Check

1. Name two features of an Excel application.
2. How do you turn on data validation for a specified cell?
3. How do you specify an input message for a cell?
4. Describe the three types of error alert messages that Excel can display when a user violates a validation rule.
5. What is a locked cell? Under what condition is the locked property enabled?
6. What is the difference between worksheet protection and workbook protection?
7. Can you rename a protected worksheet? Explain why or why not.

Session 8.2

Naming Cells and Ranges

In Nigel's report, the following statistics are displayed in the range K13:K19 of the Reporter worksheet.

- The starting and ending date of the stock history
- The starting and ending values of the stock
- The actual change and percent change between the starting and ending values
- The average volume over the course of the stock history

These values are calculated from the data stored in the History Log worksheet. The first 31 rows of the History Log sheet display the previous 30 days of activity, the first 61 rows cover the 60-day values, and the entire 91 rows record the values from the previous 90 days. Figure 8-11 lists the formulas used to calculate the statistics of the 90-day report.

Names for the Stock2 worksheet ◄ **Figure 8-11**

Name	Initial Definition	Name	Initial Definition
Date	'History Log'!A2:A91	Low	'History Log'!E2:E91
Volume	'History Log'!B2:B91	Close	'History Log'!F2:F91
Open	'History Log'!C2:C91	Starting_Date	'History Log'!A91
High	'History Log'!D2:D91	Starting_Value	'History Log'!C91

The chart on the Reporter worksheet is also based on the values stored in the History Log worksheet. One way of switching between the 30-, 60-, and 90-day reports would be to change the cell reference in each formula in the worksheet along with the chart's data source. Another approach is to use names assigned to a cell or a range.

Creating a Name

So far, in Excel, you have always referred to cells by their cell references, but you can also assign a descriptive name to represent a cell or range of cells. A **name** is a word or string of characters associated with a cell or range of cells. For example, if the range A1:A100 contains salary data for 100 employees, you can create the name "Salary" that refers to the range containing the salary data. The name, Salary, can then be used in place of the range reference (A1:A100). To calculate the average salary, you can use the formula =AVERAGE(A1:A100) or =AVERAGE(Salary). A name can also be assigned to a single cell. For example, if cell B2 contains the current sales tax rate, you can create the name "TaxRate" to refer to the cell containing the sales tax rate.

When you assign a name to a cell or range, the name must begin with a letter or the underscore character (_). The remaining characters in the name can be letters and numbers. You can include periods and underscore characters, but no other symbols or spaces. For example, names such as Net_Income or NetIncome are valid, but Net Income and Net-Income are not. Names can be up to 255 characters, although short, meaningful names of five to 15 characters are more practical. Excel is not case sensitive in regard to a named cell or range. Note that if you name one range "Salary" and later another "SALARY" the second name will overwrite the first.

There are several advantages to using names instead of cell references. A name is more descriptive than a cell reference, making it easier for you to identify the cell's content or use when creating or viewing formulas. Also, if you change the definition of the name, pointing it to a different range of cells, the value of any formula using that name will be updated automatically to reflect the new definition. The data source of any chart that uses that name will be similarly updated. Using names makes creating and defining a macro easier as well.

It is this feature of named ranges in which Nigel is interested. He proposes that you replace the cell references in several formulas with named ranges. Then, to switch between the 30-, 60-, and 90-day report, you only have to edit the definitions of the names rather than edit each formula. Figure 8-12 lists the names you'll create for Nigel, along with their initial definitions.

Figure 8-12 | **Formulas used in the reporter worksheet**

Report Value	Cell	90-day Report Formulas
Starting Date	K13	='History Log'!A9
Ending Date	K14	='History Log'!A2
Starting Value	K15	='History Log'!C91
Ending Value	K16	='History Log'!F2
Change	K17	=K16-K15
% Change	K18	=K17/K15
Average Volume (mil)	K19	=AVERAGE('History Log'!B2:B91)

Reference Window | **Creating a Name for a Cell or Range**

To create a name for cell or range:
- Select the cell or range to which you want to assign a name.
- Type the name into the Name box on the Formula bar.

or
- Click Insert on the menu bar, point to Name, click Define, enter the name of the range in the Names in workbook text box, click the Add button, and then click the OK button.

To create names for ranges in an Excel list:
- Click Insert on the menu bar, point to Name, and then click Create.
- Specify whether to create the ranges based on the first row, last row, first column, or last column in the list.
- Click the OK button.

Excel provides several ways of creating and defining names. The easiest way is to use the Name box located at the left end of the Formula bar. Try using the Name box now to create the Starting_Date name. The Starting_Date name will point to the first, or oldest, date value in the report. For the 90-day report, this is the date in cell A91 of the History Log worksheet.

To name a cell using the Name box:

1. If you took a break after the last session, make sure Excel is running and the Stock2 workbook is open. Switch to the History Log worksheet, if necessary.

2. Press the **Ctrl + ↓** keys to move to cell A91 in the History Log worksheet. The starting date for the 90-day report is 1/13/2006.

   You will assign a name to cell A91, which is the cell that contains the starting date for the 90-day report.

3. Click the Name box at the far left of the Formula bar. The cell reference A91 is automatically selected.

4. Type **Starting_Date** and then press the **Enter** key. See Figure 8-13. The name, Starting_Date, appears in the Name box instead of the cell reference A91.

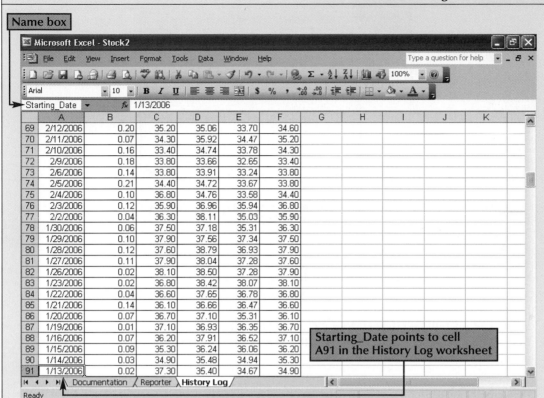

Name box

Starting_Date points to cell
A91 in the History Log worksheet

Trouble? If the text "Starting_Date" appears in cell A91, you probably didn't click the Name box before typing the name. Click the Undo button 🔄 on the Standard toolbar, and then repeat Steps 3 and 4.

The Name box, as the title implies, displays all of the names in a workbook. If you want to jump to the location of a name, you can select the name from the Name box, and the cell(s) referenced by the name will be automatically selected. A second way to create names is to use the Define Name dialog box. You will use the Define Name dialog box now to create the Starting_Value name. The Starting_Value name will point to the first, or oldest, stock value in the History Log worksheet. For the 90-day report, that value is stored in cell C91.

To name a cell using the Define Name dialog box:

1. Click cell **C91**. The cell reference C91 appears in the Name box.

2. Click **Insert** on the menu bar, point to **Name**, and then click **Define**. The Define Name dialog box opens, with a list of the names already defined in the workbook. The cell reference of the active cell appears in the Refers to box.

   You will create a name for the last value in the Open column, which is also the oldest stock value in the History Log worksheet.

3. Type **Starting_Value** in the Names in workbook text box. See Figure 8-14. Note that the Refers to box displays the complete cell reference, including the sheet name.

Figure 8-14   Creating a name with the Define Name dialog box

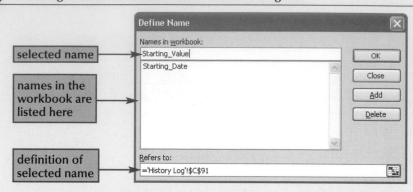

selected name

names in the workbook are listed here

definition of selected name

4. Click the **Add** button to add this name to the list, and then click the **OK** button to close the dialog box.

If your data is organized in a tabular format, you can quickly create names for each column or row in the table by using the Create Names dialog box. Excel will derive the names based on the table's row or column labels. Any blanks or parentheses in the row or column labels will be changed to underscore characters (_) in the names.

You will create names now for all of the stock values in the History Log worksheet.

To create names based on the labels in a row or column:

1. Select the range **A1:F91**. The selection includes all the column headings as well as the dates and data.

2. Click **Insert** on the menu bar, point to **Name**, and then click **Create**. The Create Names dialog box opens. From this dialog box, you can create names based on the labels entered into the top or bottom row of the list, or the left or right column of the list. By default, Excel will create names based on the top row and left column labels.

3. Deselect the **Left column** check box. See Figure 8-15. Only the Top row option is selected.

Figure 8-15   Creating names based on the list

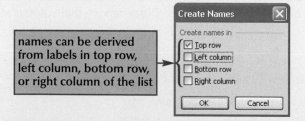

names can be derived from labels in top row, left column, bottom row, or right column of the list

4. Click the **OK** button. Excel creates names from the labels in the first row of the list.

To see the names and their definitions, you will reopen the Define Name dialog box.

5. Click **Insert** on the menu bar, point to **Name**, and then click **Define**. There are now six additional names in the workbook. Excel has derived these names based on the labels in row 1 of the History Log worksheet.

To see how Excel has defined each of these new names, you will click the name from the list.

6. Click **Close** in the list of names. The Close name points to all of the closing values of the stock contained in the range F2:F91 of the History Log worksheet. See Figure 8-16. Note that the definition of the Close name does not include the label in cell F1 because this cell was only used to derive the name.

Names in the Stock2 workbook | Figure 8-16

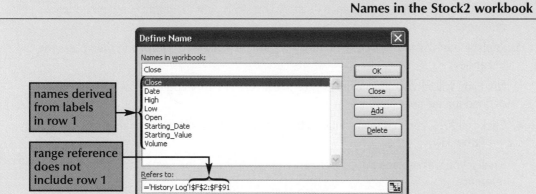

names derived from labels in row 1

range reference does not include row 1

7. Click the **OK** button to close the dialog box.

Now that you've created all of the names you need for the workbook, your next step will be to replace the cell references in the workbook with their corresponding names.

Replacing Cell References with Names

Once you have created and defined the names, you can use them in place of the cell references contained in the formulas and functions in a worksheet or workbook. You can also replace cell references used in the data series in a chart. Note that you can also replace all cell references with names by clicking Insert on the menu bar, pointing to Name, and then clicking Apply. The limitation to this approach is that the formulas must be located on the same worksheet as the cells referenced by the name. In the case of the stock report, the names refer to cells on the History Log worksheet, whereas the formulas are all located on the Reporter sheet, so you cannot use this approach.

Replacing a Cell Reference with a Name | Reference Window

- In a worksheet formula, replace the text for the cell reference with the text for the name.
or
- If the cell reference and name definition both lie in the same worksheet, click Insert on the menu bar, point to Name, and then click Apply.
- Select the names you want to apply from the Apply names list box, and then click the OK button.
or
- For cell references in charts, preface the name with the name of the workbook, separated by an exclamation point (!).

There are two locations in the workbook in which you'll need to replace the cell reference with the name: in the statistics section of the Reporter worksheet and in the data source for the embedded stock history chart.

To replace cell references with names in formulas in the Reporter worksheet:

1. Switch to the Reporter worksheet.

2. Click cell **K13**. The current formula in this cell is ='History Log'!A91.

   You will replace the cell reference ('History Log'!A91) with the name you defined for the cell reference.

3. Replace the existing formula with the new formula **=Starting_Date**, and then press the **Enter** key.

   Next you will replace the cell reference in cell K15 ('History Log'!C91) with the name you defined for the cell reference.

4. Click cell **K15**, replace the formula with the new formula **=Starting_Value**, and then press the **Enter** key.

   Finally, you will replace the cell reference in cell K19 with the name you defined for the cell reference.

5. Click cell **K19**, replace the formula with the new formula **=AVERAGE(Volume)**, and then press the **Enter** key.

Now you'll replace the cell references in the embedded chart with names. The syntax is slightly different in a chart. In the worksheet, you can simply type in the name. However, in an embedded chart, a name *must* always be prefaced by the name of the workbook. For example, to reference the closing stock values in a chart, you cannot use =*Close*. Instead, you must use =*Stock2.xls!Close*.

The stock history chart displays the opening, closing, high, and low daily values of the stock. You need to replace these cell references, as well as the cell reference for the date, with the names you created.

To insert names in the chart's data series:

1. Click the embedded chart on the Reporter worksheet, click **Chart** on the menu bar, and then click **Source Data**. The Source Data dialog box opens.

2. Click the **Series** tab to display the list of data series in the chart. Note that all the cell references point to the History Log worksheet.

3. Make sure **Volume** is selected in the Series list box.

   First, you'll replace the cell reference to the date values with the Date name. In this chart, the date values are displayed on the chart's two x-axes.

4. Click the Category (X) axis labels box, and then replace the cell reference with the name reference **=Stock2.xls!Date**. Note that you have included the workbook name. When you click in the Category (X) axis labels box, Excel switches to display the History Log worksheet. Also note that you may find it easier to replace the cell reference with the name reference by selecting the entire cell reference, pressing the Delete key, and then typing the name in the box.

5. Press the **Tab** key to move to the Second category (X) axis labels box and to automatically select its contents, and then replace the cell reference with the name reference **=Stock2.xls!Date**. The date values for the chart data source now use the Date name you specified.

   Now you'll replace the cell references for each of the five data series in the chart. The value for each series corresponds with the values from the History Log worksheet.

6. With Volume still selected in the Series list box, click in the Values box, select its contents, and then replace the cell reference with the name reference **=Stock2.xls!Volume**. Figure 8-17 shows the revised Source Data dialog box. You don't have to change the reference in the Name box, because the cell reference points to the label contained in cell B1 of the History Log worksheet.

Using names in a chart   **Figure 8-17**

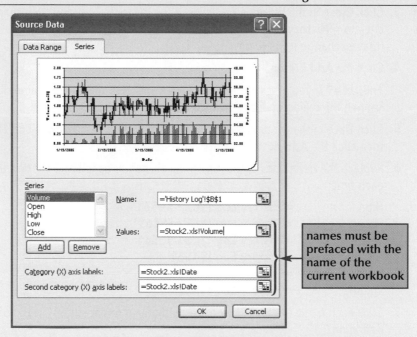

7. Click **Open** in the Series list box, and then replace the cell reference in the Values box with **=Stock2.xls!Open**.

You will replace the remaining cell references for the High, Low, and Close data series with their name references.

8. Change the Values reference for the **High** data series to **=Stock2.xls!High**. Change the Values reference for the **Low** data series to **=Stock2.xls!Low**, and change the Values reference for the **Close** data series to **=Stock2.xls!Close**.

Trouble? If you inadvertently close the Source Data dialog box by pressing the Enter key after typing a name reference, just reopen the dialog box. The information you already entered is retained.

9. Click the **OK** button.

Changing a Name Definition

With all of the names now in place, you're ready to test the names. Currently the report represents a 90-day period. Note that the chart's x-axis displays a 90-day period. Nigel proposes that you switch to a 60-day report. Rather than editing the formulas and the chart, you can switch the report by changing the definitions of the eight names so that they point to the last 60 days worth of stock market data (contained in the values up to row 61 in the History Log worksheet), rather than to the last 90 days.

To edit the name definitions:

▶ 1. Click any cell in the Reporter worksheet to deselect the chart.

▶ 2. Click **Insert** on the menu bar, point to **Name**, and then click **Define**. The Define Name dialog box opens.

First, you will change the cell reference for the Close name so the last cell in the range points to cell F61.

▶ 3. Click **Close** in the list of names, click in the Refers to box, and then change the cell reference to **='History Log'!$F$2:$F$61**. Note that you need only change the number 9 to a 6 (that is, change from 90 days to 60 days).

▶ 4. Click the **Add** button.

Trouble? If you pressed the Enter key by mistake, the Define Name dialog box closed. Reopen the dialog box, and then continue with Step 5.

▶ 5. Click **Date** in the list of names, change its definition to **='History Log'!$A$2:$A$61**, and then click the **Add** button.

▶ 6. Replace the definitions of the remaining six names as follows, clicking the **Add** button each time:

High	='History Log'!$D$2:$D$61
Low	='History Log'!$E$2:$E$61
Open	='History Log'!$C$2:$C$61
Starting_Date	='History Log'!$A$61
Starting_Value	='History Log'!$C$61
Volume	='History Log'!$B$2:$B$61

▶ 7. Click each name in the list box to verify that you replaced "91" with "61" in each range definition.

Trouble? If you make a mistake when changing a definition, do not click the Add button. Instead, click the name again, type the new definition, and then click the Add button.

▶ 8. Click the **OK** button to close the Define Name dialog box. Notice the chart's x-axis begins at 2/24/2006 instead of 1/13/2006.

▶ 9. Click cell **I12**, change the text to **60-day Statistics**, and then press the **Enter** key. The Reporter worksheet now displays the 60-day statistics and chart. See Figure 8-18.

| Figure 8-18 | 60-day report |

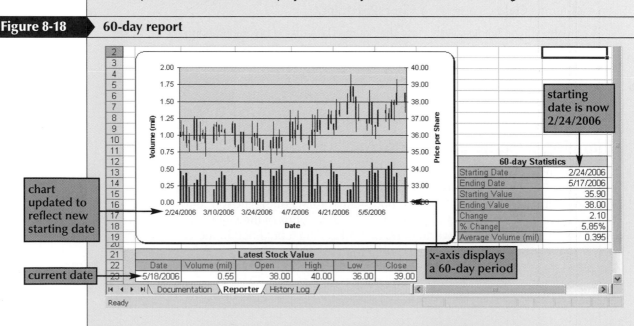

chart updated to reflect new starting date

starting date is now 2/24/2006

x-axis displays a 60-day period

current date

You are done with the Stock2 workbook for now.

▶ **10.** Save your changes to the workbook.

Editing the names has simplified the process of switching to a 60-day report, because you only have to work with a single dialog box, rather than several formulas and an embedded chart. However, Nigel wonders whether that much has been gained, since there is still a lot of typing involved in switching all of the name definitions. He wants this application to be fast and easy to use, and changing the name definitions will be a cumbersome process for some users, as well as prone to errors.

But you're not finished working with this Excel application, and in the next session, you'll learn how to save all of the keystrokes used in changing the name definitions, and then you'll learn how to replay those keystrokes with a single keystroke or click of a button.

Session 8.2 Quick Check

Review

1. What is a named cell or range? Give two advantages of using names in your workbooks.
2. Describe three ways of creating a name.
3. Which of the following is a valid name(s)?
   a. Annual_Total
   b. 3rdQtr
   c. Annual total
4. To quickly go to the cell referenced by a name, you can select the name from the

   _____ .

5. In the Report.xls workbook, the Sales name refers to a list of sales figures stored in the range B2:B100. Currently the total sales figures are calculated with the formula =SUM(B2:B100). What would a formula using the name look like?
6. The Report.xls workbook also contains a chart of sales data. What would a data source that uses the Sales name look like?

Session 8.3

Working with Macros

At the end of the last session, you were able to present Nigel with a method of switching between the 30-, 60-, and 90-day reports by modifying the definitions of several named cells and ranges, rather than editing formulas and charts. Nigel saw the value of using named cells and ranges, but was concerned about the amount of retyping that users would be required to do. Nigel would like some way of recording those actions so that users can rerun the steps without having to do all of the retyping. If you perform a task repeatedly in Excel, you can automate the task with a macro. A **macro** is a series of commands that are stored and can be run whenever you need to perform the task. For example, a macro can be created to print a worksheet, automatically insert a set of dates and values, or, in Nigel's case, automatically change the definitions of a collection of named cells and ranges. Macros carry out repetitive tasks more quickly than you can, and once the macro has been created, you don't have to worry about mistakes that may occur from simple retyping errors.

Protecting Yourself Against Macro Viruses

In the last few years, many viruses have been attached as macros to documents created in Office programs, such as Excel. Unsuspecting users open these infected workbooks, and Excel automatically runs the attached virus-infected macro. For this reason, one must use caution when opening a workbook that has a macro attached to it. You should make sure that the workbook comes from a trusted source and that the macro was inserted by a colleague or friend.

Before you can start the process of creating macros for Nigel's application, you have to define how Excel will treat the macros it encounters in open workbooks. Excel provides two safeguards against macro viruses: digital certificates and security levels.

Working with Digital Certificates

A **digital certificate** is a file attachment that vouches for the authenticity of a macro. You can obtain digital certificates from a commercial certification authority such as VeriSign Inc., or in some cases, from your system administrator. Each certificate should contain a **digital signature**, which confirms that the macro or document created by the signer has not been altered since the digital certificate was created. Your operating system stores a list of known and trusted digital certificates and signatures, so you can always be assured that the files you receive come from legitimate sources.

Macros should be signed and certified only after the file has been tested and is ready for distribution to other users, because whenever you modify a signed file, the digital signature is removed. Excel will treat a digital certificate lacking a digital signature as a possible macro virus. The combination of a valid digital certificate and signature ensures that the macro has been created by you and has not been altered by anyone else.

Setting the Security Level

You control how Excel handles macros by setting Excel's **security level**. Excel supports four levels of security: very high, high, medium, and low.

A very high security level allows only macros installed in "trusted" locations to be run. A high security level causes Excel to disable all macros either lacking a digital signature or containing an invalid digital signature. If the macro contains a valid signature from an unknown author, the user will be prompted as to whether or not to enable the macro. If the macro contains a valid signature from a known and trusted source, Excel will open the workbook and automatically enable the macro.

At a medium security level, Excel prompts the user as to whether or not to enable macros that lack a digital signature. This security level setting is not recommended because there is no protection against computer viruses masquerading as macros. Certificates with invalid signatures are still automatically disabled. Macros containing a valid signature are automatically enabled.

At a low security level, all macros are automatically enabled regardless of the status of the digital signature. You can set security using the Security dialog box that you open from the Tools Macro submenu. (You can also use the Options dialog box that you open from the Tools menu to set security for Excel.)

Reference Window | **Setting the Security Level in Excel**

- Click Tools on the menu bar, point to Macro, and then click Security.
- Click the Security Level tab.
- Select the option button for the level of security you want to set.
- Click the OK button.

Nigel does not have access to a digital certificate, so he can't set Excel's security level to high. He does not want to set Excel's security level to low because he still wants some protection against macro viruses. Nigel suggests that you set the security level to medium, which will still allow him to open files containing macros, but may warn him of possible macro viruses.

To set Excel's security level:

▶ **1.** If you took a break after the last session, make sure Excel is running. Note that you do not have to open a workbook. The security level works in conjunction with the Excel program itself.

▶ **2.** Click **Tools** on the menu bar, point to **Macro**, and then click **Security**. The Security dialog box opens.

▶ **3.** If necessary, click the **Security Level** tab.

▶ **4.** Click the **Medium** option button, as shown in Figure 8-19, if necessary.

Setting the security level in Excel ◀ **Figure 8-19**

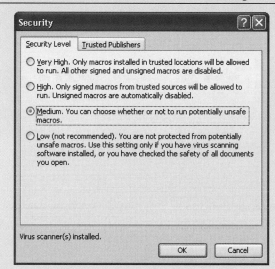

▶ **5.** Click the **OK** button. Security for the Excel application has been set to medium. The next time you open a file that contains a macro lacking a digital signature Excel will prompt you to disable or enable the macro.

If the security level is set to high when you attempt to open a workbook containing macros, you will get a message that macros are disabled. In order to open the workbook "enabled" to run macros, you first have to change the security level to medium and save the workbook. When you reopen the workbook, you will immediately see a message that indicates the file you are about to open contains macros. If you developed the workbook yourself or trust the person who sent you the workbook, click the Enable Macros button so you can run the macros in the workbook.

Now that you've set Excel's security level, you are ready to begin creating the macros that Nigel has requested.

Recording a Macro

You can create an Excel macro in one of two ways: You can use the macro recorder to record your keystrokes and mouse actions as you perform them, or you can write your own macros by entering a series of commands in the **Visual Basic for Applications (VBA)** programming language.

For new users, it's easiest to create a macro using the macro recorder. However, the recorder is limited to those actions you can perform from the keyboard or the Excel menus; thus, for more sophisticated applications, writing the code directly into the application is a better choice.

For Nigel's application, the tasks you need to perform can all be done from the keyboard and the Excel menus. There are four macros you need to create: three that will be used to switch between the 30-, 60-, and 90-day reports, and a fourth that will be used to enter new data into the History Log worksheet.

You'll start by recording the macro that displays the 30-day report. As with most complex projects, you need to plan your macro. Decide what you want to accomplish and the best way to go about it. If possible, you should practice the keystrokes or mouse actions before you actually record the macro. This may seem like extra work, but it reduces the chance of error when you actually record the macro.

Reference Window

Recording a Macro

- Click Tools on the menu bar, point to Macro, and then click Record New Macro.
- Enter a name for the macro, and specify the location in which you want to store the macro.
- Specify a shortcut key (optional).
- Enter a description of the macro (optional).
- Click the OK button to start the macro recorder.
- Perform the tasks you want to automate.
- Click the Stop Recording button on the Stop Recording toolbar (or click Tools, point to Macro, and then click Stop Recording).

After discussing the macro with Nigel, you outline the actions you need to perform the 30-day report macro. These are:

1. Unprotect the Reporter worksheet.
2. Change the definition of each name to point to the previous 30 days of stock market data.
3. Change the title in cell I12 to "30-day Statistics."
4. Set the protection for the Reporter worksheet again.

Note that the first and last actions involve turning the worksheet protection off and on. Recall that Nigel wants the workbook to be protected to keep other users from making changes to it. Currently the worksheets are not protected because in the last session you were still editing their contents, so you'll need to enable worksheet protection before recording the macro. There are other factors to consider when creating a macro.

Each macro must have a unique name. A macro name must begin with a letter and can be up to 255 characters, including letters, numbers, and the underscore symbol. No spaces or special characters are allowed. You can assign a shortcut key to the macro that can be used to run the macro directly from the keyboard. Excel creates a description that includes the date and user name. You can remove this entry or add a description of the macro that is being recorded. Finally, a macro needs to be stored somewhere. There are three options. By default, the macro is stored in the current workbook, making the macro available only to the workbook when it is open. Another option is to store the macro in the **Personal Macro workbook**. This is a hidden workbook, named Personal.xls, opened whenever you start Excel, making the macro available anytime you use Excel. The Personal Macro workbook is used to store commonly used macros that apply to many applications and is most convenient for users on stand-alone computers. Finally, you can store the macro in a new workbook. For example, an accountant might have a set of macros that help with end-of-the-month tasks which you store in a separate workbook. Remember that the new workbook you create must be opened whenever you want to use the macro. For Nigel's application, you'll store the macro in the Stock2 workbook.

To begin the macro recorder:

1. If necessary, open the **Stock2** workbook, and then switch to the Reporter worksheet.

2. Click **Tools** on the menu bar, point to **Protection**, and then click **Protect Sheet**. The Protect Sheet dialog box opens.

3. Make sure that the ability to select locked and unlocked cells are the only options selected in the list box, and then click the **OK** button.

   Now you'll start the macro recorder.

4. Click **Tools** on the menu bar, point to **Macro**, and then click **Record New Macro**. The Record Macro dialog box opens. Excel displays a default name for the macro. The default name consists of the word "Macro" and a number that is one greater than the number of macros already recorded in the workbook in the current session.

   You will change the default name to something that describes the purpose of the macro.

5. Type **Report30** in the Macro name text box, and then press the **Tab** key.

   Next, you will specify a shortcut key combination to run the macro automatically from the keyboard. Nigel suggests that the Report30 macro be run whenever the user presses the Ctrl key plus the letter a.

6. Type **a** in the Shortcut key text box, and then press the **Tab** key twice. Note that "This Workbook" is the option displayed in the Store macro in list box.

   The final text box provides a space where you can enter a description of the macro. The default description indicates the date the macro is being recorded and the name of the macro author. You will add an additional comment to this description.

7. Click at the end of the default description within the Description text box, type **.** (a period) to end the statement, and then press the **Enter** key to start a new line.

8. Type **Generates a report of stock values for the last 30 days.** Figure 8-20 shows the completed Record Macro dialog box.

Recording the Report30 macro | **Figure 8-20**

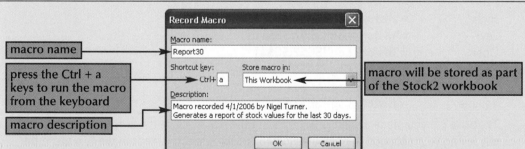

9. Click the **OK** button to start recording the macro. The Stop Recording toolbar appears, and the word "Recording" appears in the status bar.

   Trouble? If the toolbar does not appear, the macro you are recording will not be impacted so you can continue without the toolbar. Note that you will be instructed to stop recording by selecting the Stop Recording command on the Tools Macro menu.

You are now working in macro record mode. When Excel is in macro record mode, the Stop Recording toolbar appears in the workbook window. This toolbar contains two buttons: the Stop Recording button and the Relative Reference button. The Relative Reference button controls how Excel records the act of selecting a cell range in the worksheet. By default, the macro will select the same cells regardless of which cell is first selected because the macro records a selection using absolute cell references. If you want a macro to select cells regardless of the position of the active cell when you run the macro, set the macro recorder to record relative cell references. In this macro, you'll want to use the default absolute cell references, so you'll leave this button unchanged. Once you are finished recording your keystrokes, you will click the Stop Recording button.

You are now ready to record the actions of the Report30 macro. Every command and action you perform will be recorded and stored in the Report30 macro. For that reason, it's very important that you follow the instructions below precisely. You'll start by removing the protection from the Reporter worksheet.

To record the Report30 macro:

1. Click **Tools** on the menu bar, point to **Protection**, and then click **Unprotect Sheet**.

   Now you'll change the definitions of all the names so that they cover only the last 30 days of stock activity. You'll follow the same process you used in the last session when you changed the names to refer to the previous 60 days.

2. Click **Insert** on the menu bar, point to **Name**, and then click **Define** to open the Define Name dialog box.

   First, you will change the cell reference for the Close name so the last cell in the range points to cell F31.

3. Click **Close** in the list of names, and then change the definition of the name to **='History Log'!$F$2:$F$31**. Note that you only have to change the number 6 to the number 3.

4. Click the **Add** button.

   Next, you will change the cell reference for the Date range.

5. Click **Date** in the list of names, change its definition to **='History Log'!$A$2:$A$31**, and then click the **Add** button.

6. Replace the definitions of the remaining six names as follows, clicking the **Add** button each time:

High	**='History Log'!$D$2:$D$31**
Low	**='History Log'!$E$2:$E$31**
Open	**='History Log'!$C$2:$C$31**
Starting_Date	**='History Log'!$A$31**
Starting_Value	**='History Log'!$C$31**
Volume	**='History Log'!$B$2:$B$31**

   Trouble? If you made a mistake in recording the macro, close the Stock2 workbook without saving your changes. Reopen the workbook and repeat the steps in the "To begin the macro recorder" task and Steps 1 through 6 in this task.

   Before going to the next step, you will click each name to verify that the cell reference is 31.

7. Click each name to confirm that the definition now points to only the last 30 days of stock activity.

   Trouble? If any of the definitions are incorrect, click the name in the list box, correct the definition, and then click the Add button.

8. Click the **OK** button to close the Define Name dialog box.

   Next, you'll change the text of cell I12.

9. Click cell **I12**, type **30-day Statistics**, and then press the **Enter** key.

   Finally, you'll reset the protection for the Reporter worksheet.

10. Click **Tools**, point to **Protection**, click **Protect Sheet** to open the Protect Sheet dialog box, and then click the **OK** button to enable worksheet protection.

11. Click the **Stop Recording** button ◼ on the Stop Recording toolbar to stop the macro recorder. Figure 8-21 shows the 30-day report on the Maxwell Sports stock.

30-day report ◀ **Figure 8-21**

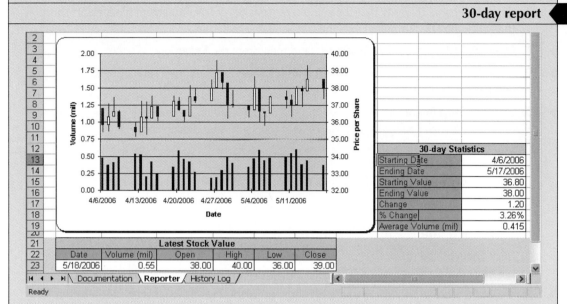

Trouble? If the Stop Recording toolbar does not appear on your screen, click Tools, point to Macro, and then click Stop Recording.

Next, you'll record the actions for the 60-day report. The steps will be the same, except that now you'll change the name definitions to cover the last 60 days of stock activity. For this macro, you'll specify the Ctrl + b shortcut key.

To record the Report60 macro:

1. Click **Tools** on the menu bar, point to **Macro**, and then click **Record New Macro**. The Record Macro dialog box opens.

2. Type **Report60** in the Macro name box, press the **Tab** key, type **b** in the Shortcut key text box, press the **Tab** key twice, and then click to position the insertion point at the end of the default description text.

3. Type **.** (a period) at the end of the description of the macro, press the **Enter** key, type **Generates a report of stock values for the last 60 days.**, and then click the **OK** button.

4. Click **Tools**, point to **Protection**, and then click **Unprotect Sheet** to disable worksheet protection.

5. Click **Insert** on the menu bar, point to **Name**, and then click **Define** to open the Define Name dialog box.

6. Change the definitions of the eight names as follows, clicking the **Add** button after each change:

Close	='History Log'!$F$2:$F$61
Date	='History Log'!$A$2:$A$61
High	='History Log'!$D$2:$D$61

Low	='History Log'!$E$2:$E$61
Open	='History Log'!$C$2:$C$61
Starting_Date	='History Log'!$A$61
Starting_Value	='History Log'!$C$61
Volume	='History Log'!$B$2:$B$61

▶ 7. Click each name to verify that the cell reference is 61, correcting errors if necessary, and then click the **OK** button to close the Define Name dialog box.

▶ 8. Click cell I12, type **60-day Statistics**, and then press the **Enter** key.

▶ 9. Click **Tools**, point to **Protection**, click **Protect Sheet** to open the Protect Sheet dialog box, and then click the **OK** button.

▶ 10. Click the **Stop Recording** button ▣ on the Stop Recording toolbar to stop the macro recorder (or click Tools, point to Macro, and then click Stop Recording).

Finally, you will record the Report90 macro, specifying the Ctrl+c shortcut key.

To record the Report90 macro:

▶ 1. Click **Tools** on the menu bar, point to **Macro**, and then click **Record New Macro** to open the Record Macro dialog box.

▶ 2. Type **Report90** in the Macro name text box, press the **Tab** key, and then type **c** in the Shortcut key text box.

▶ 3. Press the **Tab** key twice, click to position the insertion point at the end of the default description text, type **.** (a period) at the end of the description of the macro, press the **Enter** key, type **Generates a report of stock values for the last 90 days.**, and then click the **OK** button.

▶ 4. Click **Tools**, point to **Protection**, and then click **Unprotect Sheet** to disable worksheet protection.

▶ 5. Click **Insert** on the menu bar, point to **Name**, and then click **Define** to open the Define Name dialog box.

▶ 6. Change the definitions of the eight names as follows, clicking the **Add** button after each change:

Close	='History Log'!$F$2:$F$91
Date	='History Log'!$A$2:$A$91
High	='History Log'!$D$2:$D$91
Low	='History Log'!$E$2:$E$91
Open	='History Log'!$C$2:$C$91
Starting_Date	='History Log'!$A$91
Starting_Value	='History Log'!$C$91
Volume	='History Log'!$B$2:$B$91

▶ 7. Click each name to verify that the cell reference is 91, correcting any errors if necessary, and then click the **OK** button.

▶ 8. Click cell I12, type **90-day Statistics**, and then press the **Enter** key.

▶ 9. Click **Tools**, point to **Protection**, click **Protect Sheet** to open the Protect Sheet dialog box, and then click the **OK** button to enable worksheet protection.

▶ 10. Click the **Stop Recording** button ▣ on the Stop Recording toolbar to stop the macro recorder (or click Tools, point to Macro, and then click Stop Recording).

You've completed the recording of the three report macros. Now it's time to test whether they work.

Running a Macro

Currently, there are two ways of running the report macros you created. One is to use the shortcut key you specified for each report; the other is to select the Run command in the Macro dialog box.

Running a Macro

- Press the shortcut key assigned to the macro.

or

- Click Tools on the menu bar, point to Macro, and then click Macros.
- Select the macro from the list of macros, and then click the Run button.

You'll try both methods in the set of steps that follow.

To run the three report macros:

1. Click **Tools** on the menu bar, point to **Macro**, and then click **Macros**. The Macro dialog box opens, as shown in Figure 8-22. This dialog box lists all of the macros available to you in the current session. From here you can run a specific macro, or if you know the VBA programming language, you can edit the macro. You can also run the macro one step at a time, a useful feature if you're trying to fix a problem in your macro and need to slow it down to see where the problem occurs. You can also delete a macro if you discover that it is not working properly. At this point, you'll run the Report30 macro.

Three report macro | **Figure 8-22**

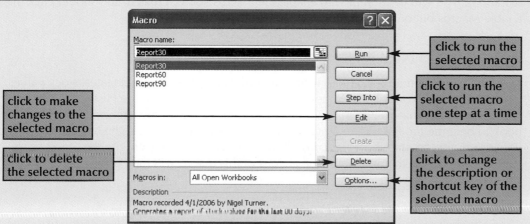

click to run the selected macro

click to run the selected macro one step at a time

click to make changes to the selected macro

click to delete the selected macro

click to change the description or shortcut key of the selected macro

2. Verify that **Report30** is highlighted in the list of macros, and then click the **Run** button. The Report30 macro runs, changing the statistics on the Reporter worksheet and updating the chart to reflect the last 30 days. Notice that the execution of the Report30 macro was very fast. More complex macros may take longer to execute and may result in some screen flicker.

   Trouble? If the Report30 macro did not run properly, you might have made a mistake in recording it. For now, continue with Step 3. You will learn how to test and fix your macro next in this session.

Now you will test the shortcut keys you specified for the other two macros. Recall that the Ctrl + a keys runs the 30-day report, the Ctrl + b keys runs the 60-day report, and the Ctrl + c keys runs the 90-day report.

3. Press and hold the **Ctrl** key and press **b** on your keyboard. The Report60 macro runs and the 60-day report is displayed with the updated chart. Note that macro shortcuts override the default Windows shortcuts for the currently open workbook. Therefore, pressing the Ctrl + b keys runs the Report60 macro; it will not apply the bold style to selected characters (which is a default Windows shortcut).

4. Press the **Ctrl + c** keys to display the 90-day report. The 90-day report is displayed with the updated chart.

Now you will test the 30-day report macro using the keyboard shortcut.

5. Press the **Ctrl + a** keys to return to the 30-day report.

Fixing Macro Errors

Hopefully, all three of the macros you recorded worked correctly. If any of the macros did not work correctly, you can fix the macro. You will also find that sometimes a mistake is made while recording the macro that is not discovered until later. In either case, you have the following options for fixing an error that might have been created:

• Rerecord the macro using the same macro name.
• Delete the recorded macro, and then record the macro again.
• Run the macro one step at a time in order to locate the source of the problem, and then use one of the previous methods to correct the problem.

You can delete or edit the macro by opening the Macro dialog box (shown earlier in Figure 8-23), selecting the macro from the list, and then clicking the appropriate button. To rerecord the macro, simply restart the macro recorder and enter the same macro name you used earlier. Excel will overwrite the previous version. If you have to reopen the Stock2 workbook, you will be prompted to enable the macros you've created. You should click the Enable Macros button to open the workbook and enable the macros.

Creating the NewData Macro

There is one more macro that you need to record. Earlier you typed the latest stock values into the Reporter worksheet, but these values were never added to the History Log worksheet. The macro that you'll create will fix that problem. Nigel does not want this workbook to become too large as new stock values are added each day, so he has decided to limit the history to only the last 90 days. Thus, you will have to overwrite the oldest set of values as you insert the new ones. The actions of this macro will then be as follows:

1. Unprotect the History Log worksheet.
2. Copy the values in the range A2:F90 of the History Log worksheet.
3. Paste the values into the range A3:F91, thus deleting the oldest values in the list.
4. Copy the values in the range B23:G23 of the Reporter worksheet.
5. Paste the values into the range A2:F2 on the History Log worksheet, thus inserting the newest values at the top of the list.
6. Reset protection on the History Log worksheet.
7. Return to the Reporter worksheet.

Nigel wants you to name this new macro "NewData." You'll assign the shortcut key Ctrl + d. Because this macro will actually be changing values in the workbook, you'll save the file before running the macro. If you make a mistake, you can go back to the saved version and start over. Before you record the macro, you will enable worksheet protection again for the History Log sheet.

To record the NewData macro:

1. Save the workbook, and then switch to the History Log worksheet.

2. Click **Tools** on the menu bar, point to **Protection**, click **Protect Sheet** to open the Protect Sheet dialog box, and then click the **OK** button.

3. Click the **Reporter** tab, click **Tools** on the menu bar, point to **Macro**, and then click **Record New Macro**. The Record Macro dialog box opens.

   Trouble? If you clicked Macros, opening the Macros dialog box in error, click the Cancel button and repeat Steps 2 and 3.

4. Type **NewData** in the Macro name box, press the **Tab** key and type the letter **d**, press the **Tab** key twice, click at the end of the description entry, type **.** (a period), press the **Enter** key, type **Inserts new data into the History Log.**, and then click the **OK** button.

5. Click the **History Log** tab, click **Tools** on the menu bar, point to **Protection**, and then click **Unprotect Sheet** to remove the worksheet protection.

   Next, you will copy the existing values in rows 2 through 90. You do not want to select row 91. When you paste the values, the oldest value (which is in row 91) will be deleted.

6. Select the range **A2:F90** (do *not* select row 91 of the worksheet).

7. Click the **Copy** button 🖺 on the Standard toolbar.

   Now you will paste the selection, beginning in row 3, moving all the values down one row.

8. Press the ↓ key to select cell A3, and then click the **Paste** button 🖺 on the Standard toolbar.

   Now you will return to the Reporter worksheet so you can copy the new set of data values, which have been entered into the range B23:G23, but have not been entered into the History Log worksheet.

9. Click the **Reporter** tab, select the range **B23:G23**, and then click the **Copy** button 🖺 on the Standard toolbar.

   To update the History Log worksheet with the latest stock values, you will return to the History Log sheet and paste these new values in row 2.

10. Click the **History Log** tab, click cell **A2**, click the **Paste** button 🖺 on the Standard toolbar, and click cell **A2** to remove the selection.

    Finally, you will enable worksheet protection and return to the Reporter worksheet.

11. Click **Tools**, point to **Protection**, click **Protect Sheet** to open the Protect Sheet dialog box, and then click the **OK** button.

12. Click the **Reporter** tab and click cell **A1**.

13. Click the **Stop Recording** button 🔲 on the Stop Recording toolbar (or click Stop Recording on the Tools Macro submenu). Figure 8-23 shows the new 30-day report with the latest data value inserted into the chart and statistics.

Figure 8-23 ▶ **Reporter worksheet after inserting the new data values**

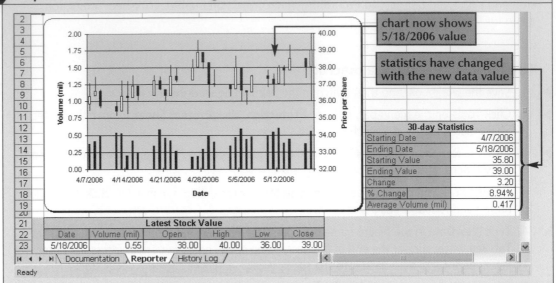

Trouble? If you make a mistake in recording the macro, close the Stock2 workbook without saving your change. Reopen the workbook and repeat Steps 1 through 13.

Nigel has some new stock market data to add to his worksheet. This is a good opportunity for you to test the NewData macro.

To test the NewData macro:

▶ 1. Click cell **B23**, type **5/19/2006**, and then press the **Tab** key.

▶ 2. Type **0.72** for the volume of shares traded, and then press the **Tab** key.

▶ 3. Enter an opening value for the stock of **39**, a high value of **39.5**, a low value of **36**, and a closing value of **36.8**. Make sure you press the Enter or Tab key after typing the closing value.

▶ 4. Press the **Ctrl + d** keys to run the NewData macro, which inserts the new data into the History Log worksheet and updates the chart and statistics. See Figure 8-24.

Figure 8-24 ▶ **Reporter worksheet after inserting the 5/19/2006 values**

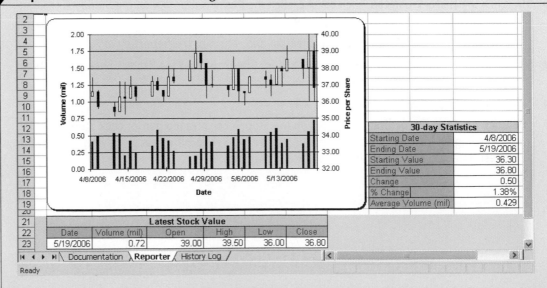

Trouble? If the macro fails to run correctly, close the Stock2 workbook without saving your changes. Reopen the Stock2 workbook and attempt to rerecord the NewData macro following the steps described earlier.

Nigel watches the operation of the NewData macro, and he's concerned about a flurry of activity that occurs when the macro is running as it switches from one worksheet to another, copying and pasting values. He thinks that this might be disconcerting to some users. Is there a way of hiding the actions of the macro as it runs through the recorded steps?

Working with the Visual Basic Editor

You discuss Nigel's problem with Cindy Dean, who is a programmer at Harris & Burton. She tells you that there is no way of hiding the intermediate steps using only the macro recorder, but hiding steps can be done with two simple VBA commands. Even though you're not a VBA programmer and don't have the time to learn the language, you realize that this would be an opportunity to "peek under the hood" at Excel's macro capability, so you agree to try to edit the macro following Cindy's instructions.

Reference Window

Editing a Macro

- Click Tools on the menu bar, point to Macro, and then click Macros.
- Select the macro in the list, and then click the Edit button.
- Use the Visual Basic Editor to edit the macro code.
- To print the macro code, click File on the menu bar, click Print, select the item to print and other print-related options, and then click the OK button.
- Click File on the menu bar, and then click Close and Return to Microsoft Excel.

To view the code of the NewData macro, you need to open the **Visual Basic Editor**, a separate application that works with Excel and all of the Office products to edit and manage VBA code. Cindy tells you that you can access the Visual Basic Editor through the Macro dialog box.

To view the code for the NewData macro:

1. Click **Tools** on the menu bar, point to **Macro**, and then click **Macros**. The Macro dialog box opens.

2. Verify that the **NewData** macro is highlighted in the list of macros, and then click the **Edit** button. The Visual Basic Editor opens as a separate program, consisting of several windows. One of the windows, the Code window, contains the VBA code generated by the macro recorder. See Figure 8-25.

Figure 8-25 ▶ **Visual Basic Editor**

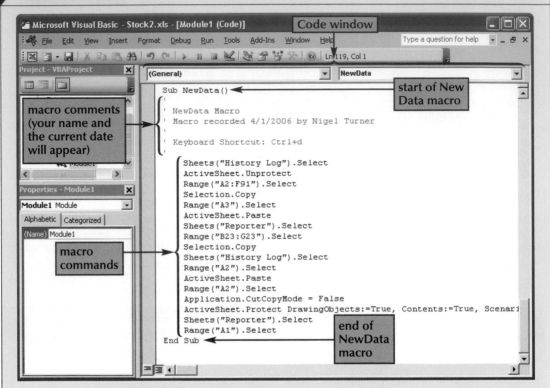

Trouble? The number of windows and their contents will vary depending on how your system is configured. At this point, you can ignore all other windows aside from the Code window. Also, depending on how you recorded the macros and whether you had to close and reopen the Stock2 workbook in the process, you may see more than one module listed in the window at the left.

3. If the Code window is not maximized in the editor, click the **Maximize** button ▣ on the Code window title bar.

Learning to interpret and write VBA code is a subject worthy of its own book. At this point, you'll just cover what you need to know to make Cindy's recommended changes.

Understanding the Structure of Macros

The VBA code shown in the Code window lists all of the actions you performed in recording the NewData macro. In VBA, macros are called **sub procedures**. Each sub procedure begins with the keyword "Sub" followed by the name of the sub procedure and a set of parentheses. In this example, the code begins with *Sub NewData()*, which provides the name of this sub procedure, "NewData"—the same name you gave the macro. The parentheses are used if you want to include any arguments in the procedure. These arguments that pass information to the sub procedure have roughly the same purpose as the arguments used in an Excel function.

If you write your own VBA code, sub procedure arguments are an important part of the programming process, but they are not used when you create macros with the macro recorder.

Following the Sub NewData() statement are comments about the macro, taken from the description you entered earlier in the Record New Macro dialog box. Note that each line appears in green and is prefaced with an apostrophe ('). This indicates that the line is a comment and does not include any actions that need to be performed by Excel.

After the comments is the body of the macro, a listing of all of the commands performed by the NewData macro as written in the language of VBA. Your list of commands might look slightly different, depending on the exact actions you performed when recording the macro. Even though you might not know VBA, some of the commands are easy to interpret. Near the top of the NewData macro, you should see the command *Sheets("History Log").Select*, which is a command that tells Excel to select the History Log worksheet, making it the active sheet in the workbook. The next command, *ActiveSheet.Unprotect*, removes worksheet protection from the active sheet, in this case the History Log sheet. At the bottom of the macro is the statement *End Sub*, which indicates the end of the NewData sub procedure.

A Code window can contain several sub procedures, with each procedure separated from the others by the *Sub ProcedureName()* statement at the beginning, and the *End Sub* statement at the end. Sub procedures are organized into **modules**. As shown in Figure 8-27, all of the macros that have been recorded are stored in the Module1 module (your window may differ).

Writing a Macro Command

Cindy wants you to insert two commands into the NewData sub procedure to hide the actions of the macro as it runs. The first command, which needs to be inserted directly after the *Sub NewData()* statement, is *Application.ScreenUpdating = False*. This command turns *off* Excel's screen updating feature, keeping any actions that run in the macro from being displayed on the screen. The second command, which needs to be inserted directly before the *End Sub* statement, is *Application.ScreenUpdating = True*. This command turns Excel's screen update feature back on, enabling the user to see the final results of the macro after it has completed running.

You have to enter these commands exactly. VBA will not be able to run a command if you mistype a word or omit part of the statement. The Visual Basic Editor does provide tools to assist you in writing error-free code. As you type a command, the editor will provide pop-up windows and text to help you insert the correct code. Try inserting these new commands now.

To insert the new commands into the macro:

1. Click the end of the Sub NewData () statement in the Code window, and then press the **Enter** key. A new blank line appears under the statement.

2. Type **Application.** (Be sure to include the period, but no spaces, in the command.) The editor displays a list box with a selection of possible keywords you could type at this point in the command. You can either scroll down the list or continue typing the command yourself. You'll continue typing.

3. Type **ScreenUpdating =**. Note that as you type the command another list box appears, and once you type the equal sign, the editor prompts you with two possible choices: True or False.

4. Type **False** to turn off the screen updating feature of Excel, and then press the **Enter** key. Figure 8-26 shows the new command inserted into the sub procedure.

Turning off screen updating in the NewData macro   Figure 8-26

Next, you'll insert a command at the end of the sub procedure to turn screen updating back on.

5. Scroll down the Code window to view the end of the NewData sub procedure.

6. Click at the beginning of the End Sub statement to position the insertion point, and then press the **Enter** key. A new blank line appears above the End Sub statement.

7. Press the ↑ key to move the insertion point up into the new blank line.

8. Type **Application.ScreenUpdating = True** and then press the **Enter** key. Note that once again the editor displayed list boxes to assist you in typing the command. The new command appears as shown in Figure 8-27.

Figure 8-27 ▶ **Turning on screen updating in the NewData macro**

```
          Sheets("Reporter").Select
          Range("A1").Select
Application.ScreenUpdating = True  ◀—  insert this
                                        line at the
End Sub                                 end of the
                                        macro
```

Printing the Macro Code

As you learn more about VBA and writing your own programs, you will find it useful to document the code generated by the macro recorder. You will print the macro code for future reference.

To print the macro code:

1. Verify that the insertion point still appears in the Code window and that the Code window is active.

2. Click **File** on the menu bar, and then click **Print**. The Print – VBAProject dialog box opens. The editor gives two choices of items to print. One is to print the current project, which refers to all of the code in any module and any other features that might be involved in this collection of macros. Printing the project is usually done for Excel applications that involve more advanced features such as customized dialog boxes. The other choice, the default, is to print only those macros in the current module. To ensure that all of the macros in this application are printed, you will choose to print the current project.

3. Click the **Current Project** option button, and verify that the **Code** check box is selected.

4. Click the **OK** button to print the macro code.

Trouble? If you need to send your output to a specific printer on your network, click the Setup button to select your printer and its settings, and then click the OK button.

Now that you've viewed, edited, and printed the macro, you will close the Visual Basic Editor and return to Excel.

5. Click **File** on the menu bar, and then click **Close and Return to Microsoft Office Excel**. The Visual Basic Editor closes, and the Stock2 workbook is redisplayed.

If you want to return to the Visual Basic Editor, you can select one of the macros in the Macro dialog box and click the Edit button again, or you can click Tools on the menu bar, point to Macro, and then click Visual Basic Editor.

Nigel has a new set of data for you to enter. This time, you'll check to see whether your commands to turn off the screen updating feature makes the macro run more smoothly. Before running the macro, you should save your work so that if the macro runs incorrectly, you can go back to the previous version.

To test the screen updating command:

▶ **1.** Save the workbook, and then click cell **B23**.

You will begin the test by entering new information for stocks.

▶ **2.** Type **5/20/2006** in cell B23, press the **Tab** key, type **0.51** in cell C23, and then press the **Tab** key.

▶ **3.** Continue inserting the new stock values into the worksheet, typing **36.8** for the opening value, **37.9** for the high value, **36.2** for the low value, and **37.1** for the closing value. Remember to press the Tab or Enter key when you're finished entering all the data.

▶ **4.** Press the **Ctrl + d** keys. The NewData macro runs, but this time the actions of the macro are hidden. The macro executed faster so only the final result is displayed.

Nigel is pleased with the change you've made to the macro. He thinks it runs more smoothly and will be less distracting to those who use this application.

Creating Macro Buttons

Another way to run a macro is to assign it to a button that is placed directly on the worksheet. Nigel wants you to add four macro buttons to the Reporter worksheet, one for each of the four macros you've created. Macro buttons are often a better way to run macros than shortcut keys. For users who are unfamiliar with the set up or details of a workbook, clicking on a button (with a descriptive label) is probably more intuitive than trying to remember a combination of keystrokes.

Creating a Macro Button

Reference Window

- Click View on the menu bar, point to Toolbars, and then click Forms.
- Click the Button tool on the Forms toolbar, and then click and drag the mouse pointer until the button is the size and shape you want.
- Release the mouse button. The button appears on the worksheet with a default label, and the Assign Macro dialog box opens.
- Select the macro you want to assign to the button. With the button still selected, type a new label.

Because the worksheet is still protected, you'll need to turn off the sheet protection before adding the four buttons to the worksheet.

To insert a button on the worksheet:

▶ **1.** Click **Tools** on the menu bar, point to **Protection**, and then click **Unprotect Sheet**.

To create the macro buttons, you will display the Forms toolbar.

▶ **2.** Click **View** on the menu bar, point to **Toolbars**, and then click **Forms**. The Forms toolbar appears. The Forms toolbar contains a variety of objects that can be placed on the worksheet. In this case, you'll work only with the Button tool.

> **Trouble?** If the tools on the Forms toolbar are grayed out, unprotect the Reporter worksheet.

▶ **3.** Click the **Button** tool ▤ on the Forms toolbar. As you move the pointer over the worksheet, the pointer changes to ✛.

▶ **4.** Drag the pointer over the range **I3:J4**, and then release the mouse button. Excel places a button on the worksheet, and the Assign Macro dialog box opens. Each macro button you create appears with a default label on it. The label on the button shown in the figure is "Button 8" (the label on your screen might differ—the numbers are sequential). See Figure 8-28.

Figure 8-28	**Macro button and the Assign Macro dialog box**

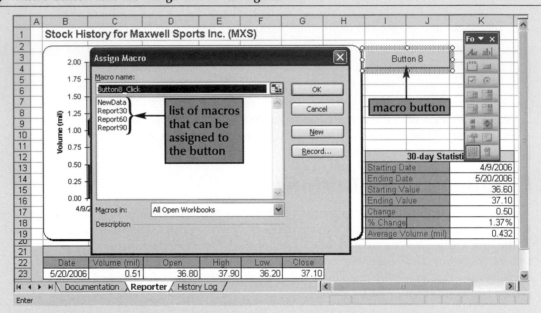

> **Trouble?** Drawing a macro button is the same as drawing any object. If the button is not the exact size of the button in the figure, you can resize it after you change the label on the button. To resize the button, first select it by right-clicking the button, and then click and drag the selection handles to resize the button. To move the button, click the selection border (not on one of the selection handles), and drag the button to a new location.

When Excel creates the macro button, the Assign Macro dialog box automatically opens. From this dialog box, you can assign a macro to the button, or you can turn on the macro recorder to record a new macro. Nigel wants you to assign the Report30 macro to this new button.

To assign a button to the Report30 macro:

▶ **1.** Click **Report30** in the list of macros, and then click the **OK** button. This action assigns the Report30 macro to the selected button, which you just created.

> You will change the default label on the button to a more descriptive one, which will indicate which macro will run when the button is clicked.

2. With the selection handles still displayed around the button, type **30-day Report** (be sure not to press the Enter key). The new label replaces the default label.

Trouble? If there are no selection handles around the button, the button is not selected. Right-click anywhere within the button to select the button and display its shortcut menu, and then click Edit Text so the insertion point appears within the button. Repeat Step 2.

Trouble? If you pressed the Enter key after entering the label on the button, press the Backspace key and then continue to Step 3.

3. Click any cell in the worksheet to deselect the macro button.

At this point, if you click the 30-day Report button, the Report30 macro will run. Of course, the worksheet is already displaying the 30-day report, so you will add the other macro buttons first.

To add the remaining macro buttons:

1. Click the **Button** tool 🔳 on the Forms toolbar, and then drag the pointer over the range **I6:J7**.

2. Select **Report60** in the Assign Macro dialog box, and then click the **OK** button.

3. Type **60-day Report** for the new button label, and then click any cell to deselect the button.

4. Click the **Button** tool 🔳 on the Forms toolbar, drag the pointer over the range **I9:J10**, select **Report90** in the Assign Macro dialog box, click the **OK** button, type **90-day Report** for the button label, and then click any cell to deselect the button.

5. Click the **Button** tool 🔳 on the Forms toolbar, drag the pointer over the range **I22:J23**, select **NewData** in the Assign Macro dialog box, click the **OK** button, type **Insert Stock Value** as the new button label, and then click any cell in the worksheet to deselect the button. Figure 8-29 shows the Reporter worksheet with the four newly inserted macro buttons.

Macro buttons in the Reporter worksheet ◄ **Figure 8-29**

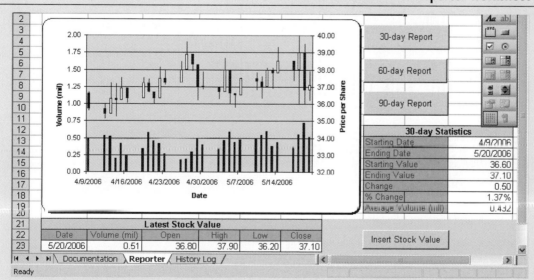

Trouble? If the macro buttons on your screen do not match the size and location of the buttons shown in the figure, you can click a button to select it, and then resize or reposition it on the worksheet.

You no longer need the Forms toolbar, so you will close it and then reset worksheet protection.

6. Click the **Close** button ✖ on the Forms toolbar.

7. Click **Tools** on the menu bar, point to **Protection**, **Protect Sheet** to open the Protect Sheet dialog box, and then click the **OK** button to enable worksheet protection.

Now you will test the macro buttons to verify that they run the macros.

To test the macro buttons:

1. Click the **60-day Report** button to display the 60-day report chart and statistics.

2. Click the **90-day Report** button to display the 90-day report chart and statistics.

3. Click the **30-day Report** button to return to the 30-day display.

Nigel has one last set of values for you to enter, so you will use the new macro button to insert these values.

4. Click cell **B23**, type **5/21/2006**, and then press the **Tab** key.

5. Complete the rest of stock values as follows: the volume is **0.25**, the opening value is **37.1**, the high value is **38.3**, the low value is **35.1**, and the closing value is **36.9**. Be sure to press the Enter or Tab key after typing the closing value.

6. Click the **Insert Stock Values** button. Excel inserts the new stock values and updates the statistics and chart. See Figure 8-30.

| Figure 8-30 | Reporter worksheet with updated values and statistics |

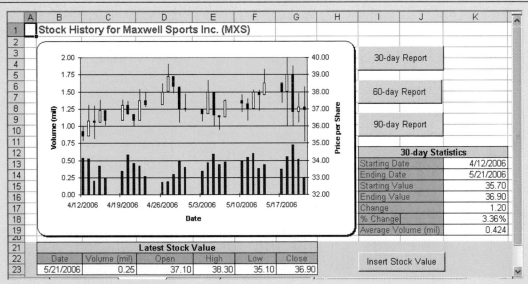

You've completed your work on the Excel application, so you will save and close the workbook and then exit Excel.

7. Save your changes to the workbook, and then close it.

Nigel is very pleased with the ease of the interface for the stock value workbook. He wants to study the Excel application some more and will get back to you with any other projects he needs to have done.

Review

Session 8.3 Quick Check

1. What is a digital signature? How does it protect you from macro viruses?
2. Discuss two ways of creating a macro.
3. What is VBA?
4. What are the three places in which you can store a macro?
5. What are the steps you follow to delete a macro?
6. What are the steps you follow to edit a macro?
7. In VBA, macros are called _____.
8. How do you insert a macro button into your worksheet?

Review

Tutorial Summary

In this tutorial, you learned how to create data validation rules that help guide users as they input data into a worksheet. You learned how to define names to make formulas easier to understand. You also learned how to protect the contents of worksheets, the worksheets themselves, and workbooks. Finally, you learned how to automate a series of actions by creating macros.

Key Terms

data validation	module	sub procedure
digital certificate	name	validation rule
digital signature	Personal Macro workbook	Visual Basic Editor
input message	protect	Visual Basic for
locked property	security level	Applications (VBA)
macro		

Practice

Review Assignments

Get hands-on practice of the skills you learned in the tutorial to answer additional questions about building macros for Harris & Burton.

Data File needed for the Review Assignments: Chart1.xls

Nigel is working on another Excel application. This application contains a chart displaying the closing value of a stock plotted against a date range. The workbook contains a list of closing stock prices for two of Harris & Burton's competitors over the last 90 days. Nigel wants users to have the ability to display any one of the stocks in the chart. He also wants them to have the ability to control the date range displayed in the chart by specifying the starting and stopping date. This way, users can look at any time interval they want within the range of dates stored in the workbook.

You've been talking to Cindy about the problem. She says that you can't change the chart's date range by using the macro recorder, but at a later date she will write up a simple VBA program that you can use in the workbook. Your job will be to create the rest of the application.

To complete this task:

1. Open the **Chart1** workbook located in the Tutorial.08\Review folder included with your Data Files, and then save the workbook as **Chart2** in the same folder.
2. Enter the current date and your name in the Documentation sheet, and then switch to the Reporter worksheet. The Reporter worksheet contains the chart and all of the stock market data. The stock market data is entered in the range $O$1:$Q$91. The two stock values are entered into the range $P$1:$P$91 for Maxwell Sports and the range $Q$1:$Q$91 for GC Records. The chart currently shows the data for Maxwell Sports.

3. Turn off the locked property for cells C23 and F23 so that users will be able to enter the starting and ending values for the chart in the worksheet. All other cells are protected so no data can be entered in these cells.
4. Create the validation rules for cells C23 and F23 as shown in Figure 8-31.

Figure 8-31

Cell	Settings	Input Message	Error Alert
C23	Start date between 1/19/06 and 5/21/06	Title: Valid Date Message: Enter a date between 1/19/06 and 5/21/06	Title: Invalid Date Style: Stop Message: The date you entered must be between 1/19/06 and 5/21/06. Please reenter the start date.
F23	End date greater than date entered in cell C23 and less than or equal to 5/21/06	*Enter an appropriate input message*	Title: Invalid Date Style: Stop Message: *Enter an appropriate error alert message*

5. Create the following names using the definitions provided:
   - Date =Reporter!$O$2:$O$91
   - Current_value =Reporter!$P$2
   - Stock_values =Reporter!$P$2:$P$91
   - Stock_name =Reporter!$P$1
6. Change the data source for the embedded chart so that the Name reference points to Stock_name, the Values reference points to Stock_values, and the Category (X) axis labels reference points to the Date name. (*Hint*: Remember that the current workbook filename must precede the cell reference.)
7. Protect the worksheet, allowing users to select locked and unlocked cells. Do not specify a password.

(*Note:* In the following steps, you'll be creating three macros. You should save your workbook before recording each macro. That way, if you make a mistake in recording the macro, you can close the workbook—without saving the changes—and then reopen it and try again. You should also read the list of tasks before you begin recording them.)

8. Create a macro named "GCR" with the shortcut key combination Ctrl + b. The macro will display the stock values (found in the range $Q$1:$Q$91) and the stock name of GC Records in the chart. Record the following tasks to create the GCR macro:
   a. Unprotect the worksheet.
   b. Change the definition of the Current_value name to "=Reporter!$Q$2".
   c. Change the definition of the Stock_name name to "=Reporter!$Q$1".
   d. Change the definition of the Stock_values name to "=Reporter!$Q$2:$Q$91".
   e. Go to cell A1.
   f. Reset worksheet protection.
9. To test the GCR macro, click cell H4 to make it the active cell. If the macro runs correctly, the chart will display GC Records data, and cell A1 will be the active cell. Now press the Ctrl + b keys to run the macro. If the macro fails to work, close the workbook without saving your changes, reopen the workbook, and record the macro again.
10. Create a macro named "MXS" with the shortcut key combination Ctrl + a. This macro should display the stock values and stock name of Maxwell Sports in the chart. Follow the same procedure that you used to create the GCR macro in Step 9, except that all of the cell references should now point to column P in the Reporter worksheet.

11. To test the MXS macro, click cell H4 to make it the active cell and then press the Ctrl + a keys to run the macro. If the macro runs correctly, the chart will display Maxwell Sports Inc. data, and cell A1 will be the active cell. If the macro fails to work, close the workbook without saving your changes, reopen the workbook, and record the macro again.

12. Edit the MXS macro so that screen updating is turned off while the macro is running and turned on when the macro ends.

13. Unprotect the worksheet so you can add two buttons to it. Create a macro button that covers the range H4:I5; assign the MXS macro to the button, and then change the button's label to "Maxwell Sports." Create a second macro button for the GCR macro, covering the range H7:I8, with the label "GC Records." Click each button and verify that the macros change the chart. If necessary, protect the worksheet and then save it.

14. Create a macro named "PrintChart" to print only the chart. Assign this macro to the shortcut keys Ctrl + c. (*Hint*: Be sure to unprotect and protect the worksheet as the first and last steps in this macro.) Create a macro button that covers the range H10:I11, and then change the default label to "Print Chart." Print your chart using the PrintChart macro.

15. Save and close the workbook.

Case Problem 1

Data File needed for this Case Problem: Popcorn1.xls

Creating a Profit Analysis for Seattle Popcorn Seattle Popcorn is a small company located in Tacoma, Washington, that produces a brand of gourmet popcorn favored by people in the Northwest. Steve Wilkes has developed a workbook that will allow him to perform a profit analysis for the company. Using this workbook, he wants to create formulas to determine the break-even point for the company—the sales volume needed so that revenues will match the anticipated monthly expenses. There are three factors in determining the break-even point: the sales price of each unit of Seattle Popcorn, the variable manufacturing cost to the company for each unit, and the fixed expenses (salaries, rent, insurance, and so on) that the company must pay each month. Steve wants to be able to explore a range of possible values for each of these factors.

- The sales price of each unit of Seattle Popcorn can vary from $5 to $15 (in whole numbers).
- The variable manufacturing cost of each unit can vary from $5 to $15 (in whole numbers).
- The fixed monthly expense for the company can vary from $15,000 to $30,000 (in whole numbers).

Figure 8-32 shows a preview of the application you'll create for Steve.

Apply

Apply the skills you've learned to define data validation rules, name cells, set worksheet protection, and create macros in a profit analysis workbook.

Figure 8-32

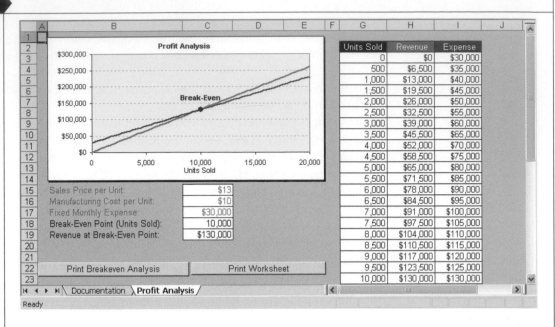

To complete this task:

1. Open the **Popcorn1** workbook located in the Tutorial.08\Cases folder included with your Data Files, enter the date and your name in the Documentation sheet, and then save the workbook as **Popcorn2** in the same folder.
2. Switch to the Profit Analysis worksheet, and then define the following names in the worksheet:
   - Price_per_Unit ='Profit Analysis'!$C$15
   - Cost_per_Unit ='Profit Analysis'!$C$16
   - Monthly_Expenses ='Profit Analysis'!$C$17
3. In the range H3:H43, enter a formula to calculate the revenue, which is determined by the units sold multiplied by the price per unit. In the range I3:I43, enter a formula to calculate the expenses, which are determined by the units sold multiplied by the cost per unit plus the fixed monthly expense. (*Note:* The named cells appear in the formulas.)
4. In cell C18, enter a formula to calculate the break-even point, which is determined by the fixed monthly expense divided by the difference between the price per unit and the cost per unit.
5. In cell C19, enter a formula to calculate the revenue at the break-even point, which is determined by the break-even point multiplied by the sale price per unit.
6. Create the validation rules for cells C15, C16, and C17 as shown in Figure 8-33.

Figure 8-33

Cell	Settings	Input Message	Error Alert
C15	Integers from 5 to 15	*Enter an appropriate input message*	Title: Sales Price Warning Style: Warning Message: *Enter an error alert appropriate message*
C16	Integers from 5 to 15	*Enter an appropriate input message*	Title: Cost Warning Style: Warning Message: *Enter an error alert appropriate message*
C17	Integers from 15000 to 30000	*Enter an appropriate input message*	Title: Fixed Monthly Expense Warning Style: Warning Message: *Enter an error alert appropriate message*

7. Protect the worksheet so the user is able to enter data only in cells C15, C16, and C17. Everything else in the worksheet should remain locked.
8. Enter the following values in the worksheet to determine how many units Seattle Popcorn must sell each month in order to break even:
   - Sales Price per Unit = $13
   - Manufacturing Cost per Unit = $10
   - Fixed Monthly Expense = $30,000

(*Note:* In the following steps, you'll be creating two macros. You should save your workbook before recording each macro. That way, if you make a mistake in recording the macro, you can close the workbook (without saving the changes) and then reopen it and try again. You should also read the list of tasks before you begin recording them.)

9. Create a macro named "PrintChart," with the shortcut key Ctrl + a, that performs the following tasks:
   a. Prints the chart and input/output area (A1:E20) in landscape orientation, centered horizontally on the page and with the text "Break-even Analysis" centered at the top of the printout and your name and date in the lower-right corner of the printout
   b. Makes cell A1 the active cell after printing is completed
10. Test the PrintChart macro by pressing the Ctrl + a keys. If the macro fails to work, close the workbook without saving your changes, reopen the workbook, and record the macro again.
11. Create a button in the range A22:B22, assign the PrintChart macro to a button, and change the default label to a more descriptive one.
12. Edit the PrintChart macro so screen updating is turned off while the macro is running and turned on when the macro ends.
13. Run the PrintChart macro again to test the button and verify that screen updating is turned off while the macro is running and on when the macro ends.
14. Create a macro named "PrintWorksheet," with shortcut key Ctrl + b, that performs the following tasks:
   a. Prints the entire worksheet on one page with text "Profit Analysis" centered at the top of the printout and your name and date in the lower-right corner of the printout
   b. Makes cell A1 the active cell after printing is completed
15. Test the PrintWorksheet macro by pressing the Crtl + b keys. If the macro fails to work, close the workbook without saving your changes, reopen the workbook, and record the macro again.
16. Create a button in the range C22:E22, assign the PrintWorksheet macro to a button, and then change the default label to a more descriptive one.
17. Edit the macro so screen updating is turned off while the macro is running and turned on when the macro ends.
18. Run the PrintWorksheet macro again to test the button and verify that screen updating is turned off while the macro is running and on when the macro ends.
19. Save and close the workbook.

Apply

Apply the skills you've learned to set data validation rules, insert a lookup table, set cell protection, and create macros in a sales data worksheet.

Case Problem 2

Data File needed for this Case Problem: HWSales1.xls

Creating a Data-Entry Form for Homeware Homeware is a company that sells specialized home cooking products. The company employs individuals to organize "Homeware Parties" in which the company's products are sold. Lisa Goodman is responsible for entering sales data from various Homeware Parties. She has asked for your help in designing an Excel workbook to act as a data-entry form. She has already created the workbook, but she needs your help setting up data validation rules, creating a table lookup, and writing the macros to enter the data.

To complete this task:

1. Open the **HWSales1** workbook located in the Tutorial.08\Cases folder included with your Data Files, and then save the workbook as **HWSales2** in the same folder.
2. Enter your name and the date in the Documentation sheet, and then switch to the Sales Form worksheet.

Explore

3. Create the following validation rules for cells C3, C4, and C7 as shown in Figure 8-34.

Figure 8-34

Cell	Settings	Input Message	Error Alert
C3	Integers from 1 to 5	*Enter an appropriate input message*	Title: Invalid Region Style: Stop Message: *Enter an appropriate error alert message*
C4	List Data source: E4:E15	*Enter an appropriate input message*	Title: Invalid Product ID Style: Stop Message: *Enter an appropriate error alert message*
C7	Positive integers	*Enter an appropriate input message*	Title: Invalid Units Sold Style: Stop Message: *Enter an appropriate error alert message*

4. Use a Lookup function to automatically display the product name (cell C5) and price (cell C6) in the sales form when the product ID is entered.
5. Enter a formula in cell C8 that calculates the total sales for the order, which is determined by the number of units sold multiplied by the price of the product.
6. Protect the Sales Form worksheet so a user can only enter data in cells C3, C4, and C7; all other cells can be selected, but no values can be entered. Protect all of the sheets in the workbook, except for the Documentation sheet.

(*Note:* In the following steps, you'll be creating several macros. You should save your workbook before recording each macro. That way, if you make a mistake in recording the macro, you can close the workbook (without saving the changes) and then reopen it and try again. You should also read the list of tasks before you begin recording them.)

7. Create a macro named "AddData," with the shortcut key Ctrl + d, that performs the following tasks:
   a. Unprotects the Sales Record and Sales Table worksheets
   b. Inserts a new blank record in the second row of the Sales Record worksheet, shifting the rest of the records down
   c. Copies the values in range C3:C8 of the Sales Form worksheet and pastes the transposed values into the new blank line of the Sales Record worksheet (*Hint*: Use the Paste Special command.)
   d. Refreshes the contents of the PivotTable on the Sales Table worksheet to include the new data
   e. Clears the values in cells C3, C4, and C7 of the Sales Form worksheet
   f. Sets worksheet protection for the Sales Record and Sales Table worksheets
8. Unprotect the Sales Form and Sales Table worksheets.

9. Create a button in the range B11:C12 in the Sales Form worksheet, and assign the AddData macro to a button. Change the default button label to "Enter New Sales."
10. Edit the AddData macro so that Excel does not display the actions of the macro as it runs.
11. Create the following macros:
    - ViewTable macro, with shortcut key Ctrl + t, that displays the contents of the Sales Table worksheet
    - ViewChart macro, with shortcut key Ctrl + c, that displays the sales chart
    - ViewForm macro, with shortcut key Ctrl + f, that displays the Sales Form worksheet
12. Add two buttons to the Sales Form worksheet to run the ViewTable and ViewChart macros. Change the default button labels to "View Sales Table" and "View Sales Chart," respectively.
13. Add a button labeled "Return to the Sales Form" to both the Sales Table worksheet and the Sales Chart worksheet. Assign the ViewForm macro to both buttons.
14. Test the data-entry form and the "Enter New Sales" button by entering the following record:
    - Region = 1, Product ID = CW, Units Sold = 5
    - Region = 3, Product ID = HR, Units Sold = 7
    - Region = 4, Product ID = OEG, Units Sold =3
15. Save and close the workbook.

Challenge

Go beyond what you've learned to define names, apply worksheet protection, and create macros in a sale reporting workbook.

Case Problem 3

Data File needed for this Case Problem: MBikes1.xls

Creating a Sales Report for Trayle Bikes Trayle Bikes specializes in mountain bikes. Pat Boland works in the accounting office of Trayle Bikes. One of her jobs is to report regional sales data for the different Trayle Bikes models. Pat is interested in creating an Excel application to display pie charts for the four different sales regions, or for all sales regions combined.

Pat envisions a set of five macro buttons placed on a worksheet. When one of the buttons is clicked, the pie chart should change, displaying values from a different sales region. Pat has asked for your help in creating this kind of application. The sales data and a pie chart have already been saved to a workbook. Your job will be to define names for cells and ranges, record the macros, and create the buttons needed for the application. Figure 8-35 shows a preview of the completed application.

Figure 8-35

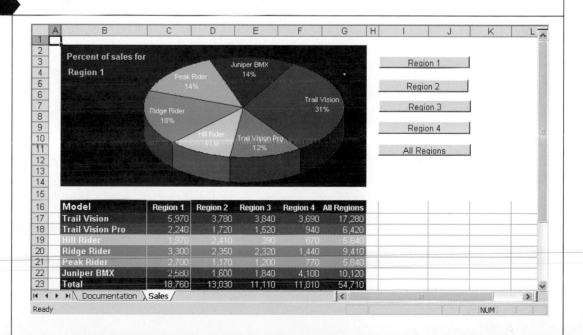

To complete this task:

1. Open the **MBikes1** workbook located in the Tutorial.08\Cases folder included with your Data Files, enter the current date and your name in the Documentation sheet, and then save the workbook as **MBikes2** in the same folder.
2. Switch to the Sales worksheet, and then create the names shown in Figure 8-36.

Figure 8-36

Name	Definition	Name	Definition
Name1	=Sales!$C$16	Region1	=Sales!$C$17:$C$22
Name2	=Sales!$D$16	Region2	=Sales!$D$17:$D$22
Name3	=Sales!$E$16	Region3	=Sales!$E$17:$E$22
Name4	=Sales!$F$16	Region4	=Sales!$F$17:$F$22
Name_All	=Sales!$G$16	Region_All	=Sales!$G$17:$G$22

Explore

3. Names can refer to other names. With this in mind, name cell C16 **Region_Name** using the name you created in Step 2. Name range C17:C22 **Region_Values** using the name you created in Step 2.
4. Edit the data source for the pie chart, changing the reference for the series name so that it points to the Region_Name range, and changing the values reference so that it points to the Region_Values reference.

Explore

5. On the pie chart there is a label with the text "Region 1." Click the Region text label in the pie chart area, and then edit the cell reference so that it points to the Region_Name name rather than cell $C$16. (*Hint*: Use the same syntax that you used when you changed the chart's data source to point to the named ranges.)
6. Protect the worksheet and the structure of the workbook, preventing users from taking any action, including selecting locked *or* unlocked cells. Do *not* set any passwords. Save the workbook.

   (*Note*: In the following steps, you'll be creating several macros. You should save your workbook before recording each macro. That way, if you make a mistake in recording the macro, you can close the workbook—without saving the changes—and then reopen it and try again. Read the list of tasks before you begin recording them.)

7. Create a macro named "Region2," and then record the following tasks:
   a. Unprotect the Sales worksheet.
   b. Change the definition of the Region_Name range so that it points to the Name2 range.
   c. Change the definition of the Region_Values range so that it points to the Region2 range.
   d. Select the range C16:G23, and then remove all borders from the selected cells.
   e. Select the range D16:D23, and then apply a yellow outline border to the range.
   f. Click cell A1.
   g. Reset protection on the Sales worksheet.
8. Run the Region2 macro to verify that it works correctly. (*Note:* The macro will appear as *Module*.Region2 in the list of macros, where *Module* is the name of a module.) If the macro does not run correctly, close the MBikes2 workbook without saving your changes. Reopen the workbook and attempt to record the macro again.
9. Record the Region3 macro, using the same procedure that you followed to create the Region2 macro, except that Region_Name should point to Name3, Region_Values should point to Region3, and the yellow outline border should apply to the range E16:E23. Test the macro.

10. Create the Region4 macro in which Region_Name points to Name4, Region_Values points to Region4, and the yellow outline border is applied to the range F16:F23. Test the macro.

11. Create the Region_All macro in which Region_Name points to Name_All, Region_Values points to Region_All, and the yellow outline border is applied to the range G16:G23. Test the macro.

12. Create the Region1 macro in which Region_Name points to Name1, Region_Values points to Region1, and a yellow border is applied to the range C16:C23. Test the macro.

13. Unprotect the worksheet, and then create a macro button for the Region1 macro, covering the range I3:J3, with the label "Region 1."

14. Create the following macro buttons (refer to Figure 8-35):
    - Region2 button placed over the range I5:J5
    - Region3 button placed over the range I7:J7
    - Region4 button placed over the range I9:J9
    - All Regions button placed over the range I11:J11

15. Select the first 14 rows of the worksheet, and then change the fill color of the selected cells to white. Click cell A1 and then set the worksheet protection again.

16. Click each of the five buttons to verify that they run the correct macro and update both the pie chart and the appearance of the table.

Explore

17. Insert a new worksheet and rename it "Names." Use the Paste Name dialog box to display a list of named cells and ranges. (*Hint*: To open the Paste Name dialog box, click Insert on the menu bar, point to Name, and then click Paste.)

18. Save and close the workbook.

Create

Figure 8-37 shows the "end result." Use your skills to create this customer billing worksheet.

Case Problem 4

There are no Data Files needed for this Case Problem.

Customer Billing for Wakefield Auto Rental Wakefield Auto Rental is the only car rental company in Wakefield, a small New England town. The company has been in business for two years. John Prescott, founder of the company, asks you to help computerize the bills he gives to customers. Figure 8-37 shows the finished application.

Figure 8-37

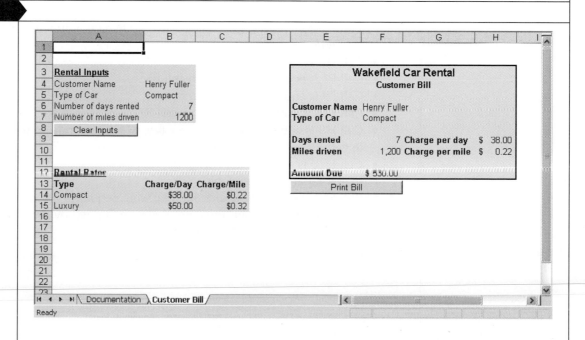

As shown in the figure, the company rents two type types of cars: compact and luxury. The current rental rates are also displayed; for example, the daily charge for a compact rental is $38 at 22¢ per mile.

To complete this worksheet:

1. Open a new blank workbook and save it as **AutoRental** in the Tutorial.08\Cases folder included with your Data Files.
2. Using Figure 8-37 as a guide, rename the first sheet "Documentation," and then enter the name of the company, your name, and the current date. Rename the second worksheet "Customer Bill," and then enter the labels and numbers for the Rental Inputs section (range A3:B7) and Rental Rates (A12:C15), and enter labels in the Customer Bill (cells in bold within the range E3:H12). Delete the third sheet.
3. Switch to the Customer Bill sheet, and then create the following names using the definitions provided:
   - Customer =B4
   - TypeCar =B5
   - DaysRented =B6
   - MilesDriven =B7
4. Create the following validation rules for cells B5, B6, and B7 as shown in Figure 8-38.

Figure 8-38

Cell	Settings	Input Message	Error Alert
B5	List Source (A14:A15)	*Enter an appropriate input message*	Title: Invalid Type Style: Stop Message: *Enter an appropriate error alert message*
B6	Integers >0 and < 30	*Enter an appropriate input message*	Title: Warning Days Rented Style: Warning Message: *Enter an appropriate error alert message*
B7	Integers > 0 and < 5000	*Enter an appropriate input message*	Title: Warning Miles Style: Warning Message: *Enter an appropriate error alert message*

5. Enter the formulas, using the names created in Step 3, to calculate the values shown in the figure.
   - Cell F6 is equal to the value in cell B4.
   - Cell F7 is equal to the value in cell B5.
   - Cell F9 is equal to the value in cell B6.
   - Cell F10 is equal to the value in cell B7.
   - Cell H9 is equal to the charge per day, which depends on the type of car entered in cell B5 and the rate table.
   - Cell H10 is equal to the charge per mile, which depends on the type of car rented in cell B5 and the rate table.
   - Cell F12 is equal to the amount due, which equals the days rented multiplied by the charge per day plus the miles driven multiplied by the charge per mile.
6. Test the worksheet using the data shown in Figure 8-37.

(*Note:* In the following steps, you'll create several macros. Save your workbook before recording each macro. That way, if you make a mistake in recording the macro or the macro doesn't run correctly, you can close the workbook—without saving the changes—and then reopen it and try again. Read the list of tasks before you begin recording them.)

7. Create a macro named "PrintBill," with the shortcut key Ctrl + p, that prints only the bill portion of the worksheet found in the range E3:H12, centered horizontally on the page, with the worksheet name in the center at the top of the printout and your name in the lower-right corner of the printout. Create a macro button that covers the range E13:F14, assign the PrintBill macro to the button, and then change the default label to "Print Bill."

8. Create a macro named "ClearInputs," with the shortcut key Ctrl + c, that clears the data in the Rental Inputs section of the worksheet (range B4:B7). Create a macro button that covers just cell A8, assign the ClearInputs macro to the button, and then change the default label to "Clear."

9. Protect the worksheet so a user may enter data only in the range B4:B7. Do not use a password to enable protection.

10. Test the worksheet using the following data: Marisa Elders, Luxury, 2 days, 150 miles.

11. Use the Print Bill macro button to print the customer bill for Marisa Elders.

12. Use the Clear macro button to remove the rental data.

13. Save the workbook, and then edit the PrintBill macro in the Visual Basic Editor so screen updating is turned off while the macro is running and turned on when the macro ends.

14. Test the revised macro using the following data: Aristo Balboni, Compact, 5 days, 635 miles.

15. Use the Print Bill macro button to print the customer bill for Aristo Balboni, and then use the Clear macro button to remove the data in the Rental Inputs section of the worksheet.

16. Save and close the workbook.

Internet Assignments

The purpose of the Internet Assignments is to challenge you to find information on the Internet that you can use to work effectively with this software. The actual assignments are updated and maintained on the Course Technology Web site. Log on to the Internet and use your Web browser to go to the Student Online Companion for New Perspectives Office 2003 at **www.course.com/np/office2003**. Click the Internet Assignments link, and then navigate to the assignments for this tutorial.

SAM Assessment and Training

If you have a SAM user profile, you may have access to hands-on instruction, practice, and assessment of the skills covered in this tutorial. Log in to your SAM account and go to your assignments page to see what your instructor has assigned.

Research

Use the Internet to find and work with data related to the topics presented in this tutorial.

Assess

Quick Check Answers

Session 8.1

1. Excel menus and actions are replaced by customized menus and commands, and the ability to control data entry.
2. Select the cell and then click Validation on the Data menu.
3. Select the cell. Open the Data Validation dialog box, select the Input Message tab, and then enter a title and text for the input message.
4. the Stop alert, which prevents the user from storing the data in the cell; the Warning alert, which, by default, rejects the invalid data but allows the user to override the rejection; and the Information alert, which, by default, accepts the invalid data but still allows the user to cancel the data entry
5. A locked cell is one in which data entry is prohibited. The locked property is only enabled when the sheet is protected.
6. Worksheet protection controls the ability of the user to make changes to the cells within the worksheet. Workbook protection controls the user's ability to change the structure of the workbook (including worksheet names) and the format of the workbook window.
7. Yes, as long as the structure of the workbook is not protected.

Session 8.2

1. A named cell or range is a name assigned to a cell or range. The name is a word or string of characters that describes a cell or range reference. Using a name for a cell or range can make interpreting your formulas easier. If you change the definition of the name, pointing it to a different range, the value of any formula using that named range will be updated automatically to reflect the new definition.
2. using the Name box, using the Define Name dialog box, and using the Create Names dialog box
3. a. Annual_Total
4. Name box
5. =SUM(Sales)
6. =Report.xls!Sales

Session 8.3

1. A digital signature is an electronic signature on a digital certificate. A digital signature confirms that the macro or document created by the signer has not been altered since the digital certificate was created.
2. You can use the macro recorder to record the exact keystrokes and commands that you want the macro to run, or you can write the macro code directly in the Visual Basic Editor with VBA macro language.
3. Visual Basic for Applications—the macro language of all Microsoft Office applications
4. You can store a macro in the current workbook, in a new workbook, or in the Personal Macro workbook, which is available whenever you use Excel.
5. Click Tools on the menu bar, point to Macro, click Macros to open the Macros dialog box, select the macro from the list of macros, and then click the Delete button.
6. Click Tools on the menu bar, point to Macro, click Macros to open the Macros dialog box, select the macro from the list of macros, and then click the Edit button.
7. sub procedures
8. Unprotect the worksheet, if necessary, and then display the Forms toolbar. Click the Button tool on the Forms toolbar, and then draw the button image on the worksheet. Assign a macro and label to the button.

Objectives

- Use IF, AND, and OR functions
- Create a nested IF function
- Calculate a conditional count
- Calculate a conditional sum
- Use advanced filters to filter a list
- Calculate summary statistics using database functions

Working with Logical Functions, Database Functions, and Advanced Filtering

Reviewing Employee Data

Case

Branco, Inc.

Maria Alba is a new financial officer at Branco, Inc., a regional superstore for kitchenware. One of Maria's jobs is to record and summarize employee information, including the total cost of employee salaries and benefits. She also tracks employee enrollment in the various benefit programs offered by the company.

Because Branco's business is expanding, the company is planning to add to its workforce. Management wants to give part-time employees and consultants the opportunity to apply for full-time positions before searching outside the company. To provide the information for which management is looking, Maria will need to review employment records using the criteria that management has defined. She needs to determine which part-time employees have worked more than two years and which consultants have worked more than one-half year and earn less than $45,000. Individuals from either group may be considered for full-time employment.

Maria has asked for your help in calculating each employee's life insurance coverage, and how much the company spends for each employee's 401(k) retirement account and health plan. She wants an Excel workbook that automatically totals the cost to the company for these benefits, and she wants the names of workers who meet specific criteria required for consideration for full-time employment.

To provide Maria with the information she wants, you'll use some of the Logical functions supported by Excel. You'll learn how to use the IF, AND, and OR functions and learn how to nest an IF function inside another IF function. You'll use the SUMIF and COUNTIF functions to calculate sums and counts based

Student Data Files

▼**Appendix.A**

▽ Tutorial folder	▽ Review folder	▽ Cases folder
Branco1.xls	Leave1.xls	Housing1.xls
		Modem1.xls

on search criteria. Finally, you'll use Excel's advanced filtering options to generate a list of potential full-time employees and then use Excel's Database functions to summarize the information in the list.

Working with Excel's Logical Functions

Branco offers three types of benefits on which Maria is focusing: life insurance, retirement, and health care. The basic life insurance coverage is equal to each employee's annual base salary. Employees may elect to purchase an additional $50,000 supplemental coverage by paying the premium. The 40l(k) retirement savings plan matches eligible employee's contributions dollar for dollar up to 3% of the employee's salary. The company supports two health plans: a family plan that costs the company $5,000 annually per employee family, and an individual employee plan that costs the company $4,000 annually for each single employee. An employee can also opt out of a health plan by showing evidence of coverage elsewhere.

Maria has created a workbook that contains descriptive data on each employee. You'll open this workbook now and review the employee information.

To open Maria's workbook:

▶ **1.** Start Excel and open the **Branco1** workbook located in the Appendix.A\Tutorial folder included with your Data Files.

▶ **2.** On the Documentation sheet, enter the *current date* and *your name*, and then save the workbook as **Branco2** in the Appendix.A\Tutorial folder.

▶ **3.** Review the contents of the workbook, and then switch to the Employee Data worksheet.

There are two sheets with which Maria needs your help. The Employee Data worksheet contains a list of employee data. Maria has recorded each employee's name and employment status (FT for full time, PT for part time, or CN for paid consultant). The worksheet also lists each employee's salary, the number of years the employee has been with the company, the type of health plan for which the employee has signed up (F for family, I for individual, or N for none), and whether the employee has additional life insurance coverage (Y for Yes, N for No). Maria needs you to insert formulas that calculate the life insurance coverage, the 401(k) contribution, and the health plan cost for each employee. Once you calculate those values, Maria wants to summarize that information on the Employee Summary worksheet, so she can report the total impact of the benefits package on the company.

Using the IF Function

There are many situations in which the value you store in a cell depends on certain conditions, for example:

- An employee's gross pay may depend on whether that employee worked overtime.
- A taxpayer's tax rate depends on his or her adjusted taxable income.
- A shipping charge depends on the size of an order.

The IF function is one of several Logical functions that are available in Excel. A Logical function works with values or expressions to test, or evaluate, whether a condition in a workbook is true or false. For example, the expression A1=10 would be true if cell A1 contains the value 10 and false if any other value is stored in the cell. The IF function allows you to evaluate a specified condition, resulting in one action if the condition is true and another action if the condition is false. The syntax of the IF function is

IF(*logical_test, value_if_true,[value_if_false]*)

where *logical_test* is an expression that is either true or false, *value_if_true* is the value displayed in the cell if the logical test is true, and *value_if_false* is the value displayed if the logical test is false. Note that the *value_if_false* argument is optional, though in most cases you'll use it so that the function covers both possibilities.

To illustrate how the IF function works, suppose you need to determine whether an employee earns a 3% or 4% commission. The commission is 4% if an employee's weekly sales are above $5,000; otherwise it's 3%. Figure A-1 shows the logic of this situation.

Flowchart illustrating logic of IF function   **Figure A-1**

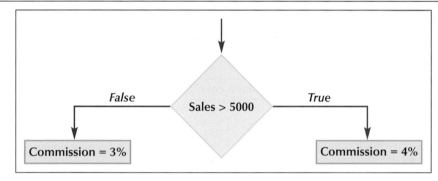

The formula *=IF(D4>5000, .04, .03)* uses the IF function to determine whether the value in cell D4 is greater than 5,000. If it is, the formula returns the value .04 (4%); otherwise, the formula returns the value .03 (3%).

You can also construct logical tests that involve **text strings**, that is, values that are text rather than values that are numbers or cell references. The formula *=IF(A1="Retail", B1, B2)* uses the IF function to determine whether cell A1 contains the text string "Retail." If it does, the formula returns the value of cell B1; otherwise, it returns the value of cell B2.

Expressions in the logical test always include a comparison operator. A comparison operator indicates the relationship between two values. Figure A-2 describes the comparison operators supported by Excel.

Comparison operators   **Figure A-2**

Operator	Example	Description
=	A1 = B1	Tests whether the value in cell A1 *is equal to* the value in cell B1
>	A1 > B1	Tests whether the value in cell A1 *is greater than* the value in cell B1
<	A1 < B1	Tests whether the value in cell A1 *is less than* the value in cell B1
>=	A1 >= B1	Tests whether the value in cell A1 is *greater than or equal to* the value in cell B1
<=	A1 <= B1	Tests whether the value in cell A1 is *less than or equal to* the value in cell B1
<>	A1 <> B1	Tests whether the value in cell A1 *is not equal to* the value in cell B1

A comparison operator is combined with an expression to form a condition. Figure A-3 illustrates several examples of conditional situations and how they can be expressed in Excel.

Figure A-3 ▶ **Examples of conditional situations**

Conditional Situation	Excel Formula

IF salesperson's sales are greater than 5000
  THEN return 0.1 (10% bonus)
  ELSE return 0.05% (5% bonus)
	=IF(B4>5000, 0.10, 0.05)
	where cell B4 stores salesperson's sales

IF region code is equal to 3
  THEN return the label East
  ELSE return the label Other
	=IF(N7=3,"East", "Other")
	where cell N7 stores region code

IF age is less than or equal to 65 rate
  THEN return amount multiplied by 65 or under rate
  ELSE return amount multiplied by over 65 rate
	=IF(A21<=65, B21*C21, B21*D21)
	where cell A21 stores age; cell B21 stores amount; cell
	C21 stores 65 or under rate; and cell D21 store over
	65 rate

Maria has sketched a flowchart, as shown in Figure A-4, which illustrates the logic needed for calculating an employee's life insurance coverage.

Figure A-4 ▶ **Flowchart illustrating logic of life insurance coverage**

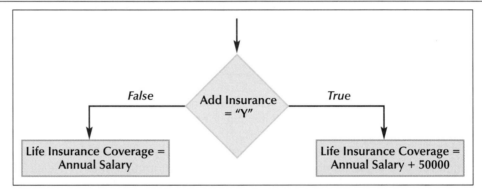

You'll now enter a formula that includes an IF function to calculate the life insurance coverage that an employee is eligible to receive.

To calculate the life insurance coverage using an IF function:

▶ 1. Click cell **G8**, and then click the **Insert Function** button 𝑓𝑥 on the Formula bar. The Insert Function dialog box opens.

▶ 2. Select **Logical** in the Or select a category list box, click **IF** in the list of functions, and then click the **OK** button. The Function Arguments dialog box for the IF function opens. You'll use this dialog box to enter the values for the IF function arguments.

▶ 3. In the Logical_test box, type **D8="Y"** and then press the **Tab** key.

▶ 4. Type **F8+50000** in the Value_if_true box. This is the value to be returned if the condition is true (that is, the salary plus $50,000).

▶ 5. Click in the Value_if_false box, and then type **F8**, the cell containing the value to be returned if the condition is false. Figure A-5 shows the completed Function Arguments dialog box.

Function Arguments dialog box for IF function

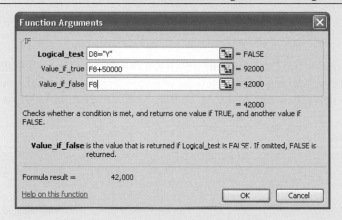

6. Click the **OK** button. The formula =IF(D8="Y",F8+50000,F8) appears in the Formula bar, and because the condition in this cell is false, the value 42,000 appears in cell G8.

7. Copy the formula in cell **G8** to the range **G9:G109**, and then click any cell to deselect the selection. The life insurance coverage for all employees is displayed in column G.

Using the AND Function

Next, you'll insert a formula to calculate the company's 401(k) contribution for each employee. To be eligible, an employee must be a full-time worker with at least one year of job experience. Maria has outlined the eligibility conditions in the flowchart shown in Figure A-6.

Flowchart illustrating logic of employee eligibility for 401(k) plan

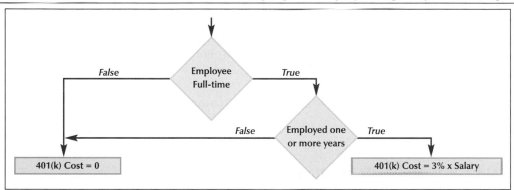

As you see in the flowchart, *both* conditions must be true for an employee to be eligible for the 401(k) plan, in which case the company contributes 3% of the employee's salary; otherwise, the employee is not eligible and the company's contribution is zero.

The IF function evaluates a single condition; however, in this case, to calculate the cost of the 401(k) plan for each employee, you need to use the AND function along with the IF function. The **AND function** returns a true value if the logical condition is true. The syntax of the AND function is

AND(*logical condition1, [logical condition2,], ...*)

where *logical condition1* and *logical condition2* are expressions that can be either true or false. If both of the logical conditions are true, the AND function returns the logical value TRUE; otherwise, the function returns the logical value FALSE. Note that you can include additional logical conditions, but they *all* must be true for the AND function to return a logical value TRUE.

Excel also supports the **OR function**, which returns a logical value TRUE if at least one of conditions is true, and the **NOT function**, which reverses the logical value of an expression. Figure A-7 lists the syntax of the AND, OR, NOT, FALSE, and TRUE functions.

Figure A-7 | **Logical functions**

Function	Description
IF(*logical_test*, *value_if_true*, [*value_if_false*])	Returns the value *value_if_true* if the *logical_test* expression is true and *value_if_false* if otherwise
AND(*logical1*, [*logical2*, *logical3*, ...])	Returns the value TRUE if all *logical* expressions in the function are true and FALSE if otherwise
OR(*logical1*, [*logical2*, *logical3*, ...])	Returns the value TRUE if any *logical* expression in the function is true and FALSE if otherwise
FALSE()	Returns the value FALSE
TRUE()	Returns the value TRUE
NOT(*logical*)	Returns the value FALSE if the *logical* expression is true and the value TRUE if the *logical* expression is false

In the Employee Data worksheet, job status is stored in column B, and years employed is stored in column E. If you want to test whether the first employee in the list fulfills the eligibility requirements, you would use the AND function in the formula =*AND(B8="FT",E8>=1)*. Therefore, if the employee works full time (B8="FT") and has worked one or more years (E8>=1), then the AND function returns the logical value TRUE; otherwise, the function returns the value FALSE.

However, to determine whether the first employee is eligible *and* to calculate the amount of the 401(k) contribution, you insert the AND function within an IF function in the formula =IF(AND(B8="FT",E8>= 1),F8*0.03,0). Then, if the employee is eligible, this formula returns the value of the employee's salary in cell F8 multiplied by .03. For any other condition, the formula returns the value 0.

You'll enter this formula using the IF and AND functions now for the first employee in Maria's list.

To use the IF and AND functions:

1. Press the **Ctrl + Home** keys to display the top of the worksheet, and then click cell **H8**.

2. Type **=IF(AND(B8="FT",E8>=1),F8*0.03,0)** and then click the **Enter** button ☑ on the Formula bar. The value 0 appears in the cell because both conditions of the logical test have not been met for the first employee. You'll copy this formula into the remaining cells in the column.

3. With cell H8 still selected, drag the fill handle over the range **H9:H109**.

4. Scroll up the worksheet window, observing the results of the formula for each record, and then click cell **H8**. Figure A-8 shows the 401(k) contributions for the first 16 employees in Maria's list.

401(k) costs

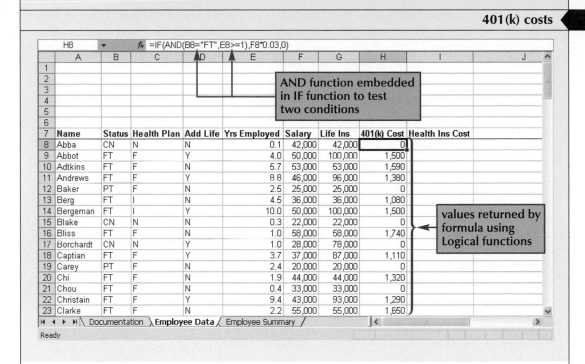

AND function embedded in IF function to test two conditions

values returned by formula using Logical functions

Next, you'll calculate the health plan cost for each employee.

Creating Nested IF Functions

At Branco, every employee, except for paid consultants, is eligible for the company's health plan. There are two health plans: the family plan (F), which costs the company $5,000 per employee, and the individual plan (I), which costs the company $4,000. Maria displays the logic for determining health plan costs in her sketch, shown in Figure A-9.

Flowchart illustrating logic of health insurance options

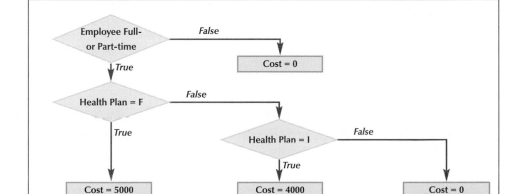

To convert this flowchart into an Excel formula, you'll work from the bottom upward. This will have the same effect as creating the formula from the inside out. First, you create an IF function to determine whether the first employee is enrolled in the individual (I) health plan. If so, the cost to the company is $4,000; otherwise, the cost is zero. The function is:

IF(C8="I",4000,0)

Next, you move up the flowchart. The employee could also have enrolled in the family plan (F) at a cost of $5,000 to Branco. For this situation, you include or "nest" one IF function in another one. The formula with a **nested IF function** appears as:

=IF(C8="F",5000,IF(C8="I",4000,0))

So, if an employee is enrolled in the family plan, the cost is $5,000; otherwise, Excel tests whether the employee is enrolled in either the individual plan (for $4,000) or no plan at all.

You are not done with the flowchart yet. You still have to determine whether the employee is eligible for the health plan in the first place. The health plan is only available for full-time or part-time employees. If the worker is not eligible for a health plan, Maria wants the field to be blank so she can easily distinguish an employee who is eligible for a health plan from one who is not eligible. You can nest the two IF functions inside yet a third IF function to determine whether the first employee is eligible. The complete formula is:

=IF(OR(B8="FT",B8="PT"),IF(C8="F",5000,IF(C8="I",4000,0)),"")

So, if the first employee is eligible, Excel determines how much the health plan will cost the company; otherwise, the cell is left blank. This is called an **empty string**. To specify the "value" of an empty string, you enter quotation marks without a space (""). Note that this formula uses the OR function to determine whether the employee is eligible. Cell B8 must be equal to "FT" *or* "PT" for the OR function to return the logical value TRUE. You'll insert this formula including the nested IF functions and the OR function to column I of the Employee Data worksheet.

To use the OR function and nested IF functions:

1. Click cell **I8**, type **=IF(OR(B8="FT",B8="PT"), IF(C8="F", 5000, IF(C8="I",4000,0)),"")** and then click the **Enter** button ☑ on the Formula bar. The entry in cell I8 is blank, because the employee has a status code of CN. There are several layers of parentheses in this function. You can keep track of the layer that you're in by viewing the color of the parentheses. The outermost layer is colored black, the next layer is green, and the innermost layer is purple.

   Now you'll copy the formula for the rest of the employees in the list.

2. With cell I8 still selected, drag the fill handle over the range **I9:I109**. Excel fills in the values.

3. Scroll up the worksheet window, and then click cell **I8**. Figure A-10 shows the health insurance costs for the first 16 employees in the list.

Health plan costs — **Figure A-10**

	A	B	C	D	E	F	G	H	I	J

I8 ▼ *fx* =IF(OR(B8="FT",B8="PT"),IF(C8="F",5000,IF(C8="I",4000,0)),"")

nested IF functions

values returned by formula using nested IF functions

	Name	Status	Health Plan	Add Life	Yrs Employed	Salary	Life Ins	401(k) Cost	Health Ins Cost	
8	Abba	CN	N	N	0.1	42,000	42,000	0		
9	Abbot	FT	F	Y	4.0	50,000	100,000	1,500	5,000	
10	Adtkins	FT	F	N	5.7	53,000	53,000	1,590	5,000	
11	Andrews	FT	F	Y	8.8	46,000	96,000	1,380	5,000	
12	Baker	PT	F	N	2.5	25,000	25,000	0	5,000	
13	Berg	FT	I	N	4.5	36,000	36,000	1,080	4,000	
14	Bergeman	FT	I	Y	10.0	50,000	100,000	1,500	4,000	
15	Blake	CN	N	N	0.3	22,000	22,000	0		
16	Bliss	FT	F	N	1.0	58,000	58,000	1,740	5,000	
17	Borchardt	CN	N	Y	1.0	28,000	78,000	0		
18	Captian	FT	F	Y	3.7	37,000	87,000	1,110	5,000	
19	Carey	PT	F	N	2.4	20,000	20,000	0	5,000	
20	Chi	FT	F	N	1.9	44,000	44,000	1,320	5,000	
21	Chou	FT	F	N	0.4	33,000	33,000	0	5,000	
22	Christain	FT	F	Y	9.4	43,000	93,000	1,290	5,000	
23	Clarke	FT	F	N	2.2	55,000	55,000	1,650	5,000	

◄ ◄ ► ►◄ \ Documentation \ **Employee Data** / Employee Summary /

Ready

You've completed your work in calculating the cost of benefits for each employee. Next, Maria wants you to summarize these results in the Employee Summary worksheet.

Calculating Conditional Counts and Sums

Excel provides the **COUNT function** to calculate the number of data values and the SUM function to calculate the total of the data values. In some situations, you may want to calculate a conditional count or sum—that is, counting or summing values for only those cells that meet a particular condition. Maria wants you to add this feature to her workbook. She wants to be able to calculate the cost of salaries for full-time and part-time employees, and consultants. She would also like to find out how many employees have signed up for the 401(k) plan and the amount paid into it.

Using the COUNTIF Function

You can calculate the number of cells in a range that match criteria you specify using the **COUNTIF function**. This is sometimes referred to as a **conditional count**. The syntax of the COUNTIF function is

COUNTIF(*range, criteria*)

where *range* is the range of cells that you want to include and *criteria* is an expression that defines which cells are to be counted. For example, Maria wants to know how many people are employed full time at Branco. The job status information is stored in column B of the Employee Data worksheet. To count the number of full-time employees, you can use the formula =COUNTIF('Employee Data'!B8:B109,"FT"), and Excel will count all of the cells in the range B8:B109 of the Employee Data worksheet that contain the text "FT." Note that because FT is a text string, you need to enclose it within a set of quotation marks. You'll enter this formula using the COUNTIF function now in the Employee Summary worksheet.

To use the COUNTIF function:

1. Switch to the Employee Summary sheet.

2. Click cell **C4**, type **=COUNTIF('Employee Data'!B8:B109,"FT")** and then press the **Enter** key. Excel returns the value 70, indicating that the company employs 70 full-time workers.

   Now you'll enter the formulas that calculate the number of part-time employees (PT) and the number of paid consultants (CN).

3. Type **=COUNTIF('Employee Data'!B8:B109,"PT")** in cell C5, and then press the **Enter** key. There are 25 part-time employees.

4. Type **=COUNTIF('Employee Data'!B8:B109,"CN")** in cell C6, and then press the **Enter** key. There are seven consultants.

5. With cell C7 the active cell, click the **AutoSum** button Σ on the Standard toolbar, and then press the **Enter** key to calculate the total number of employees at the company. There are a total of 102 people working at Branco.

Now Maria wants to know the total cost of salaries.

Using the SUMIF Function

The SUMIF function is the counterpart to the COUNTIF function. You can calculate the sum of values in a range that meet criteria you specify using the **SUMIF function**. This is called a **conditional sum**. The syntax of the SUMIF function is

SUMIF(*range*, *criteria* [, *sum_range*])

where *range* is the range of cells to which you want to apply the criteria, *criteria* contains the condition used in the range to filter the list, and *sum_range* is the range of cells that you want to sum. The *sum_range* argument is optional; if you omit it, Excel will sum the values specified in the *range* argument.

For example, Maria wants to know the total salaries paid out to full-time (FT) employees. Job status is recorded in column B of the Employee Data worksheet, and salary data is stored in column F. The formula to calculate this value is *=SUMIF('Employee Data'!B8:B109,"FT", 'Employee Data'!F8:F109)*.

Any employee whose job status is "FT" will have their salary value added to the total. You'll insert this formula into the Employee Summary sheet using the SUMIF function.

To use the SUMIF function:

1. Click cell **D4**, type **=SUMIF('Employee Data'!B8:B109,"FT", 'Employee Data'!F8:F109)**, and press the **Enter** key. Excel displays the value 3,454,000—the total salaries paid to full-time employees.

   You'll enter the formula to calculate the total salaries for part-time (PT) employees and paid consultants (CN).

2. In cell D5, enter **=SUMIF('Employee Data'!B8:B109,"PT",'Employee Data'!F8:F109)**, and then enter **=SUMIF('Employee Data'!B8:B109,"CN", 'Employee Data'!F8:F109)** in cell D6. Branco spends $342,000 per year on part-time workers and $213,000 per year on consultants.

   Now you'll calculate the total cost of all salaries.

3. With cell D7 as the active cell, click the **AutoSum** button Σ on the Standard toolbar, and then press the **Enter** key. The total cost of salaries is $4,009,000, as shown in Figure A-11.

Calculating conditional counts and sums

	A	B	C	D	E	F	G	H	I
1		Employee Summary							
2									
3		Employee Status	Number of Employees	Total Salaries					
4		Full-Time	70	3,454,000					
5		Part-Time	25	342,000					
6		Consultants	7	213,000					
7		Total	102	4,009,000					
8									
9									

You explain to Maria that as she enters new employees or edits the information on old ones, the values displayed in the Employee Summary worksheet will be automatically updated.

Advanced Filtering

Most users find that Excel's AutoFilter feature manages their filtering needs. However, users occasionally need to filter a list in a way that the AutoFilter feature cannot accommodate. For instance, you may need to perform any of the following:

- Use OR conditions across multiple fields.
- Specify more than two criteria in one field.
- Create complex criteria using functions and formulas, as well as AND/OR criteria in one filter.

In these cases, you can use Excel's Advanced Filter command to filter the data.

Setting Advanced Filtering Criteria

Before you can use advanced filters, you need to create a criteria range. The **criteria range** is an area in a worksheet, separate from the Excel list, used to specify criteria that will be used to filter the list. The criteria range consists of a row of one or more field names from the header row of the list and at least one row directly below the names where you enter the filtering criteria. When you set up a criteria range:

- There must be at least two rows in the range.
- The first row must contain field names.
- All other rows must consist of the criteria.

Criteria placed on the same row will be treated as the logical operator AND. That means all criteria on the same row must be met before a record is included in the filtered list. Criteria placed on separate rows will be treated as the logical operator OR. That means records that meet all the criteria on a row in the criteria range will be displayed independently of whether the record also satisfies the criteria in any other row.

Because the field names in the criteria range must exactly match the field name in the list, except for case, you should copy and paste the field names to the criteria range instead of typing the names into the cells. Typically, the criteria range is placed above or below the list, as placement on the same rows as the list may result in the criteria being hidden after you apply filtering commands.

You'll place the criteria range in rows 1 through 3 of the Employee Data worksheet so it will be easy to locate.

To create the criteria range:

▶ **1.** Switch to the Employee Data worksheet, select range **A7:I7**, and then click the **Copy** button 🖻 on the Standard toolbar.

▶ **2.** Click cell **A1** and then click the **Paste** button 🖺 on the Standard toolbar. The field names for the criteria range are displayed.

▶ **3.** Press the **Esc** key to deselect the range.

Now you'll enter in row 2 the criteria for consultants working more than one-half year and earning $45,000 or less.

▶ **4.** Click cell **B2**, type **CN**, and then press the **Tab** key three times to move to column E. Notice that unlike the IF function, a string constant is not enclosed in quotation marks. In the rows below the column labels, you'll enter the criteria that you want to match. All items that begin with CN will be filtered.

▶ **5.** Type **>.5** in cell E2, and then press the **Tab** key. This criterion filters records in which the value in the Yrs Employed column is greater than .5.

▶ **6.** Type **<=45000** in cell F2, and then press the **Enter** key.

Next, you'll enter the criteria for part-time employees working more than two years in the third row of the criteria range.

▶ **7.** If necessary, click cell **B3**, type **PT**, press the **Tab** key three times, type **>2** in cell E3, and then press the **Tab** key. See Figure A-12.

Figure A-12 ▶ **Criteria range**

	A	B	C	D	E	F	G	H	I	J
1	Name	Status	Health Plan	Add Life	Yrs Employed	Salary	Life Ins	401(k) Cost	Health Ins Cost	
2		CN			>.5	<=45000				
3		PT			>2					
4										
5										

Now that the criteria range is established, you can use the Advanced Filter command to filter the employee list. You can filter the records in their current location by hiding rows that don't match your criteria, as you do with the AutoFilter command, or copy the records that match your criteria to another location on the worksheet. Maria wants you to filter the records in their current location. Try filtering the list now.

To filter the list in its current location:

▶ **1.** Click any cell within the list.

▶ **2.** Click **Data** on the menu bar, point to **Filter**, and then click **Advanced Filter**. The Advanced Filter dialog box opens, as shown in Figure A-13.

Advanced Filter dialog box   **Figure A-13**

3. Make sure the **Filter the list, in-place** option button is selected, the range **$A$7:$I$109** is displayed in the List range box, and **$A$1:$I$3** is displayed in the Criteria range box, and then click the **OK** button.

4. Scroll to the top of the list. As shown in Figure A-14, the list is filtered in its current location, and 13 employee records are displayed.

Results of advanced filtering   **Figure A-14**

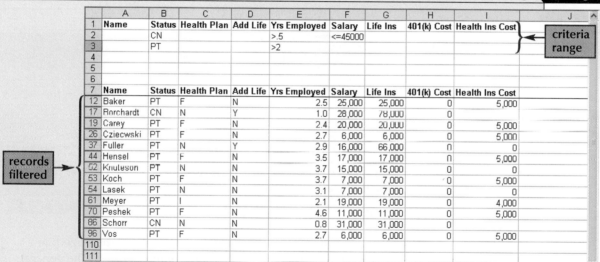

	A	B	C	D	E	F	G	H	I	J
1	Name	Status	Health Plan	Add Life	Yrs Employed	Salary	Life Ins	401(k) Cost	Health Ins Cost	
2		CN			>.5	<=45000				
3		PT			>2					
4										
5										
6										
7	Name	Status	Health Plan	Add Life	Yrs Employed	Salary	Life Ins	401(k) Cost	Health Ins Cost	
12	Baker	PT	F	N	2.5	25,000	25,000	0	5,000	
17	Borchardt	CN	N	Y	1.0	28,000	78,000	0		
19	Carey	PT	F	N	2.4	20,000	20,000	0	5,000	
26	Cziecwski	PT	F	N	2.7	6,000	6,000	0	5,000	
37	Fuller	PT	N	Y	2.9	16,000	66,000	0	0	
44	Hensel	PT	F	N	3.5	17,000	17,000	0	5,000	
52	Knuteson	PT	N	N	3.7	15,000	15,000	0	0	
53	Koch	PT	F	N	3.7	7,000	7,000	0	5,000	
54	Lasek	PT	N	N	3.1	7,000	7,000	0	0	
61	Meyer	PT	I	N	2.1	19,000	19,000	0	4,000	
70	Peshek	PT	F	N	4.6	11,000	11,000	0	5,000	
86	Schorr	CN	N	N	0.8	31,000	31,000	0		
96	Vos	PT	F	N	2.7	6,000	6,000	0	5,000	
110										
111										

criteria range

records filtered

After providing the list of eligible employees to Maria, you now want to display all records in the list, so you will remove the filter and display the complete list of records.

To show all the records in the list:

1. Click **Data** on the menu bar, point to **Filter**, and then click **Show All**. All the records in the list appear.

Copying Filtered Records to a New Location

You can change the entries in the criteria range and run the Advanced Filter command again to display a different set of filtered records. You can also specify a separate location to which the filtered records can be copied. For example, if you want the list you just filtered in a different location, you select the Copy to another location option button from the Action section of Advanced Filter dialog box and specify in the Copy to box the first cell of the range where you want the filtered records to be copied. Excel copies the filtered record to the location beginning at the cell specified in the Copy to box. If you want to copy records to a worksheet other than the sheet where the list is stored, you must make the destination worksheet the active worksheet before you choose the Advanced Filter command.

Maria wants you to provide summary statistics on employee data in the Employee Summary sheet.

Using Database Functions to Summarize an Excel List

There are a number of Excel functions that perform summary data analysis (sum, average, count, and so on) on a list of values based on criteria that you set. These functions are called **Database functions**, or **Dfunctions**. Although the SUMIF and COUNTIF functions, the total row feature of a list range, and PivotTables can achieve the same result as database functions and are often considered easier to use, there are situations in which the type of summary analysis, the placement of the summary results, or the complexity of the criteria require the use the of database functions. Figure A-15 shows a partial list of the Database functions.

Figure A-15 ▷ Database functions

Function Name	Description
DAVERAGE	Returns the average of the values that meet specified criteria
DCOUNT	Returns the number of cells containing numbers that meet specified criteria
DCOUNTA	Returns the number of nonblank cells that meet specified criteria
DMAX	Returns the maximum value in search column that meets specified criteria
DMIN	Returns the minimum value in search column that meets specified criteria
DSTDEV	Returns the estimate of standard deviation based on a sample of entries that meet the specified criteria
DSUM	Returns the sum of the values in the summary column that meet specified criteria

Dfunctions use a criteria range to specify the records that are to be summarized. In a Dfunction, the criteria range is used as one of the arguments of the function. The general syntax for any Dfunction is

DfunctionName(*list range, column to summarize, criteria range*)

where *list range* refers to the cells in which the data is located, including the header row; *column to summarize* is the column name of the field you want to summarize; and *criteria range* is the range where the criteria is specified.

You'll use Dfunctions to complete the Employee Summary worksheet, summarizing the number of participants and the total and average cost of both the 401(k) and health insurance benefits.

First, you'll set up separate criteria ranges for each benefit plan. Although the criteria range often includes all fields from the list (even those that are not required), you do not have to include all field names from the list when setting up a criteria range. In setting up the criteria range to use with the database functions, you'll use only the fields needed to specify the criteria.

To find the number of participants and the total and average cost for employees contributing to the 401(k) plan, you need to establish a criteria range to include full-time employees employed for one or more years. You'll create this criteria range in the range L11:M12 of the Employee Summary worksheet.

To establish a criteria range for employees contributing to the 401(k) plan:

▶ **1.** Switch to the Employee Summary sheet, and then scroll to the right to make column L visible. Notice that the column headers for the criteria range have already been copied from the Employee Data sheet to the Employee Summary sheet. If you want to avoid scrolling to column L, you can hide columns F, G, and H.

▶ **2.** Click cell **L12**, type **FT**, press the **Tab** key, type **>=1** in cell M12, and then press the **Enter** key. The criteria range for employees eligible for the 401(k) plan is complete. See Figure A-16.

Criteria range for 401(k) plan ◀ **Figure A-16**

Now you'll enter the database functions to get the values Marie wants.

▶ **3.** Scroll the worksheet so that column C is visible, click cell **C12**, type **=DCOUNT('Employee Data'!A7:I109,"401(k) Cost",L11:M12)** and then press the **Tab** key. There are 65 participants.

▶ **4.** Type **=DSUM('Employee Data'!A7:I109,"401(k) Cost",L11:M12)** in cell D12, and then press the **Tab** key. The contribution is $96,570.

▶ **5.** Type **=DAVERAGE('Employee Data'!A7:I109,"401(k) Cost",L11:M12)** in cell E12, and then press the **Enter** key. The average contribution is $1,486.

Before you calculate the number of participants, and the total and average health insurance costs for employees, you first will set up the criteria range for employees signed up for family or individual health plans.

To establish the criteria range for employees eligible for health insurance:

▶ **1.** Scroll to the right to make column J visible. The column header for the criteria range has already been copied from the Employee Data sheet to the Employee Summary sheet.

▶ **2.** Click cell **J12**, type **F**, press the **Enter** key, type **I** in cell J13, and then press the **Enter** key. The criteria range for employees eligible for the health plan is set up, as shown in Figure A-17.

Criteria range for health plan ◀ **Figure A-17**

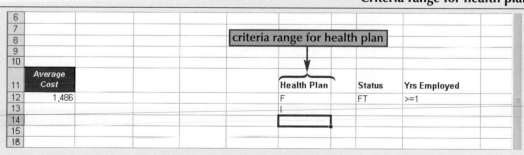

When you work with database functions, you may find that assigning named ranges (topic covered in Tutorial 8) to your Excel list and criteria range will make entering the function easier and less prone to error. With this in mind, you'll assign the name "ListRange" to the Excel list and the name "CritRngHealth" to the criteria range.

To assign a range name to the Excel list and criteria range:

▶ 1. Switch to the Employee Data worksheet, and then select the range **A7:I109**.

▶ 2. Click in the Name box to the left of the Formula bar. The cell reference A7 is automatically selected.

▶ 3. Type **ListRange** and then press the **Enter** key.

▶ 4. Switch to the Employee Summary worksheet, and then select the range **J11:J13**.

▶ 5. Click in the Name box, type **CritRngHealth** as the range name, and then press the **Enter** key.

With names assigned to the ranges, you'll use those names in the database functions you need to enter to calculate the number of participants, and the total and average health insurance costs.

To enter the database functions using range names:

▶ 1. In cell C13, type **=DCOUNT(ListRange,"Health Ins Cost",CritRngHealth)** and then press the **Tab** key. The number of participants is 89.

▶ 2. Type **=DSUM(ListRange,"Health Ins Cost",CritRngHealth)** in cell D13, and then press the **Tab** key. The total cost is $420,000.

▶ 3. Type **=DAVERAGE(ListRange,"Health Ins Cost",CritRngHealth)** in cell E13, and then click the **Enter** button ✓ on the Formula bar. The average cost is $4,719. See Figure A-18 for the results of the database functions you entered.

| Figure A-18 | Summary results using Database functions |

E13   ▼   *fx* =DAVERAGE(ListRange,"Health Ins Cost",CritRngHealth)

	A	B		D	E	F	G	H	I
3		**Employee Status**	*Number of Employees*	*Total Salaries*					
4		Full-Time	70	3,454,000	using names instead of range reference in arguments				
5		Part-Time	25	342,000					
6		Consultants	7	213,000					
7		**Total**	102	4,009,000					
8									
9									
10									
11		**Benefit**	*Number of Participants*	*Total Cost*	*Average Cost*				
12		401(k)	65	96,570	1,486				
13		Health Plan	89	420,000	4,719				
14									
15									

▶ 4. Save your changes to the workbook, and then close it.

Appendix Summary

In this appendix, you learned how to use several of Excel's logical functions (IF, AND, and OR functions), and you learned how to nest one IF function inside another IF function. You also used the SUMIF and COUNTIF functions to calculate sums and counts based on search criteria. You learned how to filter lists when more advanced filtering criteria are required. Finally, you learned how to use database functions to summarize a list based on specified criteria.

Key Terms

AND function	criteria range	NOT function
conditional count	Database function	OR function
conditional sum	Dfunction	SUMIF function
COUNT function	empty string	text string
COUNTIF function	nested IF function	

Practice the skills you learned in this appendix by creating a worksheet that tracks the amount of vacation time and family leave to which an employee is entitled.

Review Assignments

Data File needed for the Review Assignments: Leave1.xls

Maria has another workbook for which she needs your help. This workbook tracks the amount of vacation time and family leave used by each employee in the company. Maria needs to calculate how much vacation time and family leave each employee is eligible for, and then she can subtract from that amount the amount they've already used. She also wants to calculate the total number of vacation and family leave days used by all employees, as well as the total number of days remaining. Here are the eligibility requirements for the different vacation and family leave plans:

For vacation:

- 17 days for full-time employees who have worked more than 5 years
- 12 days for full-time employees who have worked more than 1 year
- 7 days for full-time employees who have worked 1 year or less
- 0 days for everyone else

For family leave:

- 5 days for full-time employees who have worked 1 or more years
- 3 days for full-time employees who have worked less than 1 year or for part-time employees who have worked more than 2 years
- 0 days for everyone else

You'll use these eligibility requirements to calculate the available vacation time and family leave for each employee. To complete this task:

1. Open the workbook **Leave1** located in the Appendix.A\Review folder included with your Data Files, and then save the workbook as **Leave2** in the same folder.
2. Enter the date and your name on the Documentation sheet, and then switch to the Employee Data worksheet
3. In column D, enter a formula using a nested IF function to determine the number of vacation days each employee is eligible for based on the employee's job status in column B and on the number of years employed in column C.

4. Subtract the amount of vacation time used from the available vacation time, displaying the remaining vacation time in column F for all employees.

5. In column G, enter a formula using a nested IF function to determine each employee's total family leave time. (*Hint*: Use the AND and OR functions.)

6. To determine the remaining family leave time, subtract the used portion of family leave from the total family leave and display the results in column I.

7. Switch to the Leave Summary worksheet. Use the COUNTIF function to calculate the total number of employees eligible for the different vacation plans. (*Hint*: An employee who is eligible for the 17-day vacation plan will have the value 17 in column D of the Employee Data worksheet.)

8. Enter a formula to calculate the total number of employees in cell C8 by summing up the employees on each vacation plan.

9. In the range D4:D7, use the SUMIF function to calculate the total number of vacation days for each vacation plan.

10. In the range E4:E7, use the DSUM function to calculate the total number of vacation days remaining.

11. In cell D8, enter a formula to calculate the total vacation days, and then, in cell E8, enter a formula to calculate the total days remaining.

12. Use advance filtering to print all full-time employees with five remaining family leave days as well as all part-time employees with three remaining family leave days.

13. Print the entire workbook. Save your changes to the workbook and close it.

Case Problem 1

Apply

Apply the skills you learned in this appendix to analyze and summarize monthly sales data for PC-Market Distribution.

Data File needed for this Case Problem: Modem1.xls

Entering Purchase Orders at PC-Market Linda Klaussen works for PC-Market Distribution, a computer supply store. She needs your help in designing an Excel workbook to enter purchase order information. She has already entered the product information on PC-Market's line of modems. She wants you to insert a lookup function to look up data from the product table. The company also supports three shipping options: Standard shipping at $5.50, Express shipping at $7.50, and Overnight shipping at $10.50. She wants the purchase order sheet to be able to calculate the total cost of the order, including the type of shipping the customer requests. She also wants to use advanced filtering to copy data on all modems under $50 to a new worksheet in order to review prices of the inexpensive items. Finally, she wants to calculate average prices for each category of modems using database functions. To complete this task:

1. Open the **Modem1** workbook located in the Appendix.A\Cases folder included with your Data Files, and then save the workbook as **Modem2** in the same folder.

2. Enter your name and the date in the Documentation sheet, and then switch to the Purchase Order worksheet.

3. A product ID number will be entered in cell B5. Create a lookup function to display the product type in cell C7, the model name in cell C8, and the price in cell C13. Product information is displayed in the Product List worksheet. (*Hint*: Refer to Tutorial 6 for information on Lookup functions.)

Explore

4. If no product ID number is entered in cell B5, then cells C7, C8, and C13 will display the #N/A error value. Linda wants these cells to display a blank value instead. Use an IF function, along with the ISNA() function, to test whether the lookup functions you created in Step 3 display the #N/A value; if so, then display a blank value (""); otherwise, display the results of the lookup function.

5. One of the three shipping options will be entered in cell B11. Use an IF statement to display the costs of the shipping in cell C14; if no shipping option is selected, then display a blank value in cell C14.

6. Display the total cost of the product and shipping in cell C16. If the sum equals an error value (#Value!), display a blank value in the cell. (*Hint*: Use an IF function, along with the ISERROR function, to determine whether an error value will be displayed.)

7. Test the worksheet using a product ID number of 1050 and the express shipping option. Print the resulting worksheet.

Explore

8. Switch to the Product List worksheet, and then use advanced filtering to copy all 56K desktop modems with a price under $50 to Sheet1. Rename the sheet "ModemsUnder50." Make sure the values in all the columns are visible, and then print the worksheet with your name and date on separate lines in the lower-right corner of the page.

9. Switch to the Summary worksheet, and then use database functions to determine the average modem price per modem type.

10. Save your changes to the workbook, and then close it.

Apply

Apply the skills you learned in this appendix to compile and summarize reports for Glenwood Realty.

Case Problem 2

Data File needed for this Case Problem: Housing1.xls

Displaying Home Data for Glenwood Realty   Tim Derkson is a realtor with Glenwood Realty. He has created a workbook containing data on homes in the local market. He has asked for your help in designing a worksheet that will display summary information on the homes he has entered. He has already set up and formatted the workbook, but he needs you to insert the correct formulas. To complete this task:

1. Open the **Housing1** workbook located in the Appendix.A\Cases folder included with your Data Files, and then save the workbook as **Housing2** in the same folder.

2. Enter the date and your name in the Documentation sheet, and then switch to the Home Summary worksheet.
   Tim has stored the housing data in the Home Data worksheet. He wants to use the Home Summary worksheet to search for information about the homes. There are two categories of homes that Tim is interested in: those in the upscale NE Sector of Glenwood and those on corner lots. In cell C3, he has created drop-down lists from which he can select the values "Yes," "No," or "Total." A value of "Yes" implies a house in the NE Sector, whereas a value of "No" indicates a house not in the NE Sector. The value "Total" indicates all of the homes in the workbook.

3. In cell C4, enter a formula that counts the number of houses listed in the Home Data worksheet. If a value of "Yes" is displayed in cell C3, count the number of NE Sector houses. If a value of "No" is displayed in cell C3, count the number of non-NE Sector houses. If a value of "Total" is displayed in cell C3, count the total number of houses. (*Hint*: You can use any numeric column in the Home Data worksheet as the basis for your count.)

Explore

4. In cells C5 through C8, enter a formula to calculate the average price, square footage, age, and annual taxes for the houses in the Home Data worksheet. Once again, the average will be based on the value chosen in cell C3: limiting the average to only NE Sector houses, non-NE Sector houses, or all of the houses that Tim has recorded. (*Hint*: To calculate the average value for either NE Sector or non-NE Sector houses, use the SUMIF function, divided by the count displayed in cell C4.)

5. Click cell C3 to display its list arrow, and then verify that the calculations in the table reflect the criteria chosen for each cell.

6. Switch to the Home Data worksheet, and then use advanced filtering to print a list of all corner lots with a price greater than $200,000 or corner lots more than 10 years old and with a square footage over 2,500. Copy the filtered data to a new sheet and rename it "Filtered List."

7. Switch to the Home Summary worksheet, and then use Database functions to complete the calculations in the range C12:F16 on the Home Summary sheet. (*Hint*: Cell C12 counts the number of houses on a corner lot, in the NE Sector. Cell D12 counts the number of houses on a corner lot, but not in the NE Sector, and so on.) Create four criteria ranges, one for each situation.

8. Print the Home Summary worksheet with your name and date on separate lines in the lower-right corner of the page.

9. Save your changes to the workbook, and then close it.

Objectives

- Learn about methods of integration using Office programs
- Link an Excel worksheet to a Word document
- Update a linked object
- Embed an object
- Modify an embedded object

Integrating Excel with Other Windows Programs

Creating Integrated Documents

Case

The Lighthouse

The Lighthouse is a charitable organization providing shelter, meal programs, and educational opportunities for the people of rural central Pennsylvania. Beth Purcell is the financial director of The Lighthouse. Each year, she sends out a financial report to the organization's supporters and contributors. Beth stores the financial data in an Excel workbook, and she uses Microsoft Word to create the report. Beth wants to be able to copy the Excel data and paste it directly into the Word document. She also wants to learn how to tie the two documents together, so that if she updates the financial information in the Excel workbook, the report in the Word document will be automatically updated as well.

Beth has asked you to help her integrate her Excel data into her Word document and link the documents, so that the data in the report is automatically updated each time Beth modifies the workbook.

Student Data Files

▼ **Appendix.B**

▽ **Tutorial folder**
Letter1.doc
LHouse1.xls

▽ **Review folder**
Request1.doc
Use1.xls

▽ **Cases folder**
Accounting.doc
Earnings.doc
Expenses.doc
Investment.doc
Omicron1.xls
Phoenix1.xls
Show1.ppt

Methods of Integration

Excel is part of a suite of programs called Microsoft Office. In addition to Excel, the Office programs include Word, a word-processing program; Access, a database entry and management program; PowerPoint, a presentation and slide show program; Outlook, a personal information manager; FrontPage, a program for creating Web pages; and Publisher, a program for creating desktop publishing projects. All of these programs share a common interface and can read each other's file formats.

Occasionally, you will need to create a document that relies on information from more than one application. This type of document is called a **compound document**. Compound documents are usually created from two or more documents. The **source document** (or documents) contains the source of the information to be shared. The **destination document** is the document (or documents) that will display the information from the source document (or documents). Compound documents are easy to create in Office because of the tight integration of the Office applications. At The Lighthouse, Beth needs to create a letter using Word that incorporates information from an Excel workbook that contains financial data.

There are three ways to duplicate data in other applications: copying and pasting, linking, and embedding. Each of these techniques can be used to create a compound document. Figure B-1 describes each of these methods, and provides examples of when each method would be appropriate.

Figure B-1 ▶ **Comparison of methods of integrating information**

Method of Integration	Description	Use when
Copying and pasting	Inserts an object into a document	You want to exchange the data between the two documents only once, and it doesn't matter if the data changes.
Linking	Displays an object in the destination document but doesn't store it there—only the location of the source document is stored in the destination document	You want to use the same data in more than one document, and you need to ensure that the data will be current and identical in each document. Any changes you make to the source document will be reflected in the destination document(s).
Embedding	Displays and stores an object in the destination document	You want the source data to become a permanent part of the destination document, or the source data will no longer be available to the destination document. Any changes you make to either the destination document or the source document will not affect the other.

Copying and Pasting Data

You can copy text, values, ranges of cells, or even charts and graphics from one program and paste it in another program using Windows' copy and paste features. The item being copied and pasted is referred to as an object. When you paste an object from the source document into the destination document, you are inserting the object so that it is now part of the destination document. The **pasted object** is static, having no connection to the source document. If you want to change the pasted object, you must do so in the destination document. For example, a range of cells pasted into a Word document can only be edited within the Word document. Any changes made in the original Excel workbook have no impact on the Word document. For this reason, pasting is only used for one-time exchanges of information.

Object Linking and Embedding

If you want to create a live connection between two documents, so that changes in the source document are automatically reflected in the destination document, you must use object linking and embedding. **Object linking and embedding (OLE)** refers to the technology that allows you to copy and paste objects, such as graphic files, cell ranges, or charts, so that information about the application that created the object is included with the object itself.

The objects are inserted into the destination document as either linked objects or embedded objects. A **linked object** is actually a separate file that is linked to the source document. If you make a change to the source document, the linked object can be automatically updated to reflect the change. An **embedded object** is information that is stored in the source document and inserted directly into the destination document. Once embedded, the object becomes part of the destination document. In the case of Office applications, embedded objects carry along their menus and toolbars. This means you can edit an Excel chart embedded in a Word document using the same tools and menu commands that are available to you in Excel. Embedded objects have no link to the source document, so that changes made to the embedded object are not reflected in the source document.

Thus, the main difference between linked and embedded objects lies in how the data is stored and how it is updated after being inserted into the destination document. Figure B-2 illustrates the difference between linking and embedding.

Embedding contrasted with linking   **Figure B-2**

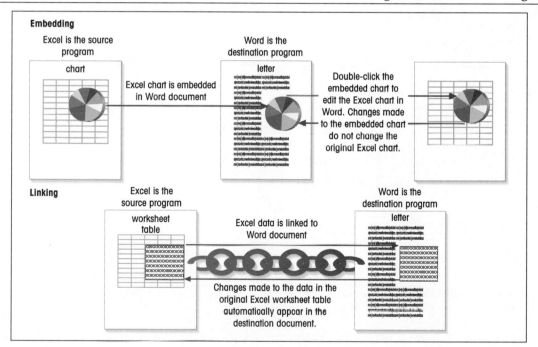

Linking an Excel Worksheet to a Word Document

Beth needs you to paste the financial data stored in her Excel workbook into a letter she has been composing for The Lighthouse's supporters. She is still working on the details of the financial report, and she might have to edit some of the values in the workbook. Rather than pasting the data each time she modifies the report, Beth wants you to create a link between her Excel workbook and her Word document, so that any changes she makes to the workbook are automatically reflected in the letter. You will open both files and link the Excel data to the Word document.

To open Beth's two files:

▶ 1. Start Excel and open the **LHouse1** workbook located in the Appendix.B\Tutorial folder included with your Data Files.

▶ 2. Enter *your name* and the *current date* in the Documentation sheet, and then save the workbook as **LHouse2** in the Appendix.B\Tutorial folder.

▶ 3. Click the **Start** button on the taskbar, point to **All Programs**, point to **Microsoft Office**, and then click **Microsoft Office Word 2003** to start Word.

▶ 4. Click the **More** link in the Getting Started task pane, navigate to the Appendix.B\Tutorial folder, and then double-click **Letter1** in the list box to open the document in the Word window.

▶ 5. Click **File** on the menu bar, click **Save As** to open the Save As dialog box, and then save the document as **Letter2** in the Appendix.B\Tutorial folder.

▶ 6. Return to the **LHouse2** workbook in Excel, and then switch to the Financial Summary worksheet. See Figure B-3.

Figure B-3	LHouse2 workbook

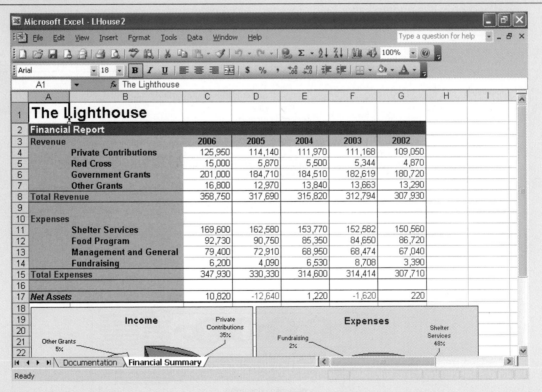

Trouble? To move between the programs, click the appropriate program button on the Windows taskbar.

The financial data that Beth wants to display in her letter is stored in the range A3:G17 of the Financial Summary worksheet. To transfer that data, you'll first copy it and then paste it as a link in the Word document.

To copy and paste the worksheet data:

1. Select the range **A3:G17**, and then click the **Copy** button 📋 on the Excel Standard toolbar.

2. Return to the **Letter2** document in Word, and then click the paragraph mark ¶ displayed below the letter's second paragraph (below the sentence that reads "Below are The Lighthouse's income and expenses for the past five years"). See Figure B-4.

Letter2 document ◄ **Figure B-4**

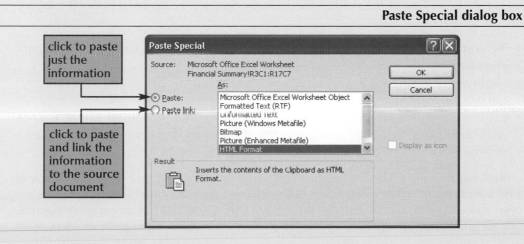

Trouble? If your document does not show paragraph marks at the end of each paragraph, click the Show/Hide button ¶ on Word's Standard toolbar.

3. Click **Edit** on the menu bar, and then click **Paste Special**. The Paste Special dialog box opens. See Figure B-5.

Paste Special dialog box ◄ **Figure B-5**

The Paste link option in the Paste Special dialog box allows you to paste information using several different formats. The default format is to insert the data as a Word table using HTML (Hypertext Markup Language). You could also paste Beth's data as a graphic image, as unformatted text, or as an embedded worksheet object. To create a link to the data in the LHouse2 workbook, you will click the Paste link option button. This will create the link that Beth wants so she can keep the data in each document in sync.

4. Verify that **HTML Format** is selected in the As list box, click the **Paste link** option button, and then click the **OK** button to paste the financial data into the letter. The financial report is pasted into the letter as shown in Figure B-6.

| Figure B-6 | Financial data pasted into the Letter2 document |

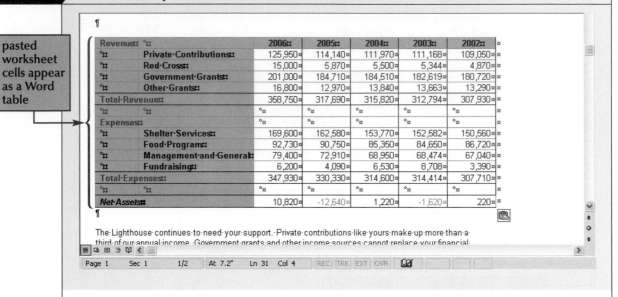

pasted worksheet cells appear as a Word table

The financial data is inserted into the Word document as a table. You can edit and format this table using any of Word's formatting features.

Updating a Linked Object

Links between different programs work the same way as links between Excel workbooks. As described in Tutorial 6, linked information will be updated under the following circumstances:

• The destination program will prompt you to update the link with the source document when you initially open the destination document.
• If both the destination and source documents are open, the link will be automatically updated whenever the information in the source document is changed.
• If only the destination document is open, you can manually update the link at any time by clicking Links on the Edit menu, selecting the link, and then clicking the Update Now button.

Beth has finished reviewing the financial summary in the LHouse2 workbook. She finds a data-entry error in the report. A $15,000 Red Cross contribution to The Lighthouse has been entered, when the amount should've been only $5,000. This is an excellent opportunity for you to test the ability to update linked data without having to paste the data again.

To update the linked information:

1. Return to the **LHouse2** workbook in Excel, and then press the **Esc** key to remove the selection border around the range A3:G17.

2. Click cell **C5**, type **5,000**, and then press the **Enter** key to insert the correct value for the Red Cross contribution.

3. Switch to the **Letter2** document in Word to verify that the value of the Red Cross contribution has automatically changed, reflecting the current value in the LHouse2 workbook.

   Trouble? f the link doesn't update automatically, right-click the table and click Update Link on the shortcut menu.

The linked information is automatically updated because both the source and destination documents are open. If this were not the case, you might have to open the Edit Links dialog box in the destination document to manually update the link. All of the Office applications use the same Edit Links dialog box to manage linked objects. You can refer to Tutorial 6 to learn more about managing linked data.

Embedding an Object

Beth also wants the letter to include a pie chart detailing the source of The Lighthouse's income. The pie chart is displayed in the LHouse2 workbook. Beth is now confident that the financial summary is correct and that no further edits are needed. Therefore, she doesn't need to create a link between her letter and the workbook's chart. Instead, she would like to embed the chart in her letter. This will allow her to use Excel's chart-editing tools from her Word document, if she chooses to modify the chart's appearance before printing the letter. You will embed the Income chart in the document now.

To embed an Excel chart in a Word document:

1. Switch to the **LHouse2** workbook in Excel, scroll down the Financial Summary worksheet so the charts are completely visible, and then click the **Income** chart to select it.

2. Click the **Copy** button 🔲 on the Excel Standard toolbar.

3. Switch to the **Letter2** document in Word, and then click the paragraph mark ¶ displayed above the letter's last paragraph (above the sentence that reads "If you would like to learn more about The Lighthouse ...").

4. Click **Edit** on the menu bar, and then click **Paste Special**. The Paste Special dialog box opens, but this time displays different format options in the As list box.

   You have two format options for charts from which to choose: One is to paste the chart as an Excel chart object; the other is to paste the chart as a graphic. Beth wants to have the ability to use Excel's chart editing tools, so you'll choose the first option.

5. Verify that **Microsoft Office Excel Chart Object** is the selected format and that the **Paste** option button (*not* the Paste link option button) is selected, and then click the **OK** button. Excel pastes the chart as an embedded object into the letter. See Figure B-7.

Figure B-7 **Chart embedded in the Letter2 document**

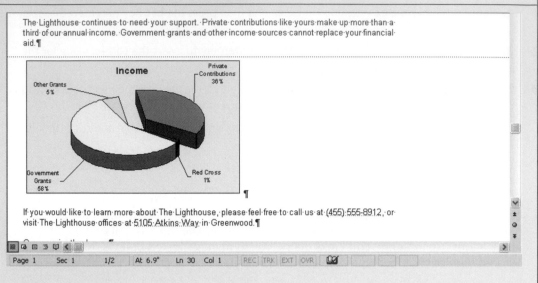

Modifying an Embedded Object

After viewing the contents of the chart, Beth wants you to change the chart's title from "Income" to "Income for 2006." You can do this by editing the chart within Word. Recall that when you make changes to an embedded object, those changes will not be reflected in the object in the source document. You will change the title of the chart that is embedded in the letter.

To edit the embedded chart:

1. Double-click the embedded chart in the Letter2 document. The hash-marked border appears around the chart, and this embedded object appears in an Excel workbook window, as shown in Figure B-8. Also note that the Chart toolbar appears and the Excel Chart menu replaces the Word Data menu.

Figure B-8 **Embedded chart selected for editing**

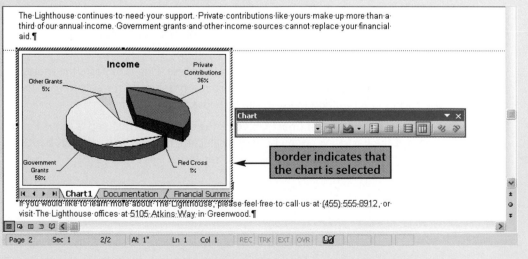

You will now edit the object using Excel's chart-editing tools within Word.

2. Click **Chart** on the menu bar, and then click **Chart Options**. The Chart Options dialog box opens in Word.

3. Click in the Chart title text box on the Titles tab, type **Income for 2006** as the new title, and then click the **OK** button. The chart title is updated.

4. Click outside the chart to deselect it. The Chart menu disappears from the Word menu bar. See Figure B-9.

Embedded chart updated with new chart title | Figure B-9

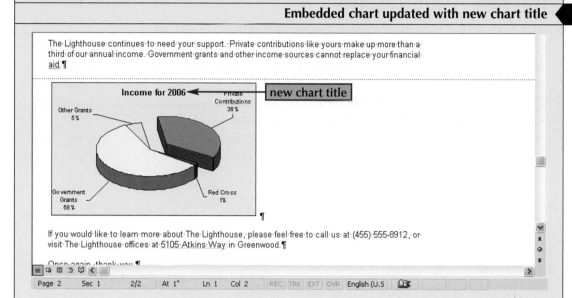

The·Lighthouse·continues·to·need·your·support.·Private·contributions·like·yours·make·up·more·than·a·third·of·our·annual·income.·Government·grants·and·other·income·sources·cannot·replace·your·financial·aid.¶

Income for 2006 ← new chart title

If·you·would·like·to·learn·more·about·The·Lighthouse,·please·feel·free·to·call·us·at·(455)·555-8912,·or·visit·The·Lighthouse·offices·at·5105·Atkins·Way·in·Greenwood.¶

Page 2   Sec 1   2/2   At 1"   Ln 1   Col 2   REC TRK EXT OVR English (U.S

Your work on both the LHouse2 workbook and the Letter2 document is complete, so you can save your changes and then exit Word.

5. Save your changes to the Letter2 document, close it, and then exit Word.

6. Save your changes to the LHouse2 workbook, and then close it.

You may have noticed in Figure B-8 that the embedded object included not just the chart sheet for the income statement, but also the other worksheets in the workbook. You could've selected one of the other worksheets in the workbook and displayed that information in place of the chart. This fact also relates to one of the disadvantages of embedded objects: They tend to greatly increase the size of the destination document. The Letter2 document now contains both the original letter and the LHouse2 workbook. For this reason, you should embed objects only when file size is not an issue.

Appendix Summary

Review

In this appendix you examined the different methods for sharing data between Office programs. You learned how to copy data from Excel to Word using pasting and linking. You saw how changes to the data in an Excel workbook are updated automatically in a linked Word document. You also learned how to embed an Excel chart within a Word document, making Excel tools available in Word.

Key Terms

compound document

destination document

embedded object

linked object

object linking and

   embedding (OLE)

pasted object

source document

Practice

Practice the skills you learned in the appendix using the same case scenario.

Review Assignments

Data Files need for the Review Assignments: Request1.doc, Use1.xls

Beth is writing a letter to the state government to report on the shelter and meal programs used at The Lighthouse. She has data in an Excel workbook and needs to incorporate the data into the letter she is composing in Word. Because the report will also include projections for the upcoming year, which she might modify, Beth wants to create a link between the information in the Excel workbook and the document in Word. She also wants to embed in the Word document a chart that she has created in her workbook. She has asked for your help in linking the two documents.

To complete this task:

1. Open the **Use1** workbook located in the Appendix.B\Review folder included with your Data Files, and then save the workbook as **Use2** in the same folder.
2. Enter the date and your name in the Documentation sheet, and then switch to the Shelter Usage sheet.
3. Start Word, open the **Request1** document located in the Appendix.B\Review folder, and then save the document as **Request2** in the same folder.
4. Return to the Use2 workbook in Excel, and then copy the range A2:G9 in the Shelter Usage sheet.
5. Return to the Request2 document in Word, and then paste the selected range as a link in Picture format below the first paragraph of Beth's letter. (*Hint*: If necessary, display the paragraph marks in the Word document.)
6. Beth has discovered that the number of client days in the domestic abuse shelter in December of 2006 was actually 75, not 72. Make this change in the Use2 workbook, and then verify that the picture in the Request2 document is automatically updated.
7. Copy the Projected Usage chart from the Shelter Usage worksheet, and then embed the chart below the second paragraph in Beth's letter (do *not* link the chart).
8. Edit the embedded chart, changing the background color of the plot area from light yellow to white.
9. Print the letter with the linked and embedded objects.
10. Save your changes to the Request2 and Use2 files, close the files, and exit the programs.

Case Problem 1

Data Files needed for this Case Problem: Accounting.doc, Earnings.doc, Expenses.doc, Investment.doc, Phoenix1.xls

Phoenix Software Kurt Walters works as an accountant for Phoenix Software. He has been asked to create an Excel workbook containing the company's income statement, cash flow statement, and balance sheet for the previous three years. Kurt wants to include some documentation in the workbook providing background details on the figures in his report. Such background details have already been entered into several Word documents. Kurt wants to embed these Word documents directly into his Excel workbook. He would like the documents to appear as icons, so that users can double-click the icons to view the document contents if they want. Kurt has asked for your help integrating the two documents. You can embed Word documents in your Excel workbooks using the Object command on Excel's Insert menu.

To complete this task:

1. Open the **Phoenix1** workbook located in the Appendix.B\Cases folder included with your Data Files, and then save the workbook as **Phoenix2** in the same folder.
2. Enter the date and your name in the Documentation sheet.
3. Switch to the Balance Sheet worksheet, and make cell E7 the active cell.

4. Open the Object dialog box from the Insert menu, click the Browse button on the Create from File tab, and then navigate to the Appendix.B\Cases folder. Insert the **Accounting** document as an icon and as a linked file. Change the icon caption to "Accounting," and then close the dialog boxes to return to the worksheet.

5. Resize the Accounting icon you created in Step 4 so that it covers the range E7:E9. Double-click the icon and verify that it opens a Word document that includes descriptions of various accounting terms used in the Balance Sheet worksheet. Close the Accounting document.
6. Repeat Steps 4 and 5 to insert the following documents (located in the Appendix.B\Cases folder) as icons (approximately the same size) into the Income Statement worksheet:
   • **Expenses** in cell E9 with the caption "Expenses"
   • **Investment** in cell E18 with the caption "Investment"
   • **Earnings** in cell E23 with the caption "Earnings"
7. Verify that the icons open the correct documents, and then close each document after it opens.
8. Save your changes to the workbook, and then exit both programs.

Challenge

Broaden your knowledge and challenge your skills by exploring how to create a slide show using Excel and PowerPoint.

Case Problem 2

Data Files needed for this Case Problem: Omicron1.xls, Show1.ppt

Omicron.com Howard Laarsen works in sales for Omicron.com, a multinational company that specializes in power and network solutions. He is preparing a slide show for an upcoming sales conference, and he wants to link some of the slides in the show to financial information contained in an Excel workbook. He has asked for your help in creating a compound document combining both an Excel worksheet and a PowerPoint slide show.

To complete this task:

1. Start Excel and then open the **Omicron1** workbook located in the Appendix.B\Cases folder included with your Data Files. Enter the date and your name in the Documentation sheet, and then save the workbook as **Omicron2** in the same folder.

Explore

2. Start PowerPoint, open the **Show1** PowerPoint presentation located in the Appendix.B\Cases folder, and then save the presentation as **Show2** in the same folder.
3. Return to the Omicron2 workbook in Excel, and then copy the range A3:B11 in the Fast Facts worksheet.

Explore

4. Return to the Show1 presentation in PowerPoint, and then paste (but don't link) the selection into the fourth slide of the presentation as a Device Independent Bitmap object. Resize the table to fit the space available in the slide.
5. Copy the range A2:F23 in the Highlights worksheet, and then paste the selection in the fifth slide of the Show2 presentation as a linked worksheet object. Resize the worksheet to fit the space available in the slide.
6. Return to the Omicron2 workbook in Excel to change the dividends paid per common share value in cell B17 from 0.50 to 0.52, and then verify that the table in the Show2 presentation has been updated.
7. Copy the chart in the Revenue Chart worksheet, and then paste the selection in the sixth slide of the Show2 presentation as an embedded chart object. Resize the chart to fit the space available in the slide.
8. Change the chart type of the embedded chart to a clustered bar chart with a 3-D visual effect. Make sure the 3-D view options are set so that the elevation is 15 degrees, the rotation is 20 degrees, and a right-angle axis is applied to the chart with auto-scaling.

Explore

9. Save your changes to the presentation, print all the slides, and then exit PowerPoint.
10. Save your changes to the Omicron2 workbook, close the file, and then exit Excel.

Glossary/Index

Task Reference

TASK	PAGE #	RECOMMENDED METHOD
3-D cell reference, enter in a formula	EX 261	See Reference Window: Entering a Formula That Contains a 3-D Reference
Absolute reference, change to relative	EX 58-59	Edit the formula, deleting the $ before the column and row references; or press the F4 key to switch to the relative reference mode
Action, redo	EX 34	Click
Action, undo	EX 34	Click
Actions, redo several	EX 34	Click , select the action(s) to redo
Actions, undo several	EX 34	Click , select the action(s) to undo
Auto Fill, copy formulas	EX 68	See Reference Window: Copying Formulas Using the Fill Handle
Auto Fill, create series	EX 71	Select the range, drag the fill handle down, release the mouse button, click , click the option button to complete the series
AutoFilter, filter list with	EX 213	See Reference Window: Filtering a List Using AutoFilter
AutoFormat, apply	EX 125	Select the range, click Format, click AutoFormat, select an AutoFormat, click OK
AutoShape, add text to	EX 183	See Reference Window: Inserting Text into an AutoShape
AutoShape, insert, reshape, resize, or rotate	EX 181	See Reference Window: Inserting an AutoShape
AutoSum, apply	EX 28	Click the cell in which you want the final value to appear, click Σ , select the AutoSum function to apply
Background color, apply	EX 112	Select the range, click the list arrow for , select a color square in the color palette
Background pattern, apply	EX 112	Open the Format Cells dialog box, click the Patterns tab, click the Pattern list arrow, click a pattern in the pattern gallery, click OK
Border, create	EX 109	Click , select a border in the border gallery
Border, draw	EX 109	Click , click , draw the border using the Pencil tool
Cell, accept or reject changes	EX 326	See Reference Window: Accepting and Rejecting Changes to Cells
Cell, clear contents of	EX 32	Click Edit, point to Clear, click Contents; or press Delete
Cell, edit	EX 34	See Reference Window: Editing a Cell
Cell, trace	EX 304	See Reference Window: Tracing Precedent and Dependent Cells
Cell, track changes	EX 323	See Reference Window: Tracking Changes to Cells
Cell reference, change	EX 59	Press the F4 key to cycle through the difference cell reference modes
Cells, delete	EX 32	Select the cell or range, click Edit, click Delete, select a delete option, click OK; or select the cell or range, right-click the selection, click Delete, select a delete option, click OK
Cells, insert	EX 31	See Reference Window: Inserting Cells into a Worksheet
Cells, merge	EX 115	Select the adjacent cells, open the Format Cells dialog box, click the Alignment tab, select the Merge cells check box, click OK
Cells, merge and center	EX 115	Select the adjacent cells, click
Cells, unlock	EX 364	Click Format, click Cells, click the Protection tab, deselect the Locked check box, click OK
Chart, add data label	EX 167	Select a data marker(s) or data series, click Chart, click Chart Options, click the Data Labels tab, select the data label type, click OK
Chart, add gridline	EX 167	Select the chart, click Chart, click Chart Options, click the Gridlines tab, click the check box for the gridline option you want to select, click OK
Chart, add, remove, or revise data series for	EX 164	See Reference Window: Editing the Data Source of a Chart

TASK	PAGE #	RECOMMENDED METHOD
Chart, change 3-D elevation	EX 180	Select a 3-D chart, click Chart, click 3-D View, enter the elevation value or click the Elevation Up or Elevation Down button, click OK
Chart, change location	EX 166	Select the chart, click Chart, click Location, specify the new location
Chart, change scale	EX 176–177	Double-click a value on the y-axis, enter the minimum and maximum values for the scale, click OK
Chart, change to 3-D	EX 179	Select the chart, click Chart, click Chart Type, select a 3-D subtype, click OK
Chart, create with Chart Wizard	EX 148	See Reference Window: Creating a Chart Using the Chart Wizard
Chart, format data marker	EX 172	Double-click the data marker, select the formatting options using the tabs in the Format Data Series dialog box
Chart, move	EX 158	Select the chart, move the pointer over the chart area, drag the chart to its new location, release the mouse button
Chart, resize	EX 158	Select the chart, move the pointer over a selection handle, drag the handle to resize the chart, release the mouse button
Chart, select	EX 157	Move the pointer over a blank area of the chart, and then click
Chart, update	EX 159	Enter new values for the chart's data source and the chart is automatically updated
Chart, use background image in	EX 175	Double-click the plot area, click the Patterns tab, click Fill Effects, click the Picture tab, click Select Picture, locate and select the background image file, click Insert, click OK twice
Chart axis title, add or edit	EX 155	Select the chart, click Chart, click Chart Options, click the Titles tab, click in the Category (X) axis text box and type the text for the title, click in the Values (Y) axis text box and type the text for the title, click OK
Chart data markers, change fill color	EX 172	Double-click the data marker, click the Patterns tab, click Fill Effects, click the Gradient tab, select the color and related color options, click OK
Chart text, format	EX 168	Select the chart label, click a button on the Formatting toolbar; or double-click the chart label, select the formatting options using the tabs in the Format Data Label dialog box
Chart text, insert new unattached	EX 171	See Reference Window: Inserting Unattached Text into a Chart
Chart title, add or edit	EX 155	Select the chart, click Chart, click Chart Options, click the Titles tab, click in the Chart title text box, type the text for the title, click OK
Chart Wizard, start	EX 148	Click 📊
Column, change width	EX 19	See Reference Window: Changing the Column Width or Row Height
Column, delete	EX 32	Select the column, click Edit, click Delete; or select the column, right-click the selection, click Delete
Column, hide	EX 116	Select the heading(s) for the column(s) you want to hide, right-click the selection, click Hide
Column, insert	EX 31	See Reference Window: Inserting a Row and Column into a Worksheet
Column, select	EX 25	Click the column heading of the column you want to select. To select a range of columns, click the first column heading in the range, hold down the Shift key and click the last column in the range.
Column, unhide	EX 116	Select the column headings left and right of the hidden column(s), right-click the selection, click Unhide
Columns, repeat in printout	EX 133	Open the Page Setup dialog box, click the Sheet tab, click in the Column to repeat at left box, click the column that contains the information you want repeated, click OK
Comment, delete	EX 323	Display the Reviewing toolbar, click 📝, click 🗑
Comment, display or hide	EX 316	Right-click the cell that contains the comment, click Show/Hide Comments or Hide Comment

TASK	PAGE #	RECOMMENDED METHOD
Comment, format	EX 316	Right-click the border of the comment box, click Format Comment, select the formatting options you want to apply, click OK; or click the comment box, click Format, click Comment
Comment, insert	EX 315	See Reference Window: Inserting a Comment
Comments, review	EX 321	Display the Reviewing toolbar, click 🔁 or 🔁
Conditional formatting, apply	EX 217	See Reference Window: Applying Conditional Formatting to Cells
Copy, across worksheets	EX 262	Select a worksheet group, select the sheet in the group containing the data you want to copy, click Edit, point to Fill, and click Across Worksheets, specify whether you want to copy all of the selected cell or just the contents or format, click OK
Count, create conditional	EX A10	Use the COUNTIF function
Custom AutoFilter, filter list with	EX 216	Click any cell in the list, click Data, point to Filter, click AutoFilter, click the list arrow in the column that contains data you want to filter, click Custom, enter criteria in the Custom AutoFilter dialog box, click OK
Data, create error alert message	EX 361	See Reference Window: Creating an Error Alert Message
Data, create input message	EX 360	See Reference Window: Creating an Input Message
Data, create validation rule	EX 358	See Reference Window: Creating a Validation Rule
Data form, add record using	EX 208	See Reference Window: Adding a Record Using a Data Form
Data form, delete record using	EX 211	See Reference Window: Deleting a Record Using a Data Form
Data form, search for record using	EX 210	Click any cell in the list, click Data, click Form, click Criteria, enter criteria, click Find Next
Database function (DFunction), insert	EX A15-A16	Use the DAVERAGE, DCOUNT, or DSUM function
Date, insert current	EX 72	Insert the TODAY() or NOW() function
Dates, fill in using Auto Fill	EX 71	Select the cell containing the initial date, drag the fill handle to fill in the rest of the dates, click 🖳, and then select an option to fill in days, weekdays, months, or years
Drawing toolbar, display	EX 181	Click View, point to Toolbars, click Drawing; or click 🎨
Excel, start	EX 5	Click Start, point to All Programs, point to Microsoft Office, click Microsoft Office Excel 2003
Find and Replace, use	EX 199-200	Click Edit, click Replace, enter the text to search for in the Find what list box, type replacement text in the Replace with list box, and then click Replace All, Replace, Find All, or Find Next
Font, change color	EX 104	Select the text, click 🅰, select a color from the color palette
Font, change size	EX 103	Click 10, click a size
Font, change style	EX 103	Click **B**, *I*, or U
Font, change typeface	EX 103	Click Arial, click a font
Format, apply Currency Style, Percent Style, or Comma Style	EX 97-99	Click $, click %, or click ; or open the Format Cells dialog box, click the Number tab, select a style, specify style-related options, click OK
Format, apply to several worksheets at once	EX 257	Group worksheets to be formatted, apply formatting options
Format, clear	EX 119	Click Edit, point to Clear, click Formats
Format, copy using Format Painter	EX 99	See Reference Window: Copying Formatting Using the Format Painter

TASK	PAGE #	RECOMMENDED METHOD
Format, decrease decimal places	EX 97	Click [icon]
Format, find and replace	EX 120	See Reference Window: Finding and Replacing a Format
Format, increase decimal places	EX 99	Click [icon]
Format Cells dialog box, open	EX 101	Click Format, click Cells
Formula, copy	EX 56	See Reference Window: Copying and Pasting a Cell or Range
Formula, copy using the fill handle	EX 68	See Reference Window: Copying Formulas Using the Fill Handle
Formula, enter using keyboard	EX 15	See Reference Window: Entering a Formula
Formula, enter using mouse	EX 15	See Reference Window: Entering a Formula
Formula, enter with worksheet reference	EX 258	See Reference Window: Entering a Formula That References Another Worksheet
Formula, insert	EX 15	See Reference Window: Entering a Formula
Formula, locate suspect	EX 312	See Reference Window: Locating Suspect Formulas
Formula, trace error	EX 309	See Reference Window: Tracing Errors
Formula, trace precedent and dependent cells	EX 304	See Reference Window: Tracing Precedent and Dependent Cells
Formula Auditing toolbar, display	EX 304	Click Tools, point to Formula Auditing, click Show Formula Auditing Toolbar
Formulas, audit	EX 304	Click Tools, point to Formula Auditing, click Show Formula Auditing Toolbar, use available buttons to audit formulas
Formulas, enter into several worksheets at once	EX 255-256	Group worksheets, enter the formulas into the appropriate cells
Formulas, show/hide	EX 42	Press the Ctrl + ` (grave accent) keys to display or hide the formulas in the worksheet cells
Freeze, row(s) and column(s)	EX 198	Click in the cell below and to the right of the row(s) and column(s) you want to freeze, click Window, click Freeze Panes
Function, create logical	EX A4-A7	Use the IF, AND, OR, or NOT function
Function, insert using Insert Function dialog box	EX 65	Click [icon] on the Formula bar, select the function from the Insert Function dialog box, complete the Function Arguments dialog box
Header/footer, create	EX 128	Open the Page Setup dialog box, click the Header/Footer tab, click the Header list arrow or the Footer list arrow, select an available header or footer, click OK
Header/footer, create custom	EX 129	Open the Page Setup dialog box, click the Header/Footer tab, click the Custom Header or Customer Footer button, complete the header/footer related boxes, click OK
Hyperlink, insert	EX 340	See Reference Window: Inserting a Hyperlink
Link, create to another workbook	EX 280	Click the cell in the destination file, type =, switch to the source file, click the cell that contains the data you want to link, complete the formula
Link, edit	EX 284	Click Edit, click Links, make the necessary changes in the Edit Links dialog box
Link, update	EX 284	Click Edit, click Links, select the link to update, click Update Values
Links, view list of	EX 283	Click Edit, click Links
List range, add record using data form	EX 208	See Reference Window: Adding a Record Using a Data Form
List range, add record using insert row	EX 208	Scroll to the insert row, click the first cell in the row, enter data
List range, calculate subtotals	EX 222	See Reference Window: Calculating Subtotals in a List
List range, calculate totals	EX 220	Click the Toggle Total Row button on the List toolbar, click a cell in the total row, click the list arrow and select a subtotal function

TASK	PAGE #	RECOMMENDED METHOD
List range, convert to normal range	EX 222	Click Data, point to List, click Convert to Range, click Yes
List range, create	EX 201	Click Data, point to List, click Create List, complete the Create List dialog box, click OK
List range, delete record using data form	EX 211	See Reference Window: Deleting a Record Using a Data Form
List range, display all records	EX 221	Click Data, point to Filter, click Show All
List range, display in outline view	EX 225	Click an Outline button located to the left of the worksheet window
List range, filter using AutoFilter	EX 213	See Reference Window: Filtering a List Using AutoFilter
List range, filter using Custom AutoFilter	EX 216	Click the column AutoFilter arrow, click Custom, specific criteria in the Custom AutoFilter dialog box, click OK
List range, search for record using data form	EX 210	Click a cell within the list, click Data, click Form, click Criteria, enter search criteria, click Find Next
List range, sort data using AutoFilter sort options	EX 204	Click the column AutoFilter arrow, click a sort option
List range, sort data using Sort commands	EX 205	See Reference Window: Sorting a List Using More Than One Sort Field
List range, sort data using toolbar buttons	EX 203	Click ⇣ or ⇡
Logical function, insert	EX 83	Use the IF function
Lookup table, create	EX 287	Create a table in a worksheet, insert compare values in the first row or column of the table, insert values to be retrieved in the rows or columns that follow
Lookup table, use functions for	EX 287	Enter the VLOOKUP or HLOOKUP function
Macro, edit	EX 389	See Reference Window: Editing a Macro
Macro, record	EX 380	See Reference Window: Recording a Macro
Macro, run	EX 385	See Reference Window: Running a Macro
Macro, set security level for	EX 378	See Reference Window: Setting the Security Level in Excel
Macro button, create	EX 393	See Reference Window: Creating a Macro Button
Macro code, print	EX 392	Open the macro in the Visual Basic Editor, click File, click Print, select the Current Project option button, select the Code check box, click OK
Magnification, change	EX 62	See Reference Window: Changing the Zoom Magnification of the Workbook Window
Mortgage, calculate interest rate of	EX 80	Use the RATE function
Mortgage, calculate monthly payment	EX 78	Use the PMT function
Mortgage, calculate number of payments	EX 80	Use the NPER function
Mortgage, calculate total value of	EX 80	Use the PV function
Name, create for range from a list	EX 370	See Reference Window: Creating a Name for a Cell or Range
Name, create for range using the Define Name dialog box	EX 370	See Reference Window: Creating a Name for a Cell or Range
Name, create for range using the Name box	EX 370	See Reference Window: Creating a Name for a Cell or Range

TASK	PAGE #	RECOMMENDED METHOD
Name, edit definition	EX 376	Click Insert, point to Name, click Define, select the range name you want to edit, change the cell reference in the Refers to box, click Add
Name range, replace cell reference with	EX 373	See Reference Window: Replacing a Cell Reference with a Name
Outline view, display or hide subtotals	EX 225	Calculate subtotals in a list, click an Outline button to display or hide levels
Page, change orientation	EX 40	Open the Page Setup dialog box, click the Page tab, click the Landscape or Portrait option button
Page, set margins	EX 127	Open the Page Setup dialog box, click the Margins tab, specify the width of the margins, click OK
Page break preview, switch to	EX 131	Click View, click Page Break Preview
Page Setup dialog box, open	EX 40	Click File, click Page Setup; or click the Setup button on the Print Preview toolbar
Pie chart, create	EX 159	Select the row or column of data values to be charted, click 📊, select Pie in the list of chart types, select a sub-type, complete the remaining Chart Wizard dialog boxes
Pie chart, explode piece(s)	EX 162	See Reference Window: Creating an Exploded Pie Chart
Pie chart, rotate	EX 161	Double-click the pie in the pie chart, click the Options tab, enter a new value in the Angle of First Slice box, click OK
PivotChart, create	EX 243	Click any cell inside the PivotTable, click 📊 on the PivotTable toolbar twice, complete the Chart Wizard dialog boxes
PivotTable, add a field	EX 237	Select the PivotTable, select a field from the PivotTable Field List, drag the field to the location on the table where you want it to appear
PivotTable, add a page view	EX 239	Click and drag a field to the Drop Page Fields Here area
PivotTable, create	EX 229	Select any cell in the list, click Data, click PivotTable and PivotChart Report, and then identify source, location, layout of data, and placement of the PivotTable
PivotTable, format numbers	EX 234	Click the PivotTable, click 📈 on the PivotTable toolbar, select an AutoFormat, click OK; or click the PivotTable, use the buttons on the Formatting toolbar
PivotTable, hide a field item	EX 240	Click the list arrow for the field button, deselect the check box for the field item you want to hide
PivotTable, layout on worksheet	EX 231	See Reference Window: Laying Out a PivotTable on a Worksheet
PivotTable, modify layout	EX 235	Click a field button on the PivotTable, drag the field button to a new location in the table
PivotTable, refresh	EX 241	Click ⚡ on the PivotTable toolbar
PivotTable, remove a field	EX 240	Click the field button, drag it to an area outside of the table
PivotTable, sort	EX 237	Click the cell that contains the field you want to sort, click ⇣ or ⇡
Print area, define	EX 131	Select the range, click File, point to Print Area, click Set Print Area
Range, copy	EX 27	Select the cell or range, hold down the Ctrl key and drag the selection to the new location, release the Ctrl key and mouse button
Range, move	EX 26	Select the cell or range, drag the selection to the new location, release the mouse button
Range, select adjacent	EX 24	See Reference Window: Selecting Adjacent or Nonadjacent Ranges of Cells
Range, select nonadjacent	EX 24	See Reference Window: Selecting Adjacent or Nonadjacent Ranges of Cells

TASK	PAGE #	RECOMMENDED METHOD
Relative reference, change to absolute	EX 58–59	Type $ before the column and row references; or press the F4 key
Review, accept and reject changes for	EX 326	See Reference Window: Accepting and Rejecting Changes to Cells
Reviewing toolbar, display	EX 321	Click View, point to Toolbars, click Reviewing
Row, change height	EX 19	See Reference Window: Changing the Column Width or Row Height
Row, delete	EX 33	Select the row, click Edit, click Delete; or select the row, right-click the selection, click Delete
Row, hide	EX 116	Select the heading(s) for the row(s) you want to hide, right-click the selection, click Hide
Row, insert	EX 31	See Reference Window: Inserting a Row or Column into a Worksheet
Row, select	EX 25	Click the heading of the row you want to select. To select a range of rows, click the first row heading in the range, hold down the Shift key and click the last row in the range
Row, unhide	EX 116	Select the row headings above and below the hidden row(s), right-click the selection, click Unhide
Rows, repeat in printout	EX 133	Open the Page Setup dialog box, click the Sheet tab, click in the Row to repeat at top box, click the row that contains the information
Sheet tab, format	EX 119	Right-click the sheet tab, click Tab Color, select a color from the color palette
Sort, single field	EX 203	Select any cell in column you want to sort by, click 🔼 or 🔽
Sort, use AutoFilter sort options	EX 204	Click the column AutoFilter arrow, click Sort Ascending or Sort Descending
Sort, use more than one sort field	EX 205	See Reference Window: Sorting a List Using More Than One Sort Field
Spelling, check	EX 38	Click 📝
Style, apply	EX 123	Select the range, click Format, click Style, select a style, click OK
Style, create	EX 122	Select the cell that contains the formatting you want to use as the basis of the new style, click Format, click Style, type a name for the style, click Modify, specify format options using the Format Cells dialog box, click OK twice
Style, modify	EX 124	Select the range, click Format, click Style, click Modify, change style attributes, click OK
Subtotals, insert in list	EX 222	See Reference Window: Calculating Subtotals in a List
Subtotals, remove from list	EX 225	Click Data, click Subtotals, click Remove All
Sum, create conditional	EX A10	Use the SUMIF function
Template, create	EX 267	See Reference Window: Saving a Workbook as a Template
Text, align within a cell	EX 105	Click ▤, click ▤, or click ▤; or open the Format Cells dialog box, click the Alignment tab, select a text alignment, click OK
Text, enter into cell	EX 11	Click the cell, type text entry, press Enter
Text, enter multiple lines in a cell	EX 12	See Reference Window: Entering Multiple Lines of Text Within a Cell
Text, enter using AutoComplete	EX 17	Type the first letter of a text entry you've entered in the worksheet, press Enter or Tab to complete the text entry displayed by AutoComplete
Text, increase or decrease indent of	EX 106	Click ▤ or ▤
Text, wrap in cell	EX 107	Open the Format Cells dialog box, click the Alignment tab, select the Wrap text check box, click OK
Total, calculate using total row	EX 220	Click the Toggle Total Row button on the List toolbar, click the cell to display its list arrow, select a subtotal function
Total, remove from list	EX 221	Click the Toggle Total Row button on the List toolbar

TASK	PAGE #	RECOMMENDED METHOD
Tracking log, show	EX 324	Click Tools, point to Track Changes, click Highlight Changes, click the List changes on a new sheet check box, click OK
Unfreeze, row(s) and column(s)	EX 198	Click Window, click Unfreeze Panes
VBA, insert a command	EX 391	Open the Visual Basic Editor, display the macro in the Code window, click at the end of a VBA command, press Enter, type the new command
VBA code, view	EX 389	Click Tools, point to Macro, click Macros, select a macro, click Edit
Visual Basic Editor, open	EX 391	Click Tools, point to Macro, click Visual Basic Editor; or click Tools, point to Macro, click Macros, select a macro, click Edit
Watch Window, use	EX 314	Select the cells to be viewed, click Tools, point to Formula Auditing, click Watch Window, use available options
Web options, define	EX 343	Click Tools, click Options, click the General tab, click Web Options, select the Web-related options that you want to define, click OK
Web page, create	EX 336	See Reference Window: Saving a Workbook as a Web Page
Web page, preview workbook as	EX 335	Click File, click Web Page Preview
Workbook, create using template	EX 267	See Reference Window: Creating a Workbook Based on a Template
Workbook, mail	EX 328	Click File, point to Send To, select an e-mail option; click 🔒
Workbook, mail for review	EX 329	Click File, point to Send To, click Mail Recipient (for Review)
Workbook, preview	EX 39	Click 🔍 ; or click the Preview button in the Print dialog box
Workbook, print	EX 39	Click 🖨 ; or click File, click Print, select printer and print-related options, click OK
Workbook, protect	EX 367	See Reference Window: Protecting a Workbook
Workbook, remove sharing from	EX 332	Click Tools, click Share Workbook, deselect the Allow changes by more than one user at the same time check box, click OK, click Yes
Workbook, route	EX 329	Click File, point to Send To, click Routing Recipient
Workbook, save	EX 22	Click File, click Save, locate the folder and drive where you want to save the file, type a filename, click Save
Workbook, save as a template	EX 269	See Reference Window: Saving a Workbook as a Template
Workbook, save as a XML file	EX 344	Click File, click Save As, click the Save as type list arrow, click XML Spreadsheet, click Save, click Yes, click the Enable the AutoRepublish feature option button, click OK
Workbook, save in a different format	EX 22	Open the Save or Save As dialog box, display the location where you want to save the file, enter a filename, click the Save as type list arrow, select the file format you want to apply, click Save
Workbook, share	EX 317	See Reference Window: Sharing a Workbook
Workbooks, merge	EX 330	See Reference Window: Merging Workbooks
Worksheet, add background image	EX 117	See Reference Window: Adding a Background Image to the Worksheet
Worksheet, copy	EX 37	See Reference Window: Moving or Copying a Worksheet
Worksheet, delete	EX 35	Click the sheet tab, click Edit, click Delete Sheet; or right-click the sheet tab, click Delete
Worksheet, insert	EX 35	Click Insert, click Worksheet; or right-click a sheet tab, click Insert, click the Worksheet icon, click OK
Worksheet, protect	EX 365	See Reference Window: Protecting a Worksheet

TASK	PAGE #	RECOMMENDED METHOD
Worksheet, remove split	EX 303	Double-click any part of the split bar that divides the worksheet
Worksheet, rename	EX 36	Double-click the sheet tab that you want to rename, type a new name, press Enter
Worksheet, split into panes	EX 302	Move the pointer over the split box, drag the split box to divide the worksheet into panes
Worksheet, unprotect	EX 368	Click Tools, point to Protection, click Unprotect Sheet
Worksheet data, copy and paste into another file	EX B5-B6	Select data, click [icon], switch to the destination file, click Edit, click Paste Special, select the HTML Format option, click the Paste link option button, click OK
Worksheet data, embed in another file	EX B7	Select data, click [icon], switch to the destination file, click Edit, click Paste Special, select the correct object format option, select the Paste option button, click OK
Worksheets, group or ungroup	EX 253	See Reference Window: Grouping and Ungrouping Worksheets
Worksheets, move	EX 37	See Reference Window: Moving or Copying a Worksheet
Worksheets, move between	EX 9	Click the sheet tab for the worksheet you want to view; or click one of the tab scrolling buttons and then click the sheet tab
Workspace, create	EX 290	Open all workbooks to be placed in the workspace, click File, Save Workspace, enter a name for the workspace, click Save
Workspace, open	EX 290	Click File, click Open, select the workspace file, click Open, click Update if prompted to update any links contained in the files

Microsoft Office Specialist Certification Grid

Standardized Coding Number	Certification Skill Activity	Courseware Requirements	Tutorial: Pages
XL03S-1	**Creating Data and Content**		
XL03S-1-1	Enter and edit cell content	Entering, editing, and clearing text, numbers and symbols in cells	Tutorial 1: 11–18, 34
		Filling series content using the fill handle tool	Tutorial 2: 68
XL03S-1-2	Navigate to specific cell content	Finding and modifying or replacing cell content or formatting	Tutorial 3: 120 Tutorial 5: 197
		Navigating to specific content (e.g., Go To)	Tutorial 1: 7–9
XL03S-1-3	Locate, select and insert supporting information	Locating supporting information in local reference materials or on the Internet using the Research tool	"Common Features" Tutorial: 16–18
		Using the Research tool to select and insert supporting text-based information	"Common Features" Tutorial: 16–18
XL03S-1-4	Insert, position, and size graphics	Inserting, positioning, and sizing graphics	Tutorial 4: 181–184
XL03S-2	**Analyzing Data**		
XL03S-2-1	Filter lists using AutoFilter	Filtering lists using AutoFilter	Tutorial 5: 211
XL03S-2-2	Sort lists	Sorting lists	Tutorial 5: 200–205
XL03S-2-3	Insert and modify formulas	Creating and editing formulas	Tutorial 1: 15 Tutorial 2: 55–56
		Entering a range within a formula by dragging	Tutorial 2: 55
		Using references (absolute and relative)	Tutorial 2: 58–60
XL03S-2-4	Use statistical, date and time, financial, and logical functions	Creating formulas using the following function categories: Statistical, Date and Time, Financial, and Logical (e.g., Sum, Min, Max, Date or Now, PMT, IF, Average)	Tutorial 2: 55, 66, 68, 73, 78, 83 Appendix A: 4, 7, 10–11, 16–17
XL03S-2-5	Create, modify, and position diagrams and charts based on worksheet data	Creating, modifying, and positioning diagrams and charts based on data contained in the active workbook	Tutorial 4: 148, 158–159, 164, 166–169, 172–174, 177
XL03S-3	**Formatting Data and Content**		
XL03S-3-1	Apply and modify cell formats	Formatting cells	Tutorial 3: 97–99, 102–104, 109–110, 112–113
		Applying AutoFormats to cells and cell ranges	Tutorial 3: 125
XL03S-3-2	Apply and modify cell styles	Applying styles (e.g., applying a style from the Format>Style list)	Tutorial 3: 122–124
XL03S-3-3	Modify row and column formats	Modifying height and width	Tutorial 1: 19
		Inserting and deleting, hiding and unhiding rows and columns	Tutorial 1: 31–33 Tutorial 3: 116
		Modifying alignment	Tutorial 3: 105–107
XL03S-3-4	Format worksheets	Formatting tab color, sheet name, and background	Tutorial 3: 112–114. 117, 119
		Hiding and unhiding worksheets	Tutorial 3: 117

Microsoft Office Specialist Certification Grid

Standardized Coding Number	Certification Skill Activity	Courseware Requirements	Tutorial: Pages
XL03S-4	**Collaborating**		
XL03S-4-1	Insert, view and edit comments	Adding and editing comments attached to worksheet cells	Tutorial 7: 315–316
XL03S-5	**Managing Workbooks**		
XL03S-5-1	Create new workbooks from templates	Creating a workbook from a template	Tutorial 6: 265, 270
XL03S-5-2	Insert, delete and move cells	Inserting and deleting selected cells	Tutorial 1: 31–32
		Cutting, copying and pasting/pasting special selected cells	Tutorial 2: 56
		Moving selected cells	Tutorial 1: 26
XL03S-5-3	Create and modify hyperlinks	Inserting and editing hyperlinks	Tutorial 7: 340–341
XL03S-5-4	Organize worksheets	Inserting worksheets into a workbook	Tutorial 1: 35
		Deleting worksheets from a workbook	Tutorial 1: 35
		Repositioning worksheets in a workbook	Tutorial 1: 37
XL03S-5-5	Preview data in other views	Previewing print and Web pages	Tutorial 7: 340
		Previewing page breaks	Tutorial 3: 131
XL03S-5-6	Customize Window layout	Splitting and arranging workbooks	Tutorial 7: 302
		Splitting, freezing/unfreezing, arranging and hiding/unhiding workbooks	Tutorial 3: 116–117 Tutorial 5: 196–197 Tutorial 7: 302
XL03S-5-7	Setup pages for printing	Setting print areas	Tutorial 3: 131
		Modifying worksheet orientation	Tutorial 1: 40
		Adding headers and footers to worksheets	Tutorial 3: 128–130
		Viewing and modifying page breaks	Tutorial 3: 131–132
		Setting Page Setup options for printing (e.g.; margins, print area, rows/columns to repeat)	Tutorial 1: 40–41 Tutorial 3: 126–128, 131, 133
XL03S-5-8	Print data	Printing selections, worksheets, and workbooks	Tutorial 1: 39
XL03S-5-9	Organize workbooks using file folders	Creating and using folders for workbook storage	Tutorial 6: 269, 271–272
		Renaming folders	Tutorial 6: 272
XL03S-5-10	Save data in appropriate formats for different uses	Converting files to different file formats for transportability (e.g., .csv, .txt)	Tutorial 1: 22
		Saving selections, worksheets or workbooks as Web pages	Tutorial 7: 336

Some of the exercises in this book require that you begin by opening a Data File. Follow one of the procedures below to obtain a copy of the Data Files you need.

Instructors

- A copy of the Data Files is on the Instructor Resources CD under the category Data Files for Students, which you can copy to your school's network for student use.

- Download the Data Files via the World Wide Web by following the instructions below.

- Contact us via e-mail at reply@course.com.

- Call Course Technology's Customer Service Department for fast and efficient delivery of the Data Files if you do not have access to a CD-ROM drive.

Students

- Check with your instructor to determine the best way to obtain a copy of the Data Files.

- Download the Data Files via the World Wide Web by following the instructions below.

Instructions for Downloading the Data Files from the World Wide Web

1. Start your browser and enter the URL www.course.com.

2. When the course.com Web site opens, click Student Downloads, and then search for your text by title or ISBN.

3. If necessary, from the Search results page, select the title of the text you are using.

4. When the textbook page opens, click the Download Student Files link, and then click the link of the compressed files you want to download.

5. If the File Download dialog box opens, make sure the Save this program to disk option button is selected, and then click the OK button. (NOTE: If the Save As dialog box opens, select a folder on your hard disk to download the file to. Write down the folder name listed in the Save in box and the filename listed in the File name box.)

6. The filename of the compressed file appears in the Save As dialog box (e.g., 3500-8.exe, 0361-1d.exe).

7. Click either the OK button or the Save button, whichever choice your browser gives you.

8. When a dialog box opens indicating the download is complete, click the OK button (or the Close button, depending on which operating system you are using). Close your browser.

9. Open Windows Explorer and display the contents of the folder to which you downloaded the file. Double-click the downloaded filename on the right side of the Windows Explorer window.

10. In the WinZip Self-Extractor window, specify the appropriate drive and a folder name to unzip the files to. Click Unzip.

11. When the WinZip Self-Extractor displays the number of files unzipped, click the OK button. Click the Close button in the WinZip Self Extractor dialog box. Close Windows Explorer.

12. Refer to the Read This Before You Begin page(s) in this book for more details on the Data Files for your text. You are now ready to open the required files.

Macintosh users should use a program to expand WinZip or PKZip archives. Students, ask your instructors or lab coordinators for assistance.

Keep Your Skills Fresh with Quick Reference CourseCards!

Thomson Course Technology CourseCards allow you to easily learn the basics of new applications or quickly access tips and tricks long after your class is complete.

Each highly visual, four-color, six-sided CourseCard features:

- **Basic Topics** enable users to effectively utilize key content.

- **Tips and Solutions** reinforce key subject matter and provide solutions to common situations.

- **Menu Quick References** help users navigate through the most important menu tools using a simple table of contents model.

- **Keyboard Shortcuts** improve productivity and save time.

- **Screen Shots** effectively show what users see on their monitors.

- **Advanced Topics** provide advanced users with a clear reference guide to more challenging content.

Over 75 CourseCards are available on a variety of topics! To order, please visit *www.courseilt.com/ilt_cards.cfm*

IF THIS BOOK DOES NOT HAVE A COURSECARD ATTACHED TO THE BACK COVER, YOU ARE NOT GETTING THE FULL VALUE OF YOUR PURCHASE.